DJ

THE
BOOK ®

Citroen ZX Diesel
Service and Repair Manual

Mark Coombs, Steve Rendle and Christopher Rogers

Models covered

(1922-4AF5-288)

All Citroen ZX Diesel and Turbo Diesel models, including Volcane Turbo Diesel; special/limited editions; Estate; 3 and 5-door Hatchback

1769 cc and 1905 cc engines

Does not cover petrol engine models
Covers major mechanical features of Commercial variants

D0434672

© Haynes Publishing 2002

ABCDE
FG

A book in the **Haynes Service and Repair Manual Series**

ISBN **1 85960 701 2**

British Library Cataloguing in Publication Data
A catalogue record for this book is available from the British Library.

Printed in the USA

Haynes Publishing
Sparkford, Nr Yeovil, Somerset BA22 7JJ, England

Haynes North America, Inc
861 Lawrence Drive, Newbury Park, California 91320, USA

Editions Haynes
4, Rue de l'Abreuvoir
92415 COURBEVOIE CEDEX, France

Haynes Publishing Nordiska AB
Box 1504, 751 45 UPPSALA, Sverige

Contents

LIVING WITH YOUR CITROEN ZX DIESEL

Introduction to the Citroen ZX Diesel   Page   0•4
Safety first!   Page   0•5

Roadside repairs
Introduction   Page   0•6
If your car won't start   Page   0•6
Jump starting   Page   0•7
Wheel changing   Page   0•8
Identifying leaks   Page   0•9
Towing   Page   0•9

Weekly checks
Introduction   Page   0•10
Underbonnet check points   Page   0•10
Engine oil level   Page   0•11
Power steering fluid level   Page   0•11
Brake fluid level   Page   0•12
Wiper blades   Page   0•12
Coolant level   Page   0•13
Screen/headlamp washer fluid level   Page   0•13
Tyre condition and pressure   Page   0•14
Battery   Page   0•15
Electrical systems   Page   0•15
Lubricants and fluids   Page   0•16
Choosing your engine oil   Page   0•16
Tyre pressures   Page   0•16

MAINTENANCE

Routine maintenance and servicing

Maintenance schedule   Page   1•3
Maintenance procedures   Page   1•5

Contents

REPAIRS & OVERHAUL

Engine and associated systems

In-car engine repair procedures   Page **2A•1**

Engine removal and general engine overhaul procedures   Page **2B•1**

Cooling, heating and ventilation systems   Page **3•1**

Fuel, exhaust and emission control systems   Page **4•1**

Engine electrical systems   Page **5•1**

Transmission

Clutch   Page **6•1**

Manual transmission   Page **7A•1**

Automatic transmission   Page **7B•0**

Driveshafts   Page **8•1**

Brakes and suspension

Braking system   Page **9•1**

Suspension and steering   Page **10•1**

Body equipment

Bodywork and fittings   Page **11•1**

Body electrical systems   Page **12•1**

Wiring diagrams   Page **12•21**

REFERENCE

Dimensions and weights   Page **REF•1**

Conversion factors   Page **REF•2**

Buying spare parts   Page **REF•3**

Vehicle identification   Page **REF•3**

General repair procedures   Page **REF•4**

Jacking and vehicle support   Page **REF•5**

Radio/cassette unit anti-theft system - precaution   Page **REF•5**

Tools and working facilities   Page **REF•6**

MOT test checks   Page **REF•8**

Fault finding   Page **REF•12**

Glossary of technical terms   Page **REF•19**

Index   Page **REF•23**

The Citroen ZX Diesel was first introduced to the UK in November 1991, being available in Reflex, Avantage and Aura versions. These first models were of a 5-door Hatchback design and equipped with a 1.9 litre normally-aspirated engine transmitting power to the front wheels via a 5-speed manual transmission.

January 1992 saw the introduction of a 4-speed automatic transmission unit, closely followed by a 3-door Hatchback body design.

In June 1992, a power steering system was introduced, this being standard on the Avantage and Aura versions.

In July 1992, a turbocharged 1.9 litre engine became available, providing remarkable performance by previous Diesel standards and being fitted to the Avantage and Aura versions, closely followed in January 1993 by the Volcane version.

May 1993 saw the incorporation of built-in side impact beams and a 2-way remote control alarm option on all models.

In March 1994, the Estate became available to the UK market in the normally-aspirated Avantage and turbocharged Aura versions. Other Estate versions soon followed, the first being the Reflex then the turbocharged Avantage.

Mid to late 1994 saw the incorporation of standard and optional modifications to all models, these being a height-adjustable driver's seat and steering wheel, seat belt pre-tensioners, a driver's airbag, a folding rear seat and revised front body styling. Late 1994 also saw the introduction of a new limited edition model, the turbocharged 1.9 litre Dimension.

June 1995 saw the discontinuation of the normally-aspirated Aura model and the introduction of a new limited edition model, the turbocharged 1.9 litre Memphis.

Three diesel engines are available, although not all of the engines are available in all markets. The engines available are 1.7 litre (not available in the UK) and 1.9 litre normally-aspirated versions, also a 1.9 litre turbocharged version. All the engines are derived from the well-proven XUD series engine which has appeared in many Citroën, Peugeot and Talbot vehicles. The engine is of 4-cylinder overhead camshaft design, mounted transversely and inclined 30° to the rear, with the transmission mounted on the left-hand side.

Fully-independent front suspension is fitted, with the components attached to a subframe assembly. The rear suspension is semi-independent, with torsion bars and trailing arms.

All models in the range are comprehensively-equipped, and an anti-lock braking system (ABS) and air conditioning system are available as options on certain models.

Provided that regular servicing is carried out in accordance with the manufacturer's recommendations, the ZX Diesel should prove reliable and very economical. The engine compartment is well-designed, and most of the items requiring frequent attention are easily accessible.

Your Citroen ZX Manual

The aim of this Manual is to help you get the best value from your vehicle. It can do so in several ways. It can help you decide what work must be done (even should you choose to get it done by a garage), provide information on routine maintenance and servicing, and give a logical course of action and diagnosis when random faults occur. However, it is hoped that you will use the Manual by tackling the work yourself. On simpler jobs it may even be quicker than booking the car into a garage and going there twice, to leave and collect it. Perhaps most important, a lot of money can be saved by avoiding the costs a garage must charge to cover its labour and overheads.

The Manual has drawings and descriptions to show the function of the various components so that their layout can be understood. Then the tasks are described and photographed in a clear step-by-step sequence.

References to the 'left' and 'right' of the vehicle are in the sense of a person sitting in the driver's seat facing forwards.

Citroen ZX Diesel Hatchback

Citroen ZX Diesel Estate

Acknowledgements

Certain illustrations are the copyright of Citroën Cars Ltd, and are used with their permission. Thanks are also due to Draper Tools Limited, who provided some of the workshop tools, and to all those people at Sparkford who helped in the production of this Manual.

Working on your car can be dangerous. This page shows just some of the potential risks and hazards, with the aim of creating a safety-conscious attitude.

General hazards

Scalding

• Don't remove the radiator or expansion tank cap while the engine is hot.
• Engine oil, automatic transmission fluid or power steering fluid may also be dangerously hot if the engine has recently been running.

Burning

• Beware of burns from the exhaust system and from any part of the engine. Brake discs and drums can also be extremely hot immediately after use.

Crushing

• When working under or near a raised vehicle, always supplement the jack with axle stands, or use drive-on ramps. *Never venture under a car which is only supported by a jack.*

• Take care if loosening or tightening high-torque nuts when the vehicle is on stands. Initial loosening and final tightening should be done with the wheels on the ground.

Fire

• Fuel is highly flammable; fuel vapour is explosive.
• Don't let fuel spill onto a hot engine.
• Do not smoke or allow naked lights (including pilot lights) anywhere near a vehicle being worked on. Also beware of creating sparks (electrically or by use of tools).
• Fuel vapour is heavier than air, so don't work on the fuel system with the vehicle over an inspection pit.
• Another cause of fire is an electrical overload or short-circuit. Take care when repairing or modifying the vehicle wiring.
• Keep a fire extinguisher handy, of a type suitable for use on fuel and electrical fires.

Electric shock

• Ignition HT voltage can be dangerous, especially to people with heart problems or a pacemaker. Don't work on or near the ignition system with the engine running or the ignition switched on.

• Mains voltage is also dangerous. Make sure that any mains-operated equipment is correctly earthed. Mains power points should be protected by a residual current device (RCD) circuit breaker.

Fume or gas intoxication

• Exhaust fumes are poisonous; they often contain carbon monoxide, which is rapidly fatal if inhaled. Never run the engine in a confined space such as a garage with the doors shut.

• Fuel vapour is also poisonous, as are the vapours from some cleaning solvents and paint thinners.

Poisonous or irritant substances

• Avoid skin contact with battery acid and with any fuel, fluid or lubricant, especially antifreeze, brake hydraulic fluid and Diesel fuel. Don't syphon them by mouth. If such a substance is swallowed or gets into the eyes, seek medical advice.
• Prolonged contact with used engine oil can cause skin cancer. Wear gloves or use a barrier cream if necessary. Change out of oil-soaked clothes and do not keep oily rags in your pocket.
• Air conditioning refrigerant forms a poisonous gas if exposed to a naked flame (including a cigarette). It can also cause skin burns on contact.

Asbestos

• Asbestos dust can cause cancer if inhaled or swallowed. Asbestos may be found in gaskets and in brake and clutch linings. When dealing with such components it is safest to assume that they contain asbestos.

Special hazards

Hydrofluoric acid

• This extremely corrosive acid is formed when certain types of synthetic rubber, found in some O-rings, oil seals, fuel hoses etc, are exposed to temperatures above 400°C. The rubber changes into a charred or sticky substance containing the acid. *Once formed, the acid remains dangerous for years. If it gets onto the skin, it may be necessary to amputate the limb concerned.*
• When dealing with a vehicle which has suffered a fire, or with components salvaged from such a vehicle, wear protective gloves and discard them after use.

The battery

• Batteries contain sulphuric acid, which attacks clothing, eyes and skin. Take care when topping-up or carrying the battery.
• The hydrogen gas given off by the battery is highly explosive. Never cause a spark or allow a naked light nearby. Be careful when connecting and disconnecting battery chargers or jump leads.

Air bags

• Air bags can cause injury if they go off accidentally. Take care when removing the steering wheel and/or facia. Special storage instructions may apply.

Diesel injection equipment

• Diesel injection pumps supply fuel at very high pressure. Take care when working on the fuel injectors and fuel pipes.

⚠️ *Warning: Never expose the hands, face or any other part of the body to injector spray; the fuel can penetrate the skin with potentially fatal results.*

Remember...

DO

• Do use eye protection when using power tools, and when working under the vehicle.

• Do wear gloves or use barrier cream to protect your hands when necessary.

• Do get someone to check periodically that all is well when working alone on the vehicle.

• Do keep loose clothing and long hair well out of the way of moving mechanical parts.

• Do remove rings, wristwatch etc, before working on the vehicle – especially the electrical system.

• Do ensure that any lifting or jacking equipment has a safe working load rating adequate for the job.

DON'T

• Don't attempt to lift a heavy component which may be beyond your capability – get assistance.

• Don't rush to finish a job, or take unverified short cuts.

• Don't use ill-fitting tools which may slip and cause injury.

• Don't leave tools or parts lying around where someone can trip over them. Mop up oil and fuel spills at once.

• Don't allow children or pets to play in or near a vehicle being worked on.

The following pages are intended to help in dealing with common roadside emergencies and breakdowns. You will find more detailed fault finding information at the back of the manual, and repair information in the main chapters.

If your car won't start and the starter motor doesn't turn

☐ If it's a model with automatic transmission, make sure the selector is in 'P' or 'N'.

☐ Open the bonnet and make sure that the battery terminals are clean and tight.

☐ Switch on the headlights and try to start the engine. If the headlights go very dim when you're trying to start, the battery is probably flat. Get out of trouble by jump starting (see next page) using a friend's car.

If your car won't start even though the starter motor turns as normal

☐ Is there fuel in the tank?

☐ Is there moisture on electrical components under the bonnet? Switch off the ignition, then wipe off any obvious dampness with a dry cloth. Spray a water-repellent aerosol product (WD-40 or equivalent) on ignition and fuel system electrical connectors like those shown in the photos. On petrol models, pay special attention to the ignition coil wiring connector and HT leads. Diesel engines are not generally as susceptible to damp problems, but all accessible wiring and connectors should still be checked.

A Check that the glow plug wire connections are clean and secure

B Check that all fuel injection pump connections are clean and secure

C The preheating system wiring plug may cause problems if dirty or not properly connected

Check that electrical connections are secure (with the ignition switched off) and spray them with a water-dispersant spray like WD-40 if you suspect a problem due to damp.

D Check the security and condition of the battery connections

E Check that all other engine-related lead connections are clean and secure

Jump starting

HAYNES HiNT *Jump starting will get you out of trouble, but you must correct whatever made the battery go flat in the first place. There are three possibilities:*

1 *The battery has been drained by repeated attempts to start, or by leaving the lights on.*

2 *The charging system is not working properly (alternator drivebelt slack or broken, alternator wiring fault or alternator itself faulty).*

3 *The battery itself is at fault (electrolyte low, or battery worn out).*

When jump-starting a car using a booster battery, observe the following precautions:

✔ Before connecting the booster battery, make sure that the ignition is switched off.

✔ Ensure that all electrical equipment (lights, heater, wipers, etc) is switched off.

✔ Take note of any special precautions printed on the battery case.

✔ Make sure that the booster battery is the same voltage as the discharged one in the vehicle.

✔ If the battery is being jump-started from the battery in another vehicle, the two vehicles MUST NOT TOUCH each other.

✔ Make sure that the transmission is in neutral (or PARK, in the case of automatic transmission).

1 Connect one end of the red jump lead to the positive (+) terminal of the flat battery

2 Connect the other end of the red lead to the positive (+) terminal of the booster battery.

3 Connect one end of the black jump lead to the negative (-) terminal of the booster battery

4 Connect the other end of the black jump lead to a bolt or bracket on the engine block, well away from the battery, on the vehicle to be started.

5 Make sure that the jump leads will not come into contact with the fan, drive-belts or other moving parts of the engine.

6 Start the engine using the booster battery and run it at idle speed. Switch on the lights, rear window demister and heater blower motor, then disconnect the jump leads in the reverse order of connection. Turn off the lights etc.

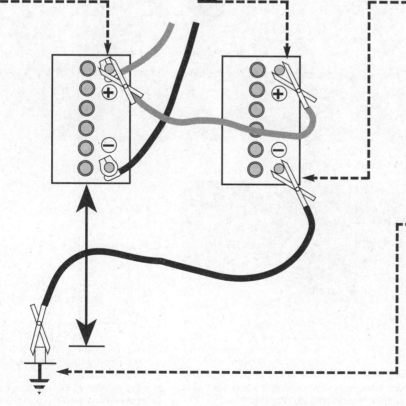

Wheel changing

Some of the details shown here will vary according to model. For instance, the location of the spare wheel and jack is not the same on all cars. However, the basic principles apply to all vehicles.

Warning: Do not change a wheel in a situation where you risk being hit by other traffic. On busy roads, try to stop in a lay-by or a gateway. Be wary of passing traffic while changing the wheel – it is easy to become distracted by the job in hand.

Preparation

- ☐ When a puncture occurs, stop as soon as it is safe to do so.
- ☐ Park on firm level ground, if possible, and well out of the way of other traffic.
- ☐ Use hazard warning lights if necessary.

- ☐ If you have one, use a warning triangle to alert other drivers of your presence.
- ☐ Apply the handbrake and engage first or reverse gear (or Park on models with automatic transmission).

- ☐ Chock the wheel diagonally opposite the one being removed – a couple of large stones will do for this.
- ☐ If the ground is soft, use a flat piece of wood to spread the load under the jack.

Changing the wheel

1 Location of wheel brace in luggage compartment - Estate shown

2 Using the wheel brace end to unscrew the spare wheel carrier retaining screw - 10 to 12 turns

3 Lowering the spare wheel carrier - chock is located within wheel

4 Removing the covered jack from the spare wheel carrier

5 Chocking the wheel diagonally opposite the one being changed

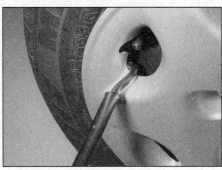

6 Using the wheel brace end to detach the wheel trim

7 Using the wheel brace to slightly loosen the wheel bolts

8 Using the jack to raise the vehicle until the wheel is clear of the ground, allowing the wheel bolts and wheel to be removed. Fit the replacement wheel and tighten the nuts to the correct torque

Finally...

- ☐ Remove the wheel chocks.
- ☐ Stow the jack and tools in the correct locations in the car.
- ☐ Check the tyre pressure on the wheel just fitted. If it is low, or you don't have a pressure gauge with you, drive slowly to the nearest garage and inflate the tyre to the right pressure.
- ☐ Have the damaged tyre or wheel repaired as soon as possible.

Identifying leaks

Puddles on the garage floor or drive, or obvious wetness under the bonnet or underneath the car, suggest a leak that needs investigating. It can sometimes be difficult to decide where the leak is coming from, especially if the engine bay is very dirty already. Leaking oil or fluid can also be blown rearwards by the passage of air under the car, giving a false impression of where the problem lies.

 Warning: Most automotive oils and fluids are poisonous. Wash them off skin, and change out of contaminated clothing, without delay.

HAYNES HiNT *The smell of a fluid leaking from the car may provide a clue to what's leaking. Some fluids are distinctively coloured.*
It may help to clean the car carefully and to park it over some clean paper overnight as an aid to locating the source of the leak.
Remember that some leaks may only occur while the engine is running.

Sump oil

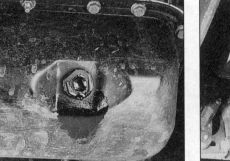

Engine oil may leak from the drain plug...

Oil from filter

...or from the base of the oil filter.

Gearbox oil

Gearbox oil can leak from the seals at the inboard ends of the driveshafts.

Antifreeze

Leaking antifreeze often leaves a crystalline deposit like this.

Brake fluid

A leak occurring at a wheel is almost certainly brake fluid.

Power steering fluid

Power steering fluid may leak from the pipe connectors on the steering rack.

Towing

When all else fails, you may find yourself having to get a tow home – or of course you may be helping somebody else. Long-distance recovery should only be done by a garage or breakdown service. For shorter distances, DIY towing using another car is easy enough, but observe the following points:

☐ Use a proper tow-rope – they are not expensive. The vehicle being towed must display an ON TOW sign in its rear window.

☐ Towing eyes are fitted to the front and rear of the vehicle for attachment of the tow rope.

On certain models, plastic covers must be unclipped from the bumpers for access to the towing eyes.

☐ Always turn the ignition key to the 'on' position when the vehicle is being towed, so that the steering lock is released, and that the direction indicator and brake lights will work.

☐ Before being towed, release the handbrake and select neutral on the transmission.

☐ Note that greater-than-usual pedal pressure will be required to operate the brakes, since the vacuum servo unit is only operational with the engine running.

☐ On models with power steering, greater-than-usual steering effort will also be required.

☐ The driver of the car being towed must keep the tow-rope taut at all times to avoid snatching.

☐ Make sure that both drivers know the route before setting off.

☐ Only drive at moderate speeds and keep the distance towed to a minimum. Drive smoothly and allow plenty of time for slowing down at junctions.

☐ On models with automatic transmission, special precautions apply. If in doubt, do not tow, or transmission damage may result.

Introduction

There are some very simple checks which need only take a few minutes to carry out, but which could save you a lot on inconvenience and expense.

These *Weekly checks* require no great skill or special tools, and the small amount of time they take to perform could well prove to be very well spent, for example;

☐ Keeping an eye on tyre condition and pressures, will not only help to stop them wearing out prematurely but could also save your life.
☐ Many breakdowns are caused by electrical problems. Battery-related faults are particularly common and a quick check on a regular basis will often prevent the majority of these.

☐ If your car develops a brake fluid leak, the first time you might know about it is when your brakes don't work properly. Checking the level regularly will give advance warning of this kind of problem.
☐ If the oil or coolant levels run low, the cost of repairing any engine damage will be far greater than fixing the leak.

Underbonnet check points

A *Engine oil level dipstick*

B *Oil filler cap*

C *Coolant filler cap*

D *Brake fluid reservoir*

E *Screen washer fluid reservoir*

F *Battery*

G *Power steering fluid reservoir*

Engine oil level

Before you start

✔ Make sure that the car is on level ground.
✔ Check the oil level before the car is driven, or at least 5 minutes after the engine has been switched off.

 HAYNES HINT *If the oil is checked immediately after driving the vehicle, some of the oil will remain in the upper engine components, resulting in an inaccurate reading on the dipstick!*

The correct oil

Modern engines place great demands on their oil. It is very important that the correct oil for your car is used (see Lubricants and Fluids).

Car Care

● If you have to add oil frequently, you should check whether you have any oil leaks. Place some clean paper under the car overnight, and check for stains in the morning. If there are no leaks, then engine may be burning oil.

● Always maintain the level between the upper and lower dipstick marks. If the level is too low, severe engine damage may occur. Oil seal failure may result if the engine is overfilled by adding too much oil.

1 The dipstick is located at the centre of the engine (see *Underbonnet Check Points* for exact location) and passes through the oil filler tube. Withdraw the dipstick.

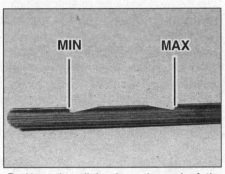

3 Note the oil level on the end of the dipstick, which should be between the upper MAX mark and the lower MIN mark. Approximately 1.3 litres of oil will raise the level from the lower mark to the upper mark.

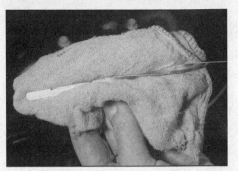

2 Using a clean rag or paper towel, wipe all oil from the dipstick. Insert the clean dipstick into its tube as far as it will go, then withdraw it again.

4 Oil is added through the filler cap orifice. A funnel may help to reduce spillage. Add the oil slowly, checking the level on the dipstick often. Do not overfill.

Power steering fluid level

Before you start:

✔ Make sure that the car is on level ground.
✔ Set the front roadwheels in the straight-ahead position.
✔ The engine must be turned off.

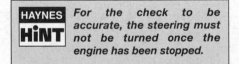 **HAYNES HINT** *For the check to be accurate, the steering must not be turned once the engine has been stopped.*

Safety First!

● If the reservoir requires repeated topping-up, there is a fluid leak somewhere in the system which should be investigated immediately.
● If a leak is suspected, the car should not be driven until the power steering system has been checked.

1 The power steering fluid reservoir is mounted forward of the right-hand suspension turret in the engine compartment. MAX and MIN level marks are indicated on the side of the reservoir and the fluid level should be maintained between these marks at all times.

2 If topping-up is necessary, first wipe the area around the filler cap with a clean rag before removing the cap. When adding fluid, pour it carefully into the reservoir to avoid spillage. Be sure to use only the specified fluid.

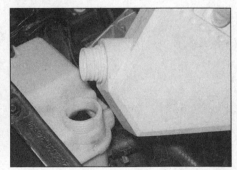

3 After filling the reservoir to the proper level, make sure that the cap is refitted securely to avoid leaks and the entry of foreign matter into the reservoir.

Brake fluid level

Warning:
● Brake fluid can harm your eyes and damage painted surfaces, so use extreme caution when handling and pouring it.
● Do not use fluid that has been standing open for some time, as it absorbs moisture from the air, which can cause a dangerous loss of braking effectiveness.

HAYNES HINT
● Make sure that your car is on level ground.
● The fluid level in the reservoir will drop slightly as the brake pads wear down, but the fluid level must never be allowed to drop below the MIN mark.

Safety First!

● If the reservoir requires repeated topping-up, this is an indication of a fluid leak somewhere in the system, which should be investigated immediately.

● If a leak is suspected, the car should not be driven until the braking system has been checked. Never take any risks where brakes are concerned.

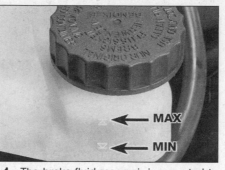

1 The brake fluid reservoir is mounted to the left of the right-hand suspension turret in the engine compartment. MAX and MIN level marks are indicated on the side of the reservoir and the fluid level should be maintained between these marks at all times.

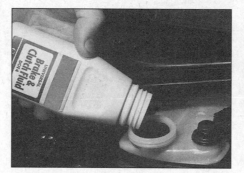

3 When adding fluid, it is a good idea to inspect the reservoir for contamination. The system should be drained and refilled if deposits, dirt particles or contamination are seen in the fluid. After filling the reservoir to the proper level, ensure that the cap is refitted securely to avoid leaks and the entry of foreign matter.

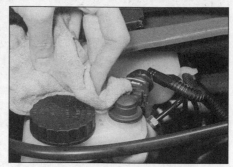

2 If topping-up is necessary, first wipe the area around the filler cap with a clean rag before removing the cap. When adding fluid, pour it carefully into the reservoir to avoid spilling it on surrounding painted surfaces. Be sure to use only the specified brake hydraulic fluid since mixing different types of fluid can cause damage to the system.

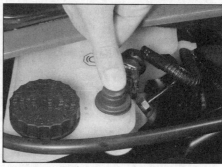

4 Test the low brake fluid warning circuit by chocking one of the wheels and releasing the handbrake. Turn the ignition on and press the button on the fluid reservoir; check the warning light on the dashboard illuminates.

Wiper blades

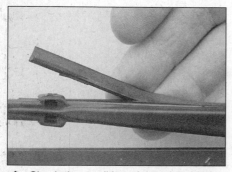

1 Check the condition of the wiper blades. If they are cracked or show any signs of deterioration, or if the glass swept area is smeared, renew them. For maximum clarity of vision, wiper blades should be renewed annually, as a matter of course.

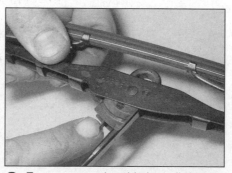

2 To remove a wiper blade, pull the arm fully away from the glass until it locks. Swivel the blade through 90º, press the locking tab with a finger nail and slide the blade out of the arm's hooked end. On refitting, ensure that the blade locks securely into the arm.

Coolant level

Car Care

● Adding coolant should not be necessary on a regular basis. If frequent topping-up is required, it is likely there is a leak. Check the radiator, all hoses and joint faces for signs of staining or wetness, and rectify as necessary.

● It is important that antifreeze is used in the cooling system all year round, not just during the winter months. Do not top up with water alone, as the antifreeze will become diluted.

1 The coolant level varies with the temperature of the engine. When the engine is cold, the coolant level should be between the MAX and MIN marks on the side of the expansion tank, which is incorporated in the right-hand side of the radiator. When the engine is hot, the level may rise slightly.

2 If topping-up is necessary, wait until the engine is cold, then cover the expansion tank with a thick layer of rag and unscrew the filler cap anti-clockwise until it reaches its first stop and a hissing sound is heard. Wait until the hissing ceases, indicating that all pressure is released, then push the cap down and turn it anti-clockwise to the second stop until it can be removed. If more hissing sounds are heard, wait until they have stopped before unscrewing the cap completely. At all times keep well away from the filler opening.

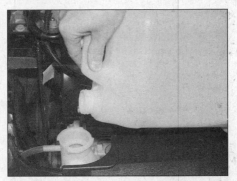

3 Add the recommended mixture of water and antifreeze through the expansion tank filler neck, until the coolant is midway between the MAX and MIN level marks. Refit the cap, turning it clockwise as far as it will go until it is secure.

Screen/headlamp washer fluid level

Car care

✔ Screenwash additives not only keep the windscreen clean during bad weather, they also prevent the washer system freezing in cold weather - which is when you are likely to need it most. Avoid top up using plain water, as the screenwash will become diluted and will freeze in cold weather.

✔ Check the operation of both screen and headlamp washers. Adjust the nozzles using a pin if necessary, aiming the spray to a point slightly above the centre of the swept area.

1 The reservoir for the windscreen/tailgate washer system is located at the rear right-hand corner of the engine compartment. Where fitted, the headlamp washer system reservoir is located under the front right-hand wing and incorporates a filler neck which extends into the engine compartment.

2 When topping-up the reservoir(s) a screenwash additive should be added in the quantities recommended on the bottle.

Tyre condition and pressure

It is very important that tyres are in good condition, and at the correct pressure - having a tyre failure at any speed is highly dangerous. Tyre wear is influenced by driving style - harsh braking and acceleration, or fast cornering, will all produce more rapid tyre wear. As a general rule, the front tyres wear out faster than the rears. Interchanging the tyres from front to rear ("rotating" the tyres) may result in more even wear. However, if this is completely effective, you may have the expense of replacing all four tyres at once! Remove any nails or stones embedded in the tread before they penetrate the tyre to cause deflation. If removal of a nail does reveal that the tyre has been punctured, refit the nail so that its point of penetration is marked. Then immediately change the wheel, and have the tyre repaired by a tyre dealer.

Regularly check the tyres for damage in the form of cuts or bulges, especially in the sidewalls. Periodically remove the wheels, and clean any dirt or mud from the inside and outside surfaces. Examine the wheel rims for signs of rusting, corrosion or other damage. Light alloy wheels are easily damaged by "kerbing" whilst parking; steel wheels may also become dented or buckled. A new wheel is very often the only way to overcome severe damage.

New tyres should be balanced when they are fitted, but it may become necessary to re-balance them as they wear, or if the balance weights fitted to the wheel rim should fall off. Unbalanced tyres will wear more quickly, as will the steering and suspension components. Wheel imbalance is normally signified by vibration, particularly at a certain speed (typically around 50 mph). If this vibration is felt only through the steering, then it is likely that just the front wheels need balancing. If, however, the vibration is felt through the whole car, the rear wheels could be out of balance. Wheel balancing should be carried out by a tyre dealer or garage.

1 *Tread Depth - visual check*
The original tyres have tread wear safety bands (B), which will appear when the tread depth reaches approximately 1.6 mm. The band positions are indicated by a triangular mark on the tyre sidewall (A).

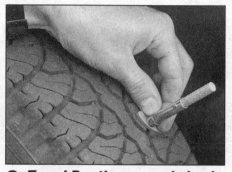

2 *Tread Depth - manual check*
Alternatively, tread wear can be monitored with a simple, inexpensive device known as a tread depth indicator gauge.

3 *Tyre Pressure Check*
Check the tyre pressures regularly with the tyres cold. Do not adjust the tyre pressures immediately after the vehicle has been used, or an inaccurate setting will result. Tyre pressures are shown on page 0•16.

Tyre tread wear patterns

Shoulder Wear

Underinflation (wear on both sides)
Under-inflation will cause overheating of the tyre, because the tyre will flex too much, and the tread will not sit correctly on the road surface. This will cause a loss of grip and excessive wear, not to mention the danger of sudden tyre failure due to heat build-up.
Check and adjust pressures
Incorrect wheel camber (wear on one side)
Repair or renew suspension parts
Hard cornering
Reduce speed!

Centre Wear

Overinflation
Over-inflation will cause rapid wear of the centre part of the tyre tread, coupled with reduced grip, harsher ride, and the danger of shock damage occurring in the tyre casing.
Check and adjust pressures

If you sometimes have to inflate your car's tyres to the higher pressures specified for maximum load or sustained high speed, don't forget to reduce the pressures to normal afterwards.

Uneven Wear

Front tyres may wear unevenly as a result of wheel misalignment. Most tyre dealers and garages can check and adjust the wheel alignment (or "tracking") for a modest charge.
Incorrect camber or castor
Repair or renew suspension parts
Malfunctioning suspension
Repair or renew suspension parts
Unbalanced wheel
Balance tyres
Incorrect toe setting
Adjust front wheel alignment
Note: *The feathered edge of the tread which typifies toe wear is best checked by feel.*

Battery

Caution: Before carrying out any work on the vehicle battery, read the precautions given in Safety first! at the start of this manual.

✔ Make sure that the battery tray is in good condition, and that the battery retaining clamp is tight. Corrosion on the tray, retaining clamp and the battery itself can be removed with a solution of water and baking soda. Thoroughly rinse all cleaned areas with water. Any metal parts damaged by corrosion should be covered with a zinc-based primer, then painted.

✔ Approximately every 3 months check the charge condition of the battery as described in Chapter 5.

✔ If the battery is flat, and you need to jump start your vehicle, see *Roadside Repairs*.

1 The battery is located in the left-hand side of the engine compartment. The exterior of the battery should be inspected periodically for damage such as a cracked case or cover.

2 Check the tightness of the battery cable clamps to ensure good electrical connections. You should not be able to move them. Also check each cable for cracks and frayed conductors.

HAYNES HINT

Battery corrosion can be kept to a minimum by applying a layer of petroleum jelly to the clamps and terminals after they are reconnected.

3 If corrosion (white fluffy deposits) is evident, remove the cables from the battery terminals, clean them with a small wire brush, then refit them. Automotive stores sell a useful tool for cleaning the battery posts . . .

4 . . . as well as the battery cable clamps.

Electrical systems

✔ Check all external lights and the horn. Refer to the appropriate Sections of Chapter 12 for details if any of the circuits are found to be inoperative.

✔ Visually check all accessible wiring connectors, harnesses and retaining clips for security, and for signs of chafing or damage.

HAYNES HINT

If you need to check your brake lights and indicators unaided, back up to a wall or garage door and operate the lights. The reflected light should show if they are working properly.

1 If a single indicator light, brake light or headlight has failed, it is likely that a bulb has blown and will need to be replaced. If both brake lights have failed, it is possible that the brake light switch operated by the brake pedal has failed.

2 If more than one indicator light or headlight has failed, it is likely that either a fuse has blown or that there is a fault in the circuit. The main fusebox is located under the facia panel, on the right-hand side. A supplementary fusebox is mounted adjacent to the battery.

3 To replace a blown fuse, pull it from position. Fit a new fuse of the same rating, available from car accessory shops. It is important to find the reason that the fuse blew.

Lubricants and fluids

Engine	Multigrade engine oil, viscosity SAE 10W/30 to 15W/50, to API CF and/or ACEA-B2/B3 *(Duckhams QXR Premium Diesel Engine Oil, or Duckhams Hypergrade Diesel Engine Oil)*
Cooling system	Ethylene glycol-based antifreeze *(Duckhams Antifreeze and Summer Coolant)*
Manual transmission	Total BV 75/80W gear oil *(Duckhams Hypoid Gear Oil 75W-80W GL-5)*
Automatic transmission	Dexron type II ATF *(Duckhams ATF Autotrans III)*
Braking system	Hydraulic fluid to SAE J1703F or DOT 4 *(Duckhams Universal Brake and Clutch Fluid)*
Power steering	Dexron type II ATF *(Duckhams ATF Autotrans III)*

Choosing your engine oil

Engines need oil, not only to lubricate moving parts and minimise wear, but also to maximise power output and to improve fuel economy. By introducing a simplified and improved range of engine oils, Duckhams has taken away the confusion and made it easier for you to choose the right oil for your engine.

HOW ENGINE OIL WORKS

• Beating friction

Without oil, the moving surfaces inside your engine will rub together, heat up and melt, quickly causing the engine to seize. Engine oil creates a film which separates these moving parts, preventing wear and heat build-up.

• Cooling hot-spots

Temperatures inside the engine can exceed 1000° C. The engine oil circulates and acts as a coolant, transferring heat from the hot-spots to the sump.

• Cleaning the engine internally

Good quality engine oils clean the inside of your engine, collecting and dispersing combustion deposits and controlling them until they are trapped by the oil filter or flushed out at oil change.

OIL CARE - FOLLOW THE CODE

To handle and dispose of used engine oil safely, always:

• **Avoid skin contact with used engine oil. Repeated or prolonged contact can be harmful.**
• **Dispose of used oil and empty packs in a responsible manner in an authorised disposal site. Call 0800 663366 to find the one nearest to you. Never tip oil down drains or onto the ground.**

Tyre pressures (cold)

Note: *Recommended tyre pressures are marked on a label attached to the driver's door edge or frame. Pressures apply to original-equipment tyres, and may vary if any other make or type of tyre is fitted; check with the tyre manufacturer or supplier for correct pressures if necessary.*

165/70 R 13 tyres	Front	Rear	
Manual transmission models	2.3 bar	2.1 bar	
Automatic transmission models	2.4 bar	2.2 bar	
175/65 R 14 tyres*			
Hatchback turbo models	2.4 bar	2.2 bar	
Hatchback non turbo models	2.2 bar	2.1 bar	
Estate models	2.4 bar	2.4 bar - lightly laden	2.8 bar - fully laden
185/60 R 14 tyres*			
All models	2.4 bar	2.2 bar	
185/65 R 14 tyres*			
Estate models	2.3 bar	2.0 bar - lightly laden	2.5 bar - fully laden

* Vehicles equipped with these tyres may have a space-saver spare wheel. Vehicles should not be driven at speeds exceeding 100 mph (160 kmh) with the spare wheel fitted.

Chapter 1
Routine maintenance and servicing

Contents

Air conditioning system check 7
Air conditioning system refrigerant check 16
Air filter renewal 26
Automatic transmission fluid level check 12
Automatic transmission fluid renewal 30
Auxiliary drivebelt check and renewal 19
Battery electrolyte level check 6
Brake check 5
Brake fluid renewal 31
Brake servo vacuum pump drivebelt check and renewal 20
Clutch adjustment check 21
Clutch control mechanism lubrication 22
Coolant renewal 32
Driveshaft gaiter check 14
Emission control system check 18
Engine oil and filter renewal 9
Front brake pad check 15
Fuel filter draining 10
Fuel filter renewal 27
Hinge and lock lubrication 28
Hose and fluid leak check 11
Idle speed and anti-stall speed check and adjustment 17
Introduction 1
Light, direction indicator and horn check 8
Lock, hinge and latch mechanism check 3
Manual transmission oil level check 29
Manual transmission oil renewal 34
Rear brake pad check 24
Rear brake shoe check 23
Regular maintenance 2
Road test 25
Seat belt check 4
Steering and suspension check 13
Timing belt renewal 33

Degrees of difficulty

| **Easy,** suitable for novice with little experience | | **Fairly easy,** suitable for beginner with some experience | | **Fairly difficult,** suitable for competent DIY mechanic | | **Difficult,** suitable for experienced DIY mechanic | | **Very difficult,** suitable for expert DIY or professional | |

Lubricants and fluids

Refer to Weekly checks

Capacities

Engine oil (including filter)
Pre-1995 models . . . . 5.0 litres
Post-1995 models . . . . 4.3 litres

Cooling system (approximate)
Non-turbo models:
  With manual transmission . . . . 8.5 litres
  With automatic transmission . . . . 9.0 litres
Turbo models . . . . 9.0 litres

Transmission
Manual transmission . . . . 2.0 litres
Automatic transmission:
  Drain and refill . . . . 2.4 litres
  From dry . . . . 6.2 litres

Fuel tank . . . . 54.0 litres

Power-assisted steering . . . . 1.7 litres

Cooling system

Antifreeze mixture:
  33% antifreeze to water . . . . Protection down to -15°C
  50% antifreeze to water . . . . Protection down to -30°C

Fuel system

Idle speed:
  Manual transmission models:
    Without air conditioning . . . . 800 ± 50 rpm
    With air conditioning . . . . 850 ± 50 rpm
  Automatic transmission models:
    Without air conditioning . . . . 850 ± 50 rpm
    With air conditioning . . . . 900 ± 50 rpm
Fast idle speed:
  1.7 litre engine . . . . 1050 ± 50 rpm
  1.9 litre engines . . . . 950 ± 50 rpm
Anti-stall speed:
  Lucas fuel injection pump:
    XUD7 (A9A) engine - with 4 mm shim (see text) . . . . 1500 ± 100 rpm
    XUD9A (D9B) engine - with 4 mm shim (see text) . . . . 1500 ± 100 rpm
    XUD9A/L (D9B) engine - with 3 mm shim (see text) . . . . 900 ± 100 rpm
  Bosch fuel injection pump:
    XUD7A (A9A) engine - with 1 mm shim (see text) . . . . 800 + 20 to 50 rpm
    XUD9A (D9B) engine - with 1 mm shim (see text) . . . . 800 + 20 to 50 rpm
    XUD9A/L (D9B) engine - with 3 mm shim (see text) . . . . 1250 ± 100 rpm
    XUD9TE/L (D8A) engine - with 1 mm shim (see text) . . . . 800 + 20 to 50 rpm
    XUD9TE/Y (DHY and DHZ) engine - with 1 mm shim (see text) . . 800 + 20 to 50 rpm
    XUD9Y (DJZ) engine - with 1 mm shim (see text) . . . . 800 + 20 to 50 rpm

Braking system

Pad friction material minimum thickness (front and rear) . . . . 2.0 mm
Shoe friction material minimum thickness . . . . 1.5 mm
Servo vacuum pump drivebelt deflection . . . . 3.0 mm under firm finger pressure at mid point between pulleys

Tyres

Refer to Weekly checks

Electrical system

Auxiliary drivebelt deflection:
  Models without power steering or air conditioning . . . . 5.0 mm under firm finger pressure at mid point between pulleys
  Models with power steering or air conditioning . . . . Twisted through 90° under firm finger pressure at mid point between power steering pump/air conditioning compressor and crankshaft pulleys
  Models with power steering and air conditioning . . . . Manual and automatic tensioner rollers - see text

Torque wrench settings

	Nm	lbf ft
Manual transmission:		
Filler/level plug	22	16
Drain plug	35	26
Roadwheel bolts	90	66

The maintenance intervals in this manual are provided with the assumption that you, not the dealer, will be carrying out the work. These are the minimum maintenance intervals recommended by us for vehicles driven daily. If you wish to keep your vehicle in peak condition at all times, you may wish to perform some of these procedures more often. We encourage frequent maintenance, because it enhances the efficiency, performance and resale value of your vehicle.

If the vehicle is driven in dusty areas, used to tow a trailer, or driven frequently at slow speeds (idling in traffic) or on short journeys, then more frequent maintenance intervals are recommended.

When the vehicle is new, it should be serviced by a factory-authorised dealer service department, in order to preserve the factory warranty.

Every 250 miles (400 km) or weekly

☐ Refer to Weekly Checks

Every 1000 miles (1500 km) or monthly

☐ Check the lock, hinge and latch mechanisms (Section 3)
☐ Check the seat belts (Section 4)
☐ Check the brakes (Section 5)
☐ Check the battery electrolyte level (Section 6)
☐ Check the air conditioning system (Section 7)
☐ Check the operation of all lights, direction indicators and horns (Section 8)

Every 6000 miles (10 000 km) or 6 months - whichever comes first

☐ Renew the engine oil and filter (Section 9)
☐ Drain any water from the fuel filter (Section 10)
☐ Check all underbonnet components and hoses for fluid leaks (Section 11)
☐ Check the automatic transmission fluid level (Section 12)
☐ Check the steering and suspension components for condition and security (Section 13)
☐ Check the condition of the driveshaft rubber gaiters (Section 14)
☐ Check the condition of the front brake pads, and renew if necessary (Section 15)

Every 12 000 miles (20 000 km) or 12 months - whichever comes first

In addition to all the items listed above, carry out the following:

☐ Check the condition of the air conditioning system refrigerant - where applicable (Section 16)
☐ Check and if necessary adjust the idle speed (Section 17)
☐ Check the condition of the emission control system hoses and components - where applicable (Section 18)

Every 12 000 miles (20 000 km) or 12 months - whichever comes first (continued)

☐ Check the condition of the auxiliary drivebelt, and renew if necessary (Section 19)
☐ Check the condition of the brake vacuum pump drivebelt - where applicable (Section 20)
☐ Check the clutch mechanism adjustment (Section 21)
☐ Lubricate the clutch control mechanism (Section 22)
☐ Check the condition of the rear brake shoes, and renew if necessary - rear drum brake models (Section 23)
☐ Check the condition of the rear disc brake pads, and renew if necessary - rear disc brake models (Section 24)
☐ Carry out a road test (Section 25)

Every 18 000 miles (30 000 km) or 18 months - whichever comes first

In addition to all the items listed above, carry out the following:

☐ Renew the air filter (Section 26)
☐ Renew the fuel filter (Section 27)
☐ Lubricate all hinges and locks (Section 28)

Every 24 000 miles (40 000 km) or 2 years - whichever comes first

In addition to all the items listed above, carry out the following:

☐ Check the manual transmission oil level, and top-up if necessary (Section 29)
☐ Renew the automatic transmission fluid (Section 30)
☐ Renew the brake fluid (Section 31)

Every 40 000 miles (60 000 km) or 2 years - whichever comes first

☐ Renew the coolant (Section 32)

Every 48 000 miles (80 000 km)

☐ Renew the timing belt (Section 33)

Note: *Although the normal interval for timing belt renewal is 72 000 miles (116 000 km), it is strongly recommended that the interval is reduced to 48 000 miles (80 000 km) on vehicles which are subjected to intensive use, ie, mainly short journeys or a lot of stop-start driving. The actual belt renewal interval is therefore very much up to the individual owner, but bear in mind that severe engine damage may result if the belt breaks.*

Every 72 000 miles (116 000 km)

☐ Renew the manual transmission oil (Section 34)

Engine compartment component locations - 1.9 litre Turbo model

1 Washer fluid reservoir filler cap
2 Suspension strut top mounting
3 Fuel system priming bulb
4 Brake fluid reservoir
5 Intercooler
6 Battery negative terminal
7 Junction box
8 Radiator top hose
9 Fuel filter housing
10 Thermostat housing
11 Fuel system water drain hose
12 Accelerator cable
13 Oil level dipstick and oil filler cap
14 Oil filter
15 Fuel injection pump
16 Alternator
17 Cooling system (expansion tank) filler cap
18 VIN plate
19 Power steering fluid reservoir
20 Right-hand engine mounting

Front underbody view - 1.9 litre turbo model with manual transmission

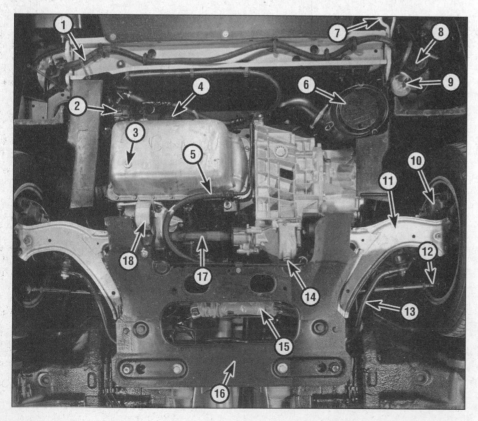

1 Wiring harness
2 Power steering pump
3 Sump drain plug
4 Oil filter
5 Power steering fluid hose
6 Air filter housing
7 Towing eye
8 Horn
9 Horn compressor
10 Brake caliper
11 Lower suspension arm
12 Track rod balljoint
13 Anti-roll bar
14 Transmission oil drain plug
15 Steering gear assembly
16 Front suspension subframe
17 Driveshaft
18 Rear engine/transmission mounting

Rear underbody view

1 Fuel tank
2 Fuel tank support bracket
3 Handbrake cables
4 Rear suspension torsion bars
5 Rear suspension tubular crossmember
6 Exhaust heat shield
7 Rear shock absorber
8 Rear suspension trailing arm
9 Brake caliper
10 Rear exhaust box
11 Spare wheel cradle retaining catch
12 Jack case
13 Rear brake pressure-regulating valves

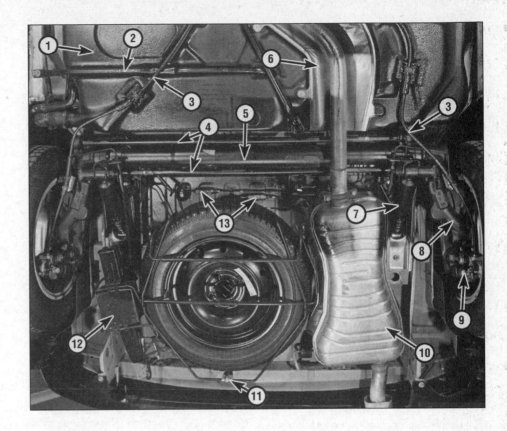

Maintenance procedures

1 Introduction

1 This Chapter is designed to help the home mechanic maintain his/her vehicle for safety, economy, long life and peak performance.
2 The Chapter contains a master maintenance schedule, followed by Sections dealing specifically with each task in the schedule. Visual checks, adjustments, component renewal and other helpful items are included. Refer to the accompanying illustrations of the engine compartment and the underside of the vehicle for the locations of the various components.
3 Servicing your vehicle in accordance with the mileage/time maintenance schedule and the following Sections will provide a planned maintenance programme, which should result in a long and reliable service life. This is a comprehensive plan, so maintaining some items but not others at the specified service intervals, will not produce the same results.

4 As you service your vehicle, you will discover that many of the procedures can - and should - be grouped together, because of the particular procedure being performed, or because of the close proximity of two otherwise-unrelated components to one another. For example, if the vehicle is raised for any reason, the exhaust can be inspected at the same time as the suspension and steering components.
5 The first step in this maintenance programme is to prepare yourself before the actual work begins. Read through all the Sections relevant to the work to be carried out, then make a list and gather together all the parts and tools required. If a problem is encountered, seek advice from a parts specialist, or a dealer service department.

2 Regular maintenance

1 If, from the time the vehicle is new, the routine maintenance schedule is followed

closely and frequent checks are made of fluid levels and high-wear items, as suggested throughout this Manual, the engine will be kept in relatively good running condition and the need for additional work will be minimised.
2 It is possible that there will be times when the engine is running poorly due to the lack of regular maintenance. This is even more likely if a used vehicle, which has not received regular and frequent maintenance checks, is purchased. In such cases, additional work may need to be carried out, outside of the regular maintenance intervals.
3 If engine wear is suspected, a compression or leakdown test will provide valuable information regarding the overall performance of the main internal components. Such a test can be used as a basis to decide on the extent of the work to be carried out. If, for example, a compression or leakdown test indicates serious internal engine wear, conventional maintenance as described in this Chapter will not greatly improve the performance of the engine and may prove a waste of time and money, unless extensive overhaul work is carried out first.

4 The following series of operations are those most often required to improve the performance of a generally poor-running engine:

Primary operations

a) Clean, inspect and test the battery (See Weekly checks).
b) Check the levels of all the engine-related fluids (See Weekly checks).
c) Check the fuel filter - drain off any water, and renew the filter if necessary (Section 10).
d) Check the condition of all hoses, and check for fluid leaks (Section 11).
e) Check and if necessary adjust the idle speed (Section 17).
f) Check the condition and tension of the auxiliary drivebelt (Section 19).
g) Check the condition of the air filter, and renew if necessary (Section 26).

Secondary operations

All items listed under *Primary operations*, plus the following:
a) Check the charging system (Chapter 5).
b) Check the preheating system (Chapter 5).
c) Check the fuel system (Chapter 4).

Every 1000 miles (1500 km) or monthly

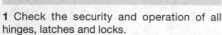

3 Lock, hinge and latch mechanism check

1 Check the security and operation of all hinges, latches and locks.
2 Check the condition and operation of the tailgate struts, renewing them if either is leaking or is no longer able to support the tailgate securely when raised.

4 Seat belt check

1 Check the webbing of each belt for signs of fraying, cuts or other damage, pulling the belt out to its full extent to check its entire length **(see illustration)**. Check the operation of the buckles by fitting the belt tongue plate and pulling hard to ensure that it remains locked, then check the retractor mechanism (inertia reel only) by pulling out the belt to the halfway point and jerking hard. The mechanism must lock immediately to prevent any further unreeling but must allow free movement during normal driving.
2 Ensure that all belt mounting bolts are securely tightened. Note that the bolts are shouldered so that the belt anchor points are free to rotate.
3 If there is any sign of damage, or any doubt about a belt's condition, it must be renewed. If the vehicle has been involved in a collision any belts in use at the time must be renewed

as a matter of course and all other belts should be checked carefully.
4 Use only warm water and non-detergent soap to clean the belts. Never use any chemical cleaners, strong detergents, dyes or bleaches. Keep the belts fully extended until they have dried naturally; do not apply heat to dry them.

5 Brake check

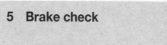

1 Make sure that the vehicle does not pull to one side when braking and that the wheels do not lock prematurely when braking hard.
2 Check that there is no vibration through the steering when braking.
3 Check that the handbrake operates correctly without excessive movement of the lever and that it holds the vehicle stationary on a slope.
4 Check the brake warning device for correct operation by switching the ignition on and releasing the handbrake. Now press the contact on the brake fluid reservoir down and get an assistant to check that the warning lamp on the instrument panel lights up **(see illustration)**.

6 Battery electrolyte level check

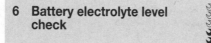

1 A 'maintenance-free' (sealed for life) battery is standard equipment on all vehicles covered

by this manual. Although this type of battery has many advantages over the older refillable type and should never require the addition of distilled water, it should still be routinely checked. On some battery types, the electrolyte level can be seen through the battery's translucent case and must be between the MINIMUM and MAXIMUM level marks. Although it should not alter in normal use, if the level has lowered (for example, due to electrolyte having boiled away as a result of overcharging) it is permissible to gently prise up the cell cover(s) and to top up the level.
2 If a conventional battery has been fitted as a replacement, the electrolyte level of each cell should be checked and, if necessary, topped up until the separators are just covered. On some batteries the case is translucent and incorporates MINIMUM and MAXIMUM level marks. The check should be made more often if the vehicle is operated in high ambient temperature conditions.
3 Top up the electrolyte level using distilled or de-ionized water. If regular topping-up becomes necessary and the battery case is not fractured, the alternator output may be excessive or the battery may be approaching the end of its life.

7 Air conditioning system check

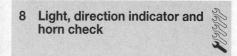

1 During winter months, operate the air conditioner for a few minutes each week to keep the system in good order.
2 Check that the condenser is free of dirt and insects. If necessary, clean it either by rinsing with a cold water hose or by blowing it clean with an air hose. Use a soft bristle brush to assist removal of dirt jammed in the condenser fins.

8 Light, direction indicator and horn check

1 Check that the horn and all vehicle lights are functioning correctly. Renew any defective bulbs.
2 The headlights and (where applicable) the foglights should be in correct alignment.

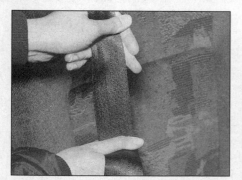

4.1 Checking the webbing of each seat belt for signs of fraying

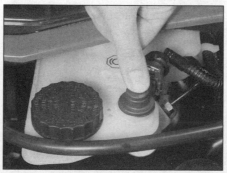

5.4 Checking the brake warning device for correct operation

Every 6000 miles (10 000 km) or 6 months - whichever comes first

9 Engine oil and filter renewal

1 Before starting, gather together all the necessary tools and materials **(see illustration)**. Also ensure that you have plenty of clean rags and newspapers handy to mop up any spills.

2 Ideally, the engine oil should be warm, as it will drain better and more built-up sludge will be removed with it. Take care, however, not to touch the exhaust or any other hot parts of the engine when working under the vehicle. To avoid any possibility of scalding, and to protect yourself from possible skin irritants and other harmful contaminants in used engine oils, it is advisable to wear gloves when draining engine oil. Access to the underside of the vehicle will be greatly improved if it can be raised on a lift, driven onto ramps or jacked up and supported on axle stands (see *Jacking and vehicle support*). Whichever method is chosen, make sure that the vehicle remains level, or if it is at an angle, that the drain plug (located at the rear right-hand corner of the sump) is at the lowest point.

3 Using a suitable square key, slacken the drain plug about half a turn **(see illustration)**. Position the draining container under the drain plug, then remove the plug completely **(see Haynes Hint)**.

4 Allow some time for the old oil to drain, noting that it may be necessary to reposition the container as the oil flow slows to a trickle.

5 After all the oil has drained, wipe off the drain plug with a clean rag. If necessary, renew the drain plug sealing washer. Clean the area around the drain plug opening, and refit the plug. Tighten the plug securely.

6 Move the container into position under the oil filter, which is located at the front right-

9.1 Tools and materials required for engine oil and filter renewal

hand side of the cylinder block, next to the alternator.

7 Using an oil filter removal tool, slacken the filter initially, then unscrew it by hand the rest of the way **(see illustration)**. Empty the oil in the old filter into the container. Check the old oil filter to make sure that the rubber sealing ring hasn't stuck to the engine. If it has, carefully remove it.

8 Use a clean rag to remove all oil, dirt and sludge from the filter sealing area on the engine.

9 Apply a light coating of clean engine oil to the sealing ring on the new filter, then screw it into position on the engine **(see illustration)**. Tighten the filter firmly by hand only - do not use any tools.

10 Remove the old oil and all tools from under the vehicle, then if applicable, lower the vehicle to the ground.

11 Remove the dipstick, then release the clips and remove the oil filler cap from the filler tube at the front of the engine. Fill the engine, using the correct grade and type of oil. An oil can spout or funnel may help to reduce spillage. Pour in half the specified quantity of oil first, then wait a few minutes for the oil to fall to the sump. Continue adding oil, a small quantity at a time, until the level is up to the lower mark on the dipstick. Adding a

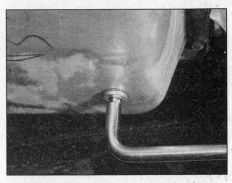

9.3 Slackening the sump drain plug

further 1.5 litres (models without air conditioning) or 1.3 litres (models with air conditioning) will bring the level up to the upper mark on the dipstick.

12 Start the engine and run it for a few minutes while checking for leaks around the oil filter seal and the sump drain plug. Note that there may be a delay of a few seconds before the low oil pressure warning light goes out when the engine is first started, as the oil circulates through the new oil filter and the engine oil galleries before the pressure builds up.

13 Switch off the engine, and wait a few minutes for the oil to settle in the sump once more. With the new oil circulated and the filter now completely full, recheck the level on the dipstick and add more oil as necessary.

14 Dispose of the used engine oil safely.

10 Fuel filter draining

1 A water drain plug and tube are provided at the base of the fuel filter housing.

2 Place a suitable container beneath the drain tube, then cover the clutch bellhousing.

3 Open the drain plug by turning it anti-clockwise. Allow fuel and water to drain until

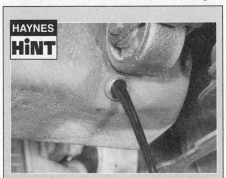

As the drain plug threads release, move it sharply away so the stream of oil issuing from the sump runs into the container, not up your sleeve

9.7 Using an oil filter removal tool to slacken the oil filter

9.9 Lubricate the oil filter sealing ring before fitting

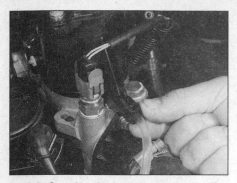

10.3 Opening the fuel filter water drain plug

A leak in the cooling system will usually show up as white- or rust-coloured deposits on the area adjoining the leak

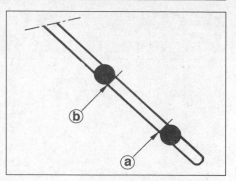

12.2 Automatic transmission fluid dipstick lower (a) and upper (b) fluid level markings

fuel which is free from water, emerges from the end of the tube **(see illustration)**. Close the drain plug.

4 Dispose of the drained fuel safely.

5 Start the engine. If difficulty is experienced, bleed the fuel system.

11 Hose and fluid leak check

1 Inspect the engine joint faces, gaskets and seals for any signs of water or oil leaks. Pay particular attention to the areas around the camshaft cover, cylinder head, oil filter and sump joint faces. Bear in mind that over a period of time, some very slight seepage from these areas is to be expected, but what you are really looking for is any indication of a serious leak. Should a leak be found, renew the offending gasket or oil seal by referring to the appropriate Chapters in this Manual.

2 Also check the security and condition of all engine-related pipes and hoses. Ensure that all cable ties or securing clips are in place and in good condition. Clips which are broken or missing can lead to chafing of the hoses, pipes or wiring, which could cause more serious problems in the future.

3 Carefully check the radiator hoses and heater hoses along their entire length. Renew any hose which is cracked, swollen or deteriorated. Cracks will show up better if the hose is squeezed. Pay close attention to the hose clips that secure the hoses to the cooling system components. Hose clips can pinch and puncture hoses, resulting in cooling system leaks. If wire-type hose clips are used, it may be a good idea to replace them with screw-type clips.

4 Inspect all the cooling system components (hoses, joint faces, etc.) for leaks **(see Haynes Hint)**. A leak in the cooling system will usually show up as white or rust-coloured deposits on the area adjoining the leak. Where any problems of this nature are found on system components, renew the component or gasket.

5 Where applicable, inspect the automatic transmission fluid cooler hoses for leaks or deterioration.

6 With the vehicle raised, inspect the fuel

tank and filler neck for punctures, cracks and other damage. The connection between the filler neck and tank is especially critical. Sometimes a rubber filler neck or connecting hose will leak due to loose retaining clamps or deteriorated rubber.

7 Carefully check all rubber hoses and metal fuel lines leading away from the tank. Check for loose connections, deteriorated hoses, crimped lines and other damage. Pay particular attention to the vent pipes and hoses, which often loop up around the filler neck and can become blocked or crimped. Follow the lines to the front of the vehicle, carefully inspecting them all the way. Renew damaged sections as necessary.

8 From within the engine compartment, check the security of all fuel hose attachments and pipe unions, and inspect the fuel hoses and vacuum hoses for kinks, chafing and deterioration.

9 Where applicable, check the condition of the power steering fluid hoses and pipes.

12 Automatic transmission fluid level check

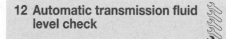

1 Take the vehicle on a short journey to warm the transmission up to normal operating temperature, then park the vehicle on level ground. Leave the engine idling and move the selector lever to the P (PARK) position. The fluid level is checked using the dipstick located at the front of the engine compartment, directly in front of the engine/transmission unit.

2 With the engine idling, move the selector lever through all the gear positions, stopping briefly at each position, then return the selector lever to the P position. With the selector lever returned to the P position, withdraw the dipstick from the tube and wipe all fluid from its end with a clean rag or paper towel. Insert the clean dipstick back into the tube as far as it will go, then withdraw it once more. Note the fluid level on the end of the dipstick. On models with two notches on the dipstick, the level should be between the upper and lower marks **(see illustration)**. On models with three notches on

the dipstick, the level should be between the two upper marks (the marks located on either side of the number 80).

3 If topping-up is necessary, add the required quantity of the specified fluid to the transmission via the dipstick tube. Use a funnel with a fine mesh gauze to avoid spillage and to ensure that no foreign matter enters the transmission. **Note:** *Never overfill the automatic transmission so that the fluid level is above the upper mark on the dipstick.*

4 After topping-up, take the vehicle on a short run to distribute the fresh fluid, then recheck the level again, topping-up if necessary.

5 Always maintain the level between the two dipstick marks. If the level is allowed to fall below the lower mark, fluid starvation may result, which could lead to severe transmission damage.

13 Steering and suspension check

Front suspension and steering

1 Raise the front of the vehicle and securely support it on axle stands.

2 Visually inspect the balljoint dust covers and the steering rack and pinion gaiters for splits, chafing or deterioration **(see illustration)**. Any wear of these components will cause loss of lubricant, together with dirt and water entry, resulting in rapid deterioration of the balljoints or steering gear.

13.2 Checking a steering gear gaiter

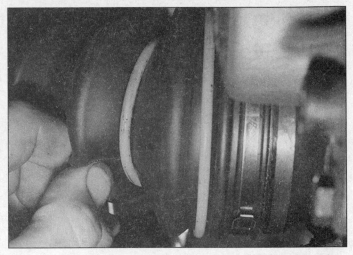

13.4 Rocking the roadwheel to check steering/suspension components

14.1 Checking driveshaft outer constant velocity (CV) joint gaiter

3 On vehicles equipped with power steering, check the fluid hoses for chafing or deterioration and the pipe and hose unions for fluid leaks. Also check for signs of fluid leakage under pressure from the steering gear rubber gaiters, which would indicate failed fluid seals within the steering gear.

4 Grasp the roadwheel at the 12 o'clock and 6 o'clock positions and try to rock it **(see illustration)**. Very slight free play may be felt, but if the movement is appreciable, further investigation is necessary to determine the source. Continue rocking the wheel while an assistant depresses the footbrake. If the movement is now eliminated or significantly reduced, it is likely that the hub bearings are at fault. If the free play is still evident with the footbrake depressed, then there is wear in the suspension joints or mountings.

5 Now grasp the wheel at the 9 o'clock and 3 o'clock positions and try to rock it as before. Any movement felt now may again be caused by wear in the hub bearings or steering track-rod balljoints. If the outer balljoint is worn, the visual movement will be obvious. If the inner joint is suspect, it can be felt by placing a hand over the rack-and-pinion rubber gaiter and gripping the track-rod. If the wheel is now rocked, movement will be felt at the inner joint if wear has taken place.

6 Using a large screwdriver or flat bar, check for wear in the suspension mounting bushes by levering between the relevant suspension component and its attachment point. Some movement is to be expected, as the mountings are made of rubber but excessive wear should be obvious. Also check the condition of any visible rubber bushes, looking for splits, cracks or contamination of the rubber.

7 With the vehicle standing on its wheels, have an assistant turn the steering wheel back and forth about an eighth of a turn each way. There should be very little, if any, lost movement between the steering wheel and roadwheels. If this is not the case, closely observe the joints and mountings previously described but in addition, check the steering column universal joints for wear and also the rack-and-pinion steering gear itself.

Suspension strut/shock absorbers

8 Check for signs of fluid leakage around the suspension strut/shock absorber body, or from the rubber gaiter around the piston rod. Should any fluid be noticed, the suspension strut/shock absorber is defective internally and should be renewed. **Note:** *Suspension struts/shock absorbers must always be renewed in pairs on the same axle.*

9 The efficiency of the suspension strut/shock absorber may be checked by bouncing the vehicle at each corner. Generally speaking, the body will return to its normal position and stop after being depressed. If it rises and returns on a rebound, the suspension strut/shock absorber is probably suspect. Examine also the suspension strut/shock absorber upper and lower mountings for any signs of wear.

14 Driveshaft gaiter check

1 With the vehicle raised and securely supported on stands, turn the steering onto full-lock then slowly rotate the roadwheel. Inspect the condition of the outer constant velocity (CV) joint rubber gaiters while squeezing the gaiters to open out the folds **(see illustration)**. Check for signs of cracking, splits or deterioration of the rubber, which may allow grease to escape and lead to water and grit entry into the joint. Also check the security and condition of the retaining clips.

2 Repeat the above checks on the inner CV joints. If any damage or deterioration is found, then renew the gaiters.

3 At the same time, check the general condition of the CV joints themselves by first holding the driveshaft and attempting to rotate the wheel. Repeat this check by holding the inner joint and attempting to rotate the driveshaft. Any appreciable movement indicates wear in the joints, wear in the driveshaft splines, or a loose driveshaft retaining nut.

15 Front brake pad check

Note: *If the friction material on any one brake pad is worn to the specified thickness or less, then all four pads must be renewed as a set.*

1 Firmly apply the handbrake, then jack up the front of the car and support it securely on axle stands. Remove the front roadwheels.

2 For a comprehensive check, the brake pads should be removed and cleaned. This will permit the operation of the caliper to be checked and the condition of the brake disc itself to be fully examined on both sides. Refer to Chapter 9 for further information **(see Haynes Hint)**.

3 On completion, refit the roadwheels and lower the car to the ground.

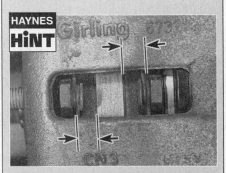

HAYNES HINT

For a quick check, the thickness of friction material remaining on each brake pad can be measured through the aperture in the caliper body

Every 12 000 miles (20 000 km) or 12 months - whichever comes first

16 Air conditioning system refrigerant check

> ⚠ **Warning: Do not attempt to open the air conditioning system refrigerant circuit. Refer to the precautions given in Chapter 3.**

1 In order to check the condition of the refrigerant, a humidity indicator and a sight glass are provided on top of the drier bottle which is located at the front right-hand corner of the engine compartment.

Humidity check

2 Check the colour of the humidity indicator **(see illustration)**. Blue indicates that the condition of the refrigerant is satisfactory. Red indicates that the refrigerant is saturated with humidity. If the indicator shows red, then the system should be drained and recharged and a new drier bottle fitted.

> ⚠ **Warning: The system should be drained and recharged only by a Citroen dealer or air conditioning specialist. Do not attempt to carry out the work yourself, as the refrigerant is a highly-dangerous substance (refer to Chapter 3).**

Flow check

3 Start the engine and switch on the air conditioning.
4 After a few minutes, inspect the sight glass and check the fluid flow. Clear fluid should be visible. If not, the following will help to diagnose the problem:
a) *Clear fluid flow - the system is functioning correctly.*
b) *No fluid flow - have the system checked for leaks by a Citroen dealer or air conditioning specialist.*
c) *Continuous stream of clear air bubbles in*

fluid - refrigerant level low. Have the system recharged by a Citroen dealer or air conditioning specialist.
d) *Milky air bubbles visible - high humidity.*

17 Idle speed and anti-stall speed check and adjustment

1 The usual type of tachometer which works from ignition system pulses cannot be used on Diesel engines. A diagnostic socket is provided for the use of Citroen test equipment but this will not normally be available to the home mechanic. If it is not felt that adjusting the idle speed 'by ear' is satisfactory, one of the following alternatives may be used:
a) *Purchase or hire of an appropriate tachometer.*

b) *Delegation of the job to a Citroen dealer or other specialist.*
2 Before making adjustments, warm-up the engine to normal operating temperature. Ensure that the accelerator cable is correctly adjusted.

Idle speed

3 Check that the engine idles at the specified speed. If necessary, adjust as follows:

Lucas CAV/Roto-Diesel injection pump
4 Loosen the locknut on the idle speed adjustment screw. Turn the screw as required and retighten the locknut **(see illustrations)**.
5 Check the anti-stall adjustment as described later in this Section.
6 Stop the engine and disconnect the tachometer, where applicable.

Bosch injection pump
7 Loosen the locknut, then unscrew the anti-

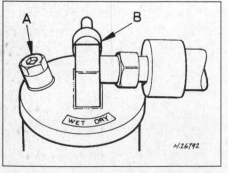

16.2 Air conditioning system refrigerant humidity indicator (A) and sight glass (B)

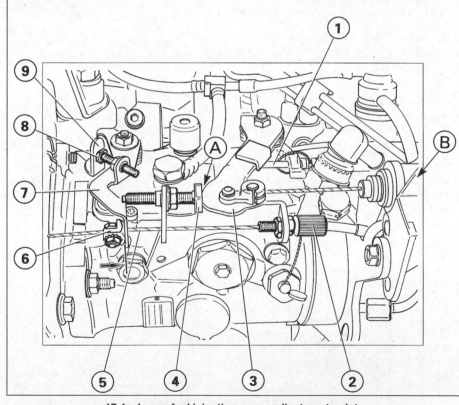

17.4a Lucas fuel injection pump adjustment points

1	*Maximum speed adjustment screw*	7 *Fast idle lever*
2	*Fast idle cable adjustment ferrule*	8 *Idle speed adjustment screw*
3	*Pump control lever*	9 *Manual stop lever*
4	*Anti-stall adjustment screw*	A *Anti-stall adjustment shim location*
5	*Fast idle cable*	B *Accelerator cable adjustment ferrule*
6	*Fast idle cable end fitting*	

17.4b Idle speed adjustment screw (arrowed) - Lucas pump

stall adjustment screw until it is clear of the pump control lever **(see illustrations)**.

8 Loosen the locknut and turn the idle speed adjustment screw as required, then retighten the locknut.

9 Make the anti-stall adjustment as described later in this Section.

10 Stop the engine and disconnect the tachometer, where applicable.

Anti-stall speed

11 Make sure that the engine is at normal operating temperature, then note the idle speed and switch off.

Lucas CAV/Roto-Diesel injection pump

12 Insert a shim or feeler blade of the specified thickness between the pump control lever and the anti-stall adjustment screw.

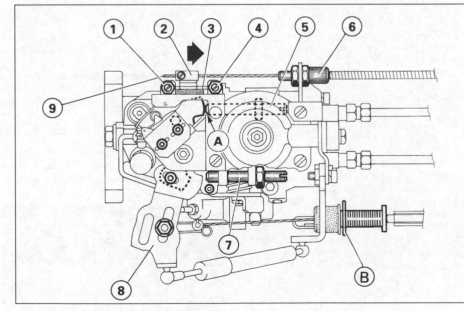

17.7a Bosch fuel injection pump adjustment points - non-turbo engines

1 Fast idle lever stop screw	7 Maximum speed adjustment screw
2 Fast idle cable end fitting	8 Pump control lever
3 Fast idle lever	9 Fast idle cable
4 Idle speed adjustment screw	A Anti-stall adjustment shim location
5 Anti-stall speed adjustment screw	B Accelerator cable adjustment ferrule
6 Fast idle cable adjustment ferrule	

13 Start the engine and allow it to idle. The engine speed should be as specified for the anti-stall speed.

14 If adjustment is necessary, loosen the locknut, turn the anti-stall adjustment screw as required, then tighten the locknut **(see illustration)**.

15 Remove the shim or feeler blade and check the idle speed as described previously.

16 Move the pump control lever to increase the engine speed to approximately 3000 rpm, then quickly release the lever. The deceleration period should be between 2.5 and 3.5 seconds and the engine speed should drop to approximately 50 rpm below idle.

17.7b Bosch fuel injection pump adjustment points - turbo engines

1 Fast idle lever stop screw	7 Maximum speed adjustment screw
2 Fast idle lever cable end fitting	8 Pump control lever
3 Fast idle lever	9 Fast idle cable
4 Idle speed adjustment screw	A Anti-stall adjustment shim location
5 Anti-stall speed adjustment screw	B Accelerator cable adjustment ferrule
6 Fast idle cable adjustment ferrule	

17.14 Anti-stall adjustment screw (arrowed) - Lucas pump

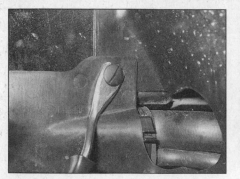

19.5a Release the securing clips . . .

19.5b . . . and remove the lower wheel arch cover . . .

19.5c . . . then unclip the coolant hoses

17 If deceleration is too fast and the engine stalls, unscrew the anti-stall adjustment screw a quarter-turn towards the control lever. If deceleration is too slow, resulting in poor engine braking, turn the screw a quarter-turn away from the lever.

18 Retighten the locknut after making an adjustment. Recheck the idle speed and adjust if necessary, as described previously.

19 With the engine idling, check the operation of the manual stop control by turning the stop lever clockwise. The engine must stop instantly.

20 Where applicable, disconnect the tachometer on completion.

Bosch injection pump

21 Insert a shim or feeler blade of the specified thickness between the pump control lever and the anti-stall adjustment screw.

22 Start the engine and allow it to idle. The engine speed should be as specified for the anti-stall speed.

23 If adjustment is necessary, loosen the locknut and turn the anti-stall adjustment screw as required. Retighten the locknut.

24 Remove the shim or feeler blade and allow the engine to idle.

25 Move the fast idle lever fully towards the flywheel end of the engine and check that the engine speed increases to the specified fast idle speed. If necessary, loosen the locknut and turn the fast idle adjusting screw as required, then retighten the locknut.

26 With the engine idling, check the operation of the manual stop control by turning the stop lever. The engine must stop instantly.

27 Where applicable, disconnect the tachometer on completion.

18 Emission control system check

1 Details of emission control system components are given in Chapter 4.

2 Checking consists simply of inspecting the system for obvious signs of damaged or leaking hoses and joints.

3 The catalytic converter should be examined for damage or corrosion and renewed if necessary.

4 Where applicable, detailed testing of the exhaust gas recirculation system and/or atmospheric pressure correction system should be entrusted to a Citroen dealer.

19 Auxiliary drivebelt check and renewal

Checking

1 On manual transmission models, select 4th or 5th gear to enable the crankshaft to be turned. On automatic transmission models, the crankshaft must be turned using a spanner on the crankshaft pulley bolt.

2 To improve access to the belt, proceed as follows.

3 Apply the handbrake. Jack up the right-hand front corner of the vehicle and support securely on an axle stand.

4 Remove the roadwheel.

5 Remove the lower wheel arch liner, then unclip the coolant hoses from the wing panel **(see illustrations)**. Lower the coolant hoses clear of the pulleys.

6 The belt should be inspected along its entire length. If the belt is found to be worn, frayed, or cracked, then it should be renewed. It is advisable to carry a spare drivebelt of the correct type in the vehicle at all times.

7 To view the entire length of the belt, it will be necessary to turn the crankshaft. This can be achieved by turning the driveshaft via the brake disc (manual transmission models) or by using a spanner on the crankshaft pulley (automatic transmission models).

8 If the condition of the belt is satisfactory, clip the coolant hoses into position then refit the wheel arch cover and roadwheel. On completion, lower the vehicle to the ground.

Renewal - models without power steering or air conditioning

Removal

9 If not already done, proceed as described in paragraphs 2 to 5.

10 Disconnect the battery negative lead.

11 Slacken the upper alternator mounting nut **(see illustration)**.

12 Back off the adjuster bolt to relieve the tension in the drivebelt, then slip the drivebelt from the pulleys.

Refitting

13 Fit the belt around the pulleys, ensuring that the belt is of the correct type if it is being renewed. Take up the slack in the belt by tightening the adjuster bolt.

14 Tension the drivebelt as described in the following paragraphs.

Tensioning

15 If not already done, proceed as described in paragraphs 2 to 5.

16 Correct tensioning of the drivebelt will ensure that it has a long life. Beware of overtightening, as this can cause excessive wear in the alternator.

17 The belt should be tensioned so that there is approximately 5.0 mm of movement under firm thumb pressure at the mid-point of the belt run between the pulleys.

18 With the upper mounting nut just holding the alternator firm, and the adjuster bolt loosened, turn the adjuster bolt until the correct tension is achieved, then tighten the upper mounting nut.

19 Reconnect the battery negative lead.

20 Clip the coolant hoses into position, refit the wheel arch liner and roadwheel, then lower the vehicle to the ground.

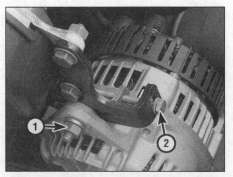

19.11 Alternator upper mounting nut (1) and adjuster bolt (2)

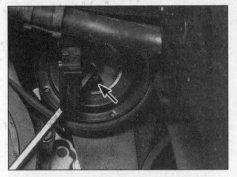

19.23 Slacken the two tensioner roller lockscrews (arrowed)

19.24a Turn the tensioner roller adjuster bolt . . .

19.24b . . . until the belt can be removed from the pulleys

Renewal - models with power steering or air conditioning

Removal

21 If not already done, proceed as described in paragraphs 2 to 5.

22 Disconnect the battery negative lead.

23 Slacken the two lockscrews securing the tensioner roller assembly **(see illustration)**.

24 Turn the tensioner roller adjuster bolt to move the tensioner roller assembly until the drivebelt can be removed from the pulleys **(see illustrations)**.

Refitting and tensioning

25 Fit the drivebelt around the pulleys in the following order:

a) *Power steering pump/air conditioning compressor.*
b) *Crankshaft.*
c) *Alternator.*
d) *Tensioner roller.*

26 Ensure that the ribs on the belt are correctly engaged with the grooves in the pulleys.

27 Tension the drivebelt by turning the tensioner roller adjuster screw, until the belt can be twisted through approximately 90° under firm thumb and finger pressure at the mid-point of the belt run between the power steering pump/air conditioning compressor and crankshaft pulleys **(see illustration)**.

28 Tighten the two lockscrews securing the tensioner roller.

19.27 It should be possible to twist the belt through 90°

29 Reconnect the battery negative lead.

30 Clip the coolant hoses into position, refit the wheel arch liner and roadwheel, then lower the vehicle to the ground.

Renewal - models with power steering and air conditioning

Note: *If a broken drivebelt is to be renewed, refer to paragraphs 47 and 48.*

Removal

31 If not already done, proceed as described in paragraphs 2 to 5.

32 Disconnect the battery negative lead.

33 Remove the upper securing screw from the power steering pump pulley shield. Push the shield to one side, to allow access to the drivebelt.

34 Slacken the two lockscrews securing the manual tensioner roller **(see illustration)**.

35 Tighten the manual tensioner roller adjuster screw until the holes in the automatic tensioner roller bracket and the power steering pump bracket are aligned.

36 Lock the automatic tensioner roller in

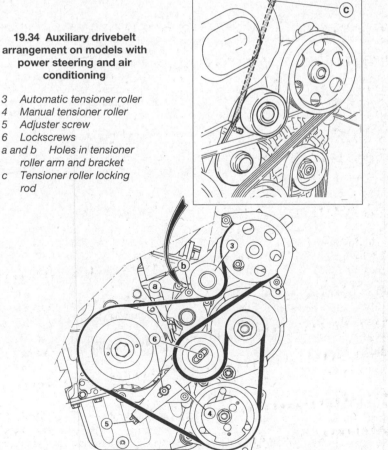

19.34 Auxiliary drivebelt arrangement on models with power steering and air conditioning

3   *Automatic tensioner roller*
4   *Manual tensioner roller*
5   *Adjuster screw*
6   *Lockscrews*
a and b   *Holes in tensioner roller arm and bracket*
c   *Tensioner roller locking rod*

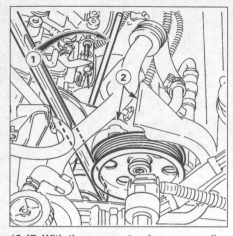

19.47 With the power steering pump pulley cover moved aside (2), lever the tensioner roller away from the power steering pump pulley (1)

position by inserting a suitable rod (such as a twist drill) through the holes in the automatic tensioner roller arm and the bracket.

37 Slacken the manual tensioner roller adjuster screw until the drivebelt can be removed from the pulleys.

Refitting and tensioning

38 Fit the drivebelt around the pulleys in the following order:
 a) Power steering pump.
 b) Automatic tensioner roller.
 c) Crankshaft.
 d) Air conditioning compressor.
 e) Alternator.
 f) Manual tensioner roller.
39 Ensure that the ribs on the belt are correctly engaged with the grooves in the pulleys.
40 Tension the drivebelt by turning the manual tensioner roller adjuster screw, until the rod inserted in paragraph 36 begins to slide.
41 Remove the rod from the holes in the automatic tensioner roller arm and the bracket.
42 Tighten the two lockscrews securing the manual tensioner roller.
43 Move the power steering pump pulley shield back into position, then refit the upper securing screw.
44 Reconnect the battery negative lead.
45 Clip the coolant hoses into position, refit the wheel arch liner and roadwheel, then lower the vehicle to the ground.

Renewing a broken drivebelt

46 Proceed as described in paragraphs 31 to 34.
47 Insert a lever between the power steering pump pulley and the automatic tensioner roller, as shown **(see illustration)**.
48 Carefully lever the tensioner roller away from the power steering pump pulley until a suitable rod can be inserted through

the holes in the automatic tensioner roller arm and the bracket, as described in paragraph 36.
49 Proceed as described in paragraphs 38 to 45 inclusive.

20 Brake servo vacuum pump drivebelt check and renewal

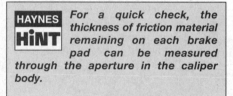

⚠ *Warning: Breakage of the brake servo vacuum pump drivebelt in service will lead to a loss of servo assistance, which will greatly reduce the efficiency of the braking system and possibly lead to an accident.*

Checking

1 Inspect the entire length of the drivebelt for signs of wear or damage. If the belt is found to be worn, frayed, or cracked, then it should be renewed.

Renewal

2 Slacken the pump adjuster bolt, pivot bolt and the adjuster strap lower mounting nut, then unhook the drivebelt from the pump pulley and remove it from the engine.
3 Locate the new drivebelt over the camshaft drive pulley and the pump pulley.
4 Tension the drivebelt by pivoting the pump around its mounting until the deflection of the drivebelt, midway between the pulleys, is approximately 3.0 mm under firm thumb or finger pressure. Holding the pump in this position, securely tighten the adjuster strap nut, and the pump pivot and adjuster bolts. Recheck the drivebelt tension, and if necessary re-adjust.

21 Clutch adjustment check

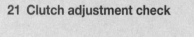

1 Check that the clutch pedal moves smoothly and easily through its full travel and that the clutch itself functions correctly, with no trace of slip or drag.
2 Adjust the clutch cable as described in Chapter 6.

22 Clutch control mechanism lubrication

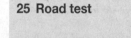

1 If excessive effort is required to operate the clutch, check first that the cable is correctly routed and undamaged, then remove the pedal to ensure that its pivot is properly greased.

23 Rear brake shoe check

1 Remove the rear brake drums and check the brake shoes for signs of wear or contamination. At the same time, inspect the wheel cylinders for signs of leakage and the brake drum for signs of wear. Refer to the relevant Sections of Chapter 9 for further information.

24 Rear brake pad check

Note: *If the friction material on any one brake pad is worn to the specified thickness or less, then all four pads must be renewed as a set.*
1 Chock the front wheels, then jack up the rear of the car and support it securely on axle stands. Remove the rear roadwheels.

HAYNES HiNT *For a quick check, the thickness of friction material remaining on each brake pad can be measured through the aperture in the caliper body.*

2 For a comprehensive check, the brake pads should be removed and cleaned. This will permit the operation of the caliper to be checked and the condition of the brake disc itself to be fully examined on both sides. Refer to Chapter 9 for further information.
3 On completion, refit the roadwheels and lower the car to the ground.

25 Road test

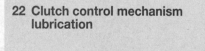

Instruments and electrical equipment

1 Check the operation of all instruments and electrical equipment.
2 Ensure all instruments read correctly and switch on all electrical equipment in turn to check that it functions properly.

Steering and suspension

3 Check for any abnormalities in the steering, suspension, handling or road feel.
4 Drive the vehicle and check that there are no unusual vibrations or noises.
5 Check that the steering feels positive with no excessive sloppiness or roughness, then check for any suspension noises when cornering and driving over bumps.

Drivetrain

6 Check the performance of the engine, clutch, transmission and driveshafts.

7 Listen for any unusual noises from the engine, clutch and transmission.

8 Make sure that the engine runs smoothly when idling and that there is no hesitation when accelerating.

9 Check that the clutch action is smooth and progressive, that the drive is taken up smoothly and that the pedal travel is not excessive. Also listen for any noises when the clutch pedal is depressed.

10 On manual transmission models, check that all gears can be engaged smoothly without noise and that the gear lever action is not abnormally vague or notchy.

11 On automatic transmission models, ensure that all gearchanges occur smoothly without snatching and without an increase in engine speed between changes. Check that all the gear positions can be selected with the vehicle at rest. If any problems are found, refer to a Citroen dealer.

12 Listen for a metallic clicking sound from the front of the vehicle, as the vehicle is driven slowly in a circle with the steering on full-lock. Carry out this check in both directions. If a clicking noise is heard, this indicates wear in a driveshaft joint which should then be renewed.

Braking system

13 Make sure that the vehicle does not pull to one side when braking and that the wheels do not lock prematurely when braking hard.

14 Check that there is no vibration through the steering when braking.

15 Check that the handbrake operates correctly without excessive movement of the lever and that it holds the vehicle stationary on a slope.

16 Test the operation of the brake servo unit as follows. Depress the footbrake four or five times to exhaust the vacuum, then start the engine. As the engine starts, there should be a noticeable give in the brake pedal as vacuum builds up. Allow the engine to run for at least two minutes and then switch it off. If the brake pedal is now depressed again, it should be possible to detect a hiss from the servo as the pedal is depressed. After about four or five applications, no further hissing should be heard and the pedal should feel considerably firmer.

Every 18 000 miles (30 000 km) or 18 months - whichever comes first

26 Air filter renewal

Non-turbo models

1 Release the clips securing the cover to the air cleaner casing (see illustration).

2 Lift off the cover, then lift out the air filter (see illustrations).

3 Refitting is a reversal of removal.

Turbo models

4 Access to the air filter is obtained from under the front of the vehicle.

5 Release the three securing clips and remove the cover from the base of the air cleaner housing (see illustration).

6 Withdraw the filter from the housing (see illustration).

7 Refitting is a reversal of removal.

26.1 Release the clips securing the air cleaner cover . . .

26.2a . . . then lift off the cover . . .

26.2b . . . and withdraw the air filter

26.5 Air cleaner cover securing clips (arrowed) - turbo models

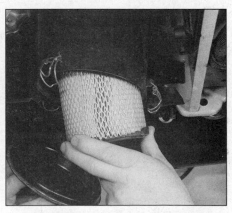

26.6 Withdrawing the air filter - turbo models

27 Fuel filter renewal

1 The fuel filter is located in a plastic housing at the front of the engine.
2 Where applicable, cover the clutch bellhousing with a piece of plastic sheeting to protect the clutch from fuel spillage.
3 Position a suitable container under the end of the fuel filter drain hose. Open the drain screw on the front of the filter housing and allow the fuel to drain completely.
4 Using a suitable Allen key or hexagon bit, remove the four filter housing cover securing screws, then lift off the cover **(see illustration)**.
5 Lift the filter from the housing **(see illustration)**.
6 Place the new filter in the housing.
7 Coat the threads of the filter cover securing bolts with thread-locking compound, then refit the cover and secure with the bolts.
8 Close the fuel filter drain screw.
9 Prime the fuel system as described in Chapter 4.
10 Open the drain screw until clean fuel flows

27.4 Lift off the fuel filter cover . . .

27.5 . . . then lift the filter from the housing

from the hose, then close the drain screw and withdraw the container from under the hose.

28 Hinge and lock lubrication

1 Work around the vehicle and lubricate the hinges of the bonnet, doors and tailgate with a light machine oil.

2 Lightly lubricate the bonnet release mechanism and exposed section of inner cable with a smear of grease.
3 Check carefully the security and operation of all hinges, latches and locks, adjusting them where required. Check the operation of the central locking system (if fitted).
4 Check the condition and operation of the tailgate struts, renewing them if either is leaking or no longer able to support the tailgate securely when raised.

Every 24 000 miles (40 000 km) or 2 years - whichever comes first

29 Manual transmission oil level check

1 Park the vehicle on a level surface. The oil level must be checked before the vehicle is driven; or at least 5 minutes after the engine has been switched off. If the oil is checked immediately after driving the vehicle, some of the oil will remain distributed around the transmission components, resulting in an inaccurate level reading.
2 Prise out the three retaining clips and remove the small access cover from the left-hand wheel arch liner **(see illustration)**.

3 Wipe clean the area around the filler/level plug, which is the largest bolt among those securing the end cover to the transmission. Unscrew the plug and clean it. Discard the sealing washer **(see illustration)**.
4 The oil level should reach the lower edge of the filler/level hole. A certain amount of oil will have gathered behind the filler/level plug and will trickle out when it is removed, this does not necessarily indicate that the level is correct. To ensure that a true level is established, wait until the initial trickle has stopped, then add oil as necessary until a trickle of new oil can be seen emerging. The level will be correct when the flow ceases. Use only good-quality oil of the specified type.

5 Refilling the transmission is an extremely awkward operation. Allow plenty of time for the oil level to settle properly before checking it. If a large amount had to be added to the transmission and a large amount flows out on checking the level, refit the filler/level plug and take the vehicle on a short journey so that the new oil is distributed fully around the transmission components, then recheck the level when it has settled again **(see illustration)**.
6 If the transmission has been overfilled so that oil flows out as soon as the filler/level plug is removed, check that the vehicle is completely level (front to rear and side to side) and allow the surplus to drain off into a suitable container.

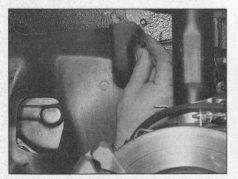

29.2 Removing the access cover from the left-hand wheel arch liner

29.3 Removing the manual transmission filler/level plug

29.5 Topping-up the manual transmission oil level

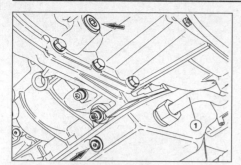

30.3 Automatic transmission fluid drain plugs (arrowed). Transmission is refilled via the dipstick tube (1)

7 When the level is correct, fit a new sealing washer and refit the filler/level plug, tightening it to the specified torque wrench setting. Wash off any spilt oil. Refit the access cover to the wheel arch liner, and secure it in position with its retaining clips.

30 Automatic transmission fluid renewal

1 Take the vehicle on a short run, to warm the transmission up to normal operating temperature.
2 Park the vehicle on level ground, switch off the ignition and apply the handbrake firmly. For improved access, jack up the front of the vehicle and support it securely on axle stands. Note that the vehicle must be lowered to the ground and be level, to ensure accuracy when refilling and checking the fluid level.
3 Remove the dipstick, then position a suitable container under the transmission. The transmission has two drain plugs, one on the sump and another on the bottom of the differential housing **(see illustration)**.

> **Warning: If the fluid is hot, take precautions against scalding.**

4 Unscrew both drain plugs and allow the fluid to drain completely into the container. Clean the drain plugs, being especially careful to wipe any metallic particles off the magnetic insert. Discard the original sealing washers which should be renewed whenever they are disturbed.
5 When the fluid has finished draining, clean the drain plug threads and those of the transmission casing, fit a new sealing washer to each drain plug and refit them to the transmission, tightening each securely. If the vehicle was raised for the draining operation, lower it to the ground.
6 Refilling the transmission is an extremely awkward operation, adding the specified type of fluid to the transmission a little at a time via the dipstick tube. Use a funnel with a fine mesh gauze, to avoid spillage and to ensure that no foreign matter enters the transmission. Allow plenty of time for the fluid level to settle properly before checking. Note that the vehicle must be parked on flat level ground when checking the fluid level.
7 Once the level is up to the MAX mark on the dipstick, refit the dipstick then start the engine and allow it to idle for a few minutes. Switch the engine off and recheck the level, topping-up if necessary. Take the vehicle on a short run to fully distribute the new fluid around the transmission, then recheck the fluid level.

31 Brake fluid renewal

> **Warning: Brake hydraulic fluid can harm your eyes and damage painted surfaces, so use extreme caution when handling**

it. Do not use fluid from a container that has been standing open for some time, as the fluid absorbs moisture from the air. Excess moisture can cause a dangerous loss of braking effectiveness.

1 This procedure is similar to that for bleeding the hydraulic system as described in Chapter 9, except that the brake fluid reservoir should be emptied by syphoning, using a clean poultry baster or similar before starting and allowance should be made for the old fluid to be expelled when bleeding a section of the circuit.
2 Working as described in Chapter 9, open the first bleed nipple in the sequence and pump the brake pedal gently until nearly all the old fluid has been emptied from the master cylinder reservoir. Top-up to the MAX level with new fluid. Continue pumping until only the new fluid remains in the reservoir and new fluid can be seen emerging from the bleed nipple. Tighten the nipple and top the reservoir level up to the MAX level line.

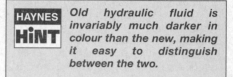

> **HAYNES HiNT** *Old hydraulic fluid is invariably much darker in colour than the new, making it easy to distinguish between the two.*

3 Work through all the remaining nipples in the sequence until new fluid can be seen at all of them. Be careful to keep the master cylinder reservoir topped-up to above the MIN level at all times, or air may enter the system and greatly increase the length of the task.
4 When the operation is complete, check that all nipples are securely tightened and that their dust caps are refitted. Wash off all traces of spilt fluid and recheck the master cylinder reservoir fluid level.
5 Check the operation of the brakes before taking the vehicle on the road.

Every 40 000 miles (60 000 km) or 2 years - whichever comes first

32 Coolant renewal

> **Warning: Wait until the engine is cold before starting this procedure. Do not allow antifreeze to come in contact with your skin or painted surfaces of the vehicle. Rinse off spills immediately with plenty of water. Never leave antifreeze lying around in an open container, or in a puddle in the driveway or on the garage floor. Children and pets are attracted by its sweet smell and antifreeze can be fatal if ingested.**

Draining

1 To drain the cooling system, remove the expansion tank filler cap. Turn the cap anti-clockwise until it reaches the first stop. Wait until any pressure remaining in the system is released then push the cap down, turn it anti-clockwise to the second stop and lift it off.
2 Position a suitable container beneath the coolant drain outlet at the lower left-hand side of the radiator. If desired, a suitable length of tubing can be attached to the outlet, to direct the flow of coolant **(see illustration)**.
3 Loosen the drain plug (there is no need to remove it completely) and allow the coolant to drain into the container.

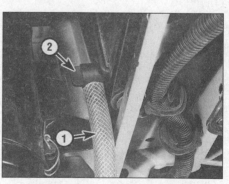

32.2 Tubing (1) attached to radiator coolant drain outlet. Drain plug (2)

32.4a Removing the radiator bleed screw

32.4b Removing the fuel filter/thermostat housing hose bleed screw

32.4c Removing the heater hose bleed screw

4 To assist draining, open the three cooling system bleed screws or caps which are located as follows:

a) At the top left-hand corner of the radiator **(see illustration)**.

b) In the coolant hose running to the top of the fuel filter/thermostat housing **(see illustration)**.

c) In the heater outlet hose (this bleed screw may be located in a bleeder extension hose to aid access) **(see illustration)**.

5 When the flow of coolant stops, reposition the container below the cylinder block drain plug, located on the rear of the cylinder block.

6 Remove the drain plug and allow the coolant to drain into the container **(see illustration)**.

7 If the coolant has been drained for a reason other than renewal, then provided it is clean and less than two years old, it can be re-used.

Flushing

8 If coolant renewal has been neglected, or if the antifreeze mixture has become diluted, then in time, the cooling system may gradually lose efficiency as the coolant passages become restricted due to rust, scale deposits and other sediment. The cooling system efficiency can be restored by flushing the system clean.

9 The radiator should be flushed independently of the engine, to avoid unnecessary contamination.

Radiator

10 To flush the radiator, first tighten the radiator drain plug and the radiator bleed screw.

11 Disconnect the top and bottom hoses from the radiator. It is only necessary to disconnect the larger radiator bottom hose.

12 Insert a garden hose into the radiator top inlet. Direct a flow of clean water through the radiator and continue flushing until clean water emerges from the radiator bottom outlet.

13 If after a reasonable period the water still does not run clear, the radiator can be flushed with a good proprietary cleaning agent. It is important that the cleaning agent manufacturer's instructions are followed

carefully. If the contamination is particularly bad, insert the hose in the radiator bottom outlet and flush the radiator in the reverse direction.

Engine

14 To flush the engine, first refit the cylinder block drain plug and tighten the cooling system bleed screws.

15 Remove the thermostat, then temporarily refit the thermostat cover.

16 With the top and bottom hoses disconnected from the radiator, insert a garden hose into the radiator top hose. Direct a clean flow of water through the engine and continue flushing until clean water emerges from the radiator bottom hose.

17 On completion of flushing, refit the thermostat and reconnect the hoses. Note that a new sealing ring should be used when reconnecting the radiator bottom hose.

Filling

18 Before attempting to fill the cooling system, ensure that all hoses and clips are in good condition and that the clips are tight. Note that an antifreeze mixture must be used all year round to prevent corrosion of the engine components. Also check that the radiator and cylinder block drain plugs are in place and tight.

19 Remove the expansion tank filler cap.

20 Open the three cooling system bleed screws.

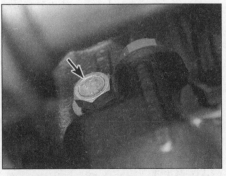

32.6 Cylinder block drain plug (arrowed)

21 Some of the cooling system hoses are positioned at a higher level than the top of the radiator expansion tank. It is therefore necessary to use a header tank when refilling the cooling system, to reduce the possibility of air being trapped in the system.

HAYNES HiNT

O-ring (1) fitted to improvised "header tank". Note clamped breather hose (2)

Although Citroen dealers use a special header tank when refilling the system, the same effect can be achieved by using a suitable bottle with a seal between the bottle and the expansion tank.

22 Clamp the expansion tank breather hose, then fit the header tank to the expansion tank and slowly fill the system **(see illustration)**. As soon as coolant free from air bubbles emerges from all three bleed screw locations,

32.22 Filing the cooling system using an improvised 'header tank'

tighten the bleed screws in the following order:
a) *Radiator.*
b) *Fuel filter/thermostat housing hose.*
c) *Heater hose.*

23 Start the engine and run it at a fast idle speed (do not exceed 2000 rpm) until the cooling fans cut in.

24 Remove the header tank, then fit the expansion tank cap.

25 Stop the engine and allow it to cool.

26 Check the coolant level, which should be up to the MAX mark on the side of the expansion tank. Top-up the level if necessary.

Antifreeze mixture

27 Antifreeze should always be renewed at the specified intervals. This is necessary not only to maintain the antifreeze properties but also to prevent corrosion, which would otherwise occur as the corrosion inhibitors become progressively less effective.

28 Always use an ethylene-glycol based antifreeze which is suitable for use in mixed-metal cooling systems. Refer to Specifications for the antifreeze mixture and level of protection.

29 Before adding antifreeze, the cooling system should be completely drained, preferably flushed and all hoses checked for condition and security.

30 After filling with antifreeze, a label should be attached to the expansion tank, stating the type and concentration of antifreeze used and the date installed. Any subsequent topping-up should be made with the same type and concentration of antifreeze.

Every 48 000 miles (80 000 km)

33 Timing belt renewal

Refer to Chapter 2A, Section 7.

Every 72 000 miles (116 000 km)

34 Manual transmission oil renewal

1 This operation is much quicker and more efficient if the vehicle is first taken on a journey of sufficient length to warm the transmission up to normal operating temperature.

34.5 Removing the manual transmission drain plug

2 Park the vehicle on level ground, switch off the ignition and apply the handbrake firmly. For improved access, jack up the front of the vehicle and support it securely on axle stands. Note that the vehicle must be lowered to the ground and be level, to ensure accuracy when refilling and checking the oil level.

3 Prise out the three retaining clips and remove the small access cover from the left-hand wheel arch liner.

4 Wipe clean the area around the filler/level plug, which is the largest bolt among those securing the end cover to the transmission, then unscrew the plug from the transmission.

5 Position a suitable container under the drain plug situated at the rear of the transmission, on the base of the differential housing, and unscrew the plug **(see illustration)**.

6 Allow the oil to drain completely into the container. If the oil is hot, take precautions against scalding. Clean both the filler/level and the drain plugs, being especially careful to wipe any metallic particles off the magnetic inserts. Discard the original sealing washers which should be renewed whenever they are disturbed.

7 When the oil has finished draining, clean the drain plug threads and those of the transmission casing. Fit a new sealing washer and refit the drain plug, tightening it to the specified torque wrench setting. If the vehicle was raised for the draining operation, now lower it to the ground.

8 Refilling the transmission is an extremely awkward operation. Above all, allow plenty of time for the oil level to settle properly before checking it. Note that the vehicle must be parked on flat level ground when checking the oil level.

9 Refill the transmission with the exact amount of the specified type of oil, then check the oil level. If the correct amount was poured into the transmission and a large amount flows out on checking the level, refit the filler/level plug and take the vehicle on a short journey so that the new oil is distributed fully around the transmission components, then check the level again on your return.

10 Once the level is correct, refit the access cover to the wheel arch liner, securing it in position with its retaining clips.

Notes

Chapter 2 Part A:
In-car engine repair procedures

Contents

Camshaft - removal, inspection and refitting	11
Camshaft cover - removal and refitting	4
Compression and leakdown tests - description and interpretation	2
Crankshaft pulley - removal and refitting	5
Cylinder head - removal and refitting	13
Engine oil and filter renewal	See Chapter 1
Engine oil level check	See "Weekly checks"
Engine/transmission mountings - removal and refitting	19
Flywheel/driveplate - removal, inspection and refitting	18
General information	1
Oil cooler - removal and refitting	20
Oil level, temperature and pressure sensors - general	17
Oil pump - removal, inspection and refitting	15
Oil seals - renewal	16
Right-hand engine mounting and timing belt tensioner - removal and refitting	9
Sump - removal and refitting	14
Timing belt - removal, inspection, refitting and tensioning	7
Timing belt covers - removal and refitting	6
Timing belt idler roller - removal and refitting	10
Timing belt sprockets - removal and refitting	8
Top dead centre (TDC) for No 1 piston - locating	3
Valve clearances - checking and adjustment	12

Degrees of difficulty

Easy, suitable for novice with little experience	**Fairly easy,** suitable for beginner with some experience	**Fairly difficult,** suitable for competent DIY mechanic	**Difficult,** suitable for experienced DIY mechanic	**Very difficult,** suitable for expert DIY or professional

Specifications

General

Engine type .... Four-cylinder in-line, water-cooled. Single belt-driven overhead camshaft, acting on bucket tappets

Manufacturer's codes:
1.7 litre non-turbo engine	XUD7 **(A9A)**
1.9 litre non-turbo non-catalyst engine (up to 1993)	XUD9A **(D9B)**
1.9 litre non-turbo non-catalyst engine (from 1993)	XUD9A/L **(D9B)**
1.9 litre non-turbo catalyst engine	XUD9/Y **(DJZ)**
1.9 litre turbo non-catalyst engine	XUD9TE/L **(D8A)**
1.9 litre turbo catalyst engine	XUD9TE/Y **(DHY or DHZ)**

No 1 cylinder location .... Flywheel end
Direction of crankshaft rotation .... Anti-clockwise (viewed from flywheel end)
Firing order .... 1-3-4-2 (No 1 at flywheel end)
Capacity:
1.7 litre engine	1769 cc
1.9 litre engines	1905 cc

Bore:
1.7 litre engine	80.0 mm
1.9 litre engines	83.0 mm

Stroke (all engines) .... 88.0 mm
Compression ratio:
A9A and D9B engines	23.0:1
DJZ engine	23.5:1
D8A, DHY and DHZ engines	21.8:1

Maximum power (DIN):
A9A engine	60 hp (44 kW) at 4600 rpm
D9B engine	71 hp (52 kW) at 4600 rpm
DJZ engine	65 hp (48 kW) at 4600 rpm
D8A engine	92 hp (68 kW) at 4000 rpm
DHY and DHZ engines	90 hp (66 kW) at 4000 rpm

Maximum torque (DIN):
A9A engine	112 Nm (83 lbf ft) at 2000 rpm
D9B engine	123 Nm (91 lbf ft) at 2000 rpm
DJZ engine	120 Nm (88 lbf ft) at 2000 rpm
D8A, DHY and DHZ engines	201 Nm (148 lbf ft) at 2250 rpm

Compression pressures (engine hot, at cranking speed)
Normal . . . . 25 to 30 bars (363 to 435 psi)
Minimum . . . . 18 bars (261 psi)
Maximum difference between any two cylinders . . . . 5 bars (73 psi)

Camshaft
Endfloat . . . . 0.07 to 0.16 mm

Valve clearances (engine cold)
Inlet (all engines) . . . . 0.15 ± 0.05 mm
Exhaust (all engines) . . . . 0.30 ± 0.05 mm

Oil pump
Type . . . . Two-gear
Pressure relief valve opens . . . . 4.0 bars (58 psi)
Gear endfloat . . . . 0.12 mm
Clearance between gear lobes and housing . . . . 0.064 mm

Torque wrench settings

	Nm	lbf ft
Camshaft cover bolts	20	15
Crankshaft pulley bolt*:		
Stage 1	40	30
Stage 2	Tighten through a further 50°	
Timing belt cover bolts	8	6
Timing belt tensioner adjustment bolt	18	13
Timing belt tensioner pivot nut	18	13
Camshaft sprocket bolt	35	26
Injection pump sprocket "puller" securing screws	10	7
Injection pump sprocket "puller" nut	50	37
Right-hand engine mounting-to-engine mounting bracket nuts	45	33
Right-hand engine mounting-to-body nut	40	30
Right-hand engine mounting bracket-to-engine bolts	18	13
Left-hand transmission mounting-to-transmission nut	80	59
Left-hand transmission mounting-to-body bolts	25	18
Lower engine/transmission mounting horizontal bracket nuts and bolts	50	37
Brake vacuum pump drive pulley bolt	35	26
Camshaft bearing cap nuts	20	15
Cylinder head bolts***:		
Non-turbo models (1992):		
Stage 1	70	52
Stage 2	Tighten through a further 140°	
Non-turbo models (1993-on):		
Stage 1	20	15
Stage 2	60	44
Stage 3	Angle tighten a further 180°	
Turbo models:		
Stage 1	20	15
Stage 2	60	44
Stage 3	Tighten through a further 220°	
Sump bolts	19	14
Oil pump mounting bolts	13	10
Crankshaft front oil seal housing bolts	16	12
Flywheel/driveplate bolts**	50	37
Big-end bearing cap nuts:		
Stage 1	20	15
Stage 2	Tighten through a further 70°	
Main bearing cap bolts	70	52

* A new bolt must be used on refitting
** Locking compound must be used on the bolt threads when refitting
*** New bolts may be required - see Section 13

1 General information

How to use this Chapter

This Part of Chapter 2 describes the repair procedures that can reasonably be carried out on the engine while it remains in the vehicle. If the engine has been removed from the vehicle and is being dismantled as described in Part B, any preliminary dismantling procedures can be ignored.

Note that, while it may be possible physically to overhaul items such as the piston/connecting rod assemblies while the engine is in the car, such tasks are not usually carried out as separate operations. Usually, several additional procedures are required (not to mention the cleaning of components and of oilways); for this reason, all such tasks are classed as major overhaul procedures, and are described in Part B of this Chapter.

Part B describes the removal of the engine/transmission unit from the car, and the full overhaul procedures that can then be carried out.

For ease of reference, relevant specifications are given in the Specifications Section at the beginning of each Part of the Chapter, with the exception of torque wrench settings, which are grouped together in the Specifications Section at the beginning of Part A of this Chapter.

Engine description

The XUD engine is a well-proven modern diesel unit which has appeared in many Citro'n, Peugeot and Talbot passenger cars and light commercial vehicles. The engine is of four-cylinder overhead camshaft design, mounted transversely and inclined 30° to the rear, with the transmission mounted on the left-hand side (see illustrations).

A toothed timing belt drives the camshaft, fuel injection pump and coolant pump. Bucket tappets are fitted between the camshaft and valves. Valve clearance adjustment is by means of selective shims. The camshaft is supported by three bearings machined directly in the cylinder head.

The crankshaft runs in five main bearings of the usual shell type. Endfloat is controlled by thrustwashers either side of number 2 main bearing.

The pistons are selected to be of matching weight, and incorporate fully-floating gudgeon pins retained by circlips.

The oil pump is chain-driven from the front of the crankshaft. An oil cooler is fitted to all engines except the 1.7 litre unit.

The design of the XUD9TE turbo engine is the same as the normally-aspirated (non-turbo) version, but components such as the crankshaft, pistons and connecting rods are uprated. It also incorporates oil jets which spray oil onto the undersides of the pistons to keep them cool.

Repair operations possible with the engine in the vehicle

The following operations can be carried out without having to remove the engine from the vehicle:

(a) Removal and refitting of the cylinder head.
(b) Removal and refitting of the timing belt and sprockets.
(c) Removal and refitting of the camshaft.
(d) Removal and refitting of the sump.
(e) Removal and refitting of the big-end bearings, connecting rods, and pistons*.
(f) Removal and refitting of the oil pump.
(g) Renewal of the engine/transmission mountings.
(h) Removal and refitting of the flywheel/driveplate.

*Although the operation marked with an asterisk can be carried out with the engine in the car after removal of the sump, it is better for the engine to be removed, in the interests of cleanliness and improved access. For this reason, the procedure is described in Part B of this Chapter.

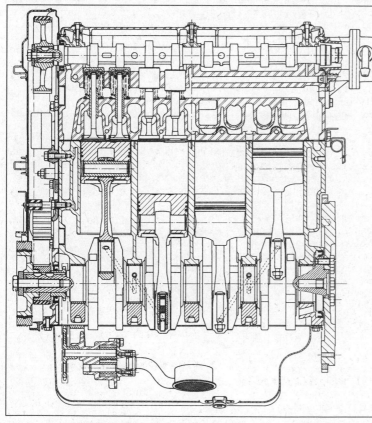

1.5a Side sectional view of a 1.9 litre turbo (XUD9TE) engine

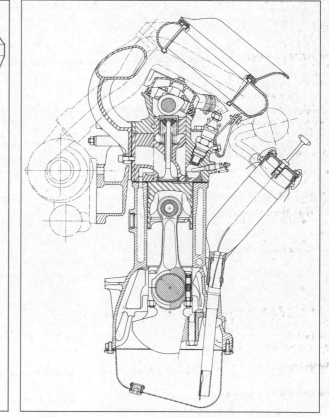

1.5b Front sectional view of a 1.9 litre turbo (XUD9TE) engine

2.2 Performing a compression test

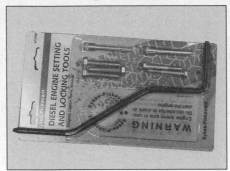

3.4a Suitable tools available for locking engine with No 1 piston at TDC

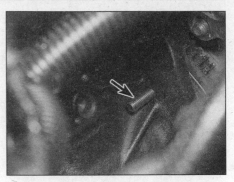

3.4b Rod (arrowed) inserted through cylinder block into TDC hole in flywheel

2 Compression and leakdown tests - description and interpretation

Compression test

Note: *A compression tester specifically designed for Diesel engines must be used for this test.*

1 When engine performance is down, or if misfiring occurs which cannot be attributed to the ignition or fuel systems, a compression test can provide diagnostic clues as to the engine's condition.

HAYNES HINT *If the compression test is performed regularly, it can give warning of trouble before any other symptoms become apparent.*

2 A compression tester specifically intended for Diesel engines must be used, because of the higher pressures involved. The tester is connected to an adaptor which screws into the glow plug or injector hole. On ZX models, an adaptor suitable for use in the injector holes will be required, due to the limited access to the glow plug holes **(see illustration)**. It is unlikely to be worthwhile buying such a tester for occasional use, but it may be possible to borrow or hire one - if not, have the test performed by a garage.

3 Unless specific instructions to the contrary are supplied with the tester, observe the following points:
(a) *The battery must be in a good state of charge, the air filter must be clean, and the engine should be at normal operating temperature.*
(b) *All the injectors or glow plugs should be removed before starting the test. If removing the injectors, also remove the flame shield washers, otherwise they may be blown out.*
(c) *The stop solenoid must be disconnected, to prevent the engine from running or fuel from being discharged.*

4 There is no need to hold the accelerator

pedal down during the test, because the Diesel engine air inlet is not throttled.

5 The actual compression pressures measured are not so important as the balance between cylinders. Values are given in the Specifications.

6 The cause of poor compression is less easy to establish on a Diesel engine than on a petrol one. The effect of introducing oil into the cylinders ("wet" testing) is not conclusive, because there is a risk that the oil will sit in the swirl chamber or in the recess on the piston crown instead of passing to the rings. However, the following can be used as a rough guide to diagnosis.

7 All cylinders should produce very similar pressures; any difference greater than that specified indicates the existence of a fault. Note that the compression should build up quickly in a healthy engine; low compression on the first stroke, followed by gradually-increasing pressure on successive strokes, indicates worn piston rings. A low compression reading on the first stroke, which does not build up during successive strokes, indicates leaking valves or a blown head gasket (a cracked head could also be the cause). Deposits on the undersides of the valve heads can also cause low compression.

8 A low reading from two adjacent cylinders is almost certainly due to the head gasket having blown between them; the presence of coolant in the engine oil will confirm this.

9 If the compression reading is unusually high, the cylinder head surfaces, valves and pistons are probably coated with carbon deposits. If this is the case, the cylinder head should be removed and decarbonised (see Chapter 2, Part B, Section 8).

Leakdown test

10 A leakdown test measures the rate at which compressed air fed into the cylinder is lost. It is an alternative to a compression test, and in many ways it is better, since the escaping air provides easy identification of where pressure loss is occurring (piston rings, valves or head gasket).

11 The equipment needed for leakdown testing is unlikely to be available to the home

mechanic. If poor compression is suspected, have the test performed by a suitably-equipped garage.

3 Top dead centre (TDC) for No 1 piston - locating

Note: *Three 8 mm diameter bolts and one 8 mm diameter rod or drill will be required for this procedure.*

1 Top dead centre (TDC) is the highest point in the cylinder that each piston reaches as the crankshaft turns. Each piston reaches TDC at the end of the compression stroke, and again at the end of the exhaust stroke. For the purpose of timing the engine, TDC refers to the position of No 1 piston at the end of its compression stroke. On all engines in this manual, No 1 piston is at the flywheel/driveplate end of the engine.

2 Remove the upper timing belt covers as described in Section 6.

3 The crankshaft must now be turned until the three bolt holes in the camshaft and injection pump sprockets (one hole in the camshaft sprocket, two holes in the injection pump sprocket) are aligned with the corresponding holes in the engine front plate. The crankshaft can be turned by using a spanner on the pulley bolt.

HAYNES HINT *Improved access to the pulley bolt can be obtained by jacking up the front right-hand corner of the vehicle (see "Jacking and vehicle support") and removing the roadwheel and the lower wheel arch cover (secured by plastic clips).*

4 Insert an 8 mm diameter rod or drill through the hole in the left-hand flange of the cylinder block by the starter motor; if necessary, carefully turn the crankshaft either way until the rod enters the TDC hole in the flywheel **(see illustrations)**.

5 Insert three M8 bolts through the holes in the camshaft and fuel injection pump

3.5a M8 bolt (arrowed) inserted through TDC hole in camshaft sprocket

3.5b M8 bolts (arrowed) inserted through TDC holes in fuel injection pump sprocket

3.7 Warning notice in place in engine compartment

sprockets, and screw them into the engine finger-tight **(see illustrations)**.

6 The crankshaft, camshaft and injection pump are now "locked" in position with No 1 piston at TDC.

7 If the engine is to be left in this state for a long period of time, it is a good idea to place suitable warning notices inside the vehicle, and in the engine compartment **(see illustration)**. This will reduce the possibility of the engine being accidentally cranked on the starter motor, which is likely to cause damage with the locking tools in place.

4 Camshaft cover - removal and refitting

Note: *A new camshaft cover gasket must be used on refitting.*

Removal

1 Remove the intercooler (Turbo models) or the air distribution housing (XUD9/A - D9B engine) where applicable, as described in Chapter 4.

2 Disconnect the breather hose from the front of the camshaft cover and, where applicable, disconnect the air hose from the top of the inlet manifold.

3 Unscrew the securing bolt and remove the fuel hose bracket from the right-hand end of the camshaft cover **(see illustration)**.

4 Note the locations of any brackets secured

by the three camshaft cover securing bolts, then unscrew the bolts. Recover the metal and fibre washers under each bolt **(see illustration)**.

5 Carefully move any hoses clear of the camshaft cover.

6 Lift off the camshaft cover, and recover the rubber gasket **(see illustration)**.

Refitting

7 Refitting is a reversal of removal, bearing in mind the following points:

(a) Use a new camshaft cover gasket.
(b) Refit any brackets in their original positions noted before removal.
(c) Where applicable, refit the intercooler or the air distribution housing, as described in Chapter 4.

5 Crankshaft pulley - removal and refitting

Note: *A new crankshaft pulley bolt will be required on refitting.*

Removal

1 Remove the auxiliary drivebelt, as described in Chapter 1, Section 19.

2 To prevent the crankshaft from turning as the pulley bolt is unscrewed, remove the starter motor (see Chapter 5) and lock the flywheel using a suitable notched tool engaged in the ring gear teeth **(see**

illustration). This tool is shown more clearly in illustration 18.3, Section 18.

3 Unscrew and remove the crankshaft pulley bolt. Note that the bolt is extremely tight. Recover the thrustwasher **(see illustration)**.

4 Remove the pulley from the end of the crankshaft, and recover the Woodruff key if it is loose. If the pulley is tight on the crankshaft, it can be removed using a puller as follows.

5 Refit the pulley bolt without the thrustwasher, but do not screw it fully home.

6 Improvise a suitable puller, using a short length of metal bar, two M6 bolts, and a large nut and bolt.

7 Pass the two M6 bolts through the bar, and screw them into the tapped holes in the pulley.

8 Tighten the large bolt, forcing it against the

4.3 Removing the fuel hose bracket from the camshaft cover

4.4 Remove the securing bolts and washers . . .

4.6 . . . and lift off the camshaft cover

5.2 Notched tool (arrowed) positioned on ring gear teeth to lock flywheel

5.3 Removing the crankshaft pulley bolt and thrustwasher

6.3 Removing the right-hand timing belt cover

6.6 Removing the left-hand timing belt cover

head of the pulley bolt while counterholding the nut, to force the pulley from the crankshaft.

Refitting

9 Where applicable, refit the Woodruff key to the end of the crankshaft, then refit the pulley.
10 Prevent the crankshaft from turning as during removal, then fit a new pulley securing bolt. Ensure that the thrustwasher is in place under the bolt head.
11 Tighten the bolt to the specified torque, and then through the specified angle (see Specifications).
12 Remove the locking tool from the flywheel ring gear, and refit the starter motor.
13 Refit and tension the auxiliary drivebelt as described in Chapter 1, Section 19.

6 Timing belt covers -
removal and refitting

Right-hand cover

Removal

1 If procedures are to be carried out which involve removal of the timing belt, remove the right-hand engine mounting-to-body bracket as described in Section 9. This will greatly improve access.
2 Release the upper spring clip from the cover.
3 Release the lower securing lug using a screwdriver, then lift the cover upwards from the engine (see illustration).

Refitting

4 Refitting is a reversal of removal, but refit and tension the auxiliary drivebelt as described in Chapter 1, Section 19.

Left-hand cover

Removal

5 Remove the right-hand outer cover as described previously.
6 Release the two securing clips, manipulate the cover over the studs on the front of the engine, then withdraw the cover upwards (see illustration). Clearance is limited, and if

desired, access can be improved by removing the engine mounting bracket (see Section 9).

Refitting

7 Refitting is a reversal of removal, noting that if the engine mounting bracket has been removed, it should be refitted with reference to Section 9.
8 On completion, refit and tension the auxiliary drivebelt as described in Chapter 1, Section 19.

Lower cover

Removal

9 Remove the crankshaft pulley as described in Section 5.
10 Unscrew the two securing bolts and remove the cover (see illustration).

Refitting

11 Refitting is a reversal of removal.

7 Timing belt - removal, inspection, refitting and tensioning

General

1 The timing belt drives the camshaft, injection pump, and coolant pump from a toothed sprocket on the front of the crankshaft. The belt also drives the brake vacuum pump indirectly via the rear ("flywheel") end of the camshaft. If the belt breaks or slips in service, the pistons are likely

6.10 Lower timing belt cover securing bolts (arrowed)

to hit the valve heads, resulting in expensive damage.
2 The timing belt should be renewed at the specified intervals, or earlier if it is contaminated with oil, or at all noisy in operation (a "scraping" noise due to uneven wear).
3 If the timing belt is being removed, it is a wise precaution to check the condition of the coolant pump at the same time (check for signs of coolant leakage). This may avoid the need to remove the timing belt again at a later stage, should the coolant pump fail.

Removal

4 Set No 1 piston to TDC, then lock the crankshaft, and the camshaft and fuel injection pump sprockets, in position as described in Section 3.
5 Remove the crankshaft pulley as described in Section 5.
6 Remove the right-hand engine mounting-to-body bracket as described in Section 9.
7 Loosen the timing belt tensioner pivot nut

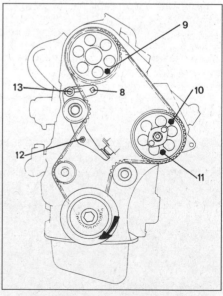

7.7 Removing the timing belt

| 8 Square hole | 12 Tensioner pivot nut |
| 9, 10 and 11 M8 bolts | 13 Adjustment bolt |

7.8a Mark the timing belt with an arrow to indicate its running direction

7.8b Removing the timing belt

7.13 Half-width of timing belt correctly engaged with camshaft sprocket

and adjustment bolt, then turn the tensioner bracket anti-clockwise to release the tension. Retighten the adjustment bolt to hold the tensioner in the released position. If available, use a 10 mm square drive extension in the hole provided, to turn the tensioner bracket against the spring tension **(see illustration)**.

8 Mark the timing belt with an arrow to indicate its running direction, if it is to be re-used. Remove the belt from the sprockets **(see illustrations)**.

Inspection

9 Inspect the belt for cracks, fraying, and damage to the teeth. Pay particular attention to the roots of the teeth. If any damage is evident, or if the belt is contaminated with oil, fuel or coolant, it must be renewed (and any leak rectified).

Refitting and tensioning

10 Commence refitting by ensuring that the M8 bolts are still fitted to the camshaft and fuel injection pump sprockets, and that the rod or drill is positioned in the TDC hole in the flywheel.

11 Locate the timing belt on the crankshaft sprocket, making sure that, where applicable, the direction of rotation arrow is facing the correct way.

12 Engage the timing belt with the crankshaft sprocket, hold it in position, then feed the belt over the remaining sprockets in the following order:

(a) Idler roller.
(b) Fuel injection pump.
(c) Camshaft.
(d) Tensioner roller.
(e) Coolant pump.

13 Be careful not to kink or twist the belt. To ensure correct engagement, locate only a half-width on the injection pump sprocket before feeding the timing belt onto the camshaft sprocket, keeping the belt taut and fully engaged with the crankshaft sprocket. Locate the timing belt fully onto the sprockets **(see illustration)**.

14 Remove the bolts from the camshaft and fuel injection pump sprockets. Remove the rod or drill from the TDC hole in the flywheel.

15 With the pivot nut loose, slacken the tensioner adjustment bolt while holding the bracket against the spring tension. Slowly release the bracket until the roller presses against the timing belt. Retighten the adjustment bolt and the pivot nut.

16 Rotate the crankshaft through two complete turns in the normal running direction (clockwise). Do not rotate the crankshaft backwards, as the timing belt must be kept tight between the crankshaft, fuel injection pump and camshaft sprockets.

17 Loosen the tensioner adjustment bolt and the pivot nut to allow the tensioner spring to push the roller against the timing belt, then tighten both the adjustment bolt and pivot nut to the specified torque.

18 Check that No 1 piston is at TDC by reinserting the sprocket locking bolts and the

rod or drill in the flywheel TDC hole, as described in Section 3. If No 1 piston is not at TDC as described, the timing belt has been incorrectly fitted (possibly one tooth out on one of the sprockets) - in this case, repeat the refitting procedure from the beginning.

19 Refit the upper timing belt covers as described in Section 6, but do not lower the vehicle to the ground until the engine mounting-to-body bracket has been refitted.

20 Refit the right-hand engine mounting-to-body bracket, with reference to Section 9.

21 Refit the crankshaft pulley as described in Section 5.

8 Timing belt sprockets - removal and refitting

Camshaft sprocket

Removal

1 Remove the upper timing belt covers as described in Section 6.

2 The camshaft sprocket bolt must now be loosened. The camshaft must be prevented from turning as the sprocket bolt is unscrewed, and this can be achieved in one of two ways, as follows **(see illustrations)**. Do not remove the camshaft sprocket bolt at this stage.

(a) Make up a tool similar to that shown, and use it to hold the sprocket stationary by means of the holes in the sprocket.

(b) Remove the camshaft cover as described in Section 4. Prevent the camshaft from turning by holding it with a suitable spanner on the lug between Nos 3 and 4 camshaft lobes.

3 Set No 1 piston to TDC, then lock the crankshaft, and the camshaft and fuel injection pump sprockets, in position as described in Section 3.

4 Loosen the timing belt tensioner pivot nut and adjustment bolt, then turn the tensioner bracket anti-clockwise to release the tension, and retighten the adjustment bolt to hold the tensioner in the released position. If available, use a 10 mm square drive extension in the hole provided, to turn the tensioner bracket against the spring tension.

8.2a Using an improvised tool to prevent the camshaft sprocket from turning

8.2b Holding the camshaft using a spanner on the lug between Nos 3 and 4 lobes

8.7 Withdrawing the camshaft sprocket

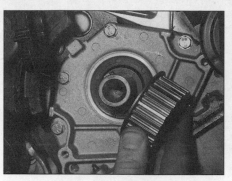

8.18a Withdrawing the crankshaft sprocket

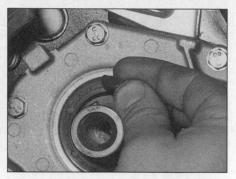

8.18b Removing the Woodruff key from the end of the crankshaft

5 Unscrew the camshaft sprocket bolt and recover the thrustwasher.

6 Withdraw the TDC locking bolt from the camshaft sprocket.

7 Withdraw the sprocket, manipulating the timing belt from it as it is withdrawn **(see illustration)**. Recover the Woodruff key from the end of the camshaft if it is loose. **Do not** allow the camshaft to rotate, otherwise the valves will strike the pistons of Nos 1 and 4 cylinders. If necessary, remove the rod or drill from the TDC hole in the flywheel, and turn the crankshaft one quarter-turn to position all the pistons halfway down the cylinders in order to prevent any damage, but release the timing belt from the injection pump sprocket first.

Refitting

8 Where applicable, refit the Woodruff key to the end of the camshaft, then refit the camshaft sprocket. Note that the sprocket will only fit one way round (with the protruding centre boss against the camshaft), as the end of the camshaft is tapered.

9 Refit the sprocket securing bolt, ensuring that the thrustwasher is in place. Tighten the bolt to the specified torque, preventing the camshaft from turning as during removal. Do not allow the camshaft to rotate, unless the crankshaft has been turned as described in paragraph 7.

10 Where applicable, refit the camshaft cover as described in Section 4.

11 Align the holes in the camshaft sprocket and the engine front plate, and refit the M8

bolt to lock the camshaft in the TDC position.

12 If the crankshaft was turned a quarter-turn from TDC in paragraph 7, turn it back by the same amount so that pistons 1 and 4 are again at TDC. Do not turn the crankshaft more than a quarter-turn, otherwise pistons 2 and 3 will pass their TDC positions, and will strike valves 4 and 6.

13 Where applicable, refit the rod or drill to the TDC hole in the flywheel.

14 Fit the timing belt around the fuel injection pump sprocket (where applicable) and the camshaft sprocket, and tension the timing belt as described in Section 7.

15 Refit the upper timing belt covers as described in Section 6.

Crankshaft sprocket
Removal

16 Remove the crankshaft pulley as described in Section 5.

17 Proceed as described in paragraphs 1, 3 and 4.

18 Withdraw the sprocket, manipulating the timing belt from it as it is withdrawn. Recover the Woodruff key from the end of the crankshaft if it is loose **(see illustrations)**. **Do not** allow the crankshaft to rotate, otherwise the valves may strike the pistons. If necessary, remove the rod or drill from the TDC hole in the flywheel, remove the flywheel locking tool, then turn the crankshaft one quarter-turn. This will position all the pistons halfway down the cylinders, in order to prevent any damage.

Refitting

19 Where applicable, refit the Woodruff key to the end of the crankshaft, then refit the crankshaft sprocket (with the flange nearest the cylinder block).

20 If the crankshaft was turned a quarter-turn from TDC in paragraph 18, turn it back by the same amount so that pistons 1 and 4 are again at TDC. Do not turn the crankshaft more than a quarter-turn, otherwise pistons 2 and 3 will pass their TDC positions, and may strike the valves.

21 Where applicable, refit the rod or drill to the TDC hole in the flywheel.

22 Fit the timing belt around the crankshaft sprocket, and tension the timing belt as described in Section 7.

23 Refit the crankshaft pulley as described in Section 5.

Fuel injection pump sprocket
Removal

24 Proceed as described in paragraphs 1, 3 and 4.

25 Make alignment marks on the fuel injection pump sprocket and the timing belt, to ensure that the sprocket and timing belt are correctly aligned on refitting.

26 Remove the M8 bolts securing the fuel injection pump sprocket in the TDC position.

27 On certain models, the sprocket may be fitted with a built-in puller, which consists of a plate bolted to the sprocket. The plate contains a captive nut (the sprocket securing nut), which is screwed onto the fuel injection pump shaft. On models not fitted with the built-in puller, a suitable puller can be made up using a short length of bar, and two M7 bolts screwed into the holes provided in the sprocket.

28 The fuel injection pump shaft must be prevented from turning as the sprocket nut is unscrewed, and this can be achieved using a tool similar to that shown **(see illustration)**. Use the tool to hold the sprocket stationary by means of the holes in the sprocket.

29 On models with a built-in puller, unscrew the sprocket securing nut until the sprocket is freed from the taper on the pump shaft, then withdraw the sprocket. Recover the Woodruff key from the end of the pump shaft if it is

8.28 Using an improvised tool to prevent the fuel injection pump sprocket from turning

8.30 Improvised puller fitted to fuel injection pump sprocket

9.3 Releasing the fuel hose and the fuel priming bulb from their support clips

9.4a Removing the engine mounting cover plate rear securing bolt and fuel priming bulb bracket

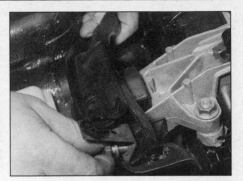

9.4b Removing the engine mounting cover plate

loose. If desired, the puller assembly can be removed from the sprocket by removing the two securing screws and washers.

30 On models not fitted with a built-in puller, partially unscrew the sprocket securing nut, then fit the improvised puller, and tighten the two bolts (forcing the bar against the sprocket nut), until the sprocket is freed from the taper on the pump shaft **(see illustration)**. Withdraw the sprocket and recover the Woodruff key from the end of the pump shaft if it is loose. Remove the puller from the sprocket.

Refitting

31 Where applicable, refit the Woodruff key to the pump shaft, ensuring that it is correctly located in its groove.

32 Where applicable, if the built-in puller assembly has been removed from the sprocket, refit it, and tighten the two securing screws to the specified torque, ensuring that the washers are in place.

33 Refit the sprocket, then tighten the securing nut to the specified torque, preventing the pump shaft from turning as during removal.

34 Make sure that the M8 TDC bolts are fitted to the camshaft and fuel injection pump sprockets, and that the rod or drill is positioned in the TDC hole in the flywheel.

35 Fit the timing belt around the fuel injection pump sprocket, ensuring that the marks made

on the belt and sprocket before removal are aligned.

36 Tension the timing belt as described in Section 7.

37 Refit the upper timing belt covers as described in Section 6.

Coolant pump sprocket

38 The coolant pump sprocket is integral with the pump, and cannot be removed.

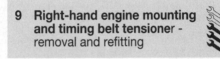

9 Right-hand engine mounting and timing belt tensioner - removal and refitting

General

1 The timing belt tensioner is operated by a spring and plunger housed in the right-hand engine mounting bracket, which is bolted to the end face of the engine. The engine mounting is attached to the mounting on the body via the engine mounting-to-body bracket.

Right-hand engine mounting-to-body bracket

Removal

2 Before removing the bracket, the engine must be supported, preferably using a

suitable hoist and lifting tackle attached to the lifting bracket at the right-hand end of the engine. Alternatively, the engine can be supported using a trolley jack and interposed block of wood beneath the sump, in which case, be prepared for the engine to tilt backwards when the bracket is removed.

3 Release the fuel hose and the fuel priming bulb from the clips attached to the engine mounting assembly and suspension top mounting, and move the hose and bulb to one side **(see illustration)**.

4 Where applicable, unscrew the two securing bolts, and remove the plate covering the engine mounting on the body. Note that the bolts also secure the fuel priming bulb and hose mounting brackets **(see illustrations)**.

5 Where applicable, lift out the rubber buffer to expose the engine mounting bracket-to-body securing nut **(see illustration)**.

6 Unscrew the three nuts securing the bracket to the engine mounting, and the single nut securing the bracket to the body, then lift off the bracket **(see illustration)**.

Refitting

7 Refitting is a reversal of removal. Tighten the bracket securing nuts to the specified torque.

Timing belt tensioner and right-hand engine mounting bracket

Note: *A suitable tool will be required to retain the timing belt tensioner plunger during this operation.*

Removal

8 Remove the engine mounting-to-body bracket as described previously in this Section, and remove the auxiliary drivebelt as described in Chapter 1, Section 19.

9 If not already done, support the engine with a trolley jack and interposed block of wood beneath the sump.

10 To prevent the engine from tilting, make a bracket from a length of stout rod, and fit the bracket between the upper alternator mounting and the body front panel **(see**

9.5 Lifting the rubber buffer from the engine mounting

9.6 Removing the engine mounting-to-body bracket

9.10 Bracket fitted between alternator mounting and body front panel to support engine

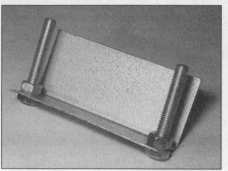

9.16 Fabricated tool for holding tensioner plunger in engine mounting bracket

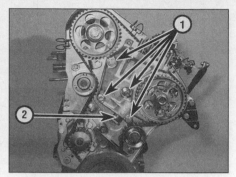

9.17a View of timing belt end of engine

1 Engine mounting bracket securing bolts
2 Timing belt tensioner plunger

illustration). Ensure that the bracket is strong enough to support the load imposed by the engine, and wrap a rag around the body panel to prevent damage to the finish.

11 Where applicable, disconnect the hoist and lifting tackle supporting the engine from the right-hand lifting bracket (this is necessary because the lifting bracket is attached to the engine mounting bracket, and must be removed).

12 Unscrew the two securing bolts and remove the engine lifting bracket.

13 Set No 1 piston to TDC, then lock the crankshaft, and the camshaft and fuel injection pump sprockets, in position as described in Section 3.

14 Loosen the timing belt tensioner pivot nut and adjustment bolt, then turn the tensioner bracket anti-clockwise until the adjustment bolt is in the middle of the slot, and retighten the adjustment bolt. If available, use a 10 mm square drive extension in the hole provided, to turn the tensioner bracket against the spring tension.

15 Mark the timing belt with an arrow to indicate its running direction, if it is to be re-used. Remove the belt from the sprockets.

16 A tool must now be obtained in order to hold the tensioner plunger in the engine mounting bracket. Citroën tool 7009-T1 is designed to slide in the two lower bolt holes of the mounting bracket. It should be straightforward to fabricate a similar tool out of sheet metal, and using M10 bolts and nuts

instead of metal dowel rods **(see illustration)**.
17 Unscrew the two lower engine mounting bracket bolts, then fit the special tool. Grease the inner surface of the tool, to prevent any damage to the end of the tensioner plunger **(see illustrations)**. Unscrew the pivot nut and adjustment bolt, and withdraw the tensioner assembly.

18 Remove the two remaining engine mounting bracket bolts, and withdraw the bracket **(see illustration)**.

19 Compress the tensioner plunger into the engine mounting bracket, remove the special tool, then withdraw the plunger and spring.

Refitting

20 Refitting is a reversal of removal, bearing in mind the following points:

(a) *Tighten all fixings to the specified torque.*
(b) *Refit and tension the timing belt as described in Section 7.*
(c) *Refit and tighten the auxiliary drivebelt as described in Chapter 1, Section 19.*

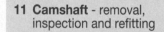

10 Timing belt idler roller - removal and refitting

Removal

1 Remove the auxiliary drivebelt as described in Chapter 1, Section 19.

2 Set No 1 piston to TDC, then lock the crankshaft, and the camshaft and fuel

injection pump sprockets, in position as described in Section 3.

3 Loosen the timing belt tensioner pivot nut and adjustment bolt, then turn the tensioner bracket anti-clockwise to release the tension, and retighten the adjustment bolt to hold the tensioner in the released position. If available, use a 10 mm square drive extension in the hole provided, to turn the tensioner bracket against the spring tension.

4 Unscrew the two bolts and the stud securing the idler roller assembly to the cylinder block, noting that the upper bolt also secures the engine mounting bracket.

5 Slightly loosen the remaining four engine mounting bolts, noting that the uppermost bolt is on the inside face of the engine front plate, and also secures the engine lifting bracket. Slide out the idler roller assembly.

Refitting

6 Refitting is a reversal of removal, bearing in mind the following points:

(a) *Tighten all fixings to the specified torque.*
(b) *Tension the timing belt as described in Section 7.*
(c) *Refit and tension the auxiliary drivebelt as described in Chapter 1, Section 19.*

11 Camshaft - removal, inspection and refitting

Note: New oil seals must be used on refitting, and suitable sealing compound will be required for the end bearing caps.

Removal

1 Remove the camshaft cover as described in Section 4.

2 Remove the camshaft sprocket as described in Section 8.

3 On models with a brake vacuum pump driven directly from the camshaft, unbolt the pump and move it to one side, with reference to Chapter 9, then proceed to paragraph 7.

4 On models with a belt-driven brake vacuum pump, remove the drivebelt as described in Chapter 1, Section 20.

5 Prevent the camshaft from turning, as

9.17b Tool in place to hold tensioner plunger in engine mounting bracket - timing belt removed for clarity

9.18 Removing the right-hand engine mounting bracket

11.7 Camshaft bearing cap identification mark (arrowed)

11.8a Progressively unscrew the nuts . . .

11.8b . . . then remove the bearing caps

described above for removing the camshaft sprocket, then unscrew the vacuum pump drive pulley bolt from the end of the camshaft and recover the thrustwasher.

6 Withdraw the pulley, and recover the Woodruff key from the end of the camshaft if it is loose.

7 The camshaft bearing caps should be numbered from the flywheel end of the engine (see illustration). If the caps are not already numbered, identify them, numbering them from the flywheel end of the engine, and making the marks on the manifold side.

8 Progressively unscrew the nuts, then remove the bearing caps (see illustrations).

9 Lift the camshaft from the cylinder head (see illustration). Remove the oil seal from the timing belt end of the camshaft.

10 Where applicable, remove the oil seal from the pulley end of the camshaft.

Inspection

11 Clean all the components, including the bearing surfaces in the cylinder head. Examine the components carefully for wear and damage. In particular, check the surface of the cams for scoring and pitting. Renew components as necessary, and obtain new oil seals.

Refitting

12 Commence reassembly by lubricating the cams and bearing journals with clean engine oil of the specified grade (see *"Lubricants and fluids"*).

13 Locate the camshaft on the cylinder head, passing it through the engine front plate, with the tips of the cams 4 and 6 facing downwards and resting on the bucket tappets. Where applicable, the cast "DIST" marking on the camshaft must be at the timing belt end of the cylinder head, and the Woodruff key slot for the camshaft sprocket should be facing upwards.

14 Fit the centre bearing cap the correct way round as previously noted, then screw on the nuts and tighten them two or three turns.

15 Apply sealing compound to the end bearing caps on the areas shown (see illustration). Fit them in the correct positions, and tighten the nuts two or three turns.

16 Tighten all the nuts progressively to the specified torque, making sure that cams 4 and 6 remain facing downwards.

17 Check that the camshaft endfloat is as given in the Specifications, using a feeler gauge. If not, the camshaft and/or the cylinder head must be renewed. To check the endfloat, push the camshaft fully towards one end of the cylinder head, and insert a feeler gauge between the thrust faces of one of the camshaft lobes and a bearing cap (see illustration).

18 If the original camshaft is being refitted, and it is known that the valve clearances are correct, proceed to the next paragraph. Otherwise, check and adjust the valve clearances as described in Section 12. Note that, because the timing belt is still

disconnected at this stage, the crankshaft *must* be turned one quarter-turn (either way) from the TDC position, so that all the pistons are halfway down the cylinders. This will prevent the valves striking the pistons when the camshaft is rotated. Remove the rod or drill from the TDC hole in the flywheel, and release the timing belt from the injection pump sprocket while turning the crankshaft.

19 Smear the lips of the new oil seals with clean engine oil, then fit them over their respective ends of the camshaft, open end first. Press the oil seal(s) in until flush with the end faces of the end camshaft bearing cap(s). The oil seal(s) can be pressed into position using an M10 bolt, washers and a suitable socket.

20 On models with a belt-driven brake vacuum pump, refit the Woodruff key to the end of the camshaft (where applicable), then refit the pump drive pulley. Refit the thrustwasher and the pulley securing bolt, and tighten the bolt to the specified torque.

21 On models with a brake vacuum pump driven directly from the camshaft, refit the pump and tighten the securing bolts.

22 If the crankshaft has been turned a quarter-turn from TDC to prevent the valves from hitting the pistons, turn it back by the same amount so that pistons 1 and 4 are again at TDC. Do not turn the engine more than a quarter-turn, otherwise pistons 2 and 3 will pass their TDC positions, and will strike valves 4 and 6.

11.9 Lifting the camshaft from the cylinder head

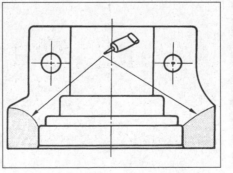

11.15 Apply sealing compound to the end camshaft bearing caps on the areas shown

11.17 Checking the camshaft endfloat using a feeler gauge

23 Refit the rod or drill to the TDC hole in the flywheel.

24 Refit the camshaft sprocket as described in Section 8.

25 Refit the camshaft cover as described in Section 4.

---

12 Valve clearances - checking and adjustment

Note: *This is not a routine operation. It should only be necessary at high mileage, after overhaul, or when investigating noise or power loss which may be attributable to the valvegear.*

Checking

1 During this procedure, the crankshaft must be turned to bring each valve in turn to a position where the clearance can be checked. On manual transmission models, this can be achieved by engaging 4th or 5th gear, applying the handbrake, then jacking up the front right-hand corner of the vehicle (support the vehicle securely on an axle stand - see *"Jacking and vehicle support"*) and turning the roadwheel. On models with automatic transmission, the crankshaft must be turned using a suitable spanner on the crankshaft pulley bolt. Note that the engine will be easier to turn if the fuel injectors or glow plugs are removed.

2 Remove the camshaft cover as described in Section 4.

3 On a piece of paper, draw the outline of the engine with the cylinders numbered from the flywheel end. Show the position of each valve, together with the specified valve clearance. Above each valve, draw lines for noting (1) the actual clearance and (2) the amount of adjustment required **(see illustration)**.

4 Turn the crankshaft until the inlet valve of No 1 cylinder (nearest the flywheel) is fully closed, with the tip of the cam facing directly away from the bucket tappet.

5 Using feeler gauges, measure the clearance between the base of the cam and the bucket tappet **(see illustration)**. Record the clearance on line (1).

6 Repeat the measurement for the other

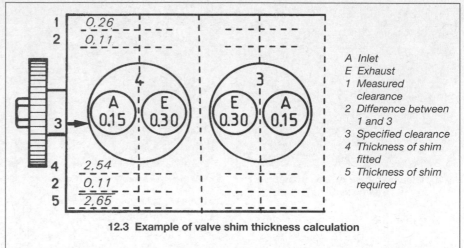

12.3 Example of valve shim thickness calculation

A Inlet
E Exhaust
1 Measured clearance
2 Difference between 1 and 3
3 Specified clearance
4 Thickness of shim fitted
5 Thickness of shim required

seven valves, turning the crankshaft as necessary so that the cam lobe in question is always facing directly away from the relevant tappet.

7 Calculate the difference between each measured clearance and the desired value, and record it on line (2). Since the clearance is different for inlet and exhaust valves, make sure that you are aware which valve you are dealing with. The valve sequence from either end of the engine is:

In - Ex - Ex - In - In - Ex - Ex - In

8 If all the clearances are within tolerance, refit the camshaft cover with reference to Section 4, and where applicable, lower the vehicle to the ground. If any clearance measured is outside the specified tolerance, adjustment must be carried out as described in the following paragraphs.

Adjustment

Note: *A micrometer will be required for this operation.*

9 Remove the camshaft as described in Section 11.

10 Withdraw the first bucket tappet and its shim. Be careful that the shim does not fall out of the tappet. Clean the shim, and measure its thickness with a micrometer **(see illustrations)**. The shims carry thickness markings, but wear may have reduced the

original thickness, so be sure to check.

11 Refer to the clearance recorded for the valve concerned. If the clearance was more than that specified, the shim thickness must be increased by the difference recorded (2). If the clearance was less than that specified, the thickness of the shim must be decreased by the difference recorded (2).

12 Draw three more lines beneath each valve on the calculation paper, as shown in illustration 12.3. On line (4) note the measured thickness of the shim, then add or deduct the difference from line (2) to give the final shim thickness required on line (5).

13 Shims are available in thicknesses between 2.950 mm and 3.500 mm, in steps of 0.025 mm. Clean new shims before measuring or fitting them.

14 Repeat the procedure given in paragraphs 10 to 12 on the remaining valves, keeping each tappet identified for position.

15 When reassembling, oil the shim and fit it on the valve stem, with the size marking face downwards. Oil the tappet and lower it onto the shim. Do not raise the tappet after fitting, as the shim may become dislodged.

16 When all the tappets are in position, complete with their shims, refit the camshaft as described in Section 11. Recheck the valve clearances before refitting the camshaft cover, to make sure they are correct.

12.5 Measuring a valve clearance using a feeler gauge

12.10a Withdrawing a bucket tappet - shim arrowed

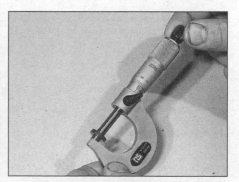

12.10b Measuring a tappet shim thickness using a micrometer

13.6 Disconnecting the vacuum hose from a direct-drive vacuum pump

13.7 Disconnecting a fuel injector leak-off hose

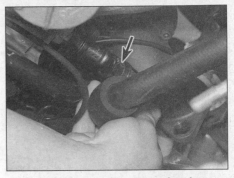

13.11 Disconnecting the coolant hose (arrowed) from the rear of the cylinder head

13 Cylinder head - removal and refitting

Note: *This is an involved procedure, and it is suggested that the Section is read thoroughly before starting work. To aid refitting, make notes on the locations of all relevant brackets and the routing of hoses and cables before removal. A new cylinder head gasket must be used on refitting, and new cylinder head bolts may be required - see text.*

Removal

1 Disconnect the battery negative lead.
2 Drain the cooling system as described in Chapter 1, Section 32.
3 Remove the intercooler (Turbo models) or the air distribution housing (XUD9A - D9B engine) where applicable, as described in Chapter 4.
4 Where applicable, release the securing clips, and disconnect the air hose connecting the air cleaner assembly to the top of the inlet manifold.
5 On models with a belt-driven brake vacuum pump, remove the drivebelt as described in Chapter 1, Section 20.
6 On models with a direct-drive brake vacuum pump, disconnect the vacuum hose from the pump **(see illustration)**.
7 Disconnect and remove the fuel injector leak-off hoses **(see illustration)**.
8 Disconnect the fuel pipes from the fuel injectors and the fuel injection pump, and

remove the pipes as described in Chapter 4.
9 Unscrew the securing nut and disconnect the feed wire from the relevant glow plug. Recover the washers.
10 Remove the inlet and exhaust manifolds as described in Chapter 4. Alternatively (particularly on Turbo models), remove the inlet manifold as described in Chapter 4, then unscrew the exhaust manifold securing nuts, remove the spacers, and remove the manifold studs from the cylinder head (using a stud extractor or two nuts locked together). The exhaust manifold can then be left in place complete with the turbocharger. Ensure that the manifold and turbocharger are adequately supported, taking particular care not to strain the turbocharger oil feed pipe.
11 Disconnect the coolant hose from the rear brake vacuum pump end of the cylinder head **(see illustration)**.
12 Disconnect the small coolant hose from the front timing belt end of the cylinder head **(see illustration)**.
13 Unclip the fuel return hose from the brackets on the cylinder head, and move it to one side **(see illustration)**.
14 Disconnect the accelerator cable from the fuel injection pump (with reference to Chapter 4 if necessary), and move the cable clear of the cylinder head.
15 Remove the fuel filter/thermostat housing as described in Chapter 4.
16 Unscrew the nut or stud securing the coolant hose bracket and the engine lifting bracket to the flywheel end of the cylinder head **(see illustration)**.

13.12 Disconnecting the coolant hose (arrowed) from the front of the cylinder head

17 Remove the camshaft sprocket as described in Section 8.
18 Remove the timing belt tensioner and the right-hand engine mounting bracket as described in Section 9.
19 Remove the timing belt idler roller as described in Section 10.
20 Remove the bolt securing the engine front plate to the fuel injection pump mounting bracket.
21 Remove the nut and bolt securing the engine front plate and the alternator mounting bracket to the fuel injection pump mounting bracket, then remove the engine front plate.
22 Progressively unscrew the cylinder head bolts, in the reverse order to that shown in illustration 13.36 (a T55 Torx bit will be required to loosen the bolts) **(see illustration)**.

13.13 Unclip the fuel return hose from its brackets

13.16 Unscrewing the coolant hose bracket/engine lifting bracket securing stud (arrowed)

13.22 Unscrewing a cylinder head bolt

13.23 Removing a cylinder head bolt and spacer

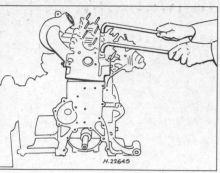

13.24 Freeing the cylinder head using angled rods

13.25 Removing the cylinder head

23 Lift out the bolts and recover the spacers **(see illustration)**.

24 Release the cylinder head from the cylinder block and location dowel by rocking it. The Citroën tool for doing this consists simply of two metal rods with 90-degree angled ends **(see illustration)**. Do not prise between the mating faces of the cylinder head and block, as this may damage the gasket faces.

25 Lift the cylinder head from the block, and recover the gasket **(see illustration)**.

Gasket selection

26 Check that the timing belt is clear of the fuel injection pump sprocket, then turn the crankshaft until pistons 1 and 4 are at TDC. Position a dial test indicator (dial gauge) on the cylinder block, and zero it on the block face. Transfer the probe to the centre of No 1 piston, then slowly turn the crankshaft back and forth past TDC, noting the highest reading on the indicator. Record this reading.

27 Repeat this measurement procedure on No 4 piston, then turn the crankshaft half a turn (180°) and repeat the procedure on Nos 2 and 3 pistons **(see illustration)**.

28 If a dial test indicator is not available, piston protrusion may be measured using a straight-edge and feeler blades or vernier calipers. However, these methods are inevitably less accurate, and cannot therefore be recommended.

29 Ascertain the greatest piston protrusion measurement, and use this to determine the correct cylinder head gasket from the following table **(see illustration)**. Note that the notches or holes on the centre-line of the gasket identify the engine capacity and type, and have no significance for the gasket thickness.

Piston protrusion	Gasket identification
0.54 to 0.65 mm	*1 notch*
0.65 to 0.77 mm	2 notches
0.77 to 0.82 mm	3 notches

Cylinder head bolt examination

30 The manufacturers recommend that the cylinder head bolts are measured, to determine whether renewal is necessary; however, some owners may wish to renew all the bolts as a matter of course. Note that, if a bolt is modified to locate the gasket (see paragraph 33), a new bolt will be required when finally refitting the cylinder head.

31 Two types of bolt have been used; type A without a protrusion and type B with a protrusion. Measure the length of each bolt from the base of the head to the end of the shank **(see illustration)**. If any bolts are longer than that shown below, they will have to be renewed.

Non-turbo models:

Bolt type	Maximum length
A	121.5 mm
B	124.5 mm

Turbo models:

Bolt type	Maximum length
A	146.5 mm
B	150.5 mm

Refitting

32 Turn the crankshaft clockwise (viewed from the timing belt end) until Nos 1 and 4 pistons pass bottom dead centre (BDC) and begin to rise, then position them halfway up their bores. Nos 2 and 3 pistons will also be at their mid-way positions, but descending their bores.

33 Fit the correct gasket the right way round on the cylinder block, with the identification notches or holes at the flywheel/driveplate end of the engine. Make sure that the locating dowel is in place at the timing belt end of the block. Note that, as there is only one locating dowel, it is possible for the gasket to move as the cylinder head is fitted, particularly when the cylinder head is fitted with the engine in the car (due to the inclination of the engine). In the worst instance, this can allow the pistons and/or the valves to hit the gasket, causing engine damage. To avoid this problem, saw the head off a cylinder head bolt, and file (or

13.27 Measuring piston protrusion

13.29 Cylinder head gasket thickness identification notches (arrowed)

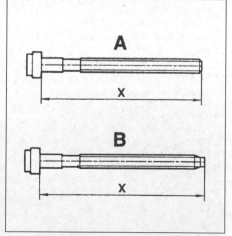

13.31 Measure the length (X) of the cylinder head bolts, to determine whether renewal is required. Note that type A does not have a protrusion whereas type B does

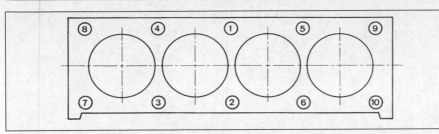

13.36 Cylinder head bolt tightening sequence

cut) a slot in the end of the bolt, to enable it to be turned with a screwdriver. Screw the bolt into one of the bolt holes at the flywheel/driveplate end of the cylinder block, then fit the gasket over the bolt and location dowel. This will ensure that the gasket is held in position as the cylinder head is fitted.

34 Lower the cylinder head onto the block.

35 Grease the threads and contact faces of the cylinder head bolts (see paragraphs 30 and 31), then insert them, together with their spacers (convex sides uppermost, where applicable). Where applicable, after fitting three or four bolts to locate the cylinder head, unscrew the modified bolt fitted in paragraph 33, and fit a new bolt in its place.

36 Tighten the cylinder head bolts in the order shown **(see illustration)**. Tighten the bolts in the stages given in the Specifications (two stages for non-turbo models, and three stages for Turbo models) - ie, tighten all bolts to the Stage 1 torque, then tighten all bolts to the Stage 2 torque (finish by tightening all bolts to the Stage 3 torque on Turbo models).

37 Refit the engine front plate, and refit the bolts and nut securing the plate to the fuel injection pump bracket.

38 Refit the timing belt idler roller.

39 Refit the timing belt tensioner and the right-hand engine mounting as described in Section 10.

40 Refit the camshaft sprocket as described in Section 9.

41 Refit the nut or stud securing the coolant hose bracket and the engine lifting bracket to the flywheel end of the cylinder head.

42 Refit the fuel filter/thermostat housing as described in Chapter 4.

43 Reconnect the accelerator cable to the fuel injection pump, and adjust if necessary, as described in Chapter 4.

44 Reposition the fuel return hose in the brackets on the cylinder head.

45 Reconnect the small coolant hose to the front timing belt end of the cylinder head.

46 Reconnect the coolant hose to the rear of the cylinder head.

47 Refit the inlet and exhaust manifolds as described in Chapter 4.

48 Reconnect the feed wire to the relevant glow plug.

49 Refit the fuel pipes to the fuel injection pump and fuel injectors as described in Chapter 4.

50 Refit the fuel injector leak-off hoses.

51 Reconnect the vacuum hose to the brake vacuum pump, or refit the vacuum pump drivebelt (Chapter 1, Section 20), as applicable.

52 Where applicable, reconnect the air hose to the top of the inlet manifold.

53 Refit the air distribution housing or the intercooler, where applicable, as described in Chapter 4.

54 Refill the cooling system as described in Chapter 1, Section 32.

55 Reconnect the battery negative lead.

56 Bleed the fuel system as described in Chapter 4.

14 Sum - removal and refitting

Note: *A new sump gasket and a new drain plug sealing washer must be used on refitting.*

Removal

1 Apply the handbrake, then jack up the front of the vehicle and support securely on axle stands (see *"Jacking and vehicle support"*).

2 Position a suitable container beneath the engine. Unscrew the sump drain plug, using a suitable square key, and allow the oil to drain into the container.

3 Wipe the drain plug clean, and refit it.

4 Unscrew the sump bolts, noting the locations of the various lengths and types of bolt. Recover the spacer plates under the bolts if they are loose.

5 Remove the sump and gasket. The sump will probably be stuck in position, in which case it will be necessary to cut it free using a thin knife.

Refitting

6 Commence refitting by cleaning the remains of the gasket from the sump and cylinder block, and wipe dry.

7 Apply a little sealing compound to the joints between the crankshaft front oil seal housing and the cylinder block.

8 Position a new gasket on the sump, then lift the sump into position, and insert the bolts, complete with spacer plates, in their correct locations.

9 Tighten the bolts progressively to the specified torque.

10 Lower the vehicle to the ground, and refill the engine with the correct grade and quantity of oil (see Chapter 1, Section 9).

15 Oil pump and drive chain - removal, inspection and refitting

Note: *A new crankshaft front oil seal and crankshaft front oil seal housing gasket must be used on refitting.*

Oil pump

Removal

1 Remove the sump as described in Section 14.

2 Unscrew the three bolts securing the oil pump to the cylinder block. Identify the bolts for position, as all three are of different lengths.

3 Withdraw the pump, disengaging the sprocket from the drive chain as it is removed **(see illustration)**.

Inspection

4 Remove the strainer by prising off the cap **(see illustration)**.

5 Remove the six bolts which hold the two halves of the oil pump together **(see illustration)**. Separate the halves, being prepared for the release of the relief valve spring and plunger. Where applicable, recover the spring seat from the cover end of the spring. Clean all the components.

6 Inspect the gears and the housings for wear and damage. Check the endfloat of the gears using a straight-edge and feeler blades. Also check the clearance between the tip of the gear lobes and the housing **(see**

15.3 Withdrawing the oil pump

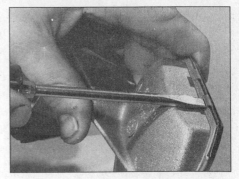

15.4a Prise off the cap, and remove the strainer

15.5 Unscrewing an oil pump cover securing bolt

15.6a Check the endfloat of the gears . . .

15.6b . . . and the clearance between the gear lobes and the housing

15.8a Refit the plunger . . .

illustrations). If any of these clearances exceeds the specified limit, renew the pump. Note that with the exception of the relief valve spring and plunger, individual components are not available.

7 If the pump is to be renewed, it is wise to renew the chain and the crankshaft sprocket also.

8 Lubricate the gears with clean engine oil of the correct grade, then reassemble the oil pump using the reverse of the dismantling procedure **(see illustrations)**. Refit the six bolts holding the two halves of the pump together, and tighten them evenly and securely.

Refitting

9 Refitting is a reversal of removal, but tighten the pump securing bolts to the specified

torque, and refit the sump as described in Section 14 **(see illustration)**.

Oil pump drive chain

Note: *A new crankshaft front oil seal and front oil seal housing gasket must be used on refitting.*

Removal

10 Remove the timing belt crankshaft sprocket, as described in Section 8.

11 Remove the oil pump as described previously in this Section.

12 Unscrew the securing bolts and remove the crankshaft front oil seal housing. Recover the gasket.

13 Remove the oil seal if it is still attached to the crankshaft.

14 Lift the chain from the crankshaft sprocket, and withdraw it from the crankcase.

15 If desired, slide the sprocket from the crankshaft. Recover the Woodruff key if it is loose.

Inspection

16 Examine the teeth on the sprockets. If the teeth are "hooked" in appearance, renew the sprockets. In the case of the pump sprocket, the complete pump must be renewed if the sprocket is significantly worn, as the sprocket cannot be removed from the pump shaft.

17 Examine the chain for wear. If the engine has completed a considerable mileage, or if when the chain is held horizontally (rollers vertical) it takes on a deeply-bowed appearance, renew it.

Refitting

18 Refitting is a reversal of removal, bearing in mind the following points:

(a) *Refit the oil seal housing using a new gasket, but without the oil seal.*

(b) *Fit a new crankshaft front oil seal with reference to Section 16.*

(c) *Refit the oil pump as described previously in this Section.*

(d) *Refit the timing belt crankshaft sprocket as described in Section 8.*

16 Oil seals - renewal

Crankshaft front (timing belt end) oil seal

1 Remove the timing belt crankshaft sprocket as described in Section 8.

2 Measure and note the fitted depth of the oil seal.

3 Pull the oil seal from the housing using a hooked instrument. Alternatively, drill a small hole in the oil seal, and use a self-tapping screw and a pair of pliers to remove it **(see illustration)**.

4 Clean the oil seal housing and the crankshaft sealing surface.

5 Dip the new oil seal in clean engine oil, and press it into the housing (open end first) to the previously-noted depth, using a suitable tube or socket. A piece of thin plastic or tape wound around the front of the crankshaft is

15.8b . . . the spring . . .

15.8c . . . and the spring seat

15.9 Tightening an oil pump securing bolt

16.3 Using a self-tapping screw and a pair of pliers to remove the crankshaft front oil seal

16.12 Removing the camshaft front oil seal

useful to prevent damage to the oil seal as it is fitted.

6 Where applicable, remove the plastic or tape from the end of the crankshaft.

7 Refit the timing belt crankshaft sprocket as described in Section 8.

Crankshaft rear (flywheel end) oil seal

8 Remove the flywheel/driveplate, as described in Section 18.

9 Proceed as described in paragraphs 2 to 6, noting that when fitted, the outer lip of the oil seal must point outwards; if it is pointing inwards, use a piece of bent wire to pull it out. Take care not to damage the oil seal.

10 Refit the flywheel/driveplate, as described in Section 18.

Camshaft front (timing belt end) oil seal

11 Remove the camshaft sprocket as described in Section 8. In principle there is no need to remove the timing belt completely, but remember that if the belt has been contaminated with oil, it must be renewed.

12 Pull the oil seal from the housing using a hooked instrument (see illustration).

Alternatively, drill a small hole in the oil seal and use a self-tapping screw and a pair of pliers to remove it.

13 Clean the oil seal housing and the camshaft sealing surface.

14 Smear the new oil seal with clean engine oil, then fit it over the end of the camshaft, open end first. A piece of thin plastic or tape wound around the front of the camshaft is useful to prevent damage to the oil seal as it is fitted.

15 Press the seal into the housing until it is flush with the end face of the cylinder head. Use an M10 bolt (screwed into the end of the camshaft), washers and a suitable tube or socket to press the seal into position (see illustration).

16 Refit the camshaft sprocket as described in Section 8.

17 Where applicable, fit a new timing belt as described in Section 7.

Camshaft rear (flywheel end) oil seal - models with belt-driven brake vacuum pump

18 For improved access, remove the intercooler (Turbo models) or the air distribution housing (XUD9/A - D9B engine) where applicable, as described in Chapter 4.

19 Remove the brake vacuum pump drive-belt as described in Chapter 1, Section 20.

20 The camshaft must now be prevented from turning as the vacuum pump drive pulley bolt is loosened. This can be achieved in one of two ways, as follows:

(a) Make up a tool similar to that shown in illustration 8.2a in Section 8, and use it to hold the sprocket stationary by means of the holes in the sprocket.

(b) Remove the camshaft cover as described in Section 4. Prevent the camshaft from turning by holding it with a suitable spanner on the lug between Nos 3 and 4 camshaft lobes (see illustration 8.2b in Section 8).

21 Remove the vacuum pump drive pulley bolt from the end of the camshaft, then withdraw the pulley. Recover the Woodruff key if it is loose.

22 Proceed as described in paragraphs 12 to 14.

23 Press the seal into the housing until it is flush with the end face of the cylinder head. Use a suitable bolt (screwed into the end of the camshaft), washers, and a suitable tube or socket to press the seal into position.

24 Further refitting is a reversal of removal, but tighten the vacuum pump pulley bolt to the specified torque, and refit and tension the pump drivebelt as described in Chapter 1, Section 20.

Camshaft rear (flywheel end) oil seal - models with direct-drive brake vacuum pump

25 No oil seal is fitted to the flywheel end of the camshaft. Sealing is provided by an O-ring fitted to the vacuum pump flange. The O-ring can be renewed after unbolting the pump from the cylinder head (see Chapter 9). Note the smaller O-ring which seals the oil feed gallery to the pump - this may also cause leakage from the pump/cylinder head mating faces if it deteriorates or fails (see illustration).

16.15 Using an M10 bolt, washers and socket to fit the camshaft front oil seal

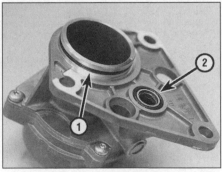

16.25 Camshaft rear oil seal (1) and oil feed gallery O-ring (2) on rear of direct-drive brake vacuum pump

18.3 Suitable tool for holding flywheel via the ring gear teeth

19.6 Remove the nut (arrowed) and bolt securing the engine mounting bracket to the horizontal bracket

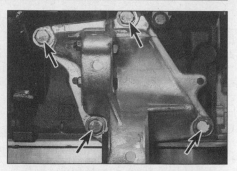

19.7 Unscrew the bolts (arrowed) securing the engine mounting bracket to the cylinder block (engine removed for clarity)

17 Oil level, temperature and pressure sensors - general

Refer to Chapter 5 for details.

18 Flywheel/driveplate - removal, inspection and refitting

Removal

Note: *Suitable locking compound will be required for the flywheel/driveplate bolts on refitting.*

Manual transmission

1 Remove the transmission as described in Chapter 7A.
2 Remove the clutch assembly as described in Chapter 6.
3 Hold the flywheel stationary, using a suitable tool applied to the flywheel ring gear teeth **(see illustration)**. Unscrew and remove the bolts, and lift the flywheel from the crankshaft. Take care, as the flywheel is heavy. Alignment marks are not required, as there is a location dowel on the crankshaft flange.

Automatic transmission

4 Remove the transmission as described in Chapter 7B.
5 Lock the driveplate using a method similar to that described in paragraph 3.
6 Mark the relationship between the torque converter plate and driveplate, then slacken all the driveplate retaining bolts.
7 Remove the retaining bolts, along with the torque converter plate and the two shims (one fitted on each side of the torque converter plate). Note that the shims are of different thickness, the thicker one being on the outside of the torque converter plate. Discard the driveplate retaining bolts as new ones must be used on refitting.
8 Remove the driveplate from the end of the crankshaft. If the locating dowel is a loose fit in the crankshaft end, remove it and store it with the driveplate for safe-keeping.

Inspection

9 If the teeth on the starter ring gear are badly worn, or if some are missing, then it will be necessary to renew the complete flywheel, as the ring gear is not available separately.
10 On manual transmission models, inspect the clutch friction disc contact surface of the flywheel for scoring, or signs of small hair cracks (caused by overheating). If evident, it may be possible to have the flywheel surface-ground, provided the overall thickness of the flywheel is not reduced too much. Consult a Citroen dealer or specialist engine repairer. If grinding is not possible, renew the flywheel complete.
11 On models with automatic transmission, check the torque converter driveplate carefully for signs of distortion. Look for any hairline cracks around the bolt holes or radiating outwards from the centre. If any sign of distortion or damage is found, then the driveplate must be renewed.

Refitting

Manual transmission

12 Commence refitting by cleaning the mating surfaces of the crankshaft and flywheel.
13 Locate the flywheel on the crankshaft dowel.
14 Apply locking fluid to the threads of the bolts (clean the old compound from the threads first), insert them, then tighten them to the specified torque while holding the flywheel stationary as during removal.
15 Refit the clutch assembly as described in Chapter 6.
16 Refit the transmission as described in Chapter 7A.

Automatic transmission

17 Clean the mating surfaces of the driveplate and crankshaft. Remove any remaining locking compound from the threads of the crankshaft holes, using the correct-size tap, if available.
18 If the new driveplate retaining bolts are not supplied with their threads already pre-coated, apply a suitable thread-locking compound to the threads of each bolt.

19 Locate the driveplate on its locating dowel.
20 Offer up the torque converter plate, with the thinner shim positioned behind the plate and the thicker shim on the outside, then align the marks made prior to removal.
21 Fit the new retaining bolts, then lock the driveplate using the method employed on dismantling. Tighten the retaining bolts to the specified torque wrench setting.
22 Remove the driveplate locking tool and refit the transmission as described in Chapter 7B.

19 Engine/transmission mountings - removal and refitting

Right-hand engine mounting

1 Refer to Section 9.

Lower engine mounting

Removal

2 The lower engine mounting also incorporates the right-hand driveshaft intermediate bearing housing.
3 Apply the handbrake, then jack up the front of the vehicle and support securely on axle stands (see *"Jacking and vehicle support"*).
4 Support the engine using a suitable hoist and lifting tackle, connected to the lifting brackets on the cylinder head. Alternatively, the engine can be supported using a suitable metal or wooden bar, securely positioned across the engine compartment..
5 Disconnect the driveshaft from the transmission, with reference to Chapter 8, Section 2. Support the end of the driveshaft by suspending it with wire or string, to avoid straining the joint.
6 Remove the nut and bolt securing the engine mounting bracket to the horizontal bracket on the subframe **(see illustration)**.
7 Unscrew the bolts securing the engine mounting bracket to the cylinder block **(see illustration)**.
8 Pull the bracket from the cylinder block, noting that the bracket locates on two dowels. Take care not to strain the driveshaft joint.

9 Slide the driveshaft intermediate bearing from the bracket, then slide the bracket from the end of the driveshaft.

10 If desired, the horizontal bracket can be removed by removing the bolt and nut securing it to the subframe.

Refitting

11 Refitting is a reversal of removal, but reconnect the driveshaft to the transmission with reference to Chapter 8, Section 2.

Left-hand engine/transmission mounting

Removal

12 Proceed as described in paragraphs 3 and 4.

13 Remove the battery and the battery tray with reference to Chapter 5.

14 On Turbo models, loosen the hose clips and disconnect the air tubing from the air cleaner, and the air tube behind the inlet manifold.

15 Unbolt the air tubing from the metal battery support plate, and lift the air tubing from the engine compartment.

16 Unclip the wiring harness from the battery support plate, noting its routing.

17 Unscrew the four securing bolts, and remove the battery support plate from the engine compartment.

18 Working at the left-hand side of the engine compartment, unscrew the nut securing the engine/transmission mounting to the body mounting bracket, and recover the washer.

19 Remove the two nuts securing the body mounting bracket to the body, and withdraw the body mounting bracket from the engine compartment. Recover the bush from the mounting stud on the transmission.

20 For details of removal and refitting of the transmission mounting stud, refer to Chapter 7, Part A, Section 7.

Refitting

21 Refitting is a reversal of removal.

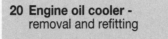

20	**Engine oil cooler -**
	removal and refitting

Removal

1 Drain the cooling system as described in Chapter 1, Section 32.

2 Position a suitable container beneath the oil filter, then unscrew the filter (using an oil filter removal tool if required), and drain the oil into the container.

3 Release the hose clips, and disconnect the coolant hoses from the oil cooler.

20.4 Oil cooler/oil filter mounting stud (A) and cooler locating notch (B)

4 Unscrew the oil cooler/oil filter mounting stud from the cylinder block, and withdraw the cooler. Note the locating notch in the cooler flange which fits over the lug on the cylinder block (**see illustration**).

Refitting

5 Refitting is a reversal of removal, bearing in mind the following points:

(a) *Ensure that the locating notch in the cooler flange engages with the notch on the cylinder block.*

(b) *Top-up the engine oil level with reference to Chapter 1, Section 9.*

(c) *Refill the cooling system as described in Chapter 1, Section 32.*

Notes

Chapter 2 Part B: Engine removal and general engine overhaul procedures

Contents

Crankshaft - inspection 14
Crankshaft - refitting and main bearing running clearance check . . . 18
Crankshaft - removal 11
Cylinder block/crankcase - cleaning and inspection 12
Cylinder head - dismantling 7
Cylinder head - reassembly 9
Cylinder head and valve components - cleaning and inspection . . . 8
Engine - initial start-up after overhaul 20
Engine and automatic transmission - removal and refitting 5
Engine and manual transmission - removal and refitting 4
Engine overhaul - dismantling sequence 6

Engine overhaul - general information 2
Engine overhaul - reassembly sequence 16
Engine removal - methods and precautions 3
General information 1
Main and big-end bearings - inspection 15
Piston/connecting rod assembly - inspection 13
Piston/connecting rod assembly - refitting and big-end bearing
   running clearance check 19
Piston/connecting rod assembly - removal 10
Piston rings - refitting 17

Degrees of difficulty

Easy, suitable for novice with little experience 	**Fairly easy,** suitable for beginner with some experience	**Fairly difficult,** suitable for competent DIY mechanic	**Difficult,** suitable for experienced DIY mechanic	**Very difficult,** suitable for expert DIY or professional

Specifications

Lubrication system
Minimum oil pressure at 90°C:
  Non-turbo models . . . . 3.5 bars at 4000 rpm
  Turbo models . . . . 3.0 bars at idle, 4.9 bars at 4000 rpm

Cylinder head
Maximum gasket face distortion:
  Non-turbo models . . . . 0.03 mm
  Turbo models . . . . 0.07 mm
Overall height . . . . 140.0 + 0.25 mm - 0.05
Swirl chamber protrusion . . . . 0 to 0.03 mm

Valves
Note: *All Specifications apply to 1.9 litre engines - no information available for 1.7 litre engine at time of writing.*
Seat angle (inclusive) . . . . 90°
Valve head diameter:
  Inlet . . . . 38.6 ± 0.2 mm
  Exhaust . . . . 33.0 ± 0.2 mm
Valve stem diameter:
  Inlet . . . . 7.99 ± 0.03 mm
  Exhaust . . . . 7.97 ± 0.1 mm
Overall length:
  Inlet . . . . 112.40 ± 0.03 mm
  Exhaust . . . . 111.85 ± 0.3 mm
Valve timing (at 0.8 mm clearance):
  Inlet opens . . . . 4°ATDC
  Inlet closes:
    Non-turbo models . . . . 35°ABDC
    Turbo models . . . . 31°ABDC
  Exhaust opens . . . . 43°BBDC
  Exhaust closes . . . . TDC
Valve clearances . . . . See Chapter 2, Part A

Cylinder block

Cylinder bore diameter:
  1.7 litre engine:
    Standard .... 80.000 to 80.018 mm
    Oversize .... 80.030 to 80.048 mm
  1.9 litre engines:
    Standard .... 83.000 to 83.018 mm
    Oversize R1 .... 83.200 to 83.218 mm
    Oversize R2 .... 83.500 to 83.518 mm
    Oversize R3 .... 83.800 to 83.818 mm

Pistons

Piston diameter:
  1.7 litre engine:
    Standard .... 79.930 ± 0.008 mm
    Oversize .... 79.960 ± 0.008 mm
  1.9 litre engines:
    Standard .... 82.930 to 82.939 mm
    Oversize R1 .... 83.130 to 83.139 mm
    Oversize R2 .... 83.430 to 83.439 mm
    Oversize R3 .... 83.730 to 83.739 mm

Connecting rods and gudgeon pins

Connecting rod length .... 145.0 ± 0.025 mm
Maximum difference in weight between connecting rods .... 4.0 g
Gudgeon pin diameter .... 25.0 + 0 mm - 0.006
Gudgeon pin length .... 72.0 + 0 mm - 0.3

Crankshaft

Endfloat .... 0.07 to 0.32 mm
Endfloat control thrustwasher thicknesses .... 2.30, 2.40, 2.45, and 2.50 mm
Main bearing journal diameter:
  Standard .... 60.0 + 0 mm - 0.019
  Undersize .... 59.7 + 0 mm - 0.019
Big-end bearing journal diameter:
  Standard .... 50.0 + 0 mm - 0.016
  Undersize .... 49.7 + 0 mm - 0.016
Maximum bearing journal out-of-round .... 0.007 mm
Main and big-end bearing running learance (typical - no values
specified by Citroën) .... 0.025 to 0.050 mm

Piston rings

End gaps:
  Upper and middle (compression) rings .... 0.20 to 0.40 mm
  Bottom (oil control) ring .... 0.25 to 0.50 mm

Torque wrench settings

Refer to Chapter 2, Part A Specifications

1 General information

Included in this part of Chapter 2 are the engine removal and general overhaul procedures for the cylinder head, cylinder block/crankcase and internal engine components.

The information ranges from advice concerning preparation for an overhaul and the purchase of replacement parts, to detailed step-by-step procedures covering removal, inspection, renovation and refitting of internal engine parts.

The following Sections have been compiled based on the assumption that the engine has been removed from the vehicle. For information concerning in-vehicle engine repair, as well as the removal and refitting of the external components necessary for the overhaul, refer to Chapter 2, Part A and to Section 6 of this Part.

2 Engine overhaul - general information

It is not always easy to determine when, or if, an engine should be completely overhauled, as a number of factors must be considered. Also bear in mind that it may prove more economical to purchase a reconditioned engine than to carry out a full overhaul; however, this cannot be accurately determined until the engine has been fully dismantled.

High mileage is not necessarily an indication that an engine overhaul is required, while low mileage does not preclude the need for an overhaul. Frequency of servicing is the most important consideration. An engine which has had regular and frequent oil and filter changes, in addition to the other specified maintenance (see Chapter 1), is likely to give many thousands of miles of reliable service. Conversely, a neglected engine may require an overhaul very early in its life.

Excessive oil consumption is an indication that piston rings, valve seals and/or valve guides are in need of attention. Make sure that oil leaks are not responsible before deciding that the piston rings and/or valve guides are worn. Perform a cylinder compression or a leakdown test, to determine the extent of the work required (see Chapter 2, Part A).

Check the oil pressure using a suitable oil pressure gauge fitted in place of the engine oil pressure switch (follow the equipment manufacturer's instructions), and compare it with the figure given in the Specifications. If the oil pressure is extremely low, the main and big-end bearings and/or the oil pump are probably worn.

Loss of power, rough running, knocking or metallic engine noises, excessive valve gear noise, or high fuel consumption may also point to the need for an overhaul, especially if all the conditions are present at the same time. If a complete service does not remedy the situation, overhaul is the only course of action available.

A full engine overhaul involves restoring the specifications (clearances, endfloats, etc) of the internal components to the standards used in a new engine. During a complete overhaul, the pistons and piston rings are renewed, and the cylinder bores are reconditioned. New main bearings and big-end bearings are generally fitted, and if necessary, the crankshaft may be reground to compensate for wear in the bearing journals. The valves should also be inspected and serviced as well, since they are usually in less-than-perfect condition if the engine has reached the stage where overhaul is required. If a complete overhaul is carried out, the end result should be to the standard of a new engine, and should provide many trouble-free miles of service. **Note:** *Critical cooling system components such as the hoses, thermostat and coolant pump should be carefully inspected, and if necessary renewed, when an engine is overhauled. The radiator should also be checked carefully, to ensure that it is not clogged or leaking.*

> **HAYNES HINT** *Always pay careful attention to the condition of the oil pump when overhauling the engine, and renew it if in any doubt as to its serviceability*

Before beginning an engine overhaul, carefully read through all the procedures involved, to familiarize yourself with the scope and requirements of the job. Overhauling an engine is not difficult if you follow all of the instructions carefully, have the necessary tools and equipment ready to hand, and pay close attention to all the recommended specifications. However, engine overhaul can be time-consuming; plan on the vehicle being off the road for a minimum of two weeks, especially if parts must be taken to an engineering works for repair or reconditioning. Check on the availability of new parts, and make sure that any necessary special tools and equipment are obtained in advance. Most work can be done with typical hand tools, although a number of precision measuring

instruments will be required to inspect some parts, in order to determine whether renewal is required. Often, an engineering works will handle the inspection of parts, and offer advice concerning reconditioning and renewal. **Note:** *Always wait until the engine has been completely dismantled and all components, especially the cylinder block, have been inspected, before deciding which service and repair operations must be entrusted to an engineering works. Since the condition of the cylinder block will be the major factor to consider when determining whether to overhaul the original engine or buy a reconditioned unit, do not purchase parts or have overhaul work done on other components until the block has been thoroughly inspected. As a general rule, time is the primary cost of an overhaul, so it does not pay to fit worn or sub-standard parts.*

As a final note, to ensure maximum life and minimum trouble from an overhauled engine, everything must be assembled with care in a spotlessly-clean environment.

3 Engine removal - methods and precautions

If you have decided to remove an engine for overhaul or major repair work, several preliminary steps should be taken.

Locating a suitable place to work is extremely important. Adequate working space, along with storage space for the vehicle, will be required. If a garage is not available, at the very least a flat, level, clean work surface is required.

Cleaning the engine compartment and engine before beginning the removal procedure will help to keep tools clean and organized.

An engine hoist or an A-frame will also be required. Make sure that the equipment is rated in excess of the combined weight of the engine and transmission. Safety is of primary importance, considering the potential hazards involved in lifting the engine out of the vehicle.

If this is the first time you have removed an engine, an assistant should ideally be available. Advice and aid from someone more experienced would also be helpful. There are many instances when one person cannot simultaneously perform all of the operations required when lifting the engine out of the vehicle.

Plan the operation carefully before beginning. Obtain all of the tools and equipment required prior to beginning the job. Equipment necessary to perform engine removal and installation safely and with relative ease includes (in addition to an engine hoist) a heavy-duty trolley jack, complete sets of spanners and sockets as described in the preliminary Sections of this manual, wooden blocks, and plenty of rags and cleaning

solvent to cope with spilled oil, coolant and fuel. If the hoist is to be hired, make sure that you arrange for it in advance, and perform all of the operations possible without it beforehand. This will save you money and time.

Plan for the vehicle to be out of use for some time. An engineering works may be required to perform some of the work which the DIY enthusiast cannot accomplish without special equipment. These establishments often have a busy schedule, so it would be a good idea to consult them before removing the engine, in order to gain a rough estimate of the amount of time required to overhaul or repair components which may require attention.

Always be extremely careful when removing and refitting the engine. Serious injury can result from careless actions. By planning ahead and taking plenty of time, the job (although a major task) can be accomplished successfully.

Due to the limited clearance in the engine compartment, it is recommended that the engine and transmission are removed together as a unit from above.

4 Engine and manual transmission - removal and refitting

Removal

1 Open the bonnet to its fully-raised position (nearly vertical), and support securely by positioning the bonnet support strut accordingly.

2 Apply the handbrake, then jack up the front of the vehicle and support securely on axle stands (see *"Jacking and vehicle support"*).

3 Remove the front roadwheels.

4 Disconnect both battery leads.

5 Drain the cooling system as described in Chapter 1.

6 Drain the engine oil as described in Chapter 1.

7 Drain the transmission oil as described in Chapter 1.

8 Where applicable, remove the intercooler (Turbo models) or the air distribution housing (XUD9/A - D9B engine) as described in Chapter 4.

9 Where applicable, release the securing clips and remove the air hose connecting the air cleaner assembly to the top of the inlet manifold.

10 On non-turbo models, unbolt the air cleaner assembly, and remove it from the engine compartment.

11 Remove the battery and the battery tray as described in Chapter 5.

12 On Turbo models, loosen the hose clips and disconnect the air tubing from the air cleaner and the air tube behind the inlet manifold.

4.13a Unbolt the air tubing from the battery support plate . . .

4.13b . . . and lift out the air tubing - Turbo models

4.21a Disconnecting the wiring plug from the oil pressure warning light switch

4.21b Transmission earth connection (arrowed)

4.22a Disconnect the wiring from the relay/junction box

13 Unbolt the air tubing from the metal battery support plate, and lift the air tubing from the engine compartment **(see illustrations)**.

14 Unclip the wiring harness from the battery support plate, noting its routing.

15 Unscrew the four securing bolts, and remove the battery support plate from the engine compartment.

16 Remove the alternator as described in Chapter 5.

17 Where applicable, remove the power steering pump as described in Chapter 10.

18 On models with air conditioning, unbolt the air conditioning compressor and move it to one side, leaving the hoses connected. *Refer to the warning in Chapter 3, Section 12 - do not attempt to disconnect any of the refrigerant pipes or hoses.*

19 Disconnect the fuel supply and return hoses from the fuel injection pump with reference to Chapter 4.

20 Disconnect the accelerator cable from the fuel injection pump, and move it clear of the engine, as described in Chapter 4.

21 Disconnect the wiring from the following components:
(a) *Starter motor (see Chapter 5).*
(b) *Alternator (see Chapter 5).*
(c) *Oil pressure warning light switch (see illustration).*
(d) *Oil level sensor - where applicable (see Chapter 5).*
(e) *Coolant sensors located in*

thermostat/fuel filter housing (see Chapter 3).
(f) *Fuel injection pump.*
(g) *Reversing light switch.*
(h) *Crankshaft TDC sensor.*
(i) *Transmission earth connection (see illustration).*
(j) *Glow plug feed wire.*

22 Lift the cover of the relay/junction box at the left-hand front corner of the engine compartment, and disconnect the wiring plugs from the relays and the connectors in the box, noting their locations. Where applicable, note the clip securing the connector block to the box. Also disconnect the wiring from the preheating system relay/timer unit at the front of the relay/junction box **(see illustrations)**.

23 Unscrew the two securing nuts, and lift the relay/junction box from the body panel **(see illustration)**.

24 Turn the locking collar anti-clockwise, and disconnect the wiring connector from the terminal block in the wing panel.

25 Release the wiring harnesses from their securing clips, noting their locations and routing, then lift the wiring harnesses from the engine compartment.

26 Disconnect the brake vacuum servo hose from the vacuum pump.

27 Disconnect the coolant hoses from the radiator, with reference to Chapter 3, Section 2.

28 Disconnect the heater hoses from the

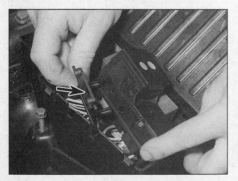

4.22b Note the clip (arrowed) securing the connector block to the box

4.22c Disconnecting the wiring from the preheating relay/timer unit

4.23 Removing a relay/junction box securing nut

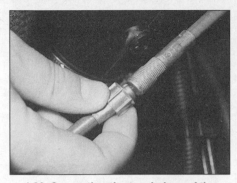

4.30 Separating the two halves of the speedometer cable connector

4.38a Unscrew the nut securing the transmission mounting to the body mounting bracket . . .

4.38b . . . and recover the washer

4.39a Remove the two securing nuts . . .

heater matrix connectors on the bulkhead, again with reference to Chapter 3, Section 2.

29 Disconnect the clutch cable from the release lever, and move the cable clear of the engine/transmission assembly, as described in Chapter 6, Section 3.

30 Separate the two halves of the speedometer cable connector below the engine compartment bulkhead **(see illustration)**.

31 On models equipped with power steering, undo the nuts securing the power steering pipe to the underside of the engine and transmission, and free the pipe from its retaining studs.

32 Disconnect the exhaust downpipe from the exhaust manifold or turbocharger, as applicable, with reference to Chapter 4, Section 24.

33 Disconnect the driveshafts from the transmission, as described in Chapter 8.

34 Disconnect the gearchange link rods from the transmission, with reference to Chapter 7, Part A, Section 3.

35 Make a final check to ensure that all relevant hoses, pipes and wires have been disconnected to facilitate engine removal.

36 Attach a suitable hoist and lifting tackle to the engine lifting brackets on the cylinder head, and position the hoist to just take the weight of the engine. Note that the engine/transmission assembly must be tilted to clear the surrounding components in the engine

compartment, and the use of adjustable lifting tackle will greatly ease this task.

37 Remove the lower engine mounting bracket as described in Chapter 2, Part A, Section 19.

38 Working at the left-hand side of the engine compartment, unscrew the nut securing the transmission mounting to the body mounting bracket, and recover the washer **(see illustrations)**.

39 Remove the two nuts securing the body mounting bracket to the body, and withdraw the body mounting bracket from the engine compartment. Recover the bush from the mounting stud **(see illustrations)**.

40 Remove the plate covering the right-hand engine mounting on the body, then lift out the rubber buffer and remove the nut securing the engine mounting bracket to the body (refer to Chapter 2, Part A, Section 9 for further details).

41 Carefully raise the hoist, and lift the engine/transmission assembly from the engine compartment. The aid of an assistant will greatly ease the process, as the assembly will have to be tilted and manipulated to clear the body panels and surrounding engine compartment components **(see illustrations)**.

42 With the engine/transmission assembly removed, support the assembly on suitable blocks of wood positioned on a workbench, or failing that, on a clean area of the workshop floor.

4.39b . . . and remove the body mounting bracket

4.39c Recover the bush from the mounting stud

4.41a Lift the engine/transmission assembly from the engine compartment

4.41b Note the angle of the engine/transmission assembly required to clear surrounding components

43 Unbolt and remove the lower flywheel cover plate from the transmission.

44 On models with a "pull-type" clutch release mechanism (see Chapter 6 for further information) withdraw the retaining pin and remove the clutch release lever from the top of the release fork shaft. This is necessary to allow the fork shaft to rotate freely, to disengage from the release bearing as the transmission is pulled away from the engine unit. Make an alignment mark across the centre of the clutch release fork shaft using a scriber, paint or similar, and mark its relative position on the transmission housing.

45 Unscrew the securing bolts and remove the starter motor.

46 Ensure that both engine and transmission are adequately supported, then unscrew and remove the engine-to-transmission bolts, noting the location of each bolt, and of any brackets which may be secured by the bolts.

47 Carefully withdraw the transmission from the engine, ensuring that the weight of the transmission is not allowed to hang on the input shaft while it is engaged with the clutch friction disc.

48 If they are loose, remove the locating dowels from the engine or transmission unit, and keep them in a safe place.

49 On models with a "pull-type" clutch, make a second alignment mark on the transmission housing, marking the relative position of the release fork mark after removal, noting the angle at which the release fork is positioned. This mark can then be used to position the release fork prior to installation, to ensure the fork correctly engages with the clutch release bearing as the transmission is installed.

Refitting

50 Fit new driveshaft oil seals to the transmission, with reference to Chapter 7, Part A, Section 4.

51 Apply a little high-melting-point grease to the splines of the transmission input shaft. Do not apply too much, otherwise there is a possibility of the grease contaminating the clutch friction plate.

52 Ensure that the locating dowels are correctly positioned in the engine or transmission prior to reconnecting the engine to the transmission.

53 On models with a "pull-type" clutch, prior to reconnecting the transmission to the engine, position the clutch release bearing so that its HAUT mark is at the top and the BAS mark is at the bottom, and align the release fork shaft mark with the second mark made on the transmission housing. This will ensure that the release fork and bearing will engage correctly as the transmission is refitted to the engine. If the bearing and fork are correctly engaged, the mark on the shaft should be aligned with the original mark made on the transmission housing when the transmission is fully engaged with the engine. *Ensure the release fork and bearing are correctly engaged before finally bolting the transmission onto the engine.*

54 Carefully offer the transmission to the engine, until the locating dowels are engaged, ensuring that the weight of the transmission is not allowed to hang on the input shaft as it is engaged with the clutch friction disc.

55 Refit the engine-to-transmission bolts and tighten them, ensuring that any brackets secured by the bolts are correctly positioned, as noted before removal.

56 Refit the starter motor and tighten the securing bolts.

57 On models with a "pull-type" clutch release mechanism, refit the clutch release lever to the top of the release fork shaft, and refit the retaining pin.

58 Refit the lower flywheel cover plate to the transmission, and tighten the securing bolts.

59 Reconnect the hoist and lifting tackle to the engine lifting brackets, and lift the assembly over the engine compartment, ensuring that the assembly is tilted as necessary to clear surrounding components, as during removal.

60 Lower the assembly into position in the engine compartment, manipulating the hoist and lifting tackle as necessary.

61 Refit the nut securing the right-hand engine mounting bracket to the body, but do not fully tighten it at this stage.

62 Refit the left-hand transmission body mounting bracket, then refit the nut securing the transmission mounting to the body mounting bracket. Again, do not fully tighten the nut at this stage.

63 Refit the lower engine mounting bracket as described in Chapter 2, Part A, Section 19.

64 Tighten the right-hand engine mounting nut and the left-hand transmission mounting nut to the specified torques, then disconnect the lifting tackle and the hoist from the engine.

65 Reconnect the gearchange link rods to the transmission, as described in Chapter 7, Part A.

66 Reconnect the driveshafts to the transmission as described in Chapter 8.

67 Reconnect the exhaust downpipe to the exhaust manifold or turbocharger, as applicable, with reference to Chapter 4, Section 24.

68 On models equipped with power steering, fit the power steering pipe to the retaining studs on the underside of the engine and transmission, and refit the securing nuts.

69 Reconnect the two halves of the speedometer cable connector.

70 Reconnect the clutch cable to the release lever, with reference to Chapter 6, Section 3, ensuring that it is routed as noted before removal.

71 Reconnect the heater hoses to the heater matrix connectors, and reconnect the coolant hoses to the radiator, with reference to Chapter 3, Section 2.

72 Reconnect the brake vacuum servo hose to the vacuum pump.

73 Refit the wiring harnesses and the relay/junction box (reconnect the wiring connector to the terminal block in the wing panel before fitting the relay/junction box), and reconnect all wiring connectors to the components listed in paragraph 21. Ensure that all wiring is routed as noted before removal.

74 Reconnect the accelerator cable to the fuel injection pump, and adjust as necessary as described in Chapter 4.

75 Reconnect the fuel supply and return hoses to the fuel injection pump.

76 Where applicable, refit the air conditioning compressor.

77 Where applicable, refit the power steering pump as described in Chapter 10.

78 Refit the alternator as described in Chapter 5.

79 Refit the battery support plate, and clip the wiring harness into position at edge of the plate.

80 On Turbo models, refit the air tubing to the air tube, battery support plate and air cleaner.

81 Refit the battery tray and the battery.

82 On non-turbo models, refit the air cleaner assembly.

83 Where applicable, refit the air hose between the air cleaner assembly and the top of the inlet manifold.

84 Where applicable, refit the intercooler or the air distribution housing.

85 Refit the roadwheels, and lower the vehicle to the ground.

86 Refill the transmission with the correct grade and quantity of oil as described in Chapter 1.

87 Refill the engine with the correct grade and quantity of oil as described in Chapter 1.

88 Refill the cooling system as described in Chapter 1.

89 Reconnect the battery leads.

90 Bleed the fuel system as described in Chapter 4.

91 Where applicable, bleed the power steering fluid circuit as described in Chapter 10.

5 Engine and automatic transmission - removal and refitting

Removal

1 Proceed as described in Section 4, paragraphs 1 to 28 inclusive.

2 Detach the kickdown inner cable from the fuel injection pump lever, then slacken the outer cable locknuts, and free the cable from its mounting bracket.

3 Release the kickdown cable from any relevant retaining clips, so that it is free to be removed with the transmission unit when the engine and transmission are separated.

4 Separate the two halves of the speedometer cable connector below the engine compartment bulkhead.

5 On models equipped with power steering, undo the nuts securing the power steering pipe to the underside of the engine and transmission, and free the pipe from its retaining studs.

6 Disconnect the exhaust downpipe from the exhaust manifold or turbocharger, as applicable, with reference to Chapter 4, Section 24.

7 Disconnect the driveshafts from the transmission, as described in Chapter 8.

8 Unscrew the union nut securing the dipstick tube to the transmission sump, then undo the bolt securing the tube to the transmission housing, and remove the dipstick from the transmission unit.

9 Disconnect the wiring connector from the starter inhibitor/reversing light switch and, where necessary, the speedometer drive housing. Undo the retaining bolt(s) and disconnect the earth strap(s) from the top of the transmission housing.

10 Slacken the retaining clips, and disconnect the coolant hoses from the transmission fluid cooler.

11 Undo the two screws securing the outer selector cable to its retaining bracket, and carefully lever the inner cable end fitting from its balljoint on the transmission selector lever. Note the transmission selector lever must not be disturbed until the cable is refitted. As a precaution, mark the position of the lever in relation to the transmission housing. Work back along the selector cable, releasing it from any relevant retaining clips, and position it clear of the transmission unit.

12 Proceed as described in Section 4, paragraphs 35 to 42 inclusive.

13 Unscrew the securing bolts and remove the starter motor.

14 Unbolt and remove the lower driveplate cover plate from the transmission, to gain access to the torque converter retaining bolts.

15 Slacken and remove the visible torque converter retaining bolt then, using a socket and extension bar to rotate the crankshaft pulley, undo the remaining bolts securing the torque converter to the driveplate as they become accessible. There are three bolts in total.

16 To ensure that the torque converter does not fall out as the transmission is removed, secure it in position using a length of metal strip bolted to one of the starter motor bolt holes.

17 Ensure that both engine and transmission are adequately supported, then unscrew and remove the engine-to-transmission bolts, noting the location of each bolt and of any brackets which may be secured by the bolts.

18 Carefully withdraw the transmission from the engine. If they are loose, remove the locating dowels from the engine or transmission unit, and keep them in a safe place.

Refitting

19 Fit new driveshaft oil seals to the transmission, with reference to Chapter 7, Part B, Section 5.

20 Ensure that the bush fitted to the centre of the crankshaft is in good condition, and apply a little Molykote G1 grease to the torque converter centring pin. Do not apply too much grease, otherwise there is a possibility of the grease contaminating the torque converter.

21 Ensure that the engine/transmission locating dowels are correctly positioned prior to reconnection.

22 Carefully offer the transmission to the engine, until the locating dowels are engaged; refit the engine-to-transmission bolts and tighten them, ensuring that any brackets secured by the bolts are correctly positioned, as noted before removal.

23 Refit the torque converter-to-driveplate bolts, and tighten them to the specified torque (see Chapter 7, Part B), then remove the torque converter retaining strip.

24 Refit the starter motor and tighten the securing bolts.

25 Refit the lower driveplate cover to the transmission, and tighten the securing bolts.

26 Proceed as described in Section 4, paragraphs 59 to 64 inclusive.

27 Reconnect and adjust the selector cable as described in Chapter 7, Part B, Section 2.

28 Reconnect the coolant hoses to the transmission fluid cooler.

29 Reconnect the earth straps to the top of the transmission housing, and reconnect the starter inhibitor/reversing light switch, and where necessary, the speedometer drive housing wiring connector.

30 Refit the dipstick tube assembly.

31 Reconnect the driveshafts to the transmission as described in Chapter 8.

32 Reconnect the exhaust downpipe to the turbocharger or exhaust manifold, as applicable, with reference to Chapter 4, Section 22.

33 Where applicable, refit the power steering pipe to the underside of the engine and transmission.

34 Reconnect the two halves of the speedometer cable connector.

35 Reconnect and adjust the kickdown cable, as described in Chapter 7, Part B, Section 7.

36 Proceed as described in Section 4, paragraphs 71 to 91 inclusive.

6 Engine overhaul - dismantling sequence

1 It is far easier to dismantle and work on the engine if it is mounted on a portable engine stand. These stands can often be hired from a tool hire shop. Depending on the type of stand used, the flywheel/driveplate may have to be removed from the engine, to allow the engine stand bolts to be tightened into the end of the cylinder block.

2 If a stand is not available, it is possible to dismantle the engine while supported on blocks on a sturdy workbench or on the floor. Be extra-careful not to tip or drop the engine when working without a stand.

3 Before starting the overhaul procedure, the external engine ancillary components must be removed (this is the case even if a reconditioned engine is to be fitted, in which case, the components from the old engine must be transferred to the reconditioned unit). These components include the following:

(a) Alternator mounting bracket (see Chapter 5).

(b) Fuel injection pump and mounting bracket, and fuel injectors and glow plugs (see Chapter 4).

(c) Inlet and exhaust manifolds (see Chapter 4).

(d) Oil filter (see Chapter 1).

(e) Oil cooler (see Chapter 2, Part A, Section 20).

(f) Engine/transmission mountings (see Chapter 2, Part A, Section 19).

(g) Oil pressure switch and oil level sensor (where applicable) (see Chapter 5).

(h) Engine lifting brackets.

(i) Coolant temperature sensor (where applicable) (see Chapter 5).

(j) Thermostat/fuel filter housing (see Chapter 3).

(k) Power steering pump mounting bracket.

(l) Wiring harnesses and brackets.

(m) Oil filler tube and dipstick.

(n) Rear coolant gallery, coolant pipe and hoses (see illustrations).

(o) TDC sensor (operates tachometer - mark the fitted position of the sensor before removal).

6.3a Rear coolant gallery and coolant pipe securing bolts (arrowed)

6.3b Recover the O-ring from the rear coolant gallery

Note: *When removing the ancillary components from the engine, pay close attention to details which may be helpful or important during refitting. Note the fitted position of gaskets, seals, spacers, washers, bolts and other small items.*

4 If a short engine is being obtained (which consists of the cylinder block, crankshaft, pistons and connecting rods all assembled as a unit), then the cylinder head, sump, and possibly other components (such as the oil pump) will have to be removed from the old unit and fitted to the new unit.

5 If a complete overhaul is being planned, the engine can be dismantled using the following sequence:

(a) *Inlet and exhaust manifolds (see Chapter 4).*
(b) *Timing belt and sprockets (see Chapter 2, Part A, Sections 7 and 8).*

7.2 Withdrawing a tappet shim

(c) *Cylinder head (see Chapter 2, Part A, Section 13).*
(d) *Flywheel/driveplate (see Chapter 2, Part A, Section 18).*
(e) *Sump (see Chapter 2, Part A, Section 14).*
(f) *Oil pump (see Chapter 2, Part A, Section 15).*
(g) *Piston/connecting rod assemblies (see Section 10).*
(h) *Crankshaft (see Section 11).*

6 Before beginning the dismantling and overhaul procedures, make sure that all of the correct tools have been obtained. Refer to the preliminary Sections at the beginning of this manual for further information.

7 Cylinder head - dismantling

Note: *New and reconditioned cylinder heads are available from the manufacturers, or from engine overhaul specialists. Due to the fact that some specialist tools are required for the dismantling and inspection procedures, and new components may not be readily available, it may be more practical and economical for the home mechanic to purchase a reconditioned head, rather than to dismantle, inspect and recondition the original head. A valve spring compressor tool will be required for this operation.*

1 With the cylinder head removed as described in Chapter 2, Part A, Section 13, clean away all external dirt, then remove the following components, if not already done:

(a) *Brake vacuum pump (direct-drive type) (Chapter 9).*
(b) *Fuel injectors (Chapter 4).*
(c) *Glow plugs (Chapter 4).*
(d) *Camshaft (Chapter 2, Part A, Section 11).*

2 Withdraw the bucket tappets, together with their respective shims, keeping them all identified for location **(see illustration)**.

3 To remove a valve, fit a valve spring compressor tool. Ensure that the arms of the compressor tool are securely positioned on the head of the valve and the spring cap. The valves are deeply recessed, so the end of the compressor may need to be extended with a tube or box section with a "window" for access **(see illustration)**.

4 Note that non-turbo models are fitted with double valve springs. Compress the valve spring(s) to relieve the pressure of the spring cap acting on the collets.

> **HAYNES HiNT** *If the spring cap sticks to the valve stem, support the compressor tool, and give the end a light tap with a soft-faced mallet to help free the spring cap.*

5 Extract the two split collets, then slowly release the compressor tool **(see illustration)**.

6 Remove the spring cap, spring(s), and the spring seat, then withdraw the valve. The valve stem oil seals (where applicable), can be removed using pliers if necessary, as they must be renewed on refitting **(see illustrations)**.

7.3 Valve spring compressor in position prior to removal of valve

7.5 Extracting the split collets

7.6a Remove the spring cap . . .

7.6b . . . spring . . .

7.6c . . . spring seat . . .

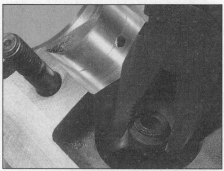

7.6d Removing a valve stem oil seal

7.7 Place each valve assembly in a labelled polythene bag

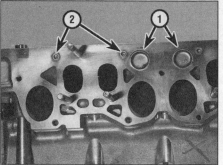

8.6 Core plugs (1) and oil gallery plugs (2) - cylinder head inverted

8.14 Checking the cylinder head gasket face for distortion

7 Repeat the procedure for the remaining valves, keeping all components in strict order, so that they can be refitted in their original positions, unless all the components are to be renewed. If the components are to be kept and used again, place each valve assembly in a labelled polythene bag or a similar small container **(see illustration)**. Note that, as with cylinder numbering, the valves are normally numbered from the flywheel end of the engine.

8 If necessary, remove the timing probe blanking plug from the timing belt end (injector side) of the cylinder head.

9 Dismantling of the cylinder head is now complete.

---

8 Cylinder head and valve components -
cleaning and inspection

1 Thorough cleaning of the cylinder head and valve components, followed by a detailed inspection, will enable a decision to be made on whether further work is necessary before reassembling the components.

Cleaning

2 Scrape away all traces of old gasket material and sealing compound from the cylinder head surfaces. Take care not to damage the cylinder head surfaces.

3 Scrape away the carbon from the surfaces of the cylinder head surrounding the valves, then wash the cylinder head thoroughly with paraffin or a suitable solvent.

4 Scrape off any heavy carbon deposits that may have formed on the valves, then use a power-operated wire brush to remove deposits from the valve heads and stems.

5 For complete cleaning, ideally the core plugs should be removed. Drill a small hole in the plugs, then insert a self-tapping screw and pull out the plugs using a pair of grips or a slide hammer.

6 Remove all oil gallery plugs. Tight plugs may have to be drilled out, in which case, use a new plug and re-cut the threads in the cylinder head on refitting **(see illustration)**.

7 If the head is extremely dirty, it should be steam-cleaned.

8 If the head has been steam-cleaned, clean all oil holes and oil galleries one more time on completion. Flush all internal passages with warm water until the water runs clear, dry the head thoroughly, and wipe all machined surfaces with a light oil. If you have access to compressed air, use it to speed the drying process, and to blow out all the oil holes and galleries.

> ⚠️ *Warning: Wear eye protection when using compressed air!*

9 If the head is relatively clean, an adequate cleaning job can be achieved with hot soapy water and a stiff brush. Take plenty of time, and do a thorough job.

> **HAYNES HiNT** *Regardless of the cleaning method used, be sure to clean all oil holes and galleries very thoroughly, dry the head completely, and coat all machined surfaces with light oil.*

10 The threaded holes in the cylinder head must be cleaned out, to ensure accurate torque readings when tightening fixings during reassembly. Run the correct-size tap (which can be determined from the size of the relevant bolt which fits in the hole) into each of the holes, to remove rust, corrosion, thread sealant or other contamination, and to restore damaged threads. If possible, use compressed air to clear the holes of debris produced by this operation. Do not forget to clean the threads of all bolts and nuts as well.

11 After coating the mating surfaces of the new core plugs with suitable sealant, fit them to the cylinder head. Make sure that they are driven in straight and seated correctly, or leakage could result. Special tools are available for this purpose, but a large socket, with an outside diameter which will just fit into the core plug, will work just as well.

12 Refit the oil gallery plugs, using new sealing washers where applicable. Tighten the plugs securely.

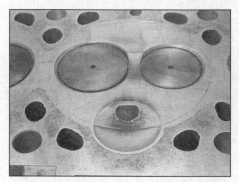

8.16 This swirl chamber shows the initial stages of cracking and burning

Inspection

Note: *Be sure to perform all the following inspection procedures before concluding that the services of a machine shop or engine overhaul specialist are required. Make a list of all items that require attention.*

Cylinder head

13 Inspect the head very carefully for cracks, evidence of coolant leakage, and other damage. If cracks are found, a new cylinder head should be obtained.

14 Use a straight-edge and feeler blade to check that the cylinder head gasket surface is not distorted **(see illustration)**. Check the head surface both diagonally, and along its edge. Do not position the straight-edge over the swirl chambers, as these may be proud of the cylinder head face. If the specified distortion limit is exceeded, machining of the gasket face is not recommended by the manufacturers, so the only course of action is to renew the cylinder head.

15 Check that the overall height of the cylinder head is within the specified limits, which will indicate if the head has been machined in a mistaken attempt to compensate for surface distortion. If the overall height is outside the specified limits, the cylinder head should be renewed.

16 Inspect the valve seats and swirl chambers for burning or cracks **(see illustration)**. Both can be renewed, but the work should be entrusted to a specialist.

8.17 Checking a swirl chamber protrusion

8.19 Measuring a valve stem with a micrometer

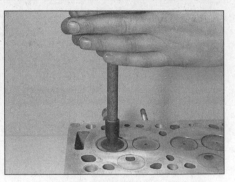

8.27 Grinding-in a valve

17 Using a dial test indicator, check that the swirl chamber protrusion is within the limits given in the Specifications. Zero the dial test indicator on the gasket surface of the cylinder head, then measure the protrusion of the swirl chamber **(see illustration)**.

18 Examine the valve seats in the cylinder head. If the seats are severely pitted, cracked or burned, then they will need to be recut or renewed by an engine overhaul specialist. If only slight pitting is evident, this can be removed by grinding the valve heads and seats together with coarse, then fine, grinding paste, as described later in this Section.

19 Check for play (side-to-side movement) of the valves in the valve guides. Excessive play in the guide may be caused by wear in either component. Measure the valve stem with a micrometer, or try the fit of a new valve, if available, to establish whether it is the valve or the guide which is worn **(see illustration)**. If the valve guides are worn, they can be renewed, but this work is best carried out by a Citroën dealer or an engine overhaul specialist.

20 Check the tappet bores in the cylinder head for wear. If excessive wear is evident, the cylinder head must be renewed.

21 Examine the camshaft bearing surfaces in the cylinder head and bearing caps. Wear here can only be corrected by renewing the head. Also examine the camshaft as described in Chapter 2, Part A, Section 11.

22 Inspect the studs for the manifolds and camshaft bearing caps. Renew them if necessary by using a proprietary stud extractor, or lock two nuts together on the exposed threads. Studs which have come out by mistake should be cleaned up and refitted using thread-locking fluid.

Valves

23 Examine the head of each valve for pitting, burning, cracks and general wear, and check the valve stem for scoring and wear ridges. Rotate the valve, and check for any obvious indication that it is bent. Look for pitting and excessive wear on the end of each valve stem. If the valve appears satisfactory at this stage, measure the valve stem diameter at several points using a micrometer. Any

significant difference in the readings obtained indicates wear of the valve stem. Should any of these conditions be apparent, the valve(s) must be renewed.

24 Note that from early 1992, modified exhaust valves were fitted to all engines. Coinciding with this modification, modified exhaust valve seats were fitted, and valve stem oil seals were fitted to both the exhaust and inlet valves. The later-type exhaust valves can be fitted to the earlier-type cylinder head, provided that the later-type exhaust valve seat is also fitted.

25 If the valves are in satisfactory condition, they should be ground (lapped) onto their respective seats, to ensure a smooth gas-tight seal.

26 Valve grinding is carried out as follows. Place the cylinder head upside-down on a bench, with a block of wood at each end to give clearance for the valve stems.

27 Smear a trace of coarse carborundum paste on the seat face in the cylinder head, and press a suction grinding tool onto the relevant valve head. With a semi-rotary action, grind the valve head to its seat, lifting the valve occasionally to redistribute the grinding paste **(see illustration)**. When a dull, matt, even surface is produced on the faces of both the valve seat and the valve, wipe off the paste and repeat the process with fine carborundum paste. A light spring placed under the valve head will greatly ease this operation. When a smooth unbroken ring of light grey matt finish is produced on both the valve and seat faces, the grinding operation is complete. Carefully clean away every trace of grinding paste, taking great care to leave none in the ports or in the valve guides. Clean the valves and valve seats with a paraffin-soaked rag, then with a clean rag, and finally, if an air line is available, blow the valves, valve guides and cylinder head ports clean.

Valve springs

28 Check that all the valve springs are intact. If any one is broken, all should be renewed.

29 If possible, check the free height of the springs against new ones, then stand each spring on a flat surface and check it for squareness. If a spring is found to be too

short, or damaged in any way, renew all the springs as a set. Springs suffer from fatigue, and it is a good idea to renew them, even if they look serviceable.

Tappets

30 Examine the surfaces of the bucket tappets for wear or scoring. If excessive wear is evident, the tappet should be renewed.

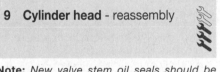

9 Cylinder head - reassembly

Note: *New valve stem oil seals should be fitted on reassembly, even if no seals were originally fitted.*

1 With all the components cleaned, starting at one end of the cylinder head, fit the valve components as follows. If the original components are being refitted, all components must be refitted in their original positions.

2 Lubricate the valve stem oil seal with clean engine oil, then fit the oil seal by pushing it into position in the cylinder head using a suitable socket **(see illustration)**. Ensure that the seal is fully engaged with the cylinder head.

3 Insert the appropriate valve into its guide (if new valves are being fitted, insert each valve into the location to which it has been ground), ensuring that the valve stem is well-lubricated

9.2 Fitting a valve stem oil seal using a socket

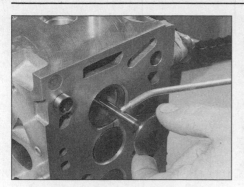

9.3 Lubricate the valves before refitting

9.11 Fitting a bucket tappet. Note shim located on top of valve (arrowed)

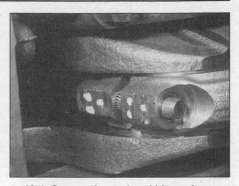

10.4 Connecting rod and big-end cap marked for identification (No 3 cylinder shown)

with clean engine oil **(see illustration)**. To prevent damage to the oil seal as the valve is installed, wind a short length of tape round the top of the valve stem, to cover the collet groove.

4 Remove the tape from the valve stem.

5 Fit the spring seat.

6 Fit the valve spring(s) (either way up) and the spring cap.

7 Fit the spring compressor tool, and compress the valve spring(s) until the spring cap passes beyond the collet groove in the valve stem.

8 Apply a little grease to the collet groove, then fit the split collets into the groove, with the narrow ends nearest the spring. The grease should hold them in the groove.

9 Slowly release the compressor tool, ensuring that the collets are not dislodged from the groove. When the compressor is fully released, give the top of the valve assembly a tap with a soft-faced mallet to settle the components.

10 Repeat the procedure for the remaining valves, ensuring that if the original components are being used, they are all refitted in their original positions.

11 Oil and insert the bucket tappets, together with their respective shims, making sure that they are fitted in the correct locations, and with the size markings facing downwards (where applicable) **(see illustration)**. Make a note of the shim thickness fitted at each position, if not already done, for reference when checking the valve clearances.

12 Where applicable, refit the timing probe blanking plug.

13 Refit the following components, as applicable (if desired, these components can be refitted after refitting the cylinder head).

(a) *Camshaft (Chapter 2, Part A, Section 11).*
(b) *Glow plugs (Chapter 4).*
(c) *Fuel injectors (Chapter 4).*
(d) *Brake vacuum pump (direct-drive type) (Chapter 9).*

10 Piston/connecting rod assembly - removal

1 Remove the cylinder head as described in Chapter 2, Part A, Section 13.

2 Remove the oil pump as described in Chapter 2, Part A, Section 15.

3 If there is a pronounced wear ridge at the top of any bore, it may be necessary to remove it with a scraper or ridge reamer, to avoid piston damage during removal. Such a ridge may indicate that reboring is necessary, which will entail new pistons in any case. See also Section 12.

4 Check that each connecting rod and big-end bearing cap is marked for position and, if not, mark them with a centre-punch or paint on the manifold side of the engine, No 1 at the flywheel end **(see illustration)**.

5 Turn the crankshaft to bring pistons 1 and 4 to BDC (bottom dead centre). Unscrew the nuts from No 1 piston big-end bearing cap, then take off the cap and recover the bottom bearing half-shell **(see illustration)**. If the bearing shells are to be re-used, tape the cap and the shell together.

6 To prevent the possibility of damage to the crankshaft bearing journals, tape or suitable lengths of tubing can be fitted to the connecting rod studs before removing the assemblies, to cover the threads **(see illustration)**.

7 Using a hammer handle, push the piston up through the bore, and remove it from the cylinder block. Recover the bearing shell, and tape it to the connecting rod if it is to be re-used.

8 Loosely refit the big-end cap to the connecting rod, and secure with the nuts, which will help to keep the components in their correct order.

9 Remove No 4 piston in the same manner.

10 Turn the crankshaft through 180° to bring pistons 2 and 3 to BDC (bottom dead centre) and remove them in the same manner.

11 Crankshaft - removal

1 Remove the flywheel/driveplate as described in Chapter 2, Part A, Section 18.

2 Remove the pistons and connecting rods, as described in Section 10. If no work is to be done on the pistons and connecting rods, there is no need to push the pistons out of the cylinder bores.

3 Unscrew the securing bolts and remove the crankshaft front oil seal housing **(see illustration)**. Recover the gasket.

4 Remove the oil seal if it is still attached to the crankshaft.

10.5 Removing a big-end bearing cap

10.6 Tape wound around connecting rod studs to protect crankshaft journals

11.3 Removing the crankshaft front oil seal housing

11.5 Removing the oil pump drive chain

11.6a Slide the oil pump drive sprocket from the crankshaft . . .

11.6b . . . and recover the Woodruff key

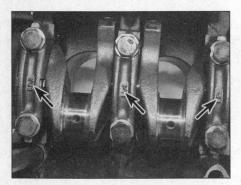

11.8 Measuring crankshaft endfloat using a feeler gauge

11.9 Main bearing cap identification markings (arrowed)

5 Lift the chain from the crankshaft sprocket, and withdraw it from the crankcase (see illustration).

6 Slide the oil pump drive sprocket from the crankshaft. Recover the Woodruff key if it is loose (see illustrations).

7 Before removing the crankshaft, check the endfloat using a dial gauge in contact with the end of the crankshaft. Push the crankshaft fully one way, and then zero the gauge. Push the crankshaft fully the other way, and check the endfloat. The result should be compared with the specified limit, and will give an indication as to whether new thrustwashers are required (the endfloat is controlled by thrustwashers either side of No 2 main bearing).

8 If a dial gauge is not available, a feeler gauge can be used to measure crankshaft endfloat. Push the crankshaft fully towards one end of the crankcase, then insert a feeler gauge between the face of one of the thrustwashers, located on either side of No 2 main bearing, and the machined surface of the crankshaft web (see illustration). Before measuring, ensure that the crankshaft is fully forced towards one end of the crankcase, to give the widest possible gap at the measuring location.

9 The main bearing caps should be numbered 1 to 5 from the flywheel end of the engine (see illustration). If not, mark them accordingly using a centre-punch. Also note the fitted depth of the rear crankshaft oil seal.

10 Invert the engine so that the crankshaft is uppermost, then unbolt and remove the main bearing caps. Recover the lower bearing half-shells, taping them to their respective caps if they are to be re-used. Also recover the lower thrustwasher halves from No 2 cap (see illustration). Recover the rubber sealing strips from the sides of No 1 main bearing cap.

11 Lift out the crankshaft. Discard the rear oil seal. Recover the upper bearing half-shells, and tape them to their respective caps if they are to be re-used (see illustrations). Also recover and identify the upper thrustwasher halves.

12 Cylinder block/crankcase - cleaning and inspection

Cleaning

1 For complete cleaning, ideally the core plugs should be removed (see illustration). Drill a small hole in the plugs, then insert a self-tapping screw, and pull out the plugs using a pair of grips or a slide hammer. Also remove all external components (senders, sensors, brackets, etc).

2 Remove the inspection plate from the flywheel end of the block, to enable cleaning of the coolant channels (see illustration). Use a new rubber sealing ring when refitting the plate.

3 Remove all oil gallery plugs (located at the

11.10 Removing the No 2 main bearing cap - note thrustwasher (arrowed)

11.11a Lifting out the crankshaft

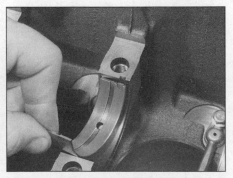

11.11b Removing a main bearing shell from the crankcase

12.1 Cylinder block core plugs (arrowed)

12.2 Remove the inspection plate (arrowed) from the flywheel end of the block

12.3a Removing an oil gallery plug

front and rear of the block and beneath the oil filter mounting) **(see illustrations)**. If the plug beneath the oil filter mounting is very tight, it may have to be drilled out, in which case, use a new plug and re-cut the threads in the cylinder block on refitting.

4 Scrape all traces of gasket from the cylinder block, taking particular care not to damage the cylinder head and sump mating faces.

5 On Turbo models, unscrew the piston oil cooling jets from the crankcase, and clean them **(see illustrations)**.

6 If the block is extremely dirty, it should be steam-cleaned.

7 If the block has been steam-cleaned, clean all oil holes and oil galleries one more time on completion. Flush all internal passages with warm water until the water runs clear, then dry the block thoroughly, and wipe all machined surfaces with a light oil. If you have access to compressed air, use it to speed the drying process, and to blow out all the oil holes and galleries.

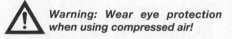

⚠ **Warning: Wear eye protection when using compressed air!**

8 If the block is relatively clean, an adequate cleaning job can be achieved with hot soapy water and a stiff brush. Take plenty of time, and do a thorough job. Regardless of the cleaning method used, be sure to clean all oil holes and galleries very thoroughly, dry the block completely, and coat all machined surfaces with light oil.

9 The threaded holes in the cylinder block must be cleaned out, to ensure accurate torque readings when tightening fixings during reassembly. Run the correct-size tap (which can be determined from the size of the relevant bolt which fits in the hole) into each of the holes, to remove rust, corrosion, thread sealant or other contamination, and to restore damaged threads **(see illustration)**. If possible, use compressed air to clear the holes of debris produced by this operation. Do not forget to clean the threads of all bolts and nuts as well.

10 After coating the mating surfaces of the new core plugs with suitable sealant, fit them to the cylinder block. Make sure that they are driven in straight and seated correctly, or leakage could result. Special tools are available for this purpose, but a large socket, with an outside diameter which will just fit into the core plug, will work just as well.

11 Refit the oil gallery plugs, using new sealing washers where applicable. Tighten the plugs securely.

12 On Turbo models, refit the piston oil cooling jets.

13 If the engine is to be left dismantled for some time, refit the main bearing caps and tighten the bolts finger-tight, and cover the cylinder block with a large plastic bag, to keep it clean and prevent corrosion.

Inspection

14 Visually check the block for cracks, rust and corrosion. Look for stripped threads in

12.3b Oil gallery plug (arrowed) located beneath oil filter mounting

the threaded holes (it may be possible to re-cut stripped threads using a suitable tap). If there has been any history of internal coolant leakage, it may be worthwhile asking an engine overhaul specialist to check the block for cracks using special equipment. If defects are found, have the block repaired if possible; otherwise, renewal may be the only solution.

15 Examine the cylinder bores for taper, ovality, scoring and scratches. Start by carefully examining the top of the cylinder bores. If they are at all worn, a very slight ridge will be found on the thrust side. This marks the top of the piston ring travel.

16 Measure the bore diameter of each cylinder at the top (just under the wear ridge), centre and bottom of the cylinder bore,

12.5a Unscrew the securing bolts (arrowed) . . .

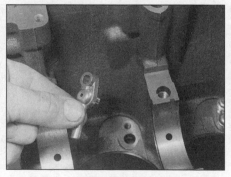

12.5b . . . and remove the piston oil cooling jets - Turbo models

12.9 Cleaning a cylinder head bolt hole in the cylinder block using a tap

parallel to the crankshaft axis. For accurate assessment, a bore micrometer is required. However, a rough measurement can be made by inserting feeler gauges between a piston (without rings) and the bore wall.

17 Next, measure the bore diameter at the same three locations, at right-angles to the crankshaft axis. Compare the results with the figures given in the Specifications.

18 Repeat the procedure for the remaining cylinders.

19 If the cylinder wear exceeds the permitted tolerances, or if the cylinder walls are badly scored or scuffed, then the cylinders will have to be rebored by a suitably-qualified specialist, and new oversize pistons will have to be fitted. A Citroën dealer or engineering workshop will normally be able to supply suitable oversize pistons when carrying out the reboring work.

20 If the bore wear is marginal, and within the specified tolerances, special piston rings can be fitted to offset the wear.

21 If this is the case, the bores should be honed, in order to allow the new rings to bed-in correctly and provide the best possible seal. The conventional type of hone has spring-loaded stones, and is used with a power drill. You will also need some paraffin or honing oil and rags. The hone should be moved up and down the cylinder bore to produce a crosshatch pattern, and plenty of honing oil should be used. Ideally, the crosshatch lines should intersect at approximately a 60° angle. Do not remove

13.2 Removing a piston ring with the aid of a feeler gauge

more material than is necessary to produce the required finish. If new pistons are being fitted, the piston manufacturers may specify a finish with a different angle, so their instructions should be followed. Do not withdraw the hone from the cylinder while it is still being turned - stop it first. After honing a cylinder, wipe out all traces of the honing oil. An engine overhaul specialist will be able to carry out this work at moderate cost.

13 Piston/connecting rod assembly - inspection

1 Before the inspection process can begin, the piston/connecting rod assemblies must be cleaned, and the original piston rings removed from the pistons.

2 Carefully expand the old rings over the top of the pistons. The use of two or three old feeler gauges will be helpful in preventing the rings dropping into empty grooves **(see illustration)**. Be careful not to scratch the piston with the ends of the ring. The rings are brittle, and will snap if they are spread too far; they are also very sharp. Note that the third ring incorporates an expander. Always remove the rings from the top of the piston. Keep each set of rings with its piston, if the old rings are to be re-used (this is not recommended).

3 Scrape away all traces of carbon from the top of the piston. A hand-held wire brush or a piece of fine emery cloth can be used once the majority of the deposits have been scraped away.

4 Remove the carbon from the ring grooves in the piston, using an old ring. Break the ring in half to do this (be careful not to cut your fingers - piston rings are sharp). Be very careful to remove only the carbon deposits - do not remove any metal, and do not nick or scratch the sides of the ring grooves.

5 Once the deposits have been removed, clean the piston/connecting rod assembly with paraffin or a suitable solvent, and dry thoroughly. Make sure that the oil return holes in the ring grooves are clear.

6 If the pistons and cylinder bores are not damaged or worn excessively. and if the

cylinder block does not need to be rebored, the original pistons can be refitted. Normal piston wear shows up as even vertical wear on the piston thrust surfaces, and slight looseness of the top ring in its groove. New piston rings should always be used when the engine is reassembled.

7 Carefully inspect each piston for cracks around the skirt, around the gudgeon pin holes, and at the piston ring lands (between the ring grooves).

8 Look for scoring and scuffing on the thrust faces of the piston skirt, holes in the piston crown, and burned areas at the edge of the crown. If the skirt is scored or scuffed, the engine may have been suffering from overheating, and/or abnormal combustion which caused excessively-high operating temperatures. The cooling and lubrication systems should be checked thoroughly. Scorch marks on the sides of the pistons show that blow-by has occurred. A hole in the piston crown, or burned areas at the edge of the piston crown, indicates that abnormal combustion (pre-ignition, knocking, or detonation) has been occurring. If any of the above problems exist, the causes must be investigated and corrected, or the damage will occur again. The causes may include incorrect injection pump timing, or a faulty injector.

9 Corrosion of the piston, in the form of pitting, indicates that coolant has been leaking into the combustion chamber and/or the crankcase. Again, the cause must be corrected, or the problem may persist in the rebuilt engine.

10 If renewing pistons without reboring, make sure that the correct size is obtained. Piston class is denoted by either an "A" mark or no mark at all on the centre of the crown. (Marks "R1", "R2" etc., denote rebore sizes.) The identical code appears also on the corner of the cylinder block at the timing belt end. The piston weight class is stamped on the crown, and must be identical on all pistons in the same engine.

11 To separate a piston from its connecting rod, prise out the circlips and push out the gudgeon pin **(see illustrations)**. Hand pressure is sufficient to remove the pin.

13.11a Prise out the gudgeon pin circlip . . .

13.11b . . . withdraw the gudgeon pin . . .

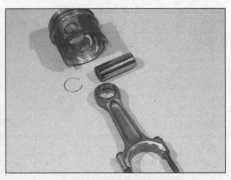

13.11c . . . and separate the piston from the connecting rod

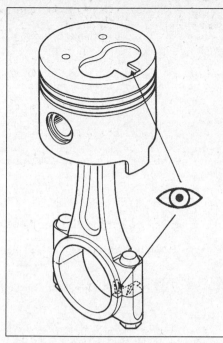

13.14 The cloverleaf recess in the crown must face the same way as the bearing shell cut-out in the connecting rod

Identify the piston and rod to ensure correct reassembly.

12 Wear between the gudgeon pin and the connecting rod small-end bush can be cured by renewing both the pin and bush. Bush renewal, however, is a specialist job, because press facilities are required and the new bush must be reamed accurately.

13 New gudgeon pins and circlips are supplied when purchasing new pistons. The connecting rods themselves should not be in need of renewal, unless seizure or some other major mechanical failure has occurred. Check the alignment of the connecting rods visually, and if the rods are not straight, take them to an engine overhaul specialist for a more detailed check.

14 Where applicable, reassemble the pistons and rods. Make sure that the pistons are fitted the right way round - the cloverleaf recess in the crown must face the same way as the bearing shell cut-out in the connecting rod **(see illustration)**. Oil the gudgeon pins before fitting them. When assembled, the piston should pivot freely on the rod.

15 Measure the piston diameters, and check that they are within limits for the corresponding bore diameters **(see illustration)**. If the piston-to-bore clearance is excessive, the block will have to be rebored, and new pistons and rings fitted.

16 Examine the mating faces of the big-end caps and connecting rods, to see if they have ever been filed, in a mistaken attempt to take up bearing wear. This is extremely unlikely, but if evident, the offending connecting rods and caps must be renewed.

13.15 Measuring a piston diameter using a micrometer

14 Crankshaft - inspection

1 Clean the crankshaft using paraffin or a suitable solvent, and dry it, preferably with compressed air, if available.

> ⚠️ **Warning: Wear eye protection when using compressed air!** *Be sure to clean the oil holes with a pipe cleaner or similar probe, to ensure that they are not obstructed*

2 Check the main and big-end bearing journals for uneven wear, scoring, pitting and cracking.

3 Big-end bearing wear is accompanied by distinct metallic knocking when the engine is running, particularly noticeable when the engine is pulling from low revs, and some loss of oil pressure.

4 Main bearing wear is accompanied by severe engine vibration and rumble - getting progressively worse as engine revs increase - and again by loss of oil pressure.

5 Check the bearing journal for roughness by running a finger lightly over the bearing surface. Any roughness (which will be accompanied by obvious bearing wear) indicates the that the crankshaft requires regrinding.

6 If the crankshaft has been reground, check for burrs around the crankshaft oil holes (the holes are usually chamfered, so burrs should not be a problem unless regrinding has been carried out carelessly). Remove any burrs with a fine file or scraper, and thoroughly clean the oil holes as described previously.

14.7 Measuring a crankshaft big-end bearing journal diameter

7 Using a micrometer, measure the diameter of the main and big-end bearing journals, and compare the results with the Specifications **(see illustration)**. By measuring the diameter at a number of points around each journal's circumference, you will be able to determine whether or not the journal is out-of-round. Take the measurement at each end of the journal, near the webs, to determine if the journal is tapered. If the crankshaft journals are damaged, tapered, out-of-round, or worn beyond the limits given in the Specifications, the crankshaft will have to be reground, and undersize bearings fitted.

8 Check the oil seal contact surfaces at each end of the crankshaft for wear and damage. If the seal has worn an excessive groove in the surface of the crankshaft, consult an engine overhaul specialist, who will be able to advise whether a repair is possible or whether a new crankshaft is necessary.

15 Main and big-end bearings - inspection

1 Even though the main and big-end bearings should be renewed during engine overhaul, the old bearings should be retained for close examination, as they may reveal valuable information about the condition of the engine. The bearing shells carry identification marks to denote their size, in the form of a code marked on the back of the shell. If the shells are to be renewed, without carrying out any crankshaft regrinding, the old shells should be taken along when obtaining new shells, to ensure that the correct shells are obtained.

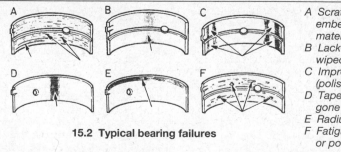

15.2 Typical bearing failures

A Scratched by dirt; dirt embedded into bearing material
B Lack of oil; overlay wiped out
C Improper seating; bright (polished) sections
D Tapered journal; overlay gone from entire surface
E Radius ride
F Fatigue failure; craters or pockets

2 Bearing failure occurs because of lack of lubrication, the presence of dirt or other foreign particles, overloading the engine, or corrosion. If a bearing fails, the cause must be found and eliminated before the engine is reassembled, to prevent the failure from happening again **(see illustration).**

3 To examine the bearing shells, remove them from the cylinder block, together with the main bearing caps, the connecting rods and the big-end bearing caps, and lay them out on a clean surface in the same order as they were fitted to the engine. This will enable any bearing problems to be matched with the corresponding crankshaft journal.

4 Dirt and other foreign particles can enter the engine in a variety of ways. Contamination may be left in the engine during assembly, or it may pass through filters or the crankcase ventilation system. Normal engine wear produces small particles of metal, which can eventually cause problems. If particles find their way into the lubrication system, it is likely that they will eventually be carried to the bearings. Whatever the source, these foreign particles often end up embedded in the soft bearing material, and are easily recognized. Large particles will not embed in the bearing, and will score or gouge the bearing and journal. To prevent possible contamination, clean all parts thoroughly, and keep everything spotlessly-clean during engine assembly. Once the engine has been installed in the vehicle, ensure that regular engine oil and filter changes are carried out at the recommended intervals.

5 Lack of lubrication (or lubrication breakdown) has a number of interrelated causes. Excessive heat (which thins the oil), overloading (which squeezes the oil from the bearing face) and oil leakage (from excessive bearing clearances, worn oil pump or high engine speeds) all contribute to lubrication breakdown. Blocked oil passages, which may be the result of misaligned oil holes in a bearing shell, will also starve a bearing of oil, and destroy it. When lack of lubrication is the cause of bearing failure, the bearing material is wiped or extruded from the steel backing of the bearing. Temperatures may increase to the point where the steel backing turns blue from overheating.

6 Driving habits can have a definite effect on bearing life. Full-throttle, low-speed operation (labouring the engine) puts very high loads on bearings, which tends to squeeze out the oil film. These loads cause the bearings to flex, which produces fine cracks in the bearing face (fatigue failure). Eventually, the bearing material will loosen in pieces and tear away from the steel backing. Regular short journeys can lead to corrosion of bearings, because insufficient engine heat is produced to drive off the condensed water and corrosive gases which form inside the engine. These products collect in the engine oil, forming acid and sludge. As the oil is carried to the bearings, the acid attacks and corrodes the bearing material.

7 Incorrect bearing installation during engine assembly will also lead to bearing failure. Tight-fitting bearings leave insufficient bearing lubrication clearance, and will result in oil starvation. Dirt or foreign particles trapped behind a bearing shell results in high spots on the bearing, which can lead to failure.

8 If new bearings are to be fitted, the bearing running clearances should be measured before the engine is finally reassembled, to ensure that the correct bearing shells have been obtained (see Sections 18 and 19). If the crankshaft has been reground, the engineering works which carried out the work will advise on the correct-size bearing shells to suit the work carried out. If there is any doubt as to which bearing shells should be used, seek advice from a Citroën dealer.

16 Engine overhaul - reassembly sequence

1 Before reassembly begins, ensure that all necessary new parts have been obtained (particularly gaskets, and various bolts which must be renewed) and that all the tools required are available. Read through the entire procedure, to familiarise yourself with the work involved, and to ensure that all items necessary for reassembly of the engine are to hand. In addition to all normal tools and materials, a thread-locking compound will be required. A tube of RTV sealing compound will also be required, to seal certain joint faces which are not fitted with gaskets.

2 In order to save time and avoid problems, engine reassembly can be carried out in the following order:

a) *Piston rings (see Section 17).*
b) *Crankshaft and main bearings (see Section 18).*
c) *Piston/connecting rod assemblies (see Section 19).*
d) *Oil pump (see Chapter 2, Part A, Section 15).*
e) *Sump (see Chapter 2, Part A, Section 14).*
f) *Cylinder head, tappets and camshaft (see Chapter 2, Part A, Sections 13 and 11).*
g) *Timing belt and sprockets (see Chapter 2, Part A, Sections 7 and 8).*
h) *Flywheel/driveplate (see Chapter 2, Part A, Section 18).*
i) *Inlet and exhaust manifolds (see Chapter 4).*
j) *Engine external components.*

17 Piston rings - refitting

1 Before refitting the new piston rings, the ring end gaps must be checked as follows.

2 Lay out the piston/connecting rod assemblies and the new piston ring sets so that the ring sets will be matched with the same piston and cylinder during the end gap

measurement and subsequent engine reassembly.

3 Insert the top ring into the first cylinder, and push it down the bore using the top of the piston. This will ensure that the ring remains square with the cylinder walls. Position the ring near the bottom of the cylinder bore, at the lower limit of ring travel.

4 Measure the end gap using feeler gauges.

5 Repeat the procedure with the ring at the top of the cylinder bore, at the upper limit of its travel, and compare the measurements with the figures given in the Specifications **(see illustration).**

6 If the gap is too small (unlikely if genuine Citroën parts are used), it must be enlarged, or the ring ends may contact each other during engine operation, causing serious damage. Ideally, new piston rings providing the correct end gap should be fitted, but as a last resort, the end gap can be increased by filing the ring ends very carefully with a fine file. Mount the file in a vice equipped with soft jaws, slip the ring over the file with the ends contacting the file face, and slowly move the ring to remove material from the ends - take care, as piston rings are sharp, and are easily broken.

7 With new piston rings, it is unlikely that the end gap will be too large, and if the gaps are too large, check that you have the correct rings for your engine and for the particular cylinder bore size.

8 Repeat the checking procedure for each ring in the first cylinder, and then for the rings in the remaining cylinders. Remember to keep rings, pistons and cylinders matched up.

9 Once the ring end gaps have been checked and if necessary corrected, the rings can be fitted to the pistons.

10 Fit the piston rings using the same technique as for removal. Fit the bottom (oil control) ring first, and work up. When fitting the oil control ring, first insert the expander, then fit the ring with its gap positioned 180° from the expander's gap. Arrange the gaps of the middle and upper rings 120° either side of the oil control ring gap. Make sure that the middle ring is fitted the correct way up. If a stepped ring is being fitted, fit the ring with the

17.5 Measuring a piston ring end gap

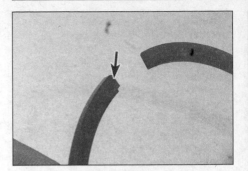

17.10 Stepped rings should be fitted with the smaller diameter of the step (arrowed) uppermost

18.8 Plastigage in place on crankshaft main bearing journal

18.12 Measuring the width of the deformed Plastigage using the card gauge

smaller diameter of the step uppermost **(see illustration)**. **Note:** *Always follow the instructions supplied with the new piston ring sets - different manufacturers may specify different procedures. Do not mix up the top and middle rings, as they have different cross sections.*

18 Crankshaft -
refitting and main bearing running clearance check

1 Refitting the crankshaft is the first step in the engine reassembly procedure. It is assumed at this point that the cylinder block and crankshaft have been cleaned, inspected, and repaired or reconditioned as necessary.
2 Position the cylinder block with the sump mating face uppermost.

Main bearing running clearance check

Note: *A vernier dial indicator, an internal micrometer, or "Plastigage" will be required for this check - see text.*
3 Clean the bearing shells and the bearing recesses in both the cylinder block and main bearing caps. If new shells are being fitted, ensure that all traces of the protective grease are cleaned off using paraffin. Wipe the shells dry with a clean lint-free cloth.
4 If the original bearing shells are being re-used, they must be refitted to their original locations in the block and caps.
5 If desired, before the crankshaft is permanently installed, the main bearing running clearance can be checked. Note that the Citroën do not specify any clearances, but a typical range is given in the Specifications. If no running clearance check is required, proceed to paragraph 16.
6 The bearing running clearance can be checked in one of two ways. One method is to fit the main bearing caps to the cylinder block, with bearing shells in place. With the cap retaining bolts tightened to the specified torque, measure the internal diameter of each assembled pair of bearing shells, using a vernier dial indicator or an internal micrometer. If the diameter of each

corresponding crankshaft journal is measured and then subtracted from the bearing internal diameter, the result will give the main bearing running clearance. The second (and more accurate) method is to use an American product known as "Plastigage". This consists of a fine thread of perfectly-round plastic, which is compressed between the bearing cap shell and the crankshaft journal. When the bearing cap is removed, the deformed plastic can be measured with a special card gauge supplied with the Plastigage kit. The running clearance is determined from this gauge. Plastigage is sometimes difficult to obtain in this country, but enquiries at one of the larger specialist chains of quality motor factors should produce the name of a stockist in your area. The procedure for using Plastigage is as follows.
7 With the upper main bearing half-shells (with the oil grooves) in place in the cylinder block (make sure that the lugs on the shells engage with the recesses in the bearing seats), carefully lay the crankshaft in position. Do not use any lubricant; the crankshaft journals and bearing shells must be perfectly clean and dry.
8 Cut several pieces of the appropriate-size Plastigage (they should be slightly shorter than the width of the main bearings) and place one piece on each crankshaft journal axis **(see illustration)**.
9 With the plain bearing half-shells in position in the caps (make sure that the lugs on the shells engage with the recesses in the bearing seats), fit the caps to their original locations. Take care not to disturb the Plastigage.
10 Starting with the centre main bearing and working outwards, tighten the main bearing cap bolts progressively to their specified torque. Do not rotate the crankshaft at any time during this operation.
11 Remove the bearing cap bolts and carefully lift off the caps, keeping them in order. Do not disturb the Plastigage or rotate the crankshaft. If any of the bearing caps are difficult to remove, free them by carefully tapping with a soft-faced mallet.
12 Compare the width of the deformed Plastigage on each journal with the scale printed on the card gauge to obtain the

main bearing running clearance **(see illustration)**.
13 If the clearance is significantly different from that expected, the bearing shells may be the wrong size (or excessively-worn, if the original shells are being re-used). Before deciding that different-size shells are required, make sure that no dirt or oil was trapped between the bearing shells and the caps or block when the clearance was measured. If the Plastigage was wider at one end than at the other, the crankshaft journal may be tapered.
14 Carefully remove all traces of the Plastigage material from the crankshaft and bearing shells, using a fingernail or an improvised tool which is unlikely to score the shells.
15 Carefully lift the crankshaft out of the cylinder block once more.

Final crankshaft refitting

16 If not already done, wipe clean the main bearing shell seats in the block and the caps. Wipe any protective coating from the new bearing shells.
17 Fit the upper main bearing half-shells (with the oil grooves) to their seats in the block. Make sure that the locating lugs on the shells engage with the corresponding recesses in the seats.
18 Fit the thrustwashers on either side of No 2 main bearing, grooved side outwards. Use a smear of grease to hold them in position **(see illustration)**.

18.18 Fitting a No 2 main bearing thrustwasher

18.19 Lubricating an upper main bearing shell - note locating lug on shell engaged with recess in seat (arrowed)

18.20 Fitting a bearing shell to a main bearing cap - ensure that the lug (arrowed) engages with the recess in the cap

18.22 Using a dial test indicator to check crankshaft endfloat

19 Lubricate the upper bearing shells using clean engine oil, then lower the crankshaft into position **(see illustration)**.

20 Fit the plain bottom bearing half-shells to their respective caps. Make sure that the locating lugs on the shells engage with the corresponding recesses in the caps **(see illustration)**.

21 Fit the thrustwashers on each side of No 2 main bearing cap, using a smear of grease to hold them in position.

22 Before fitting the bearing caps, check that the crankshaft endfloat is within limits, with reference to Section 11 **(see illustration)**.

23 Fit the main bearing caps Nos 2 to 5 to their correct locations, ensuring that they are fitted the correct way round (the bearing shell

lug recesses in the block and caps must be on the same side). Insert the bolts loosely.

24 Apply a small amount of sealant to the No 1 main bearing cap mating face on the cylinder block, around the sealing strip holes **(see illustration)**.

25 Press the sealing strips into the grooves on each side of No 1 main bearing cap. It is now necessary to obtain two thin metal strips, of 0.25 mm thickness or less, in order to prevent the strips moving when the cap is being fitted. Citroën garages use the tool shown, which acts as a clamp, but metal strips (such as old feeler blades) can be used, provided all burrs which may damage the sealing strips are first removed **(see illustrations)**.

26 Where applicable, oil both sides of the metal strips, and hold them on the sealing strips. Fit the No 1 main bearing cap, insert the bolts loosely, then carefully pull out the metal strips with a pair of pliers, in a horizontal direction **(see illustrations)**.

27 Tighten the main bearing cap bolts evenly to the specified torque **(see illustration)**.

28 Fit a new rear crankshaft (flywheel end) oil seal, with reference to Chapter 2, Part A, Section 16.

29 Refit the flywheel/driveplate as described in Chapter 2, Part A, Section 18.

30 Refit the piston/connecting rod assemblies as described in Section 19, but before refitting the oil pump and the sump, proceed as follows. Using feeler blades and a

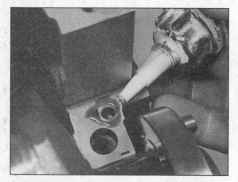

18.24 Applying sealant to the No 1 main bearing cap mating face

18.25a Fitting a sealing strip to No 1 main bearing cap

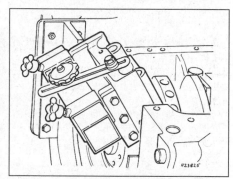

18.25b Using the Citroën special tool to fit No 1 main bearing cap

18.26a Fitting No 1 main bearing cap complete with metal strips

18.26b Removing a metal strip from number 1 main bearing cap using a pair of pliers

18.27 Tightening a main bearing cap bolt

18.30 Cutting a sealing strip on No 1 main bearing cap

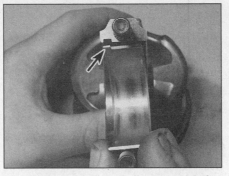

19.4 Fitting a bearing shell to a connecting rod - ensure that the lug (arrowed) engages with the recess in the connecting rod

19.7 Insert No 1 piston and connecting rod into the bore, with the cloverleaf cut-out (arrowed) towards the oil filter side of the engine

knife, cut the sealing strips on No 1 main bearing cap to 1.0 mm above the sump gasket mating surface (**see illustration**).
31 Refit the oil pump and drive chain as described in Chapter 2, Part A, Section 15.
32 Refit the cylinder head as described in Chapter 2, Part A, Section 13.

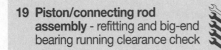

19 Piston/connecting rod assembly - refitting and big-end bearing running clearance check

Note: *New big-end bearing cap bolts and nuts must be used on refitting. A piston ring compressor tool will be required for this operation.*
1 Position the cylinder block either on its side or on the flywheel end.
2 Lay out the assembled pistons and rods in order, with the bearing shells, connecting rod caps and new bolts and nuts.
3 Clean the backs of the big-end bearing shells and the recesses in the connecting rods and big-end caps. If new shells are being fitted, ensure that all traces of protective grease are cleaned off, using paraffin. Wipe the shells, caps and connecting rods dry with a lint-free cloth.
4 Press the bearing half-shells into the connecting rods and caps in their correct positions, ensuring that the lugs on the shells engage with the corresponding recesses in

the connecting rods and caps (**see illustration**).
5 Lubricate No 1 piston and piston rings, and check that the ring gaps are positioned 120° from each other.
6 Liberally lubricate the cylinder bore with clean engine oil.
7 Fit a piston ring compressor to No 1 piston. With Nos 1 and 4 crankpins at bottom dead centre (BDC), insert No 1 piston and connecting rod into No 1 cylinder bore (at the flywheel end of the block) so that the base of the compressor stands on the block. Make sure that the cloverleaf cut-out on the piston crown is towards the oil filter side of the engine (**see illustration**).
8 Using a hammer handle, tap the piston through the ring compressor and into the bore, guiding the connecting rod onto the crankpin (**see illustration**).

Big-end bearing running clearance check

9 To measure the big-end bearing running clearance, refer to the information contained in Section 19, as the same general procedures apply. If no check on running clearance is to be made, proceed to paragraph 11. If the "Plastigage" method is being used, ensure that the big-end bearing journal and the bearing shells are clean and dry, then engage the connecting rod with the bearing journal. Lay the "Plastigage" strip on

the bearing journal, then fit the bearing cap in its original location, ensuring that it is the correct way round (make sure that the identification marks on the connecting rod and cap are both on the oil filter side of the engine). Fit the bearing cap nuts, and tighten them to the specified torque. Do not rotate the crankshaft during this operation. Remove the bearing cap, and check the running clearance by measuring the "Plastigage" as previously described (Section 18).
10 Repeat the checking procedures on the remaining piston/connecting rod assemblies.

Final piston/connecting rod assembly refitting

11 If the running clearance of the bearings has been checked, take any corrective action necessary, then clean off all traces of "Plastigage" from the bearing shells and journals.
12 Liberally lubricate the bearing journals and the bearing shells, and refit the bearing caps once more. Make sure that the caps are positioned correctly, as previously described (paragraph 9).
13 Tighten the bearing cap nuts to the specified torque, in the stages given in the Specifications; ie, tighten all bolts to Stage 1, then tighten all bolts to Stage 2 (**see illustrations**).
14 After refitting each piston/connecting rod assembly, rotate the crankshaft, and check

19.8 Tap the piston into the bore using a hammer handle

19.13a Tighten the big-end bearing cap nuts to the specified torque . . .

19.13b . . . then through the specified angle

19.15 Checking the crankshaft turning torque using a torque wrench

that it turns freely, with no signs of binding or tight spots.

15 When all four piston/connecting rod assemblies have been refitted, proceed as follows. Temporarily refit the pulley bolt to the front of the crankshaft then, using a torque wrench, check that the torque required to turn the crankshaft does not exceed 40 Nm (30 lbf ft) **(see illustration)**. Some stiffness is to be expected with new components, but any excessive tightness must be investigated

before proceeding. Dirt or grit trapped behind a bearing shell is one possible cause.

16 Refit the oil pump as described in Chapter 2, Part A, Section 15.

17 Refit the cylinder head as described in Chapter 2, Part A, Section 13.

20 Engine - initial start-up after overhaul

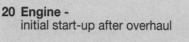

1 With the engine refitted to the vehicle, check the engine oil and coolant levels, and check that the battery is well-charged.

2 Prime the fuel system as described in Chapter 4.

3 On Turbo models, prime the turbocharger lubrication circuit by disconnecting the stop solenoid and cranking the engine on the starter motor in several ten-second bursts, pausing for half a minute or so between each burst. Reconnect the solenoid when satisfied that oil pressure has been established (ensure that the oil pressure warning light on the facia extinguishes when the engine is cranked).

4 Fully depress the accelerator pedal, turn the ignition key to position "M", and wait for the preheating warning light to go out.

5 Start the engine. Additional cranking may be necessary to bleed the fuel system before the engine starts.

6 Once started, keep the engine running at fast tickover. Check that the oil pressure light goes out, then check that there are no leaks of oil, fuel or coolant. Where applicable, check the power steering and/or automatic transmission fluid pipe/hose unions for leakage. Do not be alarmed if there are some odd smells and smoke from parts getting hot and burning off oil deposits.

7 Keep the engine idling until hot coolant is felt circulating through the radiator top hose, indicating that the engine is at normal operating temperature, then stop the engine and allow it to cool.

8 Recheck the oil and coolant levels, and top-up if necessary.

9 Check the fuel injection pump timing and the idle speed, as described in Chapter 4.

10 If new pistons, rings or bearings have been fitted, the engine must be run-in at reduced speeds and loads for the first 500 miles (800 km) or so. Do not operate the engine at full-throttle, or allow it to labour in any gear, during this period. It is beneficial to change the engine oil and filter at the end of this period.

Chapter 3
Cooling, heating and ventilation systems

Contents

Air conditioning compressor (auxiliary) drivebelt -
checking and renewal .... See Chapter 1
Air conditioning system - general information and precautions 12
Air conditioning system components - removal and refitting 13
Air conditioning system refrigerant check .... See Chapter 1
Antifreeze mixture .... See Chapter 1
Coolant level check .... See "Weekly checks"
Coolant pump - removal and refitting 7
Cooling system - draining .... See Chapter 1
Cooling system - filling .... See Chapter 1
Cooling system - flushing .... See Chapter 1

Cooling system electrical switches - testing,
removal and refitting 6
Cooling system hoses - disconnection and renewal 2
Electric cooling fan - testing, removal and refitting 5
General information and precautions 1
Heating and ventilation system - general information 9
Heater/ventilation components - removal and refitting 10
Heater/ventilation vents - removal and refitting 11
Radiator - removal, inspection and refitting 3
Thermostat - removal, testing and refitting 4
Thermostat/fuel filter housing - removal and refitting 8

Degrees of difficulty

Easy, suitable for novice with little experience	Fairly easy, suitable for beginner with some experience	Fairly difficult, suitable for competent DIY mechanic	Difficult, suitable for experienced DIY mechanic	Very difficult, suitable for expert DIY or professional

Specifications

General

System type .... Pressurised, front-mounted radiator and electric cooling fans. Coolant pump driven by timing belt

Maximum system pressure .... 1.4 bars

Thermostat

Type .... Wax
Opening temperatures:
  Starts to open:
    Non-turbo models .... 89°C
    Turbo models .... 83°C
  Fully-open:
    Non-turbo models .... 101°C
    Turbo models .... 95°C

Electric cooling fans

Cooling fans cut in:
  Non-turbo models .... 97°C
  Turbo models without air conditioning:
    1st speed .... 90.5 to 94.5°C
    2nd speed .... 95.5 to 99.5°C
  Turbo models with air conditioning:
    1st speed .... 90°C
    2nd speed .... 101°C
Cooling fans cut out:
  Non-turbo models .... 92°C
  Turbo models without air conditioning:
    1st speed .... 85.5 to 89.5°C
    2nd speed .... 90.5 to 94.5°C
  Turbo models with air conditioning:
    1st speed .... 87°C
    2nd speed .... 98°C

Torque wrench settings

	Nm	lbf ft
Coolant pump bolts	15	11
Temperature sensors (in fuel filter/thermostat housing)	18	13

1 General information and precautions

General information

The cooling system is of pressurised type, comprising a pump driven by the timing belt, an aluminium crossflow radiator with integral expansion tank, twin electric cooling fans, and a thermostat. The system functions as follows. Cold coolant in the bottom of the radiator passes through the bottom hose to the coolant pump, where it is pumped around the cylinder block and head passages, through the oil cooler, fuel filter housing and heater. After cooling the cylinder bores, combustion surfaces, valve seats, oil and fuel, the coolant reaches the underside of the thermostat, which is initially closed. The coolant passes through the heater, and is returned via the cylinder block to the coolant pump **(see illustrations)**.

When the engine is cold, the coolant circulates only through the cylinder block, cylinder head, and heater. When the coolant reaches a predetermined temperature, the thermostat opens and the coolant passes through the top hose to the radiator. As the coolant circulates through the radiator, it is cooled by the inrush of air when the car is in forward motion. Airflow is supplemented by the action of the electric cooling fans when necessary. Upon reaching the bottom of the radiator, the coolant is now cooled, and the cycle is repeated.

When the engine is at normal operating temperature, the coolant expands, and some of it is displaced into the expansion tank. This coolant collects in the tank, and is returned to the radiator when the system cools.

On models fitted with automatic transmission, a proportion of the coolant is recirculated from the bottom of the radiator through the fluid cooler mounted on the transmission.

The electric cooling fans mounted in front of the radiator are controlled by a thermostatic switch. On models without air conditioning, the switch is located in the left-hand side of the radiator. On models with air conditioning, the cooling fans are controlled by the "Bitron" sensor mounted in the fuel filter/thermostat housing. At a predetermined coolant temperature, the switch/sensor actuates the fan.

Precautions

⚠ **Warning: Do not attempt to remove the expansion tank filler cap (or disturb any part of the cooling system) while the engine is hot, as there is a high risk of scalding. If the expansion tank filler cap must be removed before the engine and radiator have fully cooled (even though this is not recommended) the pressure in the cooling system must first be relieved. Cover the** cap with a thick layer of cloth, to avoid scalding, and slowly unscrew the filler cap until a hissing sound can be heard. When the hissing has stopped, indicating that the pressure has reduced, slowly unscrew the filler cap until it can be removed; if more hissing sounds are heard, wait until they have stopped before unscrewing the cap completely. At all times, keep well away from the filler cap opening.

⚠ **Warning: Do not allow antifreeze to come into contact with skin or painted surfaces of the vehicle. Rinse off spills immediately with plenty of water. Never leave antifreeze lying around in an open container, or in a puddle in the driveway or on the garage floor. Children and pets are attracted by its sweet smell, but antifreeze can be fatal if ingested.**

⚠ **Warning: If the engine is hot, the electric cooling fan may start rotating even if the engine is not running, so be careful to keep hands, hair and loose clothing well clear when working in the engine compartment.**

⚠ **Warning: Refer to Section 12 for precautions to be observed when working on models equipped with air conditioning.**

2 Cooling system hoses - disconnection and renewal

Note: *Refer to the warnings given in Section 1 of this Chapter before proceeding. Hoses should only be disconnected once the engine has cooled sufficiently to avoid scalding.*

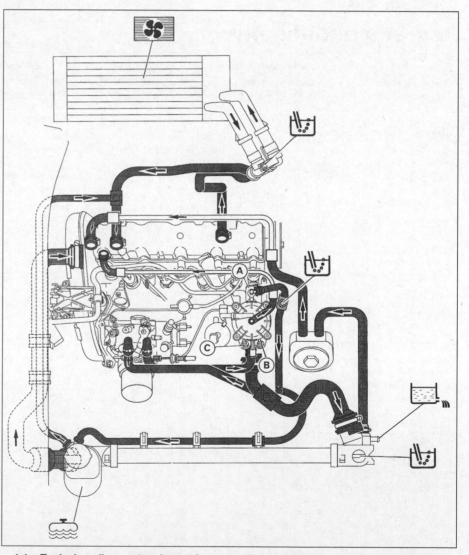

1.1a Typical cooling system layout for non-turbo model with automatic transmission

A Blanking plug
B Coolant temperature gauge sender (models with air conditioning)
C Coolant temperature gauge sender (models without air conditioning)

1 If the checks described in Chapter 1 reveal a faulty hose, it must be renewed as follows.
2 First drain the cooling system (see Chapter 1). If the coolant is not due for renewal, it may be re-used if it is collected in a clean container.
3 To disconnect a hose, proceed as follows, according to the type of hose connection.

Conventional hose-clip connections

4 The clips used to secure the hoses may be of the screw clamp type, or the disposable crimped type.
5 To disconnect a hose, use a screwdriver to slacken or release the clips, then move them along the hose, clear of the relevant inlet/outlet. Carefully work the hose free **(see illustration)**. The hoses can be removed with relative ease when new - on an older car, they may have stuck.

6 If a hose proves to be difficult to remove, try to release it by rotating the ends on the relevant inlet/outlet before attempting to free it. Gently prise the end of the hose with a blunt instrument (such as a flat-bladed screwdriver), but do not apply too much force, and take care not to damage the pipe stubs or hoses. Note in particular that the radiator inlet stub is fragile; do not use excessive force when attempting to remove the hose.

> **HAYNES HINT** *If all else fails, cut the coolant hose with a sharp knife, then slit it so that it can be peeled off in two pieces. Although this may prove expensive if the hose is otherwise undamaged, it is preferable to buying a new radiator. Check first, however, that a new hose is readily available.*

7 When fitting a hose, first slide the clips onto the hose, then work the hose into position. If crimped-type clips were originally fitted, it is a good idea to replace them with screw-type clips when refitting the hose. If the hose is stiff, use a little soapy water as a lubricant, or soften the hose by soaking it in hot water.
8 Work the hose into position, checking that it is correctly routed, then slide each clip along the hose until it passes over the flared end of the relevant inlet/outlet, before tightening the clip securely.
9 Refill the cooling system with reference to Chapter 1.
10 Check thoroughly for leaks as soon as possible after disturbing any part of the cooling system.

Radiator bottom hose

Note: *A new O-ring seal must be used when reconnecting the hose.*

Removal

11 Turn the locking ring (2) anti-clockwise until it contacts the stop (1) **(see illustration)**.
12 Press the connector away from the hose, to ensure that the two retaining lugs are free **(see illustration)**.
13 Pull the hose, complete with the connector, from the radiator.
14 Recover the O-ring from the connector.

Refitting

15 Wipe the connector and the stub on the radiator thoroughly with a clean, lint-free cloth.

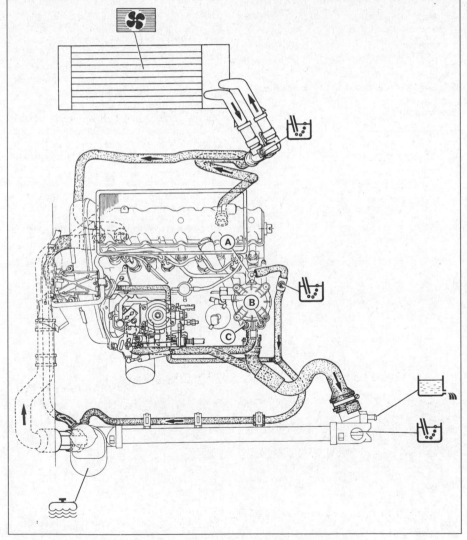

1.1b Typical cooling system layout for Turbo model

A *Blanking plug*
B *Coolant temperature gauge sender (models with air conditioning)*
C *Coolant temperature gauge sender (models without air conditioning)*

2.5 Disconnecting the top radiator hose

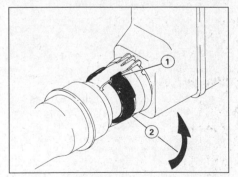

2.11 Radiator bottom hose connection
Turn the locking ring (2) until it contacts the stop (1)

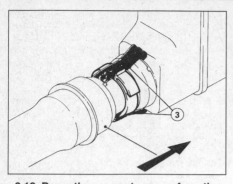

2.12 Press the connector away from the hose to ensure that the two retaining lugs (3) are free

2.16 Fit a new O-ring (arrowed)

2.18 Offer the hose to the radiator with the cut-out (arrowed) at the bottom

16 Fit a new O-ring to the male half of the connector, ensuring that it is correctly seated **(see illustration)**.
17 Turn the locking ring clockwise until it clicks.
18 Offer the hose to the stub on the radiator, with the locating cut-out in the male part of the connector located at the bottom **(see illustration)**.
19 Push the connector into the stub until both the retaining lugs click into position. Make sure that the O-ring is not trapped.
20 Pull the connector rearwards (away from the stub) to adjust the position of the retaining lugs if necessary.
21 Refill the cooling system with reference to Chapter 1.

22 Check thoroughly for leaks as soon as possible after disturbing any part of the cooling system.

Radiator bypass hose connection

Note: *A new O-ring seal must be used when reconnecting the hose.*

Removal

23 The hose is secured by means of a bayonet fit connector.
24 Turn the connector on the end of the hose anti-clockwise as far as it will go **(see illustration)**.

2.24 Turn the connector on the end of the hose anti-clockwise

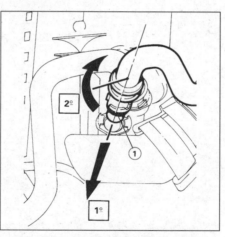

2.28 Engage the guide rails (1) with the lugs on the radiator

25 Rock the connector back and forth to release it from the radiator outlet.

Refitting

26 Wipe the connector and the stub on the radiator thoroughly with a clean, lint-free cloth.
27 Fit a new O-ring to the male half of the connector.
28 Offer the connector to the outlet on the radiator, and twist anti-clockwise to engage the guide rails on the connector with the lugs on the radiator **(see illustration)**.
29 Push the connector fully home to compress the O-ring.
30 Turn the connector clockwise as far as the stop.
31 Refill the cooling system with reference to Chapter 1.
32 Check thoroughly for leaks as soon as possible after disturbing any part of the cooling system.

Heater matrix hose connections

Removal

33 The two hoses are connected to the matrix by means of a single connector.
34 Prise the metal retaining clip from the top of the connector **(see illustration)**.
35 Release the plastic retaining clip by pushing it towards the left-hand hose connection **(see illustration)**.
36 Pull the connector assembly from the heater matrix. Recover the O-ring seals if they are loose **(see illustration)**.

2.34 Prise the metal clip from the top of the connector . . .

2.35 . . . release the plastic retaining clip . . .

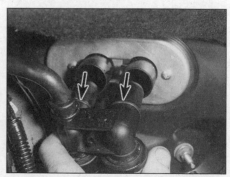

2.36 . . . and pull the connector from the heater matrix - O-rings arrowed

3.3 Removing the panel from above the radiator

3.4 Disconnecting the cooling fan switch wiring plug

3.6a Depress the securing clips . . .

Refitting

37 Refitting is a reversal of removal, but examine the condition of the O-rings seals, and renew if there is any sign of damage or deterioration.

38 Refill the cooling system with reference to Chapter 1.

39 Check thoroughly for leaks as soon as possible after disturbing any part of the cooling system.

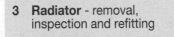

3 Radiator - removal, inspection and refitting

Note: *New sealing rings must be used when reconnecting the lower radiator hoses - see Section 2. If leakage is the reason for removing the radiator, bear in mind that minor leaks can often be cured using a radiator sealant with the radiator in situ.*

Removal

1 Disconnect the battery negative lead.

2 Drain the cooling system as described in Chapter 1.

3 Remove the securing screws, and withdraw the plastic panel from above the radiator **(see illustration)**. Unclip the air cleaner assembly from the panel, where applicable.

4 Disconnect the wiring plug from the cooling fan switch at the left-hand side of the radiator **(see illustration)**.

5 Disconnect the upper radiator hose(s) (left-hand side), and the lower radiator hoses (lower right-hand side), with reference to Section 2.

6 Depress the two securing clips, located at the top ends of the radiator, then carefully lift the radiator from the vehicle. Note the locating lugs at the bottom of the radiator which locate in the mounting rubbers in the lower body panel **(see illustrations)**.

Inspection

7 If the radiator has been removed due to suspected blockage, reverse-flush it as described in Chapter 1. Clean dirt and debris from the radiator fins, using an air line (in which case, wear eye protection) or a soft brush. Be careful, as the fins are easily damaged, and are sharp.

8 If necessary, a radiator specialist can perform a "flow test" on the radiator, to establish whether an internal blockage exists.

9 A leaking radiator must be referred to a specialist for permanent repair (also see the note at the start of this Section). Do not attempt to weld or solder a leaking radiator, as damage to the plastic components may result.

10 If the radiator is to be sent for repair or renewed, remove all hoses, and the cooling fan switch.

11 Inspect the condition of the radiator mounting rubbers, and renew them if necessary.

Refitting

12 Refitting is a reversal of removal, bearing in mind the following points.

13 Ensure that the lower lugs on the radiator are correctly engaged with the mounting rubbers in the body panel.

14 Reconnect the hoses with reference to Section 2, using new sealing rings where applicable.

15 Refill and bleed the cooling system as described in Chapter 1.

4 Thermostat - removal, testing and refitting

Removal

1 Disconnect the battery negative lead.

2 Drain the cooling system as described in Chapter 1.

3 Unscrew the three securing bolts, and carefully withdraw the thermostat housing cover to expose the thermostat. Take care not to strain the coolant hoses connected to the cover **(see illustration)**.

4 Lift the thermostat from the housing **(see illustration)**.

5 Recover the sealing ring from the thermostat flange **(see illustration)**.

Testing

6 A rough test of the thermostat may be made by suspending it with a piece of string in

3.6b . . . and withdraw the radiator

4.3 Two of the three thermostat securing bolts (arrowed)

4.4 Lifting the thermostat from the housing

4.5 Removing the sealing ring from the thermostat flange

5.6 Disconnecting the wiring plug from a cooling fan

5.8 Withdrawing a cooling fan motor assembly

a container full of water. Heat the water to bring it to the boil - the thermostat must open by the time the water boils. If not, renew it.

7 If a thermometer is available, the precise opening temperature of the thermostat may be determined, and compared with the figures given in the Specifications. The opening temperature is also marked on the thermostat.

8 A thermostat which fails to close as the water cools must also be renewed.

Refitting

9 Refitting is a reversal of removal, bearing in mind the following points.

10 Before refitting the thermostat, examine the sealing ring for signs of deterioration or damage. Renew the sealing ring if necessary.

11 Ensure that the thermostat is fitted the correct way round, with the spring(s) facing into the housing.

12 Refill and bleed the cooling system as described in Chapter 1.

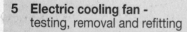

5 Electric cooling fan -
testing, removal and refitting

Testing

1 The cooling fans are supplied with current via the ignition switch (see Chapter 5) and a fuse (see Chapter 12). The circuit is completed by the cooling fan thermostatic switch, which is mounted in the left-hand side of the radiator.

2 If a fan does not appear to work, run the engine until normal operating temperature is reached, then allow it to idle. If the fan does not cut in within a few minutes (before the temperature gauge in the car enters the red section, or the warning light comes on), switch off the ignition and disconnect the wiring plug from the cooling fan switch. Bridge the two contacts in the wiring plug using a length of spare wire, and switch on the ignition. If the fan now operates, the switch is probably faulty, and should be renewed.

3 If the fan still fails to operate, check that full battery voltage is available at the feed wire to

the switch; if not, then there is a fault in the feed wire (possibly due to a fault in the fan motor, or a blown fuse). If there is no problem with the feed, check that there is continuity between the switch earth terminal and a good earth point on the body; if not, then the earth connection is faulty and must be re-made.

4 If the switch and the wiring are in good condition, the fault must lie in the motor itself. The motor can be checked by disconnecting it from the wiring loom, and connecting a 12 volt supply directly to it. If the motor is faulty, it must be renewed, as no spares are available.

Removal

5 Remove the radiator as described in Section 3.

6 Disconnect the wiring plug from the rear of the motor **(see illustration)**.

7 Unscrew the three motor securing nuts, rotating the fan blades as necessary so that the bolts can be counterheld from the front as the nuts are unscrewed.

8 Withdraw the motor assembly, complete with the fan blades, from the front of the vehicle **(see illustration)**.

9 If desired, the fan blades can be removed from the motor shaft, after removing the securing screw and washer.

10 If the motor is faulty, the complete unit must be renewed, as no spares are available.

Refitting

11 Refitting is a reversal of removal. Refit the radiator as described in Section 3.

6 Cooling system electrical switches -
testing, removal and refitting

Electric cooling fan thermostatic switch - models without air conditioning

Testing

1 Testing of the switch is described in Section 5, as part of the electric cooling fan test procedure.

Removal

2 The switch is located in the left-hand side

of the radiator. The engine and radiator should be cold before removing the switch.

3 Disconnect the battery negative lead.

4 Either partially drain the cooling system to just below the level of the switch (as described in Chapter 1), or have ready a suitable plug, which can be used to plug the switch aperture in the radiator while the switch is removed. If a plug is used, take great care not to damage the radiator, and do not use anything which will allow foreign matter to enter the radiator.

5 Disconnect the wiring plug from the switch.

6 Carefully unscrew the switch from the radiator, and recover the sealing ring (where applicable). If the system has not been drained, plug the aperture.

Refitting

7 If the switch was originally fitted using sealing compound, clean the switch threads thoroughly, and coat them with fresh sealing compound.

8 If the switch was originally fitted using a sealing ring, use a new sealing ring on refitting.

9 Refitting is a reversal of removal, but refill the cooling system as described in Chapter 1.

10 On completion, start the engine and run it until it reaches normal operating temperature, then continue to run the engine and check that the cooling fan cuts in and functions correctly.

Electric cooling fan thermostatic switch - models with air conditioning

11 The cooling fans are controlled by the "Bitron" sensor located in the fuel filter/thermostat housing - see paragraphs 26 to 28.

Coolant temperature gauge/ temperature warning light sender

Testing

Note: *On models with air conditioning, the sender provides a signal to the gauge only. The coolant temperature warning light is operated by the "Bitron" temperature sensor described later in this Section.*

6.12 Disconnecting the wiring plug from the coolant temperature gauge/temperature warning light sender

6.22 Disconnecting the wiring plug from the pre-heating system coolant temperature sensor

12 The sender is located in the top of the fuel filter/thermostat housing. On models without air conditioning, the sender is located at the right-hand front corner of the housing **(see illustration)**. On models with air conditioning, the sender is located at the left-hand front corner of the housing.

13 On models with a temperature gauge, the gauge is fed with a stabilised voltage from the instrument panel feed (via the ignition switch and a fuse), and the gauge earth is controlled by the sender. The sender contains a thermistor (an electronic component whose electrical resistance decreases at a predetermined rate as its temperature rises). When the coolant is cold, the sender resistance is high, current flow through the gauge is reduced, and the gauge needle points towards the blue (cold) end of the scale. If the sender is faulty, it must be renewed.

14 On models with a temperature warning light, the light is fed with a voltage from the instrument panel, and the light earth is controlled by the sender. The sender is effectively a switch, which operates at a predetermined temperature to earth the light. If the light is fitted in addition to a gauge, the senders for the gauge and light are incorporated in a single unit, with two wires, one each for the light and gauge earths.

15 If the gauge develops a fault, first check the other instruments; if they do not work at all, check the instrument panel electrical feed. If the readings are erratic, there may be a fault in the voltage stabiliser, which will necessitate renewal of the stabiliser (the stabiliser is integral with the instrument panel printed circuit board - see Chapter 12). If the fault lies in the temperature gauge alone, check it as follows.

16 If the gauge needle remains at the "cold" end of the scale, disconnect the sender wiring plug, and earth the relevant wire to the cylinder head. If the needle then deflects when the ignition is switched on, the sender unit is proven faulty, and should be renewed. If the needle still does not move, remove the instrument panel (Chapter 12) and check the continuity of the wire between the sender unit

and the gauge, and the feed to the gauge unit. If continuity is shown, and the fault still exists, then the gauge is faulty, and the gauge unit should be renewed.

17 If the gauge needle remains at the "hot" end of the scale, disconnect the sender wire. If the needle then returns to the "cold" end of the scale when the ignition is switched on, the sender unit is proven faulty, and should be renewed. If the needle still does not move, check the remainder of the circuit as described previously.

18 The same basic principles apply to testing the warning light. The light should illuminate when the relevant sender wire is earthed.

Removal and refitting

19 The procedure is similar to that described previously in this Section for the electric cooling fan thermostatic switch.

Pre-heating system coolant temperature sensor - Turbo models

Testing

20 The sensor forms part of the pre-heating system (see Chapter 4), and testing should be entrusted to a Citroën dealer.

Removal and refitting

21 The sensor is located at the rear of the fuel filter/thermostat housing.

22 The procedure is similar to that described previously in this Section for the electric

cooling fan thermostatic switch **(see illustration)**.

EGR system coolant temperature sensor - XUD9/Y (DJZ) engine

Testing

23 The sensor forms part of the EGR system (see Chapter 4), and testing should be entrusted to a Citroën dealer.

Removal and refitting

24 The sensor is located at the rear of the fuel filter/thermostat housing.

25 The procedure is similar to that described previously in this Section for the electric cooling fan thermostatic switch.

"Bitron" temperature sensor - models with air conditioning

Testing

26 The sensor forms part of the air conditioning "Bitron" control system (see Section 12). Testing of the sensor should be entrusted to a Citroën dealer.

Removal and refitting

27 The sender is located in the top right-hand corner of the fuel filter/thermostat housing.

28 The procedure is similar to that described previously in this Section for the electric cooling fan thermostatic switch.

7 Coolant pump - removal and refitting

Note: *A new gasket must be used when refitting the pump.*

Removal

1 Drain the cooling system as described in Chapter 1.

2 Remove the timing belt as described in Chapter 2, Part A.

3 Unscrew the two securing bolts, and remove the lower timing belt cover.

4 Unscrew the securing bolts, and withdraw the pump from the cylinder block **(see illustrations)**. Recover the gasket.

7.4a Unscrew the securing bolts (arrowed) . . .

7.4b . . . and remove the coolant pump

8.8a Unscrew the securing bolt (arrowed) . . .

8.8b . . . withdraw the plastic housing . . .

8.8c . . . and recover the O-ring

Refitting

5 Commence refitting by cleaning the mating faces of the pump and the cylinder block.
6 Fit the pump, using a new gasket, then insert the securing bolts and tighten them evenly to the specified torque.
7 Refit the lower timing belt cover.
8 Refit the timing belt as described in Chapter 2, Part A.
9 Refill the cooling system as described in Chapter 1.

8 Thermostat/fuel filter housing - removal and refitting

Removal

Note: *A new gasket must be used when refitting the main housing.*
1 Disconnect the battery negative lead.
2 Drain the cooling system as described in Chapter 1.
3 Place a plastic sheet over the transmission bellhousing and the starter motor, to prevent any fuel spilled during the following procedure from causing damage.
4 Remove the fuel filter as described in Chapter 1.
5 Disconnect the wiring plugs from the coolant sensors mounted in the top of the housing.
6 Disconnect the coolant hoses from the plastic thermostat housing.

7 Disconnect the coolant hose from the stub at the rear of the housing.
8 Unscrew the bolt securing the plastic fuel filter housing to the main housing, withdraw the plastic housing, and move it clear of the main housing. Recover the O-ring from the base of the plastic housing (see illustrations).
9 Unscrew the three securing bolts, and withdraw the main housing from the cylinder head (see illustrations). Recover the gasket.
10 Disconnect the coolant hose from the base of the housing, and remove the housing.

Refitting

11 Refitting is a reversal of removal, bearing in mind the following points.
12 Examine the condition of the O-ring on the base of the plastic housing, and renew if necessary.
13 Use a new gasket when refitting the main housing.
14 Ensure that all hoses, pipes and wires are correctly reconnected.
15 Refill the cooling system as described in Chapter 1.
16 On completion, prime the fuel system as described in Chapter 4.

9 Heating and ventilation system - general information

The heating/ventilation system consists of a four-speed blower motor (housed behind the

facia), face level vents in the centre and at each end of the facia, and air ducts to the front footwells.

The control unit is located in the facia, and the controls operate flap valves to deflect and mix the air flowing through the various parts of the heating/ventilation system. The flap valves are contained in the air distribution housing, which acts as a central distribution unit, passing air to the various ducts and vents.

Cold air enters the system through the grille at the rear of the engine compartment. If required, the airflow is boosted by the blower, and then flows through the various ducts, according to the settings of the controls. Stale air is expelled through ducts at the rear of the vehicle. If warm air is required, the cold air is passed over the heater matrix, which is heated by the engine coolant.

On models fitted with air conditioning, a recirculation switch enables the outside air supply to be closed off, while the air inside the vehicle is recirculated. This can be useful to prevent unpleasant odours entering from outside the vehicle, but should only be used briefly, as the recirculated air inside the vehicle will soon deteriorate.

10 Heater/ventilation components - removal and refitting

Heater/ventilation control unit

Removal

1 Disconnect the battery negative lead.
2 Remove the centre console as described in Chapter 11. On lower-specification models, where no centre console is fitted, undo the retaining screws, and remove the heater duct cover from the centre of the facia assembly.
3 Where a radio/cassette player is fitted, remove it as described in Chapter 12, then undo the two retaining screws and remove the mounting bracket from the radio aperture (see illustrations). Where no radio/cassette player is fitted, carefully prise out the storage box from the centre of the facia panel.
4 Undo the four centre vent panel retaining

8.9a Unscrew the three securing bolts (arrowed) . . .

8.9b . . . and withdraw the main thermostat housing

10.3a Undo the two retaining screws (arrowed) . . .

10.3b . . . and remove the mounting bracket from the radio aperture

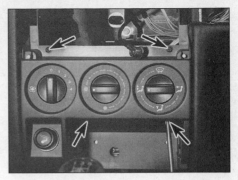

10.4a Undo the four centre vent panel retaining screws (arrowed) . . .

screws (two located above the heater controls and two directly below) then unclip the panel and withdraw it from the facia. Disconnect the wiring connectors from the cigarette lighter and ashtray illumination bulb, and remove the centre vent panel assembly from the vehicle **(see illustrations)**.

5 Undo the two heater control panel retaining screws, then release the lower panel retaining clip and manoeuvre the panel out from the centre of the facia **(see illustration)**.

6 Disconnect the control cables and the wiring connector(s) from the rear of the heater control panel, noting their locations, and withdraw the panel from the vehicle.

Refitting

7 Refitting is reversal of removal, bearing in

mind the following points.

8 Ensure that the control cables are correctly reconnected to the control panel, as noted before removal.

9 Refit the radio/cassette player with reference to Chapter 12.

Heater/ventilation control cables

Removal

10 Remove the complete heater assembly as described later in this Section.

11 The cables can now be disconnected from the heater assembly and the heater control panel **(see illustration)**. Note the locations of the cables before disconnecting them.

Refitting

12 Refitting is a reversal of removal.

Heater matrix

Removal

13 Remove the facia assembly as described in Chapter 11.

14 Remove the securing screws, and release the wiring retaining brackets from the top of the heater unit, noting their locations **(see illustration)**.

15 Working inside the vehicle, disconnect the wiring plug from the right-hand side of the heater unit **(see illustration)**.

16 Remove the lower heater assembly securing bolt **(see illustration)**.

17 Working in the engine compartment,

10.4b . . . and withdraw the panel from the facia

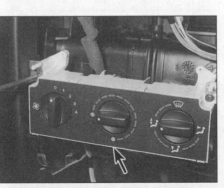

10.5 Undo the heater panel retaining screws, and release the clip (arrowed)

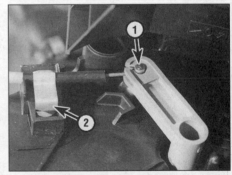

10.11 Control cable connection (1) and retaining clip (2) at heater assembly

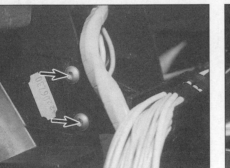

10.14 Heater unit wiring bracket securing screws (arrowed)

10.15 Disconnect the wiring plug from the right-hand side of the heater unit

10.16 Lower heater assembly securing bolt (arrowed)

10.17 Heater unit securing nut on engine compartment bulkhead

10.19a Remove the two securing screws (arrowed) . . .

10.19b . . . and withdraw the retaining plate from the hose connector

remove the two heater unit securing nuts from the bulkhead (below the heater matrix hose connector), and recover the washers **(see illustration)**.

18 Disconnect the heater hose connector from the heater matrix, with reference to Section 2.

19 Remove the two securing screws, and withdraw the retaining plate from the heater matrix hose connector **(see illustrations)**.

20 Working inside the vehicle, withdraw the heater unit, complete with the control panel **(see illustration)**.

21 Remove the securing screws, where applicable, then release the clips and withdraw the heater matrix from the heater assembly **(see illustration)**.

Refitting

22 If a new matrix is to be fitted, unbolt the hose connector elbow from the old matrix, and fit it to the new matrix using new O-rings **(see illustrations)**.

23 Refitting is a reversal of removal, but reconnect the heater hoses to the matrix with reference to Section 2, and refit the facia assembly as described in Chapter 11.

Heater blower motor
Removal

24 Working inside the vehicle, remove the facia felt undercover and the driver's side lower facia panel (left-hand-drive models) or the glovebox (right-hand-drive models), as applicable, with reference to Chapter 11.

25 Unscrew the three now-exposed blower motor securing bolts, and lower the assembly from the facia **(see illustration)**.

26 Pull off the cover and disconnect the two wiring plugs, then withdraw the assembly from the vehicle **(see illustration)**.

Refitting

27 Refitting is a reversal of removal.

Heater blower motor resistor
Removal

28 Disconnect the battery negative lead.

29 Remove the wiper arm as described in Chapter 12.

30 Open the bonnet, and remove the six

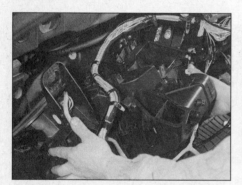

10.20 Withdrawing the heater unit

10.21 Withdrawing the heater matrix from the heater assembly

10.22a Undo the securing bolts . . .

10.22b . . . and remove the hose connector elbow from the old heater matrix

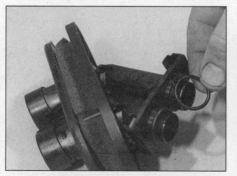

10.22c Fit the elbow to the new matrix using new O-rings

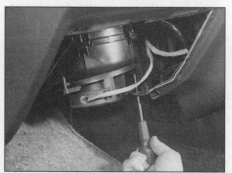

10.25 Unscrewing a heater blower motor securing bolt

10.26 Pull off the cover (arrowed) and disconnect the wiring plugs

10.32a To remove the heater blower motor resistor . . .

10.32b . . . twist the unit anti-clockwise and disconnect the wiring plug

wiper motor cover/vent panel retaining screws. Carefully ease the cover out from behind the windscreen sealing strip, then disengage its front locating pegs and manoeuvre the panel away from the vehicle.

31 Remove the heater motor vent cover, noting that it may be retained with sealant.

32 Twist the resistor anti-clockwise to release it from the bracket, then disconnect the wiring plug and withdraw the unit **(see illustrations)**.

Refitting

33 Refitting is a reversal of removal, but refit the wiper arm with reference to Chapter 12.

Complete heater assembly

Removal

34 Removal of the complete heater assembly is described in paragraphs 13 to 20, as part of the heater matrix removal and refitting procedure.

Refitting

35 Refitting is a reversal of removal, with reference to paragraph 23.

11 Heater/ventilation vents - removal and refitting

Facia side vents

Removal

1 Carefully release the relevant vent from the facia, using a screwdriver with a piece of card under the blade, to avoid damage to the facia trim, then withdraw the vent **(see illustration)**.

Refitting

2 Simply push the nozzle into its housing in the facia until the securing lugs click into place.

Facia centre vents

Removal

3 Remove the centre vent panel from the facia as described in Section 10, paragraphs 1 to 4.

4 Working at the rear of the centre vent panel, remove the securing screws, then withdraw the vent assembly from the panel.

Refitting

5 Refitting is a reversal of removal.

11.1 Withdrawing a facia side vent

12 Air conditioning system - general information and precautions

General information

An air conditioning system is available on certain models. It enables the temperature of incoming air to be lowered, and also dehumidifies the air, which makes for rapid demisting and increased comfort **(see illustration)**.

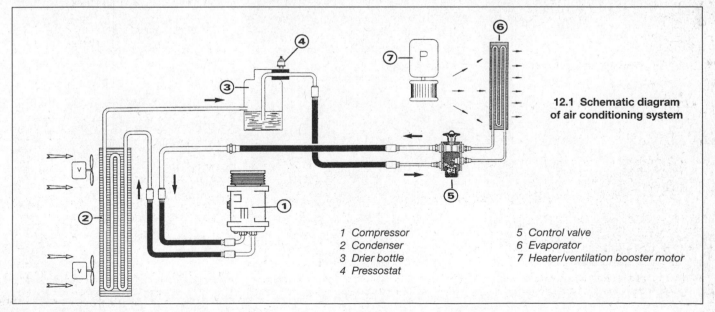

12.1 Schematic diagram of air conditioning system

1 Compressor
2 Condenser
3 Drier bottle
4 Pressostat
5 Control valve
6 Evaporator
7 Heater/ventilation booster motor

The cooling side of the system works in the same way as a domestic refrigerator. Refrigerant gas is drawn into a belt-driven compressor, and passes into a condenser mounted on the front of the radiator, where it loses heat and becomes liquid. The liquid passes through an expansion valve to an evaporator, where it changes from liquid under high pressure to gas under low pressure. This change is accompanied by a drop in temperature, which cools the evaporator. The refrigerant returns to the compressor, and the cycle begins again.

Air blown through the evaporator passes to the air distribution unit, where it is mixed with hot air blown through the heater radiator to achieve the desired temperature in the passenger compartment.

The heating side of the system works in the same way as on models without air conditioning.

The operation of the system is controlled electronically by the "Bitron" control unit, which controls the electric cooling fans, the compressor, and the facia-mounted warning light. Any problems with the system should be referred to a Citroën dealer.

Precautions

When an air conditioning system is fitted, it is necessary to observe special precautions whenever dealing with any part of the system, its associated components, and any items which necessitate disconnection of the system. If for any reason the system must be disconnected, entrust this task to your Citroën dealer or a refrigeration engineer.

⚠ *Warning: The refrigeration circuit contains a liquid refrigerant (Freon), and it is therefore dangerous to disconnect any part of the system without specialised knowledge and equipment.*

The refrigerant is potentially dangerous, and should only be handled by qualified persons. If it is splashed onto the skin, it can cause frostbite. It is not itself poisonous, but in the presence of a naked flame (including a lighted cigarette) it forms a poisonous gas. Uncontrolled discharging of the refrigerant is dangerous, and potentially damaging to the environment.

Do not operate the air conditioning system if it is known to be short of refrigerant, as this may damage the compressor.

13 Air conditioning system components - removal and refitting

⚠ *Warning: Do not attempt to open the refrigerant circuit. Refer to the precautions given in Section 12.*

The only operation which can be carried out easily without discharging the refrigerant is renewal of the compressor drivebelt, which is covered in Chapter 1, Section 19. All other operations must be referred to a Citroën dealer or an air conditioning specialist.

If necessary, the compressor can be unbolted and moved aside, *without disconnecting its flexible hoses*, after removing the drivebelt.

Chapter 4
Fuel, exhaust and emission control systems

Contents

Accelerator cable - removal, refitting and adjustment 11
Accelerator pedal - removal and refitting 12
Air distribution housing (XUD9A/D9B engine) -
  removal and refitting 21
Air filter renewal . . . . See Chapter 1
Emission control systems - general information 23
Emission control systems - testing and component renewal 24
Emission control system check . . . . See Chapter 1
Exhaust system - general information and component renewal 22
Fuel filter renewal . . . . See Chapter 1
Fuel filter water draining . . . . See Chapter 1
Fast idle thermostatic sensor - removal, refitting and adjustment . . 4
Fuel injection pump - removal and refitting 6
Fuel injectors - testing, removal and refitting 10
Fuel level sender - removal and refitting 13
Fuel pick-up unit - removal and refitting 14
Fuel system - priming and bleeding 25

Fuel tank - removal, repair and refitting 15
General information 1
Idle speed and anti-stall speed checking and
  adjustment . . . . See Chapter 1
Injection timing - checking methods and adjustment 7
Injection timing (Bosch fuel injection pump) -
  checking and adjustment 9
Injection timing (Lucas fuel injection pump) -
  checking and adjustment 8
Intercooler - removal and refitting 20
Manifolds - removal and refitting 16
Maximum speed - checking and adjustment 3
Precautions 2
Stop solenoid - description, removal and refitting 5
Turbocharger - description and precautions 17
Turbocharger - examination and renovation 19
Turbocharger - removal and refitting 18

Degrees of difficulty

Easy, suitable for novice with little experience	**Fairly easy,** suitable for beginner with some experience	**Fairly difficult,** suitable for competent DIY mechanic	**Difficult,** suitable for experienced DIY mechanic	**Very difficult,** suitable for expert DIY or professional

Specifications

General

System type . . . .   Rear-mounted fuel tank,distributor fuel injection pump with integral transfer pump, indirect injection. Turbocharger and intercooler on XUD9TE engines

Firing order . . . .   1-3-4-2 (No 1 at flywheel end)

Fuel tank capacity . . . .   56 litres

Maximum speed

No-load:
  1.7 litre engine . . . .   5100 ± 125 rpm
  1.9 litre non-turbo engines . . . .   5150 ± 125 rpm
  1.9 litre Turbo engines . . . .   5050 ± 125 rpm
Full-load:
  All non-turbo models . . . .   4600 ± 80 rpm
  Turbo models . . . .   4500 ± 80 rpm

Injection pump (Lucas CAV/Roto-Diesel)

Direction of rotation . . . .   Clockwise, viewed from sprocket end
Static timing:
  Engine position . . . .   No 4 piston at TDC (see Section 8)
  Pump position . . . .   Value shown on pump (see Section 8)
Dynamic timing (at idle speed):
  XUD7 (A9A) engine . . . .   12° ± 1°
  XUD9A (D9B) engine . . . .   14.5° ± 1°
  XUD9A/L (D9B) engine . . . .   12.5° ± 1°

Injection pump (Bosch)

Direction of rotation .... Clockwise, viewed from sprocket end
Static timing:
   Engine position .... No 4 piston at TDC (see Section 9)
   Pump position:
      XUD7 (A9A) engine .... 0.90 mm ABDC
      XUD9A (D9B) and XUD9A/L (D9B) engines .... 1.07 mm ABDC
      XUD9Y (DJZ) engine .... 0.77 mm ABDC
      XUD9TE/L (D8A) and XUD9TE/Y (DHY and DHZ) engines .... 0.66 mm ABDC
Dynamic timing (at idle speed):
   XUD7 (A9A) engine .... 15.5° ± 1°
   XUD9A (D9B) and XUD9A/L (D9B) engines .... 17.5° ± 1°
   XUD9Y (DJZ) engine .... 14° ± 1°
   XUD9TE/L (D8A) and XUD9TE/Y (DHY and DHZ) engines .... 12.5° ± 1°

Injectors

Type .... Pintle
Opening pressure:
   Models with Lucas CAV/Roto-Diesel fuel injection pump:
      No mark on injector body .... 113 to 118 bars
      Green mark on injector body .... 117 to 122 bars
      Pink mark on injector body .... 123 to 128 bars
      Pink and green marks on injector body .... 127 to 132 bars
   Models with Bosch fuel injection pump:
      All non-turbo engines .... 130 bars
      Turbo engines .... 175 bars

Turbocharger

Type .... KKK K14, or Garrett T2
Boost pressure (full-load) .... 0.8 to 0.9 bars
Speed of rotation .... Approximately 150 000 rpm

Torque wrench settings

	Nm	lbf ft
Injectors to cylinder head	90	66
Fuel pipe union nuts	20	15
No 4 cylinder TDC blanking plug	30	22
Injection pump timing hole blanking plug:		
Lucas pump	6	4
Bosch pump	15	11
Injection pump front mounting nuts	18	13
Injection pump rear mounting nut	22	16
Injection pump sprocket nut	50	37
Injection pump sprocket puller bolts	10	7
Turbocharger mounting bolts	55	41
Turbocharger oil pipe unions	20	15

1 General information

1 The fuel system consists of a rear-mounted fuel tank, a fuel filter with integral water separator, a fuel injection pump, injectors and associated components. Before passing through the filter, the fuel is heated by coolant flowing through the base of the fuel filter/thermostat housing. A turbocharger and intercooler are fitted to the XUD9TE (D8A and DHY) engines. The exhaust system is either a 2-section conventional type or 3-section type on vehicles fitted with a catalytic converter.

2 Fuel is drawn from the fuel tank to the fuel injection pump by a vane-type transfer pump incorporated in the fuel injection pump. Before reaching the pump, the fuel passes through a fuel filter, where foreign matter and water are removed. Excess fuel lubricates the moving components of the pump, and is then returned to the tank.

3 The fuel injection pump is driven at half-crankshaft speed by the timing belt. The high pressure required to inject the fuel into the compressed air in the swirl chambers is achieved by a cam plate acting on a single piston on the Bosch pump, or by two opposed pistons forced together by rollers running in a cam ring on the Lucas/CAV pump. The fuel passes through a central rotor with a single outlet drilling which aligns with ports leading to the injector pipes.

4 Fuel metering is controlled by a centrifugal governor, which reacts to accelerator pedal position and engine speed. The governor is linked to a metering valve, which increases or decreases the amount of fuel delivered at each pumping stroke. On turbocharged models, a separate device also increases fuel delivery with increasing boost pressure.

5 Basic injection timing is determined when the pump is fitted. When the engine is running, it is varied automatically to suit the prevailing engine speed by a mechanism which turns the cam plate or ring.

6 The four fuel injectors produce a homogeneous spray of fuel into the swirl chambers located in the cylinder head. The injectors are calibrated to open and close at critical pressures to provide efficient and even combustion. Each injector needle is lubricated by fuel, which accumulates in the spring chamber and is channelled to the injection pump return hose by leak-off pipes.

7 Bosch or Lucas CAV/Roto-Diesel fuel system components may be fitted, depending on model. Components from the latter

1.9a Hand-operated stop lever (arrowed) - Lucas pump

1.9b Hand-operated stop lever (arrowed) - Bosch pump

manufacturer are marked either "CAV", "Roto-Diesel" or "Con-Diesel", depending on their date and place of manufacture. With the exception of the fuel filter assembly, replacement components must be of the same make as those originally fitted.

8 Cold starting is assisted by preheater or "glow" plugs fitted to each swirl chamber. A thermostatic sensor in the cooling system operates a fast idle lever on the injection pump to increase the idling speed when the engine is cold. On turbocharged models, the injection timing is advanced when the engine is cold by a temperature-controlled solenoid.

9 A stop solenoid cuts the fuel supply to the injection pump rotor when the ignition is switched off, and there is also a hand-operated stop lever for use in an emergency **(see illustrations)**.

10 Provided that the specified maintenance is carried out, the fuel injection equipment will give long and trouble-free service. The injection pump itself may well outlast the engine. The main potential cause of damage to the injection pump and injectors is dirt or water in the fuel.

11 Servicing of the injection pump and injectors is very limited for the home mechanic, and any dismantling or adjustment other than that described in this Chapter must be entrusted to a Citroën dealer or fuel injection specialist.

2 Precautions

Fuel - Warning

Many of the procedures given in this Chapter involve the disconnection of fuel pipes and system components which may result in some fuel spillage. Before carrying out any operation on the fuel system, refer to the precautions given in the *Safety first!* Section at the beginning of this Manual and follow them implicitly.

Tamperproof adjustment screws - caution

Certain adjustment points in the fuel system

may be protected by tamperproof caps, plugs or seals. The purpose of such tamperproofing is to discourage adjustment by unqualified operators.

In some EEC countries it is an offence to drive a vehicle with missing or broken tamperproof seals. Before disturbing a tamperproof seal, satisfy yourself that you will not be breaking local or national anti-pollution regulations by doing so. Fit a new seal when adjustment is complete when this is required by law.

Do not break tamperproof seals on a vehicle which is still under warranty.

Turbocharger

The internal components of a turbocharger rotate at very high speed and as such are very sensitive to contamination. A great deal of damage can be caused by small particles of dirt, particularly if they strike the delicate turbine blades. To prevent the ingress of dirt during maintenance, thoroughly clean the area around all connections before disturbing them. Always store dismantled components in a sealed container to prevent contamination. Cover the turbocharger air inlet ducts to prevent the ingress of debris and use lint-free cloths only when cleaning.

Never run the engine with the turbocharger air inlet hose disconnected. Depression at the inlet can build up very suddenly if the engine speed is raised, thereby increasing the risk of foreign objects being sucked in and ejected at very high speed.

Catalytic converter

The catalytic converter is a reliable and simple device which needs no maintenance in itself, but there are some facts of which an owner should be aware if the converter is to function properly for its full service life:

(a) There is no need to worry about using leaded/unleaded fuel in a vehicle equipped with a catalytic converter and a Diesel engine - no Diesel fuel has added lead.

(b) Always keep the fuel system well-maintained in accordance with the manufacturer's schedule. Ensure that the air cleaner filter element and the fuel filter are renewed at the correct intervals. If the

intake air/fuel mixture is allowed to become too rich due to neglect, the unburned surplus will enter and burn in the catalytic converter, overheating the element and eventually destroying the converter.

(c) If the engine develops a misfire, do not drive the vehicle at all (or at least as little as possible) until the fault is cured. A misfire will allow unburned fuel to enter the converter, which will result in its overheating, as noted above. For the same reason do not persist if the engine ever refuses to start. Either trace the problem and cure it yourself or have the vehicle checked immediately by a qualified mechanic. Never allow the vehicle to run out of fuel.

(d) DO NOT push-or tow-start the vehicle - this will soak the catalytic converter in unburned fuel, causing it to overheat when the engine does start.

(e) Try to avoid repeated successive cold starts with short journeys. If the converter is never allowed to reach its proper working temperature it will gather unburned fuel, allowing some to pass into the atmosphere and the rest to soak the element with unburned fuel thereby causing it to overheat when the engine does start.

(f) DO NOT use fuel or engine oil additives as these may contain substances harmful to the catalytic converter.

(g) NEVER use silicon-based sealants on any part of the air intake/inlet manifold, or any kind of sealant on exhaust system joints forward of the catalytic converter. If pieces of sealant (however small) should break off, they will be carried into the converter and cause it to overheat locally.

(h) DO NOT continue to use the vehicle if the engine burns oil to the extent of leaving a visible trail of blue smoke. Unburned carbon deposits will clog the converter passages and reduce its efficiency; in severe cases the element will overheat.

(i) Remember that the catalytic converter operates at very high temperatures (hence the heat shields on the vehicle's underbody) and the casing will become hot enough to ignite combustible materials which brush against it. DO NOT, therefore, park the vehicle in dry undergrowth, over long grass or piles of dead leaves.

(j) Remember that the catalytic converter is FRAGILE - do not strike it with tools during servicing work, take great care when working on the exhaust system, ensure that the converter is well clear of any jacks or other lifting gear used to raise the vehicle and do not drive the vehicle over rough ground, roadhumps, etc., in such a way as to ground the exhaust system.

(k) The catalytic converter, used on a well-maintained and well-driven vehicle, should

3.3a Maximum speed adjustment screw (arrowed) - Turbo models with Bosch fuel injection pump

last for between 50 000 and 100 000 miles. From this point on, careful checks should be made at all specified service intervals to ensure that the converter is still operating efficiently. If the converter is no longer effective it must be renewed.

Working procedures

When working on fuel system components, scrupulous cleanliness must be observed, and care must be taken not to introduce any foreign matter into fuel lines or components. Care should be taken not to disturb any components unnecessarily. Before attempting work, ensure that the relevant spares are available. If persistent problems are encountered, it is recommended that the advice of a Citroen dealer or a Specialist is sought.

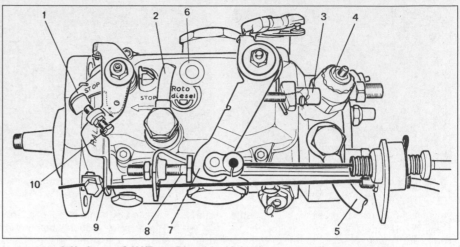

3.3b Lucas CAV/Roto-Diesel fuel injection pump adjustment points

1 Manual stop lever	4 Stop solenoid	8 Anti-stall adjustment screw
2 Fuel return pipe	5 Fuel inlet	9 Fast idle lever
3 Maximum speed adjustment screw	6 Timing access plug	10 Idle speed adjustment screw
	7 Control (accelerator) lever	

3 Maximum speed - checking and adjustment

Caution: The maximum speed adjustment screw is sealed by the manufacturers at the factory, using paint or a locking wire and a lead seal. There is no reason why it should require adjustment. Do not disturb

the screw if the vehicle is still within the warranty period, otherwise the warranty will be invalidated. This adjustment requires the use of a tachometer - refer to Chapter 1, Section 17 for alternative methods.

1 Run the engine to normal operating temperature.
2 Have an assistant fully depress the accelerator pedal, and check that the maximum engine speed is as given in the Specifications. Do not keep the engine at maximum speed for more than two or three seconds.
3 If adjustment is necessary, stop the engine, then loosen the locknut, turn the maximum speed adjustment screw as necessary, and retighten the locknut **(see illustrations)**.
4 Repeat the procedure in paragraph 2 to check the adjustment.
5 Stop the engine and disconnect the tachometer.

4 Fast idle thermostatic sensor - removal, refitting and adjustment

Removal

Note: A new sealing washer must be used when refitting the sensor.

1 The thermostatic sensor is located in the side of the thermostat/fuel filter housing.
2 If desired, for improved access, remove the intercooler (Turbo models - see Section 20) or the air distribution box (XUD9/A - D9B engine - see Section 21), where applicable. Similarly, disconnect the air hose from the top of the inlet manifold, and disconnect the breather hose from the engine oil filler tube, where applicable.
3 Drain the cooling system as described in Chapter 1.

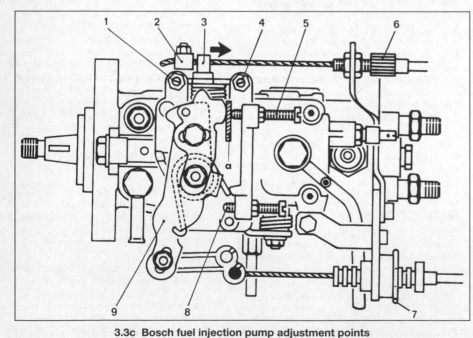

3.3c Bosch fuel injection pump adjustment points

1 Fast idle adjustment screw	5 Anti-stall adjustment screw	8 Maximum speed adjustment screw
2 Cable end fitting	6 Fast idle cable adjustment ferrule	9 Control (accelerator) lever
3 Fast idle lever	7 Accelerator cable adjustment ferrule	a Shim for anti-stall adjustment
4 Idle speed adjustment screw		

4.4a Fast idle cable end fitting clamp nut (arrowed) - Lucas pump

4.4b Loosening the fast idle cable end fitting clamp screw (arrowed) - Bosch pump

4.5 Sliding the fast idle cable from the adjustment ferrule - Bosch pump

4 Loosen the clamp screw or nut (as applicable), and disconnect the fast idle cable end fitting from the inner cable at the fuel injection pump fast idle lever **(see illustrations)**.

5 Slide the cable from the adjustment ferrule located in the bracket on the fuel injection pump **(see illustration)**.

6 Using a suitable open-ended spanner, unscrew the thermostatic sensor from the fuel filter/thermostat housing, and withdraw the sensor complete with the cable **(see illustration)**. Recover the sealing washer, where applicable.

Refitting

7 If sealing compound was originally used to fit the sensor in place of a washer, thoroughly clean all traces of old sealing compound from the sensor and housing. Ensure that no traces of sealant are left in the internal coolant passages of the housing.

8 Fit the sensor, using suitable sealing compound or a new washer as applicable, and tighten it.

9 Insert the adjustment ferrule into the bracket on the fuel injection pump, and screw on the locknut finger-tight.

10 Insert the inner cable through the fast idle lever, and position the end fitting on the cable, but do not tighten the clamp screw or nut (as applicable).

11 Adjust the cable as described in the following paragraphs.

Adjustment

12 With the engine cold, push the fast idle lever fully towards the flywheel end of the engine. Tighten the clamp screw or nut with the cable end fitting touching the lever.

13 Adjust the ferrule to ensure that the fast idle lever is touching its stop, then tighten the ferrule locknut.

14 Measure the exposed length of the inner cable.

15 Where applicable, refit the intercooler or the air distribution box, and reconnect the breather hose to the engine oil filler tube.

16 Refill the cooling system as described in Chapter 1, and run the engine to its normal operating temperature.

17 Check that the fast idle cable is slack. If not, it is likely that the sensor is faulty.

18 With the engine hot, check that the exposed length of the inner cable has increased by at least 6.0 mm, indicating that the thermostatic sensor is functioning correctly.

19 Check that the engine speed increases when the fast idle lever is pushed towards the flywheel end of the engine. With the lever against its stop, the fast idle speed should be as specified (refer to Chapter 1, Section 17 for details of how to check engine speed accurately).

20 Stop the engine.

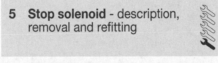

5 Stop solenoid - description, removal and refitting

Caution: Be careful not to allow dirt into the injection pump during this procedure.

Description

1 The stop solenoid is located on the end of the fuel injection pump **(see illustrations)**. Its purpose is to cut the fuel supply when the ignition is switched off. If an open-circuit occurs in the solenoid or supply wiring, it will be impossible to start the engine, as the fuel will not reach the injectors. The same applies if the solenoid plunger jams in the "stop" position. If the solenoid jams in the "run"

4.6 Fast idle thermostatic sensor (arrowed)

position, the engine will not stop when the ignition is switched off.

2 If the solenoid has failed and the engine will not run, a temporary repair may be made by removing the solenoid as described in the following paragraphs. Refit the solenoid body without the plunger and spring. Tape up the wire so that it cannot touch earth. The engine can now be started as usual, but it will be necessary to use the manual stop lever (see Section 1, paragraph 9) on the fuel injection pump (or to stall the engine in gear) to stop it.

Removal

3 Disconnect the battery negative lead.

4 On models fitted with a Bosch fuel injection pump, it may be necessary to unbolt the fast idle cable support bracket from the side of the

5.1a Removing the stop solenoid wiring cover (arrowed) - Bosch pump

5.1b Removing the stop solenoid wiring cover - Lucas pump

6.9a Disconnecting the fuel pump fuel supply banjo union. Note sealing washers (arrowed) - Bosch pump

6.9b Refitting the fuel supply banjo bolt with a small section of fuel hose (arrowed) to prevent dirt ingress - Bosch pump

6.10 Injection pump fuel return pipe banjo union (arrowed) - Bosch pump

fuel injection pump, to improve access. Refer to Section 4 if it proves necessary to disconnect the cable from the bracket.

5 Withdraw the rubber boot (where applicable), then unscrew the terminal nut and disconnect the wire from the top of the solenoid.

6 Carefully clean around the solenoid, then unscrew and withdraw the solenoid, and recover the sealing washer or O-ring (as applicable). Recover the solenoid plunger and spring if they remain in the pump. Operate the hand-priming pump as the solenoid is removed, to flush away any dirt.

Refitting

7 Refitting is a reversal of removal, using a new sealing washer or O-ring.

8 If the fast idle cable was disconnected, reconnect it with reference to Section 4.

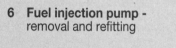

6 Fuel injection pump - removal and refitting

Caution: Be careful not to allow dirt into the injection pump or injector pipes during this procedure. New sealing rings should be used on the fuel pipe banjo unions when refitting.

Removal

1 Disconnect the battery negative lead.

2 Cover the alternator with a plastic bag, as a precaution against spillage of diesel fuel.

3 For improved access, remove the intercooler (Turbo models - see Section 20) or the air distribution box (XUD9/A - D9B engine - see Section 21), where applicable. Similarly, disconnect the air hose from the top of the inlet manifold, where applicable.

4 On manual transmission models, jack up the front right-hand corner of the vehicle until the wheel is just clear of the ground. Support the vehicle on an axle stand (see *"Jacking and vehicle support"*) and engage 4th or 5th gear. This will enable the engine to be turned easily by turning the right-hand wheel. On automatic transmission models, turn the engine using a spanner on the crankshaft pulley bolt. It will be easier to turn the engine if the glow plugs are removed (see Chapter 5).

5 Remove the upper timing belt covers with reference to Chapter 2, Part A.

6 On XUD9/Y (DJZ) engines, disconnect the hoses from the vacuum converter on the end of the fuel injection pump.

7 Disconnect the accelerator cable from the fuel injection pump, with reference to Section 11. On models with automatic transmission, also disconnect the kickdown cable.

8 Disconnect the fast idle cable from the fuel injection pump, with reference to Section 4.

9 Loosen the clip, or undo the banjo union, and disconnect the fuel supply hose. Recover the sealing washers from the banjo union,

where applicable. Cover the open end of the hose, and refit and cover the banjo bolt to keep dirt out **(see illustrations)**.

10 Disconnect the main fuel return pipe and the injector leak-off return pipe banjo union **(see illustration)**. Recover the sealing washers from the banjo union. Again, cover the open end of the hose and the banjo bolt to keep dirt out. Take care not to get the inlet and outlet banjo unions mixed up.

11 Disconnect all relevant wiring from the pump. Note that on certain Bosch pumps, this can be achieved by simply disconnecting the wiring connectors at the brackets on the pump **(see illustration)**. On some pumps, it will be necessary to disconnect the wiring from the individual components (some connections may be protected by rubber covers).

12 Unscrew the union nuts securing the injector pipes to the fuel injection pump and injectors. Counterhold the unions on the pump, while unscrewing the pipe-to-pump union nuts. Remove the pipes as a set. Cover open unions to keep dirt out, using small plastic bags, or fingers cut from discarded (but clean!) rubber gloves **(see illustrations)**.

13 Turn the crankshaft until the two bolt holes in the fuel injection pump sprocket are aligned with the corresponding holes in the engine front plate.

14 Insert two M8 bolts through the holes, and hand-tighten them. Note that the bolts must retain the sprocket while the fuel injection

6.11 Disconnecting a fuel injection pump wiring plug - Bosch pump

6.12a Unscrewing a fuel pipe-to-injector union

6.12b Cover the open end of the injector to prevent dirt ingress

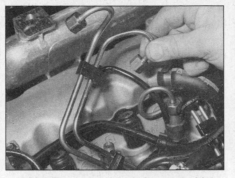

6.12c Unscrewing a fuel pipe-to-pump union - Bosch pump

6.12d Removing a fuel pipe assembly

6.14 M8 bolts inserted through timing holes in injection pump sprocket

6.15 Mark the injection pump in relation to the mounting bracket (arrowed)

6.16a Unscrewing an injection pump front mounting nut - Bosch pump

6.16b Unscrewing an injection pump rear mounting nut (arrowed) - Bosch pump

pump is removed, thereby making it unnecessary to remove the timing belt **(see illustration)**.

15 Mark the fuel injection pump in relation to the mounting bracket, using a scriber or felt tip pen **(see illustration)**. This will ensure the correct pump timing is retained when refitting.

16 Unscrew the three front mounting nuts, and recover the washers. Unscrew and remove the rear mounting nut and bolt, noting the locations of the washers, and support the injection pump on a block of wood **(see illustrations)**.

17 Release the injection pump sprocket from the pump shaft, as described in Chapter 2, Part A, Section 8. Note that the sprocket can be left engaged with the timing belt as the pump is withdrawn from its mounting bracket.

Refit the M8 bolts to retain the sprocket in position while the pump is removed.

18 Carefully withdraw the pump. Recover the Woodruff key from the end of the pump shaft if it is loose, and similarly recover the bush from the rear of the mounting bracket **(see illustrations)**.

Refitting

19 Commence refitting the injection pump by fitting the Woodruff key to the shaft groove (if removed).

20 Offer the pump to the mounting bracket, and support on a block of wood, as during removal.

21 Engage the pump shaft with the sprocket, and refit the sprocket as described in Chapter 2, Part A, Section 8. Ensure that the

Woodruff key does not fall out of the shaft as the sprocket is engaged.

22 Align the marks made on the pump and mounting bracket before removal. If a new pump is being fitted, transfer the mark from the old pump to give an approximate setting.

23 Refit and lightly tighten the pump mounting nuts and bolt.

24 Set up the injection timing, as described in Sections 7, 8 and 9, as applicable.

25 Refit and reconnect the injector fuel pipes.

26 Reconnect all relevant wiring to the pump.

27 Reconnect the fuel supply and return hoses, and tighten the unions, as applicable. Use new sealing washers on the banjo unions.

28 Reconnect the fast idle cable, and adjust it as described in Section 4.

29 Reconnect and adjust the accelerator cable with reference to Section 11. Also reconnect the kickdown cable where applicable.

30 On XUD9/Y (DJZ) engines, reconnect the hoses to the vacuum converter.

31 Refit the upper timing belt covers.

32 Lower the vehicle to the ground.

33 Where applicable, refit the intercooler or the air distribution housing.

34 Remove the plastic bag used to cover the alternator.

35 Reconnect the battery negative lead.

36 Bleed the fuel system as described in Section 25.

37 Start the engine, and check the fuel injection pump adjustments as described in Chapter 1, Section 17.

6.18a Removing an injection pump - Bosch pump

6.18b Recover the bush from the rear of the pump mounting bracket

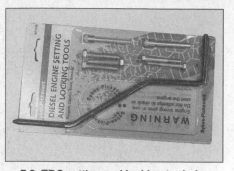

7.3 TDC setting and locking tools for setting injection timing on Citroën diesel engines

7 Injection timing - checking methods and adjustment

1 Checking the injection timing is not a routine operation. It is only necessary after the injection pump has been disturbed.

2 Dynamic timing equipment does exist, but it is unlikely to be available to the home mechanic. The equipment works by converting pressure pulses in an injector pipe into electrical signals. If such equipment is available, use it in accordance with its maker's instructions.

3 Static timing as described in this Chapter gives good results if carried out carefully. A dial test indicator will be needed, with probes and adaptors appropriate to the type of injection pump (see illustration). Read through the procedures before starting work, to find out what is involved.

8 Injection timing (Lucas fuel injection pump) - checking and adjustment

Caution: The maximum engine speed and transfer pressure settings, together with timing access plugs, are sealed by the manufacturers at the factory using locking wire and lead seals. Do not disturb the wire if the vehicle is still within the warranty

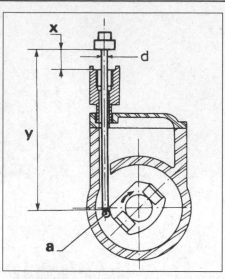

8.9 Timing probe details - Lucas pump

a Timing piece
d 7.0 mm
x Timing value (on disc or tag)
y 95.5 ± 0.01 mm

period, otherwise the warranty will be invalidated. Also do not attempt the timing procedure unless accurate instrumentation is available. Suitable special tools for carrying out pump timing are available from motor factors, and a dial test indicator will be required regardless of the method used.

1 Disconnect the battery negative lead.

2 Cover the alternator with a plastic bag, as a precaution against spillage of diesel fuel.

3 On manual transmission models, jack up the front right-hand corner of the vehicle until the wheel is just clear of the ground. Support the vehicle on an axle stand, and engage 4th or 5th gear. This will enable the engine to be turned easily by turning the right-hand wheel.

4 On automatic transmission models, use an open-ended spanner on the crankshaft pulley bolt.

5 For improved access, remove the air distribution housing (XUD9/A - D9B engine) where applicable, as described in Section 21. Similarly, disconnect the air hose from the top of the inlet manifold, where applicable.

6 Note that the engine is timed with *No 4 piston* at TDC on the compression stroke. Disconnect the feed wire, and unscrew the glow plug from cylinder No 4 (timing belt end). Alternatively, the blanking plug can be removed from the top of the cylinder head (located above No 4 cylinder, next to the cylinder head bolt).

7 The pump timing is now carried out at TDC. Turn the engine to bring No 4 cylinder to TDC on compression. To determine whether the cylinder is on compression, if the glow plug has been removed, place a finger over the glow plug hole. It should be possible to feel the pressure building up as the piston approaches TDC on the compression stroke. Alternatively, if the blanking plug has been removed from the cylinder head, probe the hole revealed by removing the blanking plug, using a long rod. By resting the rod on the top of the piston, it should be possible to determine when the piston is approaching TDC at the upper limit of its travel.

8 Insert an 8 mm diameter rod or drill through the hole in the left-hand flange of the cylinder block by the starter motor. If necessary, carefully turn the crankshaft either way until the rod enters the TDC hole in the flywheel.

9 A dial test indicator will now be required, and if a suitable special probe (designed specifically for the Lucas pump, and available from motor factors) is not available, an alternative should be made up to the dimensions shown (see illustration).

10 Remove the inspection plug from the top of the pump (see illustration). Position a dial test indicator so that it can read the movement of the probe inserted into the hole. **Note**: *A gauge mounted other than on the pump will also measure pump movement.*

11 Insert the probe into the inspection hole, so that the tip of the probe rests on the rotor timing piece. Position the dial test indicator to read the movement of the probe (see illustration).

12 Remove the TDC locking rod or drill from the flywheel. Turn the engine approximately a quarter-turn backwards. Zero the dial test indicator.

13 Turn the engine forwards slowly until the TDC locking tool can be re-inserted. Read the

8.10 Removing the injection pump timing inspection plug - Lucas pump

8.11 Dial test indicator positioned to read injection pump timing - Lucas pump

8.13a Pump timing value (x) marked on plastic disc - Lucas pump

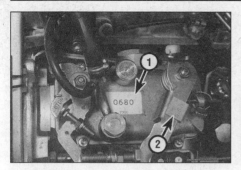

8.13b Pump timing values marked on label (1) and tag (2) - Lucas pump

9.6 Removing the timing aperture blanking plug from the cylinder head

9.8 Inserting a suitable cranked rod into the flywheel TDC hole

dial test indicator; the reading should correspond to the value marked on the pump. The timing value may be marked on a plastic disc on the front of the pump, or alternatively may appear on a label attached to the top of the pump, or a tag attached to the accelerator pump lever **(see illustrations)**.

14 If the reading is not as specified, proceed as follows.

15 Unscrew the union nuts securing the injector pipes to the fuel injection pump. Counterhold the unions on the pump, when unscrewing the nuts. Cover open unions to keep dirt out, using small plastic bags or fingers cut from discarded (but clean!) rubber gloves.

16 Slacken the four pump mounting nuts (three front and one rear), and swing the pump away from the engine. Zero the dial test indicator.

17 With the engine still at TDC, slowly swing the pump back towards the engine until the dial test indicator displays the value marked on the front face of the pump. In this position, tighten the pump mountings (the reading on the dial test indicator should not change as the pump mountings are tightened), then remove the TDC locking tool and recheck the timing as just described.

18 When the timing is correct, reconnect the injector fuel pipes and remove the dial test indicator. Remove the probe from the

inspection hole, and refit the inspection plug. Remove the TDC locking tool from the flywheel.

19 Refit the glow plug and connect the wire, or refit the blanking plug to the top of the cylinder head, as applicable.

20 Refit the intercooler or the air distribution housing, where applicable.

21 Lower the car to the ground, and reconnect the battery negative lead. Remove the plastic bag used to cover the alternator.

22 Bleed the fuel system as described in Section 25.

23 Check and if necessary adjust the idle speed and the anti-stall speed as described in Chapter 1, Section 17.

9 Injection timing (Bosch fuel injection pump) - checking and adjustment

Caution: Some of the injection pump settings and access plugs may be sealed by the manufacturers at the factory, using paint or locking wire and lead seals. Do not disturb the seals if the vehicle is still within the warranty period, otherwise the warranty will be invalidated. Also do not attempt the timing procedure unless accurate instrumentation is available.

1 Disconnect the battery negative lead.

2 Cover the alternator with a plastic bag, as a precaution against spillage of diesel fuel.

3 On manual transmission models, jack up the front right-hand corner of the vehicle until the wheel is just clear of the ground. Support the vehicle on an axle stand, and engage 4th or 5th gear. This will enable the engine to be turned easily by turning the right-hand wheel.

4 On automatic transmission models, use an open-ended spanner on the crankshaft pulley bolt.

5 For improved access, remove the intercooler (Turbo models - Section 20) or the air distribution housing (XUD9/A - D9B engine - Section 21), where applicable. Similarly, disconnect the air hose from the top of the inlet manifold, where applicable.

6 Note that the engine is timed with *No 4 piston* at TDC on the compression stroke. Disconnect the feed wire, and unscrew the glow plug from cylinder No 4 (timing belt end). Alternatively, the blanking plug can be removed from the top of the cylinder head (located above No 4 cylinder, next to the cylinder head bolt) **(see illustration)**.

7 The pump timing is now carried out at TDC. Turn the engine to bring No 4 cylinder to TDC on compression. To determine whether the cylinder is on compression, if the glow plug has been removed, place a finger over the glow plug hole. It should be possible to feel the pressure building up as the piston approaches TDC on the compression stroke. Alternatively, if the blanking plug has been removed from the cylinder head, probe the hole revealed by removing the blanking plug, using a long rod. By resting the rod on the top of the piston, it should be possible to determine when the piston is approaching TDC at the upper limit of its travel.

8 Insert an 8 mm diameter rod or drill through the hole in the left-hand flange of the cylinder block by the starter motor. If necessary, carefully turn the crankshaft either way until the rod enters the TDC hole in the flywheel **(see illustration)**.

9 A dial test indicator will now be required, along with a suitable special probe and adaptor to screw into the hole in the rear of the pump (designed specifically for the Bosch pump, and available from motor factors) **(see illustration)**.

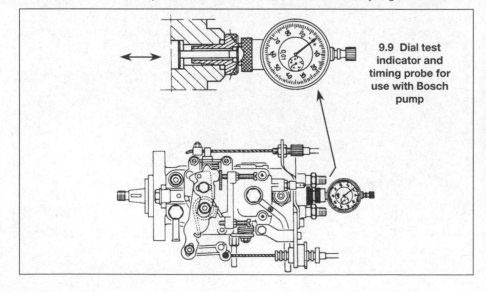

9.9 Dial test indicator and timing probe for use with Bosch pump

10 On XUD9/Y (DJZ) engines, disconnect the vacuum hoses from the vacuum converter on the top of the fuel injection pump.

11 Unscrew the union nuts securing the injector pipes to the fuel injection pump. Counterhold the unions on the pump while unscrewing the nuts **(see illustration)**. Cover open unions to keep dirt out, using small plastic bags, or fingers cut from discarded (but clean!) rubber gloves.

12 Unscrew the blanking plug from the end of the injection pump between the injector pipe connections. Be prepared for the loss of some fuel.

13 Insert the probe, and connect it to the dial test indicator positioned directly over the hole.

14 Remove the TDC locking tool from the flywheel, and turn the engine approximately a quarter-turn backwards until the needle on the dial test indicator no longer moves. Zero the dial test indicator.

15 Turn the engine forwards slowly until the TDC locking tool can be re-inserted into the flywheel. Read the dial test indicator; the value should correspond to that given in the Specifications **(see illustration)**.

16 If the reading is not as specified, proceed as follows.

17 Slacken the four pump mounting nuts (three front and one rear), and swing the pump away from the engine. Zero the dial test indicator.

18 With the engine still at TDC, slowly swing the pump back towards the engine until the dial test indicator displays the value given in the Specifications. In this position, tighten the pump mountings (the reading on the dial test indicator should not change as the pump mountings are tightened), then remove the TDC locking tool and recheck the timing as just described.

19 When the timing is correct, remove the dial test indicator, and the probe and adaptor, and reconnect the injector fuel pipes.

20 Refit the blanking plug to the end of the pump, and remove the TDC locking tool from the flywheel.

21 Refit the glow plug and connect the wire, or refit the blanking plug to the top of the cylinder head, as applicable.

9.11 Unscrewing an injector pipe-to-fuel pump union

9.15 Dial test indicator positioned to read injection pump timing - Bosch pump

22 Where applicable, reconnect the hoses to the vacuum converter on the top of the fuel injection pump.

23 Refit the intercooler or the air distribution housing, where applicable.

24 Lower the car to the ground, and reconnect the battery negative lead. Remove the plastic bag used to cover the alternator.

25 Bleed the fuel system as described in Section 25.

26 Check and if necessary adjust the idle speed and the anti-stall speed as described in Chapter 1, Section 17.

10 Fuel injectors - testing, removal and refitting

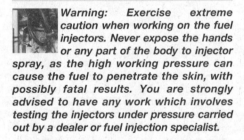 *Warning: Exercise extreme caution when working on the fuel injectors. Never expose the hands or any part of the body to injector spray, as the high working pressure can cause the fuel to penetrate the skin, with possibly fatal results. You are strongly advised to have any work which involves testing the injectors under pressure carried out by a dealer or fuel injection specialist.*

Testing

1 Injectors do deteriorate with prolonged use, and it is reasonable to expect them to need reconditioning or renewal after 60 000 miles (100 000 km) or so. Accurate testing, overhaul and calibration of the injectors must be left to

a specialist. A defective injector which is causing knocking or smoking can be located without dismantling as follows.

2 Run the engine at a fast idle. Slacken each injector union in turn, placing rag around the union to catch spilt fuel, and being careful not to expose the skin to any spray. When the union on the defective injector is slackened, the knocking or smoking will stop.

Removal

3 For improved access, remove the intercooler (Turbo models - Section 20) or the air distribution housing (XUD9/A - D9B engine - Section 21) where applicable. Similarly, disconnect the air hose from the top of the inlet manifold, where applicable.

4 Carefully clean around the injectors and injector pipe union nuts.

5 Pull the leak-off pipes from the injectors **(see illustration)**.

6 Unscrew the union nuts securing the injector pipes to the fuel injection pump. Counterhold the unions on the pump when unscrewing the nuts. Cover open unions to keep dirt out, using small plastic bags, or fingers cut from discarded (but clean!) rubber gloves.

7 Unscrew the union nuts and disconnect the pipes from the injectors **(see illustration)**. If necessary, the injector pipes may be completely removed. Note carefully the locations of the pipe clamps, for use when refitting. Cover the ends of the injectors, to prevent dirt ingress.

8 Unscrew the injectors using a deep socket or box spanner (27 mm across-flats), and remove them from the cylinder head **(see illustrations)**.

10.5 Pulling a leak-off pipe from a fuel injector

10.7 Unscrewing an injector pipe union nut

10.8a Unscrew the injectors . . .

10.8b . . . and remove them from the cylinder head

10.9a Removing a fuel injector copper washer . . .

10.9b . . . fire seal washer . . .

10.9c . . . and sleeve

9 Recover the copper washers and fire seal washers from the cylinder head. Also recover the sleeves if they are loose **(see illustrations)**.

Refitting

10 Obtain new copper washers and fire seal washers. Also renew the sleeves, if they are damaged.
11 Take care not to drop the injectors, or allow the needles at their tips to become damaged. The injectors are precision-made to fine limits, and must not be handled roughly. In particular, never mount them in a bench vice.
12 Commence refitting by inserting the sleeves (if removed) into the cylinder head, followed by the fire seal washers (convex face uppermost), and copper washers.

13 Insert the injectors, and tighten them to the specified torque.
14 Refit the injector pipes, and tighten the union nuts. Make sure the pipe clamps are in their previously-noted positions. If the clamps are wrongly positioned or missing, problems may be experienced with pipes breaking or splitting.
15 Reconnect the leak-off pipes.
16 Refit the intercooler or air distribution housing where applicable.
17 Start the engine. If difficulty is experienced, bleed the fuel system as described in Section 25.

11 Accelerator cable - removal, refitting and adjustment

Removal

1 Working in the engine compartment, operate the accelerator lever on the fuel injection pump, and release the cable inner from the lever **(see illustration)**.
2 Pull the cable outer from the grommet in the fuel injection pump bracket **(see illustration)**.
3 Release the cable from the remaining clips and brackets in the engine compartment, noting its routing **(see illustration)**.
4 Working in the passenger compartment, release the securing clips, and remove the felt trim panel from under the facia in the driver's footwell.

5 Release the securing clips, and remove the driver's side lower facia panel.
6 Release the securing clip, and disconnect the cable inner from the pedal **(see illustration)**.
7 Slide the cable outer grommet from the bracket on the pedal.
8 Carefully feed the cable through the bulkhead grommet from the engine compartment into the vehicle interior, and remove it from the vehicle.

Refitting

9 Refitting is a reversal of removal, but ensure that the cable is routed as noted before removal, and on completion, adjust the cable as follows.

11.1 Releasing the accelerator cable inner from the accelerator lever on the injection pump

11.2 Pulling the accelerator cable outer from the bracket

11.3 Accelerator cable/coolant hose clip (arrowed) at rear of engine compartment

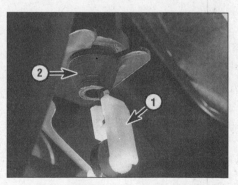

11.6 Accelerator cable inner securing clip (1) and cable outer grommet (2)

12.2 Unscrewing the nut from the accelerator pedal pivot shaft

12.3a Pull the pedal and pivot shaft assembly from the bracket (arrowed) . . .

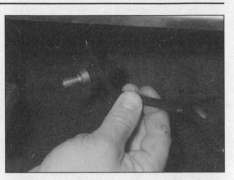

12.3b . . . and withdraw it from the vehicle

13.3 Removing the fuel level sender plastic cover

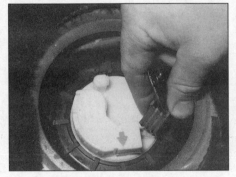

13.4 Disconnecting the wiring plug from the fuel level sender unit

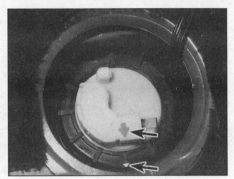

13.5 Alignment arrows (arrowed) on sender unit and locking ring

Adjustment

10 Have an assistant fully depress the accelerator pedal, then check that the accelerator lever on the injection pump is touching the maximum speed adjustment screw. If not, pull the spring clip from the adjustment ferrule, reposition the ferrule, and fit the spring clip in the groove next to the metal washer.

11 With the accelerator pedal fully released, check that the accelerator lever is touching the anti-stall adjustment screw.

12 Accelerator pedal - removal and refitting

Removal

1 Disconnect the accelerator cable from the pedal, with reference to Section 11.
2 Unscrew the nut from the end of the pedal pivot shaft, while counterholding the pivot shaft on the flats provided (see illustration).
3 Pull the pedal and pivot shaft assembly from the support bracket (see illustrations).
4 If desired, the pivot shaft can be unscrewed from the pedal.

Refitting

5 Refitting is a reversal of removal, but reconnect the accelerator cable to the pedal, and adjust if necessary as described in Section 11.

13 Fuel level sender - removal and refitting

Removal

1 Disconnect the battery negative lead.
2 For access to the sender unit, tilt or remove the rear seats, according to model, as described in Chapter 11.
3 Using a screwdriver, carefully prise the plastic cover from the floor to expose the sender unit (the sender unit is located under the left-hand cover, viewed facing towards the front of the vehicle) (see illustration).
4 Disconnect the wiring plug from the sender unit (see illustration).

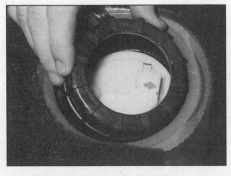

13.7a Unscrew the locking ring . . .

5 Note the alignment arrows on the sender unit and the locking ring (see illustration).
6 The locking ring which secures the sender unit in the fuel tank must now be unscrewed. This is best accomplished by using a screwdriver on the raised ribs of the locking ring. Carefully tap the screwdriver to turn the ring anti-clockwise until it can be unscrewed by hand.
7 Unscrew the locking ring, and carefully lift the sender unit from the top of the fuel tank. Take care not to spill fuel into the interior of the vehicle. Recover the rubber sealing ring if it is loose (see illustrations).

Refitting

8 Before refitting the sender unit, examine the condition of the sealing ring, and renew if necessary.

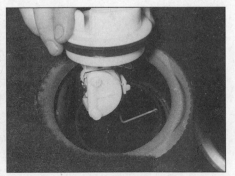

13.7b . . . and lift the sender unit from the fuel tank

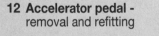

13.7c Removing the sealing ring from the sender unit

14.4 Note the flow direction arrows (arrowed) on the fuel pick-up unit

14.5 Alignment arrows (arrowed) on fuel pick-up unit and locking ring

9 Refitting is a reversal of removal, but ensure that the arrows on the sender unit and the locking ring are aligned as noted before removal (tighten the locking ring using a screwdriver as during removal).

14 Fuel pick-up unit - removal and refitting

Removal

1 Disconnect the battery negative lead.
2 For access to the pick-up unit, tilt or remove the rear seats, according to model, as described in Chapter 11.
3 Using a screwdriver, carefully prise the plastic cover from the floor to expose the pick-up unit (the unit is located under the right-hand cover, viewed facing towards the front of the vehicle).
4 Disconnect the fuel hoses from the unit, noting their locations **(see illustration)**. Be prepared for fuel spillage, and take care not to spill fuel into the interior of the vehicle.
5 Note the alignment arrows on the pick-up unit and the locking ring **(see illustration)**.
6 The locking ring which secures the unit in the fuel tank must now be unscrewed. This is best accomplished by using a screwdriver on the raised ribs of the locking ring. Carefully tap the screwdriver to turn the ring anti-

clockwise until it can be unscrewed by hand **(see illustration)**.
7 Unscrew the locking ring, and carefully lift the unit from the top of the fuel tank. Recover the rubber sealing ring if it is loose **(see illustrations)**.

Refitting

8 Before refitting, examine the condition of the sealing ring, and renew if necessary. Similarly examine the condition of the filter at the end of the pick-up pipe, and clean or renew as necessary.
9 Refitting is a reversal of removal, ensuring that the hoses are correctly reconnected, as noted before removal. Also ensure that the arrows on the pick-up unit and the locking ring are aligned as previously noted (tighten the locking ring using a screwdriver as during removal).

15 Fuel tank - removal, repair and refitting

Removal

1 Disconnect the battery negative lead.
2 Siphon out any remaining fuel in the tank through the filler pipe. Siphon the fuel into a suitable metal or plastic container which can be sealed.
3 For access to the fuel level sender unit and

14.6 Releasing the fuel pick-up unit locking ring using a screwdriver

the pick-up unit, tilt or remove the rear seats, according to model, as described in Chapter 11.
4 Using a screwdriver, prise the plastic cover from the floor, then disconnect the wiring plug from the sender unit (see Section 13).
5 Remove the exhaust system as described in Section 22.
6 Remove the plastic nuts securing the rear exhaust heat shield to the fuel tank and, where applicable, loosen the two screws securing the front edge of the heat shield **(see illustration)**. Withdraw the heat shield.
7 Disconnect the two handbrake cables from the handbrake lever adjuster, as described in Chapter 9, Section 19.

14.7a Lifting the fuel pick-up unit from the tank

14.7b Recovering the sealing ring

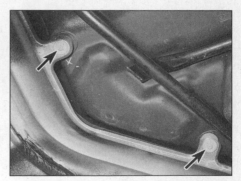

15.6 Two of the plastic nuts (arrowed) securing the exhaust heat shield to the fuel tank

15.8 Handbrake cable securing clip (arrowed) on fuel tank

15.9 Disconnect the fuel inlet and return hoses (arrowed)

15.12a Front left-hand fuel tank securing screw

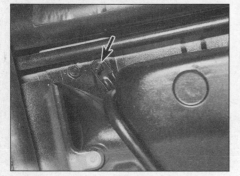

15.12b Fuel tank support rod securing nut (arrowed)

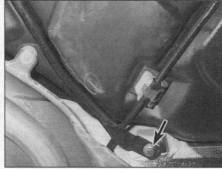

15.12c Fuel tank strap securing bolt (arrowed)

8 Release the handbrake cables from the clips on the fuel tank, and move the cables clear of the tank **(see illustration)**.

9 Working at the right-hand side of the fuel tank, disconnect the fuel inlet and return hoses **(see illustration)**.

10 Disconnect the fuel supply and return hoses from the pipes under the floor of the vehicle.

11 Support the fuel tank on a trolley jack with an interposed block of wood.

12 Remove the three fuel tank securing screws, the single nut, and the two support rods **(see illustrations)**.

13 Lower the fuel tank slightly, and disconnect the vent pipe.

14 Lower the tank, and remove it from under the vehicle.

Repair

15 The tank is made of plastic. If it is damaged, it should be renewed. Proprietary repair kits are available, but check that they are suitable for use on plastic tanks. A fuel leak is not just expensive, it is dangerous.

Refitting

16 Refitting is a reversal of removal, bearing in mind the following points:

(a) Ensure that the vent hose is reconnected before raising the tank into its final position.

(b) Ensure that all hoses are correctly reconnected, as noted before removal.

(c) Reconnect the handbrake cables to the handbrake adjuster, and adjust the cables as described in Chapter 9, Section 17.

(d) Refit the exhaust system as described in Section 22.

(e) On completion, check all hose connections for leaks.

16 Manifolds - removal and refitting

1 On certain models, the inlet and exhaust manifolds share the same gasket. Where this is the case, it is recommended that both manifolds are removed, whenever one is removed, in order that the gasket can be renewed. It is possible to remove the manifolds individually, in which case the original gasket would be re-used, but this is not recommended.

Inlet manifold

Note: *Renew the manifold gasket(s) when refitting.*

Removal

2 Disconnect the battery negative lead.

3 For improved access, remove the intercooler (Turbo models - Section 20) or the air distribution housing (XUD9/A - D9B engine - Section 21), where applicable. Similarly, disconnect the air hose from the top of the inlet manifold, where applicable.

4 Disconnect the end of the accelerator cable from the fuel injection pump, with reference to Section 11. Release the cable from its clips, noting their locations, and position the cable to one side, clear of the manifolds.

5 Similarly, disconnect the brake servo vacuum hose from the vacuum pump, and move the hose to one side. On models fitted with an exhaust gas recirculation (EGR) system (see Section 23), disconnect the vacuum hose from the flow valve.

6 On Turbo models, release the hose clips and disconnect the air hoses from the air tube which connects the turbocharger to the air cleaner tubing. Manipulate the air tube from the inlet manifold, and remove it from the engine compartment **(see illustrations)**. Push a wad of (clean!) rag into the open end of the turbocharger air hose (or the turbocharger

16.6a Release the hose clips (one arrowed) . . .

16.6b . . . and remove the air tube - Turbo models

16.7 Removing the intercooler air hose - Turbo models

16.8 Inlet manifold securing bolts (A) and hex bolt (B - loosen, do not remove) on Turbo models - viewed with engine removed for clarity

16.9 Withdrawing the inlet manifold from the cylinder head

itself, if the hose has been removed completely), to prevent the possibility of dirt ingress.

7 On Turbo models, release the securing clip, and remove the intercooler air hose from the turbocharger **(see illustration)**.

8 Using a suitable hexagon bit or Allen key, remove the six bolts securing the inlet manifold. Loosen, but do not remove, the central hexagon manifold securing bolt - the manifold is slotted **(see illustration)**.

9 Withdraw the manifold from the cylinder head **(see illustration)**.

Refitting

10 Refitting is a reversal of removal, bearing in mind the following points.

11 Renew the gasket(s) when refitting the manifold.

12 Tighten all fixings to the specified torques, where applicable.

13 Reconnect the accelerator cable to the fuel injection pump. Adjust the cable if necessary, with reference to Section 11.

14 Ensure that all relevant hoses and pipes are correctly reconnected and routed.

Exhaust manifold

Note: *Renew the manifold gasket(s) when refitting.*

Removal

15 For improved access, remove the inlet manifold as described previously in this Section. This is essential on Turbo models.

16 If the inlet manifold is to be left in place, proceed as described in paragraphs 2 to 5, then proceed as follows.

17 On non-turbo models, disconnect the exhaust downpipe from the manifold, with reference to Section 22.

18 On Turbo models, remove the turbocharger as described in Section 18.

19 On certain models, it may be necessary to unbolt the resonator chamber from the manifold, to allow sufficient clearance for the manifold to be removed. On models fitted with an exhaust gas recirculation (EGR) system (see Section 23), disconnect the vacuum hose from the recirculation valve.

20 Unscrew the six exhaust manifold securing nuts, and recover the spacers from the studs **(see illustration)**.

21 Lift the exhaust manifold from the cylinder head, and recover the gasket **(see illustration)**.

22 It is possible that some of the manifold studs may be unscrewed from the cylinder head when the manifold securing nuts are unscrewed. In this event, the studs should be screwed back into the cylinder head once the manifolds have been removed, using two manifold nuts locked together.

Refitting

23 Refitting is a reversal of removal, bearing in mind the following points.

24 Renew the manifold gasket(s) on refitting.

25 Where applicable, refit the turbocharger as described in Section 18.

26 Where applicable, reconnect the exhaust

downpipe to the exhaust manifold as described in Section 22.

27 Tighten all fixings to the specified torque, where applicable.

28 Reconnect the accelerator cable to the fuel injection pump. Adjust the cable if necessary, with reference to Section 11.

29 Ensure that all relevant hoses and pipes are correctly reconnected and routed.

17 Turbocharger - description and precautions

Description

1 A turbocharger is fitted to the XUD9TE/L (D8A) and XUD9TE/Y (DHY and DHZ) engines. It increases engine efficiency by raising the pressure in the inlet manifold above atmospheric pressure. Instead of the air simply being sucked into the cylinders, it is forced in. Additional fuel is supplied by the injection pump in proportion to the increased air intake.

2 Energy for the operation of the turbocharger comes from the exhaust gas. The gas flows through a specially-shaped housing (the turbine housing) and in so doing, spins the turbine wheel. The turbine wheel is attached to a shaft, at the end of which is another vaned wheel known as the compressor wheel. The compressor wheel spins in its own housing, and compresses the inlet air on the way to the inlet manifold.

3 Between the turbocharger and the inlet manifold, the compressed air passes through an intercooler. This is an air-to-air heat exchanger, mounted over the engine, and supplied with cooling air ducted through the bonnet insulation. The purpose of the intercooler is to remove from the inlet air some of the heat gained in being compressed. Because cooler air is denser, removal of this heat further increases engine efficiency.

4 Boost pressure (the pressure in the inlet manifold) is limited by a wastegate, which diverts the exhaust gas away from the turbine wheel in response to a pressure-sensitive actuator. A pressure-operated switch operates

16.20 Exhaust manifold securing nuts (arrowed) on Turbo models - viewed with engine removed for clarity

16.21 Lifting the exhaust manifold and gasket from the cylinder head

18.2 Disconnecting the oil feed pipe from the turbocharger

18.5 Remove the hose (arrowed) connecting the turbocharger oil return pipe to the pipe on the cylinder block

18.6 Remove the screw (arrowed) securing the oil feed pipe

a warning light on the instrument panel in the event of excessive boost pressure developing.
5 The turbo shaft is pressure-lubricated by an oil feed pipe from the main oil gallery. The shaft "floats" on a cushion of oil. A drain pipe returns the oil to the sump.

Precautions

6 The turbocharger operates at extremely high speeds and temperatures. Certain precautions must be observed, to avoid premature failure of the turbo, or injury to the operator.
7 Do not operate the turbo with any of its parts exposed, or with any of its hoses removed. Foreign objects falling onto the rotating vanes could cause excessive damage, and (if ejected) personal injury.
8 Do not race the engine immediately after start-up, especially if it is cold. Give the oil a few seconds to circulate.
9 Always allow the engine to return to idle speed before switching it off - do not blip the throttle and switch off, as this will leave the turbo spinning without lubrication.
10 Allow the engine to idle for several minutes before switching off after a high-speed run.
11 Observe the recommended intervals for oil and filter changing, and use a reputable oil of the specified quality. Neglect of oil changing, or use of inferior oil, can cause carbon formation on the turbo shaft, leading to subsequent failure.

18 Turbocharger -
removal and refitting

Removal

1 Remove the inlet manifold as described in Section 16.
2 Unscrew the union nut, and disconnect the oil feed pipe from the top of the turbocharger (see illustration).
3 Apply the handbrake, then jack up the front of the vehicle and support securely on axle stands (see "Jacking and vehicle support").
4 Disconnect the exhaust downpipe from the turbocharger, with reference to Section 22.
5 Working under the vehicle, loosen the

securing clips, and remove the hose connecting the turbocharger oil return pipe to the pipe on the cylinder block (see illustration).
6 Remove the screw securing the oil feed pipe to the support bracket at the rear of the cylinder block (see illustration).
7 Unscrew the union nut securing the oil feed pipe to the cylinder block, then withdraw the oil feed pipe from above the engine (see illustrations).
8 Remove the filter from the cylinder block end of the oil feed pipe, and examine it for contamination (see illustration). Clean or renew if necessary.
9 Working under the vehicle, unscrew and remove the two lower turbocharger securing bolts (see illustration).

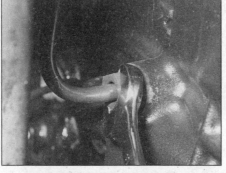

18.7a Unscrew the union nut . . .

18.7b . . . and withdraw the oil feed pipe

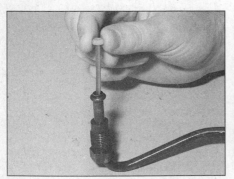

18.8 Removing the filter from the oil feed pipe

18.9 Lower turbocharger securing bolts (arrowed) - viewed from underneath

18.10 Unscrewing the upper turbocharger securing bolt

10 Support the turbocharger, then remove the upper turbocharger securing bolt, and recover the spacer **(see illustration)**.
11 Carefully manipulate the turbocharger out through the top of the engine compartment **(see illustration)**. If it is to be refitted, store the turbocharger carefully, and plug its openings to prevent dirt ingress.

Refitting

12 Refitting is a reversal of removal, bearing in mind the following points:
(a) *If a new turbocharger is being fitted, change the engine oil and filter. Also renew the filter in the oil feed pipe.*
(b) *Do not fully tighten the oil feed pipe unions until both ends of the pipe are in place. When tightening the oil return pipe union, position it so that the return hose is not strained.*
(c) *Before starting the engine, prime the turbo lubrication circuit by disconnecting the stop solenoid lead at the fuel pump, and cranking the engine on the starter for three ten-second bursts.*

19 Turbocharger -
examination and renovation

1 With the turbocharger removed, inspect the housing for cracks or other visible damage.

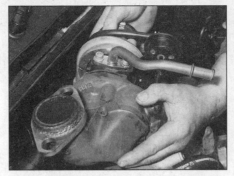

18.11 Withdrawing the turbocharger

2 Spin the turbine or the compressor wheel, to verify that the shaft is intact and to feel for excessive shake or roughness. Some play is normal, since in use, the shaft is "floating" on a film of oil. Check that the wheel vanes are undamaged.
3 On the KKK turbo, the wastegate and actuator are integral, and cannot be checked or renewed separately. On the Garrett turbo, the wastegate actuator is a separate unit. Consult a Citroën dealer or other specialist if it is thought that testing or renewal is necessary.
4 If the exhaust or induction passages are oil-contaminated, the turbo shaft oil seals have probably failed. (On the induction side, this will also have contaminated the intercooler,

20.1a Disconnect the hose (arrowed) from the front edge of the intercooler

which should if necessary be flushed with a suitable solvent.)
5 No DIY repair of the turbo is possible. A new unit may be available on an exchange basis.

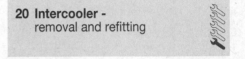

20 Intercooler -
removal and refitting

Removal

1 To remove the intercooler, follow the procedure shown in the accompanying sequence of photographs **(see illustrations)**.

Refitting

2 Refitting is a reversal of removal.

20.1b Disconnect the two hoses (arrowed) from the valve on the left-hand side of the intercooler

20.1c Disconnect the hose from the right-hand end of the intercooler

20.1d Lift the surround from the top of the intercooler

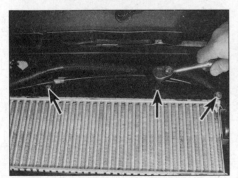

20.1e Unscrew the three upper securing bolts (arrowed) . . .

20.1f . . . and the two front securing bolts . . .

20.1g . . . and remove the intercooler

21.2 Front air distribution housing securing bolt (arrowed)

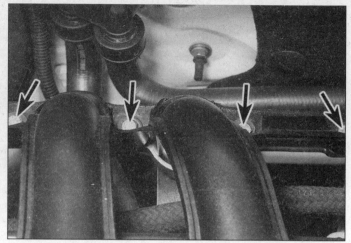

21.3 Air distribution housing-to-inlet manifold bolts (arrowed)

21 Air distribution housing (XUD9A/D9B engine) - removal and refitting

Removal

1 Disconnect the air hose and the crankcase breather hose from the front of the air distribution housing.

2 Unscrew the two bolts securing the housing to the front mounting brackets **(see illustration)**. Recover the spacer plates.

3 Unscrew the four bolts securing the housing to the inlet manifold. Recover the washers **(see illustration)**.

4 Lift the housing from the inlet manifold, and recover the four O-ring seals.

Refitting

5 Refitting is a reversal of removal, but examine the condition of the O-ring seals, and renew if necessary.

22 Exhaust system - general information and component renewal

1 The exhaust system consists of two sections on models with a conventional system, and three sections on models fitted with a catalytic converter **(see illustrations)**.

2 Each part of the system can be removed independently, although to remove the centre section on three-piece systems, it is recommended that the complete system is removed, to avoid straining the individual sections.

3 To remove the complete system or part of the system, first jack up the front or rear of the vehicle, as applicable (both, if the complete

system is to be removed), and support on axle stands (see *"Jacking and vehicle support"*).

Front section

4 To remove the front section, first disconnect the downpipe from the manifold or turbocharger (as applicable), as follows.

5 Unscrew the two nuts securing the downpipe to the manifold or turbocharger, while counterholding the bolts. Recover the

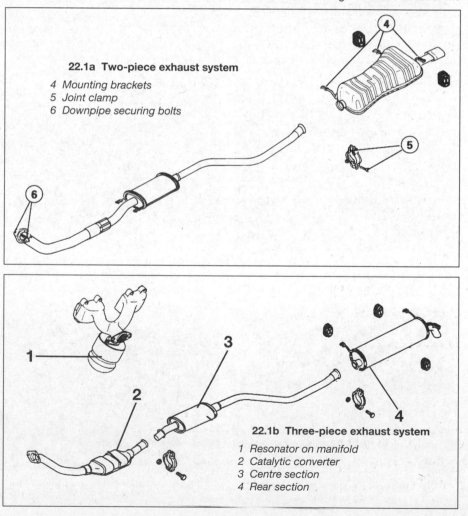

22.1a Two-piece exhaust system

4 *Mounting brackets*
5 *Joint clamp*
6 *Downpipe securing bolts*

22.1b Three-piece exhaust system

1 *Resonator on manifold*
2 *Catalytic converter*
3 *Centre section*
4 *Rear section*

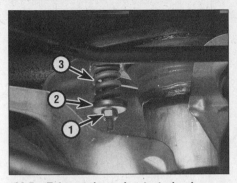

22.5a Exhaust downpipe-to-turbocharger securing nut (1), spring seat (2) and spring (3) - viewed from underneath vehicle

22.5b Exhaust downpipe-to-turbocharger securing bolts (arrowed) - viewed from engine compartment

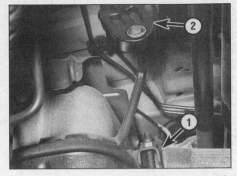

22.14 Exhaust rear section joint clamp (1) and mounting rubber (2)

springs, spring seats and washers, noting their locations **(see illustrations)**.

6 Recover the wire mesh sealing ring from the downpipe or manifold, as applicable.

7 Support the front of the system, then unscrew the nuts and bolts, and remove the clamp securing the front section to the centre or rear section, as applicable.

8 Unhook the exhaust front section from the mounting rubbers, and remove it from under the vehicle.

9 Refitting is a reversal of removal, but use a new wire mesh sealing ring when reconnecting the downpipe to the manifold, and tighten the downpipe-to-manifold nuts until they contact the shoulders on the bolts.

Centre section

10 Unscrew the nuts and bolts, and remove the clamp securing the exhaust centre section to the front section.

11 Support the rear of the front section, and the front of the centre section, and repeat the procedure on the rear clamp.

12 Lower the centre section from under the vehicle.

13 Refitting is a reversal of removal.

Rear section

14 Unscrew the nuts and bolts, and remove the clamp securing the rear section to the front section or centre section, as applicable **(see illustration)**.

15 Support the rear of the front section or centre section, as applicable, then unhook the rear section from the mounting rubbers, and lower it from the vehicle.

16 Refitting is a reversal of removal.

23 Emission control systems - general information

1 Certain engines in the ZX Diesel range are equipped with systems designed to reduce the emission of harmful by-products of the combustion process into the atmosphere.

2 The following systems may be fitted, according to model.

Crankcase emission control system - all models

3 A crankcase ventilation system is fitted to all models.

4 Oil fumes and piston blow-by gases (combustion gases which have passed by the piston rings) are drawn from the crankcase and the camshaft cover through the oil filler tube, into the air inlet tract. The oil filler tube contains an oil separator. The gases are then drawn into the engine for combustion.

Exhaust emission control system - XUD9/Y (DJZ) and XUD9TE/Y (DHY and DHZ) engines

5 To minimise the level of exhaust gas pollutants released into the atmosphere, a catalytic converter is fitted, located in the exhaust system.

6 The catalytic converter consists of a canister containing a fine mesh impregnated with a catalyst material, over which the exhaust gases pass. The catalyst speeds up the oxidation of harmful carbon monoxide, unburnt hydrocarbons and soot, effectively reducing the quantity of harmful products reaching the atmosphere.

Exhaust gas recirculation system - XUD9/Y (DJZ) engine

7 This system is designed to recirculate small quantities of exhaust gas into the inlet tract, and therefore into the combustion process **(see illustration)**. This process reduces the level of oxides of nitrogen present in the final exhaust gas which is released into the atmosphere.

8 The volume of exhaust gas recirculated is controlled by vacuum supplied from the brake

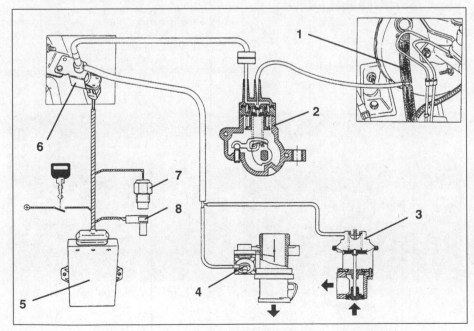

23.7 Schematic view of exhaust gas recirculation system

1 Brake servo vacuum hose
2 Vacuum converter (fitted to fuel injection pump)
3 Recirculation valve (fitted to exhaust manifold)
4 Flow valve/butterfly housing (fitted to inlet manifold)
5 Electronic control unit
6 Solenoid valve
7 Coolant temperature sensor
8 TDC sensor

servo vacuum pump, via a solenoid valve controlled by the system electronic control unit. Before reaching the solenoid valve, the vacuum from the brake servo passes to a vacuum converter mounted on the fuel injection pump. The purpose of the vacuum converter is to modify the vacuum supplied to the solenoid valve according to engine load. The converter uses the position of the accelerator lever on the pump to operate a cam, springs and valve, to vary the amount of vacuum as the load on the engine varies.

9 A vacuum-operated valve is fitted to the exhaust manifold, to regulate the quantity of exhaust gas recirculated. The valve is operated by the vacuum supplied by the solenoid valve.

10 Additionally, a butterfly valve mounted on the inlet manifold allows the ratio of air-to-recirculated exhaust gas to be controlled. The butterfly valve also enables the exhaust gases to be drawn into the inlet manifold at idle or under light load, when the valve on the exhaust manifold is fully open. Without the butterfly valve, the inlet manifold would be effectively at atmospheric pressure, and the vacuum created by the opening of the inlet valves would not be sufficient to cause the exhaust gas to circulate.

11 The system is controlled by an electronic control unit, which receives information on coolant temperature and engine speed (via the TDC sensor).

Atmospheric pressure correction system - XUD9TE/Y (DHY and DHZ) engine

12 This system allows the timing advance function of the fuel injection pump to be cancelled, in order to reduce smoke emissions at predetermined combinations of engine temperature and atmospheric pressure. The system operates in conjunction with the preheating system (see Chapter 5), according to information supplied by a coolant temperature sensor and an atmospheric pressure switch.

24 Emission control systems - testing and component renewal

Crankcase emission control system components

Testing

1 If the system is thought to be faulty, first check that the hoses are unobstructed. On high-mileage vehicles, particularly those regularly used for short journeys, a jelly-like deposit may be evident inside the crankcase

emission control system hoses. If excessive deposits are present, the relevant hose(s) should be removed and cleaned.

2 Periodically inspect the system hoses for security and damage, and renew them as necessary. Note that damaged or loose hoses can cause various engine running problems (erratic idle speed, stalling, etc) which can be difficult to trace.

Component renewal

3 Renewal procedures for the hoses and oil filler tube are self-evident.

Exhaust emission control system

Testing

4 The system can only be tested accurately using a suitable exhaust gas analyser.

Component renewal

5 The catalytic converter is fitted in the exhaust system between the manifold and centre sections.

6 Removal and refitting are as described for the exhaust front section in Section 22.

Exhaust gas recirculation system

Testing

7 Testing of the system should be entrusted to a Citroën dealer.

Component renewal

8 At the time of writing, no specific information was available regarding removal and refitting of the system components.

Atmospheric pressure correction system

Testing

9 Testing of the system should be entrusted to a Citroën dealer.

Component renewal

10 Refer to Chapter 3, Section 6 for details of the coolant temperature sensor.

25.3 Automatic fuel system bleed valve (arrowed)

11 Refer to Chapter 5, Section 17 for details of the preheating system relay/timer unit.

12 No details were available for the atmospheric pressure switch at the time of writing.

25 Fuel system - priming and bleeding

1 After disconnecting part of the fuel supply system or running out of fuel, it is necessary to prime the system and bleed off any air which may have entered the system components.

2 All models are fitted with a hand-operated priming pump, consisting of a rubber bulb located on the right-hand side of the engine compartment.

3 An automatic bleed valve is fitted, which bleeds air from the low-pressure fuel circuit when it is primed (see illustration).

4 To prime the system, switch on the ignition so that the stop solenoid is energised. Pump the rubber priming bulb until resistance is felt, indicating that air has been expelled from the fuel injection pump (see illustration). It should be possible to hear the fuel circulating through the pump when the all the air has been expelled.

5 If air has reached the injectors, the high-pressure circuit must be bled as follows.

6 Place wads of clean rag around the fuel pipe unions at the injectors to absorb spilt fuel, then slacken the fuel pipe unions.

7 Crank the engine on the starter motor until fuel emerges from the unions, then stop cranking the engine and tighten the unions. Mop up any spilt fuel.

8 Start the engine with the accelerator pedal fully depressed. Additional cranking may be necessary to finally bleed the system before the engine starts.

25.4 Hand-operated fuel system priming pump

Chapter 5 Engine electrical systems

Contents

Alternator - removal and refitting 7
Alternator brushes and regulator - inspection and renewal 8
Alternator drivebelt - removal, refitting and tensioning 6
Battery - removal and refitting 4
Battery - testing and charging 3
Battery check ....See "Weekly checks" and Chapter 1
Charging system - testing 5
Electrical fault finding - general information 2
Electrical system check ....See "Weekly checks" and Chapter 1
Engine electrical systems - general information and precautions ... 1
Glow plugs - removal, inspection and refitting 16
Ignition switch - removal and refitting 12
Oil level sensor - removal and refitting 14
Oil pressure warning light switch - removal and refitting 13
Preheating system - description and testing 15
Preheating system relay/timer unit - removal and refitting 17
Starter motor - brush renewal 11
Starter motor - removal and refitting 10
Starting system - testing 9

Degrees of difficulty

Easy, suitable for novice with little experience	**Fairly easy,** suitable for beginner with some experience	**Fairly difficult,** suitable for competent DIY mechanic	**Difficult,** suitable for experienced DIY mechanic	**Very difficult,** suitable for expert DIY or professional

Specifications

System type	12-volt, negative earth

Battery

Type	Fulmen, Delco or Steco
Charge condition:	
Poor	12.5 volts
Normal	12.6 volts
Good	12.7 volts

Alternator

Type	Valeo

Starter motor

Type	Valeo or Mitsubishi reduction-gear

Torque wrench setting	**Nm**	**lbf ft**
Glow plugs	22	16

1 Engine electrical system - general information and precautions

General information

The engine electrical system includes all charging, starting and pre-heating components and engine oil sensors. Because of their engine-related functions, these components are covered separately from the body electrical devices such as the lights, instruments, etc (which are covered in Chapter 12).

The electrical system is of the 12-volt negative earth type.

The battery is of the low-maintenance or "maintenance-free" ("sealed for life") type,

and is charged by the alternator, which is belt-driven from a crankshaft-mounted pulley.

The starter motor is of the pre-engaged reduction-gear type, incorporating an integral solenoid. On starting, the solenoid moves the drive pinion into engagement with the flywheel ring gear before the starter motor is energised. Once the engine has started, a one-way clutch prevents the motor armature being driven by the engine until the pinion disengages from the flywheel. The motor is fitted with a reduction gear mechanism, in order to achieve the high torque necessary to turn the engine against the high compression pressures encountered in a Diesel engine.

Precautions

Further details of the various systems are given in the relevant Sections of this Chapter.

While some repair procedures are given, the usual course of action is to renew the component concerned. The owner whose interest extends beyond mere component renewal should obtain a copy of the "Automobile Electrical & Electronic Systems Manual", available from the publishers of this manual.

It is necessary to take extra care when working on the electrical system, to avoid damage to semi-conductor devices (diodes and transistors), and to avoid the risk of personal injury. In addition to the precautions given in "Safety first!" at the beginning of this manual, observe the following when working on the system:

Always remove rings, watches, etc before working on the electrical system. Even with the battery disconnected, capacitive discharge could occur if a component's live terminal is earthed through a metal object. This could cause a shock or nasty burn.

Do not reverse the battery connections. Components such as the alternator, pre-heating electronic control unit, or any other components having semi-conductor circuitry could be irreparably damaged.

If the engine is being started using jump leads and a slave battery, connect the batteries *positive-to-positive* and *negative-to-negative* (see *"Booster battery (jump) starting"*). This also applies when connecting a battery charger.

Never disconnect the battery terminals, the alternator, any electrical wiring or any test instruments when the engine is running.

Do not allow the engine to turn the alternator when the alternator is not connected.

Never "test" for alternator output by "flashing" the output lead to earth.

Never use an ohmmeter of the type incorporating a hand-cranked generator for circuit or continuity testing.

Always ensure that the battery negative lead is disconnected when working on the electrical system.

Before using electric-arc welding equipment on the car, disconnect the battery, alternator, and components such as the pre-heating electronic control unit, to protect them from the risk of damage.

The radio/cassette unit fitted as standard equipment by Citroën is equipped with a built-in security code, to deter thieves. If the power source to the unit is cut, the anti-theft system will activate. Even if the power source is immediately reconnected, the radio/cassette unit will not function until the correct security code has been entered. Therefore, if you do not know the correct security code for the radio/cassette unit, *do not* disconnect the battery negative terminal of the battery, or remove the radio/cassette unit from the vehicle. Refer to the *"Radio/cassette unit anti-theft system precaution"* Section at the beginning of this manual for details of how to enter the security code.

2 Electrical fault finding - general information

Refer to Chapter 12, Section 2.

3 Battery - testing and charging

Standard and low-maintenance battery - testing

1 If the vehicle covers a small annual mileage, it is worthwhile checking the specific gravity of the electrolyte every three months, to determine the state of charge of the battery.

Use a hydrometer to make the check, and compare the results with the following table **(see illustration)**. Note that the specific gravity readings assume an electrolyte temperature of 15°C (60°F); for every 10°C (18°F) below 15°C (60°F), subtract 0.007. For every 10°C (18°F) above 15°C (60°F), add 0.007.

	Ambient temperature above 25°C (77°F)
Fully-charged	*1.210 to 1.230*
70%-charged	*1.170 to 1.190*
Fully-discharged	*1.050 to 1.070*
	Ambient temperature below 25°C (77°F)
Fully-charged	*1.270 to 1.290*
70%-charged	*1.230 to 1.250*
Fully-discharged	*1.100 to 1.130*

2 If the battery condition is suspect, first check the specific gravity of electrolyte in each cell. A variation of 0.040 or more between any cells indicates loss of electrolyte, or deterioration of the internal plates.

3 If the specific gravity variation is 0.040 or more, the battery should be renewed. If the cell variation is satisfactory but the battery is discharged, it should be charged as described later in this Section.

Maintenance-free battery - testing

4 In cases where a "sealed for life" maintenance-free battery is fitted, topping-up and testing of the electrolyte in each cell is not possible. The condition of the battery can therefore only be tested using a battery condition indicator or a voltmeter.

5 Certain models my be fitted with a "Delco" type maintenance-free battery, with a built-in charge condition indicator. The indicator is located in the top of the battery casing, and indicates the condition of the battery from its colour. If the indicator shows green, then the battery is in a good state of charge. If the indicator turns darker, eventually to black, then the battery requires charging, as described later in this Section. If the indicator shows clear/yellow, then the electrolyte level in the battery is too low to allow further use, and the battery should be renewed. **Do not** attempt to charge, load or jump-start a battery when the indicator shows clear/yellow.

6 If testing the battery using a voltmeter, connect the voltmeter across the battery, and compare the result with the figures given in the Specifications under "charge condition". The test is only accurate if the battery has not been subjected to any kind of charge for the previous six hours. If this is not the case, switch on the headlights for 30 seconds, then wait four to five minutes before testing the battery after switching off the headlights. All other electrical circuits must be switched off, so check that the doors and tailgate are fully shut when making the test.

7 If the voltage reading is less than 12.2 volts, then the battery is discharged, whilst a reading of 12.2 to 12.4 volts indicates a partially-discharged condition.

8 If the battery is to be charged, remove it

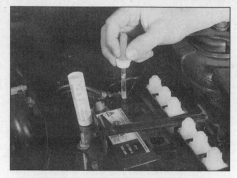

3.1 Using a hydrometer to check the battery electrolyte specific gravity

from the vehicle (Section 4) and charge it as described later in this Section.

Standard and low-maintenance battery - charging

Note: *The following is intended as a guide only. Always refer to the battery manufacturer's recommendations (often printed on a label attached to the battery) before charging.*

9 Charge the battery at a rate of 3.5 to 4 amps, and continue to charge the battery at this rate until no further rise in specific gravity is noted over a four-hour period.

10 Alternatively, a trickle-charger, charging at the rate of 1.5 amps, can safely be used overnight.

11 Special rapid "boost" charges (which are claimed to restore the power of the battery in 1 to 2 hours) are not recommended, as they can cause serious damage to the battery plates through overheating.

12 While charging the battery, note that the temperature of the electrolyte should never exceed 37.8°C (100°F).

Maintenance-free battery - charging

Note: *The following is intended as a guide only. Always refer to the battery manufacturer's recommendations (often printed on a label attached to the battery) before charging.*

13 This battery type takes considerably longer to fully recharge than the standard type, the time taken being dependent on the extent of discharge, but it can take anything up to three days.

14 A constant-voltage type charger is required, to be set, when connected, to 13.9 to 14.9 volts, with a charger current below 25 amps. Using this method, the battery should be usable within three hours, giving a voltage reading of 12.5 volts, but this is for a partially-discharged battery and, as mentioned, full charging can take considerably longer.

15 If the battery is to be charged from a fully-discharged state (condition reading less than 12.2 volts), have it recharged by your Citroën dealer or local automotive electrician, as the charge rate is higher, and constant supervision during charging is necessary.

4 Battery - removal and refitting

Removal

1 The battery is located on the left-hand side of the engine compartment.
2 Disconnect the lead(s) at the negative (earth) terminal by unscrewing the retaining nut and removing the terminal clamp.
3 Disconnect the positive terminal lead(s) in the same way.
4 Unscrew the nut and the bolt securing the battery clamp plate, then lift the clamp plate from the top of the battery **(see illustration)**.
5 Lift the battery from the plastic tray.
6 If desired, the plastic tray can be lifted from the metal support plate, after unclipping any relevant hoses and wiring from its sides **(see illustration)**.

Refitting

7 Refitting is a reversal of removal, but smear petroleum jelly on the terminals when reconnecting the leads, and always reconnect the positive lead first, and the negative lead last.

5 Charging system - testing

Note: *Refer to the warnings given in "Safety first!" and in Section 1 of this Chapter before starting work.*

1 If the alternator (no-charge) warning light fails to illuminate when the ignition is switched on, first check the alternator wiring connections for security. If satisfactory, check that the warning light bulb has not blown, and that the bulbholder is secure in its location in the instrument panel. If the light still fails to illuminate, check the continuity of the warning light feed wire from the alternator to the bulbholder. If all is satisfactory, the alternator is at fault, and should be taken to an auto-electrician for testing and repair, or else renewed.

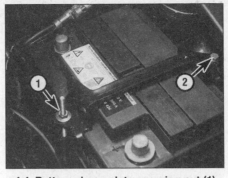

4.4 Battery clamp plate securing nut (1) and bolt (2)

2 If the warning light illuminates when the engine is running, stop the engine and check that the drivebelt is correctly tensioned (Chapter 1, Section 19) and that the alternator connections are secure. If all is so far satisfactory, check the alternator brushes and slip rings (see Section 8). If the fault persists, the alternator should be taken to an auto-electrician for testing and repair, or else renewed.
3 If the alternator output is suspect even though the warning light functions correctly, the regulated voltage may be checked as follows.
4 Connect a voltmeter across the battery terminals, and start the engine.
5 Increase the engine speed until the voltmeter reading remains steady; the reading should be approximately 12 to 13 volts, and no more than 14 volts.
6 Switch on as many electrical accessories (eg, the headlights, heated rear window and heater blower) as possible, and check that the alternator maintains the regulated voltage at around 13 to 14 volts.
7 If the regulated voltage is not as stated, the fault may be due to worn brushes, weak brush springs, a faulty voltage regulator, a faulty diode, a severed phase winding, or worn or damaged slip rings. The brushes and slip rings may be checked (see Section 8), but if the fault persists, the alternator should be taken to an auto-electrician for testing and repair, or else renewed.

4.6 Removing the plastic battery tray

6 Alternator drivebelt - removal, refitting and tensioning

Refer to the procedure given for the auxiliary drivebelt in Chapter 1.

7 Alternator - removal and refitting

Removal

1 Disconnect the battery negative lead.
2 Slacken the auxiliary drivebelt as described in Chapter 1, Section 19.
3 Remove the rubber covers, where applicable, then unscrew the securing nuts and disconnect the wiring from the rear of the alternator **(see illustrations)**.
4 Unscrew the nut and bolt securing the alternator to the upper mounting bracket **(see illustration)**.
5 Unscrew the lower mounting through-bolt (there is no need to remove it completely), and withdraw the alternator from the engine compartment **(see illustration)**.

Refitting

6 Refitting is a reversal of removal, but tension the auxiliary drivebelt as described in Chapter 1, Section 19.

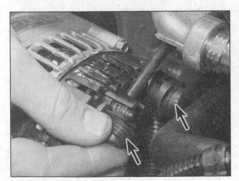

7.3a Remove the rubber covers (arrowed) . . .

7.3b . . . then disconnect the wiring from the rear of the alternator

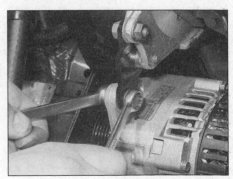

7.4 Unscrew the upper alternator securing nut and bolt

7.5 Unscrew the lower through-bolt (arrowed) and withdraw the alternator

8.2 Alternator rear cover securing nuts (arrowed)

8.3 Withdrawing the alternator rear cover

8 Alternator brushes and regulator - inspection and renewal

Note: *At the time of writing, it is unclear whether new alternator brushes are available as separate items. It is advisable to check on the availability of new components before proceeding.*

1 Remove the alternator as described in Section 7.

2 Where applicable, scrape the sealing compound from the rear plastic cover, to expose the three rear cover securing nuts **(see illustration)**.

8.4 Alternator brush/regulator assembly securing nuts (1) and screw (2)

3 Remove the securing nuts, and withdraw the rear cover **(see illustration)**.

4 If necessary, scrape the sealing compound from the rear of the alternator, to expose the brush/regulator assembly fixings. The brush regulator assembly is secured by two nuts and a single screw **(see illustration)**.

5 Pull the plastic cover from the rear of the armature shaft **(see illustration)**.

6 Unscrew the nuts and screw, and withdraw the brush/regulator assembly from the rear of the alternator **(see illustration)**.

7 Measure the protrusion of each brush from the brush holder. No minimum dimension is specified by the manufacturers, but excessive wear should be self-evident. If either brush requires renewal, check to see whether replacement brushes are available. If not, the complete brush/regulator assembly must be renewed.

8 If new brushes are to be fitted, unsolder the old brush leads from the brush/regulator assembly, and solder on the new leads in exactly the same place.

9 Check that the new brushes move freely in their guides.

10 If the brushes are still serviceable, clean them with a petrol-moistened cloth. Check that the brush spring tension is equal for both brushes, and provides a reasonable pressure. The brushes must move freely in their holders.

11 Clean the alternator slip-rings with a petrol-moistened cloth **(see illustration)**. Check for signs of scoring, burning or severe

pitting on the surface of the slip-rings. It may be possible to have the slip rings renovated by an electrical specialist.

12 Refit the brush/regulator assembly using a reverse of the removal procedure.

13 Refit the alternator as described in Section 7.

9 Starting system - testing

Note: *Refer to the precautions given in "Safety first!" and in Section 1 of this Chapter before starting work.*

1 If the starter motor fails to operate when the ignition key is turned to the appropriate position, the following possible causes may be to blame:

(a) The battery is faulty.

(b) The electrical connections between the switch, solenoid, battery and starter motor are somewhere failing to pass the necessary current from the battery through the starter to earth.

(c) The solenoid is faulty.

(d) The starter motor is mechanically or electrically defective.

2 To check the battery, switch on the headlights. If they dim after a few seconds, this indicates that the battery is discharged - recharge (see Section 3) or renew the battery. If the headlights glow brightly, operate the

8.5 Pulling the cover from the armature shaft

8.6 Removing the brush/regulator assembly

8.11 Clean the alternator slip-rings (arrowed)

10.2 Unscrew the two securing nuts (arrowed) and disconnect the wiring from the rear of the starter motor

10.3 Unscrew the starter motor securing bolts (1). Note the location of the bracket (2)

10.4 Withdrawing the starter motor

ignition switch and observe the lights. If they dim, then this indicates that current is reaching the starter motor, therefore the fault must lie in the starter motor. If the lights continue to glow brightly (and no clicking sound can be heard from the starter motor solenoid), this indicates that there is a fault in the circuit or solenoid - refer to the following paragraphs. If the starter motor turns slowly when operated, but the battery is in good condition, then this indicates that either the starter motor is faulty, or there is considerable resistance somewhere in the circuit.

3 If a fault in the circuit is suspected, disconnect the battery leads (including the earth connection to the body), the starter/solenoid wiring and the engine/transmission earth strap. Thoroughly clean the connections, and reconnect the leads and wiring, then use a voltmeter or test lamp to check that full battery voltage is available at the battery positive lead connection to the solenoid, and that the earth is sound.

> **HAYNES HINT** *Smear petroleum jelly around the battery terminals to prevent corrosion - corroded connections are among the most frequent causes of electrical system faults.*

4 If the battery and all connections are in good condition, check the circuit by disconnecting the wire from the solenoid blade terminal. Connect a voltmeter or test lamp between the wire end and a good earth (such as the battery negative terminal), and check that the wire is live when the ignition switch is turned to the "start" position. If it is, then the circuit is sound - if not, check the circuit using the information in Chapter 12, Section 2.

5 The solenoid contacts can be checked by connecting a voltmeter or test lamp between the battery positive feed connection on the starter side of the solenoid, and earth. When the ignition switch is turned to the "start" position, there should be a reading or lighted bulb, as applicable. If there is no reading or

lighted bulb, the solenoid is faulty, and should be renewed.

6 If the circuit and solenoid are proved sound, the fault must lie in the starter motor. Begin checking the starter motor by removing it (see Section 10), and checking the brushes (see Section 11). If the fault does not lie in the brushes, the motor windings must be faulty. In this event, it may be possible to have the starter motor overhauled by a specialist, but check on the availability and cost of spares before proceeding, as it may prove more economical to obtain a new or exchange motor.

10 Starter motor - removal and refitting

Removal

1 Disconnect the battery negative lead.

2 Unscrew the two securing nuts, and disconnect the wiring from the rear of the starter motor. Recover the washers under the nuts **(see illustration)**.

3 Working at the rear of the starter motor, unscrew the three securing bolts, supporting the motor as the bolts are withdrawn. Recover the washers under the bolt heads, and note the locations of any wiring or hose brackets secured by the bolts **(see illustration)**. Note that the top securing bolt may foul the clutch

release mechanism as it is withdrawn, but there is no need to withdraw it completely to remove the starter motor.

4 Withdraw the starter motor from the engine **(see illustration)**.

Refitting

5 Refitting is a reversal of removal, ensuring that any wiring or hose brackets are in place under the bolt heads, as noted before removal.

11 Starter motor - brush renewal

Valeo starter motor

1 Note that no minimum brush length is specified by the manufacturers, but it should be self-evident if the brushes are worn to the extent where renewal is required. With the motor removed as described in Section 10, proceed as follows.

2 Carefully prise the plastic cap from the end of the armature shaft, using a screwdriver or similar tool **(see illustration)**.

3 Prise the C-clip from the end of the armature shaft, and recover the shim **(see illustrations)**.

4 Unscrew the two through-bolts, then withdraw the end cover from the motor

11.2 Removing the plastic cap from the end of the starter motor armature shaft

11.3a Prise the C-clip from the end of the armature shaft . . .

11.3b . . . and recover the shim

11.4a Remove the through-bolts . . .

11.4b . . . then withdraw the end cover, and recover the shim (arrowed)

11.5 Carefully pull the brushplate from the end of the armature

11.6a Using a screwdriver . . .

casing, and recover the shim from the armature shaft **(see illustrations)**. Do not mix up the shim with the one removed in the previous paragraph.

5 Carefully pull the brush plate from the end of the armature **(see illustration)**.

6 Using a suitable screwdriver, release the brush retainers, and withdraw the brushes from the brush holders **(see illustrations)**.

7 Unsolder the brush leads, or release them from the clips on the brush plate, as applicable.

8 Fit the new brushes. Solder the leads into position, or secure them to the brush plate by bending the securing clips into position, as applicable.

9 Fit the brush plate over the end of the armature shaft, leaving enough clearance to fit the brushes. Note that when finally fitted, the lug on the brush plate must locate in the corresponding hole in the motor casing.

10 Push the brushes into their holders, so that they rest against the commutator on the armature shaft.

11 Carefully fit the brush retainers, complete with springs, and secure them to retain the brushes.

12 Check that the brushes are seated on the commutator, then slide the brush plate down the armature shaft until the lug on the brush plate engages with the hole in the motor casing.

13 Further refitting is a reversal of removal, ensuring that the shims are fitted to the armature shaft as noted before removal.

Mitsubishi starter motor

14 At the time of writing, no specific information was available for the Mitsubishi starter motor. Although the components differ in detail, the same basic principles outlined previously for the Valeo starter motor are equally applicable.

12 Ignition switch -
removal and refitting

The ignition switch is integral with the steering column lock, and can be removed as described in Chapter 10, Section 21.

13 Oil pressure warning light
switch - removal and refitting

Removal

Note: If the switch was originally fitted using a sealing ring, a new sealing ring should be used on refitting.

1 The switch is located at the front of the cylinder block, above the oil filter mounting.

2 Disconnect the battery negative lead.

3 Remove the protective sleeve from the wiring plug (where applicable), then disconnect the wiring from the switch **(see illustration)**.

4 Unscrew the switch from the cylinder block,

11.6b . . . release the brush retainers . . .

11.6c . . . and withdraw the brushes from the brush holders

13.3 Disconnecting the wiring plug from the oil pressure warning light switch

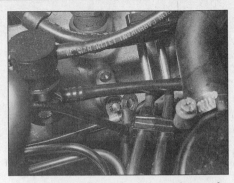

14.2 Removing the oil level sensor - viewed with engine removed for clarity

16.3a Unscrew the nut . . .

16.3b . . . and disconnect the main supply cable (No 2 cylinder plug only) . . .

and recover the sealing ring, where applicable; be prepared for oil spillage. If the switch is to be left removed from the engine for any length of time, plug the hole in the cylinder block.

Refitting

5 If the switch was originally fitted using sealing compound, clean the switch threads thoroughly, then coat them with fresh sealing compound.

6 If the switch was originally fitted using a sealing ring, use a new ring on refitting.

7 Refitting is a reversal of removal.

14 Oil level sensor - removal and refitting

1 The sensor is located at rear left-hand side of the cylinder block.

2 The removal and refitting procedure is as described for the oil pressure switch in Section 13 **(see illustration)**. Access is most easily obtained from underneath the vehicle.

15 Preheating system - description and testing

1 Each swirl chamber has a heater plug (commonly called a glow plug) screwed into it. The plugs are electrically-operated before and during start-up when the engine is cold. Electrical feed to the glow plugs is controlled by a relay/timer unit.

2 On certain models, the glow plugs provide a "post-heating" function, whereby the glow plugs remain switched on for a period after the engine has started. Once the starter has been switched off, the glow plugs begin a timed 3-minute "post-heating" cycle. The operation of the plugs cannot be cancelled for the first 15 seconds, but after the first 15 seconds, the supply to the plugs will be interrupted by:

(a) *Operation of the accelerator pedal beyond a travel of 13 mm for a duration of more than 2.5 seconds.*

(b) *A coolant temperature of more than 60ºC.*

3 A warning light in the instrument panel tells the driver that preheating is taking place. When the light goes out, the engine is ready to be started. The voltage supply to the glow plugs continues for several seconds after the light goes out. If no attempt is made to start, the timer then cuts off the supply, in order to avoid draining the battery and overheating the glow plugs.

4 If the system malfunctions, testing is ultimately by substitution of known good units, but some preliminary checks may be made as follows.

5 Connect a voltmeter or 12-volt test lamp between the glow plug supply cable and earth (engine or vehicle metal). Make sure that the live connection is kept clear of the engine and bodywork.

6 Have an assistant switch on the ignition, and check that voltage is applied to the glow plugs. Note the time for which the warning light is lit, and the total time for which voltage is applied before the system cuts out. Switch off the ignition.

7 At an under-bonnet temperature of 20ºC, typical times noted should be 5 or 6 seconds for warning light operation, followed by a further 10 seconds supply after the light goes out. Warning light time will increase with lower temperatures and decrease with higher temperatures.

8 If there is no supply at all, the relay or associated wiring is at fault.

9 To locate a defective glow plug, first remove the intercooler (Turbo models) or the air distribution housing (XUD9/A - D9B engine) where applicable, as described in Chapter 4. Similarly, disconnect the air hose from the top of the inlet manifold, where applicable. Disconnect the main supply cable and the interconnecting wire or strap from the top of the glow plugs. Be careful not to drop the nuts and washers.

10 Use a continuity tester, or a 12-volt test lamp connected to the battery positive terminal, to check for continuity between each glow plug terminal and earth. The resistance of a glow plug in good condition is very low (less than 1 ohm), so if the test lamp does not light or the continuity tester shows a high resistance, the glow plug is certainly defective.

11 If an ammeter is available, the current draw

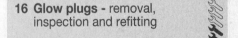

16.3c . . . and the interconnecting wire from the glow plug

of each glow plug can be checked. After an initial surge of 15 to 20 amps, each plug should draw 12 amps. Any plug which draws much more or less than this is probably defective.

12 As a final check, the glow plugs can be removed and inspected as described in the following Section.

16 Glow plugs - removal, inspection and refitting

Removal

⚠️ *Caution: If the preheating system has just been energised, or if the engine has been running, the glow plugs may be very hot.*

1 Disconnect the battery negative lead.

2 For improved access, remove the intercooler (Turbo models) or the air distribution housing (XUD9/A - D9B engine) where applicable, as described in Chapter 4. Similarly, disconnect the air hose which connects the air cleaner assembly to the top of the inlet manifold, where applicable.

3 Unscrew the nuts from the glow plug terminals, and recover the washers. Note that the main supply cable is connected to one of the glow plugs (normally No 2 or 3 cylinder glow plug), and is secured by a Nyloc nut. Remove the interconnecting wire from the top of the glow plugs **(see illustrations)**.

4 Carefully move any obstructing pipes or

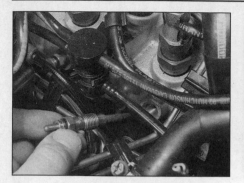

16.5 Removing a glow plug

17.5 Preheating system relay/timer unit wiring plug (1) and securing bolt (2)

wires to one side, to gain access to the glow plugs.

5 Unscrew the glow plugs and remove them from the cylinder head **(see illustration)**. Note that on certain models, access to No 4 cylinder glow plug is extremely limited, and the plug is most easily removed using a cranked spanner. Alternatively, it may be possible to remove the plug, after it has been initially slackened, using two screwdrivers acting on opposing flats of the plug.

Inspection

6 Inspect the glow plugs for physical damage. Burnt or eroded glow plug tips can be caused by a bad injector spray pattern. Have the injectors checked if this sort of damage is found.

7 If the glow plugs are in good physical condition, check them electrically using a 12-volt test lamp or continuity tester, as described in the previous Section.

8 The glow plugs can be energised by applying 12 volts to them, to verify that they heat up evenly and in the required time. Observe the following precautions:

(a) Support the glow plug by clamping it carefully in a vice or self-locking pliers. Remember, the plug will become red-hot.

(b) Make sure that the power supply or test lead incorporates a fuse or overload trip, to protect against damage from a short-circuit.

(c) After testing, allow the glow plug to cool for several minutes before attempting to handle it.

9 A glow plug in good condition will start to glow red at the tip after drawing current for 5 seconds or so. Any plug which takes much longer to start glowing, or which starts glowing in the middle, instead of at the tip, is defective.

Refitting

10 Refit by reversing the removal operations. Apply a smear of copper-based anti-seize compound to the plug threads, and tighten the glow plugs to the specified torque. Do not overtighten, as this can damage the glow plug element.

---

17 Preheating system relay/timer unit - removal and refitting

Removal

1 The unit is located on the front of the relay/junction box at the front left-hand corner of the engine compartment.

2 Disconnect the battery negative lead.

3 Disconnect the wiring plug from the base of the relay/timer unit.

4 Unscrew the two securing nuts, and disconnect the leads from the terminals on the base of the unit.

5 Unscrew the securing bolt, and withdraw the unit from the relay/junction box **(see illustration)**.

Refitting

6 Refitting is a reversal of removal.

Chapter 6 Clutch

Contents

Clutch - adjustment 2
Clutch assembly - removal, inspection and refitting 5
Clutch cable - removal and refitting 3
Clutch pedal - removal and refitting 4
Clutch release mechanism - removal, inspection and refitting 6
General check . . . . See Chapter 1
General information 1

Degrees of difficulty

Easy, suitable for novice with little experience	Fairly easy, suitable for beginner with some experience	Fairly difficult, suitable for competent DIY mechanic	Difficult, suitable for experienced DIY mechanic	Very difficult, suitable for expert DIY or professional

Specifications

Type	Single dry plate with diaphragm spring. Cable-operated "push-type" or "pull-type" release mechanism (depeding on model)
Clutch pedal travel	150 to 160 mm

Friction plate diameter

Turbo models	215 mm
Non-turbo models	200 mm

Torque wrench settings	Nm	lbf ft
Pressure plate retaining bolts	20	15
Clutch pedal pivot bolt	25	18

1 General information

The clutch consists of a friction plate, a pressure plate assembly, a release bearing and the release mechanism; all of these components are contained in the large cast-aluminium alloy bellhousing, sandwiched between the engine and the transmission. The release mechanism is mechanical, being operated by a cable.

The friction plate is fitted between the engine flywheel and the clutch pressure plate, and is allowed to slide on the transmission input shaft splines. It consists of two circular facings of friction material riveted in position to provide the clutch bearing surface, and a spring-cushioned hub to damp out transmission shocks.

The pressure plate assembly is bolted to the engine flywheel, and is located by three dowel pins. When the engine is running, drive is transmitted from the crankshaft, via the flywheel, to the friction plate (these components being clamped securely together by the pressure plate assembly) and from the friction plate to the transmission input shaft.

To interrupt the drive, the spring pressure must be relaxed. On the models covered in this manual, there are two different types of clutch release mechanism used; a conventional "push-type" mechanism, where an independent clutch release bearing, fitted concentrically around the transmission input shaft, is pushed onto the pressure plate assembly, and a "pull-type" mechanism, where the clutch release bearing is an integral part of the pressure plate assembly, and is lifted away from the friction plate.

On models with the conventional "push-type" mechanism, at the transmission end of the clutch cable, the outer cable is retained by a fixed mounting bracket, and the inner cable is attached to the release fork lever. Depressing the clutch pedal pulls the control cable inner wire, and this in turn rotates the release fork by acting on the lever at the fork's upper end, above the bellhousing. The release fork then acts on the release bearing, pressing it against the fingers at the centre of the pressure plate diaphragm spring. Since the spring is held by rivets between two annular fulcrum rings, the pressure at its centre causes it to deform so that it flattens, and thus releases the clamping force it exerts at its periphery, on the pressure plate.

On models with the "pull-type" mechanism, at the transmission end of the clutch cable, the inner cable is attached to a fixed mounting bracket, and the outer cable acts against the release fork lever. Depressing the clutch pedal pulls the outer cable towards the fixed end of the inner cable, and this in turn rotates the release fork by acting on the lever at the fork's upper end, above the bellhousing. The release fork then lifts the release bearing, which is attached to the pressure plate springs, away from the friction plate, and thus releases the clamping force exerted at the pressure plate periphery.

As the friction plate facings wear, the pressure plate moves towards the flywheel; this causes the diaphragm spring fingers to push against the release bearing, thus reducing the clearance which must be present in the mechanism. To ensure correct operation, the clutch cable must be regularly adjusted.

2 Clutch - adjustment

1 The clutch adjustment is checked by measuring the clutch pedal travel.
2 Ensure that there are no obstructions beneath the clutch pedal. Depress the clutch pedal fully to the floor, and measure the distance that the centre of the clutch pedal

2.2 To check clutch cable adjustment, measure the clutch pedal travel as described in text

2.4 Adjusting the clutch cable (air cleaner duct removed for clarity)

3.2a Slacken the clutch cable locknut and adjuster nut, then free the inner cable end fittings . . .

pad travels through, from the at-rest position to the floor **(see illustration)**. If this is less than the distance given in the Specifications at the start of this Chapter, adjust the clutch as follows.

3 The clutch cable is adjusted by means of the adjuster nut on the transmission end of the cable. On some models, access to the locknut is limited and, if required, the relevant air cleaner duct/housing component can be removed or disconnected to improve access. Refer to Chapter 4 for further information.

4 Working in the engine compartment, slacken the locknut from the end of the clutch cable. Adjust the position of the adjuster nut, then re-measure the clutch pedal travel. Repeat this procedure until the clutch pedal travel is as specified **(see illustration)**.

5 Once the adjuster nut is correctly positioned, and the pedal travel is correctly set, securely tighten the cable locknut. Where necessary, refit any disturbed air cleaner duct/housing components as described in Chapter 4.

3 Clutch cable - removal and refitting

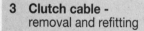

Removal

1 Working in the engine compartment, fully slacken the locknut and adjuster nut from the end of the clutch cable. On some models,

3.2b . . . and outer cable end fittings from the release lever and mounting bracket

access to these nuts is limited and, if required, the relevant air cleaner duct/housing component can be removed or disconnected to improve access. Refer to Chapter 4 for further information.

2 Release the inner cable and outer cable fittings from the clutch release lever and mounting bracket, and free the cable from the transmission housing **(see illustrations)**.

3 Working inside the vehicle, release the fasteners by turning them through a quarter of a turn, and remove the driver's side lower facia panel. Remove the heater duct which is situated behind the panel.

4 Release the facia felt undercover retaining clips, and peel back the material to gain access to the upper end of the clutch pedal.

5 Depress the metal retaining clip, and free the inner cable from the plastic retainer fitted to the upper end of the clutch pedal **(see illustration)**.

6 Return to the engine compartment, and withdraw the cable forwards through the bulkhead, releasing it from any relevant retaining clips and guides. Note its correct routing, and remove it from the vehicle.

7 Examine the cable, looking for worn end fittings or a damaged outer casing, and for signs of fraying of the inner wire. Check the cable's

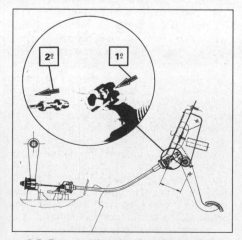

3.5 Depress the clutch pedal retainer clip (1) and release the inner cable end fitting (2) from the pedal

operation; the inner wire should move smoothly and easily through the outer casing. Remember that a cable that appears serviceable when tested off the car may well be much heavier in operation when compressed into its working position. Renew the cable if it shows any signs of excessive wear or any damage.

Refitting

8 Apply a thin smear of multi-purpose grease to the cable end fittings, then pass the cable through the engine compartment bulkhead.

9 From inside the vehicle, engage the inner cable with the plastic retainer on the clutch pedal, and check that it is securely retained by the metal clip. Clip the felt undercover back into position, then refit the heater duct, ensuring it is correctly located at both ends, and install the lower facia panel.

10 Refit the plastic locating collar to the release lever, and ensure the rubber spacer is correctly located on the transmission end of the outer cable.

11 Ensuring that the cable is correctly routed and retained by all the relevant retaining clips and guides, pass the lower end through the release lever/mounting bracket, and engage the inner cable with the clutch release lever/mounting bracket (as applicable). Refit the rubber spacer and flat washer to the end of the inner cable, and screw on the adjuster nut and locknut.

12 Adjust the clutch cable as described in Section 2.

4 Clutch pedal - removal and refitting

Removal

1 Remove the pedal bracket assembly from the vehicle, as described in Section 14 of Chapter 9.

2 With the pedal bracket assembly on the bench, slacken the nut, withdraw the clutch pedal pivot bolt, and separate the pedal and bracket. Slide the pivot bush and spring off the left-hand end of the pedal, and remove the spacer and pivot bushes from the pedal bore.

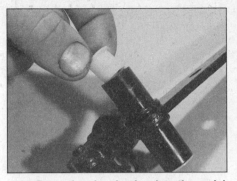

4.4a Press the pivot bushes into the pedal bore . . .

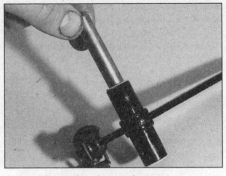

4.4b . . . then insert the spacer . . .

4.4c . . . and refit the pedal spring

3 Carefully clean all components, and renew any that are worn or damaged; check the bearing surfaces of the pivot bushes and spacer with particular care; the bushes can be renewed separately if worn.

Refitting

4 Press the pivot bushes into the pedal bore, then apply a smear of multi-purpose grease to their bearing surfaces, and slide in the spacer. Install the spring and pivot bush on the end of the pedal pivot, ensuring that the inner end of the spring is correctly hooked over the pedal **(see illustrations)**.

5 Refit the pedal to the bracket, ensuring that the outer end of the pedal spring is correctly located in the slot on the pedal mounting bracket, and install the pivot bolt. Refit the pivot bolt nut, and tighten it to the specified torque setting **(see illustrations)**.

6 Check that the pedal pivots smoothly, then refit the pedal bracket assembly to the vehicle as described in Section 14 of Chapter 9.

5 Clutch assembly - removal, inspection and refitting

Warning: Dust created by clutch wear and deposited on the clutch components may contain asbestos, which is a health hazard. DO NOT blow it out with compressed air, or inhale any of it. DO NOT use petrol or petroleum-based solvents to clean off the dust. Brake system cleaner or methylated spirit should be used to flush the dust into a suitable receptacle. After the clutch components are wiped clean with rags, dispose of the contaminated rags and cleaner in a sealed, marked container.
Note: Although some friction materials may no longer contain asbestos, it is safest to assume that they do, and to take precautions accordingly.

Removal

1 Unless the complete engine/transmission unit is to be removed from the car and separated for major overhaul (see Chapter 2), the clutch can be reached by removing the transmission as described in Chapter 7, Part A.

2 Before disturbing the clutch, use chalk or a marker pen to mark the relationship of the pressure plate assembly to the flywheel.
3 Working in a diagonal sequence, slacken the pressure plate bolts by half a turn at a time, until spring pressure is released and the bolts can be unscrewed by hand.
4 Prise the pressure plate assembly off its locating dowels, and collect the friction plate, noting which way round the friction plate is fitted.

Inspection

Note: Due to the amount of work necessary to remove and refit clutch
components, it is usually considered good practice to renew the clutch friction plate, pressure plate assembly and release bearing as a matched set, even if only one of these is actually worn enough to require renewal.
5 Remove the clutch assembly.
6 When cleaning clutch components, read first the warning at the beginning of this Section; remove dust using a clean, dry cloth, and working in a well-ventilated atmosphere.
7 Check the friction plate facings for signs of wear, damage or oil contamination. If the friction material is cracked, burnt, scored or damaged, or if it is contaminated with oil or grease (shown by shiny black patches), the friction plate must be renewed.
8 If the friction material is still serviceable, check that the centre boss splines are unworn, that the torsion springs are in good condition and securely fastened, and that all

the rivets are tight. If any wear or damage is found, the friction plate must be renewed.
9 If the friction material is fouled with oil, this must be due to an oil leak from the crankshaft left-hand oil seal, from the sump-to-cylinder block joint, or from the transmission input shaft. Renew the seal or repair the joint, as appropriate, as described in Chapter 2 or 7, before installing the new friction plate.
10 Check the pressure plate assembly for obvious signs of wear or damage; shake it to check for loose rivets or worn or damaged fulcrum rings, and check that the drive straps securing the pressure plate to the cover do not show signs (such as a deep yellow or blue discoloration) of overheating. If the diaphragm spring is worn or damaged, or if its pressure is in any way suspect, the pressure plate assembly should be renewed.
11 Examine the machined bearing surfaces of the pressure plate and of the flywheel; they should be clean, completely flat, and free from scratches or scoring. If either is discoloured from excessive heat, or shows signs of cracks, it should be renewed - although minor damage of this nature can sometimes be polished away using emery paper.
12 Check that the release bearing contact surface rotates smoothly and easily, with no sign of noise or roughness. Also check that the surface itself is smooth and unworn, with no signs of cracks, pitting or scoring. If there is any doubt about its condition, the bearing must be renewed. On clutches with a "pull-type" release mechanism, this means that the complete pressure plate assembly must be renewed.

4.5a Refit the pedal to the bracket, ensuring that the spring is correctly engaged in the bracket, and hooked over the pedal (arrowed)

4.5b Install the pedal pivot bolt, and tighten it to the specified torque

Refitting

13 On reassembly, ensure that the bearing surfaces of the flywheel and pressure plate are completely clean, smooth, and free from oil or grease. Use solvent to remove any protective grease from new components.

14 Fit the friction plate so that its spring hub assembly faces away from the flywheel; there may also be a marking showing which way round the plate is to be refitted **(see illustration)**.

15 Refit the pressure plate assembly, aligning the marks made on dismantling (if the original pressure plate is re-used), and locating the pressure plate on its three locating dowels. Fit the pressure plate bolts, but tighten them only finger-tight, so that the friction plate can still be moved.

16 The friction plate must now be centralised, so that when the transmission is refitted, its input shaft will pass through the splines at the centre of the friction plate.

17 Centralisation can be achieved by passing a screwdriver or other long bar through the friction plate and into the hole in the crankshaft; the friction plate can then be moved around until it is centred on the crankshaft hole.

> **HAYNES HINT** *A clutch-aligning tool can be used to eliminate guesswork; these can be obtained from most accessory shops. A home-made aligning tool can be fabricated from a length of metal rod or wooden dowel which fits closely inside the crankshaft hole, and has insulating tape wound around it to match the diameter of the friction plate splined hole.*

18 When the friction plate is centralised, tighten the pressure plate bolts evenly and in a diagonal sequence to the specified torque setting **(see illustration)**.

19 Apply a thin smear of molybdenum disulphide grease to the splines of the friction plate and the transmission input shaft, and also to the release bearing bore and release fork shaft.

20 Refit the transmission as described in Chapter 7, Part A.

5.14 Ensure the friction plate is fitted the correct way around, then install the pressure plate

6 Clutch release mechanism - removal, inspection and refitting

Note: *Refer to the warning concerning the dangers of asbestos dust at the beginning of Section 5.*

Removal

1 Unless the complete engine/transmission unit is to be removed from the car and separated for major overhaul (see Chapter 2), the clutch release mechanism can be reached by removing the transmission only, as described in Chapter 7, Part A.

2 On models with a conventional "push-type" release mechanism, unhook the release bearing from the fork, and slide it off the input shaft. Drive out the roll pin, and remove the release lever from the top of the release fork shaft. Discard the roll pin - a new one must be used on refitting.

3 On both types of clutch, depress the retaining tabs, then slide the upper bush off the end of the release fork shaft. Disengage the shaft from its lower bush, and manoeuvre it out from the transmission. Depress the retaining tabs, and remove the lower pivot bush from the transmission housing.

Inspection

4 Check the release mechanism, renewing any component which is worn or damaged.

5.18 Once the friction plate is centralised, tighten the pressure plate retaining bolts to the specified torque

Carefully check all bearing surfaces and points of contact.

5 When checking the release bearing itself, note that it is often considered worthwhile to renew it as a matter of course. Check that the contact surface rotates smoothly and easily, with no sign of noise or roughness, and that the surface itself is smooth and unworn, with no signs of cracks, pitting or scoring. If there is any doubt about its condition, the bearing must be renewed. On models with a "pull-type" release mechanism, this means that the complete pressure plate assembly must be renewed, as described in Section 5.

Refitting

6 Apply a smear of molybdenum disulphide grease to the shaft pivot bushes and the contact surfaces of the release fork.

7 Locate the lower pivot bush in the transmission, ensuring it is securely retained by its locating tangs, and refit the release fork. Slide the upper bush down the shaft, and clip it into position in the transmission housing **(see illustrations)**.

8 On models with a conventional "push-type" release mechanism, refit the release lever to the shaft. Align the lever with the shaft hole, and secure it in position by tapping a new roll pin fully into position. Slide the release bearing onto the input shaft, and engage it with the release fork.

9 Refit the transmission as described in Chapter 7, Part A.

6.7a Clip the lower pivot bush into position in the transmission housing . . .

6.7b . . . then locate the release fork shaft in the lower bush . . .

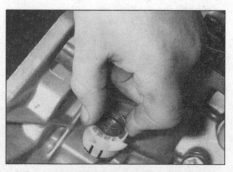

6.7c . . . and slide the upper pivot down the release fork shaft, and into position in the transmission housing

Chapter 7 Part A: Manual transmission

Contents

Gearchange linkage - general information and adjustment 2
Gearchange linkage - removal and refitting 3
General information 1
Manual transmission oil level check . . . . See Chapter 1
Manual transmission overhaul - general information 8
Manual transmission - removal and refitting 7
Manual transmission oil renewal . . . . See Chapter 1
Oil seals - renewal 4
Reversing lamp switch - testing, removal and refitting 5
Speedometer drive - removal and refitting 6

Degrees of difficulty

Easy, suitable for novice with little experience	**Fairly easy,** suitable for beginner with some experience	**Fairly difficult,** suitable for competent DIY mechanic	**Difficult,** suitable for experienced DIY mechanic	**Very difficult,** suitable for expert DIY or professional

Specifications

General

Type	Manual, five forward speeds and reverse. Synchromesh on all forward speeds
Designation	BE3

Transmission code:

1.7 litre engine (A9A)	CL 28
1.9 litre non-turbo engines (D9B and DJZ):	
Models not equipped with ABS	CL 29
Models equipped with ABS	CL 45
1.9 litre Turbo engines (D8A, DHY and DHZ)	CL 32 or CL 79

Lubrication

Recommended oil	See *"Lubricants and fluids"*
Recommended gearchange linkage grease	Esso Norva 275 or Total Multis G6

Torque wrench settings

	Nm	lbf ft
Gearchange linkage bellcrank pivot bolt	28	21
Oil filler/level plug	22	16
Oil drain plug	35	26
Clutch release bearing guide sleeve bolts	12	9
Right-hand driveshaft intermediate bearing retaining bolt nuts	10	7
Lower suspension arm balljoint retaining nuts	45	33
Reversing light switch	25	18
Left-hand engine/transmission mounting:		
Mounting bracket-to-body bolts	25	18
Mounting stud	50	37
Centre nut	80	59
Engine-to-transmission unit fixing bolts	50	37
Clutch cable bracket retaining bolts ("pull-type" clutch only)	18	13
Roadwheel bolts	90	66

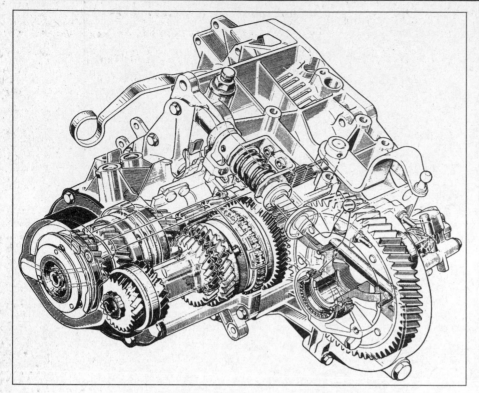

1.1 Cutaway view of the BE3 manual transmission

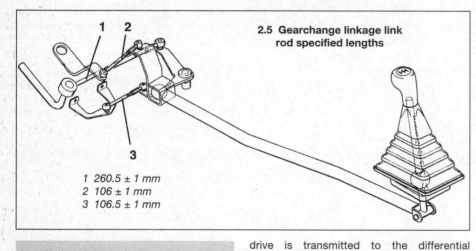

2.5 Gearchange linkage link rod specified lengths

1 260.5 ± 1 mm
2 106 ± 1 mm
3 106.5 ± 1 mm

1 General information

The transmission is contained in a cast-aluminium alloy casing bolted to the engine's left-hand end, and consists of the gearbox and final drive differential - often called a transaxle.

Drive is transmitted from the crankshaft via the clutch to the input shaft, which has a splined extension to accept the clutch friction plate, and rotates in sealed ball-bearings. From the input shaft, drive is transmitted to the output shaft, which rotates in a roller bearing at its right-hand end, and a sealed ball-bearing at its left-hand end. From the output shaft, the drive is transmitted to the differential crownwheel, which rotates with the differential case and planetary gears, thus driving the sun gears and driveshafts. The rotation of the planetary gears on their shaft allows the inner roadwheel to rotate at a slower speed than the outer roadwheel when the car is cornering.

The input and output shafts are arranged side by side, parallel to the crankshaft and driveshafts, so that their gear pinion teeth are in constant mesh. In the neutral position, the output shaft gear pinions rotate freely, so that drive cannot be transmitted to the crownwheel **(see illustration)**.

Gear selection is via a floor-mounted lever and selector rod mechanism. The selector rod causes the appropriate selector fork to move its respective synchro-sleeve along the shaft, to lock the gear pinion to the synchro-hub. Since the synchro-hubs are splined to the output shaft, this locks the pinion to the shaft, so that drive can be transmitted. To ensure that gear-changing can be made quickly and quietly, a synchro-mesh system is fitted to all forward gears, consisting of baulk rings and spring-loaded fingers, as well as the gear pinions and synchro-hubs. The synchro-mesh cones are formed on the mating faces of the baulk rings and gear pinions.

2 Gearchange linkage - general information and adjustment

General information

1 If a stiff, sloppy or imprecise gearchange leads you to suspect that a fault exists within the linkage, first dismantle it completely and check it for wear or damage as described in Section 3. Reassemble it, applying a smear of the special grease to all bearing surfaces.

2 If this does not cure the fault, the car should be examined by an expert, as the fault must lie within the transmission itself. There is no adjustment as such in the linkage; note that, while the length of the link rods can be altered, this is for initial setting-up only, and is not intended to provide a form of compensation for wear.

3 If the link rods have been renewed, or if the length of the originals is incorrect, adjust them as follows.

Adjustment

4 Firmly apply the handbrake, then jack up the front of the vehicle and support it on axle stands. Access to the link rods is poor, but they can be reached both from above and below the vehicle. On Turbo models, to improve access from above, remove the intercooler and air intake duct as described in Chapter 4.

5 Referring to illustration 2.5, working in (or under) the engine compartment, measure the length of each link rod, and compare this to the relevant length specified. Note the measurements given are the distances between the centre points of the link rod balljoints, and not the total length of the rod **(see illustration)**.

6 If adjustment is necessary, slacken the locknut, then carefully lever the relevant link rod off its balljoint on the transmission unit. Screw or unscrew (as applicable) the end of the rod until the specified distance between the link rod balljoint centres is obtained, then press the disconnected end of the rod firmly back onto its balljoint. Securely tighten the link rod locknut.

7 Once all link rod lengths are correctly set, check that all gears can be selected, and that the gearchange lever returns properly to its correct at-rest position. Where necessary, refit any components which were removed to improve access.

3.3 Disconnect the three gearchange linkage link rods (arrowed) from their transmission balljoints

3.7a Slacken and remove the four retaining nuts . . .

3.7b . . . then remove the gearchange lever from underneath the vehicle

3 Gearchange linkage - removal and refitting

Removal

1 Firmly apply the handbrake, then jack up the front of the vehicle and support it on axle stands.

2 Slacken and remove the nut, and withdraw the pivot bolt securing the selector rod to the base of the gearchange lever.

3 Using a flat-bladed screwdriver, carefully lever the three link rods off their balljoints on the transmission **(see illustration)**. Disengage the selector rod from the bellcrank pivot, and remove it from underneath the vehicle.

4 Undo the two retaining screws, and unclip the heat shield from the top of the steering gear assembly.

5 Carefully prise the plastic cap off the bolt securing the gearchange linkage bellcrank to the subframe.

6 Slacken and remove the bellcrank pivot bolt and washer, then manoeuvre the bellcrank and link rod out from under the vehicle, and recover the spacer and pivot bushes from the centre of the bellcrank.

7 Where a leather gaiter is fitted to the lever, carefully prise the gearchange lever trim panel out from the centre console, then release the pop fastener and velcro strip and remove the gaiter. Where a rubber gaiter is fitted, unscrew the knob from the gearchange lever, and

remove the knob and gaiter assembly, noting that it may also be necessary to undo the two retaining screws and remove the small centre console with the gaiter. Undo the four retaining nuts, lower the gearchange lever out of position, and remove it from underneath the vehicle **(see illustrations)**.

8 Inspect all the linkage components for signs of wear or damage, paying particular attention to the pivot bushes and link rod balljoints, and renew worn components as necessary.

9 Peel back the lower gaiter from the base of the gearchange lever. Disengage the lever mounting plate, and slide the upper gaiter up the lever to gain access to the gearchange lever pivot ball. Examine the lever components for signs of wear or damage, paying particular attention to the rubber gaiters, and renew components as necessary. The lever can be separated from its baseplate after the retaining ring has been unclipped **(see illustrations)**.

Refitting

10 Refitting is a reversal of the removal procedure, noting the following points:

(a) Prior to refitting, check and if necessary adjust the link rod lengths as described in Section 2.

(b) Apply a smear of the special grease (see Specifications) to the gearchange lever pivot ball, the link rod balljoints and the bellcrank ball and pivot bushes.

3.9a Peel back the lower gaiter . . .

(c) Ensure the gearchange lever rubber gaiters are correctly seated prior to refitting the lever assembly to the vehicle.

(d) Tighten the bellcrank pivot bolt to the specified torque setting, and ensure the link rods are securely pressed onto their balljoints.

4 Oil seals - renewal

Driveshaft oil seals

1 Chock the rear wheels, firmly apply the handbrake, then jack up the front of the car and support it on axle stands. Remove the appropriate front roadwheel.

3.9b . . . then disengage the mounting plate . . .

3.9c . . . and peel the upper gaiter away from the lever baseplate

3.9d The lever and baseplate can be separated once the retaining ring has been unclipped

4.7 Use a large flat-bladed screwdriver to prise the driveshaft oil seals out of position

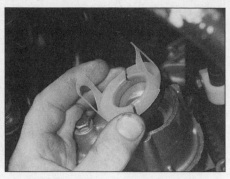

4.8a Fit the new seal to the transmission, noting the plastic seal protector . . .

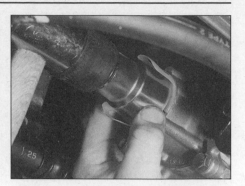

4.8b . . . and tap it into position using a suitable tubular drift

2 Drain the transmission oil as described in Chapter 1.

3 Slacken and remove the three nuts securing the balljoint to the lower suspension arm, then withdraw the bolts and free the balljoint from the arm. Discard the nuts - new ones must be used on refitting. Proceed as described under the relevant sub-heading.

Right-hand seal

4 Loosen the two intermediate bearing retaining bolt nuts, then rotate the bolts through 90º so that their offset heads are clear of the bearing outer race.

5 Carefully pull the swivel hub assembly outwards, and pull on the inner end of the driveshaft to free the intermediate bearing from its mounting bracket.

6 Once the driveshaft end is free from the transmission, slide the dust seal off the inner end of the shaft, noting which way around it is fitted, and support the inner end of the driveshaft to avoid damaging the constant velocity joints or gaiters.

7 Carefully prise the oil seal out of the transmission, using a large flat-bladed screwdriver **(see illustration)**.

8 Remove all traces of dirt from the area around the oil seal aperture, then apply a smear of grease to the outer lip of the new oil seal. Fit the new seal into its aperture, and drive it squarely into position using a suitable tubular drift (such as a socket) which bears only on the hard outer edge of the seal, until it abuts its locating shoulder. If the seal was

supplied with a plastic protector sleeve, leave this in position until the driveshaft has been refitted **(see illustrations)**.

9 Thoroughly clean the driveshaft splines, then apply a thin film of grease to the oil seal lips and to the driveshaft inner end splines.

10 Slide the dust seal into position on the end of the shaft, ensuring that its flat surface is facing the transmission.

11 Carefully locate the inner driveshaft splines with those of the differential sun gear, taking great care not to damage the oil seal, then align the intermediate bearing with its mounting bracket, and push the driveshaft fully into position. If necessary, use a soft-faced mallet to tap the outer race of the bearing into position in the mounting bracket.

12 Ensure the intermediate bearing is correctly seated, then rotate its retaining bolts back through 90º so that their offset heads are resting against the bearing outer race, and tighten the retaining nuts to the specified torque. Remove the plastic seal protector (where supplied), and slide the dust seal tight up against the oil seal.

13 Align the balljoint with the lower arm, and fit the three retaining bolts. Fit new retaining nuts to the bolts, and tighten them to the specified torque setting.

14 Refit the roadwheel, then lower the vehicle to the ground and tighten the roadwheel bolts to the specified torque.

15 Refill the transmission with the specified type and amount of oil, and check the level using the information given in Chapter 1.

Left-hand seal

16 Carefully pull the swivel hub assembly outwards, and withdraw the driveshaft inner constant velocity joint from transmission, taking great care not to damage the driveshaft oil seal. Support the driveshaft, to avoid damaging the constant velocity joints or gaiters.

17 Renew the oil seal as described above in paragraphs 7 to 9.

18 Carefully locate the inner constant velocity joint splines with those of the differential sun gear, taking great care not to damage the oil seal, and push the driveshaft fully into position. Where fitted, remove the plastic protector from the oil seal.

19 Carry out the operations described above in paragraphs 13 to 15.

Input shaft oil seal

20 Remove the transmission from the car as described in Section 7.

21 Undo the three bolts securing the clutch release bearing guide sleeve in position, and slide the guide off the input shaft, along with its O-ring or gasket (as applicable). Recover any relevant thrustwashers which have stuck to the rear of the guide sleeve, and refit them to the input shaft.

22 Carefully lever the oil seal out of the guide using a suitable flat-bladed screwdriver **(see illustration)**.

23 Before fitting a new seal, check the input shaft's seal rubbing surface for signs of burrs, scratches or other damage, which may have

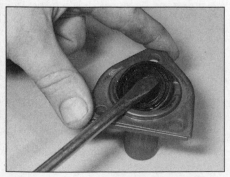

4.22 Removing the input shaft seal from the guide sleeve

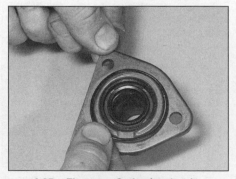

4.25a Fit a new O-ring/gasket (as applicable) . . .

4.25b . . . then carefully refit the guide sleeve over the input shaft . . .

4.25c . . . and secure it in position with its three retaining bolts

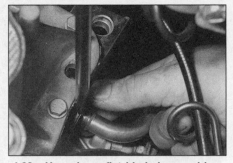

4.29a Use a large flat-bladed screwdriver to prise the selector shaft seal out of position . . .

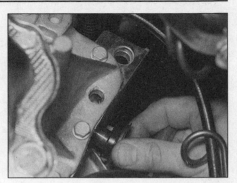

4.29b . . . then slide the seal off the shaft

caused the seal to fail in the first place. It may be possible to polish away minor faults of this sort using fine abrasive paper; however, more serious defects will require the renewal of the input shaft. Ensure that the input shaft is clean and greased, to protect the seal lips on refitting.

24 Dip the new seal in clean oil, and fit it to the guide sleeve.

25 Fit a new O-ring or gasket (as applicable) to the rear of the guide sleeve, then carefully slide the sleeve into position over the input shaft. Refit the retaining bolts and tighten them to the specified torque setting **(see illustrations)**.

26 Refit the transmission to the car as described in Section 7.

Selector shaft oil seal

27 Park the car on level ground, firmly apply the handbrake, then jack up the front of the vehicle and support it on axle stands. Remove the left-hand front roadwheel, and unclip the access cover from the centre of the wheel arch liner.

28 Using a large flat-bladed screwdriver, carefully lever the link rod balljoint off the transmission selector shaft, and disconnect the link rod.

29 Carefully prise the selector shaft seal out of the housing, and slide it off the end of the shaft **(see illustrations)**.

30 Before fitting a new seal, check the selector shaft's seal rubbing surface for signs of burrs, scratches or other damage, which

may have caused the seal to fail in the first place. It may be possible to polish away minor faults of this sort using fine abrasive paper; however, more serious defects will require the renewal of the selector shaft.

31 Apply a smear of grease to the new seal's outer edge and sealing lip, then carefully slide the seal along the selector rod. Press the seal fully into position in the transmission housing.

32 Reconnect the link rod to the selector shaft, ensuring that its balljoint is pressed firmly onto the shaft. Lower the car to the ground.

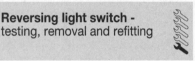

5 Reversing light switch - testing, removal and refitting

Testing

1 The reversing light circuit is controlled by a plunger-type switch that is screwed into the top of the transmission casing. If a fault develops in the circuit, first ensure that the circuit fuse has not blown.

2 To test the switch, disconnect the wiring connector, and use a multimeter (set to the resistance function) or a battery-and-bulb test circuit to check that there is continuity between the switch terminals only when reverse gear is selected. If this is not the case, and there are no obvious breaks or other damage to the wires, the switch is faulty, and must be renewed.

Removal

3 To remove the switch, disconnect its wiring connector, then unscrew it from the transmission casing along with its sealing washer **(see illustration)**.

Refitting

4 Fit a new sealing washer to the switch, then screw it back into position in the top of the transmission housing and tighten it to the specified torque setting. Reconnect the wiring connector, and test the operation of the circuit.

6 Speedometer drive - removal and refitting

Removal

1 Chock the rear wheels, firmly apply the handbrake, then jack up the front of the car and support it on axle stands. The speedometer drive is situated on the rear of the transmission housing, next to the inner end of the right-hand driveshaft.

2 Pull out the speedometer cable retaining pin, and disconnect the cable from the speedometer drive. Where necessary, disconnect the wiring connector from the speedometer drive.

3 Slacken and remove the retaining bolt, along with the heat shield (where fitted), and withdraw the speedometer drive and driven pinion assembly from the transmission housing, along with its O-ring **(see illustrations)**.

5.3 Disconnecting the wiring connector from the reversing light switch (arrowed)

6.3a Slacken and remove the retaining bolt . . .

6.3b . . . then withdraw the speedometer drive from the transmission (shown with transmission removed for clarity)

6.5a Undo the three retaining bolts . . .

6.5b . . . and remove the housing, O-ring and drive pinion from the transmission (shown with transmission removed for clarity)

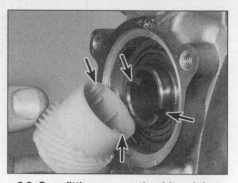

6.6 On refitting, ensure the drive pinion dogs are correctly engaged with the gear slots (arrowed)

4 If necessary, the pinion can be slid out of the housing, and the oil seal can be removed from the top of the housing. Examine the pinion for signs of damage, and renew if necessary. Renew the housing O-ring as a matter of course.

5 If the driven pinion is worn or damaged, also examine the drive pinion in the transmission housing for similar signs. To remove the drive pinion, first disengage the right-hand driveshaft from the transmission, as described in paragraphs 1 to 7 of Section 4. Undo the three retaining bolts, and remove the speedometer drive housing from the transmission, along with its O-ring. Remove the drive pinion from the differential gear, and recover any relevant adjustment shims from the gear **(see illustrations)**.

Refitting

6 Where the drive pinion has been removed, refit the adjustment shims to the differential gear, then locate the speedometer drive on the gear, ensuring it is correctly engaged in the gear slots **(see illustration)**. Fit a new O-ring to the rear of the speedometer drive housing, then refit the housing to the transmission and securely tighten its retaining screws. Inspect the driveshaft oil seal for signs of wear, and renew if necessary. Refit the driveshaft to the transmission, using the information given in Section 4.

7 Where necessary, apply a smear of grease

to the lips of the seal and driven pinion shaft, and slide the pinion into position in the speedometer drive.

8 Fit a new O-ring to the speedometer drive, and refit it to the transmission, ensuring the drive and driven pinions are correctly engaged.

9 Refit the retaining bolt and the heat shield (where fitted), and securely tighten the bolt. Where necessary, reconnect the wiring connector to the speedometer drive.

10 Apply a smear of oil to the speedometer cable O-rings, then reconnect the cable to the drive, and secure it in position with the rubber retaining pin. Lower the vehicle to the ground.

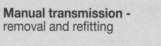

7 Manual transmission - removal and refitting

Removal

1 Chock the rear wheels, then firmly apply the handbrake. Jack up the front of the vehicle, and securely support it on axle stands. Remove both front roadwheels.

2 Drain the transmission oil as described in Chapter 1, then refit the drain and filler plugs, and tighten them to their specified torque settings.

3 Remove the battery and battery tray as described in Chapter 5. Slacken and remove the battery support tray retaining bolts, then free the wiring from its retaining clips on the

edge of the tray, and remove the tray **(see illustrations)**.

4 Remove the starter motor as described in Chapter 5.

5 Remove the air cleaner housing and intake duct as described in Chapter 4. On Turbo models, also remove the intercooler.

6 On models equipped with a belt-driven vacuum pump for the braking system, and where the pump is mounted on the top of the transmission housing, remove the pump as described in Chapter 9.

7 Fully slacken the clutch cable locknut and adjuster nut, then free the inner and outer cable end fittings from the mounting bracket and release lever. Release the cable from any relevant retaining clips, and position it clear of the transmission.

8 Disconnect the wiring connector from the reversing light switch and, where necessary, the speedometer drive housing. Undo the retaining bolts, and disconnect the earth straps from the top of the transmission housing **(see illustration)**.

9 Disconnect the wiring connector from the TDC sensor, which is situated on the rear of the cylinder block, and release the wiring from its clip on the top of the transmission housing.

10 Using a flat-bladed screwdriver, carefully lever the three gearchange mechanism link rods off their respective balljoints on the transmission **(see illustration)**. Position the rods clear of the transmission unit.

7.3a Undo the four retaining bolts . . .

7.3b . . . and remove the battery support tray. Note the wiring retaining clip (arrowed)

7.8 Slacken and remove the bolts (arrowed) and disconnect the earth straps from the transmission

7.10 Carefully lever the gearchange link rods off their transmission balljoints using a large flat-bladed screwdriver

7.11a On models equipped with power steering, undo the retaining nuts . . .

7.11b . . . and free the power steering pipe from its mountings on the underside of the transmission

11 On models equipped with power steering, undo the nuts securing the power steering pipe to the underside of the transmission, and free the pipe from its retaining studs **(see illustrations)**.

12 Undo the retaining bolts, and remove the lower flywheel cover plate from the transmission **(see illustration)**.

13 Withdraw the rubber retaining pin, disconnect the speedometer cable from the drive housing, and free it from any relevant retaining clips **(see illustrations)**.

14 Slacken and remove the three nuts securing the balljoint to the left-hand lower suspension arm, then withdraw the bolts and free the balljoint from the arm. Discard the nuts - new ones must be used on refitting.

Repeat the procedure on the right-hand side.

15 Release the inner end of the right-hand driveshaft from the transmission, as described in paragraphs 4 to 6 of Section 4.

16 To release the left-hand driveshaft inner constant velocity joint from the transmission, pull the swivel hub assembly outwards and withdraw the joint from transmission, taking great care not to damage the driveshaft oil seal. Support the driveshaft, to avoid damaging the constant velocity joints or gaiters.

17 Place a jack with interposed block of wood beneath the engine, to take the weight of the engine. Alternatively, attach a couple of lifting eyes to the engine, and fit a hoist or support bar to take the engine weight.

18 Place a jack and block of wood beneath the transmission, and raise the jack to take the weight of the transmission.

19 Slacken and remove the centre nut and washer from the left-hand engine/transmission mounting. Undo the two bolts securing the mounting bracket assembly to the vehicle body, and remove the mounting bracket assembly, along with its spacer. Unscrew the mounting stud from the top of the transmission housing, and remove it, along with its washer. If the mounting stud is tight, a universal stud extractor can be used to unscrew it **(see illustrations)**.

20 On models with a "pull-type" clutch release mechanism (see Chapter 6 for further information) withdraw the retaining pin, and

7.12 Removing the flywheel lower cover plate

7.13a Withdraw the rubber retaining pin (arrowed) . . .

7.13b . . . and disconnect the speedometer cable from the transmission

7.19a Remove the centre nut and washer from the left-hand mounting . . .

7.19b . . . then undo the two retaining bolts and remove mounting bracket assembly . . .

7.19c . . . and slide the spacer off the mounting stud

7.19d If the mounting stud is tight, use a universal stud extractor to unscrew it

7.20a On models with a "pull-type" clutch, withdraw the retaining pin . . .

7.20b . . . then remove the clutch release lever . . .

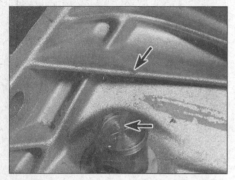

7.20c . . . and make an alignment mark between the release fork shaft and transmission housing (arrowed)

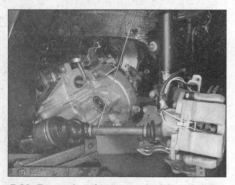

7.23 Removing the transmission unit from the vehicle

remove the clutch release lever from the top of the release fork shaft. This is necessary to allow the fork shaft to rotate freely, to disengage from the release bearing as the transmission is pulled away from the engine. Make an alignment mark across the centre of the clutch release fork shaft using a scriber, paint or similar, and mark its relative position on the transmission housing **(see illustrations)**. Undo the retaining bolts, and remove the clutch cable bracket from the top of the transmission housing.

21 With the jack positioned beneath the transmission taking the weight, slacken and remove the remaining bolts securing the transmission housing to the engine unit. Note the correct fitted positions of each bolt, and the necessary brackets, as they are removed, to use as a reference on refitting. Make a final check that all necessary components have been disconnected, and are positioned clear of the transmission unit so that they will not hinder the removal procedure.

22 With the bolts removed, move the trolley jack and transmission to the left, to free it from its locating dowels.

23 Once the transmission is free, lower the jack and manoeuvre the unit out from under the car **(see illustration)**. If they are loose, remove the locating dowels from the transmission or engine unit, and keep them in a safe place.

24 On models with a "pull-type" clutch, make a second alignment mark on the transmission housing, marking the relative position of the release fork mark after removal, noting the angle at which the release fork is positioned **(see illustration 7.25a)**. This mark can then be used to position the release fork prior to installation, to ensure the fork correctly engages with the clutch release bearing as the transmission is installed.

Refitting

25 The transmission is refitted by a reversal of the removal procedure, bearing in mind the following points:

(a) *Apply a little high-melting-point grease to the splines of the transmission input shaft. Do not apply too much, otherwise there is a possibility of the grease contaminating the clutch friction plate.*

(b) *Ensure the locating dowels are correctly positioned prior to installation.*

(c) *On models with a "pull-type" clutch, prior to refitting, position the clutch release bearing so that its HAUT mark is at the top, and the BAS mark is at the bottom, and align the release fork shaft mark with the second mark made on the transmission housing (see illustrations). This will ensure that the release fork and bearing will engage correctly as the transmission is refitted to the engine. If*

7.25a On models with a "pull-type" clutch, prior to refitting the transmission, align the release fork mark with the second mark made on removal . . .

7.25b . . . and position the release bearing so that its HAUT mark is at the top, and the BAS mark at the bottom

7.25c Prior to refitting, apply thread-locking fluid to the mounting stud threads

the bearing and fork are correctly engaged, the mark on the shaft should be aligned with the original mark made on the transmission housing. **Ensure the release fork and bearing are correctly engaged before bolting the transmission onto the engine.**

(d) Apply thread-locking fluid to the left-hand engine/transmission mounting stud threads, prior to refitting it to the transmission **(see illustration)**. Tighten the stud to the specified torque.

(e) Tighten all nuts and bolts to the specified torque (where given).

(f) Renew the driveshaft oil seals and refit the driveshafts to the transmission, using the information given in Section 4.

(g) On completion, refill the transmission with the specified type and quantity of lubricant, as described in Chapter 1.

8 Manual transmission overhaul - general information

Overhauling a manual transmission unit is a difficult and involved job for the DIY home mechanic. In addition to dismantling and reassembling many small parts, clearances must be precisely measured and, if necessary, changed by selecting shims and spacers. Internal transmission components are also often difficult to obtain, and in many instances, extremely expensive. Because of this, if the transmission develops a fault or becomes noisy, the best course of action is to have the unit overhauled by a specialist repairer, or to obtain an exchange reconditioned unit.

Nevertheless, it is not impossible for the more experienced mechanic to overhaul the transmission, provided the special tools are available, and the job is done in a deliberate step-by-step manner, so that nothing is overlooked.

The tools necessary for an overhaul include internal and external circlip pliers, bearing pullers, a slide hammer, a set of pin punches, a dial test indicator, and possibly a hydraulic press. In addition, a large, sturdy workbench and a vice will be required.

During dismantling of the transmission, make careful notes of how each component is fitted, to make reassembly easier and more accurate.

Before dismantling the transmission, it will help if you have some idea what area is malfunctioning. Certain problems can be closely related to specific areas in the transmission, which can make component examination and replacement easier. Refer to the Fault diagnosis Section at the beginning of this manual for more information.

Chapter 7 Part B: Automatic transmission

Contents

Automatic transmission - removal and refitting 12
Automatic transmission fluid level check . . . . See Chapter 1
Automatic transmission fluid renewal . . . . See Chapter 1
Automatic transmission overhaul - general information 13
Fluid cooler - removal and refitting 9
General information 1
Kickdown cable - adjustment 5
Kickdown cable - renewal 6
Oil seals - renewal 8

Selector cable - adjustment 2
Selector cable - removal and refitting 3
Selector lever assembly - removal and refitting 4
Selector lever position display switch -
  removal, refitting and adjustment 11
Speedometer drive - removal and refitting 7
Starter inhibitor/reversing light switch - removal, testing
  and refitting 10

Degrees of difficulty

Easy, suitable for novice with little experience	**Fairly easy,** suitable for beginner with some experience	**Fairly difficult,** suitable for competent DIY mechanic	**Difficult,** suitable for experienced DIY mechanic	**Very difficult,** suitable for expert DIY or professional

Specifications

General

Type	Automatic, four forward speeds and reverse
Designation	4 HP 14
Transmission code	GZ 57

Lubrication

Recommended fluid	See "Lubricants and fluids"

Torque wrench settings

	Nm	lbf ft
Selector cable fixings:		
Outer cable locknuts	10	7
Mounting bracket-to-transmission bolts	20	15
Cable-to-mounting bracket screws	10	7
Selector lever retaining nuts	7	5
Transmission selector lever retaining nut	30	22
Fluid cooler centre bolt	50	36
Left-hand engine/transmission mounting:		
Mounting bracket-to-body bolts	25	18
Mounting stud	50	37
Centre nut	80	59
Engine-to-transmission unit securing bolts	40	30
Torque converter-to-driveplate bolts	35	26
Dipstick tube-to-sump union nut	45	33

1 General information

Some models covered in this manual were offered with the option of a four-speed fully-automatic transmission, consisting of a torque converter, an epicyclic geartrain, and hydraulically-operated clutches and brakes **(see illustration)**.

The torque converter provides a fluid coupling between engine and transmission, which acts as an automatic clutch, and also provides a degree of torque multiplication when accelerating.

The epicyclic geartrain provides either of the four forward or one reverse gear ratios, according to which of its component parts are held stationary or allowed to turn. The components of the geartrain are held or released by brakes and clutches which are activated by a hydraulic control unit. A fluid pump within the transmission provides the necessary hydraulic pressure to operate the brakes and clutches.

Driver control of the transmission is by a seven-position selector lever. The transmission has a "drive" position, and a "hold" facility on the first three gear ratios. The "drive" position "A" provides automatic changing throughout the range of all four gear ratios, and is the one to select for normal driving. An automatic kickdown facility shifts the transmission down a gear if the accelerator pedal is fully depressed. The "hold" facility is very similar, but limits the number of gear ratios available - ie when the selector lever is in the "3" position, only the first three ratios can be selected; in the "2" position, only the first two can be selected, and so on. The lower ratio "hold" is useful for providing engine braking when travelling down steep gradients, or for preventing unwanted selection of top gear on twisty roads. Note, however, that the transmission should *never* be shifted down a position if the engine speed exceeds 4000 rpm.

Due to the complexity of the automatic transmission, any repair or overhaul work must be left to a Citroën dealer with the necessary special equipment for fault diagnosis and repair. The contents of the following Sections are therefore confined to supplying general information, and any service information and instructions that can be used by the owner.

2 Selector cable - adjustment

1 Position the selector lever firmly against its detent mechanism in the "N" position.
2 To improve access to the transmission end of the selector cable, remove the battery and battery tray as described in Chapter 5, then unbolt the support tray and remove it from the top of the transmission. On some models, it may also be necessary to remove the air cleaner housing and/or intake duct as described in Chapter 4.
3 Using a large flat-bladed screwdriver, carefully lever the selector cable end fitting off the transmission selector lever balljoint, whilst ensuring that the lever does not move.
4 First ensure that the cable end fitting is screwed onto at least 5 mm of the inner cable thread.
5 With both the selector levers in the "N" (neutral) position, the selector cable end fitting should be correctly aligned with the transmission lever balljoint, so that the cable

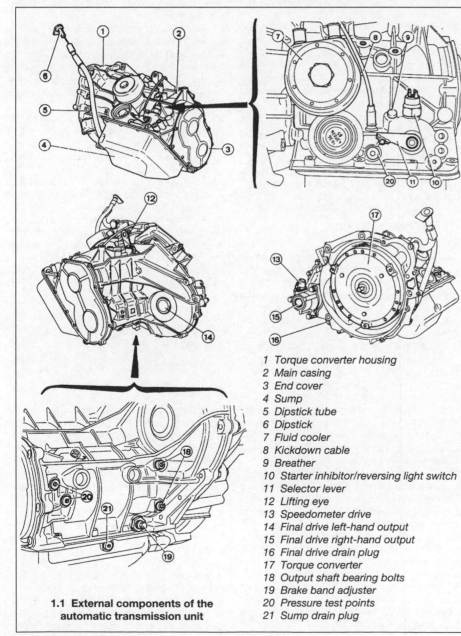

1 Torque converter housing
2 Main casing
3 End cover
4 Sump
5 Dipstick tube
6 Dipstick
7 Fluid cooler
8 Kickdown cable
9 Breather
10 Starter inhibitor/reversing light switch
11 Selector lever
12 Lifting eye
13 Speedometer drive
14 Final drive left-hand output
15 Final drive right-hand output
16 Final drive drain plug
17 Torque converter
18 Output shaft bearing bolts
19 Brake band adjuster
20 Pressure test points
21 Sump drain plug

1.1 External components of the automatic transmission unit

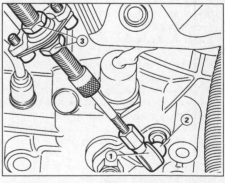

2.5 Selector cable transmission end fixings

1 Cable end fitting
2 Selector lever balljoint
3 Outer cable locknuts

can be connected to the lever without the balljoint moving. If necessary, adjust the position of the end fitting by screwing or unscrewing it (as applicable) on the cable thread, bearing in mind the point made above in paragraph 4. If this proves impossible, further adjustments can be made by slackening the locknuts securing the outer cable to its mounting bracket **(see illustration)**. Reposition the nuts as required until the end fitting and balljoint are correctly aligned, then tighten the nuts to the specified torque.

6 Once the end fitting is correctly positioned, press it firmly onto the balljoint, and check that it is securely retained.

7 Refit the battery support tray, and securely tighten its retaining bolts. Refit the battery tray and battery as described in Chapter 5. Also refit any disturbed air cleaner/duct components as described in Chapter 4.

8 Check the operation of the selector lever position display panel and, if necessary, adjust the switch using the information given in Section 11.

---

3 Selector cable - removal and refitting

Removal

1 Firmly apply the handbrake, then jack up the front of the vehicle and support it on axle stands. Position the selector lever in the "N" position.

2 Remove the battery and battery tray as described in Chapter 5. Slacken and remove the battery support tray retaining bolts, then free the wiring from its retaining clip on the side of the tray, and remove the tray from the vehicle.

3 Remove the exhaust system as described in Chapter 4, and remove the heat shield(s) to gain access to the base of the selector lever assembly.

4 Working on the transmission end of the cable, undo the two screws securing the outer cable to its retaining bracket, and carefully lever the inner cable end fitting off its balljoint on the transmission selector lever. Note the transmission selector lever must not be disturbed until the cable is refitted. As a precaution, mark the position of the lever in relation to the transmission housing.

5 Work back along the selector cable, releasing it from any relevant retaining clips, and noting its correct routing.

6 Working from inside the vehicle, carefully prise the selector lever trim panel out from the centre console, and fold the gaiter back over the selector lever.

7 Slacken and remove the four screws securing the handle to the shaft of the selector lever. Depress the selector lever handle detent knob, then rotate the handle through 90° anti-clockwise, lift the assembly up, and rotate it back 90° clockwise to release

the detent button from the selector lever pushrod. With the handle removed, withdraw the detent button and spring from the handle.

8 Slide the gaiter off the selector lever shaft, then undo the four nuts securing the selector lever to the floor. Disengage the position display switch from the selector lever studs, and position it clear of the lever.

9 Working underneath the vehicle, disengage the selector lever assembly from the body, and remove the lever and cable assembly, noting the correct routing of the cable.

10 With the assembly on the bench, prise the rubber dust cover from the base of the lever, and slide it along the cable.

11 Slacken the outer cable retaining nut, then remove the retaining clip. Carefully prise the selector cable end fitting off its balljoint on the base of the selector lever, and separate the cable and lever assembly.

12 Examine the cable, looking for worn end fittings or a damaged outer casing, and for signs of fraying of the inner cable. Check the cable's operation; the inner cable should move smoothly and easily through the outer casing. Renew the cable if it shows any signs of excessive wear or any damage.

> **HAYNES HINT** *Remember that a cable that appears serviceable when tested off the car may well be much heavier in operation when compressed into its working position*

Refitting

13 Apply a smear of the special grease (Mobil Temp G9, available from your Citroën dealer) to the exposed sections of the inner cable and balljoints, and to the detent mechanism of the selector lever. In the absence of the specified grease, a good-quality molybdenum disulphide grease can be used.

14 Insert the selector cable into the selector lever housing, ensuring that the outer cable flange holes are correctly located on the pegs on the housing. Secure the cable in position with the retaining clip, ensuring that the outer ends of the clip are correctly located in the slots in the lever housing, and the inner ends are correctly hooked over the base of the housing. Tighten the outer cable retaining nut to the specified torque.

15 Press the inner cable end fitting firmly onto the lever balljoint. Check that the balljoint connection is securely made, then slide the rubber dust cover back into position over the selector lever base.

16 Ensuring that the cable is correctly routed, manoeuvre the lever and cable assembly back into position from underneath the vehicle.

17 From inside the vehicle, pull the lever up into position, and fit its two right-hand retaining nuts, tightening them finger-tight only at this stage.

18 Refit the position display switch onto the left-hand selector lever studs, ensuring that the switch lug is correctly engaged with the selector lever shaft. Refit the two left-hand nuts, then tighten all four selector lever retaining nuts to the specified torque.

19 Refit the gaiter to the selector lever.

20 Refit the spring and detent button to the selector lever handle, and press the button fully into the handle. Keeping the button depressed, slide the handle assembly onto the lever then, exerting light downward pressure on the handle, rotate the handle through 90° clockwise, then back 90° anti-clockwise to engage the detent button with the lever pushrod. Release the detent button, then refit the four handle retaining screws and tighten them securely. Check the operation of the selector lever detent button before proceeding further.

21 From underneath the vehicle, work along the length of the selector cable, ensuring that it is retained by all the relevant clips. Align the outer cable bracket with its mounting bracket on the transmission, then refit its retaining bolts and tighten them to the specified torque setting.

22 Ensure the selector lever is in the "N" position and the transmission selector lever is still in the neutral position, then adjust the cable and connect it to the transmission lever as described in paragraphs 4 to 6 of Section 2.

23 Refit the heat shield(s) and exhaust system as described in Chapter 4, then lower the vehicle to the ground.

24 Refit the battery support tray, and securely tighten its retaining bolts. Clip the wiring onto the side of the tray, and refit the battery tray and battery as described in Chapter 5.

25 Check and, if necessary, adjust selector lever display switch using the information given in Section 11.

---

4 Selector lever assembly - removal and refitting

Removal

1 Firmly apply the handbrake, then jack up the front of the vehicle and support it on axle stands. Position the selector lever in the "N" position.

2 Remove the exhaust system as described in Chapter 4, and remove the heat shield(s) to gain access to the base of the selector lever assembly.

3 Carry out the procedures described in paragraphs 6 to 8 of Section 3.

4 Working again from underneath the vehicle, disengage the selector lever assembly from the body, and lower it out of position.

5 Prise the rubber dust cover from the base of the lever, and slide it along the cable.

6 Slacken the outer cable retaining nut, then remove the retaining clip. Carefully prise the selector cable end fitting off its balljoint on the base of the selector lever, and remove the lever assembly from underneath the vehicle.

Refitting

7 Carry out the operations described in paragraphs 13 to 20 of Section 3.

8 Refit the heat shield(s) and exhaust system as described in Chapter 4, then lower the vehicle to the ground.

9 On completion, check the selector cable adjustment as described in Section 2.

5 Kickdown cable - adjustment

1 Warm the engine up to its normal operating temperature, then check that the engine idle speed is correctly set. If necessary, adjust the idle speed as described in Chapter 4.

2 Detach the kickdown inner cable from the injection pump then, referring to Chapter 4, check that the accelerator cable is correctly adjusted.

3 Pull the kickdown inner cable fully out of its outer cable, and measure the distance between the end of the lug on the inner cable and the threaded end of the outer cable **(see illustration)**. This should be approximately 39 mm. If necessary, slacken the two outer cable

locknuts, and position the nuts as required so that the distance is as specified.

4 Reconnect the kickdown cable to the injection pump, then check the clearance once more between the inner cable lug and the threaded end of the outer cable. Ensuring that the pump throttle lever is fully against its stop, there should a gap of 0.5 to 1.0 mm **(see illustration)**. If not, adjust the gap by repositioning the outer cable locknuts as required. Once the outer cable is correctly positioned and the gap is as specified, securely tighten the cable locknuts.

6 Kickdown cable - renewal

1 Renewal of the kickdown cable is a complex task, which should be entrusted to a Citroën dealer. To detach the cable at the transmission end requires removal of the hydraulic valve block, which is a task that should not be undertaken by the home mechanic.

7 Speedometer drive - removal and refitting

Refer to Chapter 7A, Section 6.

8 Oil seals - renewal

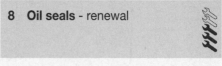

Driveshaft oil seals

1 Refer to the information given in Section 4 of Chapter 7A.

Selector shaft oil seal

2 Position the selector lever firmly against its detent mechanism in the "N" position.

3 To improve access to the transmission end of the selector cable, remove the battery and battery tray as described in Chapter 5, then unbolt the support tray and remove it from the top of the transmission. On some models, it may also be necessary to remove the air cleaner housing and/or intake duct as described in Chapter 4.

4 Undo the two screws securing the outer cable to its retaining bracket, and carefully lever the inner cable end fitting off its balljoint on the transmission selector lever. Note the transmission selector shaft must not be disturbed until the cable is refitted. As a precaution, mark the position of the lever in relation to the transmission housing.

5 Undo the retaining nut, and remove the lever from the transmission selector shaft.

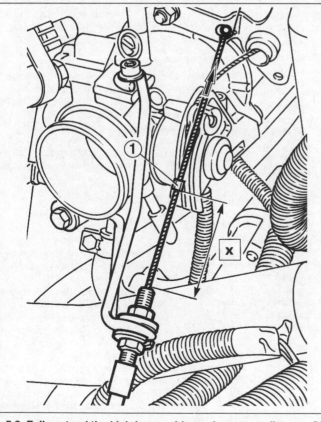

5.3 Fully extend the kickdown cable, and measure distance (X) between the cable lug (1) and the outer cable end - petrol engine shown, Diesel engine similar

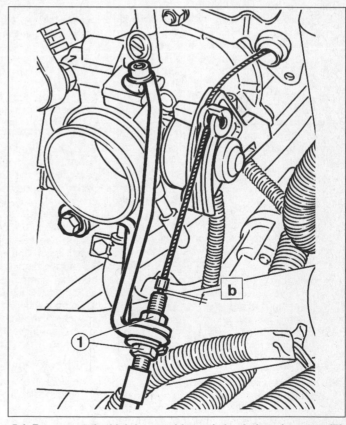

5.4 Reconnect the kickdown cable, and check that clearance (B) is as given in the text. If necessary, adjust by repositioning the locknuts (1) - petrol engine shown, Diesel engine similar

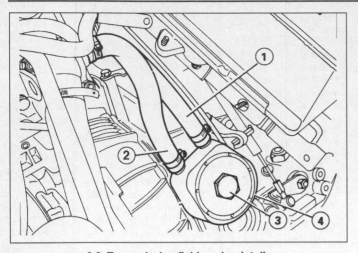

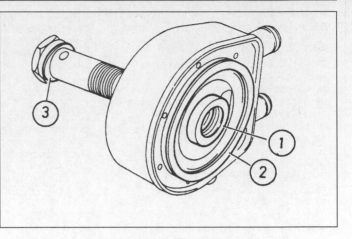

9.2 Transmission fluid cooler details

1 Coolant hose   2 Coolant hose   3 Centre bolt   4 Fluid cooler

9.5 Transmission fluid cooler seals

1 Cooler inner seal   2 Cooler outer seal
3 Centre bolt seal

6 Punch or drill two small holes opposite each other in the seal. Screw a self-tapping screw into each, and pull on the screws with pliers to extract the seal.

7 Clean the seal housing, and polish off any burrs or raised edges, which may have caused the seal to fail in the first place. Small imperfections can be removed using emery paper, but larger defects will require the renewal of the selector shaft.

8 Lubricate the lips of the new seal with clean engine oil, and carefully ease the seal into position over the end of the shaft, taking great care not to damage its sealing lip. Tap the seal into position until it is flush with the transmission casing, using a suitable tubular drift (such as a socket) which bears only on the hard outer edge of the seal. Note that the seal lips should face inwards.

9 Refit the selector lever to the shaft, and tighten its retaining nut to the specified torque setting.

10 Align the outer cable bracket with its mounting bracket on the transmission, then refit its retaining bolts and tighten them to the specified torque setting.

11 Ensure the selector lever is in the "N" position and the transmission selector lever is still in the neutral position, then adjust the cable and connect it to the transmission lever as described in paragraphs 4 to 8 of Section 2.

9   Fluid cooler -
removal and refitting

Removal

1 The fluid cooler is mounted onto the top of the transmission housing. To gain access to the fluid cooler, remove the air intake duct and, where necessary, the air cleaner housing as described in Chapter 4.

2 Using a hose clamp or similar, clamp both the fluid cooler coolant hoses to minimise

coolant loss during the subsequent operation **(see illustration)**.

3 Slacken the retaining clips, and disconnect both coolant hoses from the fluid cooler - be prepared for some coolant spillage. Wash off any spilt coolant immediately with cold water, and dry the surrounding area before proceeding further.

4 Slacken and remove the fluid cooler centre bolt, and remove the cooler from the transmission. Remove the seal from the centre bolt, and the two seals fitted to the base of the cooler, and discard them; new ones must be used on refitting.

Refitting

5 Lubricate the new seals with clean automatic transmission fluid, then fit the two new seals to the base of the fluid cooler, and a new seal to the centre bolt **(see illustration)**.

6 Locate the fluid cooler on the top of transmission housing, ensuring its flat edge is parallel to the mating surface of the transmission/driveplate housing. Refit the centre bolt, and tighten it to the specified torque setting.

7 Reconnect the coolant hoses to the fluid cooler, and securely tighten their retaining clips. Remove the hose clamp.

8 Refit the disturbed intake duct/air cleaner housing components (as applicable) as described in Chapter 4.

9 On completion, top-up the cooling system and check the automatic transmission fluid level as described in Chapter 1.

10   Starter inhibitor/reversing
light switch - removal, testing and refitting

1 The starter inhibitor/reversing light switch is a dual-function switch which is screwed into the top of the transmission housing. The inhibitor function of the switch ensures that the

engine can only be started with the selector lever in either the "N" or "P" positions, therefore preventing the engine being started with the transmission in gear. This is achieved by the switch cutting the supply to the starter motor solenoid. If at any time it is noted that the engine can be started with the selector lever in any position other than "P" or "N", then it is likely that the inhibitor function of the switch is suspect. The switch also performs the function of the reversing light switch, illuminating the reversing lights whenever the selector lever is in the "R" position.

Removal

2 To gain access to the switch, remove the battery and battery tray as described in Chapter 5, then unbolt the support tray from the top of the transmission.

3 Trace the wiring back from the switch, and disconnect it at the wiring connector.

4 Unscrew the switch, and remove it from the top of the transmission housing, along with its washer.

Testing

5 Temporarily reconnect the battery and reconnect the switch wiring.

6 With the ignition switched on and the starter inhibitor/reversing light switch plunger pressed fully in, check that the reversing lights are illuminated.

7 With the switch plunger released, check that it is possible to start the engine.

8 With the switch plunger in the mid-position check that it is not possible to start the engine and that the reversing lights are not illuminated.

9 If the switch does not operate as described, check the security and continuity of the switch wiring connections. If the wiring is satisfactory, the switch should be renewed.

Refitting

10 Fit a new washer to the switch, screw it back into the transmission, and tighten it securely. Note that washers of various thicknesses are available in the form of a shim kit from Citroen dealers. If the original switch is being refitted, a washer 0.2 mm thicker than the original should be used. If a new switch is being fitted, a washer at least 1.4 mm thick should be used.

11 Temporarily reconnect the battery, reconnect the switch wiring and carry out the following tests.

12 Firmly apply the handbrake and footbrake and check that it is possible to start the engine with the selector lever in the "P" and "N" positions, but not in any other positions.

13 Check that it is not possible to start the engine with the selector lever moved half way between the "N" and "R" positions and "N" and "D" positions.

14 Check that the reversing lights are only illuminated with the selector lever in the "R" position.

15 If the switch does not operate as described, fit a slightly thicker washer and repeat the procedure until the correct operation is achieved.

16 On completion, refit the support tray and securely tighten its retaining bolts.

17 Refit the battery tray and battery as described in Chapter 5.

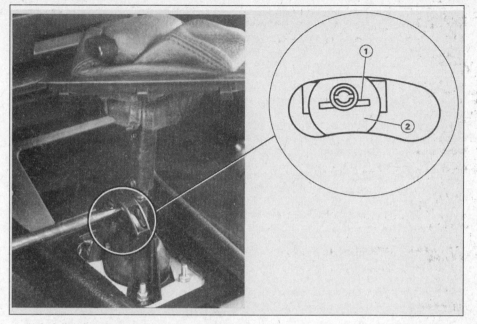

11.6 Adjusting the selector lever position display switch. Insert a screwdriver in the slot (1) and rotate the eccentric adjuster (2) so that the switch performs as described in the text

11 Selector lever position display switch - removal, refitting and adjustment

Removal

1 Working from inside the vehicle, carefully prise the selector lever trim panel out from the centre console, and fold the gaiter back over the selector lever.

2 Trace the wiring back from the switch, and disconnect it at its wiring connector.

3 Undo the two left-hand retaining nuts securing the selector lever to the floor, then disengage the position display switch from the selector lever studs and remove it from the vehicle.

Refitting and adjustment

4 Refit the position display switch onto the left-hand selector lever studs, ensuring that the switch lug is correctly engaged with the selector lever shaft. Refit the two left-hand selector lever retaining nuts, and tighten them to the specified torque.

5 Reconnect the wiring connector, then switch on the ignition and check the operation of the selector lever position display panel.

6 Move the selector lever throughout its range, and check that the corresponding position on the position display panel illuminates as each position is selected. If necessary, the switch can be adjusted by rotating the switch eccentric adjuster using a flat-bladed screwdriver **(see illustration)**.

7 Once the switch is correctly adjusted, fold the gaiter back down over the selector lever, and clip the trim panel back into position.

12 Automatic transmission - removal and refitting

Removal

1 Chock the rear wheels, firmly apply the handbrake, and place the selector lever in the "N" (neutral) position. Jack up the front of the vehicle, and securely support it on axle stands. Remove both front roadwheels.

2 Drain the transmission fluid as described in Chapter 1, then refit the drain plugs, tightening them securely.

3 Remove the battery and battery tray as described in Chapter 5. Slacken and remove the support tray retaining bolts, then release the wiring from its retaining clip on the side of the tray, and remove the tray from the top of the transmission.

4 Remove the starter motor as described in Chapter 5.

5 Remove the air cleaner housing and intake duct as described in Chapter 4. On Turbo models, also remove the intercooler.

6 Undo the union nut securing the dipstick tube to the transmission sump, then undo the bolt securing the tube to the transmission housing, and remove the dipstick from the transmission unit.

7 Disconnect the wiring connector from the starter inhibitor/reversing light switch and, where necessary, the speedometer drive housing. Undo the retaining bolt(s) and disconnect the earth strap(s) from the top of the transmission housing.

8 Disconnect the wiring connector from the

TDC sensor, which is situated at the rear of the cylinder block.

9 Using a hose clamp or similar, clamp both the fluid cooler coolant hoses to minimise coolant loss. Slacken the retaining clips and disconnect both coolant hoses from the fluid cooler - be prepared for some coolant spillage. Wash off any spilt coolant immediately with cold water.

10 Undo the two screws securing the outer selector cable to its retaining bracket, and carefully lever the inner cable end fitting off its balljoint on the transmission selector lever. Note that the transmission selector lever must not be disturbed until the cable is refitted. As a precaution, mark the position of the lever in relation to the transmission housing. Work back along the selector cable, releasing it from any relevant retaining clips, and position it clear of the transmission unit.

11 Detach the kickdown inner cable from the injection pump lever, then slacken the outer cable locknuts and free the cable from its mounting bracket. Release the kickdown cable from any relevant retaining clips, so that it is free to be removed with the transmission unit.

12 On models equipped with power steering, undo the nut securing the power steering pipe to the underside of the transmission, and free the pipe from its retaining stud.

13 Undo the retaining bolts and remove the lower driveplate cover plate from the transmission, to gain access to the torque converter retaining bolts. Slacken and remove the visible bolt then, using a socket and extension bar to rotate the crankshaft pulley, undo the remaining bolts securing the torque converter to the driveplate as they become accessible. There are three bolts in total.

14 To ensure that the torque converter does not fall out as the transmission is removed, secure it in position using a length of metal strip bolted to one of the starter motor bolt holes.

15 Withdraw the rubber retaining pin, disconnect the speedometer cable from the drive, and free it from any relevant retaining clips.

16 Slacken and remove the three nuts securing the balljoint to the left-hand lower suspension arm, then withdraw the bolts and free the balljoint from the arm. Discard the nuts - new ones must be used on refitting. Repeat the procedure on the right-hand side.

17 Release the inner end of the right-hand driveshaft from the transmission, as described in paragraphs 4 to 6 of Section 4 of Chapter 7A.

18 To release the left-hand driveshaft inner constant velocity joint from the transmission, pull the swivel hub assembly outwards, and withdraw the joint from transmission, taking great care not to damage the driveshaft oil seal. Support the driveshaft to avoid damaging the constant velocity joints or gaiters.

19 Place a jack with interposed block of wood beneath the engine, to take the weight of the engine. Alternatively, attach a couple of lifting eyes to the engine, and fit a hoist or support bar to take the weight of the engine.

20 Place a jack and block of wood beneath the transmission, and raise the jack to take the weight of the transmission.

21 Slacken and remove the centre nut and washer from the left-hand engine/ transmission mounting. Undo the two bolts securing the mounting bracket assembly to the vehicle body, and remove the mounting

bracket assembly, along with its spacer. Unscrew the mounting stud from the top of the transmission housing, and remove it, along with its washer.

22 With the jack positioned beneath the transmission taking the weight, slacken and remove the remaining bolts securing the transmission housing to the engine unit. Note the correct fitted positions of each bolt as it is removed, to use as a reference on refitting. Make a final check that all necessary components have been disconnected, and positioned clear of the transmission unit so that they will not hinder the removal procedure.

23 With the bolts removed, move the trolley jack and transmission to the left, to free it from its locating dowels.

24 Once the transmission is free, lower the jack and manoeuvre the unit out from under the car. If they are loose, remove the locating dowels from the transmission or engine unit, and keep them in a safe place.

Refitting

25 The transmission is refitted by a reversal of the removal procedure, bearing in mind the following points:

(a) *Ensure the bush fitted to the centre of the crankshaft is in good condition, and apply a little Molykote G1 grease to the torque converter centring pin. Do not apply too much, otherwise there is a possibility of the grease contaminating the torque converter.*

(b) *Ensure the engine/transmission locating dowels are correctly positioned prior to installation.*

(c) *Once the transmission and engine are correctly joined, refit the securing bolts,*

tightening them to the specified torque setting, then remove the metal strip used to retain the torque converter.

(d) *Apply thread-locking fluid to the left-hand engine/transmission mounting stud threads prior to refitting it to the transmission. Tighten the stud to the specified torque.*

(e) *Tighten all nuts and bolts to the specified torque (where given).*

(f) *Renew the driveshaft oil seals and refit the driveshafts to the transmission, using the information given in Section 4 of Chapter 7A.*

(g) *Adjust the selector cable and kickdown cable as described in Sections 2 and 5 of this Chapter.*

(h) *On completion, top-up the cooling system, then refill the transmission with the specified type and quantity of fluid as described in Chapter 1.*

13 Automatic transmission overhaul - general information

In the event of a fault occurring with the transmission, it is first necessary to determine whether it is of an electrical, mechanical or hydraulic nature, and to do this, special test equipment is required. It is therefore essential to have the work carried out by a Citroën dealer if a transmission fault is suspected.

Do not remove the transmission from the car for possible repair before professional fault diagnosis has been carried out, since most tests require the transmission to be in the vehicle.

Chapter 8 Driveshafts

Contents

Driveshaft overhaul - general information 4
Driveshaft rubber gaiter and constant
   velocity (CV) joint check . . . . See Chapter 1
Driveshaft rubber gaiters - renewal 3
Driveshafts - removal and refitting 2
General information 1
Right-hand driveshaft intermediate bearing - renewal 5

Degrees of difficulty

Easy, suitable for novice with little experience	Fairly easy, suitable for beginner with some experience	Fairly difficult, suitable for competent DIY mechanic	Difficult, suitable for experienced DIY mechanic	Very difficult, suitable for expert DIY or professional

Specifications

Type . . . . Unequal-length driveshafts, with ball-and-cage type outer constant velocity (CV) joint, and tripod-type inner joint

Lubrication (overhaul only - see text)
Lubricant type/specification . . . . Use only special grease supplied in sachets with gaiter kits - joints are otherwise pre-packed with grease and sealed

Torque wrench settings	Nm	lbf ft
Driveshaft retaining nut	320	236
Right-hand driveshaft intermediate bearing retaining bolt nuts	10	7
Lower suspension arm balljoint retaining nuts	45	33
Roadwheel bolts	90	66

1 General information

Drive is transmitted from the differential to the front wheels by means of two solid-steel driveshafts of unequal length.

Both driveshafts are splined at their outer ends, to accept the wheel hubs, and are threaded so that each hub can be fastened by a large nut. The inner end of each driveshaft is splined, to accept the differential sun gear.

Constant velocity (CV) joints are fitted to each end of the driveshafts, to ensure the smooth and efficient transmission of power at all suspension and steering angles. The outer constant velocity joints are of the ball-and-cage type, and the inner constant velocity joints are of the tripod type.

On the right-hand side, due to the length of the driveshaft, the inner constant velocity joint is situated approximately halfway along the shaft's length, and an intermediate support bearing is mounted in the rear engine/transmission mounting bracket. The inner end of the driveshaft passes through the bearing (which prevents any lateral movement of the driveshaft inner end) and the inner constant velocity joint outer member.

2 Driveshafts - removal and refitting

Removal

1 Chock the rear wheels of the car, firmly apply the handbrake, then jack up the front of the car and support it on axle stands. Remove the appropriate front roadwheel.

2 Drain the transmission oil as described in Chapter 1.

3 On models equipped with ABS, trace the wiring connector back from the wheel sensor, freeing it from its retaining clips, and disconnect it at its wiring connector.

4 Withdraw the R-clip and remove the locking cap from the driveshaft retaining nut.

5 Refit at least two roadwheel bolts to the front hub, and tighten them securely. Have an assistant firmly depress the brake pedal to prevent the front hub from rotating, then using a socket and extension bar, slacken and remove the driveshaft retaining nut.

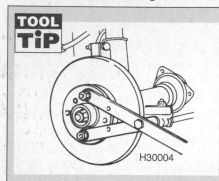

A tool to hold the front hub stationary can be fabricated from two lengths of steel strip (one long, one short) and a nut and bolt; the nut and bolt forming the pivot of a forked tool. Bolt the tool to the hub using two wheel bolts, and hold the tool to prevent the hub from rotating as the driveshaft retaining nut is undone.

6 Slacken and remove the three nuts securing the balljoint to the lower suspension arm, then withdraw the bolts and free the balljoint from the arm. Discard the nuts - new ones must be used on refitting.

Left-hand driveshaft

7 Carefully pull the swivel hub assembly outwards, and withdraw the driveshaft outer constant velocity joint from the hub assembly. If necessary, the shaft can be tapped out of the hub using a soft-faced mallet.

8 Support the driveshaft, then withdraw the inner constant velocity joint from the transmission, taking great care not to damage the driveshaft oil seal. Remove the driveshaft from the vehicle.

Right-hand driveshaft

9 Loosen the two intermediate bearing retaining bolt nuts, then rotate the bolts through 90°, so that their offset heads are clear of the bearing outer race **(see illustrations)**.

10 Carefully pull the swivel hub assembly outwards, and withdraw the driveshaft outer constant velocity joint from the hub assembly. If necessary, the shaft can be tapped out of the hub using a soft-faced mallet.

11 Support the outer end of the driveshaft, then pull on the inner end of the shaft to free the intermediate bearing from its mounting bracket.

12 Once the driveshaft end is free from the

transmission, slide the dust seal off the inner end of the shaft, noting which way around it is fitted, and remove the driveshaft from the vehicle.

Refitting

13 Before installing the driveshaft, examine the driveshaft oil seal in the transmission for signs of damage or deterioration and, if necessary, renew it, referring to Chapter 7A for further information.

14 Thoroughly clean the driveshaft splines, and the apertures in the transmission and hub assembly. Apply a thin film of grease to the oil seal lips, and to the driveshaft splines and shoulders. Check that all gaiter clips are securely fastened.

Left-hand driveshaft

15 Offer up the driveshaft, and locate the joint splines with those of the differential sun gear, taking great care not to damage the oil seal. Push the joint fully into position.

16 Locate the outer constant velocity joint splines with those of the swivel hub, and slide the joint back into position in the hub.

17 Align the balljoint with the lower arm, and fit the three retaining bolts. Fit new retaining nuts to the bolts, and tighten them to the specified torque setting.

18 Lubricate the inner face and threads of the driveshaft retaining nut with clean engine oil, and refit it to the end of the driveshaft. Use the method employed on removal to prevent the hub from rotating, and tighten the driveshaft retaining nut to the specified torque setting. Check that the hub rotates freely, then engage the locking cap with the driveshaft nut so that one of its cut-outs is aligned with driveshaft hole, and secure it in position with the R-clip **(see illustrations)**.

19 Where necessary, reconnect the ABS wheel sensor wiring connector, ensuring that the wiring is correctly routed and retained by all the necessary clips and ties.

20 Refit the roadwheel, then lower the vehicle to the ground and tighten the roadwheel bolts to the specified torque.

21 Refill the transmission unit with the specified type and amount of fluid/oil, and check the level using the information given in Chapter 1.

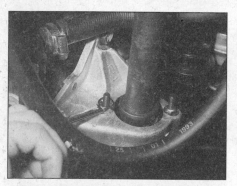

2.9a On the right-hand driveshaft, slacken the two intermediate bearing retaining bolt nuts . . .

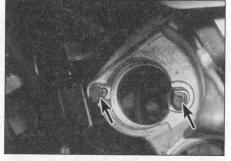

2.9b . . . then rotate the bolts through 90° to disengage their offset heads (arrowed) from the bearing (shown with driveshaft removed)

2.18a Tighten the driveshaft retaining nut to the specified torque . . .

2.18b . . . then refit the locking cap . . .

2.18c . . . and secure it in position with the R-clip

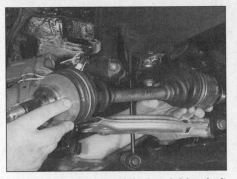

2.24a Manoeuvre the right-hand driveshaft into position . . .

2.24b . . . and locate the dust seal to its inner end, ensuring it is fitted the correct way round

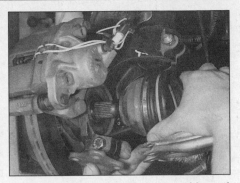

2.26 Pull out the swivel hub assembly, and locate the outer constant velocity joint splines with those of the swivel hub

Right-hand driveshaft

22 Check that the intermediate bearing rotates smoothly, without any sign of roughness or undue free play between its inner and outer races. If necessary, renew the bearing as described in Section 5. Examine the dust seal for signs of damage or deterioration, and renew if necessary.

23 Apply a smear of grease to the outer race of the intermediate bearing, and to the inner lip of the dust seal.

24 Pass the inner end of the shaft through the bearing mounting bracket, then carefully slide the dust seal into position on the driveshaft, ensuring that its flat surface is facing the transmission **(see illustrations)**.

25 Carefully locate the inner driveshaft splines with those of the differential sun gear, taking great care not to damage the oil seal. Align the intermediate bearing with its mounting bracket, and push the driveshaft fully into position. If necessary, use a soft-faced mallet to tap the outer race of the bearing into position in the mounting bracket.

26 Locate the outer constant velocity joint splines with those of the swivel hub, and slide the joint back into position in the hub **(see illustration)**.

27 Ensure the intermediate bearing is correctly seated, then rotate its retaining bolts back through 90°, so that their offset heads are resting against the bearing outer race. Tighten

the retaining nuts to the specified torque. Ensure that the dust seal is tight against the driveshaft oil seal **(see illustration)**.

28 Carry out the operations described above in paragraphs 17 to 21.

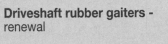

3 Driveshaft rubber gaiters - renewal

Outer joint

1 Remove the driveshaft from the car as described in Section 2.

2 Secure the driveshaft in a vice equipped with soft jaws, and release the two rubber gaiter retaining clips. If necessary, the gaiter retaining clips can be cut to release them.

3 Slide the rubber gaiter down the shaft, to expose the outer constant velocity joint. Scoop out the excess grease.

4 Using a hammer and suitable soft metal drift, sharply strike the inner member of the outer joint to drive it off the end of the shaft. The outer joint is retained on the driveshaft by a circlip, and striking the joint in this manner forces the circlip into its groove, so allowing the joint to slide off.

5 Once the joint assembly has been removed, remove the circlip from the groove in the driveshaft splines, and discard it. A new circlip must be fitted on reassembly.

6 Withdraw the rubber gaiter from the driveshaft, and slide off the gaiter inner end plastic bush.

7 With the constant velocity joint removed from the driveshaft, thoroughly clean the joint using paraffin, or a suitable solvent, and dry it thoroughly. Carry out a visual inspection of the joint.

8 Move the inner splined driving member from side to side, to expose each ball in turn at the top of its track. Examine the balls for cracks, flat spots, or signs of surface pitting.

9 Inspect the ball tracks on the inner and outer members. If the tracks have widened, the balls will no longer be a tight fit. At the same time, check the ball cage windows for wear or cracking between the windows.

10 If on inspection any of the constant velocity joint components are found to be worn or damaged, it will be necessary to renew the complete joint assembly (where available), or even the complete driveshaft (where no joint components are available separately). Refer to your Citroën dealer for further information on parts availability. If the joint is in satisfactory condition, obtain a repair kit consisting of a new gaiter, circlip, retaining clips, and the correct type and quantity of grease.

11 To install the new gaiter, refer to the accompanying illustrations, and perform the operations shown **(see illustrations 3.11a to 3.11k)**. Be sure to stay in order, and follow the

2.27 Secure the intermediate bearing in position, then slide the dust seal up tight against the driveshaft oil seal

3.11a Fit the hard plastic rings to the outer CV joint gaiter . . .

3.11b . . . then slide on the new plastic bush (arrowed), and seat it in its recess in the shaft. Slide the gaiter onto the shaft . . .

3.11c . . . and seat the gaiter inner end on top of the plastic bush

3.11d Fit the new circlip to its groove in the driveshaft splines . . .

3.11e . . . then locate the joint outer member on the splines, and slide it into position over the circlip. Ensure that the joint is securely retained by the circlip before proceeding

3.11f Pack the joint with the grease supplied, working it well into the ball tracks while twisting the joint, then locate the gaiter outer lip in its groove on the outer member

3.11g Fit the outer gaiter retaining clip and, using a hook fabricated out of welding rod and a pair of pliers, pull the clip tightly to remove all slack

3.11h Bend the clip end back over the buckle, then cut off the excess clip

3.11i Fold the clip end underneath the buckle . . .

3.11j . . . then fold the buckle firmly down onto the clip to secure the clip in position

3.11k Carefully lift the gaiter inner end to equalize air pressure in the gaiter, then secure the inner gaiter retaining clip in position using the same method

3.15a Release the inner gaiter retaining clips, and remove the joint outer member

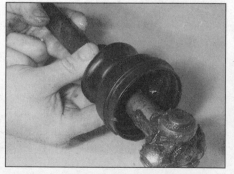

3.15b Slide the gaiter off the end of the driveshaft . . .

3.15c . . . and remove the plastic bush

captions carefully. Note that the hard plastic rings are not fitted to all gaiters, and the gaiter retaining clips supplied with the repair kit may be different to those shown in the sequence. To secure this other type of clip in position, lock the ends of the clip together, then remove any slack in the clip by carefully compressing the raised section of the clip using a pair of side cutters.

12 Check that the constant velocity joint moves freely in all directions, then refit the driveshaft to the car as described in Section 2.

Inner joint

13 Remove the outer constant velocity joint as described above in paragraphs 1 to 5.

14 Tape over the splines on the driveshaft, and carefully remove the outer constant velocity joint rubber gaiter, and the gaiter inner end plastic bush. It is recommended that the outer joint gaiter is also renewed, regardless of its apparent condition.

15 Release the retaining clips, then slide the gaiter off the shaft, and remove its plastic bush. As the gaiter is released, the joint outer member will also be freed from the end of the shaft **(see illustrations)**.

16 Thoroughly clean the joint using paraffin, or a suitable solvent, and dry it thoroughly. Check the tripod joint bearings and joint outer member for signs of wear, pitting or scuffing on their bearing surfaces. Check that the bearing rollers rotate smoothly and easily around the tripod joint, with no traces of roughness.

17 If on inspection, the tripod joint or outer member reveal signs of wear or damage, it will be necessary to renew the complete driveshaft assembly, since the joint is not available separately. If the joint is in satisfactory condition, obtain a repair kit consisting of a new gaiter, retaining clips, and the correct type and quantity of grease. Although not strictly necessary, it is also recommended that the outer constant velocity joint gaiter is renewed, regardless of its apparent condition.

18 On reassembly, pack the inner joint with the grease supplied in the gaiter kit. Work the grease well into the bearing tracks and rollers, while twisting the joint.

19 Clean the shaft, using emery cloth to remove any rust or sharp edges which may

damage the gaiter, then slide the plastic bush and inner joint gaiter along the driveshaft. Locate the plastic bush in its recess on the shaft, and seat the inner end of the gaiter on top of the bush.

20 Fit the outer member over the end of the shaft, and locate the gaiter in the groove on the joint outer member. Push the outer member onto the joint, so that its spring-loaded plunger is compressed, then lift the outer edge of the gaiter to equalise air pressure in the gaiter. Fit both the inner and outer retaining clips, securing them in position using the information given in paragraph 11. Ensure the gaiter retaining clips are securely tightened, then check that the joint moves freely in all directions.

21 Refit the outer constant velocity joint components using the information given above in paragraph 11.

4 Driveshaft overhaul - general information

1 If any of the checks described in Chapter 1 reveal wear in any driveshaft joint, first remove the roadwheel trim or centre cap (as appropriate). If the R-clip is fitted, the driveshaft nut should be correctly tightened; if in doubt, remove the R-clip and locking cap, and use a torque wrench to check that the nut is securely fastened. Once tightened, refit the locking cap and R-clip, then refit the centre cap or trim. Repeat this check on the remaining driveshaft nut. Refer to Section 2 for further information.

2 Road test the vehicle, and listen for a metallic clicking from the front as the vehicle is driven slowly in a circle on full-lock. If a clicking noise is heard, this indicates wear in the outer constant velocity joint. This means that the joint must be renewed; reconditioning is not possible.

3 If vibration, consistent with road speed, is felt through the car when accelerating, there is a possibility of wear in the inner constant velocity joints.

4 To check the joints for wear, remove the driveshafts, then dismantle them as described in Section 3; if any wear or free play is found, the affected joint must be renewed. In the case of the inner joints (and on some models,

the outer joints), this means that the complete driveshaft assembly must be renewed, as the joints are not available separately. Refer to your Citroën dealer for information on the availability of driveshaft components.

5 Right-hand driveshaft intermediate bearing - renewal

Note: A suitable bearing puller will be required, to draw the bearing and collar off the driveshaft end.

1 Remove the right-hand driveshaft as described in Section 2 of this Chapter.

2 Check that the bearing outer race rotates smoothly and easily, without any signs of roughness or undue free play between the inner and outer races. If necessary, renew the bearing as follows.

3 Using a long-reach universal bearing puller, carefully draw the collar and intermediate bearing off the driveshaft inner end **(see illustration)**. Apply a smear of grease to the inner race of the new bearing, then fit the bearing over the end of the driveshaft. Using a hammer and suitable piece of tubing which bears only on the bearing inner race, tap the new bearing into position on the driveshaft, until it abuts the constant velocity joint outer member. Once the bearing is correctly positioned, tap the bearing collar onto the shaft until it contacts the bearing inner race.

4 Check that the bearing rotates freely, then refit the driveshaft as described in Section 2.

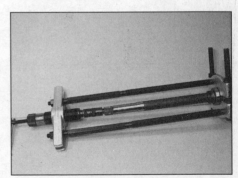

5.3 Using a long-reach bearing puller to remove the intermediate bearing from the right-hand driveshaft

Notes

Chapter 9 Braking system

Contents

Anti-lock Braking System (ABS) - general information 23
Anti-lock Braking System (ABS) components -
  removal and refitting 24
Brake pedal - removal and refitting 14
Front brake caliper - removal, overhaul and refitting 10
Front brake disc - inspection, removal and refitting 7
Front brake pad wear check .... See Chapter 1
Front brake pads - renewal 4
General information 1
Handbrake - adjustment 17
Handbrake cables - removal and refitting 19
Handbrake lever - removal and refitting 18
Hydraulic fluid level check ....See "Weekly checks"
Hydraulic fluid renewal .... See Chapter 1
Hydraulic pipes and hoses - renewal 3
Hydraulic system - bleeding 2
Master cylinder - removal, overhaul and refitting 13

Rear brake caliper - removal, overhaul and refitting 11
Rear brake disc - inspection, removal and refitting 8
Rear brake drum - removal, inspection and refitting 9
Rear brake pad wear check .... See Chapter 1
Rear brake pads - renewal 5
Rear brake pressure compensator (Estate models) -
  adjustment, removal and refitting 21
Rear brake pressure-regulating valves - removal and refitting 20
Rear brake shoe wear check .... See Chapter 1
Rear brake shoes - renewal 6
Rear wheel cylinder - removal and refitting 12
Stop-light switch - removal, refitting and adjustment 22
Vacuum pump - removal and refitting 25
Vacuum pump - testing and overhaul 26
Vacuum servo unit - testing, removal and refitting 15
Vacuum servo unit check valve - removal,
  testing and refitting 16

Degrees of difficulty

Easy, suitable for novice with little experience	**Fairly easy,** suitable for beginner with some experience	**Fairly difficult,** suitable for competent DIY mechanic	**Difficult,** suitable for experienced DIY mechanic	**Very difficult,** suitable for expert DIY or professional

Specifications

System type ...... Dual hydraulic circuit, split diagonally. Anti-lock braking system (ABS) available as an option. Front disc brakes on all models. Rear disc or drum brakes fitted to Hatchback models. Rear drum brakes on all Estate models. Vacuum servo-assistance on all models, vacuum provided by pump driven by camshaft (either direct-drive or belt-driven). Pressure compensator on Estate models. Cable-operated handbrake on rear brakes

ABS system
Wheel sensor-to-reluctor ring air gap .... 0.3 to 1.2 mm

Rear brakes
Type:
  Hatchback:
    Some higher-specification models, and all models with ABS .... Disc, with single-piston sliding caliper
    All other non-ABS models .... Single leading shoe drum
  Estate:
    ABS and non-ABS models .... Single leading shoe drum
Drum brakes:
  Drum diameter:
    Hatchback:
      New ...... 180 mm
      Maximum diameter after machining ...... 182 mm
    Estate:
      New ...... 228.6 mm
      Maximum diameter after machining ...... 229.8 mm
Disc brakes:
  Disc diameter ...... 247 mm
  Disc thickness:
    New ...... 8.0 mm
    Minimum thickness ...... 6.0 mm
  Maximum disc run-out ...... 0.2 mm
  Brake pad minimum thickness ...... 2.0 mm

Front brakes

Type	Disc, with single-piston sliding caliper
Disc diameter	247 mm
Disc thickness:	
New:	
Solid disc	10 mm
Ventilated disc	20.4 mm
Minimum thickness:	
Solid disc	8.0 mm
Ventilated disc	18.4 mm
Maximum disc run-out	0.2 mm
Brake pad minimum thickness	2.0 mm

Torque wrench settings

	Nm	lbf ft
Front brake caliper:		
Guide pin bolts (CJN48 caliper)	35	26
Mounting bracket-to-swivel hub bolts	120	89
Rear brake caliper mounting bolts	120	89
Rear hub nut:		
Models with rear drum brakes	200	148
Models with rear disc brakes	180	133
Master cylinder-to-servo unit nuts	10	7
Brake pedal pivot bolt	25	18
Pedal bracket retaining nuts	5	4
Vacuum servo unit mounting nuts	20	15
ABS wheel sensor retaining bolts	9	7
Roadwheel bolts	90	66

1 General information

The braking system is of the servo-assisted, dual-circuit hydraulic type. The arrangement of the hydraulic system is such that each circuit operates one front and one rear brake from a tandem master cylinder. Under normal circumstances, both circuits operate in unison. However, in the event of hydraulic failure in one circuit, full braking force will still be available at two wheels.

As with all Diesel engines, since there is insufficient vacuum in the inlet manifold to operate the braking system servo unit, a vacuum pump is fitted to the engine, to provide the required vacuum. Depending on the type of engine/transmission unit which is fitted to the vehicle, the pump is either mounted on the end of the cylinder head, and driven directly off the end of the camshaft, or it is mounted on the top of the transmission housing, and driven off the end of the camshaft via a drivebelt and pulley arrangement.

Some high-specification Hatchback models were equipped with disc brakes all round as standard, whereas all other Hatchback models not equipped with ABS were fitted with front disc brakes and rear drum brakes. Both ABS and non-ABS Estate models were equipped with rear drum brakes of a larger diameter than those fitted to Hatchback models. An Anti-lock Braking System (ABS) was offered as an option on all models; on models with ABS, disc brakes are fitted at both the front and rear.

The front disc brakes are actuated by single-piston sliding type calipers, which ensure that equal pressure is applied to each disc pad.

On models with rear drum brakes, the rear brakes incorporate leading and trailing shoes which are actuated by twin-piston wheel cylinders. The wheel cylinders incorporate integral pressure-regulating valves, which control the hydraulic pressure applied to the rear brakes. The regulating valves help to prevent rear wheel lock-up during emergency braking. A self-adjust mechanism is incorporated, to automatically compensate for brake shoe wear. As the brake shoe linings wear, the footbrake operation automatically operates the adjuster mechanism, which effectively lengthens the shoe strut and repositions the brake shoes to remove the lining-to-drum clearance.

On models with rear disc brakes, the brakes are actuated by single-piston sliding calipers which incorporate mechanical handbrake mechanisms. A pressure-regulating valve is situated in the brake line to each rear caliper. The regulating valve is similar to that fitted to the rear wheel cylinders (on rear drum brake models), and helps to prevent rear wheel lock-up during emergency braking. On Estate models, a braking system pressure compensator is incorporated. This varies the hydraulic pressure applied to the rear brakes, depending on the load carried.

On all models, the handbrake provides an independent mechanical means of rear brake application.

Note: *When servicing any part of the system, work carefully and methodically; also observe scrupulous cleanliness when overhauling any part of the hydraulic system. Always renew components (in axle sets, where applicable) if in doubt about their condition, and use only genuine Citroën replacement parts, or at least those of known good quality. Note the warnings given in "Safety first" and at relevant points in this Chapter concerning the dangers of asbestos dust and hydraulic fluid.*

2 Hydraulic system - bleeding

Note: *Hydraulic fluid is poisonous; wash off immediately and thoroughly in the case of skin contact, and seek immediate medical advice if any fluid is swallowed or gets into the eyes. Certain types of hydraulic fluid are inflammable, and may ignite when allowed into contact with hot components; when servicing any hydraulic system, it is safest to assume that the fluid is inflammable, and to take precautions against the risk of fire as though it is petrol that is being handled. Finally, it is hygroscopic (it absorbs moisture from the air) - old fluid may be contaminated and unfit for further use. When topping-up or renewing the fluid, always use the recommended type, and ensure that it comes from a freshly-opened sealed container.*

> **HAYNES HiNT** *Hydraulic fluid is an effective paint stripper, and will attack plastics; if any is spilt, it should be washed off immediately, using copious quantities of fresh water*

General

1 The correct operation of any hydraulic system is only possible after removing all air from the components and circuit; this is achieved by bleeding the system.
2 During the bleeding procedure, add only clean, unused hydraulic fluid of the recommended type; never re-use fluid that has already been bled from the system. Ensure that sufficient fluid is available before starting work.

3 If there is any possibility of incorrect fluid being already in the system, the brake components and circuit must be flushed completely with uncontaminated, correct fluid, and new seals should be fitted to the various components.

4 If hydraulic fluid has been lost from the system, or air has entered because of a leak, ensure that the fault is cured before proceeding further.

5 Park the vehicle on level ground, switch off the engine and select first or reverse gear, then chock the wheels and release the handbrake.

6 Check that all pipes and hoses are secure, unions tight and bleed screws closed. Clean any dirt from around the bleed screws.

7 Unscrew the master cylinder reservoir cap, and top the master cylinder reservoir up to the "MAX" level line; refit the cap loosely, and remember to maintain the fluid level at least above the "MIN" level line throughout the procedure, or there is a risk of further air entering the system.

8 There are a number of one-man, do-it-yourself brake bleeding kits currently available from motor accessory shops. It is recommended that one of these kits is used whenever possible, as they greatly simplify the bleeding operation, and also reduce the risk of expelled air and fluid being drawn back into the system. If such a kit is not available, the basic (two-man) method must be used, which is described in detail below.

9 If a kit is to be used, prepare the vehicle as described previously, and follow the kit manufacturer's instructions, as the procedure may vary slightly according to the type being used; generally, they are as outlined below in the relevant sub-section.

10 Whichever method is used, the same sequence must be followed (paras 11 and 12) to ensure the removal of all air from the system.

Bleeding sequence

11 If the system has been only partially disconnected, and suitable precautions were taken to minimise fluid loss, it should be necessary only to bleed that part of the system (ie the primary or secondary circuit).

12 If the complete system is to be bled, then it should be done working in the following sequence:

Non-ABS models
(a) Left-hand rear brake.
(b) Right-hand front brake.
(c) Right-hand rear brake.
(d) Left-hand front brake.

ABS models
(a) Left-hand front brake.
(b) Right-hand front brake.
(c) Left-hand rear brake.
(d) Right-hand rear brake.

Note: *If difficulty is experienced in bleeding the braking circuit on models with ABS, try bleeding the complete system working in the reverse of the specified sequence, starting*

with the right-hand rear brake and finishing with the left-hand front brake.

Bleeding - basic (two-man) method

13 Collect a clean glass jar, a suitable length of plastic or rubber tubing which is a tight fit over the bleed screw, and a ring spanner to fit the screw. The help of an assistant will also be required.

14 Remove the dust cap from the first screw in the sequence. Fit the spanner and tube to the screw, place the other end of the tube in the jar, and pour in sufficient fluid to cover the end of the tube.

15 Ensure that the master cylinder reservoir fluid level is maintained at least above the "MIN" level line throughout the procedure.

16 Have the assistant fully depress the brake pedal several times to build up pressure, then maintain it on the final stroke.

17 While pedal pressure is maintained, unscrew the bleed screw (approximately one turn) and allow the compressed fluid and air to flow into the jar. The assistant should maintain pedal pressure, following it down to the floor if necessary, and should not release it until instructed to do so. When the flow stops, tighten the bleed screw again, release the pedal slowly, and recheck the reservoir fluid level.

18 Repeat the steps given in paragraphs 16 and 17 until the fluid emerging from the bleed screw is free from air bubbles. If the master cylinder has been drained and refilled, and air is being bled from the first screw in the sequence, allow approximately five seconds between cycles for the master cylinder passages to refill.

19 When no more air bubbles appear, tighten the bleed screw securely, remove the tube and spanner, and refit the dust cap. Do not overtighten the bleed screw.

20 Repeat the procedure on the remaining screws in the sequence, until all air is removed from the system and the brake pedal feels firm again.

Bleeding - using a one-way valve kit

21 As their name implies, these kits consist of a length of tubing with a one-way valve fitted, to prevent expelled air and fluid being drawn back into the system; some kits include a translucent container, which can be positioned so that the air bubbles can be more easily seen flowing from the end of the tube.

22 The kit is connected to the bleed screw, which is then opened. The user returns to the driver's seat, depresses the brake pedal with a smooth, steady stroke, and slowly releases it; this is repeated until the expelled fluid is clear of air bubbles **(see illustration)**.

23 Note that these kits simplify work so much that it is easy to forget the master cylinder reservoir fluid level; ensure that this is maintained at least above the "MIN" level line at all times.

2.22 Bleeding a rear brake caliper using a one-way valve kit

Bleeding - using a pressure-bleeding kit

24 These kits are usually operated by the reservoir of pressurised air contained in the spare tyre. However, note that it will probably be necessary to reduce the pressure to a lower limit than normal; refer to the instructions supplied with the kit.

25 By connecting a pressurised, fluid-filled container to the master cylinder reservoir, bleeding can be carried out simply by opening each screw in turn (in the specified sequence), and allowing the fluid to flow out until no more air bubbles can be seen in the expelled fluid.

26 This method has the advantage that the large reservoir of fluid provides an additional safeguard against air being drawn into the system during bleeding.

27 Pressure-bleeding is particularly effective when bleeding "difficult" systems, or when bleeding the complete system at the time of routine fluid renewal.

All methods

28 When bleeding is complete, and firm pedal feel is restored, wash off any spilt fluid, tighten the bleed screws securely, and refit their dust caps.

29 Check the hydraulic fluid level, and top-up if necessary (*"Weekly checks"*).

30 Discard any hydraulic fluid that has been bled from the system; it will not be fit for re-use.

31 Check the feel of the brake pedal. If it feels at all spongy, air must still be present in the system, and further bleeding is required. Failure to bleed satisfactorily after a reasonable repetition of the bleeding procedure may be due to worn master cylinder seals.

3 Hydraulic pipes and hoses - renewal

Note: *Before starting work, refer to the note at the beginning of Section 2 concerning the dangers of hydraulic fluid.*

1 If any pipe or hose is to be renewed, minimise fluid loss by first removing the master cylinder reservoir cap, then tightening it down onto a piece of polythene to obtain an

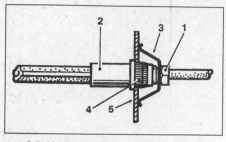

3.2 Hydraulic pipe-to-flexible hose connection

1 Union nut   4 Splined end fitting
2 Flexible hose   5 Mounting bracket
3 Spring clip support

4.2 Disconnecting the pad wear sensor wiring from its connector

4.4 On the CJN48 caliper, retain the guide pin with an open-ended spanner whilst slackening the guide pin bolt

airtight seal. Alternatively, flexible hoses can be sealed, if required, using a proprietary brake hose clamp; metal brake pipe unions can be plugged (if care is taken not to allow dirt into the system) or capped immediately they are disconnected. Place a wad of rag under any union that is to be disconnected, to catch any spilt fluid.

2 If a flexible hose is to be disconnected, unscrew the brake pipe union nut before removing the spring clip which secures the hose to its mounting bracket **(see illustration)**.

3 To unscrew the union nuts, it is preferable to obtain a brake pipe spanner of the correct size; these are available from most large motor accessory shops. Failing this, a close-fitting open-ended spanner will be required, though if the nuts are tight or corroded, their flats may be rounded-off if the spanner slips. In such a case, a self-locking wrench is often the only way to unscrew a stubborn union, but it follows that the pipe and the damaged nuts must be renewed on reassembly. Always clean a union and surrounding area before disconnecting it. If disconnecting a component with more than one union, make a careful note of the connections before disturbing any of them.

4 If a brake pipe is to be renewed, it can be obtained, cut to length and with the union nuts and end flares in place, from Citroën dealers. All that is then necessary is to bend it to shape, following the line of the original, before fitting it to the car. Alternatively, most

motor accessory shops can make up brake pipes from kits, but this requires very careful measurement of the original, to ensure that the replacement is of the correct length. The safest answer is usually to take the original to the shop as a pattern.

5 On refitting, do not overtighten the union nuts. It is not necessary to exercise brute force to obtain a sound joint.

6 Ensure that the pipes and hoses are correctly routed, with no kinks, and that they are secured in the clips or brackets provided. After fitting, remove the polythene from the reservoir, and bleed the hydraulic system as described in Section 2. Wash off any spilt fluid, and check carefully for fluid leaks.

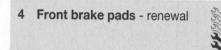

4 Front brake pads - renewal

⚠️ *Warning: Renew both sets of front brake pads at the same time - never renew the pads on only one wheel, as uneven braking may result. Note that the dust created by wear of the pads may contain asbestos, which is a health hazard. Never blow it out with compressed air, and don't inhale any of it. An approved filtering mask should be worn when working on the brakes. DO NOT use petrol or petroleum-based solvents to clean brake parts; use brake cleaner or methylated spirit only.*

1 Apply the handbrake, then jack up the front of the vehicle and support it on axle stands. Remove the front roadwheels.

2 Trace the brake pad wear sensor wiring back from the pads, and disconnect it from the wiring connector **(see illustration)**. Note the routing of the wiring, and free it from any relevant retaining clips.

3 Push the piston into its bore by pulling the caliper outwards. There are two different types of front brake caliper fitted to the models covered in this manual. The Girling CJN48 caliper has only a small aperture to view the pads through, whereas on the Girling J48 caliper, the whole pad can be viewed from the top of the caliper, the pads being retained by two pins. Identify the caliper type, and proceed as described under the relevant sub-heading.

Girling CJN48 caliper

4 Slacken and remove the upper and lower caliper guide pin bolts, using a slim open-ended spanner to prevent the guide pin itself from rotating **(see illustration)**. Where possible, new guide pin bolts should be used on refitting, otherwise clean the old ones thoroughly.

5 With the guide pin bolts removed, lift the caliper away from the brake pads and mounting bracket, and tie it to the suspension strut using a suitable piece of wire. Do not allow the caliper to hang unsupported on the flexible brake hose.

6 Withdraw the two brake pads from the caliper mounting bracket, and examine them as follows.

7 First measure the thickness of the friction material of each brake pad **(see illustration)**. If either pad is worn at any point to the specified minimum thickness or less, all four pads must be renewed as a complete set. Also, the pads should be renewed if any are fouled with oil or grease; there is no satisfactory way of degreasing friction material, once contaminated. If any of the brake pads are worn unevenly, or fouled with oil or grease, trace and rectify the cause before reassembly. New brake pad kits are available from Citroën dealers.

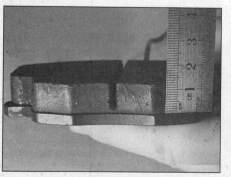

4.7 Measuring brake pad friction material thickness

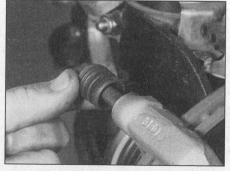

4.9 Whilst the caliper is removed, check the condition of the guide pins and gaiters

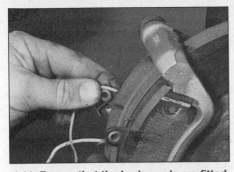

4.11 Ensure that the brake pads are fitted the correct way round, with friction material facing the disc . . .

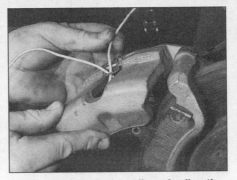

4.12 . . . then refit the caliper, feeding the pad wiring through the caliper aperture

4.18 On J48 caliper, note the correct fitted positions of pads and pad springs prior to removal

8 If the brake pads are still serviceable, carefully clean them using a clean, fine wire brush or similar, paying particular attention to the sides and back of the metal backing. Clean out the grooves in the friction material, and pick out any large embedded particles of dirt or debris. Carefully clean the pad locations in the caliper body/mounting bracket.

9 Prior to fitting the pads, check that the guide pins are free to slide easily in the caliper body/mounting bracket, and check that the rubber guide pin gaiters are undamaged **(see illustration)**. Brush the dust and dirt from the caliper and piston, but **do not** inhale it, as it is injurious to health. Inspect the dust seal around the piston for damage, and the piston for evidence of fluid leaks, corrosion or damage. If attention to any of these components is necessary, refer to Section 10.

10 If new brake pads are to be fitted, the caliper piston must be pushed back into the cylinder to make room for them. Either use a G-clamp or similar tool, or use suitable pieces of wood as levers. Provided that the master cylinder reservoir has not been overfilled with hydraulic fluid, there should be no spillage, but keep a careful watch on the fluid level while retracting the piston. If the fluid level rises above the "MAX" level line at any time, the surplus should be syphoned off, or ejected via a plastic tube connected to the bleed screw (see Section 2). **Note:** *Do not syphon the fluid by mouth, as it is poisonous; use a syringe or an old poultry baster.*

11 Install the pads in the caliper mounting bracket, ensuring that the friction material of each pad is against the brake disc **(see illustration)**.

12 Position the caliper over the pads, and pass the pad warning sensor wiring through the caliper aperture and underneath the retaining clip **(see illustration)**. If the threads of the guide pin bolts are not already coated with locking compound, apply a suitable thread-locking compound to them. Press the caliper into position, then install the guide pin bolts, tightening them to the specified torque setting whilst retaining the guide pins with an open-ended spanner.

13 Reconnect the brake pad wear sensor wiring connectors, ensuring that the wiring is correctly routed through the loop of the caliper bleed screw cap.

14 Depress the brake pedal repeatedly until the pads are pressed into firm contact with the brake disc, and normal (non-assisted) pedal pressure is restored.

15 Repeat the above procedure on the remaining front brake caliper.

16 Refit the roadwheels, then lower the vehicle to the ground and tighten the roadwheel bolts to the specified torque setting.

17 Check the hydraulic fluid level as described in *"Weekly checks"*.

Girling J48 caliper

18 Prior to removing the pads, make a note the correct fitted positions of the pad springs,

noting the difference between the inner and outer pad **(see illustration)**.

19 Using a small screwdriver, prise the pad retaining pin spring clip out of each pin, and remove the clip. Also prise the inner pad anti-rattle spring off the pad retaining pin.

20 Using a hammer and pin punch, tap both the pad retaining pins out of the caliper.

21 Using pliers if necessary, withdraw the inner and outer pads from the caliper body, along with the pad shim (were fitted).

22 Examine the pads and caliper as described above in paragraphs 7 to 10. If there are signs of corrosion on the pad retaining pins, these should also be renewed, along with their retaining clips; these components are available as a kit from Citroën dealers.

23 Slide the pads into position in the caliper body, ensuring that the inner and outer pads are fitted in their correct positions, and the pad shim (where fitted) is correctly positioned. Also ensure that the friction material of each pad is facing the disc.

24 Slide the pad retaining pins into the caliper and through the brake pad holes, and tap them fully into position. Ensure that the outer pad anti-rattle spring is correctly positioned underneath both retaining pins, and the inner pad anti-rattle spring is clipped onto the relevant pin **(see illustrations)**.

25 Secure the retaining pins in position with the spring clip, ensuring the clip ends are correctly located in the retaining pin holes **(see illustration)**.

4.24a Tap in the retaining pins, ensuring that the outer pad anti-rattle spring (arrowed) is correctly located underneath both pins . . .

4.24b . . . then clip the inner pad anti-rattle spring onto the retaining pin

4.25 Ensure the retaining pin spring clip ends are correctly located in the pin holes (arrowed)

5.2a Extract the spring clip . . .

5.2b . . . then slide out the pad retaining plate . . .

5.3 . . . and withdraw the brake pads from the caliper

26 Pass both the pad wear warning sensor wires underneath the retaining pin spring clip, and reconnect them to the wiring connector.

27 Depress the brake pedal repeatedly until the pads are pressed into firm contact with the brake disc, and normal (non-assisted) pedal pressure is restored.

28 Repeat the above procedure on the remaining front brake caliper.

29 Refit the roadwheels, then lower the vehicle to the ground and tighten the roadwheel bolts to the specified torque setting.

30 Check the hydraulic fluid level as described in *"Weekly checks"*.

5 Rear brake pads - renewal

⚠ *Warning: Renew both sets of rear brake pads at the same time - never renew the pads on only one wheel, as uneven braking may result. Note that the dust created by wear of the pads may contain asbestos, which is a health hazard. Never blow it out with compressed air, and don't inhale any of it. An approved filtering mask should be worn when working on the brakes. DO NOT use petrol or petroleum-based solvents to clean brake parts; use brake cleaner or methylated spirit only.*

1 Chock the front wheels, then jack up the rear of the vehicle and support it on axle stands. Remove the rear wheels.

2 Extract the small spring clip from the pad retaining plate, and then slide the plate out of the caliper **(see illustrations)**. Discard the spring clip - a new one must be used on refitting.

3 Using pliers if necessary, withdraw both the inner and outer pads from the caliper **(see illustration)**. Make a note of the correct fitted position of the anti-rattle springs, and remove the springs from each pad.

4 First measure the thickness of the friction material of each brake pad. If either pad is worn at any point to the specified minimum thickness or less, all four pads must be renewed. Also, the pads should be renewed if any are fouled with oil or grease; there is no satisfactory way of degreasing friction material, once contaminated. If any of the brake pads are worn unevenly, or fouled with oil or grease, trace and rectify the cause before reassembly. New brake pads and spring kits are available from Citroën dealers.

5 If the brake pads are still serviceable, carefully clean them using a clean, fine wire brush or similar, paying particular attention to the sides and back of the metal backing. Clean out the grooves in the friction material, and pick out any large embedded particles of dirt or debris. Carefully clean the pad locations in the caliper body/mounting bracket.

6 Prior to fitting the pads, check that the guide sleeves are free to slide easily in the caliper body, and check that the rubber guide sleeve gaiters are undamaged. Brush the dust and dirt from the caliper and piston, but **do**

not inhale it, as it is injurious to health. Inspect the dust seal around the piston for damage, and the piston for evidence of fluid leaks, corrosion or damage. If attention to any of these components is necessary, refer to Section 11.

7 If new brake pads are to be fitted, it will be necessary to retract the piston fully into the caliper bore, by rotating it in a clockwise direction. This can be achieved using a suitable square-section bar, such as the shaft of a screwdriver, which locates snugly in the caliper piston slots **(see illustration)**. Provided that the master cylinder reservoir has not been overfilled with hydraulic fluid, there should be no spillage, but keep a careful watch on the fluid level while retracting the piston. If the fluid level rises above the "MAX" level line at any time, the surplus should be syphoned off, or ejected via a plastic tube connected to the bleed screw (see Section 2). **Note:** *Do not syphon the fluid by mouth, as it is poisonous; use a syringe or an old poultry baster.*

8 Position the caliper piston so that its piston slot is horizontal; this is necessary to ensure that the lug on the inner pad will locate with the caliper piston slot on installation **(see illustration)**.

9 The brake pad with the lug on its backing plate is the inner pad. Refit the anti-rattle springs to the pads, so that when the pads are installed in the caliper, the spring end will be located at the opposite end of the pad, in relation to the pad retaining plate **(see illustration)**.

5.7 Retract the piston using a square-section bar . . .

5.8 . . . and position the piston so that its slot (arrowed) is horizontal to the ground

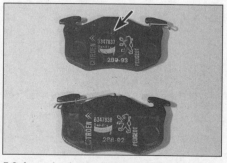

5.9 Inner brake pad can be identified by its locating lug (arrowed). Note the correct fitted positions of the anti-rattle springs

10 Locate the outer brake pad in the caliper body, ensuring that its friction material is against the brake disc. Slide the inner pad into position in the caliper, ensuring that the lug on its backing plate is aligned with the slot in the caliper piston (**see illustration**).

11 Ensure that the anti-rattle spring ends on both pads are correctly positioned, then slide the retaining plate into place, and secure it in position with a new spring clip. It may be necessary to file an entry chamfer on the edge of the retaining plate, to enable it to be fitted without difficulty.

12 Depress the brake pedal repeatedly until the pads are pressed into firm contact with the brake disc, and normal (non-assisted) pedal pressure is restored. Check that the inner pad lug is correctly engaged with one of the caliper piston slots.

13 Repeat the above procedure on the remaining rear brake caliper.

14 Check the handbrake cable adjustment as described in Section 17, then refit the roadwheels and lower the vehicle to the ground. Tighten the roadwheel bolts to the specified torque setting.

15 Check the hydraulic fluid level as described in "Weekly checks".

6 Rear brake shoes - renewal

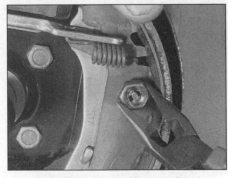

5.10 Install the inner pad, ensuring its locating lug is correctly engaged in the piston slot

⚠️ **Warning: Brake shoes must be renewed on both rear wheels at the same time - never renew the shoes on only one wheel, as uneven braking may result. Also, the dust created by wear of the shoes may contain asbestos, which is a health hazard. Never blow it out with compressed air, and don't inhale any of it. An approved filtering mask should be worn when working on the brakes. DO NOT use petrol or petroleum-based solvents to clean brake parts; use brake cleaner or methylated spirit only.**

1 Remove the brake drum as described in Section 9.

2 Working carefully, and taking the necessary precautions, remove all traces of brake dust from the brake drum, backplate and shoes.

3 Measure the thickness of the friction material of each brake shoe at several points; if either shoe is worn at any point to the specified minimum thickness or less, all four shoes must be renewed as a set. The shoes should also be renewed if any are fouled with oil or grease; there is no satisfactory way of degreasing friction material, once contaminated.

4 If any of the brake shoes are worn unevenly, or fouled with oil or grease, trace and rectify the cause before reassembly.

5 To renew the brake shoes, proceed as described under the relevant sub-heading.

Bendix brake shoes - Hatchback

6 Using a pair of pliers, remove the shoe retainer spring cups by depressing and turning them through 90° (**see illustrations**). With the cups removed, lift off the springs and withdraw the retainer pins.

7 Ease the shoes out one at a time from the lower pivot point, to release the tension of the return spring, then disconnect the lower return spring from both shoes (**see illustration**).

8 Ease the upper end of both shoes out from their wheel cylinder locations, taking great care not to damage the wheel cylinder seals, and disconnect the handbrake cable from the trailing shoe. The brake shoe and adjuster strut assembly can then be manoeuvred out of position and away from the backplate. Do not depress the brake pedal until the brakes are reassembled; wrap a strong elastic band around the wheel cylinder pistons to retain them.

9 With the shoe and adjuster strut assembly on a bench, make a note of the correct fitted positions of the springs and adjuster strut, to use as a guide for reassembly. Release the handbrake lever stop-peg (if not already done), then carefully detach the adjuster strut bolt retaining spring from the leading shoe. Disconnect the upper return spring, then detach the leading shoe and return spring from the trailing shoe and strut assembly. Unhook the spring securing the adjuster strut to the trailing shoe, and separate the two.

10 If genuine Citroën brake shoes are being installed, it will be necessary to remove the handbrake lever from the original trailing shoe,

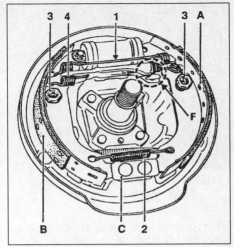

6.6a Correct fitted positions of the Bendix rear brake components

A Leading shoe
B Trailing shoe
C Lower pivot point
F Adjuster strut mechanism
1 Upper return spring
2 Lower return spring
3 Retaining pin, spring and spring cup
4 Adjuster strut-to-trailing shoe spring

and install it on the new shoe. Secure the lever in position with a new retaining clip. All return springs should be renewed, regardless of their apparent condition; spring kits are also available from Citroën dealers.

11 Withdraw the adjuster bolt from the strut, and carefully examine the assembly for signs of wear or damage. Pay particular attention to the threads of the adjuster bolt and the knurled adjuster wheel, and renew if necessary. Note that left-hand and right-hand struts are not interchangeable - they are marked "G" (gauche) and "D" (droit) respectively. Also note that the strut adjuster bolts are not interchangeable; the left-hand strut bolt has a left-handed thread, and the right-hand bolt a right-handed thread.

12 Ensure the components on the end of the strut are correctly positioned, then apply a little high-melting-point grease to the threads

6.6b Removing a shoe retainer spring cup

6.7 On Bendix rear brake shoes, ease the shoes out of the lower pivot point, and disconnect the lower return spring

6.12 Correct fitted position of Bendix adjuster strut components

6.16 Apply a little high-melting-point grease to the shoe contact points on the backplate

of the adjuster bolt **(see illustration)**. Screw the adjuster wheel onto the bolt until only a small gap exists between the wheel and the head of the bolt, then install the bolt in the strut.

13 Fit the adjuster strut retaining spring to the trailing shoe, ensuring that the shorter hook of the spring is engaged with the shoe. Attach the adjuster strut to the spring end, then ease the strut into position in its slot in the trailing shoe.

14 Engage the upper return spring with the trailing shoe, then hook the leading shoe onto the other end of the spring, and lever the leading shoe down until the adjuster bolt head

is correctly located in its groove. Once the bolt is correctly located, hook its retaining spring into the slot on the leading shoe.

15 Peel back the rubber protective caps, and check the wheel cylinder for fluid leaks or other damage; check that both cylinder pistons are free to move easily. Refer to Section 12, if necessary, for information on wheel cylinder renewal.

16 Prior to installation, clean the backplate, and apply a thin smear of high-temperature brake grease or anti-seize compound to all those surfaces of the backplate which bear on the shoes, particularly the wheel cylinder pistons and lower pivot point **(see illustration)**. Do not allow the lubricant to foul the friction material.

17 Ensure the handbrake lever stop-peg is correctly located against the edge of the trailing shoe, and remove the elastic band fitted to the wheel cylinder.

18 Manoeuvre the shoe and strut assembly into position on the vehicle, and locate the upper end of both shoes with the wheel cylinder pistons. Attach the handbrake cable to the trailing shoe lever. Fit the lower return spring to both shoes, and ease the shoes into position on the lower pivot point.

19 Tap the shoes to centralise them with the backplate, then refit the shoe retainer pins and springs, and secure them in position with the spring cups.

20 Using a screwdriver, turn the strut adjuster wheel to expand the shoes until the brake drum just slides over the shoes.

21 Refit the brake drum as described in Section 9.

22 Repeat the above procedure on the remaining rear brake.

23 Once both sets of rear shoes have been renewed, adjust the lining-to-drum clearance by repeatedly depressing the brake pedal. Whilst depressing the pedal, have an assistant listen to the rear drums, to check that the adjuster strut is functioning correctly; if so, a clicking sound will be emitted by the strut as the pedal is depressed.

24 Check and, if necessary, adjust the handbrake as described in Section 17.

25 On completion, check the hydraulic fluid level as described in *"Weekly checks"*.

Bendix brake shoes - Estate

26 Although of larger diameter, the Bendix rear drum brake assembly fitted to the Estate model is generally similar to that fitted to the Hatchback and a similar renewal procedure should be followed **(see illustration)**.

27 To remove each shoe retainer spring, use a close fitting rod to slightly tilt the spring so that it disconnects from its retaining bracket **(see illustration)**.

Girling brake shoes

28 Make a note of the correct fitted positions

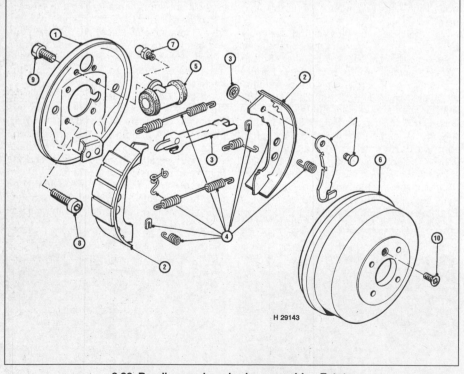

H 29143

6.26 Bendix rear drum brake assembly - Estate

1 *Brake plate*	5 *Wheel cylinder*	8 *Screw*
2 *Brake shoe*	6 *Brake drum*	9 *Bolt*
3 *Spacer*	7 *Bleed screw*	10 *Screw*
4 *Spring set*		

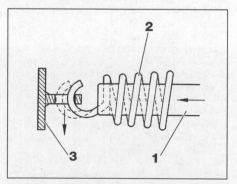

6.27 Use a close fitting rod (1) to slightly tilt each shoe retainer spring (2) so that it disconnects from its retaining bracket (3)

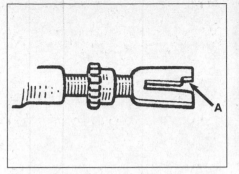

6.39 On Girling rear brake shoes, adjuster strut fork cut-out (A) must engage with leading shoe adjusting lever on refitting

7.3 Using a micrometer to measure disc thickness

7.4 Checking disc run-out using a dial gauge

of the springs and adjuster strut, to use as a guide on reassembly.

29 Carefully unhook both the upper and lower return springs, and remove them from the brake shoes.

30 Using a pair of pliers, remove the leading shoe retainer spring cup by depressing it and turning through 90°. With the cup removed, lift off the spring, then withdraw the retainer pin and remove the shoe from the backplate. Unhook the adjusting lever spring, and remove it from the leading shoe.

31 Detach the adjuster strut, and remove it from the trailing shoe.

32 Remove the trailing shoe retainer spring cup, spring and pin as described above, then detach the handbrake cable and remove the shoe from the vehicle. Do not depress the brake pedal until the brakes are reassembled; wrap a strong elastic band around the wheel cylinder pistons to retain them.

33 If genuine Citroën brake shoes are being installed, it will be necessary to remove the adjusting lever from the original leading shoe, and install it on the new shoe. All return springs should be renewed, regardless of their apparent condition; spring kits are also available from Citroën dealers.

34 Withdraw the forked end from the strut, and carefully examine the assembly for signs of wear or damage. Pay particular attention to the threads and the knurled adjuster wheel, and renew if necessary. Note that left-hand and right-hand struts are not interchangeable; the left-hand fork has a right-handed thread, and the right-hand fork a left-handed thread.

35 Peel back the rubber protective caps, and check the wheel cylinder for fluid leaks or other damage; check that both cylinder pistons are free to move easily. Refer to Section 12, if necessary, for information on wheel cylinder renewal.

36 Prior to installation, clean the backplate, and apply a thin smear of high-temperature brake grease or anti-seize compound to all those surfaces of the backplate which bear on the shoes, particularly the wheel cylinder pistons and lower pivot point. Do not allow the lubricant to foul the friction material.

37 Ensure the handbrake lever stop-peg is correctly located against the edge of the trailing shoe, and remove the elastic band fitted to the wheel cylinder.

38 Locate the upper end of the trailing shoe in the wheel cylinder piston, then refit the retainer pin and spring, and secure it in position with the spring cup. Connect the handbrake cable to the lever.

39 Screw in the adjuster wheel until the minimum strut length is obtained, then hook the strut into position on the trailing shoe. Rotate the adjuster strut forked end, so that the cut-out of the fork will engage with the leading shoe adjusting lever once the shoe is installed **(see illustration)**.

40 Fit the spring to the leading shoe adjusting lever, so that the shorter hook of the spring engages with the lever.

41 Slide the leading shoe assembly into position, ensuring that it is correctly engaged with the adjuster strut fork, and that the fork cut-out is engaged with the adjusting lever. Ensure the upper end of the shoe is located in the wheel cylinder piston, then secure the shoe in position with the retainer pin, spring and spring cup.

42 Install the upper and lower return springs, then tap the shoes to centralise them with the backplate.

43 Using a screwdriver, turn the strut adjuster wheel to expand the shoes until the brake drum just slides over the shoes.

44 Refit the brake drum as described in Section 9.

45 Repeat the above procedure on the remaining rear brake.

46 Once both sets of rear shoes have been renewed, adjust the lining-to-drum clearance by repeatedly depressing the brake pedal. Whilst depressing the pedal, have an assistant listen to the rear drums, to check that the adjuster strut is functioning correctly; if so, a clicking sound will be emitted by the strut as the pedal is depressed.

47 Check and, if necessary, adjust the handbrake as described in Section 17.

48 On completion, check the hydraulic fluid level as described in "Weekly checks".

7 Front brake disc - inspection, removal and refitting

Note: *Before starting work, refer to the note at the beginning of Section 4 concerning the dangers of asbestos dust.*

Inspection

Note: *If either disc requires renewal, BOTH should be renewed at the same time, to ensure even and consistent braking.*

1 Firmly apply the handbrake, then jack up the front of the car and support it on axle stands. Remove the appropriate front roadwheel.

2 Slowly rotate the brake disc so that the full area of both sides can be checked; remove the brake pads if better access is required to the inboard surface. Light scoring is normal in the area swept by the brake pads, but if heavy scoring is found, the disc must be renewed.

3 It is normal to find a lip of rust and brake dust around the disc's perimeter; this can be scraped off if required. If, however, a lip has formed due to excessive wear of the brake pad swept area, then the disc's thickness must be measured using a micrometer **(see illustration)**. Take measurements at several places around the disc, at the inside and outside of the pad swept area; if the disc has worn at any point to the specified minimum thickness or less, the disc must be renewed.

4 If the disc is thought to be warped, it can be checked for run-out. Either use a dial gauge mounted on any convenient fixed point, while the disc is slowly rotated, or use feeler gauges to measure (at several points all around the disc) the clearance between the disc and a fixed point, such as the caliper mounting bracket **(see illustration)**. If the measurements obtained are at the specified maximum or beyond, the disc is excessively warped, and must be renewed; however, it is worth checking first that the hub bearing is in good condition (Chapters 1 and/or 10). Also try the effect of removing the disc and turning it through 180°, to reposition it on the hub; if the run-out is still excessive, the disc must be renewed.

5 Check the disc for cracks, especially

7.6a Undo the two mounting bolts . . .

7.6b . . . then slide the caliper assembly off the disc . . .

7.6c . . . and tie it to the suspension strut, to avoid placing any strain on the flexible hose

around the wheel bolt holes, and any other wear or damage, and renew if necessary.

Removal

6 Unscrew the two bolts securing the brake caliper to the swivel hub, and discard them - new bolts must be used on refitting. Slacken and remove the bolt securing the wiring retaining bracket to the swivel hub, then slide the caliper assembly off the disc. Using a piece of wire or string, tie the caliper to the front suspension coil spring, to avoid placing any strain on the hydraulic brake hose **(see illustrations)**.

7 Use chalk or paint to mark the relationship of the disc to the hub, then remove the screws securing the brake disc to the hub, and remove the disc **(see illustration)**. If it is tight, lightly tap its rear face with a hide or plastic mallet.

Refitting

8 Refitting is the reverse of the removal procedure, noting the following points:
(a) Ensure that the mating surfaces of the disc and hub are clean and flat.
(b) Align (if applicable) the marks made on removal, and securely tighten the disc retaining screws.
(c) If a new disc has been fitted, use a suitable solvent to wipe any preservative coating from the disc, before refitting the caliper.
(d) If the threads of the new caliper mounting bolts are not already pre-coated with

locking compound, apply a suitable locking compound to them. Refit the caliper, and tighten the mounting bolts to the specified torque setting **(see illustration)**.
(e) Refit the roadwheel, then lower the vehicle to the ground and tighten the roadwheel bolts to the specified torque. On completion, repeatedly depress the brake pedal until normal (non-assisted) pedal pressure returns.

8 Rear brake disc - inspection, removal and refitting

Note: Before starting work, refer to the note at the beginning of Section 5 concerning the dangers of asbestos dust.

Inspection

Note: If either disc requires renewal, BOTH should be renewed at the same time, to ensure even and consistent braking.

1 Firmly chock the front wheels, then jack up the rear of the car and support it on axle stands. Remove the appropriate rear roadwheel.
2 Inspect the disc as described in paragraphs 2 to 5 of Section 7.

Removal

3 Remove the brake pads as described in paragraphs 2 and 3 of Section 5.

4 Use chalk or paint to mark the relationship of the disc to the hub, then remove the screw securing the brake disc to the hub, and remove the disc **(see illustration)**. If it is tight, lightly tap its rear face with a hide or plastic mallet.

Refitting

5 Refitting is the reverse of the removal procedure, noting the following points:
(a) Ensure that the mating surfaces of the disc and hub are clean and flat.
(b) Align (if applicable) the marks made on removal, and securely tighten the disc retaining screws.
(c) If a new disc has been fitted, use a suitable solvent to wipe any preservative coating from the disc, before refitting the caliper.
(d) Refit the brake pads as described in paragraphs 8 to 12 of Section 5.
(e) Refit the roadwheel, then lower the vehicle to the ground and tighten the roadwheel bolts to the specified torque.

9 Rear brake drum - removal, inspection and refitting

Note: Before starting work, refer to the note at the beginning of Section 6 concerning the dangers of asbestos dust.

7.7 Undo the two retaining screws and remove the disc

7.8 On refitting, tighten the caliper mounting bolts to the specified torque setting

8.4 Removing the rear brake disc

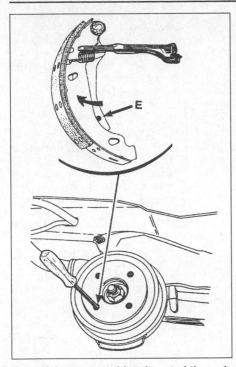

9.6a Using a screwdriver inserted through the brake drum to release the handbrake operating lever

E Handbrake operating lever stop-peg location

Removal

1 Chock the front wheels, then jack up the rear of the vehicle and support it on axle stands. Remove the appropriate rear wheel.
2 Using a hammer and suitable large flat-bladed screwdriver, carefully tap and prise the cap out of the centre of the brake drum. Discard the cap - a new one must be used on refitting. Using a hammer and suitable chisel-nosed tool, tap up the staking securing the hub retaining nut to the groove in the stub axle.
3 Using a socket and long bar, slacken and remove the rear hub nut, and withdraw the thrustwasher. Discard the hub nut - a new nut must used on refitting.
4 It should now be possible to withdraw the brake drum and hub bearing assembly from the stub axle by hand. It may be difficult to remove the drum due to the tightness of the hub bearing on the stub axle, or due to the brake shoes binding on the inner circumference of the drum. If the brake shoes are binding, first check that the handbrake is fully released, then proceed as follows.

> **HAYNES HINT** *If the bearing is tight, tap the periphery of the drum using a hide or plastic mallet, or use a universal puller, secured to the drum with the wheel bolts, to pull it off.*

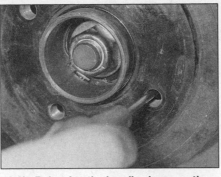

9.6b Releasing the handbrake operating lever

5 Referring to Section 17 for further information, fully slacken the handbrake cable adjuster nut, to obtain maximum free play in the cable.
6 Insert a screwdriver through one of the wheel bolt holes in the brake drum, so that it contacts the handbrake operating lever on the trailing brake shoe. Push the lever until the stop-peg slips behind the brake shoe web, allowing the brake shoes to retract fully **(see illustrations)**. The brake drum can now be withdrawn, and the seal slid off the stub axle.

Inspection

Note: *If either drum requires renewal, BOTH should be renewed at the same time, to ensure even and consistent braking.*
7 Working carefully, remove all traces of brake dust from the drum, but *avoid inhaling the dust, as it is injurious to health.*
8 Scrub clean the outside of the drum, and check it for obvious signs of wear or damage, such as cracks around the roadwheel bolt holes; renew the drum if necessary.
9 Examine carefully the inside of the drum. Light scoring of the friction surface is normal, but if heavy scoring is found, the drum must be renewed. It is usual to find a lip on the drum's inboard edge which consists of a mixture of rust and brake dust; this should be scraped away, to leave a smooth surface which can be polished with fine (120- to 150-grade) emery paper. If, however, the lip is due to the friction surface being recessed by excessive wear, then the drum must be renewed.
10 If the drum is thought to be excessively worn, or oval, its internal diameter must be measured at several points using an internal micrometer. Take measurements in pairs, the second at right-angles to the first, and compare the two, to check for signs of ovality. Provided that it does not enlarge the drum to beyond the specified maximum diameter, it may be possible to have the drum refinished by skimming or grinding; if this is not possible, the drums on both sides must be renewed. Note that if the drum is to be skimmed, BOTH drums must be refinished, to maintain a consistent internal diameter on both sides.

Refitting

11 If a new brake drum is to be installed, use

9.12 Check that the handbrake lever stop-peg is correctly positioned against the shoe edge

a suitable solvent to remove any preservative coating that may have been applied to its interior. Note that it may also be necessary to shorten the adjuster strut length, by rotating the strut wheel, to allow the drum to pass over the brake shoes.
12 Ensure that the handbrake lever stop-peg is correctly repositioned against the edge of the brake shoe web **(see illustration)**, then apply a smear of clean engine oil to the stub axle, and slide on the seal and brake drum.
13 Fit the thrustwasher and new hub nut, and tighten the hub nut to the specified torque. Stake the nut firmly into the groove on the stub axle, to secure it in position, then tap the new hub cap into place in the centre of the brake drum.
14 Depress the footbrake several times to operate the self-adjusting mechanism.
15 Repeat the above procedure on the remaining rear brake assembly (where necessary), then check and, if necessary, adjust the handbrake cable as described in Section 17.
16 On completion, refit the roadwheel(s), then lower the vehicle to the ground and tighten the wheel bolts to the specified torque.

10 Front brake caliper - removal, overhaul and refitting

Note: *Before starting work, refer to the note at the beginning of Section 2 concerning the dangers of hydraulic fluid, and to the warning at the beginning of Section 4 concerning the dangers of asbestos dust.*

Removal

1 Apply the handbrake, then jack up the front of the vehicle and support it on axle stands. Remove the appropriate roadwheel.
2 Minimise fluid loss by first removing the master cylinder reservoir cap, and then tightening it down onto a piece of polythene, to obtain an airtight seal. Alternatively, use a brake hose clamp, a G-clamp or a similar tool to clamp the flexible hose. Referring to the information given in paragraph 3 of Section 4, identify the type of caliper fitted, and proceed as described under the relevant sub-heading.

Girling CJN48 caliper

3 Clean the area around the hose union, then loosen the brake hose union nut. Disconnect the pad wear warning sensor wiring from the connector.

4 Slacken and remove the upper and lower caliper guide pin bolts, using a slim open-ended spanner to prevent the guide pin itself from rotating. Discard the guide pin bolts - new bolts must be used on refitting. With the guide pin bolts removed, lift the caliper away from the brake disc, then unscrew the caliper from the end of the brake hose. Note that the brake pads need not be disturbed, and can be left in position in the caliper mounting bracket.

Girling J48 caliper

5 Remove the brake pads as described in paragraphs 18 to 21 of Section 4.

6 Clean the area around the union, then loosen the brake hose union nut.

7 Slacken and remove the two bolts securing the caliper mounting bracket to the swivel hub. Discard the bolts - new ones should be used on refitting. Slide the caliper assembly off the brake disc, and unscrew it from the end of the brake hose.

Overhaul

8 With the caliper on the bench, wipe away all traces of dust and dirt, but *avoid inhaling the dust, as it is injurious to health*.

9 Where necessary, use a small flat-bladed screwdriver to carefully prise the dust seal retaining clip out of the caliper bore.

10 Withdraw the partially-ejected piston from the caliper body, and remove the dust seal. The piston can be withdrawn by hand, or if necessary pushed out by applying compressed air to the brake hose union hole. Only low pressure should be required, such as is generated by a foot pump.

11 Using a small screwdriver, extract the piston hydraulic seal, taking great care not to damage the caliper bore.

12 On the CJN48 type caliper, withdraw the guide pins from the caliper mounting bracket, and remove the rubber gaiters. On the J48 type caliper, slide the mounting bracket out of the caliper body, and remove the rubber gaiters.

13 Thoroughly clean all components, using only methylated spirit, isopropyl alcohol or clean hydraulic fluid as a cleaning medium. Never use mineral-based solvents such as petrol or paraffin, as they will attack the hydraulic system's rubber components. Dry the components immediately, using compressed air or a clean, lint-free cloth. Use compressed air to blow clear the fluid passages.

14 Check all components, and renew any that are worn or damaged. Check particularly the cylinder bore and piston; these should be renewed (note that this means the renewal of the complete body assembly) if they are scratched, worn or corroded in any way. Similarly check the condition of the guide pins and their bores in the caliper body/mounting bracket (as applicable); both pins should be undamaged and (when cleaned) a reasonably tight sliding fit in the

body/mounting bracket bores. If there is any doubt about the condition of any component, renew it. On the J48 type caliper, wear of the guide pins and/or their bores will necessitate the renewal of the complete caliper and mounting bracket assembly.

15 If the assembly is fit for further use, obtain the appropriate repair kit; the components are available from Citroën dealers in various combinations.

16 Renew all rubber seals, dust covers and caps disturbed on dismantling as a matter of course; these should never be re-used.

17 On reassembly, ensure that all components are absolutely clean and dry.

18 Soak the piston and the new piston (fluid) seal in clean hydraulic fluid. Smear clean fluid on the cylinder bore surface.

19 Fit the new piston (fluid) seal, using only the fingers to manipulate it into the cylinder bore groove. Fit the new dust seal to the piston, and refit it to the cylinder bore using a twisting motion, and ensure that the piston enters squarely into the bore. Press the piston fully into the bore, then press the dust seal into the caliper body.

20 Where fitted, install the dust seal retaining clip, ensuring that it is correctly seated in the caliper groove.

21 Apply the grease supplied in the repair kit, or a good quality high-temperature brake grease or anti-seize compound to the guide pins and their bores. On the CJN48 type caliper, fit the rubber gaiters and guide pins to the caliper mounting bracket, ensuring that the gaiters are correctly located in the grooves on both the pin and mounting bracket. On the J48 type caliper, fit the gaiters to the mounting bracket pins, then refit the bracket to the caliper, ensuring the gaiters are correctly located in the grooves on the bracket and caliper body.

Refitting

Girling CJN48 caliper

22 Screw the caliper body fully onto the flexible hose union nut, then check that the brake pads are still correctly fitted in the caliper mounting bracket.

23 Position the caliper over the pads, and pass the pad warning sensor wiring through the caliper aperture. If the threads of the new guide pin bolts are not already pre-coated with locking compound, apply a suitable locking compound to them. Fit the new lower guide pin bolt, then press the caliper into position and fit the new upper guide pin bolt. Securely tighten both the guide pin bolts, whilst retaining the guide pin with an open-ended spanner.

24 Reconnect the brake pad wear sensor wiring connectors, ensuring that the wiring is correctly routed through the loop of the caliper bleed screw cap.

25 Tighten the brake hose union nut securely, then remove the brake hose clamp or polythene, where fitted, and bleed the hydraulic system as described in Section 2. Note that, providing the precautions described were taken to minimise brake fluid

loss, it should only be necessary to bleed the relevant front brake.

26 Depress the brake pedal repeatedly until the pads are pressed into firm contact with the brake disc, and normal (non-assisted) pedal pressure is restored.

27 Refit the roadwheel, then lower the vehicle to the ground and tighten the roadwheel bolts to the specified torque.

Girling J48 caliper

28 Screw the caliper fully onto the flexible hose union nut, then slide the caliper into position on the brake disc. If the threads of the new caliper mounting bolts are not already pre-coated with locking compound, apply a suitable locking compound to them. Install the mounting bolts, and tighten them to the specified torque setting.

29 Tighten the brake hose union nut securely, then refit the brake pads as described in paragraphs 23 to 26 of Section 4.

30 Remove the brake hose clamp or polythene, where fitted, and bleed the hydraulic system as described in Section 2. Note that, providing the precautions described were taken to minimise brake fluid loss, it should only be necessary to bleed the relevant front brake.

31 Refit the roadwheel, then lower the vehicle to the ground and tighten the roadwheel bolts to the specified torque.

11 Rear brake caliper - removal, overhaul and refitting

Note: *Before starting work, refer to the note at the beginning of Section 2 concerning the dangers of hydraulic fluid, and to the warning at the beginning of Section 5 concerning the dangers of asbestos dust.*

Removal

1 Chock the front wheels, then jack up the rear of the vehicle and support on axle stands. Remove the relevant rear wheel.

2 Remove the brake pads as described in paragraphs 2 and 3 of Section 5.

3 Ensure the handbrake is fully released, then free the handbrake inner cable from the caliper handbrake operating lever. Tap the outer cable out of its bracket on the caliper body **(see illustrations)**.

11.3a Disconnect the handbrake inner cable from the caliper lever . . .

11.3b . . . then tap the outer cable out from the caliper body

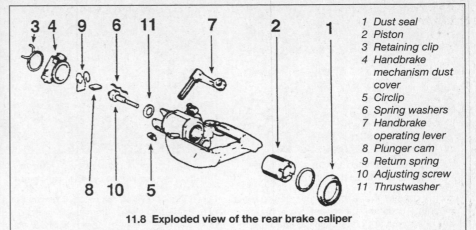

1 Dust seal
2 Piston
3 Retaining clip
4 Handbrake mechanism dust cover
5 Circlip
6 Spring washers
7 Handbrake operating lever
8 Plunger cam
9 Return spring
10 Adjusting screw
11 Thrustwasher

11.8 Exploded view of the rear brake caliper

4 Minimise fluid loss by first removing the master cylinder reservoir cap, and then tightening it down onto a piece of polythene, to obtain an airtight seal. Alternatively, use a brake hose clamp, a G-clamp or a similar tool to clamp the flexible hose at the nearest convenient point to the brake caliper.

5 Wipe away all traces of dirt around the brake pipe union on the caliper, and slacken the union nut.

6 Slacken the two bolts securing the caliper assembly to the trailing arm, and remove them along with the mounting plate, noting which way around the plate is fitted. Lift the caliper assembly away from the brake disc, and unscrew it from the end of the brake hose. Discard the caliper mounting bolts - they should be renewed whenever they are disturbed.

Overhaul

7 With the caliper on the bench, wipe away all traces of dust and dirt, but *avoid inhaling the dust, as it is injurious to health*.

8 Using a small screwdriver, carefully prise out the dust seal from the caliper bore, taking great care not to damage the piston **(see illustration)**.

9 Remove the piston from the caliper bore by rotating it in an anti-clockwise direction. This can be achieved using a suitable square-section bar, such as the shaft of a screwdriver, which locates snugly in the caliper piston slots. Once the piston turns freely but does not come out any further, the piston can be withdrawn by hand, or if necessary pushed out by applying compressed air to the union bolt hole. Only low pressure should be required, such as is generated by a foot pump.

10 Using a small screwdriver, extract the piston hydraulic seal, taking great care not to damage the caliper bore.

11 Withdraw the guide sleeves from the caliper body, and remove the guide sleeve gaiters.

12 Inspect all the caliper components as described in Section 10, paragraphs 13 to 17, and renew as necessary, noting that the inside of the caliper piston must **not** be dismantled. If necessary, the handbrake

mechanism can be overhauled as described in the following paragraphs; if it is not wished to overhaul the handbrake mechanism, proceed straight to paragraph 16.

13 Release the handbrake dust cover retaining clip, and peel the cover away from the rear of the caliper; make a note of the correct fitted positions of the relative components, to use as a guide on reassembly. Remove the circlip from the base of the operating lever shaft, then compress the adjusting screw spring washers, and withdraw the operating lever and dust cover from the caliper body. With the lever withdrawn, remove the return spring, plunger cam, adjusting screw and spring washers, and thrustwasher from the rear of the caliper body. Using a suitable pin punch, carefully tap the adjusting screw bush out of the caliper body, and remove the O-ring.

14 Clean all the handbrake components in methylated spirit, and examine them for wear. If there is any sign of wear or damage, the complete handbrake mechanism assembly should be renewed; a kit is available from your Citroën dealer. On reassembly, ensure that all components are absolutely clean and dry.

15 Install the O-ring, then press the adjusting screw bush into position in the rear of the caliper body until its outer edge is flush with the caliper body; if necessary, tap the bush into position using a suitable tubular drift. Fit the thrustwasher, then install the adjusting screw and spring washers, ensuring that the washers are correctly positioned **(see illustration)**. Locate the plunger cam in the end of the adjusting screw, and position the return spring in the caliper housing. Fit the new dust cover to the operating lever, then compress the adjusting screw spring washers and insert the lever shaft through the caliper body, ensuring that it is correctly engaged with the return spring and plunger cam. Secure the operating lever in position with the circlip, then release the spring washers and check the operation of the handbrake mechanism. Apply a smear of high-melting-point grease to the operating lever shaft and adjusting screw, then slide the dust cover over the caliper body, and secure it in position with a cable tie.

16 Soak the piston and the new piston (fluid) seal in clean hydraulic fluid. Smear clean fluid on the cylinder bore surface.

17 Fit the new piston (fluid) seal, using only the fingers to manipulate it into the cylinder bore groove, and refit the piston assembly. Turn the piston in a clockwise direction, using the method employed on dismantling, until it is fully retracted into the caliper bore.

18 Fit the dust seal to the caliper, ensuring that it is correctly located in the caliper and also the groove on the piston.

19 Apply the grease supplied in the repair kit, or a good quality high-temperature brake grease or anti-seize compound to the guide sleeves. Fit the guide sleeves to the caliper body, and fit the new gaiters, ensuring that the gaiters are correctly located in the grooves on both the guide sleeve and caliper body.

Refitting

20 Screw the caliper fully onto the brake hose, then position the caliper over the brake disc. If the threads of the new caliper mounting bolts are not already pre-coated with locking compound, apply a suitable locking

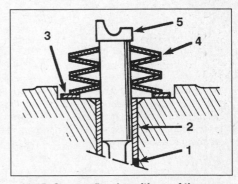

11.15 Correct fitted positions of the rear brake caliper handbrake mechanism adjuster screw and associated components

1 O-ring
2 Adjusting screw bush
3 Thrustwasher
4 Correct arrangement of spring washers
5 Adjusting screw

12.3 To minimise fluid loss, fit a brake hose clamp to the flexible hose

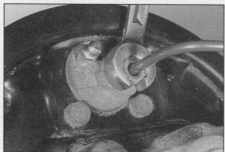

12.4 Using a brake pipe spanner to unscrew the wheel cylinder union nut

compound to them. Install the new caliper mounting bolts and the mounting plate, noting that the mounting plate must be fitted so that its bend curves away from the caliper body. With the plate correctly positioned, tighten the caliper bolts to the specified torque setting.

21 Tighten the brake hose union securely, then remove the clamp from the flexible brake hose, or the polythene from the master cylinder reservoir (as applicable).

22 Insert the handbrake cable through its bracket on the caliper, and tap the outer cable into position using a hammer and suitable pin punch. Reconnect the inner cable to the caliper operating lever.

23 Refit the brake pads as described in paragraphs 8 to 12 of Section 5.

24 Bleed the hydraulic system as described in Section 2. Note that, providing the precautions described were taken to minimise brake fluid loss, it should only be necessary to bleed the relevant rear brake.

25 Repeatedly apply the brake pedal until normal (non-assisted) pedal pressure returns, then check and, if necessary, adjust the handbrake cable as described in Section 17.

26 Refit the roadwheel, then lower the vehicle to the ground and tighten the wheel bolts to the specified torque. On completion, check the hydraulic fluid level as described in "Weekly checks".

12 Rear wheel cylinder - removal and refitting

Note: *Before starting work, refer to the note at the beginning of Section 2 concerning the dangers of hydraulic fluid, and to the warning at the beginning of Section 6 concerning the dangers of asbestos dust.*

Removal

1 Remove the brake drum as described in Section 9.

2 Using pliers, carefully unhook the upper brake shoe return spring, and remove it from both brake shoes. Pull the upper ends of the shoes away from the wheel cylinder to disengage them from the pistons.

3 Minimise fluid loss by first removing the master cylinder reservoir cap, and then

tightening it down onto a piece of polythene, to obtain an airtight seal. Alternatively, use a brake hose clamp, a G-clamp or a similar tool to clamp the flexible hose at the nearest convenient point to the wheel cylinder **(see illustration)**.

4 Wipe away all traces of dirt around the brake pipe union at the rear of the wheel cylinder, and unscrew the union nut **(see illustration)**. Carefully ease the pipe out of the wheel cylinder, and plug or tape over its end to prevent dirt entry. Wipe off any spilt immediately.

5 Unscrew the two wheel cylinder retaining bolts from the rear of the backplate, and remove the cylinder, taking great care not to allow surplus hydraulic fluid to contaminate the brake shoe linings.

6 Note that it is not possible to overhaul the cylinder, since no components are available separately. If faulty, the complete wheel cylinder assembly must be renewed.

Refitting

7 Ensure the backplate and wheel cylinder mating surfaces are clean, then spread the brake shoes and manoeuvre the wheel cylinder into position.

8 Engage the brake pipe, and screw in the union nut two or three turns to ensure that the thread has started.

9 Insert the two wheel cylinder retaining bolts, and tighten them securely. Now fully tighten the brake pipe union nut.

10 Remove the clamp from the flexible brake hose, or the polythene from the master cylinder reservoir (as applicable).

11 Ensure the brake shoes are correctly

located in the cylinder pistons, then carefully refit the brake shoe upper return spring, using a screwdriver to stretch the spring into position.

12 Refit the brake drum as described in Section 9.

13 Bleed the brake hydraulic system as described in Section 2. Providing suitable precautions were taken to minimise loss of fluid, it should only be necessary to bleed the relevant rear brake.

13 Master cylinder - removal, overhaul and refitting

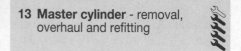

Note: *Before starting work, refer to the warning at the beginning of Section 2 concerning the dangers of hydraulic fluid.*

Removal

1 On left-hand-drive models, remove the battery and battery tray as described in Chapter 5.

2 On right-hand-drive Turbo models, if required, remove the intercooler to improve access to the master cylinder, referring to Chapter 4 for further information.

3 On all models, remove the master cylinder reservoir cap, and syphon the hydraulic fluid from the reservoir. **Note:** *Do not syphon the fluid by mouth, as it is poisonous; use a syringe or an old poultry baster.* Alternatively, open any convenient bleed screw in the system, and gently pump the brake pedal to expel the fluid through a plastic tube connected to the screw (see Section 2). Disconnect the wiring connector from the brake fluid level sender unit **(see illustration)**.

4 Wipe clean the area around the brake pipe unions on the side of the master cylinder, and place absorbent rags beneath the pipe unions to catch any surplus fluid. Make a note of the correct fitted positions of the unions, then unscrew the union nuts and carefully withdraw the pipes **(see illustration)**. Plug or tape over the pipe ends and master cylinder orifices, to minimise the loss of brake fluid, and to prevent the entry of dirt into the system. Wash off any spilt fluid immediately with cold water.

13.3 Disconnecting the wiring connector from the master cylinder fluid level sender

13.4 Using a brake pipe spanner to unscrew the master cylinder union nut

13.5 Master cylinder retaining nuts (arrowed)

5 Slacken and remove the two nuts securing the master cylinder to the vacuum servo unit, then withdraw the unit from the engine compartment **(see illustration)**. Remove the O-ring from the rear of the master cylinder, and discard it.

Overhaul

6 Slacken the fluid reservoir retaining clamp screw, then unhook the clamp and remove the fluid reservoir and reservoir seals from the master cylinder body.

7 Using a wooden dowel, press the piston assembly into the master cylinder body, then extract the circlip from the end of the master cylinder bore.

8 Noting the order of removal, and the direction of fitting of each component, withdraw the washer, and the piston assemblies with their springs and seals, tapping the body on to a clean wooden surface to dislodge them. If necessary, clamp the master cylinder body in a vice (fitted with soft jaw covers) and use compressed air (applied through the secondary circuit fluid port) to assist the removal of the secondary piston assembly.

9 Thoroughly clean all components, using only methylated spirit, isopropyl alcohol or clean hydraulic fluid as a cleaning medium. Never use mineral-based solvents such as petrol or paraffin, as they will attack the hydraulic system's rubber components. Dry the components immediately, using compressed air or a clean, lint-free cloth.

10 Check all components, and renew any that are worn or damaged. Check particularly the cylinder bores and pistons; the complete assembly should be renewed if these are scratched, worn or corroded. If there is any doubt about the condition of the assembly or of any of its components, renew it. Check that the body's fluid passages are clear.

11 If the assembly is fit for further use, obtain a repair kit from your Citroën dealer; the kit consists of both piston assemblies and springs, as well as a new circlip. Renew all seals and sealing O-rings disturbed on dismantling as a matter of course; these should never be re-used.

12 On reassembly, soak the pistons and the new seals in clean hydraulic fluid. Smear clean fluid into the cylinder bore.

13 Insert the pistons into the bore, using a twisting motion to avoid trapping the seal lips. Ensure that all components are refitted in the correct order and the right way round, then fit the washer to the end of the primary piston.

14 Press the piston assemblies fully into the bore using a clean wooden dowel, and secure them in position with the new circlip. Ensure the circlip is correctly located in the groove in the cylinder bore.

15 Fit the new mounting seals to the master cylinder body, then refit the reservoir. Clip the retaining clamp onto the reservoir, and securely tighten its clamp screw.

Refitting

16 Before refitting the master cylinder, clean the mounting faces, and check the distance between the tip of the master cylinder end of the pushrod and front of the servo unit, using the information given in Section 15, paragraph 9.

17 Remove all traces of dirt from the master cylinder and servo unit mating surfaces, and fit a new O-ring to the groove on the master cylinder body.

18 Fit the master cylinder to the servo unit, ensuring that the servo unit pushrod enters the master cylinder bore centrally. Refit the master cylinder mounting nuts, and tighten them to the specified torque.

19 Wipe clean the brake pipe unions, then refit them to the master cylinder ports and tighten them securely.

20 On left-hand-drive models, refit the battery tray and battery as described in Chapter 5.

21 On right-hand-drive Turbo models, refit the intercooler (where removed) as described in Chapter 4.

22 On all models, refill the master cylinder reservoir with new fluid, and bleed the complete hydraulic system as described in Section 2.

14 Brake pedal - removal and refitting

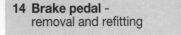

Removal

1 Remove the steering column as described in Chapter 10.

2 Remove the vacuum servo unit as described in Section 15.

3 On models with manual transmission, referring to Chapter 6 for further information, slacken the clutch cable adjuster nut to obtain maximum cable free play. From inside the vehicle, depress the metal retaining clip, and free the inner cable from the plastic retainer fitted to the upper end of the clutch pedal.

4 Disconnect the wiring connector from the stop-light switch.

5 Slacken and remove the six pedal bracket retaining nuts, then return to the engine compartment and manoeuvre the pedal bracket assembly out from the vehicle, noting its rubber seal **(see illustration)**.

6 With the pedal bracket assembly on the bench, slacken the nut, then withdraw the pedal pivot pin, and separate the pedal from the bracket. Slide the spacer out from the centre of the pedal bore, and remove the pivot bushes **(see illustrations)**.

7 Carefully clean all components, and renew any that are worn or damaged; check the bearing surfaces of the pivot bushes and spacer with particular care; the bushes can be renewed separately if worn.

Refitting

8 Press the pivot bushes into the pedal bore, then apply a smear of multi-purpose grease to their bearing surfaces, and slide in the spacer.

14.5 Removing the pedal bracket assembly from the bulkhead

14.6a Withdraw the spacer from the brake pedal . . .

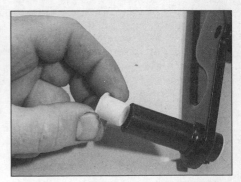

14.6b . . . and remove the pedal pivot bushes

14.9a Locate the pedal in the bracket, and insert the pivot bolt . . .

14.9b . . . then refit the nut, and tighten it to the specified torque setting

15.7 Servo unit pushrod clevis pin spring clip (arrowed)

9 Refit the pedal to the bracket, and install the pivot bolt. Refit the pivot bolt nut, and tighten it to the specified torque setting **(see illustrations)**. Check that the pedal pivots smoothly before proceeding further.

10 Ensure that the seal is correctly located, then manoeuvre the pedal bracket assembly back into position from the engine compartment. Refit the pedal bracket retaining nuts, and tighten them to the specified torque setting.

11 Where necessary, feed the clutch cable back through the bracket, and engage the inner cable with the plastic retainer on the clutch pedal. Check that it is securely retained by the metal clip. Adjust the clutch cable as described in Chapter 6.

12 Connect the wiring connector to the stop-light switch.

13 Refit the servo unit as described in Section 15.

14 Refit the steering column as described in Chapter 10. Prior to refitting the lower facia panel, check and, if necessary, adjust the stop-light switch as described in Section 22.

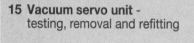

15 Vacuum servo unit -
testing, removal and refitting

Testing

1 To test the operation of the servo unit, depress the footbrake several times to exhaust the vacuum, then start the engine whilst keeping the pedal firmly depressed. As the engine starts, there should be a noticeable "give" in the brake pedal as the vacuum builds up. Allow the engine to run for at least two minutes, then switch it off. If the brake pedal is now depressed it should feel normal, but further applications should result in the pedal feeling firmer, with the pedal stroke decreasing with each application.

2 If the servo does not operate as described, first inspect the servo unit check valve as described in Section 16, then check the operation of the vacuum pump as described in Section 26.

3 If the servo unit still fails to operate satisfactorily, the fault lies within the unit itself.

Repairs to the unit are not possible - if faulty, the servo unit must be renewed.

Removal

Note: *On right-hand-drive models, to gain the clearance required to remove the servo unit, it may prove necessary to split the right-hand engine/transmission mounting and move the engine unit forward slightly; this is due to the lack of clearance between the servo unit and the rear of the inlet manifold. If this proves necessary, refer to Chapter 2A, Section 9 for further information on supporting the engine unit and dismantling the mounting.*

4 Remove the master cylinder as described in Section 13, noting that on turbocharged right-hand-drive models, it will definitely be necessary to remove the intercooler as described in Chapter 4.

5 Slacken the retaining clip (where fitted) and disconnect the vacuum hose from the servo unit check valve.

6 From inside the vehicle, release the panel fasteners by rotating them through a quarter of a turn, and remove the driver's side lower facia panel. Release the heater duct, and remove the duct to improve access to the rear of the servo unit.

7 Prise off the spring clip, then withdraw the clevis pin securing the servo unit pushrod to the brake pedal **(see illustration)**.

8 Undo the four retaining nuts securing the servo unit to the pedal mounting bracket, then return to the engine compartment and manoeuvre the servo unit out of position, noting the gasket which is fitted to the rear of the unit **(see illustration)**.

15.8 Removing the servo unit

Refitting

9 Prior to refitting, check the servo unit dimensions as follows. With the gasket removed, check that the pushrod protrusion from the rear of the unit, dimension "L", (measured from the rear of the servo unit to the centre of the pushrod clevis pin hole), and the distance between the tip of the master cylinder end of the pushrod and front of the unit, dimension "X", are as shown in **illustration 15.9a**. Where possible, dimension "L" can be altered by slackening the locknut and repositioning the pushrod clevis (C). Dimension "X" can be altered by repositioning the nut (P) **(see illustrations)**. After adjustment, ensure the clevis locknut is securely tightened. Note that on some servo units adjustment is not possible.

10 Check the servo unit check valve sealing grommet for signs of damage or deterioration, and renew if necessary.

11 Fit a new gasket to the rear of the servo

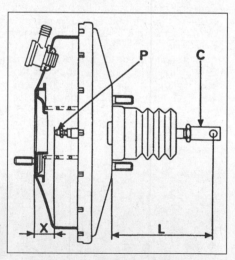

15.9a Vacuum servo unit adjustment dimensions

C *Pushrod clevis*
P *Pushrod nut*
L *Non-ABS models: 22.3 ± 0.1 mm*
  ABS models: 24.8 ± 0.1 mm
X *Bendix servo unit: 88.0 + 0.5 mm*
  Teves servo unit: 86.0 + 0.5 mm

15.9b Servo unit pushrod adjustment nut

15.11 Prior to refitting, fit a new sealing gasket to the rear of the servo unit

16.2 Servo unit check valve is a push fit in its sealing grommet (master cylinder removed for clarity)

unit, and reposition the unit in the engine compartment **(see illustration)**.

12 From inside the vehicle, ensure that the servo unit pushrod is correctly engaged with the brake pedal, then refit the servo unit mounting nuts and tighten them to the specified torque setting.

13 Refit the servo unit pushrod-to-brake pedal clevis pin, and secure it in position with the spring clip.

14 Refit the heater duct, ensuring it is securely connected at either end, then refit the lower facia panel.

15 Reconnect the vacuum hose to the servo unit check valve and, where necessary, securely tighten its retaining clip.

16 Refit the master cylinder as described in Section 13 of this Chapter.

17 On completion, start the engine and check for air leaks at the vacuum hose-to-servo unit connection; check the operation of the braking system.

16 Vacuum servo unit check valve - removal, testing and refitting

Removal

1 Slacken the retaining clip (where fitted), and disconnect the vacuum hose from the servo unit check valve.

2 Withdraw the valve from its rubber sealing grommet, using a pulling and twisting motion. Remove the grommet from the servo **(see illustration)**.

Testing

3 Examine the check valve for signs of damage, and renew if necessary. The valve may be tested by blowing through it in both directions. Air should flow through the valve in one direction only - when blown through from the servo unit end of the valve. Renew the valve if this is not the case.

4 Examine the rubber sealing grommet and flexible vacuum hose for signs of damage or deterioration, and renew as necessary.

Refitting

5 Fit the sealing grommet into position in the servo unit.

6 Carefully ease the check valve into position, taking great care not to displace or damage the grommet. Reconnect the vacuum hose to the valve and, where necessary, securely tighten its retaining clip.

7 On completion, start the engine and check the check valve-to-servo unit connection for signs of air leaks.

17 Handbrake - adjustment

1 To check the handbrake adjustment, first apply the footbrake firmly several times to establish correct shoe-to-drum/pad-to-disc clearance, then apply and release the handbrake several times to ensure the self-adjust mechanism is fully adjusted. Applying

normal moderate pressure, pull the handbrake lever to the fully-applied position, counting the number of clicks emitted from the handbrake ratchet mechanism. If adjustment is correct, there should be between 4 and 7 clicks before the handbrake is fully applied. If this is not the case, adjust as follows.

2 Open up the rear ashtray, then depress the retaining tang and remove the ashtray from the handbrake lever cover panel. Slacken and remove the rear retaining nut and the two front retaining screws, then manoeuvre the cover panel off the handbrake lever **(see illustrations)**.

3 Chock the front wheels, then jack up the rear of the vehicle and support it on axle stands.

4 With the handbrake set on the first notch of the ratchet mechanism, rotate the adjusting nut until only a slight drag can be felt when the rear wheels/hubs are turned **(see illustration)**. Once this is so, fully release the

17.2a Remove the ashtray from the rear of the handbrake cover, then undo the retaining nut (arrowed) . . .

17.2b . . . and the two front retaining screws . . .

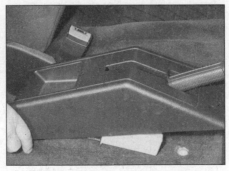

17.2c . . . and lift the cover off the handbrake lever

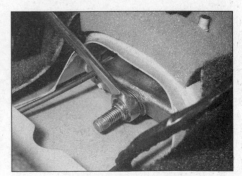

17.4 Adjusting the handbrake

18.4 Handbrake lever is retained by three nuts (arrowed)

handbrake lever, and check that the wheels/hubs rotate freely. Check the adjustment by applying the handbrake fully, counting the clicks emitted from the handbrake ratchet and, if necessary, re-adjust.

5 Refit the cover panel over the lever, and securely tighten its retaining screws and nut. Clip the rear ashtray back into position, then lower the vehicle to the ground.

18 Handbrake lever - removal and refitting

Removal

1 Remove the handbrake lever cover panel as described in paragraph 2 of Section 17.

2 Slacken the handbrake lever adjusting nut to obtain maximum free play in the cables, and disengage the inner cables from the handbrake lever plate.

3 On models with central locking, undo the nut and free the central locking control unit from the handbrake lever mounting studs.

4 Slacken and remove the three handbrake lever retaining nuts, and remove the lever from the vehicle (see illustration).

Refitting

5 Refitting is a reversal of the removal. Prior to refitting the handbrake lever cover panel,

19.5 Handbrake cable trailing arm bracket

adjust the handbrake as described in Section 17.

19 Handbrake cables - removal and refitting

Removal

1 Remove the handbrake lever cover panel as described in paragraph 2 of Section 17. The handbrake cable consists of two sections, a right- and a left-hand section, which are linked to the lever by an equalizer plate. Each section can be removed individually.

2 Slacken the handbrake lever adjusting nut to obtain maximum free play in the cable(s), and disengage the inner cables from the handbrake lever plate.

3 Firmly chock the front wheels, then jack up the rear of the vehicle and support it on axle stands.

4 Slacken and remove the retaining nuts, then release the exhaust system rear heat shield from the vehicle underbody, to gain access to the front of the relevant handbrake cable. Free the front end of the outer cable from the body, and withdraw the cable from its support guide.

5 Working back along the length of the cable, prise off the retaining clip and free it from its guide, then depress the retaining tangs and free the cable from its trailing arm bracket (see illustration).

6 On models with rear drum brakes, remove the rear brake shoes from the relevant side as described in Section 6. Using a hammer and pin punch, carefully tap the outer cable out from the brake backplate, and remove it from underneath the vehicle (see illustration).

7 On models with rear disc brakes, disengage the inner cable from the caliper handbrake lever then, using a hammer and pin punch, tap the outer cable out of its mounting bracket on the caliper, and remove the cable from underneath the vehicle (see illustration).

Refitting

8 Refitting is a reversal of the removal procedure, adjusting the handbrake as described in Section 17.

20 Rear brake pressure-regulating valves - removal and refitting

Note: *Before starting work, refer to the warning at the beginning of Section 2 concerning the dangers of hydraulic fluid.*

Removal

1 Firmly chock the front wheels, then jack up the rear of the vehicle and support it on axle stands. The pressure-regulating valves are located just in front of the rear axle assembly; there are two valves, one for each rear brake caliper (see illustration).

2 Minimise fluid loss by first removing the master cylinder reservoir cap, and then tightening it down onto a piece of polythene, to obtain an airtight seal.

3 Wipe clean the area around the brake pipe unions on the relevant valve, and place absorbent rags beneath the pipe unions to catch any surplus fluid. Retain the relevant pressure-regulating valve with a suitable open-ended spanner, then slacken the union nuts, disconnect both brake pipes, and remove the valve from underneath the vehicle. Plug or tape over the pipe ends and valve orifices, to minimise the loss of brake fluid, and to prevent the entry of dirt into the

19.6 On drum brake models, drive the outer cable out from the brake backplate

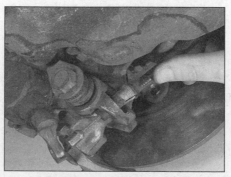

19.7 On disc brake models, disconnect the cable from the brake caliper

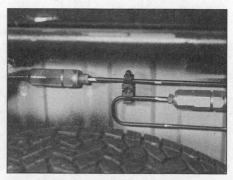

20.1 Rear disc brake pressure-regulating valves

21.1 Location of brake pressure compensator

system. Wash off any spilt fluid immediately with cold water.

Refitting

4 Refitting is a reverse of the removal procedure, ensuring that the pipe union nuts are securely tightened. On completion, bleed the complete braking system as described in Section 2.

21 Rear brake pressure compensator (Estate models) - adjustment, removal and refitting

Note: *Refer to the warning at the beginning of Section 2 concerning the dangers of hydraulic fluid.*

Adjustment

1 The brake pressure compensator is located beneath the rear of the vehicle, adjacent to the right-hand suspension unit **(see illustration)**.
Full access to the compensator can be obtained by removal of the spare wheel from its carrying rack.

2 To adjust the brake pressure compensator, it is first necessary to obtain Citroen tool nos. 9515-TM2, 9515-TM1, 4140-T and 2305-T. In view of the difficulty and expense connected with obtaining these tools and the fact that Citroen state that under no circumstances should the plastic adjusting nut on the end of the compensator be turned, we strongly advise that you entrust the adjustment procedure to your Citroen dealer.

Removal and refitting

3 Any attempt to fit a replacement compensator will result in it having to be adjusted, which will present the same difficulty as stated above. Again, we strongly advise that you entrust this procedure to your Citroen dealer.

22 Stop-light switch - removal, refitting and adjustment

Removal

1 The stop-light switch is located on the pedal bracket behind the facia.
2 To remove the switch, release the driver's side lower facia panel fasteners by rotating them through a quarter of a turn, and remove the panel. Release the heater duct, and remove the duct to gain access to the switch.
3 Disconnect the wiring connector, and unscrew the switch from its mounting bracket.

Refitting and adjustment

4 Screw the switch back into position in the mounting bracket, until the gap between the end of the main body of the switch and the lug on the brake pedal is approximately 2 to 3 mm.

5 Once the stop-light switch is correctly positioned, reconnect the wiring connector, and check the operation of the stop-lights. The stop-lights should illuminate after the brake pedal has travelled approximately 5 mm.
6 Refit the heater duct, ensuring it is securely connected at either end. Refit the lower facia panel, and secure it in position by rotating its fasteners through a quarter of a turn.

23 Anti-lock braking system (ABS) - general information

ABS is available as an option on all models covered in this manual. The system comprises a modulator block which contains the ABS computer, the hydraulic solenoid valves and accumulators, the electrically-driven return pump, and four roadwheel sensors; one fitted to each wheel. The purpose of the system is to prevent the wheel(s) locking during heavy braking. This is achieved by automatic release of the brake on the relevant wheel, followed by re-application of the brake.

The solenoids are controlled by the computer, which itself receives signals from the four wheel sensors (one fitted on each hub), which monitor the speed of rotation of each wheel. By comparing these speed signals from the four wheels, the computer can determine the speed at which the vehicle is travelling. It can then use this speed to determine when a wheel is decelerating at an abnormal rate, compared to the speed of the vehicle, and therefore predicts when a wheel is about to lock. During normal operation, the system functions in the same way as a non-ABS braking system **(see illustration)**.

If the computer senses that a wheel is about to lock, the ABS system enters the

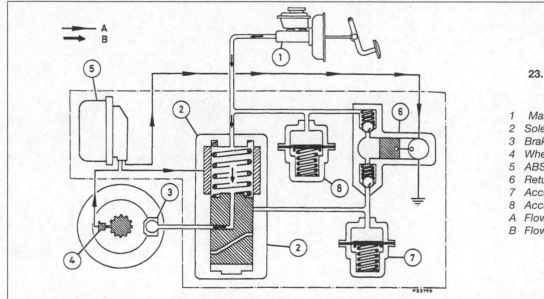

23.1a ABS system normal operation

1 Master cylinder
2 Solenoid valve
3 Brake caliper
4 Wheel sensor and reluctor ring
5 ABS computer
6 Return pump
7 Accumulator
8 Accumulator
A Flow of electrical signal
B Flow of hydraulic fluid

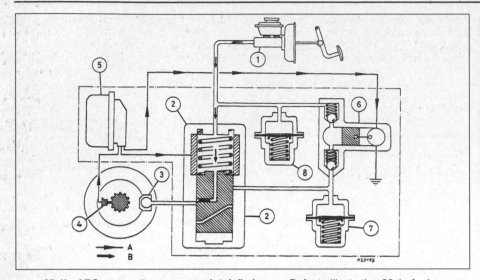

23.1b ABS system "pressure-maintain" phase *Refer to illustration 22.1a for key*

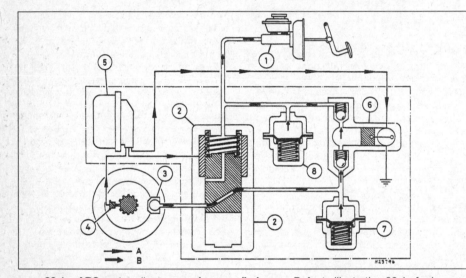

23.1c ABS system "pressure-decrease" phase *Refer to illustration 22.1a for key*

"pressure-maintain" phase **(see illustration)**. The computer operates the relevant solenoid valve in the modulator block, which then isolates the brake caliper on the wheel which is about to lock from the master cylinder, effectively sealing-in the hydraulic pressure.

If the speed of rotation of the wheel continues to decrease at an abnormal rate, the ABS system then enters the "pressure-decrease" phase **(see illustration)**, where the electrically-driven return pump operates and pumps the hydraulic fluid back into the master cylinder, releasing pressure on the brake caliper so that the brake is released. Once the speed of rotation of the wheel returns to an acceptable rate, the pump stops; the solenoid valve opens, allowing the hydraulic master cylinder pressure to return to the caliper, which then re-applies the brake. This cycle can be carried out at up to 10 times a second.

The action of the solenoid valves and return pump creates pulses in the hydraulic circuit.

When the ABS system is functioning, these pulses can be felt through the brake pedal.

The solenoid valves connected to the front calipers operate independently, but the valve connected to the rear calipers operates both calipers simultaneously. Since the braking circuit is split diagonally, a separate mechanical plunger valve in the modulator block divides the rear solenoid valve hydraulic outlet into two separate circuits; one for each rear brake.

The operation of the ABS system is entirely dependent on electrical signals. To prevent the system responding to any inaccurate signals, a built-in safety circuit monitors all signals received by the computer. If an inaccurate signal or low battery voltage is detected, the ABS system is automatically shut down, and the warning light on the instrument panel is illuminated, to inform the driver that the ABS system is not operational. Normal braking should still be available, however.

If a fault does develop in the ABS system, the vehicle must be taken to a Citroën dealer for fault diagnosis and repair.

24 Anti-lock braking system (ABS) components - removal and refitting

Modulator assembly

Note: *Before starting work, refer to the note at the beginning of Section 2 concerning the dangers of hydraulic fluid.*

Removal

1 Disconnect the battery negative terminal.
2 Undo the retaining screw, and remove the relay cover from the modulator assembly.
3 Disconnect the large 15-pin connector, the square 4-pin connector, and the return pump earth lead, from the modulator **(see illustration)**.
4 Unscrew the master cylinder reservoir filler cap, then place a piece of polythene over the filler neck, and securely refit the cap. This will minimise brake fluid loss during subsequent operations. As a precaution, place absorbent rags beneath the modulator brake pipe unions.
5 Wipe clean the area around the modulator brake pipe unions, then make a note of how the pipes are arranged, to use as a reference on refitting; the four modulator outlet unions are marked, to aid refitting. Unscrew the union nuts, and carefully withdraw the pipes **(see illustration)**. Plug or tape over the pipe ends

24.3 Disconnecting the large wiring connector from ABS modulator computer (square connector arrowed)

24.5 ABS modulator block brake pipe unions (arrowed)

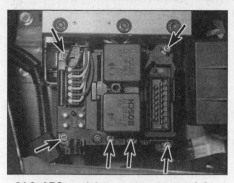

24.9 ABS modulator computer retaining screws (arrowed)

24.12 Remove the shield from the top of the front wheel sensor . . .

24.13 . . . then trace the sensor wiring back to its wiring connector, and disconnect it

and valve orifices, to minimise the loss of brake fluid, and to prevent the entry of dirt into the system. Wash off any spilt fluid immediately with cold water.

6 Slacken the mounting nuts, and remove the modulator assembly from the engine compartment. Note that the nuts do not need to be removed, since the mounting bracket bolt holes are slotted. **Note:** *Do not attempt to dismantle the modulator block hydraulic assembly. Overhaul of the unit is a complex job, which if necessary should be entrusted to a Citroën dealer.*

Refitting

7 Refitting is the reverse of the removal procedure, noting the following points:

(a) *Tighten the modulator block mounting nuts securely.*

(b) *Refit the brake pipes to their respective unions, and securely tighten the union nuts.*

(c) *Ensure the wiring is correctly routed, and the connectors firmly pressed into position.*

(d) *On completion, and prior to refitting the battery, bleed the complete braking system as described in Section 2. Ensure the system is bled in the correct order, to prevent air entering the modulator return pump.*

ABS computer

Removal

8 Disconnect the battery negative terminal,

then slacken the retaining screw, and remove the relay cover from the modulator assembly.

9 Disconnect the three wiring connectors from the computer unit, then slacken and remove the six Torx retaining screws, and lift the computer away from the modulator assembly **(see illustration)**.

Refitting

10 Refitting is a reversal of the removal procedure, ensuring that the computer retaining screws are securely tightened and the wiring connectors are firmly reconnected.

Front wheel sensor

Removal

11 Chock the rear wheels, then firmly apply the handbrake, jack up the front of the vehicle and support on axle stands. Remove the appropriate front roadwheel.

12 Slacken and remove the bolt securing the wiring retaining bracket to the top of the swivel hub assembly, then undo the retaining nut and remove the shield from the top of the sensor **(see illustration)**.

13 Trace the wiring back from the sensor to the connector, freeing it from all the relevant retaining clips, and disconnect it from the main loom **(see illustration)**.

14 Slacken and remove the bolt securing the sensor to the swivel hub, and remove the sensor and lead assembly from the vehicle **(see illustrations)**.

Refitting

15 Prior to refitting, apply a thin coat of multi-purpose grease to the sensor tip.

16 Ensure that the sensor and swivel hub sealing faces are clean, then fit the sensor to the hub. Apply a few drops of locking fluid to the sensor bolt, then refit the bolt and tighten it to the specified torque.

17 Rotate the hub until one of the reluctor ring teeth is correctly aligned with the sensor tip. Using feeler gauges, measure the air gap between the tooth and sensor tip **(see illustration)**. Rotate the hub, and repeat the procedure on several other teeth. If the air gap is not within the specified range given in the Specifications at the start of this Chapter, then the advice of a Citroën dealer must be sought.

18 Ensure the sensor wiring is correctly routed and retained by all the necessary clips, and reconnect it to its wiring connector.

19 Refit the roadwheel, then lower the vehicle to the ground and tighten the roadwheel bolts to the specified torque.

Rear wheel sensor

Removal

20 Chock the front wheels, then jack up the rear of the vehicle and support it on axle stands. Remove the appropriate roadwheel.

21 Trace the wiring back from the sensor to its wiring connector, which is situated just in front

24.14a Slacken and remove the retaining bolt . . .

24.14b . . . and remove the sensor from the swivel hub

24.17 Checking the front wheel sensor air gap

24.21 Rear wheel sensor wiring connectors are located just in front of the rear axle

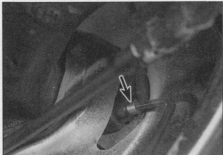

24.23 Undo the retaining bolt (arrowed) and remove the rear wheel sensor from the trailing arm

24.31 Undo the retaining screw and lift the relay cover off the modulator block to gain access to the ABS relays

of the rear axle **(see illustration)**. Free the connector from its retaining clip, and disconnect the wiring from the main wiring loom.

22 Work back along the sensor wiring, and free it from any relevant retaining clips.

23 Slacken and remove the bolt securing the sensor unit to the trailing arm, and remove the sensor and lead assembly from the vehicle **(see illustration)**.

Refitting

24 Prior to refitting, apply a thin coat of multi-purpose grease to the sensor tip.

25 Ensure that the sensor and trailing arm sealing faces are clean, then fit the sensor and tighten its retaining bolt to the specified torque.

26 Rotate the disc until one of the reluctor ring teeth is correctly aligned with sensor tip. Using feeler gauges, measure the air gap between the tooth and sensor tip. Note that this may prove difficult with the disc shield in position. Rotate the disc, and repeat the procedure on several other teeth. If the air gap is not within the specified range given in the Specifications at the start of this Chapter, then the advice of a Citroën dealer must be sought.

27 Ensure the sensor wiring is correctly routed and retained by all the necessary retaining clips, and reconnect it to the wiring connector.

28 Refit the roadwheel, then lower the vehicle to the ground and tighten the roadwheel bolts to the specified torque.

Front reluctor rings

29 The front reluctor rings are an integral part of the driveshaft outer constant velocity (CV) joints, and cannot be renewed separately. Examine the rings for damage such as chipped or missing teeth. If renewal is necessary, the complete outer constant velocity joint must be renewed as described in Chapter 8.

Rear reluctor rings

30 The rear reluctor rings are an integral part of the rear hub assembly, and cannot be renewed separately. Examine the rings for signs of damage such as chipped or missing teeth, and renew as necessary. If renewal is

necessary, the rear hub assembly must be renewed as described in Chapter 10.

Relays

31 Both the solenoid relay and return pump relay are located in the modulator block assembly. To gain access to them, undo the relay cover retaining screw and lift off the cover. Either relay can then be simply pulled out of position **(see illustration)**. Refer to Chapter 12 for further information on relays.

---

25 Vacuum pump - removal and refitting

Removal

1 Two different types of vacuum pump may be fitted, depending on the engine/transmission unit used. The direct-drive pump is mounted on the end of the cylinder head, and driven off the end of the camshaft; the belt-driven pump is mounted on the top of the transmission, and driven by the camshaft, via a drivebelt and pulley arrangement. Determine which pump is fitted, then proceed as described under the relevant sub-heading.

Direct drive pump

2 On Turbo models, to improve access to the

25.3 On the direct-drive vacuum pump, slacken the retaining clip and disconnect the vacuum hose . . .

pump, remove the intercooler as described in Chapter 4.

3 Release the retaining clip, and disconnect the vacuum hose from the top of the pump **(see illustration)**.

4 Slacken and remove the three bolts and washers securing the pump to the left-hand end of the cylinder head, then remove the pump, along with its two O-rings **(see illustration)**. Discard the O-rings - new ones must be used on refitting.

Belt-driven pump

5 Make identification marks between one of the hoses and the pump body, then release the retaining clips (where fitted) and disconnect the vacuum and discharge hoses from the pump.

6 Slacken and remove the pump adjuster bolt, and recover the washers which are fitted on either side of the pump adjuster strap. Unhook the drivebelt, and remove it from the engine unit.

7 Unscrew the nut and washer from the pump pivot bolt, then withdraw the bolt and remove the vacuum pump from the engine compartment.

Refitting

Direct-drive pump

8 Fit new O-rings to the pump recesses, then align the drive dog with the slot in the camshaft end, and refit the pump to the

25.4 . . . then undo the retaining bolts and remove the pump from the end of the cylinder head

25.8a Fit new O-rings (arrowed) to the pump recesses . . .

25.8b . . . then refit the pump to the engine, ensuring that its drive dog is correctly aligned with the camshaft slot (arrowed)

cylinder head, ensuring that the O-rings remain correctly seated **(see illustrations)**.

9 Refit the pump mounting bolts and washers, and tighten them securely.

10 Reconnect the vacuum hose to the pump, and securely tighten its retaining clip.

11 Where necessary, refit the intercooler as described in Chapter 4.

Belt-driven pump

12 Manoeuvre the pump into position, and insert the pivot bolt. Refit the pivot bolt nut and washer, tightening it by hand only at this stage.

13 Position a washer on either side of the adjuster strap, then refit the adjuster bolt.

14 Slacken the adjuster strap lower mounting nut, then refit the drivebelt over the pulleys. Tension the drivebelt by pivoting the pump around its mounting, until the deflection of the drivebelt (measured midway between the pulleys) is approximately 3 mm, under firm thumb or finger pressure. Hold the pump in this position, and securely tighten the adjuster strap nut and the pump pivot and adjuster bolts. Recheck the drivebelt tension, and adjust as necessary.

15 Reconnect the vacuum and discharge hoses to the pump body, using the marks made on removal to ensure that they are connected to the correct pump union, and securely tighten their retaining clips (where fitted).

16 With the pump installed on the vehicle, unscrew the oil level plug from the side of the

pump, and check that the level is up to the lower edge of the hole. If necessary, top-up the oil level using clean engine oil.

26 Vacuum pump - testing and overhaul

Testing

1 The operation of the braking system vacuum pump can be checked using a vacuum gauge.

2 Disconnect the vacuum pipe from the pump, and connect the gauge to the pump union using a suitable length of hose. On the belt-driven pump, ensure the drivebelt is correctly tensioned.

3 Start the engine and allow it to idle, then measure the vacuum created by the pump. As a guide, after one minute, a minimum of approximately 500 mm Hg should be recorded. If the vacuum registered is significantly less than this, it is likely that the pump is faulty. However, seek the advice of a Citroën dealer before condemning the pump.

Overhaul
Direct-drive pump

4 Overhaul of the direct-drive pump is not possible, since no components are available separately for it. If faulty, the complete pump assembly must be renewed.

Belt-driven pump

5 Remove the pump as described in Section 25.

6 Undo the two screws securing the cover to the top of the pump, then lift off the cover. Remove the three valves from the top of the pump, along with their seals, making careful note of which way round the valves are fitted.

7 Make alignment marks between the pump upper body and the main pump body. Undo the retaining screws, then lift off the upper body.

8 Unscrew the retaining nut, and remove the diaphragm and support plates from the pump piston. Remove the O-ring from its recess in the top of the piston.

9 Turn the pulley until the piston is at the top of its stroke, then check the piston-to-bore wear by moving the piston from side to side. If wear is excessive, the complete vacuum pump assembly must be renewed.

10 If the piston wear is acceptable, examine the pump diaphragm and valves for signs of splitting and deterioration, and renew as necessary. It is recommended that the diaphragm and valves are renewed as a matter of course whenever the pump is stripped. Repair kits are available from Citroën dealers.

11 Ensure all components are clean, and fit the new O-ring to the top of the piston.

12 Position a support plate on either side of the diaphragm, ensuring that the flat surfaces of each plate are facing the diaphragm, and the larger of the two support plates is at the bottom. Refit the diaphragm and support plate assembly to the piston, and secure it in position with the retaining nut. Ensure the diaphragm holes are correctly aligned with those of the pump body, then securely tighten the retaining nut.

13 Refit the upper body, aligning the marks made on dismantling, and securely tighten all the cover retaining screws.

14 Fit the valve seals to the upper body, then install the valves, ensuring they are fitted the correct way around. Refit the valve cover, and securely tighten its retaining screws.

15 Refit the vacuum pump as described in Section 25.

Notes

Chapter 10 Suspension and steering

Contents

Front hub bearings - renewal 3
Front swivel hub assembly - removal and refitting 2
Front suspension and steering check .... See Chapter 1
Front suspension anti-roll bar - removal and refitting 8
Front suspension anti-roll bar connecting
  link - removal and refitting 9
Front suspension lower arm balljoint - removal and refitting 7
Front suspension lower arm - removal, overhaul and refitting 6
Front suspension strut - overhaul 5
Front suspension strut - removal and refitting 4
Front suspension subframe - removal and refitting 10
General information 1
Ignition switch/steering column lock - removal and refitting 21
Power steering pump - removal and refitting 25
Power steering pump drivebelt check,
  adjustment and renewal .... See Chapter 1
Power steering fluid level check .... See "Weekly checks"
Power steering system - bleeding 24

Rear axle assembly - removal and refitting 17
Rear hub assembly - removal and refitting 11
Rear hub bearings - renewal 12
Rear shock absorber - removal, testing and refitting 13
Rear suspension anti-roll bar - removal and refitting 16
Rear suspension torsion bar - removal and refitting 14
Rear suspension trailing arm - removal and refitting 15
Steering column - removal, inspection and refitting 20
Steering gear assembly - removal, overhaul and refitting 22
Steering gear rubber gaiters - renewal 23
Steering wheel - removal and refitting 19
Track rod - removal and refitting 27
Track rod balljoint - removal and refitting 26
Vehicle ride height - checking and adjustment 18
Wheel alignment and steering angles - general information 28
Wheel and tyre maintenance and tyre pressure
  checks .... See "Weekly checks"

Degrees of difficulty

Easy, suitable for novice with little experience	**Fairly easy,** suitable for beginner with some experience	**Fairly difficult,** suitable for competent DIY mechanic	**Difficult,** suitable for experienced DIY mechanic	**Very difficult,** suitable for expert DIY or professional

Specifications

Steering

Type .... Rack-and-pinion, power-assisted on some models
Power steering fluid type .... Dexron type II ATF

Wheel alignment and steering angles

Front wheel camber angle:
  Unladen .... 0° 30' ± 40'
  Fully-laden* .... 0° ± 40'
Castor angle:
  Unladen:
    Manual steering .... 0° 30' ± 40'
    Power-assisted steering .... 2° ± 40'
  Fully-laden*:
    Manual steering .... 1° 30' ± 40'
    Power-assisted steering .... 3° ± 40'
Steering axis inclination/kingpin inclination .... 10° 45' ± 40'
Front wheel toe setting:
  Unladen:
    Manual steering .... 0.5 to 2.5 mm (toe-out)
    Power-assisted steering .... -1.5 to -3.5 mm (toe-in)
  Fully-laden*:
    Manual steering .... 1 to 3 mm (toe-out)
    Power-assisted steering .... -1 to -3 mm (toe-in)
Rear wheel camber setting .... -1° ± 40'
Rear wheel toe setting:
  Unladen .... -2 (toe-in) to 2 mm (toe-out)
  Fully-laden* .... -2.5 to -6.0 mm (toe-in)

* Fully-laden is defined as 4 occupants and 40 kg of luggage in the vehicle

Front suspension

Type	Independent by MacPherson struts, with inclined coil springs and integral shock absorbers. Anti-roll bar linked either to the lower arms or struts (depending on model)

Front ride height:
Unladen .... 198 ± 10 mm
Fully-laden* .... 177 ± 10 mm
Fully-laden is defined as 4 occupants and 40 kg of luggage in the vehicle

Rear suspension

Type	Trailing arms with transverse torsion bars and telescopic shock absorbers. Rear anti-roll bar linking both trailing arms

Rear ride height:
Unladen .... 272 ± 10 mm
Fully-laden* .... 201 ± 10 mm
Fully-laden is defined as 4 occupants and 40 kg of luggage in the vehicle

Roadwheels

Type .... Pressed-steel or aluminium alloy (depending on model)
Size .... 5B x 13, 5J x 13 and 5.5J x 14 (depending on model)
Maximum run-out at rim .... 1.2 mm
Maximum eccentricity on tyre bead locating surface .... 0.8 mm

Tyres

Tyre size .... 165/70 R 13, 175/65 R 14, 185/60 R 14 or 185/65 R 14 (depending on model)
Tyre pressures .... See *Weekly checks*

Torque wrench settings

	Nm	lbf ft
Steering		
Track rod balljoint-to-swivel hub nut	35	26
Track rod-to-steering rack	50	37
Steering gear mounting bolts	40	30
Steering wheel nut	35	26
Steering column mounting nuts	17	13
Universal joint clamp bolt	25	18
Power-assisted steering gear fluid unions:		
Feed pipe	25	18
Return pipe	20	15
Front suspension		
Strut-to-swivel hub bolt (see text Section 2):		
Standard swivel hub	55	41
Modified swivel hub	45	33
Strut upper mounting bolts	20	15
Strut upper mounting retaining nut	45	33
Lower arm balljoint clamp bolt	40	30
Lower arm balljoint retaining nuts	45	33
Lower arm front pivot bolt	60	44
Lower arm rear pivot bush mounting bolts:		
8 mm bolt	27	20
10 mm bolt	55	41
Anti-roll bar (models with anti-roll bar connected to lower arm):		
Mounting clamp bolts	55	41
Bar-to-connecting link nuts	30	22
Connecting link-to-bracket bolt	40	30
Bracket-to-lower arm bolts	20	15
Anti-roll bar (models with anti-roll bar connected to strut):		
Mounting clamp bolts	55	41
Connecting link nuts	40	30
Subframe mounting bolts	84	62

Rear suspension

Shock absorber upper mounting bolt	75	55
Shock absorber lower mounting bolt	70	52
Rear hub nut:		
Models with rear drum brakes	200	148
Models with rear disc brakes	180	133
Torsion bar Torx retaining screw	20	15
Anti-roll bar retaining bracket bolt	35	26
Brake backplate bolts (drum brakes only)	37	27
Rear axle mountings:		
Front mounting-to-body nuts	55	41
Front mounting-to-crossmember bolts	70	52
Rear mounting nuts	45	33

Roadwheels

Wheel bolts	90	66

1 General information

The independent front suspension is of the MacPherson strut type, incorporating coil springs and integral telescopic shock absorbers. The MacPherson struts are located by transverse lower suspension arms, which utilise rubber inner mounting bushes, and incorporate a balljoint at the outer ends. The front swivel hubs, which carry the wheel bearings, brake calipers and the hub/disc assemblies, are bolted to the MacPherson struts, and connected to the lower arms via the balljoints. A front anti-roll bar is fitted to all models. The anti-roll bar is rubber-mounted onto the subframe, and is either connected to both lower suspension arms or directly to the front suspension struts, depending on the model **(see illustration)**.

• The rear suspension is of the independent trailing arm type, which consists of two trailing arms, linked by a tubular crossmember. Torsion bars linking the trailing arms are situated in front of and behind the crossmember, and an anti-roll bar linking the arms passes through the centre of the crossmember **(see illustration)**.

The complete rear axle assembly is mounted onto the vehicle underbody by four "self-steering" rubber mountings. These mountings are designed to move slightly under extreme cornering forces. This movement of the rear axle assembly has the effect of actually turning the rear wheels slightly, to help steer the vehicle in the required direction. This improves the handling of the vehicle when cornering at extreme speeds.

The steering column has a universal joint

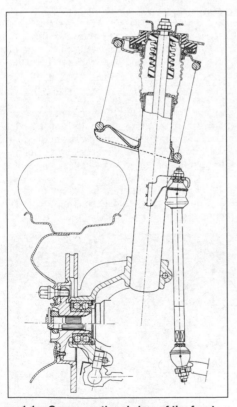

1.1a Cross-sectional view of the front suspension components

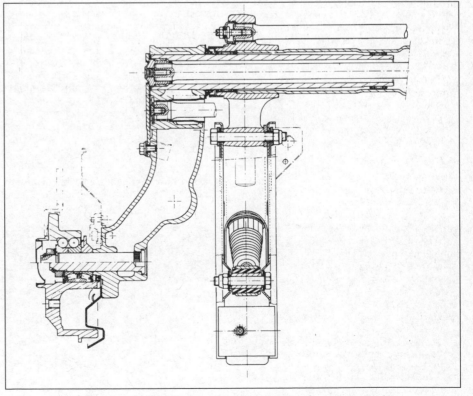

1.1b Cross-sectional view of the rear suspension components

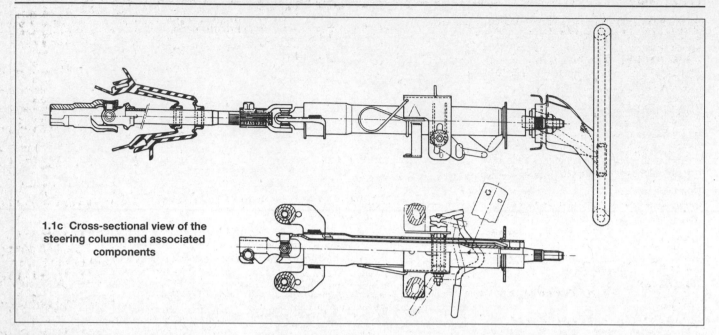

1.1c Cross-sectional view of the steering column and associated components

fitted in the centre of its length, which is connected to an intermediate shaft having a second universal joint at its lower end. The lower universal joint is clamped to the steering gear pinion by means of a clamp bolt **(see illustration)**.

The steering gear is mounted onto the front subframe, and is connected by two track rods, with balljoints at their outer ends, to the steering arms projecting rearwards from the swivel hubs. The track rod ends are threaded, to facilitate adjustment.

Power-assisted steering is fitted as standard on most models, and is available as an option on all others. The hydraulic steering system is powered by a belt-driven pump, which is driven off the crankshaft pulley.

2 Front swivel hub assembly - removal and refitting

Removal

1 Chock the rear wheels, then firmly apply the handbrake. Jack up the front of the vehicle, and support it on axle stands. Remove the appropriate front roadwheel.
2 Withdraw the R-clip, and remove the locking cap from the driveshaft retaining nut.
3 Refit at least two roadwheel bolts to the front hub, and tighten them securely. Have an assistant firmly depress the brake pedal, to prevent the front hub from rotating, then using a socket and extension bar, slacken and remove the driveshaft retaining nut.

> **TOOL TIP** *A tool to hold the hub stationary can be fabricated from two lengths of steel strip (one long, one short) and a nut and bolt; the nut and bolt forming the pivot of a forked tool. Bolt the tool to the hub using two wheel bolts, and hold the tool to prevent the hub from rotating as the driveshaft nut is undone (see Chapter 8, Section 2).*

4 If the hub bearings are to be disturbed, remove the brake disc as described in Chapter 9. If not, unscrew the two bolts securing the

brake caliper assembly to the swivel hub, and slide the caliper assembly off the disc. Using a piece of wire or string, tie the caliper to the front suspension coil spring, to avoid placing any strain on the hydraulic brake hose. Discard the caliper mounting bolts - they must be renewed whenever they are disturbed.
5 Slacken and remove the bolt securing the wiring retaining bracket to the top of the swivel hub **(see illustration)**.
6 On models with ABS, remove the wheel sensor as described in Chapter 9.
7 On all models, slacken and remove the nut securing the steering gear track rod balljoint to the swivel hub, and release the balljoint tapered shank using a universal balljoint separator.
8 Slacken and remove the three nuts securing the balljoint to the lower suspension arm, then withdraw the bolts and free the balljoint from the arm **(see illustration)**.
9 Undo the nut and withdraw the swivel hub to suspension strut clamp bolt, noting which way around it is fitted.
10 Free the swivel hub assembly from the end of the strut, then release it from the outer constant velocity joint splines, and remove it

2.5 Slacken and remove the bolt securing the wiring retaining bracket to the swivel hub

2.8 Undo the three lower suspension arm balljoint retaining nuts

2.10 Removing the swivel hub assembly. Note the use of the screwdriver to open up the hub clamp

2.13a On refitting, ensure the swivel hub clamp is aligned with the lug (arrowed) on the strut prior to inserting the clamp bolt

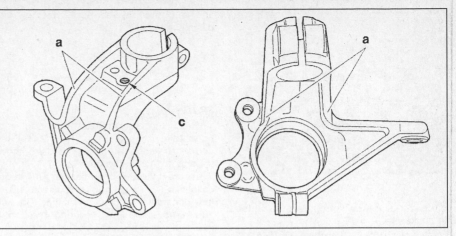

2.13b Standard type front swivel hub assembly

a H-shaped ribbing   c Wiring bracket mounting bolt hole

from the vehicle. If the swivel hub is a tight fit on the strut, use a large flat-bladed screwdriver to carefully open up the clamp a little **(see illustration)**.

Refitting

11 Note that all Nyloc nuts disturbed on removal must be renewed as a matter of course. These nuts have threads which are pre-coated with locking compound (this is only effective once), and include the track rod balljoint nut, lower suspension arm balljoint nuts, and the swivel hub clamp bolt nut.
12 Ensure the driveshaft outer constant velocity joint and hub splines are clean, then slide the hub fully onto the driveshaft splines.
13 Slide the hub assembly fully onto the suspension strut, aligning the split in the hub clamp with the lug on the base of the strut. Also ensure that the stop bosses on the strut are in contact with the top surface of the swivel hub. Insert the swivel hub-to-suspension strut clamp bolt from the rear side of the strut, then fit a new nut to the clamp bolt, and tighten it to the specified torque **(see illustration)**. Note that later models are fitted with a modified swivel hub assembly which can be identified by its tubular shape, and the lack of the H-shaped ribbing around the periphery **(see**

illustrations)**. If working on the modified assembly, note that the torque setting for the swivel hub-to-suspension strut clamp bolt has altered. Ensure that the correct torque setting is used according to swivel hub type.
14 Align the balljoint with the lower arm, and fit the three retaining bolts. Fit new retaining nuts to the bolts, and tighten them to the specified torque setting.
15 Engage the track rod balljoint in the swivel hub, then fit a new retaining nut and tighten it to the specified torque setting.
16 Where necessary, refit the brake disc to the hub, referring to Chapter 9 for further information. If the threads of the new caliper mounting bolts are not already pre-coated with locking compound, apply a suitable locking compound to them. Slide the caliper assembly into position over the disc, then fit the mounting bolts and tighten them to the specified torque setting (see Chapter 9).
17 Where necessary, refit the ABS wheel sensor as described in Chapter 9.
18 Refit the wiring retaining bracket to the top of the swivel hub, and tighten its retaining bolt securely.

19 Lubricate the inner face and threads of the driveshaft retaining nut with clean engine oil, and refit it to the end of the driveshaft. Use the method employed on removal to prevent the hub from rotating, and tighten the driveshaft retaining nut to the specified torque setting (see Chapter 8). Check that the hub rotates freely, then engage the locking cap with the driveshaft nut so that one of its cut-outs is aligned with driveshaft hole, and secure it in position with the R-clip.
20 Refit the roadwheel, then lower the vehicle to the ground and tighten the roadwheel bolts to the specified torque.

3 Front hub bearings - renewal

Note: *The bearing is a sealed, pre-adjusted and pre-lubricated, double-row roller type, and is intended to last the car's entire service life without maintenance or attention. Never overtighten the driveshaft nut beyond the specified torque wrench setting in an attempt to "adjust" the bearing.*
Note: *A press will be required to dismantle and rebuild the assembly; if such a tool is not available, a large bench vice and suitable spacers (such as large sockets) will serve as an adequate substitute. The bearing's inner races are an interference fit on the hub; if the inner race remains on the hub when it is pressed out of the hub carrier, a suitable knife-edged bearing puller will be required to remove it.*
1 Remove the swivel hub assembly as described in Section 2.
2 Support the swivel hub securely on blocks or in a vice. Using a suitable tubular spacer which bears only on the inner end of the hub flange, press the hub flange out of the bearing. If the bearing's outboard inner race remains on the hub, remove it using a suitable bearing puller (see note above).
3 Extract the bearing retaining circlip from the

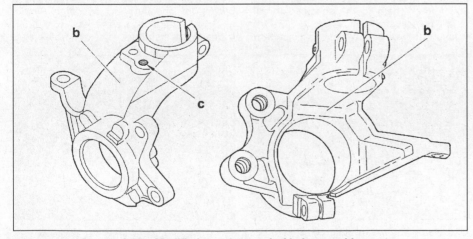

2.13c Modified type front swivel hub assembly

b Tubular shaped area   c Wiring bracket mounting bolt hole

3.3 Front hub bearing retaining circlip

inner end of the swivel hub assembly **(see illustration)**.

4 Where necessary, refit the inner race back in position over the ball cage, and securely support the inner face of the swivel hub. Using a suitable tubular spacer which bears only on the inner race, press the complete bearing assembly out of the swivel hub.

5 Thoroughly clean the hub and swivel hub, removing all traces of dirt and grease, and polish away any burrs or raised edges which might hinder reassembly. Check both for cracks or any other signs of wear or damage, and renew them if necessary. Renew the circlip, regardless of its apparent condition.

6 On reassembly, apply a light film of oil to the bearing outer race and hub flange shaft, to aid installation of the bearing.

7 Securely support the swivel hub, and locate the bearing in the hub. Press the bearing fully into position, ensuring that it enters the hub squarely, using a suitable tubular spacer which bears only on the bearing outer race.

8 Once the bearing is correctly seated, secure the bearing in position with the new circlip, ensuring that it is correctly located in the groove in the swivel hub.

9 Securely support the outer face of the hub flange, and locate the swivel hub bearing inner race over the end of the hub flange. Press the bearing onto the hub, using a suitable tubular spacer which bears only on the inner race of the hub bearing, until it seats against the hub shoulder. Check that the hub flange rotates freely, and wipe off any excess oil or grease.

10 Refit the swivel hub assembly as described in Section 2.

4 Front suspension strut - removal and refitting

Removal

1 Chock the rear wheels, firmly apply the handbrake, then jack up the front of the vehicle and support on axle stands. Remove the appropriate roadwheel.

2 Unscrew the two bolts securing the brake caliper to the swivel hub, and discard them; new bolts must be used on refitting. Slacken and remove the bolt securing the wiring retaining bracket to the swivel hub, then slide the caliper assembly off the disc. Using a piece of wire or string, tie the caliper to the front suspension lower arm, to avoid placing any strain on the hydraulic brake hose.

3 On models where the anti-roll bar is connected to the suspension strut body, undo the nut and washer securing the connecting link to the strut, and position the link clear of the strut **(see illustration)**. Discard the nut - a new one must be used on refitting.

4 Undo the nut and withdraw the swivel hub-to-suspension strut clamp bolt, noting which way around it is fitted. Discard the nut - a new one must be used on refitting.

5 Slacken and remove the two suspension strut upper mounting bolts.

6 Release the strut from the swivel hub, and withdraw it from under the wheel arch. If the swivel hub is a tight fit on the strut, use a large flat-bladed screwdriver to carefully open up the clamp a little **(see illustration)**.

Refitting

7 Manoeuvre the strut assembly into position, ensuring that the top mounting plate locating pin is correctly located in its hole. Engage the lower end of the strut with the swivel hub, aligning the split in the hub clamp with the lug on the base of the strut.

8 Insert the two strut upper mounting bolts, and tighten them to the specified torque setting **(see illustration)**.

9 Insert the swivel hub-to-suspension strut

clamp bolt from the front side of the strut. Fit a new nut to the clamp bolt, and tighten it to the specified torque setting.

10 Where necessary, refit the anti-roll bar connecting link to the strut. Fit a new nut to the connecting link, and tighten it to the specified torque setting.

11 Slide the brake caliper into position over the disc. If the threads of the new caliper mounting bolts are not already pre-coated with locking compound, apply a suitable locking compound to them. Install the bolts and tighten them to the specified torque setting (see Chapter 9).

12 Refit the roadwheel, then lower the vehicle to the ground and tighten the roadwheel bolts to the specified torque setting.

5 Front suspension strut - overhaul

Note: *Before attempting to dismantle the front suspension strut, a suitable tool to hold the coil spring in compression must be obtained. Adjustable coil spring compressors are readily-available, and are recommended for this operation. Any attempt to dismantle the strut without such a tool is likely to result in damage or personal injury.*

1 With the strut removed from the car as described in Section 4, clean away all external dirt, then mount it upright in a vice.

2 Fit the spring compressor, and compress the coil spring until all tension is relieved from the upper mounting seat.

3 Remove the rubber cap, then slacken the upper mounting retaining nut whilst retaining the strut piston with an Allen key.

4 Remove the nut and washer, then lift off the collar, mounting plate, bearing, upper spring seat and flat washer. Remove the coil spring, then slide off the damper piston dust cover and rubber damper stop.

5 With the strut assembly now completely dismantled, examine all the components for wear, damage or deformation, and check the bearing for smoothness of operation. Renew any of the components as necessary.

6 Examine the strut for signs of fluid leakage.

4.3 Where the anti-roll bar is linked to the strut, undo the retaining nut and free the connecting link from the strut body

4.6 Removing the front suspension strut

4.8 Tighten the suspension strut upper mounting bolts to the specified torque. Note upper mounting locating pin (arrowed)

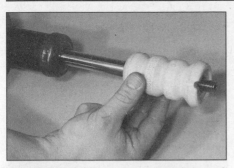

5.9a Ensure all components are clean and dry, then slide the rubber damper stop . . .

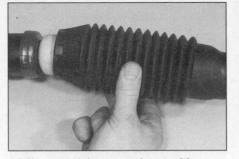

5.9b . . . and dust cover into position on the strut

5.9c Refit the coil spring, ensuring the spring end is correctly located against its stop on the lower seat (arrowed)

5.9d Fit the flat washer to the top of the strut piston . . .

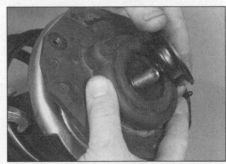

5.9e . . . then locate the upper spring seat on the spring, ensuring that the spring seat stop (arrowed) is correctly located against the spring end

5.9f Refit the bearing to the upper spring seat, ensuring that it is fitted the correct way around

5.9g Locate the upper mounting plate on the spring seat . . .

5.9h . . . and refit the collar to the mounting plate

or if there is any visible sign of wear or damage to the strut, renewal is necessary.

7 If any doubt exists about the condition of the coil spring, carefully remove the spring compressors, and check the spring for distortion and signs of cracking. Renew the spring if it is damaged or distorted, or if there is any doubt as to its condition.

8 Inspect all other components for signs of damage or deterioration, and renew any that are suspect.

9 To reassemble the strut, follow the accompanying photos, beginning with **illustration 5.9a.** Be sure to stay in order, and carefully read the caption underneath each **(see illustrations).**

10 Refit the rubber cap to the top of the strut piston, then refit the strut to the vehicle as described in Section 4.

Check the strut piston for signs of pitting along its entire length, and check the strut body for signs of damage. While holding it in an upright position, test the operation of the strut by

moving the piston through a full stroke, and then through short strokes of 50 to 100 mm. In both cases, the resistance felt should be smooth and continuous. If the resistance is jerky, or uneven,

5.9i Refit the washer and upper mounting retaining nut, and tighten the nut to the specified torque setting

5.9j Ensure that the spring ends are still correctly located against the seat stops, then release the spring compressors and remove them from the strut

5.9k With the compressors removed, push the rubber bump stop and gaiter upwards until they are correctly seated inside the upper mounting plate

6.3 Removing the lower suspension arm balljoint clamp bolt

6.4 Release the balljoint from the swivel hub, and remove the protector plate from the balljoint shank

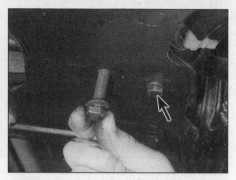

6.5b . . . and the two rear mounting bush bolts (second bolt arrowed) . . .

6 Front suspension lower arm - removal, overhaul and refitting

Removal

1 Chock the rear wheels, firmly apply the handbrake, then jack up the front of the vehicle and support on axle stands. Remove the appropriate front roadwheel.

2 On models where the anti-roll bar is mounted onto the lower suspension arm, slacken and remove the two nuts securing the mounting bracket to the lower arm, then withdraw then retaining bolts and free the bracket from the arm. Discard the nuts - new ones must be used on refitting.

3 Slacken and remove the nut, then withdraw the lower arm balljoint clamp bolt from the swivel hub **(see illustration)**. Discard the nut - a new one must be used on refitting.

4 Lever the arm downwards to release the balljoint from the swivel hub, and remove the protector plate which is fitted to the balljoint shank **(see illustration)**.

5 Slacken and remove the lower arm front pivot bolt and nut, then undo the two bolts securing the rear mounting bush to the subframe (the larger of which is also the anti-roll bar mounting clamp bolt), and recover the nut from the top of the subframe. Manoeuvre the lower arm assembly out from underneath the vehicle **(see illustrations)**.

Overhaul

6 Thoroughly clean the lower arm and the area around the arm mountings, removing all traces of dirt and underseal if necessary, then check carefully for cracks, distortion or any other signs of wear or damage, paying particular attention to the pivot bushes, and renew components as necessary.

7 Check that the lower arm balljoint moves freely, without any sign of roughness; check also that the balljoint gaiter shows no sign of deterioration, and is free from cracks and splits. If renewal is necessary, slacken and remove its retaining bolts, and remove the balljoint from the arm. Fit the new balljoint, and insert its retaining bolts. Fit new retaining nuts to the bolts, and tighten them to the specified torque.

8 Examine the shank of the pivot bolt for signs of wear or scoring, and renew if necessary.

Refitting

9 Manoeuvre the lower arm assembly into position, and refit the front pivot bolt, tightening it finger-tight only. Refit the two rear pivot bush retaining bolts, and tighten both to their specified torque settings.

10 Refit the protector plate to the lower arm balljoint, then locate the balljoint shank in the swivel hub, ensuring that the lug on the protector plate is correctly located in the clamp split. Insert the balljoint clamp bolt, then fit the new retaining nut and tighten it to the specified torque.

11 Where necessary, align the anti-roll bar mounting bracket with the lower arm, and insert its retaining bolts. Fit new nuts to the bolts, and tighten them to the specified torque setting.

12 Refit the roadwheel, then lower the vehicle and tighten the roadwheel bolts to the specified torque. Rock the vehicle to settle the disturbed components in position, then tighten the lower arm front pivot bolt to the specified torque **(see illustration)**.

7 Front suspension lower arm balljoint - removal and refitting

Removal

1 Carry out the operations described in paragraphs 1 to 4 of Section 6.

2 Slacken and remove the three nuts, then withdraw the balljoint retaining bolts and remove the balljoint from the lower arm **(see illustrations)**. Discard the nuts - new ones must be used on refitting.

3 Check that the lower arm balljoint moves freely, without any sign of roughness; check also that the balljoint gaiter shows no sign of

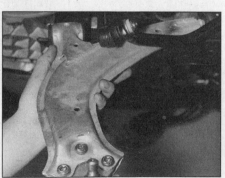

6.5c . . . then remove the lower arm from the vehicle

6.12 With the vehicle resting on its wheels, tighten the lower arm front pivot bolt to the specified torque setting

7.2a Remove the three retaining bolts . . .

7.2b . . . and remove the lower arm balljoint

8.10 Slacken and remove the bolt and nut (arrowed) and remove the anti-roll bar mounting clamp

deterioration, and is free from cracks and splits, and renew if necessary.

Refitting

4 Locate the balljoint in the end of the suspension arm, and insert the three retaining bolts. Fit new nuts to the bolts, and tighten them to the specified torque setting.
5 Carry out the operations described in paragraphs 10 to 12 of Section 6.

8 Front suspension anti-roll bar - removal and refitting

Removal

1 Chock the rear wheels, firmly apply the handbrake, then jack up the front of the vehicle and support on axle stands. Remove both front roadwheels.
2 On models where the anti-roll bar is mounted onto the lower suspension arm, slacken and remove the two nuts and bolts securing the mounting bracket to the left-hand lower arm, then undo the nut securing the connecting link to the anti-roll bar, and remove the connecting link and bracket assembly. Repeat the procedure on the right-hand side.
3 On models where the anti-roll bar is connected to the suspension strut body, undo the nut and washer securing the left-hand connecting link to the anti-roll bar, and position the link clear of the bar. Repeat the procedure on the right-hand side.
4 On models with power steering, using brake hose clamps, clamp both the supply and return hoses near the power steering fluid reservoir. This will minimise fluid loss during subsequent operations. Mark the unions to ensure they are correctly positioned on reassembly, then unscrew the feed and return pipe union nuts from the steering gear assembly; be prepared for fluid spillage, and position a suitable container beneath the pipes whilst unscrewing the union nuts. Disconnect both pipes, and plug the pipe ends and steering gear orifices, to prevent excessive fluid leakage and the entry of dirt into the hydraulic system.
5 On all models, using a hammer and punch, white paint or similar, mark the exact

relationship between the intermediate shaft universal joint and the steering gear drive pinion. Slacken and remove the clamp bolt securing the joint to the pinion, and free the intermediate shaft from the steering gear.
6 Slacken and remove the nut securing the left-hand steering gear track rod balljoint to the swivel hub, and release the balljoint tapered shank using a universal balljoint separator. Repeat the procedure on the right-hand side.
7 On models with manual transmission, using a large screwdriver, carefully lever the three gearchange linkage link rods off their balljoints on the transmission unit.
8 Slacken and remove the rear engine/transmission through-bolt and nut.
9 Slacken and remove the four front subframe mounting bolts which are situated at the rear of the subframe. Loosen the two front subframe mounting bolts by a few turns, until it is possible to lower the rear edge of the subframe approximately 65 mm. Wedge a block of wood between the rear of the subframe and vehicle underbody, to hold the subframe in this position.
10 Slacken the two anti-roll bar mounting clamp retaining bolts, and recover the nuts from the top of the clamps **(see illustration)**. Remove both clamps from the subframe.
11 Manoeuvre the anti-roll bar out from underneath the vehicle, and remove the mounting bushes from the bar.
12 Carefully examine the anti-roll bar components for signs of wear, damage or deterioration, paying particular attention to the mounting bushes. Renew worn components as necessary.

Refitting

13 Fit the rubber mounting bushes to the anti-roll bar, ensuring that the recess on the inside of each bush engages with the lugs on the anti-roll bar. Rotate each bush so that its marking is aligned the paint mark on the anti-roll bar.
14 Offer up the anti-roll bar, and manoeuvre it into position on the subframe. Refit the mounting clamps, ensuring that their ends are correctly located in the hooks on the subframe, and refit the retaining bolts. Ensure that the bush markings are still aligned with the paint marks on the bars, then tighten the

mounting clamp retaining bolts to the specified torque setting.
15 The remainder of the refitting is a direct reversal of the removal procedure, noting the following points:
(a) *All Nyloc nuts disturbed on removal must be renewed as a matter of course. These nuts have threads which are pre-coated with locking compound (this is only effective once), and include the track rod balljoint nuts, connecting link nuts, engine mounting bolt nut, and the intermediate shaft clamp bolt nut. The intermediate shaft clamp bolt nut is retained by a metal cage; release the cage retaining tangs, then remove the old nut from inside the cage and install the new one. Refit the cage to the shaft, and secure it in position with the retaining tangs.*
(b) *Tighten all nuts and bolts to the specified torque settings (where given).*
(c) *Align the marks made on removal when reconnecting the intermediate shaft to the steering gear splines.*
(d) *On models with power steering, bleed the hydraulic system as described in Section 24.*
(e) *On completion check and, if necessary, adjust the front wheel alignment as described in Section 28.*

9 Front suspension anti-roll bar connecting link - removal and refitting

Removal

1 Firmly apply the handbrake, then jack up the front of the car and support it on axle stands.
2 On models where the anti-roll bar is connected to the lower suspension arms, slacken and remove the nut and bolt securing the link to the lower arm bracket, then undo the nut and washer securing the link to the anti-roll bar. Disengage the connecting link from the end of the anti-roll bar, and remove it from the vehicle.
3 On models where the anti-roll bar is connected to the strut, slacken and remove the upper and lower connecting link retaining nuts and washers, and remove the link from the vehicle **(see illustrations)**.

9.3a Anti-roll bar connecting link lower retaining nut . . .

9.3b ... and upper retaining nut - models with the anti-roll bar connected to the suspension strut body

10.7 Power steering pipe-to-subframe retaining clip

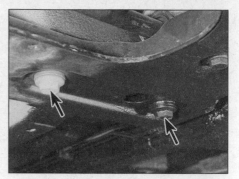

10.9a Front subframe left-hand rear mounting bolts (arrowed) ...

4 Examine the connecting link for signs of damage, paying particular attention to the mounting bushes or balljoints (as applicable), and renew if necessary. It is not possible to renew the bushes or balljoints separately. Note that the connecting link retaining nuts must be renewed as a matter of course.

Refitting

5 Refitting is a reversal of the removal procedure, using new retaining nuts and tightening them to the specified torque setting.

10 Front suspension subframe - removal and refitting

Removal

1 Chock the rear wheels, firmly apply the handbrake, then jack up the front of the vehicle and support it on axle stands. Remove both front roadwheels.
2 Remove the anti-roll bar connecting links as described in Section 9.
3 Slacken and remove the rear engine/transmission through-bolt and nut, then undo the nut and bolt securing the mounting bracket to the subframe and remove the bracket.
4 Slacken and remove the three nuts, then withdraw the balljoint retaining bolts and disengage the left-hand balljoint from the lower arm. Repeat the procedure on the right-hand side.
5 Slacken the steering gear mounting bolts,

and recover the nuts. Withdraw the mounting bolts, and recover the spacers from the subframe apertures.
6 On models with manual transmission, using a large screwdriver, carefully lever the three gearchange linkage link rods off their balljoints on the transmission unit. Slacken and remove the pivot bolt securing the selector rod to the gearchange lever.
7 On models with power steering, undo the nut securing the steering gear pipe to its mounting bracket on the subframe, and free both pipes from any subframe retaining clips **(see illustration)**.
8 On right-hand-drive models, undo the nut securing the clutch cable retaining clip to the subframe, and disengage the cable from its retaining clips on either side of the subframe.
9 Slacken and remove the four rear front subframe mounting bolts and the two front mounting bolts, then carefully lower the subframe assembly out of position and remove it from underneath the vehicle **(see illustrations)**. On models with power steering, take great care to ensure the subframe assembly does not catch the power steering pipes as it is lowered out of position.

Refitting

10 Refitting is a reversal of the removal procedure, noting the following points:
(a) All Nyloc nuts disturbed on removal must be renewed as a matter of course. These nuts have threads which are pre-coated with locking compound (this is only effective once), and include the

10.9b ... and front mounting bolt

connecting link nuts, lower arm balljoint nuts, engine mounting bolt nuts and steering gear bolt nuts.
(b) Tighten all nuts and bolts to the specified torque settings (where given).
(c) On completion check and, if necessary, adjust the front wheel alignment as described in Section 28.

11 Rear hub assembly - removal and refitting

Models with rear drum brakes

1 On models with rear drum brakes, the rear hub is an integral part of the brake drum. Refer to Chapter 9 for drum removal and refitting details.

Models with rear disc brakes

Note: Do not remove the hub assembly unless it is absolutely necessary. A suitable puller will be required to draw the hub assembly off the stub axle, and the hub bearing will almost certainly be damaged by the removal procedure.

Removal

2 Remove the rear brake disc as described in Chapter 9.
3 Using a hammer and suitable large flat-bladed screwdriver, carefully tap and prise the cap out of the centre of the hub. Discard the cap - a new one must be used on refitting. Using a hammer and suitable chisel-nosed tool, tap up the staking securing the hub retaining nut to the groove in the stub axle **(see illustrations)**.

11.3a Tap off the hub centre cap ...

11.3b ... then tap up the rear hub staking using a hammer and suitable punch

11.5 Use a suitable legged puller to draw the hub assembly off the stub axle

11.11a Fit the thrustwasher and new hub nut . . .

11.11b . . . and tighten the nut to the specified torque setting

4 Using a socket and long bar, slacken and remove the rear hub nut, and withdraw the thrustwasher. Discard the hub nut - a new nut must used on refitting.

5 Using a suitable puller, draw the hub assembly off the stub axle, along with the outer bearing race **(see illustration)**. With the hub removed, use the puller to draw the inner bearing race off the stub axle, then remove the hub spacer, noting which way around it is fitted.

6 Refit the races to the hub bearing, and check the hub bearing for signs of roughness. It is recommended that the bearing should be renewed as a matter of course, as it is likely to have been damaged during removal. This means that the complete hub assembly must be renewed, since it is not possible to obtain the bearing separately.

7 With the hub removed, examine the stub axle shaft for signs of wear or damage, and if necessary renew it. The stub axle is an interference fit in the trailing arm, and can either be tapped out of position, using a suitable hammer and soft-metal drift, or pushed out using a suitable heavy-duty bearing puller. When installing the new stub axle, align its splines with those of the trailing arm, and drift or press it fully into position in the arm.

Refitting

8 Lubricate the stub axle shaft with clean engine oil, then slide on the spacer, ensuring it is fitted the correct way around.

9 Fit the new bearing inner race, and tap it fully onto the stub axle using a hammer and

suitable tubular drift which bears only on the flat inside edge of the race.

10 Ensure that the bearing is packed with grease, then slide the hub assembly onto the stub axle. Fit the new outer bearing race, and tap it into position using the tubular drift.

11 Fit the thrustwasher and new hub nut, and tighten the hub nut to the specified torque. Stake the nut firmly into the groove on the stub axle to secure it in position, then tap the new hub cap into place in the centre of the hub **(see illustrations)**.

12 Refit the rear brake disc as described in Chapter 9.

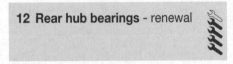

12 Rear hub bearings - renewal

Note: *The bearing is intended to last the car's entire service life without maintenance or attention. Never overtighten the hub nut beyond the specified torque wrench setting, in an attempt to "adjust" the bearings.*

Models with rear drum brakes

1 Remove the rear brake drum as described in Chapter 9.

2 Using a suitable flat-bladed screwdriver, lever the spacer out of the rear of the brake drum, noting which way around it is fitted.

3 Using circlip pliers, extract the bearing

retaining circlip from the centre of the brake drum.

4 Securely support the drum hub, then press or drift the bearing out of position, using a suitable tubular drift which bears on the bearing inner race.

5 Thoroughly clean the hub, removing all traces of dirt and grease, and polish away any burrs or raised edges which might hinder reassembly. Check the hub for cracks or any other signs of wear or damage, and renew them if necessary. The bearing and its circlip must be renewed whenever they are disturbed. Note that a replacement bearing kit is available from Citroën dealers, which consists of the bearing, circlip and spacer.

6 Examine the stub axle shaft for signs of wear or damage, and if necessary renew it. The stub axle is an interference fit in the trailing arm, and can either be tapped out of position, using a suitable hammer and soft-metal drift, or pushed out using a suitable heavy-duty bearing puller. When installing the new stub axle, align its splines with those of the trailing arm, and drift or press it fully into position in the arm.

7 On reassembly, apply a light film of clean engine oil to the bearing outer race, to aid installation of the bearing.

8 Securely support the drum, and locate the bearing in the hub. Press the bearing fully into position, ensuring that it enters the hub squarely, using a suitable tubular spacer which bears only on the bearing outer race.

11.11c Using a hammer and suitable punch . . .

11.11d . . . stake the hub nut firmly into the stub axle groove . . .

11.11e . . . then fit the new hub cap

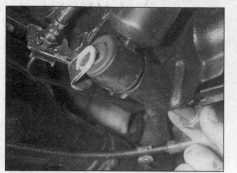

13.5a Withdraw the shock absorber lower mounting bolt . . .

13.5b . . . and the upper mounting bolt (arrowed) . . .

13.5c . . . and remove the shock absorber from underneath the vehicle

9 Ensure the bearing is correctly seated against the hub shoulder, and secure it in position with the new circlip. Ensure that the circlip is correctly seated in its hub groove.

10 Fit the new spacer to the drum, ensuring it is fitted the correct way around, and use a suitable tubular spacer to press it into squarely into position.

11 Refit the brake drum as described in Chapter 9.

Models with rear disc brakes

12 On models with rear disc brakes, it is not possible to renew the rear hub bearing separately. If the bearing is worn, the complete rear hub assembly must be renewed. Refer to Section 11 for hub removal and refitting procedures.

13 Rear shock absorber - removal, testing and refitting

Removal

1 Chock the front wheels, then jack up the rear of the vehicle and support it on axle stands. Remove the relevant rear roadwheel.

2 If the left-hand shock absorber is to be removed, first remove the exhaust tailpipe and tailpipe heat shield as described in Chapter 4.

3 Using a trolley jack, raise the trailing arm slightly until the shock absorber is slightly compressed.

4 Free the handbrake cable from its retaining clip on the bottom of the trailing arm. Slacken and remove the nuts and washers from both the upper and lower shock absorber mounting bolts, and free the brake hose mounting bracket from the lower mounting bolt.

5 Withdraw the mounting bolts, noting which way around they are fitted, and manoeuvre the shock absorber out from underneath the vehicle **(see illustrations)**.

Testing

6 Examine the shock absorber for signs of fluid leakage or damage. Test the operation of the strut, while holding it in an upright

position, by moving the piston through a full stroke and then through short strokes of 50 to 100 mm. In both cases, the resistance felt should be smooth and continuous. If the resistance is jerky, or uneven, or if there is any visible sign of wear or damage to the strut, renewal is necessary. Also check the rubber mounting bushes for damage and deterioration. Renew the complete unit if any damage or excessive wear is evident; the mounting bushes are not available separately. Inspect the shanks of the mounting bolts for signs of wear or damage, and renew as necessary.

Refitting

7 Prior to refitting the shock absorber, mount it upright in the vice, and operate it fully through several strokes in order to prime it. Apply a smear of multi-purpose grease to both the shock absorber mounting bolts.

8 Manoeuvre the shock absorber into position, and insert its mounting bolts; ensure that the upper bolt is inserted from the inside of the trailing arm, and the lower bolt from the outside.

9 Refit the nuts and washers to the mounting bolts, not forgetting to refit the brake hose bracket to the lower bolt, tightening them by hand only at this stage. Clip the handbrake cable onto the trailing arm bracket.

10 Refit the roadwheel, then lower the car to ground and tighten the roadwheel bolts to the specified torque.

11 With the car standing on its wheels, rock the car to settle the shock absorber in position, then tighten both the upper and lower mounting bolts to their specified torque settings.

12 Where necessary, refit the heat shield and tailpipe as described in Chapter 4.

14 Rear suspension torsion bar - removal and refitting

Note: *To ensure the trailing arm is correctly positioned prior to refitting the torsion bar, a special bracket is required. This bracket (special tool number 9501-T.G3) can be obtained from a Citroën dealer, or alternatively, a home-made substitute can be fabricated; the dimensions of the Citroën tool are shown in* **illustration 14.0.**

Note that the substitute bracket must be accurately fabricated to be suitable.

Removal

1 Chock the front wheels, then jack up the rear of the vehicle and support it on axle stands. Remove both rear roadwheels, then proceed as described under the relevant sub-heading.

Front torsion bar

2 Remove the right-hand shock absorber as described in Section 13.

3 With the trailing arm unsupported, measure the distance between the centres of the upper and lower shock absorber mounting bolt holes, on the side from which the shock absorber has been removed, and note this down; this measurement will be needed on refitting.

4 Position a trolley jack underneath the end of the trailing arm, and raise the jack until it is supporting the weight of the trailing arm. Alternatively, a tool similar to that shown in **illustration 14.4** can be fabricated from a length of threaded bar, and attached to the shock absorber mounting bolt holes to hold the trailing arm in position. It is necessary to support the trailing arm, to prevent it moving as the torsion bar is removed. Excess trailing arm movement will place strain on the brake lines, which could cause them to fracture.

5 Slacken and remove the Torx screw and washer from the right-hand end of the torsion bar. Using a punch or scriber, make alignment marks between the torsion bar and trailing arm. Unscrew the retaining nut from the left-hand end of the torsion bar, and remove the washer.

6 The torsion bar can now be withdrawn from the right-hand side, using a slide-hammer which is screwed into the 8 mm threaded hole in the end of the bar **(see illustration 14.6).**

> **HAYNES HINT** *It is possible to improvise by screwing a long bolt with a flat washer into the torsion bar, and placing the jaws of a spanner against the washer. Striking the spanner sharply with a hammer should free the torsion bar.*

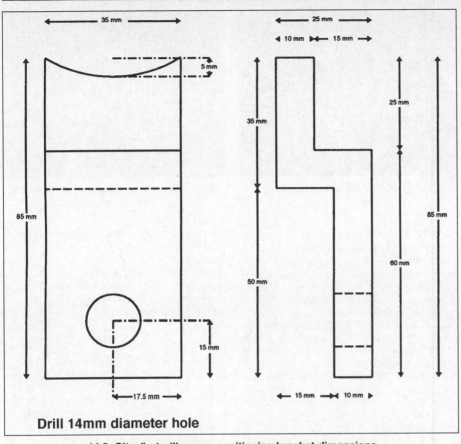

Drill 14mm diameter hole

14.0 Citroën trailing arm positioning bracket dimensions

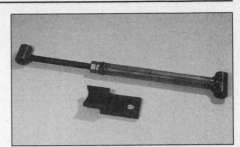

14.4 Home-made versions of the special Citroën trailing arm position bracket and dummy shock absorber used for holding the trailing arm stationary whilst the torsion bar is removed

washer from the left-hand end of the torsion bar. Using a punch or scriber, make alignment marks between the torsion bar and trailing arm. Unscrew the retaining nut from the right-hand end of the torsion bar, and remove the washer.

12 Withdraw the torsion bar from the left-hand side, using the information given above in paragraphs 6 and 7.

Refitting

Front torsion bar

13 Ensure that the trailing arm and torsion bar splines are clean and dry, then lubricate the splines with molybdenum disulphide grease. Where a new torsion bar is being installed, unscrew the threaded stud from the original bar, and screw it fully into the smaller-diameter end of the new bar.

14 Ensure the distance between the upper and lower shock absorber mounting bolt holes is still as measured prior to removal, and adjust as necessary. Attach the positioning bracket (see note above) to the shock absorber lower mounting bolt hole as shown in **illustration 14.14a**. Using feeler blades, check that the clearance between the inner edge of the bracket and the edge of the tubular crossmember is 0.05 mm. If necessary, adjust the position of the trailing arm by tapping it lightly with a soft-faced

7 Once the splines of the torsion bar are free, the bar can be withdrawn completely from its location. Note that the front and rear torsion bars are not interchangeable; the bars can be identified by the markings on their shafts. The front bar has one band painted around the left-hand end of its shaft, and the rear bar has two bands painted around its right-hand end.

Rear torsion bar

8 Remove the left-hand shock absorber as described in Section 13.
9 Carry out the operations described above in paragraphs 3 and 4.

10 Slacken and remove the bolt securing the anti-roll bar retaining bracket to the left-hand trailing arm, and unscrew the plastic plug from the centre of the bracket. Obtain a 12 x 1.5 mm bolt which is at least 70 mm in length, then lubricate its threads and screw it into the bracket. The bolt can then be used as a jacking bolt, to draw the bracket out of position **(see illustration)**. Once the bracket is free from the anti-roll bar splines, remove it from the trailing arm, along with its sealing rings. Discard the sealing rings - new ones should be used on refitting.

11 Slacken and remove the Torx screw and

14.6 Using a slide-hammer to withdraw a torsion bar

14.10 Using a jacking bolt to draw the retaining bracket off the end of the anti-roll bar

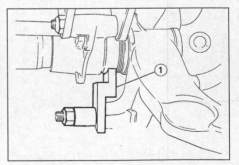

14.14a Attach the position bracket (1) to the shock absorber lower mounting bolt hole as shown, using the mounting bolt and nut and a suitable spacer

14.14b Using a feeler blade to check the positioning bracket-to-crossmember clearance

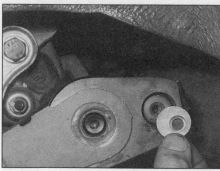

14.17a Refit the offset washer . . .

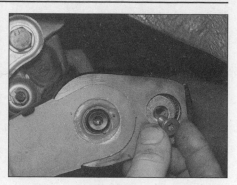

14.17b . . . and retaining screw to the end of the torsion bar . . .

mallet until the 0.05 mm feeler blade is a light, sliding fit **(see illustrations)**.

15 Where the original torsion bar is being installed, rotate the bar until the marks made on removal are aligned, then slide the bar into position. The bar should engage freely with the trailing arm splines for the first 8 to 10 mm, and can then be tapped fully into position using a hammer and suitable soft metal drift.

16 If a new bar is being installed, rotate the bar until the position is found where the bar can be freely engaged with the first 8 to 10 mm of the trailing arm splines. Having found this position, tap the bar fully home using a hammer and suitable soft metal drift.

17 Once the torsion bar is fully home, refit the washer and Torx screw to the end of the torsion bar, and tighten it to the specified torque **(see illustrations)**.

18 Ensure the trailing arm is still correctly positioned, then unscrew the threaded stud from the opposite end of the torsion bar until its shoulder contacts the trailing arm cup; do not force the stud against the cup. Refit the washer and nut to the stud, and securely tighten the nut whilst retaining the stud with a small flat-bladed screwdriver **(see illustrations)**.

19 Refit the rear shock absorber as described in Section 13, then check and, if necessary, adjust the vehicle ride height as described in Section 18.

Rear torsion bar

20 Refit the torsion bar as described above in paragraphs 13 to 19.

21 Unscrew the plastic plug from the centre of the opposite anti-roll bar retaining bracket, and screw a short 8 mm bolt and washer into the end of the anti-roll bar. Securely tighten the bolt to hold the anti-roll bar in position.

22 Apply a smear of the special grease (Mobil Temp G9, available from your Citroën dealer) to the new sealing rings, and fit them to the anti-roll bar bracket. In the absence of the special grease, a good-quality molybdenum disulphide grease can be used.

23 Insert the retaining bracket into position in the trailing arm, aligning its retaining bolt hole with that of the trailing arm, and engage it with the anti-roll bar splines. Using a soft-faced mallet, tap the bracket into position until the clearance between the inside of the bracket and the trailing arm is 1.0 mm; this can be checked using a suitable feeler blade. If the bracket is a tight fit on the anti-roll bar splines, screw a long 8 mm bolt, nut and washer into the end of the anti-roll bar. The bracket can then be drawn into position by tighten the nut **(see illustration 16.13b)**.

24 Once the bracket is correctly positioned, refit its retaining bolt, not forgetting to position the handbrake cable bracket underneath it, and tighten it to the specified torque setting. Unscrew the bolt(s) from the end(s) of the anti-roll bar, then wipe clean the threads of the

retaining bracket holes. Apply a smear of sealant to the plugs, and refit them to the brackets.

25 Refit the rear shock absorber as described in Section 13, then check and, if necessary, adjust the vehicle ride height as described in Section 18.

15 Rear suspension trailing arm - removal and refitting

Note: *To ensure the trailing arm is correctly positioned on refitting, a special bracket is required. This bracket (special tool number 9501-T.G3) can be obtained from a Citroën dealer, or alternatively, a home-made substitute can be fabricated; the dimensions of the Citroën tool are shown in illustration 14.0. Note that the substitute bracket must be accurately fabricated to be suitable.*

Removal

1 Chock the front wheels, then jack up the rear of the vehicle and support it on axle stands. Remove both rear roadwheels.

2 Remove the relevant shock absorber as described in Section 13.

3 Slacken and remove the bolt securing the anti-roll bar retaining bracket to the left-hand trailing arm, and unscrew the plastic plug from

14.17c . . . and tighten the screw to the specified torque setting

14.18a Screw the threaded stud out from the end of the opposite end of the bar until it just contacts the cup

14.18b Refit the washer and retaining nut, and securely tighten the nut whilst retaining the stud with the screwdriver

the centre of the bracket. Obtain a 12 x 1.5 mm bolt which is at least 70 mm in length, then lubricate its threads and screw it into the bracket. The bolt can then be used as a jacking bolt, to draw the bracket out of position. Once the bracket is free from the anti-roll bar splines, remove it from the trailing arm, along with its sealing rings. Discard the sealing rings - new ones should be used on refitting. Proceed as described under the relevant sub-heading.

Models with rear drum brakes

4 Remove the brake drum as described in Chapter 9.

5 Work back along the length of the brake pipe/hose, and remove any retaining clips securing it to the trailing arm. Note that on some models, it may be necessary to split the brake hose at its union in order to free it from the trailing arm bracket; refer to Chapter 9, Section 3 for further information.

6 Undo the four bolts and washers securing the brake backplate to the trailing arm. Carefully ease the backplate assembly over the end of the stub axle, and position it clear of the trailing arm. Tie the backplate assembly to the vehicle underbody, to prevent undue strain being placed on the brake pipe.

7 Remove the relevant torsion bar as described in Section 14.

8 The trailing arm can then be withdrawn from the crossmember, and removed from the vehicle.

9 Inspect the trailing arm bearings, axle tube tracks and crossmember outer sleeves for signs of wear and damage. If renewal is necessary, the task should be entrusted to a Citroën dealer. The bearing renewal procedure involves the use of numerous special tools to remove the original bearings and install the new ones. Attempting to install the bearings without these special tools will almost certainly lead to the bearings being damaged during fitting.

Models with rear disc brakes

10 Work back along the length of the brake hose/pipe, and remove any retaining clips securing it to the trailing arm. Note that on some models, it may be necessary to split the brake hose at its union in order to free it from the trailing arm bracket; refer to Chapter 9, Section 3 for further information. On models with ABS, trace the wiring back from the wheel sensor, and disconnect it at the wiring connector.

11 Slacken the two bolts securing the caliper assembly to the trailing arm, and remove them along with the mounting plate, noting which way around the plate is fitted. Discard the caliper mounting bolts - they should be renewed whenever they are disturbed.

12 Slide the caliper assembly off the brake disc. Where the brake hose/pipe has not been split, tie the caliper to the vehicle underbody, to prevent any undue strain being placed on the brake hose.

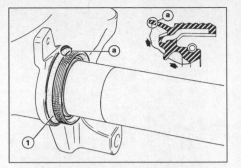

15.15 Ensure the seal (1) is fitted the correct way around, and is correctly located on the trailing arm shoulder (a)

13 Remove the relevant torsion bar as described in Section 14.

14 The trailing arm can then be withdrawn from the crossmember, and examined as described above in paragraph 9.

Refitting

15 Prior to refitting, inspect the trailing arm seal for signs of wear or damage, and renew if necessary. Ensure the new seal is installed the correct way around, and is pressed fully onto the trailing arm **(see illustration)**.

16 Coat the lips of the seal, and the bearing and bearing tracks, with a smear of the special grease (Total Multis G6, available from your Citroën dealer). In the absence of the special grease, a good-quality molybdenum disulphide grease can be used.

17 Slide the trailing arm into position in the crossmember, until its seal is against the crossmember sleeve. Support the trailing arm so that the distance between the upper and lower mounting bolt holes is as noted prior to removal.

18 Refit the torsion bar as described in paragraphs 13 to 18 of Section 14.

Models with rear drum brakes

19 Ensure the mating surfaces of the brake backplate and trailing arm are clean and dry. Locate the backplate over the stub axle, then refit its retaining bolts and tighten them to the specified torque setting.

20 Refit the anti-roll bar retaining bracket as described in paragraphs 21 to 24 of Section 14.

21 Reconnect the brake pipe/hose (where split), and ensure the brake pipe/hose and handbrake cable are securely retained by all the necessary fasteners. Refit the brake drum, referring to the relevant Sections of Chapter 9.

22 Refit the rear shock absorber as described in Section 13, then check and, if necessary, adjust the vehicle ride height as described in Section 18.

Models with rear disc brakes

23 Slide the caliper into position over the brake disc.

24 If the threads of the new caliper mounting bolts are not already pre-coated with locking compound, apply a suitable locking

compound to them. Install the new caliper mounting bolts and the mounting plate, noting that the mounting plate must be fitted so that its bend curves away from the caliper body. With the plate correctly positioned, tighten the caliper bolts to the specified torque setting (see Chapter 9).

25 Refit the anti-roll bar retaining bracket as described in paragraphs 21 to 24 of Section 14.

26 Reconnect the brake pipe/hose (where split), and ensure the brake hose/pipe and handbrake cable are securely retained by all the necessary fasteners. Where necessary, reconnect the ABS wheel sensor wiring connector, referring to the relevant Sections of Chapter 9 for further information.

27 Refit the rear shock absorber as described in Section 13, then check and, if necessary, adjust the vehicle ride height as described in Section 18.

---

16 Rear suspension anti-roll bar - removal and refitting

Removal

1 Chock the front wheels, then jack up the rear of the vehicle and support it on axle stands. Remove both rear roadwheels.

2 Slacken and remove the bolt securing the anti-roll bar retaining bracket to the right-hand trailing arm, and unscrew the plastic plug from the centre of the bracket. Obtain a 12 x 1.5 mm bolt which is at least 70 mm in length, then lubricate its threads and screw it into the bracket. The bolt can then be used as a jacking bolt, to draw the bracket out of position. Once the bracket is free from the anti-roll bar splines, remove it from the trailing arm, along with its sealing rings. Discard the sealing rings - new ones should be used on refitting.

3 Slacken and remove the bolt securing the anti-roll bar retaining bracket to the left-hand trailing arm, and unscrew the plastic plug from the centre of the bracket.

4 The anti-roll bar and right-hand retaining bracket assembly can now be withdrawn from the left-hand side, using a slide-hammer which is screwed into the 8 mm threaded hole in the end of the anti-roll bar. It is possible to improvise by screwing a long bolt with a flat washer into the bar, and placing the jaws of a spanner against the washer. Striking the spanner sharply with a hammer should free the torsion bar.

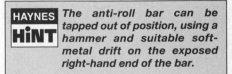

HAYNES HiNT *The anti-roll bar can be tapped out of position, using a hammer and suitable soft-metal drift on the exposed right-hand end of the bar.*

16.5a Slide the inner . . .

16.5b . . . and outer sealing rings off the anti-roll bar

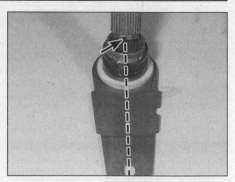

16.9 If a new anti-roll bar is being installed, align the cut-out (arrowed) with the bracket retaining bolt hole

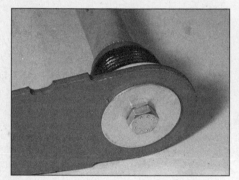

16.10 Secure the left-hand bracket in position with a short 8 mm bolt and washer, prior to refitting the anti-roll bar to the vehicle

16.11a Refit the anti-roll bar and bracket assembly to the vehicle . . .

16.11b . . . then refit the retaining bracket bolt, and tighten it to the specified torque setting

5 Remove the sealing rings from the left-hand end of the bar (see illustrations).

6 If it is wished, the anti-roll bar and left-hand retaining bracket can be separated using the jacking bolt (see paragraph 2). Prior to separation, make alignment marks between the bar and bracket.

7 Inspect the anti-roll bar and retaining brackets for signs of wear or damage, and renew if necessary. The sealing rings should be renewed as a matter of course.

Refitting

8 Ensure the splines of the anti-roll bar and retaining bracket(s) are clean and dry, then apply a smear of the special grease (Mobil Temp G9, available from your Citroën dealer) to them and the new sealing rings. In the absence of the special grease, a good-quality molybdenum disulphide grease can be used.

9 If the left-hand retaining bracket and anti-roll bar were separated, refit the bracket to the bar, aligning the marks made on removal. If a new bar or bracket is being fitted, align the bracket retaining bolt hole with the cut-out on the end of the anti-roll bar. Tap the bracket fully onto the splines using a soft-faced mallet (see illustration).

10 Screw a short 8 mm bolt and washer into the left-hand end of the anti-roll bar, and tighten it securely (see illustration). This will

ensure that the bar and bracket will stay correctly engaged during the refitting procedure.

11 Slide the new sealing rings onto the anti-roll bar, then slide the bar into position from the left-hand side of the vehicle. Refit the retaining bracket bolt, not forgetting to position the handbrake cable bracket underneath it, and tighten it to the specified torque setting (see illustrations).

TOOL TiP

If the retaining bracket is a tight fit on the anti-roll bar splines, screw a long 8 mm bolt, nut and washer into the end of the anti-roll bar. The bracket can then be drawn into position by tightening the nut.

12 Fit the new sealing rings to the right-hand retaining bracket.

13 Insert the right-hand retaining bracket into position in the trailing arm, aligning its retaining bolt hole with that of the trailing arm, and engage it with the anti-roll bar splines. Using a soft-faced mallet, tap the bracket into position until the clearance between the inside of the bracket and the trailing arm is 1.0 mm; this can be checked using a suitable feeler blade. If the bracket is a tight fit on the anti-roll bar splines, screw a long 8 mm bolt, nut and washer into the end of the anti-roll bar. The bracket can then be drawn into position by tightening the nut (see illustrations).

16.13a Fit the new sealing rings to the right-hand retaining bracket, then refit the bracket to the anti-roll bar

16.13b Using a nut and bolt arrangement to draw the right-hand bracket into position, whilst using a feeler blade to measure bracket-to-arm clearance

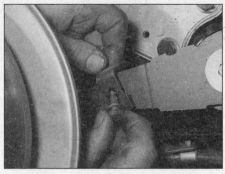

16.14a Refit the handbrake cable bracket to the trailing arm, then refit the retaining bracket bolt . . .

16.14b . . . and tighten it to the specified torque setting

14 Once the bracket is correctly positioned, refit its retaining bolt, not forgetting to position the handbrake cable bracket underneath it, and tighten it to the specified torque setting **(see illustrations)**.

15 Unscrew the bolt(s) from the end(s) of the anti-roll bar, then wipe clean the threads of the retaining bracket holes. Apply a smear of sealant to the threads of the plastic plugs, and refit them to the brackets **(see illustration)**.

16 Refit the roadwheels, then lower the car to ground and tighten the roadwheel bolts to the specified torque.

17 Rear axle assembly - removal and refitting

Removal

1 Remove the rear seat assembly as described in Chapter 11.

2 Firmly chock the front wheels, then jack up the rear of the vehicle and support it on axle stands. Remove both rear roadwheels, then lower the spare wheel out from underneath the rear of the vehicle, and unhook the wheel carrier.

3 Remove the exhaust system and heat shield(s) as described in Chapter 4.

4 Referring to Section 17 of Chapter 9 for further information, remove the handbrake lever cover, and fully slacken the handbrake cable adjuster nut.

5 On models with rear drum brakes, disconnect both cables from the handbrake lever. From underneath the vehicle, work along the length of each cable, and free them from any relevant retaining clips which secure them to the vehicle underbody.

6 On models with rear disc brakes, free the end of the handbrake inner cable from the caliper handbrake lever, then tap the outer cable out of the caliper using a suitable hammer and punch. Where necessary, disconnect the ABS wheel sensors at the

wiring connectors, and free them from any relevant retaining clips.

7 Trace the brake pipes back from the caliper/backplate to their unions, which are situated just in front of the rear axle assembly. Slacken the union nuts, and disconnect the pipes. Plug the pipe ends, to minimise fluid loss and prevent the entry of dirt into the hydraulic system. Remove any relevant retaining clips securing the rear section of the pipe to the vehicle underbody.

8 Make a final check that all necessary components have been disconnected and positioned so that they will not hinder the removal procedure, then position a trolley jack beneath the centre of the rear axle assembly. Raise the jack until it is supporting the weight of the axle.

9 Remove the luggage compartment lower side trim panels, as described in Chapter 11, then lift up the rear luggage compartment carpet to gain access to the rear axle retaining nuts. Slacken and remove the two retaining nuts and washers from each front mounting assembly, and the single nut and washer securing each rear mounting assembly to the vehicle.

10 Carefully lower the jack and axle assembly out of position, and remove it from underneath the vehicle.

11 Examine the rear axle mountings for signs or damage or deterioration of the mounting rubber, and renew if necessary. Note that all four mountings should be renewed as a set; do not renew the mountings individually.

Refitting

12 Refitting is a reverse of the removal procedure, bearing in mind the following points:

(a) Raise the rear axle assembly into position, and tighten the mounting retaining nuts to their specified torque settings.

(b) Ensure the brake pipes, handbrake cables and wiring (as applicable) are correctly routed, and retained by all the necessary retaining clips.

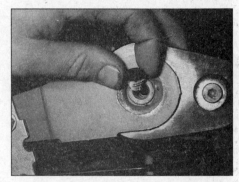

16.15 Apply a smear of sealant to the threads of the plastic plugs, and refit them to the retaining brackets

(c) Securely tighten the brake pipe union nuts.

(d) Adjust the handbrake cable as described in Chapter 9.

(e) On completion, lower the vehicle to the ground, and bleed the braking system hydraulic circuit as described in Chapter 9.

(f) Check and, if necessary, adjust the vehicle ride height as described in Section 18.

18 Vehicle ride height - checking and adjustment

Checking

1 Position the unladen vehicle on a level surface, with the tyres correctly inflated and approximately 1 gallon (5 litres) of fuel in the fuel tank. Roll the vehicle backwards and forwards, to relieve any stress in the suspension components.

2 The front vehicle ride height is measured from the centre of the front lower suspension arm pivot and the ground; the rear ride height measurement is taken between the lower edge of the 58 mm section of the tubular

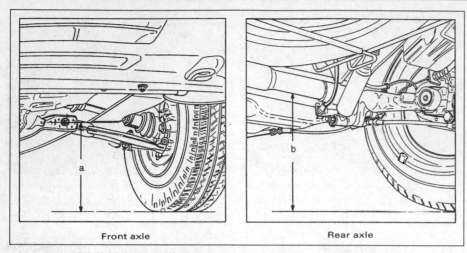

18.2 Vehicle front (a) and rear (b) ride height measurement points

crossmember and the ground **(see illustration).**

3 Take three measurements on the right-hand side of the vehicle, then take the average of these three to be the correct right-hand height. Repeat the procedure on the left-hand side, to find the correct left-hand height. Note that the maximum permissible difference between the left- and right-hand side is 10 mm. Add both the left- and right-hand side averages together, and divide by two to obtain the correct vehicle ride height.

4 Compare the measurement obtained with those given in the Specifications at the start of this Chapter.

5 If the rear ride differs from that specified, adjust it as described below.

6 If the front ride height differs significantly from that specified, one of the suspension components must be worn or damaged; no adjustment is possible. Inspect all the front suspension components for signs of wear or damage, such as worn bushes, and renew components as necessary. If no sign of damage can be found, the vehicle should be taken to a Citroën dealer for a more detailed examination.

Adjustment (rear ride height only)

7 First measure the ride height, and determine the amount of adjustment required. The rear suspension height can be adjusted in multiples of 3.0 mm, by rotating the rear torsion bars. If adjustment is necessary, determine the number of splines the torsion bar must be moved, noting that one spline is equal to roughly 3.0 mm of ride height. For example, if the ride height needs adjusting by 10.0 mm, the torsion bar should be moved by three splines. If the left- and right-hand ride height difference was excessive, compensate for this during the adjustment procedure.

8 Chock the front wheels, then jack up the rear of the vehicle and support it on axle stands. Remove both rear roadwheels.

9 Working first on the left-hand side, remove the rear torsion bar as described in Section 14.

10 Noting that a 2 mm change in distance between the rear shock absorber mounting bolt holes equals a 3 mm change in ride height, or one spline of torsion bar movement, raise or lower the trailing arm by the required amount. Note that increasing the distance between the bolt holes increases ride height, and decreasing the distance lowers the ride height; if the ride needs lowering by 9 mm, decrease the distance between the shock absorber mounting bolt holes by 6 mm by raising the trailing arm.

11 Rotate the torsion bar by the required number of splines in the required direction, and relocate it with the trailing arm splines. The bar should engage freely with the trailing arm splines for the first 8 to 10 mm, and can then be tapped into fully into position using a hammer and suitable soft metal drift.

12 Refit the anti-roll bar retaining bracket as described in Section 14.

13 Remove the front torsion bar as described in Section 14, and repeat the procedure described in paragraphs 10 and 11 on the right-hand side. Secure the bar in position as described in Section 14.

14 Refit the roadwheels, then lower the car to ground and tighten the roadwheel bolts to the specified torque.

15 With the car standing on its wheels, rock the car to settle the disturbed suspension components in position, then tighten the shock absorber mounting bolts to the specified torque settings.

16 Recheck the vehicle ride heights as described earlier in this Section and, if necessary, repeat the adjustment procedure. Note that after adjustment, it may be necessary to adjust the headlight beam alignment, referring to Chapter 12 for further information.

19 Steering wheel - removal and refitting

Models without airbag

Removal

1 Set the front wheels in the straight-ahead position, and release the steering lock by inserting the ignition key.

2 Carefully ease off the steering wheel centre pad, then slacken and remove the steering wheel retaining nut **(see illustrations).**

3 Mark the steering wheel and steering column shaft in relation to each other, then lift the steering wheel off the column splines. If it is tight, tap it up near the centre, using the palm of your hand, or twist it from side to side, whilst pulling upwards to release it from the shaft splines.

Refitting

4 Refitting is a reversal of removal, noting the following points:

(a) Check the indicator cancelling lug fitted to the rear of steering wheel is in good condition, and if necessary renew it. The lug is retained by a circlip **(see illustration).**

(b) Prior to refitting, ensure that the indicator switch stem is in its central position. Failure to do this could lead to the

19.2a Remove the centre pad . . .

19.2b . . . then slacken and remove the steering wheel retaining nut

19.4a Indicator cancelling lug is secured to the base of the steering wheel by a circlip

19.4b Tighten the steering wheel retaining nut to the specified torque setting

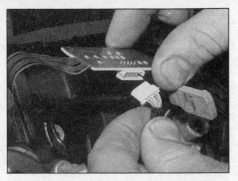

19.6 Disconnecting the wiring plug from the radio/cassette player remote control circuit board

steering wheel lug breaking the switch tab as the steering wheel is refitted.

(c) On refitting, align the marks made on removal, and tighten the retaining nut to the specified torque (see illustration).

Models with air bag

Note: *The air bag electronic control unit is integral with the steering wheel. Take care not to damage the unit during removal, and store the wheel carefully once removed.*

Removal

5 Remove the air bag unit as described in Chapter 12.

6 Where applicable, disconnect the wiring plug from the radio/cassette player remote control circuit board located in the slot at the top of the steering wheel (see illustration).

7 Unclip the air bag wiring connector from the steering wheel, and separate the two halves of the connector (see illustration).

8 Unscrew the steering wheel securing nut. Refer to paragraph 3 and withdraw the steering wheel (see illustration). Feed the wiring through the centre of the steering wheel as it is withdrawn.

9 Store the wheel carefully, taking care not to damage the air bag electronic control unit.

Refitting

10 Refitting is a reversal of removal, bearing in mind the following points:

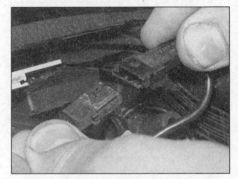

19.7 Disconnecting the air bag wiring connector

(a) Make sure that the wiring is correctly routed through the wheel.
(b) Tighten the steering wheel securing nut to the specified torque.
(c) Refit the air bag unit as described in Chapter 12.

19.8 Unscrewing the steering wheel securing nut

2 Remove the steering wheel as described in Section 19.

3 Release the panel fasteners by rotating them through a quarter of a turn, and remove the driver's side lower facia panel.

4 Slacken and remove the five screws which secure the two halves of the steering column shrouds together, then remove both the upper and lower shroud (see illustrations).

5 Release the facia felt undercover retaining clips, and peel back the material. Release the heater duct, and remove the duct to gain access to the steering column mountings.

6 Tilt the steering column fully downwards, and disconnect the wiring connectors from the steering column combination switches and the three wiring connectors from the

20 Steering column - removal, inspection and refitting

Removal

1 Disconnect the battery negative terminal.

20.4a Undo the five steering column shroud retaining screws (arrowed) . . .

20.4b . . . then remove the both the lower . . .

20.4c . . . and upper shroud sections

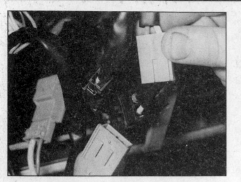

20.6 Disconnecting the ignition switch wiring connectors

ignition switch **(see illustration)**. Free the wiring from any relevant retaining clips.

7 Make alignment marks between the universal joint on the base of the steering column and the intermediate shaft, then slacken and remove the universal joint clamp bolt.

8 Slacken and remove the four steering column mounting nuts, then release the steering column from its mountings, and recover the column mounting spacers from the lower mounting studs **(see illustration)**. Disengage the universal joint from the intermediate shaft, and remove the steering column assembly from the vehicle.

9 To remove the intermediate shaft, firmly apply the handbrake, then jack up the front of the vehicle and support it on axle stands. Disengage the rubber gaiter from the floor, and slide it off the end of the shaft. Make alignment marks between the universal joint on the base of the intermediate shaft and steering gear pinion, then slacken and remove the universal joint clamp bolt **(see illustrations)**. Release the shaft from the pinion splines, and remove it from the vehicle.

Inspection

10 The steering column incorporates a telescopic safety feature. In the event of a front-end crash, the shaft collapses and prevents the steering wheel injuring the driver. Before refitting the steering column, examine the column and mountings for signs of damage and deformation, and renew as necessary.

11 Check the steering shaft for signs of free play in the column bushes, and check the universal joints for signs of damage or roughness in the joint bearings. If any damage or wear is found on the steering column universal joints or shaft bushes, the column must be renewed as an assembly. Inspect the column lower mounting rubbers for signs of damage or deterioration, and renew if necessary.

12 The steering column nuts (and, where disturbed, the intermediate shaft clamp bolt nuts) must be renewed as a matter of course. Each nut is retained by a metal cage; release the cage retaining tangs, then remove the old nut from inside the cage and install the new one. Refit the cage, and secure it in position with the retaining tangs **(see illustration)**.

Refitting

13 Where removed, refit the intermediate shaft, aligning the marks made prior to removal, and engaging the universal joint with the steering gear drive pinion splines. Refit the shaft clamp bolt, and tighten it to the specified torque setting. Slide the rubber gaiter down the intermediate shaft, and locate it in the floorpan.

14 Manoeuvre the steering column assembly into position then, aligning the marks made prior to removal, engage the universal joint with the intermediate shaft splines.

15 Fit the column over its mounting studs, and refit the steering column mounting nuts, not forgetting the lower mounting stud spacers, and tighten them to the specified torque **(see illustrations)**.

16 Position the column universal joint on the intermediate shaft, so that the top of the steering shaft protrudes from the top of the

20.8 Steering column lower mounting nuts (arrowed)

20.9a From inside the vehicle, slide the rubber gaiter off the intermediate shaft . . .

20.9b . . . then slacken and remove the universal joint clamp bolt, and free the shaft from the steering gear

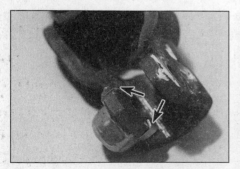

20.12 Ensure the universal joint clamp bolt nut cage is securely held in position by its retaining tangs (arrowed)

20.15a Ensure the mounting rubbers and spacers are correctly positioned on the column lower mountings . . .

20.15b . . . then refit the steering column to the vehicle

20.16 Adjust the position of the steering shaft as described in text prior to tightening the universal joint clamp bolt

21.5 Ignition switch/steering column lock retaining screw (arrowed)

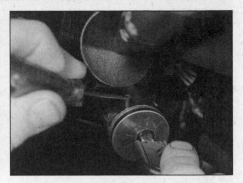

21.6a Insert the key, positioning it as described in the text, then depress the lock retaining lug . . .

steering column by 58 mm **(see illustration)**. Once correctly positioned, refit the clamp bolt and tighten it to the specified torque setting.

17 Ensuring that the wiring is correctly routed and retained by any necessary retaining clips, reconnect the wiring connectors to the combination switches and the ignition switch.

18 Refit the heater duct, ensuring that it is correctly seated at each end, and clip the undercover back into position.

19 Position the upper and lower column shrouds around the steering column, then refit the retaining screws and tighten them securely.

20 Refit the lower facia panel, and secure it in position by rotating the fasteners through a quarter of a turn.

21 Refit the steering wheel as described in Section 18.

22 Release the column tilt lever, check that the column moves freely, then lock the lever and check the column is securely held. If adjustment is necessary, working through the aperture in the lower shroud, slacken the lever locknut, then slacken the adjuster nut until the column moves freely with the lever released and locks securely with the lever locked. Note that on some models, a single Nyloc nut is used instead of the locknut and adjuster nut arrangement. Where necessary, hold the adjuster nut stationary and securely tighten the locknut. Check the operation of the lever and, if necessary, repeat the adjustment procedure. If a Nyloc nut is fitted, it may be

necessary to renew it, to restore its effectiveness.

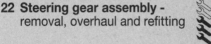

21 Ignition switch/steering column lock - removal and refitting

Removal

1 Disconnect the battery negative terminal.

2 Working inside the car, release the panel fasteners by rotating them through a quarter of a turn, and remove the driver's side lower facia panel.

3 Slacken and remove the five screws which secure the two halves of the steering column shrouds together, then remove the lower shroud.

4 Tilt the steering column fully downwards, then trace the wiring back from the ignition switch, and disconnect its three wiring connectors from the main wiring loom.

5 Slacken and remove the lock retaining screw and washer from the side of the lock **(see illustration)**.

6 Insert the key, and rotate it so that is aligned with the mark positioned between the "A" and "S" marks on the barrel. Using a small flat-bladed screwdriver, depress the lock retaining lug, then withdraw the lock assembly from the steering column **(see illustrations)**.

Refitting

7 Refitting is a direct reversal of the removal procedure, ensuring that the lock assembly is

securely held in position by its retaining lug. Prior to refitting the column shroud, remove the ignition key and check that the steering lock functions correctly.

22 Steering gear assembly - removal, overhaul and refitting

Removal

1 Chock the rear wheels, firmly apply the handbrake, then jack up the front of the vehicle and support on axle stands. Remove both front roadwheels.

2 Slacken and remove the nuts securing the steering gear track rod balljoints to the swivel hubs, and release the balljoint tapered shanks using a universal balljoint separator.

3 Mark the exact relationship between the intermediate shaft universal joint and the steering gear drive pinion. Slacken and remove the clamp bolt securing the joint to the pinion, and free the intermediate shaft from the steering gear **(see illustration)**.

4 Undo the two lower retaining screws, then unclip the heat shield and remove it from the top of the steering gear assembly.

Manual steering gear

5 Slacken the steering gear mounting bolts, and recover the nuts. Withdraw the mounting bolts, and recover the spacers from the subframe apertures **(see illustrations)**.

21.6b . . . and withdraw the lock assembly from the steering column

22.3 Intermediate shaft universal joint clamp bolt (arrowed) viewed from underneath

22.5a Slacken and remove the two steering gear retaining bolts (viewed underneath the front of the vehicle) . . .

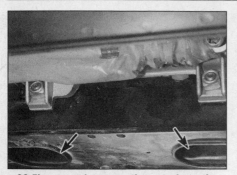

22.5b . . . and recover the nuts from the rear of the steering gear, and the spacers from the subframe apertures (arrowed)

6 The steering gear assembly can then be manoeuvred out from underneath the right-hand wheel arch. Note that on some left-hand-drive models with manual transmission, it may be necessary to disconnect the three gearchange linkage link rods from their balljoints on the transmission unit, to gain the necessary clearance required to withdraw the steering gear.

Power-assisted steering gear

7 Using brake hose clamps, clamp both the supply and return hoses near the power steering fluid reservoir. This will minimise fluid loss during subsequent operations.

8 Mark the unions to ensure they are correctly positioned on reassembly, then unscrew the feed and return pipe union nuts from the steering gear assembly; be prepared for fluid spillage, and position a suitable container beneath the pipes whilst unscrewing the union nuts. Disconnect both pipes, and plug the pipe ends and steering gear orifices, to prevent excessive fluid leakage and the entry of dirt into the hydraulic system.

9 Free the power steering pipes from any relevant retaining clips, and position them clear of the steering gear so that they will not hinder the removal procedure.

10 Remove the steering gear as described above in paragraphs 5 and 6.

Overhaul

11 Examine the steering gear assembly for signs of wear or damage, and check that the rack moves freely throughout the full length of its travel, with no signs of roughness or excessive free play between the steering gear pinion and rack. It is possible to overhaul the steering gear assembly housing components, but this task should be entrusted to a Citroën dealer. The only components which can be renewed easily by the home mechanic are the steering gear gaiters, the track rod balljoints and the track rods. Track rod, track rod balljoint and steering gear gaiter renewal procedures are covered in Sections 27, 26 and 23 respectively.

12 On models with power steering, inspect all the steering gear fluid unions for signs of leakage, and check that all union nuts are

securely tightened. Also examine the steering gear hydraulic ram for signs of fluid leakage or damage, and if necessary renew it.

Refitting

13 Note that all Nyloc nuts disturbed on removal must be renewed as a matter of course. These nuts have threads which are pre-coated with locking compound (this is only effective once), and include the track rod balljoint nuts, steering gear mounting bolt nuts, and the intermediate shaft clamp bolt nut. The intermediate shaft clamp bolt nut is retained by a metal cage; release the cage retaining tangs, then remove the old nut from inside the cage and install the new one. Refit the cage to the shaft, and secure it in position with the retaining tangs (see illustration 20.12).

14 Manoeuvre the steering gear assembly into position from the right-hand side of the vehicle.

15 Position the spacers in the subframe apertures, then insert the mounting bolts. Fit the new nuts onto the steering gear, then tighten the mounting bolts to the specified torque setting. Where necessary, clip the gearchange linkage link rods onto their balljoints.

16 Clip the heat shield onto the top of the steering gear, and securely tighten its two retaining screws.

17 Aligning the marks made prior to removal, engage the intermediate shaft universal joint with the steering gear pinion splines. Refit the clamp bolt with a new nut, and tighten it to the specified torque.

18 Engage the track rod balljoints in the swivel hubs, then fit a new retaining nut to each one. Tighten the nuts to the specified torque setting.

19 On models with power steering, wipe clean the feed and return pipe unions, then refit them to their respective positions on the steering gear, and tighten the union nuts to their specified torque settings. Ensure the pipes are correctly routed, and are securely held by all the necessary retaining clips.

20 On all models, refit the roadwheels, then lower the vehicle to the ground and tighten the roadwheel bolts to the specified torque.

21 Where necessary, remove the hose clamps from the power steering hoses, then top-up the fluid reservoir and bleed the hydraulic system as described in Section 24.

22 On completion check and, if necessary, adjust the front wheel alignment as described in Section 28.

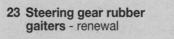

23 Steering gear rubber gaiters - renewal

Manual steering gear

1 Remove the track rod balljoint as described in Section 26.

2 Mark the correct fitted position of the gaiter on the track rod, then release the retaining clips and slide the gaiter off the steering gear housing and track rod end.

3 Thoroughly clean the track rod and the steering gear housing, using fine abrasive paper to polish off any corrosion, burrs or sharp edges, which might damage the new gaiter's sealing lips on installation. Scrape off all grease from the old gaiter, and apply to the track rod inner balljoint.

4 Carefully slide the new gaiter onto the track rod end, and locate it on the steering gear housing. Align the outer edge of the gaiter with the mark made on the track rod prior to removal, then secure it in position with new retaining clips.

5 Refit the track rod balljoint as described in Section 26.

Power-assisted steering gear

6 On power-assisted steering gear assemblies, it is only possible to renew the gaiter nearest the drive pinion, ie. the right-hand gaiter on right-hand-drive models, and the left-hand gaiter on left-hand-drive models. This can be renewed as described above in paragraphs 1 to 5.

7 The task of renewing the opposite gaiter should be entrusted to a Citroën dealer. This is necessary since it is not possible to pass the gaiter over the steering rack stud to which the hydraulic ram is fixed. Therefore, the steering gear must be dismantled and the rack removed from the housing to allow the gaiter to be renewed.

8 The only task on this end of the assembly which can be carried out by the home mechanic is the renewal of the track rod inner balljoint dust cover. The dust cover can be renewed once the track rod balljoint has been removed as described in Section 26. On refitting, ensure the dust cover is correctly located on the track rod and steering rack, then refit the balljoint.

24 Power steering system - bleeding

1 This procedure will only be necessary when any part of the hydraulic system has been disconnected.

2 Referring to *"Weekly checks"*, remove the fluid reservoir filler cap, and top-up the fluid level to the maximum mark, using only the specified fluid.

3 With the engine stopped, slowly move the steering from lock-to-lock several times to purge out the trapped air, then top-up the level in the fluid reservoir. Repeat this procedure until the fluid level in the reservoir does not drop any further.

4 Start the engine, then slowly move the steering from lock-to-lock several times to purge out any remaining air in the system.

25.3 Undo the retaining nut (arrowed), and free the feed pipe from the rear of the power steering pump. Fluid supply hose retaining clip also arrowed

25.5a The front two power steering pump retaining bolts can be accessed through holes in the drive pulley

25.5b Upper power steering pump mounting bolts (viewed from above)

26.4 Using a universal balljoint separator to free the balljoint shank from the swivel hub

Repeat this procedure until bubbles cease to appear in the fluid reservoir.

5 If, when turning the steering, an abnormal noise is heard from the fluid lines, it indicates that there is still air in the system. Check this by turning the wheels to the straight-ahead position and switching off the engine. If the fluid level in the reservoir rises, then air is present in the system, and further bleeding is necessary.

6 Once all traces of air have been removed from the power steering hydraulic system, turn the engine off and allow the system to cool. Once cool, check that fluid level is up to the maximum mark on the power steering fluid reservoir, topping-up if necessary.

25 Power steering pump - removal and refitting

Removal

1 Release the drivebelt tension as described in Chapter 1, and unhook the drivebelt from the pump pulley. The power steering pump is either mounted directly above or directly below the alternator, depending on the engine type and specification level of the vehicle.

2 Using brake hose clamps, clamp both the supply and return hoses near the power steering fluid reservoir. This will minimise fluid loss during subsequent operations.

3 Undo the retaining nut, and free the power steering hose retaining clip from the rear of the pump (see illustration).

4 Slacken the retaining clip, and disconnect the fluid supply hose from the rear of the pump. If the original Citroën clip is still fitted, cut the clip and discard it; replace it with a standard worm-drive hose clip on refitting. Slacken the union nut, and disconnect the feed pipe from the pump, along with its O-ring. Be prepared for some fluid spillage as the pipe and hose are disconnected, and plug the hose/pipe end and pump unions, to minimise fluid loss and prevent the entry of dirt into the system.

5 Slacken and remove the three bolts securing the power steering pump, and remove the pump from the engine compartment (see illustrations).

Refitting

6 Manoeuvre the pump into position, then refit its mounting bolts and tighten them securely.

7 Fit a new O-ring to the feed pipe union, then reconnect the pipe to the pump and securely tighten the union nut. Refit the supply pipe to the pump, and securely tighten its retaining clip. Remove the brake hose clamps used to minimise fluid loss.

8 Refit the fluid hose retaining clip to the rear of the pump, and securely tighten its retaining nut.

9 Refit the drivebelt to the pump pulley, and tension it as described in Chapter 1.

10 On completion, bleed the hydraulic system as described in Section 24.

26 Track rod balljoint - removal and refitting

Removal

1 Apply the handbrake, then jack up the front of the vehicle and support it on axle stands. Remove the appropriate front roadwheel.

2 If the balljoint is to be re-used, use a straight-edge and a scriber, or similar, to mark its relationship to the track rod.

3 Hold the track rod, and unscrew the balljoint locknut by a quarter of a turn. Do not move the locknut from this position, as it will serve as a handy reference mark on refitting.

4 Slacken and remove the nut securing the track rod balljoint to the swivel hub, and release the balljoint tapered shank using a universal balljoint separator (see illustration). Discard the nut - a new one must be used of refitting.

5 Counting the **exact** number of turns necessary to do so, unscrew the balljoint from the track rod end.

6 Count the number of exposed threads

between the end of the balljoint and the locknut, and record this figure. If a new balljoint is to be fitted, unscrew the locknut from the old balljoint.

7 Carefully clean the balljoint and the threads. Renew the balljoint if its movement is sloppy or too stiff, if excessively worn, or if damaged in any way; carefully check the stud taper and threads. If the balljoint gaiter is damaged, the complete balljoint assembly must be renewed; it is not possible to obtain the gaiter separately.

Refitting

8 If a new balljoint is to be fitted, screw the locknut onto its threads, and position it so that the same number of exposed threads are visible, as was noted prior to removal.

9 Screw the balljoint into the track rod by the number of turns noted on removal. This should bring the balljoint locknut to within a quarter of a turn from the locknut, with the alignment marks that were made on removal (if applicable) lined up.

10 Refit the balljoint shank to the swivel hub, then fit a new retaining nut and tighten it to the specified torque setting.

11 Refit the roadwheel, then lower the vehicle to the ground and tighten the roadwheel bolts to the specified torque setting.

12 Check and, if necessary, adjust the front wheel toe setting as described in Section 28, then securely tighten the balljoint locknut.

27 Track rod - removal and refitting

Removal

1 Remove the track rod balljoint as described in Section 26.

2 Referring to Section 23 for further information, either release the retaining clips and slide the steering gear gaiter off the end of the track rod, or release the track rod balljoint dust cover from rack, and slide it off the track rod (as applicable).

3 Unscrew the track rod inner balljoint from the steering rack end, whilst preventing the steering rack from turning by holding the

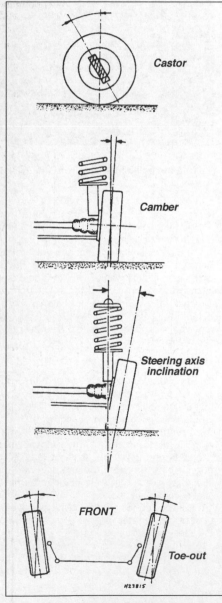

28.1 Wheel alignment and steering angle measurements

balljoint lock washer with a pair of grips. Take great care not to mark the surfaces of the rack and balljoint.

4 Remove the track rod assembly, and discard the lock washer - a new one must be used on refitting.

5 Examine the track rod inner balljoint for signs of slackness or tight spots, and check that the track rod itself is straight and free from damage. If necessary, renew the track rod; it is also recommended that the steering gear gaiter/dust cover is renewed.

Refitting

6 Locate the new lock washer assembly on the end of the steering rack, and apply a few drops of locking fluid to the track rod inner balljoint threads.

7 Screw the balljoint into the steering rack, and tighten it to the specified torque whilst retaining the lock washer with a suitable pair of grips. Again, take great care not to damage or mark the track rod balljoint or steering rack.

8 Where a gaiter was removed, carefully slide on the new gaiter, and locate it on the steering gear housing. Turn the steering fully from lock-to-lock, to check that the gaiter is correctly positioned on the track rod, then secure it in position with new retaining clips.

9 Where a dust cover was removed, carefully slide on the new cover, and locate it in its grooves on the steering rack collar and track rod.

10 Refit the track rod balljoint as described in Section 26.

28 Wheel alignment and steering angles - general information

Wheel alignment and steering angles - general

1 A car's steering and suspension geometry is defined in four basic settings - all angles are expressed in degrees (toe settings are also expressed as a measurement); the steering axis is defined as an imaginary line drawn through the axis of the suspension strut, extended where necessary to contact the ground **(see illustration)**.

2 **Camber** is the angle between each roadwheel and a vertical line drawn through its centre and tyre contact patch, when viewed from the front or rear of the car. Positive camber is when the roadwheels are tilted outwards from the vertical at the top; negative camber is when they are tilted inwards.

3 Camber is not adjustable, is given for reference only; while it can be checked using a camber checking gauge, if the figure obtained is significantly different from that specified, the vehicle must be taken for careful checking by a professional, as the fault can only be caused by wear or damage to the body or suspension components.

4 **Castor** is the angle between the steering axis and a vertical line drawn through each roadwheel's centre and tyre contact patch, when viewed from the side of the car. Positive castor is when the steering axis is tilted so that it contacts the ground ahead of the vertical; negative castor is when it contacts the ground behind the vertical.

5 Castor is not adjustable, and is given for reference only; while it can be checked using a castor checking gauge, if the figure obtained is significantly different from that specified, the vehicle must be taken for careful checking by a professional, as the fault can only be caused by wear or damage to the body or suspension components.

6 **Steering axis inclination/SAI** - also known as **kingpin inclination/KPI** - is the angle between the steering axis and a vertical line drawn through each roadwheel's centre and tyre contact patch, when viewed from the front or rear of the car.

7 SAI/KPI is not adjustable, and is given for reference only.

8 **Toe** is the difference, viewed from above, between lines drawn through the roadwheel centres and the car's centre-line. "Toe-in" is when the roadwheels point inwards, towards each other at the front, while "toe-out" is when they splay outwards from each other at the front.

9 The front wheel toe setting is adjusted by screwing the balljoints in or out of their track rods, to alter the effective length of the track rod assemblies.

10 Rear wheel toe setting is not adjustable, and is given for reference only. While it can be checked, if the figure obtained is significantly different from that specified, the vehicle must be taken for careful checking by a professional, as the fault can only be caused by wear or damage to the body or suspension components.

Checking - general

11 Due to the special measuring equipment necessary to check the wheel alignment, and the skill required to use it properly, the checking and adjustment of these settings is best left to a Citroën dealer or similar expert; note that most tyre-fitting shops now possess sophisticated checking equipment.

12 For **accurate** checking, the vehicle **must** be at the kerb weight, ie. fully unladen with a full tank of fuel, and the vehicle ride height must be correct (see Section 18).

13 Before starting work, always check first that the tyre sizes and types are as specified, then check the pressures and tread wear, the roadwheel run-out, the condition of the hub bearings, the steering wheel free play, and the condition of the front suspension components (Chapter 1). Correct any faults found.

14 Park the vehicle on level ground, check that the front roadwheels are in the straight-ahead position, then rock the rear and front ends to settle the suspension. Release the handbrake, and roll the vehicle backwards 1 metre, then forwards again, to relieve any stresses in the steering and suspension components.

Toe setting - checking and adjusting

Front wheel toe setting

15 The front wheel toe setting is checked by measuring the distance between the front and rear inside edges of the roadwheel rims.

16 Prepare the vehicle as described in paragraphs 12 to 14 above.

17 If the measurement procedure is being used, carefully measure the distance between the front edges of the wheel rims and the rear edges of the rims. Subtract the rear measurement from the front measurement, and check that the result is within the specified range.

18 If adjustment is necessary, apply the handbrake, then jack up the front of the vehicle and support it securely on axle stands. Turn the steering wheel onto full-left lock, and record the number of exposed threads on the right-hand track rod end. Now turn the steering onto full-right lock, and record the number of threads on the left-hand side. If there are the same number of threads visible on both sides, then subsequent adjustment should be made equally on both sides. If there are more threads visible on one side than the other, it will be necessary to compensate for this during adjustment. **Note:** *It is most important that after*

adjustment, the same number of threads are visible on each track rod end.

19 First clean the track rod threads; if they are corroded, apply penetrating fluid before starting adjustment. Release the rubber gaiter outboard clips (where necessary), and peel back the gaiters; apply a smear of grease to the inside of the gaiters, so that both are free, and will not be twisted or strained as their respective track rods are rotated.

20 Use a straight-edge and a scriber or similar to mark the relationship of each track rod to its balljoint then, holding each track rod in turn, unscrew its locknut fully.

21 Alter the length of the track rods, bearing in mind the note made in paragraph 18. Screw them into or out of the balljoints, rotating the track rod using an open-ended spanner fitted to the flats provided on the track rod; shortening the track rods (screwing them into their balljoints) will reduce toe-in/increase toe-out **(see illustration)**.

22 When the setting is correct, hold the track rods and securely tighten the balljoint locknuts. Check that the balljoints are seated correctly in their sockets, and count the exposed threads to check the length of both track rods. If they are not the same, then the adjustment has not been made equally, and problems will be encountered with tyre scrubbing in turns; also, the steering wheel spokes will no longer be horizontal when the wheels are in the straight-ahead position.

28.21 Adjusting the front wheel alignment

23 If the track rod lengths are the same, check that the toe setting has been correctly adjusted by lowering the vehicle to the ground and re-checking the toe setting; re-adjust if necessary. If the setting is correct, securely tighten the track rod balljoint locknuts. Ensure that the rubber gaiters are seated correctly, and are not twisted or strained, and secure them in position with new retaining clips (where necessary).

Rear wheel toe setting

24 The procedure for checking the rear toe setting is same as described for the front in paragraph 17. The setting is not adjustable - see paragraph 10.

Notes

Chapter 11 Bodywork and fittings

Contents

Body exterior fittings - removal and refitting 23
Bonnet - removal, refitting and adjustment 8
Bonnet lock - removal and refitting 10
Bonnet release cable - removal and refitting 9
Central locking components - removal and refitting 17
Centre console - removal and refitting 27
Door - removal, refitting and adjustment 11
Door inner trim panel - removal and refitting 12
Door handle and lock components - removal and refitting 13
Door window glass and regulator - removal and refitting 14
Electric window components renewal - general information 18
Exterior mirrors and associated components - removal
  and refitting 19
Facia panel assembly - removal and refitting 28
Front bumper - removal and refitting 6
General information 1

Interior trim - removal and refitting 26
Maintenance - bodywork and underframe 2
Maintenance - upholstery and carpets 3
Major body damage - repair 5
Minor body damage - repair 4
Rear bumper - removal and refitting 7
Rear quarter window (three-door models) - removal
  and refitting 21
Seat belt components - removal and refitting 25
Seats - removal and refitting 24
Sunroof - general information 22
Tailgate and support struts - removal and refitting 15
Tailgate lock components - removal and refitting 16
Windscreen, tailgate and fixed rear quarter window glass -
  general information 20

Degrees of difficulty

Easy, suitable for novice with little experience	**Fairly easy**, suitable for beginner with some experience	**Fairly difficult**, suitable for competent DIY mechanic	**Difficult**, suitable for experienced DIY mechanic	**Very difficult**, suitable for expert DIY or professional

1 General information

The bodyshell is made of pressed-steel sections, and is available in both three- and five-door Hatchback versions as well as in Estate form. Most components are welded together, but some use is made of structural adhesives; the front wings are bolted on.

The bonnet, door, and some other vulnerable panels are made of zinc-coated metal, and are further protected by being coated with an anti-chip primer prior to being sprayed.

Extensive use is made of plastic materials, mainly in the interior, but also in exterior components. The front and rear bumpers, front grille and tailgate assembly are injection-moulded from a synthetic material which is very strong and yet light. Plastic components such as wheel arch liners are fitted to the underside of the vehicle, to improve the body's resistance to corrosion.

2 Maintenance - bodywork and underframe
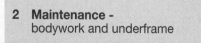

The general condition of a vehicle's bodywork is the one thing that significantly affects its value. Maintenance is easy, but needs to be regular. Neglect, particularly after minor damage, can lead quickly to further deterioration and costly repair bills. It is important also to keep watch on those parts of the vehicle not immediately visible, for instance the underside, inside all the wheel arches, and the lower part of the engine compartment.

The basic maintenance routine for the bodywork is washing - preferably with a lot of water, from a hose. This will remove all the loose solids which may have stuck to the vehicle. It is important to flush these off in such a way as to prevent grit from scratching the finish. The wheel arches and underframe need washing in the same way, to remove any accumulated mud, which will retain moisture and tend to encourage rust. Paradoxically enough, the best time to clean the underframe and wheel arches is in wet weather, when the mud is thoroughly wet and soft. In very wet weather, the underframe is usually cleaned of large accumulations automatically, and this is a good time for inspection.

Periodically, except on vehicles with a wax-based underbody protective coating, it is a good idea to have the whole of the underframe of the vehicle steam-cleaned, engine compartment included, so that a thorough inspection can be carried out to see what minor repairs and renovations are necessary. Steam-cleaning is available at many garages, and is necessary for the removal of the accumulation of oily grime, which sometimes is allowed to become thick in certain areas. If steam-cleaning facilities are not available, there are some excellent grease solvents available which can be brush-applied; the dirt can then be simply hosed off. Note that these methods should not be used on vehicles with wax-based underbody protective coating, or the coating will be removed. Such vehicles should be inspected annually, preferably just prior to Winter, when the underbody should be washed down, and any damage to the wax coating repaired. Ideally, a completely fresh coat should be applied. It would also be worth considering the use of such wax-based protection for injection into door panels, sills, box sections, etc, as an additional safeguard against rust damage, where such protection is not provided by the vehicle manufacturer.

After washing paintwork, wipe off with a chamois leather to give an unspotted clear finish. A coat of clear protective wax polish will give added protection against chemical pollutants in the air. If the paintwork sheen has dulled or oxidised, use a cleaner/polisher combination to restore the brilliance of the shine. This requires a little effort, but such dulling is usually caused because regular washing has been neglected. Care needs to be taken with metallic paintwork, as special non-abrasive cleaner/polisher is required to avoid damage to the finish. Always check that the door and ventilator opening drain holes and pipes are completely clear, so that water can be drained out. Brightwork should be treated in the same way as paintwork. Windscreens and windows can be kept clear of the smeary film which often appears, by the use of proprietary glass cleaner. Never use any form of wax or other body or chromium polish on glass.

3 Maintenance - upholstery and carpets

Mats and carpets should be brushed or vacuum-cleaned regularly, to keep them free of grit. If they are badly stained, remove them from the vehicle for scrubbing or sponging, and make quite sure they are dry before refitting. Seats and interior trim panels can be kept clean by wiping with a damp cloth. If they do become stained (which can be more apparent on light-coloured upholstery), use a little liquid detergent and a soft nail brush to scour the grime out of the grain of the material. Do not forget to keep the headlining clean in the same way as the upholstery. When using liquid cleaners inside the vehicle, do not over-wet the surfaces being cleaned. Excessive damp could get into the seams and padded interior, causing stains, offensive odours or even rot.

HAYNES HiNT *If the inside of the vehicle gets wet accidentally, it is worthwhile taking some trouble to dry it out properly, particularly where carpets are involved. Do not leave oil or electric heaters inside the vehicle for this purpose.*

4 Minor body damage - repair

Note: *For more detailed information about bodywork repair, Haynes Publishing produce a book by Lindsay Porter called "The Car Bodywork Repair Manual". This incorporates information on such aspects as rust treatment, painting and glass-fibre repairs, as well as details on more ambitious repairs involving welding and panel beating.*

Repairs of minor scratches in bodywork

If the scratch is very superficial, and does not penetrate to the metal of the bodywork, repair is very simple. Lightly rub the area of the scratch with a paintwork renovator, or a very fine cutting paste, to remove loose paint from the scratch, and to clear the surrounding bodywork of wax polish. Rinse the area with clean water.

Apply touch-up paint to the scratch using a fine paint brush; continue to apply fine layers of paint until the surface of the paint in the scratch is level with the surrounding paintwork. Allow the new paint at least two weeks to harden, then blend it into the surrounding paintwork by rubbing the scratch area with a paintwork renovator or a very fine cutting paste. Finally, apply wax polish.

Where the scratch has penetrated right through to the metal of the bodywork, causing the metal to rust, a different repair technique is required. Remove any loose rust from the bottom of the scratch with a penknife, then apply rust-inhibiting paint to prevent the formation of rust in the future. Using a rubber or nylon applicator, fill the scratch with bodystopper paste. If required, this paste can be mixed with cellulose thinners to provide a very thin paste which is ideal for filling narrow scratches. Before the stopper-paste in the scratch hardens, wrap a piece of smooth cotton rag around the top of a finger. Dip the finger in cellulose thinners, and quickly sweep it across the surface of the stopper-paste in the scratch; this will ensure that the surface of the stopper-paste is slightly hollowed. The scratch can now be painted over as described earlier in this Section.

Repairs of dents in bodywork

When deep denting of the vehicle's bodywork has taken place, the first task is to pull the dent out, until the affected bodywork almost attains its original shape. There is little point in trying to restore the original shape completely, as the metal in the damaged area will have stretched on impact, and cannot be reshaped fully to its original contour. It is better to bring the level of the dent up to a point which is about 3 mm below the level of the surrounding bodywork. In cases where the dent is very shallow anyway, it is not worth trying to pull it out at all. If the underside of the dent is accessible, it can be hammered out gently from behind, using a mallet with a wooden or plastic head. Whilst doing this, hold a suitable block of wood firmly against the outside of the panel, to absorb the impact from the hammer blows and thus prevent a large area of the bodywork from being "belled-out".

Should the dent be in a section of the bodywork which has a double skin, or some other factor making it inaccessible from behind, a different technique is called for. Drill several small holes through the metal inside the area - particularly in the deeper section. Then screw long self-tapping screws into the holes, just sufficiently for them to gain a good purchase in the metal. Now the dent can be pulled out by pulling on the protruding heads of the screws with a pair of pliers.

The next stage of the repair is the removal of the paint from the damaged area, and from an inch or so of the surrounding "sound" bodywork. This is accomplished most easily by using a wire brush or abrasive pad on a power drill, although it can be done just as effectively by hand, using sheets of abrasive paper. To complete the preparation for filling, score the surface of the bare metal with a screwdriver or the tang of a file, or alternatively, drill small holes in the affected area. This will provide a really good "key" for the filler paste.

To complete the repair, see the Section on filling and respraying.

Repairs of rust holes or gashes in bodywork

Remove all paint from the affected area, and from an inch or so of the surrounding "sound" bodywork, using an abrasive pad or a wire brush on a power drill. If these are not available, a few sheets of abrasive paper will do the job most effectively. With the paint removed, you will be able to judge the severity of the corrosion, and therefore decide whether to renew the whole panel (if this is possible) or to repair the affected area. New body panels are not as expensive as most people think, and it is often quicker and more satisfactory to fit a new panel than to attempt to repair large areas of corrosion.

Remove all fittings from the affected area, except those which will act as a guide to the original shape of the damaged bodywork (eg headlight shells etc). Then, using tin snips or a hacksaw blade, remove all loose metal and any other metal badly affected by corrosion. Hammer the edges of the hole inwards, in order to create a slight depression for the filler paste.

Wire-brush the affected area to remove the powdery rust from the surface of the remaining metal. Paint the affected area with rust-inhibiting paint, if the back of the rusted area is accessible, treat this also.

Before filling can take place, it will be necessary to block the hole in some way. This can be achieved by the use of aluminium or plastic mesh, or aluminium tape.

Aluminium or plastic mesh, or glass-fibre matting, is probably the best material to use for a large hole. Cut a piece to the approximate size and shape of the hole to be filled, then position it in the hole so that its edges are below the level of the surrounding bodywork. It can be retained in position by several blobs of filler paste around its periphery.

Aluminium tape should be used for small or very narrow holes. Pull a piece off the roll, trim it to the approximate size and shape required, then pull off the backing paper (if used) and stick the tape over the hole; it can be overlapped if the thickness of one piece is insufficient. Burnish down the edges of the tape with the handle of a screwdriver or similar, to ensure that the tape is securely attached to the metal underneath.

Bodywork repairs - filling and respraying

Before using this Section, see the Sections on dent, deep scratch, rust holes and gash repairs.

Many types of bodyfiller are available, but generally speaking, those proprietary kits which contain a tin of filler paste and a tube of resin hardener are best for this type of repair. A wide, flexible plastic or nylon applicator will be found invaluable for imparting a smooth and well-contoured finish to the surface of the filler.

Mix up a little filler on a clean piece of card or board - measure the hardener carefully (follow the maker's instructions on the pack), otherwise the filler will set too rapidly or too slowly. Using the applicator, apply the filler paste to the prepared area; draw the applicator across the surface of the filler to achieve the correct contour and to level the surface. As soon as a contour that approximates to the correct one is achieved, stop working the paste - if you carry on too long, the paste will become sticky and begin to "pick-up" on the applicator. Continue to add thin layers of filler paste at 20-minute intervals, until the level of the filler is just proud of the surrounding bodywork.

Once the filler has hardened, the excess can be removed using a metal plane or file. From then on, progressively-finer grades of abrasive paper should be used, starting with a 40-grade production paper, and finishing with a 400-grade wet-and-dry paper. Always wrap the abrasive paper around a flat rubber, cork, or wooden block - otherwise the surface of the filler will not be completely flat. During the smoothing of the filler surface, the wet-and-dry paper should be periodically rinsed in water. This will ensure that a very smooth finish is imparted to the filler at the final stage.

At this stage, the "dent" should be surrounded by a ring of bare metal, which in turn should be encircled by the finely "feathered" edge of the good paintwork. Rinse the repair area with clean water, until all of the dust produced by the rubbing-down operation has gone.

Spray the whole area with a light coat of primer - this will show up any imperfections in the surface of the filler. Repair these imperfections with fresh filler paste or bodystopper, and once more smooth the surface with abrasive paper. Repeat this spray-and-repair procedure until you are satisfied that the surface of the filler, and the feathered edge of the paintwork, are perfect. Clean the repair area with clean water, and allow to dry fully.

> **HAYNES HINT**
> If bodystopper is used, it can be mixed with cellulose thinners, to form a really thin paste which is ideal for filling small holes.

The repair area is now ready for final spraying. Paint spraying must be carried out in a warm, dry, windless and dust-free atmosphere. This condition can be created artificially if you have access to a large indoor working area, but if you are forced to work in the open, you will have to pick your day very carefully. If you are working indoors, dousing the floor in the work area with water will help to settle the dust which would otherwise be in the atmosphere. If the repair area is confined to one body panel, mask off the surrounding panels; this will help to minimise the effects of a slight mis-match in paint colours. Bodywork fittings (eg chrome strips, door handles etc) will also need to be masked off. Use genuine masking tape, and several thicknesses of newspaper, for the masking operations.

Before commencing to spray, agitate the aerosol can thoroughly, then spray a test area (an old tin, or similar) until the technique is mastered. Cover the repair area with a thick coat of primer; the thickness should be built up using several thin layers of paint, rather than one thick one. Using 400-grade wet-and-dry paper, rub down the surface of the primer until it is really smooth. While doing this, the work area should be thoroughly doused with water, and the wet-and-dry paper periodically rinsed in water. Allow to dry before spraying on more paint.

Spray on the top coat, again building up the thickness by using several thin layers of paint. Start spraying at one edge of the repair area, and then, using a side-to-side motion, work until the whole repair area and about 2 inches of the surrounding original paintwork is covered. Remove all masking material 10 to 15 minutes after spraying on the final coat of paint.

Allow the new paint at least two weeks to harden, then, using a paintwork renovator, or a very fine cutting paste, blend the edges of the paint into the existing paintwork. Finally, apply wax polish.

Plastic components

With the use of more and more plastic body components by the vehicle manufacturers (eg bumpers, spoilers, and in some cases major body panels), rectification of more serious damage to such items has become a matter of either entrusting repair work to a specialist in this field, or renewing complete components. Repair of such damage by the DIY owner is not really feasible, owing to the cost of the equipment and materials required for effecting such repairs. The basic technique involves making a groove along the line of the crack in the plastic, using a rotary burr in a power drill. The damaged part is then welded back together, using a hot-air gun to heat up and fuse a plastic filler rod into the groove. Any excess plastic is then removed, and the area rubbed down to a smooth finish. It is important that a filler rod of the correct plastic is used, as body components can be made of a variety of different types (eg polycarbonate, ABS, polypropylene).

Damage of a less serious nature (abrasions, minor cracks etc) can be repaired by the DIY owner using a two-part epoxy filler repair material. Once mixed in equal proportions, this is used in similar fashion to the bodywork filler used on metal panels. The filler is usually cured in twenty to thirty minutes, ready for sanding and painting.

If the owner is renewing a complete component himself, or if he has repaired it with epoxy filler, he will be left with the problem of finding a suitable paint for finishing which is compatible with the type of plastic used. At one time, the use of a universal paint was not possible, owing to the complex range of plastics encountered in body component applications. Standard paints, generally speaking, will not bond to plastic or rubber satisfactorily. However, it is now possible to obtain a plastic body parts finishing kit which consists of a pre-primer treatment, a primer and coloured top coat. Full instructions are normally supplied with a kit, but basically, the method of use is to first apply the pre-primer to the component concerned, and allow it to dry for up to 30 minutes. Then the primer is applied, and left to dry for about an hour before finally applying the special-coloured top coat. The result is a correctly-coloured component, where the paint will flex with the plastic or rubber, a property that standard paint does not normally posses.

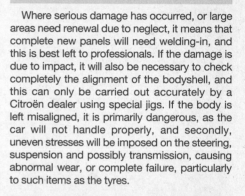

5 Major body damage - repair

Where serious damage has occurred, or large areas need renewal due to neglect, it means that complete new panels will need welding-in, and this is best left to professionals. If the damage is due to impact, it will also be necessary to check completely the alignment of the bodyshell, and this can only be carried out accurately by a Citroën dealer using special jigs. If the body is left misaligned, it is primarily dangerous, as the car will not handle properly, and secondly, uneven stresses will be imposed on the steering, suspension and possibly transmission, causing abnormal wear, or complete failure, particularly to such items as the tyres.

6 Front bumper - removal and refitting

Removal

1 Apply the handbrake, then jack up the front of the vehicle and support it on axle stands.
2 Remove both the right- and left-hand headlights as described in Chapter 12.
3 Working through the headlamp apertures, slacken and remove the four bolts (two on either side) securing the upper ends of the bumper to the vehicle.
4 Slacken and remove the five bolts securing the bottom edge of the bumper to the vehicle.
5 Working from underneath the vehicle, undo the two bolts (one on either end) securing the lower ends of the bumper to the vehicle. Where necessary, disconnect the wiring connectors from the front foglamps.
6 Release both the left- and right-hand ends of the bumper, and pull the bumper away from the vehicle in a forwards direction.

Refitting

7 Refitting is a reverse of the removal procedure, ensuring that the bumper mounting bolts are securely tightened.

7.2 Unscrew the wheel brace retaining clip from its mounting stud in the luggage compartment

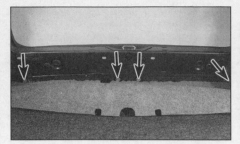

7.3 Peel back the carpet to gain access to the rear bumper retaining bolts (arrowed)

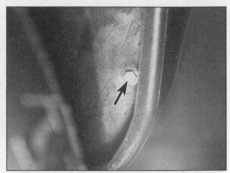

7.5 Slacken and remove the bolts securing the rear bumper to the wheel arch liners (arrowed) . . .

7 Rear bumper - removal and refitting

Removal

Hatchback

1 Remove the luggage compartment rear trim panels (where fitted) as described in Section 26.

2 On five-door models, remove the wheel brace, and unscrew the wheel brace clip from the rear right-hand corner of the luggage compartment **(see illustration)**. Remove the retaining nut and clip from the same position on the left-hand side.

7.6a . . . and the vehicle body . . .

3 Release the retaining clips and peel back the luggage compartment carpet, then slacken and remove the four bumper retaining bolts **(see illustration)**.

4 Chock the front wheels, then jack up the rear of the vehicle and support it on axle stands.

5 Working from underneath the vehicle, undo the two bolts (one either side) securing the ends of the bumper to the wheel arch liner **(see illustration)**.

6 Undo the two bolts securing the bumper to the underside of the vehicle, then release the left- and right-hand ends of the bumpers from their mountings, and pull the bumper away from the vehicle in a rearwards direction **(see illustrations)**.

Estate

7 Remove the rear light cluster on each side as described in Chapter 12.

8 Undo the two bumper upper retaining nuts, one each side, located at the base of the light cluster apertures.

9 Chock the front wheels, then jack up the rear of the vehicle and support it on axle stands. Remove the rear roadwheels.

10 Undo the screws and release the clips securing the rear wheel arch liners to the bumper and body on both sides.

11 Working from underneath the vehicle, undo the two bolts, one each side, securing the sides of the bumper to the body.

12 Work along the lower edge of the bumper and remove the two lower retaining bolts.

13 With the help of an assistant, pull the bumper rearwards, disconnect the rear foglight wiring connectors, and remove the bumper from the vehicle.

Refitting

14 Refitting is a reverse of the removal procedure, ensuring that all disturbed fasteners are securely tightened.

8 Bonnet - removal, refitting and adjustment

Removal

1 Open the bonnet and get an assistant to support it, then, using a pencil or felt tip pen, mark the outline position of each bonnet hinge relative to the bonnet, to use as a guide on refitting.

2 Disconnect the windscreen washer supply pipe from its non-return valve on the right-hand side, then undo the bonnet retaining bolts and, with the help of an assistant, carefully lift the bonnet clear. Store the bonnet out of the way in a safe place **(see illustrations)**.

3 Inspect the bonnet hinges for signs of wear and free play at the pivots, and if necessary renew. Each hinge is secured to the body by two pivot bolts. On refitting, apply a smear of multi-purpose grease to the shanks of the hinge pivot bolts, and tighten them securely.

7.6b . . . then remove the bumper from the rear of the vehicle

8.2a Slacken and remove the bonnet-to-hinge retaining bolts . . .

8.2b . . . then, with the aid of an assistant, lift off the bonnet

9.5 Removing the bonnet release lever retaining bolts

10.1 Undo the three retaining screws, and remove the plastic cover to gain access to the bonnet lock

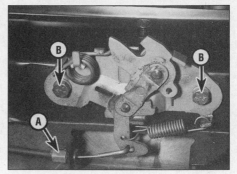

10.2 Unclip the release cable (A), then undo the retaining bolts (B) and remove the bonnet lock

Refitting and adjustment

4 With the aid of an assistant, offer up the bonnet and loosely fit the retaining bolts. Align the hinges with the marks made on removal, then tighten the retaining bolts securely, and reconnect the windscreen washer supply pipe.

5 Close the bonnet, and check for alignment with the adjacent panels. If necessary, slacken the hinge bolts and re-align the bonnet to suit. Once the bonnet is correctly aligned, tighten the hinge bolts to the specified torque.

6 Once the bonnet is correctly aligned, check that the bonnet fastens and releases in a satisfactory manner. If adjustment is necessary, slacken the bonnet lock retaining bolts, and adjust the position of the lock to suit. Once the lock is operating correctly, securely tighten its retaining bolts.

9 Bonnet release cable - removal and refitting

Removal

1 Open up the bonnet, then undo the three retaining screws, and remove the plastic cover to gain full access to the bonnet lock.

2 Unclip the bonnet release outer cable from the lock bracket, then release the inner cable from the lock lever.

3 Work back along the length of the cable, noting its correct routing, and free it from all the relevant retaining clips and ties. Tie a length of string to the end of the cable.

4 From inside the vehicle, release the panel fasteners by rotating them through a quarter of a turn, and remove the driver's side lower facia panel.

5 Slacken and remove the two retaining bolts, then free the bonnet release lever from its retaining bracket, and withdraw the cable **(see illustration)**. Once the cable is free, untie the string and leave it in position in the vehicle; the string can then be used to draw the new cable back into position.

Refitting

6 Tie the inner end of the string to the end of the cable, then use the string to draw the bonnet release cable through into the engine compartment. Once the cable is through, untie the string.

7 Manoeuvre the bonnet release lever back into position, and securely tighten its retaining bolts.

8 Ensure the cable is correctly routed, and secured to all the relevant retaining clips. Connect the end of the inner cable to the lock lever, then clip the outer cable into position in the lock bracket.

9 Operate the bonnet release lever, and check that the lock operates smoothly, without any sign of undue resistance. Check that the bonnet fastens and releases in a satisfactory manner. If adjustment is necessary, slacken the bonnet lock retaining bolts, and adjust the position of the lock to suit. Once the lock is operating correctly, securely tighten its retaining bolts and refit the lock cover.

10 Refit the lower facia panel, and secure it in position by rotating its fasteners through a quarter of a turn.

10 Bonnet lock - removal and refitting

Removal

1 Open up the bonnet, then undo the three retaining screws, and remove the plastic cover to gain full access to the bonnet lock **(see illustration)**. Mark the outline of the bonnet lock on the body, to use as a guide on refitting.

2 Unclip the bonnet release outer cable from the lock bracket, then release the inner cable from the lock lever **(see illustration)**.

3 Undo the two retaining bolts, and remove the lock assembly from the vehicle.

Refitting

4 Refit the lock to the vehicle, aligning it with

the marks made on removal, and securely tighten its retaining bolts.

5 Connect the end of the inner cable to the lock lever, then clip the outer cable into position in the lock bracket.

6 Check that the bonnet fastens and releases in a satisfactory manner. If adjustment is necessary, slacken the bonnet lock retaining bolts, and adjust the position of the lock to suit. Once the lock is operating correctly, securely tighten its retaining bolts and refit the lock cover.

11 Door - removal, refitting and adjustment

Removal

1 Open the door, to gain access to the wiring connector which is fitted to the front edge of the door.

2 Where a circular wiring connector is used, unscrew the connector locking ring until its tab is located between the lugs on the connector, then disconnect the wiring connector from the door **(see illustration)**. Where a rectangular connector is used, pull out the locking clip to release it, then disconnect the connector from the door.

3 Undo the two bolts securing the check link

11.2 On circular wiring connectors, unscrew the locking ring until its tab is located between the connector lugs (arrowed), then pull it away from the door

to the pillar (see illustration). On models where the bolts are not accessible, using a hammer and suitable punch, drive out the check link roll pin.

4 Loosen the two hinge pin grub bolts, then, with the aid of an assistant, lift the door upwards to release it from the hinge pins, and remove it from the vehicle (see illustration).

5 Examine the hinges for signs of wear or damage, and if necessary renew. The hinges are welded to the door and pillar, and if renewal is necessary, the task should be entrusted to a Citroën dealer.

Refitting

6 Apply a smear of multi-purpose grease to the hinge pins, then, with the aid of an assistant, refit the door to the vehicle. Once the door is correctly positioned, securely tighten the hinge grub bolts.

7 Align the check link with the door pillar, and securely tighten its retaining bolts. Where the check link roll pin was removed, align the link with its retaining bracket, and secure it in position by tapping in the roll pin.

8 Reconnect the wiring connector, and secure it in position by tightening its retaining ring, or by pressing in its retaining clip (as applicable).

Adjustment

9 Adjustment of the door position is not possible by the home mechanic. However, small adjustments can be made by slightly bending the hinge pin using a special Citroën

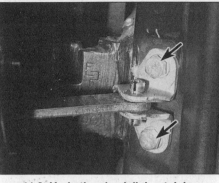

11.3 Undo the check link retaining bolts . . .

service tool. This task should be entrusted to a Citroën dealer.

12 Door inner trim panel - removal and refitting

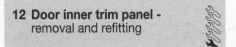

Removal

Front door

1 Open the door, and carefully prise out and remove the exterior mirror inner trim panel (see illustration).

2 Lift the door inner handle, then carefully prise the escutcheon out from the door panel and remove it (see illustration).

3 On models with manual windows, pull the

11.4 . . . then slacken the hinge grub pins (arrowed), and lift the door upwards and away from the vehicle

handle off the spindle, and remove the regulator escutcheon.

4 On models with electric windows, carefully prise the window switch out of the armrest, taking great care not to mark the switch or armrest. Disconnect the wiring connector, and remove the switch (see illustration).

5 Lift up the inner door lock operating button, then, using a small flat-bladed screwdriver, depress the retaining tab, and slide off the button (see illustration).

6 Slacken and remove the armrest retaining screws, and remove the armrest from the door (see illustration).

7 Remove the speaker as described in Chapter 12.

8 Release the door trim panel studs, carefully levering between the panel and door with a

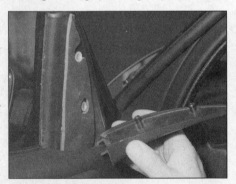

12.1 Unclip the exterior mirror inner trim panel from the door

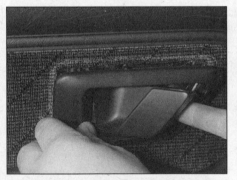

12.2 Lift the door inner handle, and remove the escutcheon from the door

12.4 On models with electric windows, remove the switch from the armrest

12.5 Depress the retaining tab, and slide the inner lock button off its link rod

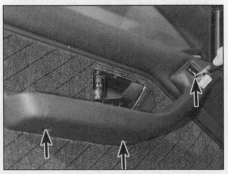

12.6 Undo the retaining screws (arrowed), and remove the armrest from the door

12.8 Removing the inner trim panel from the front door

12.10 Removing the small inner trim panel from the rear door

12.11 Pull the window winder handle and trim collar off the regulator spindle

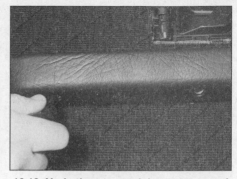

12.13 Undo the two retaining screws, and remove the armrest from the rear door

12.14 Undo the two retaining screws (arrowed) located behind the speaker grille

12.15 Unclip the inner trim panel, and remove it from the rear door

12.16 Refitting a door lock operating button. Note the locating tab (arrowed) engaged in the lower of the two button holes

suitable flat-bladed screwdriver. Work around the outside of the panel, and when all the studs are released, slide the panel upwards and away from the door **(see illustration)**.

Rear door

9 Lift the door inner handle, then carefully prise the escutcheon out from the door panel and remove it.

10 Carefully prise off the small inner trim panel from the rear of the door **(see illustration)**.

11 Pull the window winder handle off the spindle, and remove it, along with its trim collar **(see illustration)**.

12 Lift up the inner door lock operating button, then, using a small flat-bladed screwdriver, depress the retaining tab, and slide off the button **(see illustration 12.5)**.

13 Slacken and remove the armrest retaining

screws, and remove the armrest from the door **(see illustration)**.

14 Prise off the speaker grille, and slacken and remove the two retaining screws securing the trim panel to the door **(see illustration)**.

15 Release the door trim panel studs, carefully levering between the panel and door with a suitable flat-bladed screwdriver. Work around the outside of the panel, and when all the studs are released, lift the panel upwards and away from the door **(see illustration)**.

Refitting

16 Refitting of the trim panel is the reverse sequence of removal, noting the following points:

(a) Prior to refitting, check whether any of the trim panel retaining studs were broken on removal, and renew them as necessary.

(b) To refit the inner door lock operating button, first lock the door, to ensure that the link rod is in its lowest position. Position the button locating tab in the lower of the its two holes, then firmly push the button onto the rod, until it clips into position and the retaining tab appears in the upper hole (see illustration).

13 Door handle and lock components - removal and refitting

Removal

1 Remove the door inner trim panel as described in Section 12, then proceed as described under the relevant sub-heading.

Interior door handle

2 Unclip the interior handle from the door, and disconnect it from the link rod.

Exterior door handle

3 Carefully cut the rubber insulating panel away from the rear of the door, to gain access to the rear of the handle.

4 Undo the three screws securing the lock assembly to the door, then drop the lock assembly slightly to disengage it from the handle.

5 On five-door models, working through the door aperture, slacken and remove the retaining nut, then free the handle from the lock assembly, and withdraw it from the door **(see illustrations)**.

13.5a On five-door models, undo the retaining nut from the inside of the door . . .

13.5b . . . then remove the exterior handle

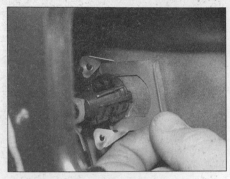

13.9a Slide out the retaining clip . . .

13.9b . . . then withdraw the lock cylinder, and disconnect it from its link rod

13.15a Undo the three retaining screws . . .

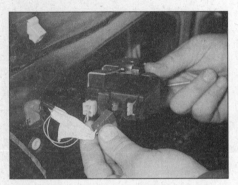

13.15b . . . then manoeuvre the lock assembly out of the door, and (where necessary) disconnect the wiring connector from the servo unit

6 On three-door models, slacken and remove the two bolts securing the handle to the outside of the door, then free the handle from the lock assembly and remove it from the door.

Front door lock cylinder

7 Carefully cut the rubber insulating panel away from the rear of the door, to gain access to the rear of the lock cylinder.
8 Undo the three screws securing the lock assembly to the door, and drop the lock assembly slightly to improve access to the lock cylinder.
9 Using a pair of pliers, slide out the lock cylinder retaining clip, then withdraw the lock

cylinder from the outside of the door, and free it from its link rod **(see illustrations)**.

Front door lock

10 Remove the interior lock handle as described in paragraph 2.
11 Remove the lock cylinder as described in paragraphs 7 to 9.
12 Manoeuvre the lock and link rod assembly out through the door aperture. On models with central locking, it will be necessary to disconnect the wiring connector from the servo motor as the lock is removed.

Rear door lock

13 Remove the interior door handle as described in paragraphs 1 and 2.
14 Carefully cut the rubber insulating panel away from the rear of the door, to gain access to the rear of the lock assembly.
15 Slacken and remove the three lock retaining screws, then manoeuvre the lock and link rod assembly out through the door aperture. On models with central locking, it will be necessary to disconnect the wiring connector from the servo motor as the lock is removed **(see illustrations)**.

Refitting

16 Refitting is the reverse of the removal sequence, noting the following points:
(a) *Ensure that all link rods are securely held in position by their retaining clips.*
(b) *Apply grease to all lock and link rod pivot points.*

(c) *Before installing the inner trim panel, thoroughly check the operation of all the door lock handles and, where applicable, the central locking system, and ensure that the rubber insulating panel is correctly positioned.*

14 Door window glass and regulator - removal and refitting

Removal

1 Remove the door inner trim panel as described in Section 12.
2 Carefully cut the rubber insulating panel away from the edge of the door, remove the panel, then proceed as described under the relevant sub-heading **(see illustration)**.

Front door window glass

3 With the window in the fully-raised position, slacken and remove the upper and lower window guide retaining bolts, and remove the guide from the front of the door **(see illustrations)**.
4 Temporarily refit the handle (or reconnect the switch, as applicable), and lower the window glass approximately halfway.
5 Working from inside the door, release the clip securing the window glass to the regulator peg by rotating it through 45°, then

14.2 Removing the rubber insulating panel from the front door

14.3a Undo the two retaining bolts (arrowed) . . .

14.3b . . . and remove the window guide from the door

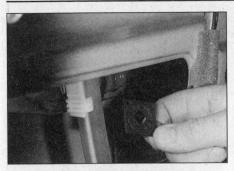

14.5 Remove the retaining clip as described in the text, and free the window glass from the regulator peg

14.6 Removing the window glass from the front door

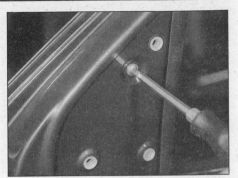

14.7a Undo the retaining screw . . .

slide off the clip, and free the glass from the regulator mechanism **(see illustration)**.

6 Fully lower the glass, and free the upper window guide from the rear of the sealing strip, then carefully manoeuvre the window glass out through the top of the door **(see illustration)**.

Rear door window glass

7 Undo the retaining screw from the inside, then remove the small outer trim panel from the door **(see illustrations)**.

8 Temporarily refit the handle, and lower the window glass.

9 Working around the edge of the strip, carefully ease the sealing strip out from the door, and remove it from the vehicle **(see illustration)**.

10 Release the window glass from the regulator mechanism as described above in paragraph 5, then carefully manoeuvre the glass out through the top of the door **(see illustrations)**.

Window regulator

11 Remove the window glass as described above.

12 Slacken and remove the five regulator retaining nuts, then carefully manoeuvre the regulator assembly out through the largest door panel aperture. On models with electric windows, it will be necessary to disconnect the wiring connector from the regulator motor as it becomes accessible **(see illustrations)**.

14.7b . . . and remove the trim panel from the outside of the rear door

14.9 Work around the edge of the sealing strip, freeing it from the door, and remove the strip

14.10a Remove the retaining clip, then free the window glass from the regulator . . .

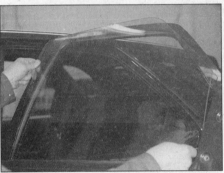

14.10b . . . and remove it from the top edge of the door

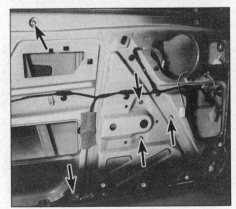

14.12a Undo the five regulator retaining nuts (arrowed) . . .

14.12b . . . and withdraw the regulator assembly through the largest door panel aperture

14.12c On models with electric windows, disconnect the wiring connector from the motor as the regulator is removed

15.2a Undo the retaining screw (arrowed) and remove the vent grille . . .

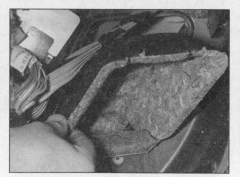

15.2b . . . and duct from each side of the luggage compartment

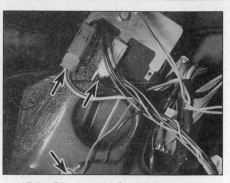

15.3a Disconnect the tailgate wiring connectors and earth lead connection (arrowed) - left-hand side shown . . .

Refitting

Front door window glass

13 Manoeuvre the window glass back into position through the top of the door.

14 Lower the window glass to the base of the door, and engage the upper guide with the rear of the sealing strip.

15 Raise the glass, and locate it on the regulator mechanism peg. Slide the retaining clip onto the regulator peg, and secure it in position by rotating it through 45°.

16 Fully raise the window glass, then refit the front window guide, tightening its retaining screws securely.

17 Check that the window glass can be raised and lowered smoothly, then refit the rubber insulating panel to the door.

18 Ensure the insulating panel is securely stuck to the door, and refit the inner trim panel as described in Section 12.

Rear door window glass

19 Manoeuvre the window glass back into position through the top of the door, and locate it on the regulator mechanism peg. Slide the retaining clip onto the regulator peg, and secure it in position by rotating it through 45°.

20 Engage the front edge of the sealing strip with the upper window glass guide, then work around the edge of the strip, and seat it back into position in the door. Refit the outer trim panel, and securely tighten its retaining screw.

21 Check that the window glass can be

raised and lowered smoothly, then refit the rubber insulating panel to the door.

22 Ensure the insulating panel is securely stuck to the door, and refit the inner trim panel as described in Section 12.

Window regulator

23 Reconnect the wiring connector (where applicable), and manoeuvre the regulator assembly back into position in the door. Refit the five retaining nuts, and tighten them securely.

24 Refit the window glass as described above.

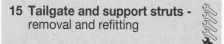

15 Tailgate and support struts - removal and refitting

Removal

Tailgate - Hatchback

1 Remove both the left- and right-hand rear light units as described in Chapter 12.

2 Undo the retaining screw, and remove the vent grilles and ducts which are situated on the left- and right-hand sides of the luggage compartment **(see illustrations)**.

3 Disconnect the tailgate wiring connectors, situated on the left- and right-hand sides, from the main wiring loom, and unscrew the bolt securing the earth lead to the vehicle body. Withdraw the wiring connectors from

15.3b . . . then withdraw the wiring looms from the rear of the vehicle, and free them from underneath the tailgate sealing strip

the rear of the body, then work back along the length of each loom, and release them from underneath the outside of the tailgate sealing strip, and from any relevant retaining clips **(see illustrations)**.

4 Release the rear screen washer supply pipe from underneath the top of the tailgate sealing strip, and disconnect it at its non-return valve **(see illustration)**.

5 Have an assistant support the tailgate, then raise the spring clips and pull the support struts off their balljoint mountings on the tailgate. Carefully prise out the hinge pin retaining clips, then tap both hinge pins out of position, and remove the tailgate from the vehicle **(see illustrations)**.

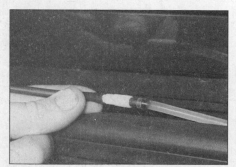

15.4 Release the tailgate washer pipe from underneath the sealing strip, and disconnect it at its non-return valve

15.5a Remove the retaining clips . . .

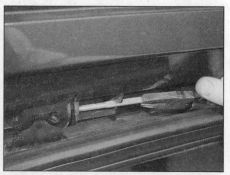

15.5b . . . and withdraw the tailgate hinge pins

6 Examine the hinge pins for signs of wear or damage, and renew if necessary.

Tailgate - Estate

7 Open the tailgate and undo the screws around the periphery of the tailgate trim panel. Undo the two screws located in the grab handle apertures, release the upper clip each side and remove the trim panel.
8 Disconnect the wiring harness from the tailgate inner panel.
9 Disconnect the rear screen washer supply pipe.
10 Have an assistant support the tailgate, then raise the spring clips and pull the support struts off their balljoint mountings on the tailgate.
11 Carefully prise out the hinge pin retaining clips, then tap both hinge pins out of position and remove the tailgate from the vehicle.
12 Examine the hinge pins for signs of wear or damage and renew as necessary.

Support struts

13 Support the tailgate in the open position, using a stout piece of wood, or with the help of an assistant.
14 Raise the spring clip, and pull the support strut off its balljoint mounting on the tailgate. Using a flat-bladed screwdriver, prise out the retaining clip, then carefully lever the strut off its balljoint, and remove it from the vehicle (see illustrations).

Refitting

Tailgate

15 Refitting is a reversal of the removal procedure, noting the following points:
(a) *Prior to refitting, apply a smear of multi-purpose grease to the hinge pins.*
(b) *Ensure that the hinge pins are securely retained by their retaining clips, and that the support struts are securely held in position by their spring clips.*
(c) *Ensure that the washer jet pipe and wiring looms are correctly located behind the tailgate sealing strip.*

Support struts

16 Refitting is a reverse of the removal procedure, ensuring that the strut is securely retained by its spring clip and retaining clip.

16 Tailgate lock components - removal and refitting

Removal

Tailgate lock - Hatchback

1 Open up the tailgate, then undo the two retaining bolts and remove the lock (see illustrations).

Tailgate lock - Estate

2 At the time of writing, no detailed information was available on removal and refitting of the tailgate lock assembly fitted to

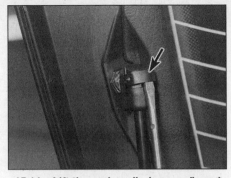
15.14a Lift the spring clip (arrowed), and free the support strut from the tailgate . . .

Estate models. However, the procedure is likely to be similar to that for Hatchback models.

Tailgate lock cylinder - Hatchback

3 Remove the tailgate wiper motor as described in Chapter 12.
4 Using a pair of pliers, slide out the lock retaining clip, and withdraw the lock cylinder and handle from the tailgate (see illustrations).

Refitting

5 Refitting is a reversal of the removal procedure.

16.1a Undo the two retaining bolts . . .

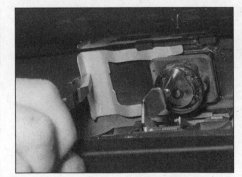
16.4a Slide out the retaining clip . . .

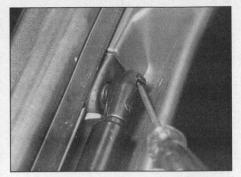
15.14b . . . then prise out the retaining clip, and free the strut from the body

17 Central locking components - removal and refitting

Electronic control unit

1 Open up the rear ashtray, then depress the retaining tang and remove the ashtray from the handbrake lever cover panel. Slacken and remove the rear retaining nut and the two front retaining screws, then manoeuvre the cover panel off the handbrake lever.
2 Undo the nut securing the control unit to the handbrake lever mounting stud, then

16.1b . . . and remove the lock from the base of the tailgate

16.4b . . . then withdraw the lock cylinder and handle assembly from the tailgate

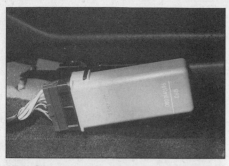

17.2 Central locking electronic control unit is mounted onto one of the handbrake lever studs

17.5 Removing a central locking servo unit from a lock assembly

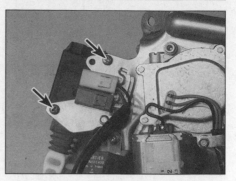

17.8 Tailgate lock servo motor is retained by two screws

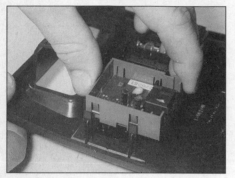

17.11 Removing the central locking receiver unit from the overhead console

17.13 Prise the two halves of the transmitter unit apart, and remove the batteries

disconnect the wiring connector and remove the unit from the vehicle **(see illustration)**.
3 Refitting is the reverse of removal.

Door lock servo unit

4 Remove the relevant door lock as described in Section 13.
5 The servo unit is a bayonet fit on the lock assembly. To remove it, twist it slightly to release it from the lock bracket, and disengage it from the lock peg **(see illustration)**.
6 On refitting, ensure that the servo unit is securely clipped in position, and that it is correctly engaged with the lock peg.

Tailgate lock servo unit

7 Remove the tailgate wiper motor as described in Chapter 12.
8 Undo the two retaining screws, and remove

the servo unit from wiper motor bracket **(see illustration)**.
9 Refitting is the reverse of the removal procedure.

Remote receiver unit

10 Carefully prise the courtesy light out from the overhead console, and disconnect it from its wiring connector. Remove the two console retaining screws, then lower the console out of position, and disconnect it from its wiring connectors.
11 Release the retaining clips, and remove the receiver unit from the top of the console **(see illustration)**.
12 Refitting is the reverse of removal.

Transmitter batteries

13 Using a small screwdriver, carefully prise the two halves of the transmitter apart, and

remove the two batteries, noting which way around they are fitted **(see illustration)**.
14 Fit the two batteries, ensuring that they are fitted the correct way around, and then clip the transmitter back together; the battery and transmitter terminals are marked "+" and "-" to avoid confusion.

18 Electric window components renewal - general information

Window switches
1 Refer to Chapter 12.

Window winder motors
2 The window winder electric motor is an integral part of the regulator mechanism, and cannot be renewed separately. Refer to Section 14 for regulator removal and refitting details.

19 Exterior mirrors and associated components - removal and refitting

Removal
Manually-operated mirror
1 Carefully prise off the mirror interior trim panel **(see illustration)**.
2 Unscrew the two retaining screws, then slacken and remove the adjusting lever grub screw, and slide the retaining plate off the mirror adjusting lever **(see illustrations)**.

19.1 On manually-operated mirrors, prise off the inner trim panel . . .

19.2a . . . then slacken and remove the two retaining screws . . .

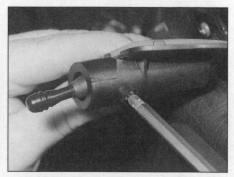

19.2b . . . and the adjusting lever grub screw . . .

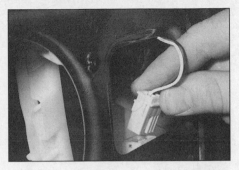

19.2c ... and remove the retaining plate from the adjusting lever

19.3 Undo the three retaining screws (arrowed), and remove the mirror assembly from the door

19.5 On electrically operated mirrors, remove the door inner trim panel to gain access to the mirror wiring connector

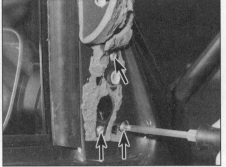

19.6a Peel back the rubber insulating foam ...

19.6b ... then undo the three retaining screws (arrowed) ...

19.6c ... and remove the mirror assembly from the door

3 Remove the rubber insulating foam, then slacken and remove the three retaining screws, and remove the mirror assembly from the door **(see illustration)**.

Electrically-operated mirror

4 Remove the door inner trim panel as described in Section 12.
5 Carefully cut the rubber insulating panel away from the front edge of the door, to gain access to the mirror wiring connector, and disconnect the connector from the main wiring loom **(see illustration)**.
6 Remove the rubber insulating foam, then slacken and remove the three retaining screws, and remove the mirror assembly from the door **(see illustrations)**.

Mirror glass

7 The mirror glass is stuck onto the mirror assembly, and removal will almost certainly lead to the glass being broken. Therefore, the mirror glass should not be removed unless it is to be replaced.
8 To ease removal, gently warm the glass with a hairdryer, then carefully lever the glass out of position.

Mirror switch (electrically-operated mirror)

9 Refer to Chapter 12.

Refitting

Manually-operated mirror

10 Offer up the mirror, and securely tighten its three retaining screws.

11 Refit the insulating foam, then slide the retaining plate over the adjusting lever, and secure it in position with its two retaining screws. Refit the adjusting lever grub screw, and check the operation of the lever.
12 If all is well, refit the inner trim panel to the door.

Electrically-operated mirror

13 Offer up the mirror, feeding its wiring connector through the door, and securely tighten its retaining screws.
14 Reconnect the mirror wiring connector, ensuring that the wiring loom is correctly routed.
15 Refit the insulating foam and panel to the door, and refit the inner trim panel as described in Section 12.

Mirror glass

16 Prior to fitting the new glass, use a solvent to remove all traces of old adhesive from the mounting plate. Remove the backing from the new mirror, then warm the adhesive gently, and press the glass firmly onto its mounting plate.

Mirror switch

17 Refitting is the reverse of removal.

20 Windscreen, tailgate and fixed rear quarter window glass - general information

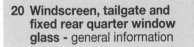

These areas of glass are secured by the tight fit of the weatherstrip in the body

aperture, and are bonded in position with a special adhesive. The removal and refitting of these areas of fixed glass is difficult, messy and time-consuming task, which is beyond the scope of the home mechanic. It is difficult, unless one has plenty of practice, to obtain a secure, waterproof fit. Furthermore, the task carries a high risk of breakage; this applies especially to the laminated glass windscreen. In view of this, owners are strongly advised to have this sort of work carried out by one of the many specialist windscreen fitters.

21 Rear quarter window (three-door models) - removal and refitting

At the time of writing, no information was available on removal and refitting of the rear quarter window on three-door models. Therefore, this task should be entrusted to a Citroën dealer.

22 Sunroof - general information

A manual or electric sunroof was fitted is standard equipment on most models, and is available as an option on other models.
Due to the complexity of the sunroof mechanism, considerable expertise is needed to repair, replace or adjust the sunroof

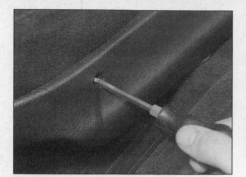

24.1a Undo the trim panel retaining screws . . .

24.1b . . . and peel back the trim panel to improve access to the front seat mounting bolts

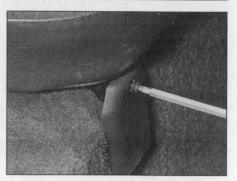

24.4a Undo the retaining screws . . .

components successfully. Removal of the roof first requires the headlining to be removed, which is a complex and tedious operation, and not a task to be undertaken lightly (see Section 26). Therefore, any problems with the sunroof should be referred to a Citroën dealer.

On models with an electric sunroof, if the sunroof motor fails to operate, first check the relevant fuse. If the fault cannot be traced and rectified, the sunroof can be opened and closed manually using a suitable Allen key to turn the motor spindle. To gain access to the motor spindle, carefully prise the courtesy light out of the overhead console, then undo the two console retaining screws, and drop the console assembly out of position. Insert the Allen key in the motor spindle, and rotate the key to move the sunroof to the required position. A suitable wrench is supplied with the vehicle, and should be located behind the driver's side lower facia panel, where it is clipped onto the fusebox.

23 Body exterior fittings - removal and refitting

Wheel arch liners and body under-panels

1 The various plastic covers fitted to the underside of the vehicle are secured in

24.4b . . . and remove the trim covers to gain access to the rear seat front retaining nuts

position by a mixture of screws and retaining clips, and removal will be fairly obvious on inspection. Work methodically around the panel, removing its retaining screws and releasing its retaining clips until the panel is free and can be removed from the underside of the vehicle.

2 On refitting, renew any retaining clips that may have been broken on removal, and ensure that the panel is securely retained by all the relevant clips and screws.

Body trim strips and badges

3 The various body trim strips and badges are held in position with a special adhesive tape. Removal requires the trim/badge to be heated, to soften the adhesive, and then cut away from the surface. Due to the high risk of damage to the vehicle's paintwork during this operation, it is recommended that this task should be entrusted to a Citroën dealer.

24 Seats - removal and refitting

Front seats

⚠️ **Warning: On models with seat belt pre-tensioners, observe the following precautions before attempting to remove the seat:**

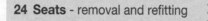

24.5 On models with a sliding rear seat assembly, unclip the trim panel from the base of the seat, to gain access to the rear seat rear mounting bolts

(a) Remove the ignition key.
(b) Disconnect the battery negative lead, and wait for ten minutes before carrying out any further work.
(c) Disconnect the pre-tensioner wiring plug (located under the seat).
Do not tamper with the pre-tensioner unit in any way, and do not attempt to test the unit. Note that the unit is triggered if the mechanism is supplied with an electrical current (including via an ohmmeter), or if the assembly is subjected to a temperature of greater than 100°C.

Removal

1 Slide the seat fully backwards, then undo the two Torx bolts securing the front of the seat slides to the floor. Where necessary, to improve access to the bolts, undo the retaining screws, and prise the trim covers back from the base of the seat **(see illustrations)**.

2 Slide the seat fully forwards, then undo the two Torx bolts securing the rear of the seat slides to the floor, and remove the seat from the car.

Refitting

3 Refitting is a reverse of the removal procedure, ensuring that the seat mounting bolts are securely tightened.

Rear seat

Removal - fixed and sliding types

4 Undo the retaining screws, and remove the plastic trim covers from each of the three seat front mounting points. With the covers removed, slacken and remove the seat front retaining nuts **(see illustrations)**.

5 On models with a sliding rear seat assembly, slide the seat fully forwards, and remove the rear parcel shelf; unclip the trim cover from the base of the seat, to gain access to the rear mounting bolts **(see illustration)**. On models with a fixed rear seat assembly, remove the parcel shelf, then release the trim fasteners and peel back the carpet from the rear of the seat, to gain access to the rear mounting bolts.

6 Slacken and remove the three rear mounting bolts, and recover the spacers

24.6 Slacken and remove the rear mounting bolts, and recover the spacers (arrowed) from underneath the seat mounting brackets

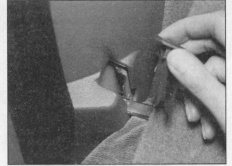

24.8 Removing a folding rear seat retaining bar end cover

24.10 The central hinged mounting point of a split-type folding rear seat

which are positioned beneath the seat mounting brackets **(see illustration)**.

7 Feed the rear seat belts back through the gap between the seat back and cushion, and manoeuvre the seat assembly out of the vehicle.

Removal - folding types

8 There are two types of folding rear seats fitted, the bench type or split type. On both types, pivot the seat base forwards so that it rests against the back of the front seats. Now pivot the back of the seat forwards to expose its retaining bar end covers. Remove these covers **(see illustration)**.

9 The back of the seat can now be removed by positioning it vertically and pulling it upwards so that the retaining bar clears its end slots in the vehicle bodywork.

10 Repositioning the seat base in its normal position will expose its hinged mounting points **(see illustration)**. To remove the base, remove each mounting point retaining nut then move the base forward to release it.

Refitting

11 Refitting is a reverse of the removal procedure, ensuring that all seat mounting bolts and nuts are securely tightened.

---

25 Seat belt components - removal and refitting

Note: *Take note of the positions of any washers and spacers on the seat belt anchors, and ensure that they are refitted in their original positions.*

Removal

Front seat belt - five-door models

1 Prise off the trim cap from the lower belt anchorage bolt, then slacken and remove the bolt and washers, and free the seat belt from its lower anchorage.

2 Prise the trim cover off the upper seat belt mounting bolt, then undo the bolt and release the seat belt.

3 Undo the two retaining screws from the base of the lower door pillar trim panel, then carefully prise the panel away from the pillar, and remove it from the vehicle.

4 Pull the knob off the seat belt upper mounting height adjuster lever. Slacken and remove the retaining screw, then unclip the upper trim panel from the door pillar, and remove it from the vehicle.

5 Slacken and remove the inertia reel retaining bolt(s), and remove the seat belt from the vehicle.

Front seat belt - three-door models

6 Remove the centre door pillar upper trim panel, as described in paragraphs 27 to 30 of Section 26.

7 Carefully drill out the rivet securing the seat belt guide to the door pillar.

8 Slacken and remove the bolt and washers securing the lower seat belt mounting rail to the floor, and disengage the rail from the belt.

9 Slacken and remove the inertia reel retaining bolt(s), and remove the seat belt from the vehicle.

Front seat belt stalk - models without seat belt pre-tensioners

10 Remove the seat as described in Section 24.

11 Slacken and remove the bolt securing the stalk to the seat, and remove the stalk.

Front seat belt stalk - models with seat belt pre-tensioners

Warning: Observe the following precautions before attempting to remove the seat belt stalk assembly:

(a) Remove the ignition key.

(b) Disconnect the battery negative lead, and wait for ten minutes before carrying out any further work.

(c) Disconnect the pre-tensioner wiring plug (located under the seat).

Do not tamper with the pre-tensioner unit in any way, and do not attempt to test the unit. Note that the unit is triggered if the mechanism is supplied with an electrical current (including via an ohmmeter), or if the assembly is subjected to a temperature of greater than 100°C.

12 The seat belt stalk is an integral part of the seat belt tensioner mechanism.

13 Remove the securing screws or release the clips, as applicable, and remove the trim panel from the side of the seat.

14 Unclip the tensioner wiring harness from the bottom of the seat **(see illustration)**.

15 Slacken the front tensioner securing screw and remove the rear tensioner securing bolt **(see illustration)**.

16 Withdraw the tensioner mechanism from the seat.

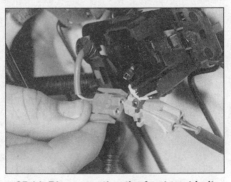

25.14 Disconnecting the front seat belt pre-tensioner wiring plug - seat tilted for clarity

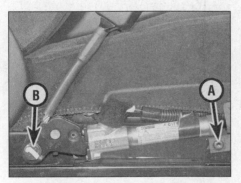

25.15 Seat belt pre-tensioner front securing screw (A) and rear securing bolt (B)

25.21 Front seat belt pre-tensioner electronic control unit securing nuts (arrowed)

25.23a Rear seat side belt inertia reel bolt, and upper belt mounting bolt (arrowed) - five-door model shown

25.23b Rear seat side belt lower mounting bolt

25.25 Rear seat centre belt/buckle retaining bolt

Warning: Do not hold the tensioner by the buckle or by the cable - only hold the unit around the tensioner body.

Front seat belt pre-tensioner electronic control unit

17 This unit is located under the centre console.

18 Disconnect the battery negative lead, and wait for at least ten minutes before carrying out any further work.

19 Remove the centre console.

20 Disconnect the wiring connectors, noting the routing of the wiring.

21 Unscrew the four securing nuts, and withdraw the unit from the mounting bracket **(see illustration)**.

Rear seat side belt

22 Remove the lower and upper luggage compartment side trim panels as described in Section 26.

23 Slacken and remove the upper and lower seat belt mounting bolts and washers, if not already having done so, then undo the inertia reel retaining bolt and remove the seat belt from the vehicle **(see illustrations)**.

Rear seat centre belt and buckles

24 On models with a sliding rear seat, slide the rear seat fully forwards then unclip the trim panel from the base of the rear of the seat. On models with a fixed rear seat, release the trim fasteners and peel back the carpet from the rear of the seat. On models with a folding rear

seat, pivot the seat base forwards so that it rests against the back of the front seats.

25 Slacken and remove the bolt and washers securing the centre belt and/or buckle assembly to the floor, and remove it from the vehicle **(see illustration)**.

Refitting

26 Refitting is a reversal of the removal procedure, ensuring that all the seat belt mounting bolts are securely tightened, and all disturbed trim panels are securely retained by all the relevant retaining clips.

27 On front seat belt stalks equipped with seat belt pre-tensioners, observe the following precautions:

(a) *Before refitting, ensure that the battery negative lead is disconnected and that the ignition is switched off.*

(b) *Do not touch the seat belt buckle when the ignition is first switched on.*

28 When refitting a front seat belt pre-tensioner electronic control unit, reverse the removal procedure but ensure that the unit wiring connectors are reconnected before reconnecting the battery negative lead.

---

26 Interior trim - removal and refitting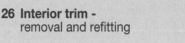

Interior trim panels

Door trim panels

1 Refer to Section 12.

Rear seat side trim panels - three-door models

2 Remove the rear seat assembly as described in Section 24.

3 Remove the speaker as described in Chapter 12.

4 Slacken and remove the three retaining screws, then remove the plastic panel from the trim panel.

5 Peel the sealing strip away from the front edge of the trim panel, then release the panel studs by carefully levering between the panel and body with a suitable flat-bladed screwdriver. Work around the outside of the panel, and when all the studs are released, slide the panel upwards and away from the body.

6 Refitting is the reversal of the removal, renewing any broken retaining studs/clips prior to refitting the panel.

Luggage compartment rear trim panels - Hatchback

7 Open up the tailgate, then slacken and remove the bump-stop retaining screws, and remove both tailgate bump-stops **(see illustration)**.

8 Undo the three retaining screws securing the right- or left-hand (as applicable) rear luggage compartment trim panel to the floor, noting the correct fitted positions of the luggage clips, and remove the panel **(see illustration)**. If necessary, repeat the procedure and remove the remaining trim panel.

26.7 Removing a tailgate bump-stop from the rear of the vehicle

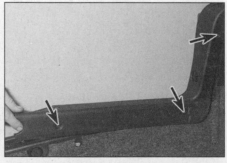

26.8 Removing a rear trim panel from the luggage compartment (retaining screw locations arrowed)

26.12 On five-door models, the wheel brace clip unscrews from the body

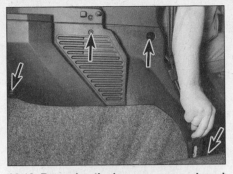

26.13 Removing the luggage compartment side trim panel retaining clip (retaining screw locations arrowed)

26.14 Removing a side trim panel from the luggage compartment

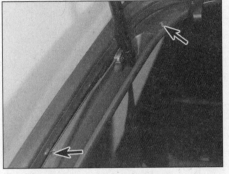

26.19a Slacken and remove the two upper retaining screws (arrowed) . . .

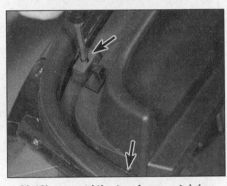

26.19b . . . and the two lower retaining screws (arrowed) . . .

26.19c . . . then remove the rear section of the upper trim panel

9 Refitting is a reversal of the removal procedure.

Luggage compartment lower side trim panel - Hatchback

10 Slide the rear seat fully forwards (where possible), and fold down the rear seat backs.
11 Where necessary, remove the relevant half of the rear trim panel as described above.
12 On five-door models, if the right-hand panel is being removed, remove the wheel brace, and unscrew the wheel brace clip from the rear right-hand corner of the luggage compartment (**see illustration**). If the left-hand panel is being removed, remove the retaining nut and clip from the same position on the left-hand side.
13 Slide the retaining clip, located just

behind the base of the rear seat cushion, out of the trim panel (**see illustration**).
14 Slacken and remove the four trim panel retaining screws, carefully release the edges of the panel from its surrounding components, then remove it from the vehicle (**see illustration**). If the left-hand panel is being removed, it will be necessary to disconnect the wiring connector from the luggage compartment light as it becomes accessible.
15 Refitting is the reverse of removal, ensuring that all fasteners are securely tightened.

Luggage compartment upper side trim panel - Hatchback

16 Remove the relevant lower side trim panel as described above in paragraphs 10 to 14.

17 On three-door models, prise the trim cover the rear seat belt upper mounting point, then slacken and remove the mounting bolts and washer(s), and free the belt from the panel.
18 Undo the two upper side trim panel lower retaining screws.
19 Slacken and remove the four retaining screws and rubber bump-stop from the rear section of the upper panel. Peel back the tailgate sealing strip from the side of the panel rear section, then remove the panel. Where necessary, disconnect the wiring connector from the luggage compartment light switch as it becomes accessible (**see illustrations**).
20 Undo the two retaining screws located behind the rear section of the trim panel, then free the panel from the side of the body (**see illustrations**). On five-door models, to remove

26.20a Undo the upper retaining screw . . .

26.20b . . . and the lower retaining screw . . .

26.20c . . . and free the upper trim panel from the luggage compartment - five-door model shown

26.41 On refitting, ensure the windscreen trim pegs are correctly located in the facia (viewed through the windscreen)

the panel from the vehicle, slacken and remove the rear seat belt lower mounting bolt and washer, and feed the belt back through the slot in the panel.

21 Refitting is a reversal of the removal procedure. Ensure that the tailgate wiring is correctly positioned beneath the sealing strip prior to pressing the sealing strip onto the vehicle.

Luggage compartment upper side trim panel - Estate

22 Remove the back of the rear seat as described in Section 24.

23 Undo the six screws and remove the lower trim strip from the base of the tailgate aperture.

24 Undo the bolts and remove the tailgate bump stop and centring stop on the side concerned.

25 Undo the two screws on the inner face of the tailgate aperture side trim. Peel back the rubber sealing strip around the side of the tailgate aperture then remove the side trim.

26 Suitably support the tailgate, then raise the spring clips and pull the support strut off the balljoint mounting on the body. Undo the upper trim panel retaining screw adjacent to the support strut balljoint mounting.

27 Undo the two upper trim panel retaining screws above the luggage compartment storage box, and the two screws below the side window.

28 Undo the retaining screw at the extreme rear edge of the upper trim panel (exposed after removal of the side trim).

29 Undo the screws and remove the parcel shelf rear support.

30 Carefully release the retaining clips and withdraw the trim panel from its location.

31 Open the rear side door and peel back the rubber sealing strip from the rear of the door aperture.

32 Undo the screw at the base of the door aperture trim panel, release the clips and remove the panel.

33 Undo the now accessible seat belt lower mounting bolt and feed the belt through the opening in the upper side trim panel. The panel can now be removed from the luggage compartment.

34 Refitting is a reversal of the removal procedure.

Luggage compartment lower side trim panel - Estate

35 Remove the upper side trim panel as described previously.

36 Undo the rear seat belt upper mounting and inertia reel mounting bolts and remove the seat belt.

37 Lift up the luggage tie-down rings and lift out the luggage compartment floor covering.

38 Carefully release the retaining clips and remove the lower side trim panel from the luggage compartment.

39 Refitting is a reversal of the removal procedure.

Windscreen pillar trim panel

40 Unclip the trim panel from the windscreen pillar and, where necessary, release the alarm sensor from the clip on the top of the panel.

41 Prior to refitting, check the panel retaining clips, and renew any that are broken. Where necessary, ensure the alarm sensor wire is correctly routed, and refit the sensor to its retaining clip. Clip the panel back into position, ensuring that the pegs on the base of the panel are correctly located in the facia panel **(see illustration)**.

Front footwell side trim panel

42 Undo the two retaining screws, and remove the trim panel from the side of the footwell.

43 Refitting is a reverse of the removal procedure.

Centre door pillar trim panels - five-door models

44 Refer to the information given in paragraphs 1 to 4 of Section 25.

Centre door pillar upper trim panel - three-door models

45 Remove the rear seat side trim panel as described in paragraphs 2 to 5 of this Section.

46 Prise the trim cover off the upper seat belt mounting bolt, then slacken and remove the bolt and washer(s), and release the seat belt.

47 Undo the retaining screw from the base of the upper trim panel.

48 Peel back the sealing strip from the front edge of the panel, carefully prise the panel away from the pillar, and remove it from the vehicle.

49 Refitting is a reversal of the removal procedure.

Glovebox

50 Remove the two retaining clips, and release the felt undercover from the underside of the glovebox.

51 Open up the glovebox, then slacken and remove the four retaining screws situated along its upper edge, and the six retaining screws located along its lower edge, and slide the glovebox out of position.

52 Refitting is the reverse of the removal procedure, ensuring that the retaining screws are securely tightened.

Carpets

53 The passenger compartment floor carpet is in one piece, and is secured at its edges by screws or clips - usually the same fasteners used to secure the various adjoining trim panels.

54 Carpet removal and refitting is reasonably straightforward, but very time-consuming, due to the fact that all adjoining trim panels must be removed first, as must components such as the seats, the centre console and seat belt lower anchorages.

Headlining

55 The headlining is clipped to the roof, and can be withdrawn only once all fittings such as the grab handles, sun visors, sunroof (if fitted), windscreen and rear quarter windows, and related trim panels, have been removed. The door, tailgate and sunroof aperture sealing strips will also have to be prised clear.

56 Note that headlining removal requires considerable skill and experience if it is to be carried out without damage, and is therefore best entrusted to an expert.

---

27 Centre console - removal and refitting

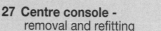

Removal

Low-specification models

1 Undo retaining the two retaining screws, then free the console from the gearchange lever gaiter, and lift it over the lever.

High-specification models

2 Undo the left-hand front side panel retaining screw, then disengage the panel from the centre console, and remove it from the vehicle **(see illustration)**. Repeat the procedure and remove the right-hand panel.

3 On models with manual transmission, carefully prise the gear lever trim panel out from the centre console. Where a leather gaiter is fitted to the lever, release the pop fastener and velcro strip, and remove the

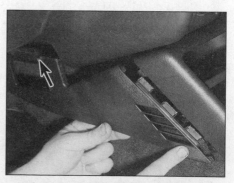

27.2 Removing the centre console left-hand front side panel - retaining screw location arrowed

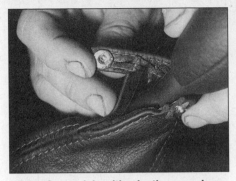

27.3a On models with a leather gear lever gaiter, release the pop fastener and velcro strip . . .

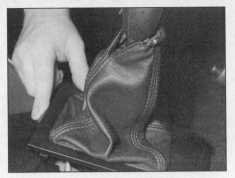

27.3b . . . then unclip the trim panel from the centre console

27.5a Depress the retaining tang (arrowed), and slide out the ashtray . . .

gaiter **(see illustrations)**. Where a rubber gaiter is fitted, unscrew the knob from the gear lever, and remove the knob and gaiter assembly.

4 On models with automatic transmission, carefully prise the selector lever trim panel out from the centre console, and fold the gaiter back over the selector lever. Slacken and remove the four screws securing the handle to the shaft of the selector lever. Depress the selector lever handle detent knob, then rotate the handle through 90° anti-clockwise, lift the assembly up and rotate it back 90° clockwise, to release the detent button from the selector lever pushrod. With the handle removed, withdraw the detent button and spring from the handle.

5 Depress the retaining tang, and slide the ashtray out from the centre facia panel, then slacken and remove the two front centre console retaining screws, located behind the ashtray **(see illustrations)**.

6 Slacken and remove the retaining nut from the rear of the centre console, then manoeuvre the console over the gear lever, and remove it from the vehicle **(see illustrations)**.

Refitting
Low-specification models

7 Locate the gaiter back in the console base,

then refit the two retaining screws, tightening them securely.

High-specification models

8 Manoeuvre the centre console back into position over the gear lever, ensuring that the heater ducts fitted to either side of the console are correctly located with the heater unit outlets at the front of the console.

9 Refit the two front retaining screws and the rear retaining nut, and tighten them securely. Slide the ashtray back into the centre facia panel.

10 On models with manual transmission, either screw the lever and gaiter back onto the gearchange lever, or locate the gaiter over the lever, and secure it in position with the velcro strip and pop fastener (as applicable). Clip the gaiter trim panel back into position in the centre console.

11 On models with automatic transmission, refit the spring and detent button to the selector lever handle, and press the button fully into the handle. Keeping the button depressed, slide the handle assembly onto the lever, then, exerting light downward pressure on the handle, rotate the handle through 90° clockwise, then back 90° anti-clockwise, to engage the detent button with the lever pushrod. Release the detent button, then refit the four handle retaining screws and tighten them securely. Check the operation of the selector lever detent button, then clip the

trim panel back into position in the centre console.

12 Refit the side panels to the front of the console, and secure them in position with their retaining screws.

28 Facia panel assembly - removal and refitting

Note: *Label each wiring connector as it is disconnected from its relevant component. The labels will prove useful on refitting, when routing the wiring and feeding the wiring through the facia apertures.*

Removal

1 Disconnect the battery negative terminal.

2 Remove the instrument panel assembly and clock, as described in the relevant Sections of Chapter 12.

3 Remove the steering column assembly as described in Chapter 10.

4 On high-specification models, remove the centre console as described in Section 27. On lower-specification models where only a small centre console is fitted, undo the retaining screws, and remove the heater duct cover from the centre of the facia assembly (where fitted).

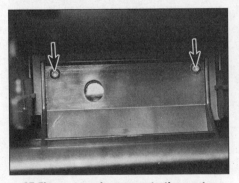

27.5b . . . to gain access to the centre console front retaining screws (arrowed)

27.6a Undo the rear retaining nut . . .

27.6b . . . then lift the centre console over the gear lever, and remove it from the vehicle

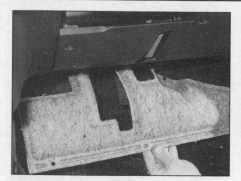

28.5 Removing the driver's side facia felt undercover

28.6a Unclip both the left-hand switch panel . . .

28.6b . . . and right-hand switch panel, and remove them from the facia (right-hand-drive model shown)

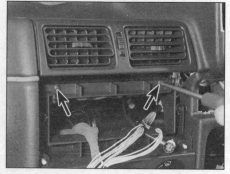

28.7a On models fitted with a radio/cassette player, undo the two retaining screws (arrowed) . . .

28.7b . . . and remove the mounting bracket

5 Unclip both the left- and right-hand felt undercovers from underneath the facia, and remove them from the vehicle **(see illustration)**.

6 Carefully prise the switch panels, located on either side of the instrument panel, out of the facia, taking care not to mark either the panel or facia. Disconnect the wiring connectors, and remove the panels **(see illustrations)**.

7 Where a radio/cassette player is fitted, remove it as described in Chapter 12, then undo the two retaining screws, and remove the mounting bracket from the radio aperture **(see illustrations)**. Where no radio/cassette player is fitted, carefully prise out the storage box from the centre of the facia panel.

8 Undo the four centre vent panel retaining screws (two located above the heater controls, and two directly below), then unclip the panel and withdraw it from the facia. Disconnect the wiring connectors from the cigarette lighter and ashtray illumination bulb, and remove the centre vent panel assembly from the vehicle **(see illustrations)**.

9 Undo the two heater control panel retaining screws, then release the lower panel retaining clip, and manoeuvre the panel out from the centre of the facia. Slacken and remove the facia mounting bolt and retaining screw which are located behind the heater control panel **(see illustrations)**.

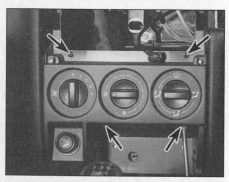

28.8a Undo the four retaining screws (arrowed) . . .

28.8b . . . then unclip the centre vent panel from the facia . . .

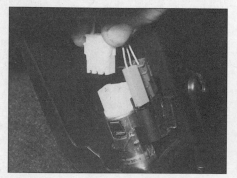

28.8c . . . and disconnect the wiring connectors from the cigarette lighter and illumination bulb

28.9a Undo the retaining screws, and release the heater control panel from the facia (retaining clip location arrowed) . . .

28.9b . . . to gain access to the facia mounting bolt . . .

28.9c . . . and retaining screw located behind the panel

28.10 Removing a facia panel end retaining screw

28.11 Facia retaining nuts located beneath instrument panel aperture

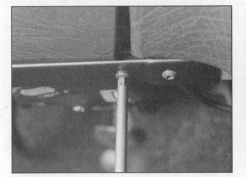

28.12 Removing the facia retaining screw situated underneath the glovebox

28.13 On right-hand-drive models, remove the retaining screw from beneath the centre of the facia panel

28.14 Undo the retaining nut, and free the earth strap from the base of the centre of the facia panel

10 Slacken and remove the retaining screw from each end of the facia panel **(see illustration)**.

11 Undo the two facia retaining nuts located on the lower edge of the instrument panel aperture **(see illustration)**.

12 Unscrew the retaining screw, located underneath the inner corner of the glovebox, securing the facia in position **(see illustration)**.

13 On right-hand-drive models, slacken and

remove the retaining screw from the centre of the facia - accessed from underneath **(see illustration)**.

14 Where necessary, undo the nut and release the earth lead from the stud at the base of the centre of the facia **(see illustration)**.

15 Remove the windscreen wiper motor as described in Chapter 12.

16 With the wiper motor removed, slacken and remove the three retaining nuts and

washers securing the facia panel to the bulkhead **(see illustration)**.

17 From inside the vehicle, unclip the trim panels from the front roof pillars. Where necessary, release the alarm sensors from the clips on the top of each trim panel, and remove the panels.

18 The facia panel is now free to be removed. Pull the panel away from the bulkhead to release it from its retaining pins, then remove the facia assembly, noting the correct routing of the wiring harnesses, and feeding the wiring back through the facia apertures **(see illustration)**.

Refitting

19 Refitting is a reversal of the removal procedure, noting the following points:

(a) Manoeuvre the facia into position and, using the labels stuck on during removal, ensure the wiring is correctly routed and fed through the relevant facia apertures.

(b) Clip the facia back into position, then refit all the facia fasteners, and tighten them securely.

(c) On completion, reconnect the battery and check that all the electrical components and switches function correctly.

28.16 Centre facia-to-bulkhead retaining nut and wiring bracket

28.18 Removing the facia assembly

Notes

Chapter 12
Body electrical systems

Contents

Air bag system components - removal and refitting 27
Air bag system - general information, precautions and
  system de-activation 26
Anti-theft alarm system - general information 24
Battery check and maintenance . . See *"Weekly checks"* and Chapter 1
Battery - removal and refitting . . . . See Chapter 5
Bulbs (exterior lights) - renewal 5
Bulbs (interior lights) - renewal 6
Cigarette lighter - removal and refitting 13
Clock - removal and refitting 11
"Dim-dip" lighting system (UK models only) -
  general information 25
Door-open warning display - general information 12
Electrical fault finding - general information 2
Exterior light units - removal and refitting 7
Fuses and relays - general information 3
General information and precautions 1
Headlight beam alignment - general information 8
Horn - removal and refitting 15
Instrument panel components - removal and refitting 10
Instrument panel - removal and refitting 9
"Lights-on" warning buzzer - general information 14

Loudspeakers - removal and refitting 22
Radio aerial - removal and refitting 23
Radio/cassette player - removal and refitting 21
Reversing light switch (models with manual
  transmission) - removal and refitting . . . . See Chapter 7A
Selector lever position display switch (models with automatic
  transmission) - removal, refitting and adjustment . . See Chapter 7B
Speedometer drive cable - removal and refitting 16
Starter inhibitor/reversing light switch (models with automatic
  transmission) - removal and refitting . . . . See Chapter 7B
Stop-light switch - removal, refitting and adjustment . See Chapter 9
Switches - removal and refitting 4
Tailgate wiper motor - removal and refitting 19
Windscreen/headlight washer system check
  and adjustment . . . . See *"Weekly checks"*
Windscreen/tailgate washer system components -
  removal and refitting 20
Windscreen/tailgate wiper blade check and
  renewal . . . . See *"Weekly checks"*
Windscreen wiper motor and linkage - removal and refitting 18
Wiper arm - removal and refitting 17
Wiring diagrams - explanatory notes 28

Degrees of difficulty

Easy, suitable for novice with little experience	Fairly easy, suitable for beginner with some experience	Fairly difficult, suitable for competent DIY mechanic	Difficult, suitable for experienced DIY mechanic	Very difficult, suitable for expert DIY or professional

Specifications

System type . . . . 12-volt, negative earth

Facia fusebox fuses (1991 to 1992)

Fuse	Rating (amps)	Circuit(s) protected
F1	30	Headlamp washers, electric mirrors and heated seats
F2	30	Low fuel level, brake pad wear and battery charge warning lamps. Front and rear wipers. High pressure pump. Radio/cassette
F3	30	Heated rear window relay, electric front window relay, indicators
F4	25	Central locking
F5	30	Heated rear screen and heated exterior mirror
F6	10	Hazard warning lights
F7	10	Reversing lights, facia panel lights and instrument panel warning lights
F8	20	Radio/cassette, interior lights, cigarette lighter, luggage compartment light and clock
F9	30	Electric windows, sunroof and seat adjustment
F10	20	Horn
F11	5	High intensity rear foglight
F12	5	Right-hand front and rear sidelights, ashtray and cigarette lighter illumination, "lights-on" buzzer and switch illumination
F13	5	Left-hand front and rear sidelights, number plate light, interior lighting and side lamp warning light

Facia fusebox fuses (1992 to 1994)

Fuse	Rating (amps)	Circuit(s) protected
F1	30	Heater blower motor, headlamp washers, electric mirrors, air conditioning relay, headlamp washer timer and heated seats
F2	10	Radio/cassette, instrument panel, stop-lights, front and rear wash/wipe and "lights-on" buzzer
F3	30	Heated rear window relay, electric window relay, indicators and cooling fan relay(s)
F4	25	Central locking and anti-theft alarm
F5	25	Heated rear window and heated exterior mirror
F6	10	Hazard warning lights
F7	10	Reversing lights, facia panel lights and instrument panel warning lights
F8	20	Radio/cassette, interior lights, cigarette lighter, luggage compartment light, clock and remote central locking receiver
F9	30	Electric windows, sunroof, seat adjustment and map reading light
F10	20	Horn
F11	5	High intensity rear foglight
F12	5	Right-hand front and rear sidelights, ashtray and cigarette lighter illumination, "lights-on" buzzer and switch illumination
F13	5	Left-hand front and rear sidelights, number plate light

Facia fusebox fuses (1995-on)

Fuse	Rating (amps)	Circuit(s) protected
F1	30	Electric windows, sunroof and seat adjustment
F2	25	Heater blower controls and air conditioning switch
F3	25	Heated seat control, cooling fan relay(s), heated rear screen switch and timer, heated rear view mirrors
F4	25	Warning lamps for: battery charge, pad wear, low fuel. Lights on audible warning, control for sunroof and front windows, front and rear wash wipe.
F5	25	Heated rear window and heated exterior mirror
F6	10	Hazard warning lights, alarm switch and warning lamp, coded anti-theft keypad
F7	10	Dash lighting rheostat, tachometer, dash warning lamps, alarm unit, anti-theft keypad, cigar lighter relay, ABS, reverse lamp, reduced lighting
F8	30	Radio/cassette, interior lights, cigarette lighter, luggage compartment light, clock and remote central locking receiver, sunroof and window control, alarm and siren
F9	30	Headlamp wash, rear view mirror, indicators, STOP switch, Automatic display and map reading light
F10	20	Horn and cigar lighter
F11	5	High intensity rear foglight and warning lamp
F12	10	Right-hand front and rear sidelights, dash switch and radio illumination, ashtray illumination, "lights-on" buzzer, foglamp
F13	5	Left-hand front and rear sidelights, number plate light, side lamp warning light, alarm switch

Junction box fuses (two-fuse arrangement)

Fuse	Rating (amps)	Circuit protected
F1	-	Unused
F2	-	Unused
F3	5	Cooling fan relay
F4	30	Cooling fan

Junction box fuses (four-fuse arrangement)

Fuse	Rating (amps)	Circuit protected
F1	15	Front foglights
F2	30	Heater blower motor and air conditioning controls
F3	30	Supplementary cooling fan
F4	30	Cooling fan

Note: *Not all items fitted to all models*

Bulbs

	Fitting	Wattage
Headlights:		
Dip/main beam bulb	H4	60/55
Individual main beam (where fitted)	H1	55
Front foglights	H3	55

Bulbs (continued)

	Fitting	Wattage
Front sidelights	Capless	5
Direction indicators	Bayonet	21
Direction indicator side repeaters	Capless	5
Interior lights	Capless	5
Luggage boot light	Capless	5
Heater control panel illumination	Capless	1.2
Instrument panel warning lights/illumination	Integral with holder	1.2
Clock illumination	Integral with holder	1.2
Stop/tail lights	Bayonet	21/5
Rear foglight	Bayonet	21
Reversing lights	Bayonet	21

1 General information and precautions

⚠️ **Warning: Before carrying out any work on the electrical system, read through the precautions given in "Safety first!" at the beginning of this manual, and in Chapter 5.**

The electrical system is of 12-volt negative earth type. Power for the lights and all electrical accessories is supplied by a lead/acid type battery, which is charged by the alternator.

This Chapter covers repair and service procedures for the various electrical components not associated with engine. Information on the battery, alternator and starter motor can be found in Chapter 5.

It should be noted that, prior to working on any component in the electrical system, the battery negative terminal should first be disconnected, to prevent the possibility of electrical short-circuits and/or fires.

Caution: If the radio/cassette player fitted to the vehicle is one with an anti-theft security code, as the standard unit is, refer to the information given in the preliminary Sections of this manual before disconnecting the battery.

2 Electrical fault finding - general information

Note: *Refer to the precautions given in "Safety first!" and in Section 1 of this Chapter before starting work. The following tests relate to testing of the main electrical circuits, and should not be used to test delicate electronic circuits (such as anti-lock braking systems), particularly where an electronic control module is used.*

General

1 A typical electrical circuit consists of an electrical component, any switches, relays, motors, fuses, fusible links or circuit breakers related to that component, and the wiring and connectors which link the component to both the battery and the chassis. To help to pinpoint a problem in an electrical circuit, wiring diagrams are included at the end of this manual.

2 Before attempting to diagnose an electrical fault, first study the appropriate wiring diagram, to obtain a more complete understanding of the components included in the particular circuit concerned. The possible sources of a fault can be narrowed down by noting whether other components related to the circuit are operating properly. If several components or circuits fail at one time, the problem is likely to be related to a shared fuse or earth connection.

3 Electrical problems usually stem from simple causes, such as loose or corroded connections, a faulty earth connection, a blown fuse, a melted fusible link, or a faulty relay (refer to Section 3 for details of testing relays). Visually inspect the condition of all fuses, wires and connections in a problem circuit before testing the components. Use the wiring diagrams to determine which terminal connections will need to be checked, in order to pinpoint the trouble-spot.

4 The basic tools required for electrical fault-finding include a circuit tester or voltmeter (a 12-volt bulb with a set of test leads can also be used for certain tests); a self-powered test light (sometimes known as a continuity tester); an ohmmeter (to measure resistance); a battery and set of test leads; and a jumper wire, preferably with a circuit breaker or fuse incorporated, which can be used to bypass suspect wires or electrical components. Before attempting to locate a problem with test instruments, use the wiring diagram to determine where to make the connections.

5 To find the source of an intermittent wiring fault (usually due to a poor or dirty connection, or damaged wiring insulation), a "wiggle" test can be performed on the wiring. This involves wiggling the wiring by hand, to see if the fault occurs as the wiring is moved. It should be possible to narrow down the source of the fault to a particular section of wiring. This method of testing can be used in conjunction with any of the tests described in the following sub-Sections.

6 Apart from problems due to poor connections, two basic types of fault can occur in an electrical circuit - open-circuit, or short-circuit.

7 Open-circuit faults are caused by a break somewhere in the circuit, which prevents current from flowing. An open-circuit fault will prevent a component from working, but will not cause the relevant circuit fuse to blow.

8 Short-circuit faults are caused by a "short" somewhere in the circuit, which allows the current flowing in the circuit to "escape" along an alternative route, usually to earth. Short-circuit faults are normally caused by a breakdown in wiring insulation, which allows a feed wire to touch either another wire, or an earthed component such as the bodyshell. A short-circuit fault will normally cause the relevant circuit fuse to blow.

Finding an open-circuit

9 To check for an open-circuit, connect one lead of a circuit tester or voltmeter to either the negative battery terminal or a known good earth.

10 Connect the other lead to a connector in the circuit being tested, preferably nearest to the battery or fuse.

11 Switch on the circuit, bearing in mind that some circuits are live only when the ignition switch is moved to a particular position.

12 If voltage is present (indicated either by the tester bulb lighting or a voltmeter reading, as applicable), this means that the section of the circuit between the relevant connector and the battery is problem-free.

13 Continue to check the remainder of the circuit in the same fashion.

14 When a point is reached at which no voltage is present, the problem must lie between that point and the previous test point with voltage. Most problems can be traced to a broken, corroded or loose connection.

Finding a short-circuit

15 To check for a short-circuit, first disconnect the load(s) from the circuit (loads are the components which draw current from a circuit, such as bulbs, motors, heating elements, etc).

16 Remove the relevant fuse from the circuit, and connect a circuit tester or voltmeter to the fuse connections.

17 Switch on the circuit, bearing in mind that some circuits are live only when the ignition switch is moved to a particular position.

18 If voltage is present (indicated either by the tester bulb lighting or a voltmeter reading, as applicable), this means that there is a short-circuit.

19 If no voltage is present, but the fuse still blows with the load(s) connected, this indicates an internal fault in the load(s).

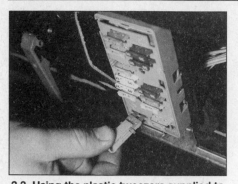

3.3 Using the plastic tweezers supplied to remove a fuse from the main fusebox

Finding an earth fault

20 The battery negative terminal is connected to "earth" - the metal of the engine/transmission unit and the car body - and most systems are wired so that they only receive a positive feed, the current returning via the metal of the car body. This means that the component mounting and the body form part of that circuit. Loose or corroded mountings can therefore cause a range of electrical faults, ranging from total failure of a circuit, to a puzzling partial fault. In particular, lights may shine dimly (especially when another circuit sharing the same earth point is in operation), motors (eg wiper motors or the radiator cooling fan motor) may run slowly, and the operation of one circuit may have an apparently-unrelated effect on another. Note that on many vehicles, earth straps are used between certain components, such as the engine/transmission and the body, usually where there is no metal-to-metal contact between components, due to flexible rubber mountings, etc.

21 To check whether a component is properly earthed, disconnect the battery, and connect one lead of an ohmmeter to a known good earth point. Connect the other lead to the wire or earth connection being tested. The resistance reading should be zero; if not, check the connection as follows.

22 If an earth connection is thought to be faulty, dismantle the connection, and clean back to bare metal both the bodyshell and the wire terminal or the component earth connection mating surface. Be careful to

3.7a Engine compartment junction box relays. Fuses are located beneath the small cover (arrowed)

remove all traces of dirt and corrosion, then use a knife to trim away any paint, so that a clean metal-to-metal joint is made. On reassembly, tighten the joint fasteners securely; if a wire terminal is being refitted, use serrated washers between the terminal and the bodyshell, to ensure a clean and secure connection. When the connection is remade, prevent the onset of corrosion in the future by applying a coat of petroleum jelly or silicone-based grease, or by spraying on (at regular intervals) a proprietary ignition sealer or a water-dispersant lubricant.

3 Fuses and relays - general information

Fuses

1 Most of the fuses are located behind the driver's side lower facia panel, with a few odd fuses on some models being located in the junction box on the left-hand side of the engine compartment.

2 To gain access to main fusebox, release the three fasteners by rotating them through 90º, then remove the driver's side lower facia panel. To gain access to those in the junction box, unclip the junction box lid, then release the retaining clip, and lift the small cover situated inside the box **(see illustration 3.7a)**.

3 The fuse number is marked on the fusebox next to each fuse; a list of the circuits each fuse protects is given in the Specifications at the start of this Chapter. Plastic tweezers are also clipped into the fusebox, and can be used to remove and fit the fuses **(see illustration)**.

4 To remove a fuse, first switch off the circuit concerned (or the ignition), then fit the tweezers and pull the fuse out of its terminals. Slide the fuse sideways from the tweezers. The wire within the fuse is clearly visible; if the fuse is blown, it will be broken or melted.

5 Always renew a fuse with one of an identical rating; never use a fuse with a different rating from the original, or substitute anything else. Never renew a fuse more than once without tracing the source of the trouble. The fuse rating is stamped on top of the fuse; note that the fuses are also colour-coded for easy recognition.

6 If a new fuse blows immediately, find the cause before renewing it again; a short to earth as a result of faulty insulation is most likely. Where a fuse protects more than one circuit, try to isolate the defect by switching on each circuit in turn (if possible) until the fuse blows again. Always carry a supply of spare fuses of each relevant rating in the vehicle.

Relays

7 The main relays are located to the rear of the fusebox, behind the facia on the drivers side. Other relays are in the junction box located on the left-hand side of the engine

compartment **(see illustration)**. The exceptions to this are as follows:
(a) *Sunroof relay - located behind the overhead console.*
(b) *Tailgate wiper motor relay - fitted to the wiper motor bracket.*
(c) *Cooling fan relay(s) - in the rear of the fan shroud on models with twin fans, or at the side of the radiator where only one fan is fitted* **(see illustration)**.

8 The flasher relay is located to the rear of the fusebox, behind the facia trim panel on the driver's side **(see illustrations 9.3a and 14.2)**. Refer to the appropriate Chapters for further information, and to the relevant wiring diagram for details of wiring connections.

9 If a circuit or system controlled by a relay develops a fault and the relay is suspect, operate the system; if the relay is functioning, it should be possible to hear it click as it is energized. If this is the case, the fault lies with the components or wiring of the system. If the relay is not being energized, then either the relay is not receiving a main supply or a switching voltage, or the relay itself is faulty. Testing is by the substitution of a known good unit, but be careful; while some relays are identical in appearance and in operation, others look similar but perform different functions.

10 To renew a relay, first ensure that the ignition switch is off. The relay can then simply be pulled out from the socket, and the new relay pressed in.

4 Switches - removal and refitting

Note: *Disconnect the battery negative lead before removing any switch, and reconnect the lead after refitting the switch.*

Ignition switch/steering column lock

1 Refer to Chapter 10, Section 21.

Steering column combination switches

2 Remove the steering wheel as described in Chapter 10.

3.7b Cooling fan relay(s) are located in the rear of the fan shroud

4.5a Undo the three retaining screws (arrowed) . . .

4.5b . . . then disconnect the wiring connectors, and slide off the combination switch assembly

4.6a Undo the two retaining screws . . .

3 Release the panel fasteners by rotating them through a quarter of a turn, and remove the driver's side lower facia panel.

4 Slacken and remove the five screws which secure the two halves of the steering column shrouds together, then remove both the upper and lower shroud.

5 Undo the three retaining screws, then disconnect the wiring connectors from the rear of the combination switches, and lift the switch assembly off the steering column (see illustrations).

6 Unscrew the two retaining screws, and slide the relevant switch assembly out of position (see illustrations).

7 Refitting is a reversal of the removal procedure.

Instrument panel dimmer switch, exterior mirror switch, alarm switch and air conditioning switch

8 Using a suitable flat-bladed screwdriver, carefully prise the relevant switch panel out of the facia, taking great care not to mark either the panel or facia.

9 Disconnect the wiring connector from the switch, then depress the retaining tangs, and slide the switch out of the panel (see illustration).

10 Slide the switch back into the panel until it clicks into position. Reconnect the wiring connector, then clip the panel back into the facia.

Instrument shroud switches

11 Release the panel fasteners by rotating them through a quarter of a turn, and remove the driver's side lower facia panel.

12 Slacken and remove the five screws which secure the two halves of the steering column shrouds together, then remove both the upper and lower shroud.

13 Slacken and remove the four instrument panel shroud retaining screws, then remove the shroud, disconnecting the switch wiring connectors as they become accessible.

14 Depress the retaining tangs, and slide the relevant switch out of the shroud (see illustration).

15 Refitting is a reverse of the removal procedure.

Courtesy light switches

16 Open up the door, then prise the rubber gaiter from the courtesy switch.

17 Undo the retaining screw, then withdraw the switch from the pillar, disconnecting its wiring connector as it becomes accessible. Tie a piece of string to the wiring, to prevent it falling back into the door pillar.

18 Refitting is a reverse of the removal procedure, ensuring that the rubber gaiter is correctly seated on the switch.

Luggage compartment light switch

19 Open up the tailgate, then carefully prise the switch out from the left-hand trim panel, and disconnect its wiring connector (see illustrations). Tie a piece of string to the

4.6b . . . and slide the relevant switch assembly out from the combination switch bracket

wiring, to prevent it falling back behind the trim panel.

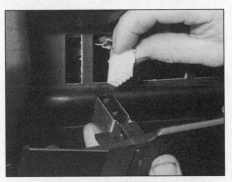

4.9 Removing the instrument panel dimmer switch

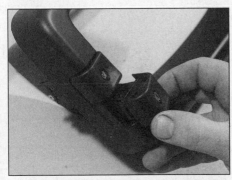

4.14 Removing an instrument shroud switch

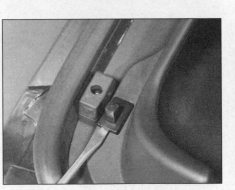

4.19a Prise the luggage compartment light switch out of the trim panel . . .

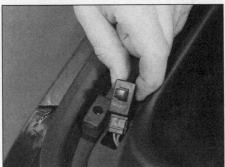

4.19b . . . then withdraw the switch and disconnect its wiring connector

4.22 Handbrake warning light switch retaining screw (arrowed)

4.24a Carefully prise the window switch out of the armrest . . .

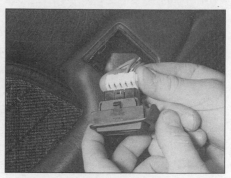

4.24b . . . and disconnect it from its wiring connector

20 Reconnect the wiring connector, and clip the switch back into position in the trim panel.

Handbrake warning light switch

21 Open up the rear ashtray, then depress the retaining tang and remove the ashtray from the handbrake lever cover panel. Slacken and remove the rear retaining nut and the two front retaining screws, then manoeuvre the cover panel off the handbrake lever.
22 Disconnect the wiring connector from the handbrake switch, then undo the retaining screw and remove the switch from the side of the handbrake lever **(see illustration)**.
23 Refitting is a reverse of the removal procedure.

Electric window switches

24 Carefully prise the window switch out of the armrest, taking great care not to mark the switch or the armrest, and disconnect the wiring connector **(see illustrations)**.
25 On refitting, connect the wiring connector, and clip the switch back into position in the armrest.

Electric sunroof switch

26 Carefully prise the courtesy light out from the overhead console, and disconnect it from its wiring connector. Remove the two console retaining screws, then lower the console out of position, and disconnect it from its wiring connectors.
27 Depress the retaining tangs, and slide the sunroof switch out of the console **(see illustration)**.

28 Refitting is a reverse of the removal procedure.

---

5 Bulbs (exterior lights) - renewal

General

1 Whenever a bulb is renewed, note the following points:
(a) *Disconnect the battery negative lead before starting work.*
(b) *Remember that, if the light has just been in use, the bulb may be extremely hot.*
(c) *Always check the bulb contacts and holder, ensuring that there is clean metal-to-metal contact between the bulb and its live(s) and earth. Clean off any corrosion or dirt before fitting a new bulb.*
(d) *Wherever bayonet-type bulbs are fitted (see Specifications) ensure that the live contact(s) bear firmly against the bulb contact.*
(e) *Always ensure that the new bulb is of the correct rating, and that it is completely clean before fitting it; this applies particularly to headlight/foglight bulbs (see below).*

Headlight

2 Working in the engine compartment, remove the relevant plastic cover from the rear of the headlight unit.

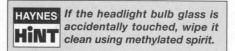

4.27 Depress the retaining tangs, and slide out the sunroof switch

3 Disconnect the wiring connectors, then press together the ends of the bulb retaining clip, and release it from the rear of the light **(see illustrations)**.
4 Withdraw the bulb **(see illustration)**.
5 When handling the new bulb, use a tissue or clean cloth, to avoid touching the glass with the fingers; moisture and grease from the skin can cause blackening and rapid failure of this type of bulb.

> **HAYNES HiNT** *If the headlight bulb glass is accidentally touched, wipe it clean using methylated spirit.*

6 Install the new bulb, ensuring that its locating tabs are correctly located in the light cut-outs. Secure the bulb in position with the retaining clip, and reconnect the wiring connectors.

5.3a Disconnect the wiring connectors from the headlight bulb . . .

5.3b . . . then release the retaining clip . . .

5.4 . . . and withdraw the bulb from the rear of the light unit

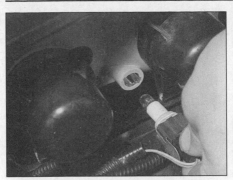

5.8 Removing the sidelight bulbholder from the rear of the headlight unit

5.11 Unhook the retaining spring from within the engine compartment . . .

5.12 . . . then withdraw the direction indicator from the front of the vehicle, and release its bulbholder

5.15 Push the direction indicator side repeater towards the rear of the vehicle, to release its retaining clips . . .

5.16a . . . then withdraw the light from the wing, and disengage it from its bulbholder

5.16b Side repeater bulb is of the capless type, being a push-fit in the holder

7 Slide the plastic cover back into position, ensuring that it is correctly seated on the rear of the light unit.

Front sidelight

8 Working in the engine compartment, twist the bulbholder anti-clockwise, then withdraw it from the headlight unit **(see illustration)**. Note that on some models, it will be necessary to displace the plastic cover from the rear of the unit to gain access to the bulbholder.
9 The bulb is of the capless (push-fit) type, and can be removed by simply pulling it out of the bulbholder.
10 Refitting is the reverse of the removal procedure, ensuring that the bulbholder seal is in good condition.

Front direction indicator

11 Working in the engine compartment, from behind the light, unhook the retaining spring and withdraw the light unit from the front of the vehicle **(see illustration)**.
12 Twist the bulbholder in a clockwise direction to free it from the light, and remove the light unit **(see illustration)**.
13 The bulb is a bayonet fit in the holder, and can be removed by pressing it and twisting in an anti-clockwise direction.
14 Refitting is a reverse of the removal procedure, ensuring that the light unit is correctly located and securely retained by its spring.

Front direction indicator side repeater

15 Push the light unit towards the rear of the

vehicle, to free its retaining clips, then withdraw it from the wing **(see illustration)**.
16 Pull the bulbholder out of the light unit, then pull the capless (push-fit) bulb out of its holder **(see illustrations)**.
17 Refitting is a reverse of the removal procedure.

Front foglight

18 Undo the two retaining screws, and withdraw the lens unit from the front of the light **(see illustration)**.
19 Release the retaining clip, and withdraw the bulb from the rear of the unit. Unclip the plastic insulator cover, then disconnect the bulb wiring connector and remove the bulb **(see illustrations)**.
20 When handling the new bulb, use a tissue or clean cloth, to avoid touching the glass

5.18 Undo the two retaining screws, and withdraw the lens unit from the foglight

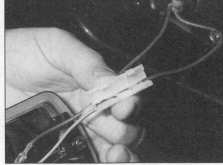

5.19a Unclip the plastic insulator cover . . .

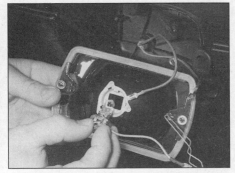

5.19b . . . then disconnect the wiring connector and withdraw the foglight bulb

5.22 Prior to refitting the foglight lens, ensure that the plastic insulator (arrowed) is correctly positioned underneath the retaining clip

5.24a Rear light cluster lens is retained by two screws

5.24b Removing a rear light cluster lens - Estate

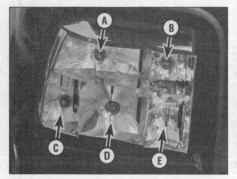

5.25a Rear light cluster bulbs - Hatchback

A Direction indicator   *D Sidelight*
B Reversing light   *E Foglight (where fitted)*
C Stop/tail light

with the fingers; moisture and grease from the skin can cause blackening and rapid failure of this type of bulb. If the glass is accidentally touched, wipe it clean using methylated spirit.
21 Connect the new bulb to the wiring connector, and refit the plastic insulator cover to the connector.
22 Install the bulb in the rear of the lens, ensuring that its locating tabs are correctly located in the cut-outs. Secure the bulb in position with the retaining clip, ensuring that the wiring insulator is correctly located underneath the clip **(see illustration)**.
23 Refit the lens to the light unit, taking great care not trap the wiring, and securely tighten its retaining screws.

5.25b Removing a rear direction indicator bulb - Estate

Rear light cluster

24 Open up the tailgate, then undo the two retaining screws and remove the lens from the rear light cluster, noting its rubber seal **(see illustrations)**.
25 The relevant bulb can then be renewed - all bulbs have a bayonet fitting **(see illustrations)**. Note that the stop/tail light bulb has offset locating pins, to prevent it being installed incorrectly.
26 Refitting is the reverse of the removal sequence, noting that the rubber lens seal must be renewed if damaged.

Rear foglight - Estate

27 Ease a thin blade between the side of the light unit and its housing in the bumper to depress the light retaining clip. With the clip depressed, pull the light from position.

5.31 Pulling a number plate light bulb from its holder - Estate

28 Withdraw the bulb from the rear of the unit.
29 Push in the new bulb and push the light back into position.

Number plate light

30 Raise the tailgate slightly to improve access to the light, then carefully prise out the light lens to gain access to the bulb.
31 The bulb is of the capless (push-fit) type, and is simply pulled out of position **(see illustration)**.
32 Push in the new bulb, and clip the lens back into position.

6 Bulbs (interior lights) - renewal

General

1 Refer to Section 5, paragraph 1.

Courtesy lights

2 Carefully prise the light unit out of position, then twist the bulbholder in an anti-clockwise direction, and remove it from the rear of the light unit **(see illustrations)**.
3 The bulb is of the capless (push-fit) type; pull the old bulb out of the holder, and press the new one into position.
4 Refit the bulbholder to the rear of the light unit, and clip the light unit back into position.

6.2a Prise the courtesy light out of position . . .

6.2b . . . and twist the bulbholder anti-clockwise to release it from the rear of the light unit

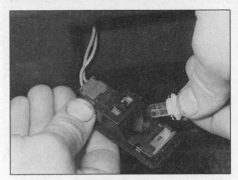

6.5 Removing the luggage compartment light bulbholder

6.6a Carefully prise the map reading light out of the overhead console . . .

6.6b . . . and disconnect it from its wiring connector

6.7 Align the bulbholder with the arrow on the light unit, and pull in the direction of the arrow to remove the bulbholder

6.8 The map reading light bulb is of the capless type

6.11 Removing an instrument panel bulb from the rear of the panel

Luggage compartment light

5 Refer to the information given above in paragraphs 2 to 5 **(see illustration)**.

Map reading light

6 Carefully prise the map reading light unit out of the headlining, then disconnect the wiring connector and remove the light unit **(see illustrations)**.

7 Swivel the bulbholder unit fully away from the wiring connector, then pull the bulbholder lever in the direction of the arrow cast on the light unit, to disengage the holder from the light unit **(see illustration)**.

8 The bulb is of the capless (push-fit) type; pull the old bulb out of the holder, and press the new one into position **(see illustration)**.

9 Slide the bulbholder back onto its pivot in the light unit, then connect the wiring

connector, and clip the light unit back into position in the headlining.

Instrument panel lights

10 Remove the instrument panel as described in Section 9.

11 Twist the relevant bulbholder anti-clockwise, and withdraw it from the rear of panel **(see illustration)**.

12 All bulbs are integral with their holders. Be very careful to ensure that the new bulbs are of the correct rating, the same as those removed; this is especially important in the case of the alternator/no-charge warning light.

13 Refit the bulbholder to the rear of the instrument panel, then refit the instrument panel as described in Section 9.

Selector lever position display bulbs - models with automatic transmission

14 Remove the centre console as described in Chapter 11.

15 Twist the relevant bulbholder anti-clock-wise, and withdraw it from the rear of the panel.

16 The bulbs are of the capless (push-fit) type; pull the old bulb out of the holder, and press the new one into position.

17 Refit the bulbholder to the rear of the panel, then refit the centre console as described in Chapter 11.

Clock illumination bulb

18 Remove the clock as described in Section 11.

19 Twist the bulbholder anti-clockwise, and withdraw it from the rear of the clock **(see illustration)**. The bulb is integral with its holder.

20 Refit the bulbholder to the rear of the clock, then refit the clock as described in Section 11.

Cigarette light/ashtray illumination bulb

21 Remove the centre console as described in Chapter 11.

22 Where a radio/cassette player is fitted, remove it as described in Section 21, then undo the two retaining screws and remove the mounting bracket from the radio aperture. Where no radio/cassette player is fitted, carefully prise out the storage box from the centre of the facia panel.

6.19 Removing the clock illumination bulb

6.24 Removing the cigarette lighter/ashtray illumination bulb

6.28a Where required, unclip the heater vents from the centre facia panel . . .

6.28b . . . and use a screwdriver to disengage the retaining clip(s)

6.29a Carefully release the retaining lugs . . .

6.29b . . . and unclip the heater control facia, complete with the control knobs

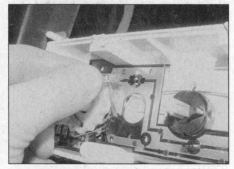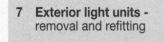

6.30 The capless bulbs can then be pulled from their holders

23 Undo the four centre vent panel retaining screws (two located above the heater controls, and two directly below), then unclip the panel and withdraw it from the facia **(see illustrations 13.3a and 13.3b).**
24 Slide the illumination bulbholder out of the panel, and renew the bulb **(see illustration).** The bulbs is of the capless (push-fit) type; pull the old bulb out of the holder, and press the new one into position.
25 Slide the illumination bulbholder back into position, and refit the panel by reversing the removal procedure.

Heater control panel illumination bulb

26 Remove the centre console as described in Chapter 11, Section 27.
27 Carry out the operation described above in paragraphs 22 and 23.
28 If required, unclip the air vents from the

top of the heater facia panel and release the retaining clips **(see illustrations)** to release the top of the panel.
29 Using a flat-bladed screwdriver, carefully unclip the heater control panel facia complete with control knobs from the heater control panel assembly **(see illustrations).** Note the position of the heater control knobs for refitting.
30 The bulbs are of the capless (push-fit) type; pull the old bulb out of the holder, and press the new one into position **(see illustration).**
31 Refitting is a reverse of the removal procedure.

Switch illumination bulbs

32 All of the switches are fitted with illuminating bulbs; some are also fitted with a bulb to show when the circuit concerned is operating. These bulbs are an integral part of the switch assembly, and cannot be obtained

separately. Bulb replacement will therefore require the renewal of the complete switch assembly.

7 Exterior light units - removal and refitting

Note: *Disconnect the battery negative lead before removing any light unit, and reconnect the lead after refitting the light.*

Headlight

1 Open the bonnet, then slacken and remove the three retaining screws, and remove the plastic cover from the bonnet lock. Slacken the three retaining screws, and remove the radiator grille **(see illustration).**
2 Remove the direction indicator light as described below.
3 Remove the plastic cover(s) from the rear of the headlight unit, and disconnect the wiring connectors from both the headlight and sidelight bulbs (and, where fitted, from the headlight adjustment motor).
4 Using pliers, slide out the retaining clip from the top headlight mounting point (where fitted) **(see illustration).**
5 Pull the headlight forwards, to release it from its two retaining spring clips, and remove the headlight from the vehicle **(see illustrations).**
6 Refitting is a direct reversal of the removal procedure. On completion, check the headlight beam alignment, using the information given in Section 8.

7.1 Radiator grille is retained by three screws (arrowed)

7.4 Using pliers remove the retaining clip from the top headlight mounting point

7.5a Pull the headlight forwards, to release it from its retaining spring clips . . .

7.5b . . . and withdraw the headlight unit from the vehicle

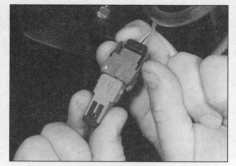

7.13 Disconnect the wiring connector . . .

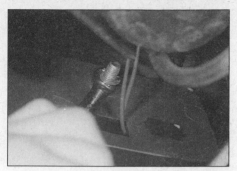

7.14a . . . then slacken and remove the retaining nut . . .

Front direction indicator light

7 Open the bonnet, and from within the engine compartment, unhook the indicator light retaining spring from the vehicle body.
8 Withdraw the light unit from the front of the vehicle, and disconnect its wiring connector.
9 Refitting is the reverse of removal.

Front direction side repeater light

10 Push the light unit towards the rear of the vehicle, to free its retaining clips, then withdraw it from the wing and disconnect its wiring connector.
11 On refitting, reconnect the wiring connector to the light, then clip it back into position on the wing.

Front foglight

12 Jack up the front of the vehicle, and support it on axle stands.
13 Trace the wiring back from the rear of the foglight, and disconnect it at the wiring connector **(see illustration)**.
14 Slacken and remove the foglight retaining nut, and withdraw the light unit from the front of the bumper **(see illustrations)**.
15 Refitting is the reverse of removal.

Rear light cluster

16 Remove the luggage compartment lower side trim panel as described in Chapter 11, Section 26.
17 Slacken and remove the rear light cluster retaining nut, then free the light cluster from the rear of the vehicle, and disconnect its

wiring connector **(see illustrations)**.
18 Refitting is a reversal of the removal procedure.

Rear foglight - Estate

19 Ease a thin blade between the side of the light unit and its housing in the bumper to depress the light retaining clip. With the clip depressed, pull the light from position.
20 Refitting is a reversal of the removal procedure. Ensure that the light is pushed fully back into position.

Number plate light

21 Raise the tailgate slightly to improve access to the light, then carefully prise out the light lens and disconnect its wiring connector.
22 On refitting, reconnect the wiring connector, and clip the light back into position.

8 Headlight beam alignment - general information

1 Accurate adjustment of the headlight beam is only possible using optical beam-setting equipment, and this work should therefore be carried out by a Citroën dealer or suitably-equipped workshop.
2 For reference, the headlights can be adjusted using a suitable-sized Allen key to rotate the adjuster assemblies fitted to the top of each light unit. The outer adjuster alters the vertical height of the beam, whilst the inner adjuster alters the horizontal position of the

beam. Prior to adjustment, ensure that the vehicle is unladen, and the adjuster units (see below) are both set to position "0".
3 Each headlight unit is equipped with a four-position adjuster unit - this can be used to adjust the headlight beam, to compensate for the relevant load which the vehicle is carrying. The adjuster units are incorporated into the vertical beam adjuster; access to them can be gained with the bonnet open. Position "0" is the standard position, positions "1" and "2" for when the vehicle is partly-laden, and position "3" for when the vehicle is fully-laden. Ensure that both adjusters are set to the same position, and be sure to reset to position "0" once the load has been removed.

9 Instrument panel - removal and refitting

Removal

1 Disconnect the battery negative terminal.
2 Remove the steering wheel as described in Chapter 10.
3 Release the panel fasteners by rotating them through a quarter of a turn, and remove the driver's side lower facia panel. Release the heater duct, and remove it from behind the panel **(see illustrations)**.
4 Slacken and remove the five screws which secure the two halves of the steering column shrouds together, then remove both the upper and lower shroud. Release the steering column, and lock it in its lowest position.

7.14b . . . and withdraw the foglight from the front of the bumper

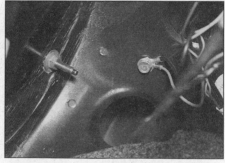

7.17a Undo the retaining nut situated on the inside of the luggage compartment . . .

7.17b . . . then remove the rear light unit from the rear of the vehicle, and disconnect its wiring connector

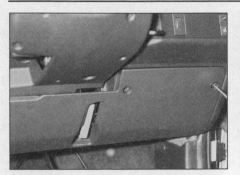

9.3a Remove the driver's side lower facia panel . . .

9.3b . . . and remove the heater duct from behind the panel

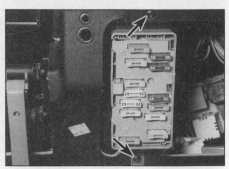

9.5 Fusebox retaining screws (arrowed)

9.6 Undo the two bonnet release lever retaining bolts, and free the lever from its bracket. Heater duct retaining screw is arrowed

9.7a Slacken and remove the instrument panel shroud retaining screws (arrowed) . . .

9.7b . . . then disconnect the switch wiring connectors and remove the shroud

9.9a Undo the retaining screws (arrowed) . . .

9.9b . . . then withdraw the instrument panel from the facia . . .

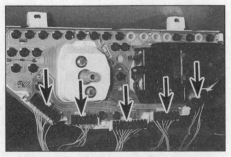
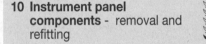

9.9c . . . and disconnect the wiring connectors (arrowed) from the rear of the panel

5 Undo the two retaining screws, and free the fusebox from the facia panel **(see illustration)**.
6 Slacken and remove the two bolts securing the bonnet release lever to the facia, and free the release lever assembly from the facia. Undo the heater duct retaining screw, located directly beneath the bonnet release lever, then manoeuvre the heater duct out from the behind the facia **(see illustration)**.
7 Slacken and remove the four instrument panel shroud retaining screws, then remove the shroud, disconnecting the switch wiring connectors as they become accessible **(see illustrations)**.
8 Reaching in through the lower facia aperture, reach up behind the instrument panel, then depress the retaining tangs and detach the speedometer cable from the rear of the panel.
9 Undo the two lower retaining screws, then withdraw the instrument panel assembly from the facia. Disconnect the wiring connectors from the rear of the panel, and remove the assembly from the vehicle **(see illustrations)**.

Refitting

10 Refitting is a reversal of the removal procedure. On completion, reconnect the battery and check the operation of all the panel warning lights and the instrument panel shroud switches, to ensure that they are functioning correctly.

10 Instrument panel components - removal and refitting

General

1 Remove the instrument panel as described in Section 9, then proceed as described under the relevant sub-heading.

Speedometer

2 Slacken and remove the three panel front cover retaining screws from the rear of the instrument panel. Carefully release the six retaining clips situated around the outside of the cover, then separate the cover and instrument panel **(see illustrations)**.
3 Undo the two retaining screws from the front of the speedometer face, then undo the two retaining bolts from the rear of the panel, and withdraw the speedometer **(see illustrations)**.
4 Refitting is a reverse of the removal procedure. Do not overtighten the instrument panel fasteners, as the plastic is easily cracked.

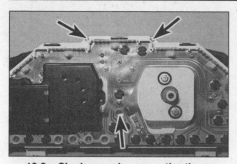

10.2a Slacken and remove the three instrument panel cover retaining screws (arrowed) . . .

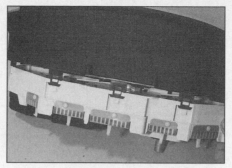

10.2b . . . then release the retaining clips, and separate the panel and cover

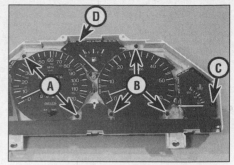

10.3a Instrument panel component front fasteners

A Speedometer screws
B Tachometer screws
C Temperature gauge screw
D Fuel gauge screw

Tachometer

5 Remove the panel front cover as described in paragraph 2.

6 Undo the two screws and remove the cover from the rear of panel, disconnecting its wiring connector as it becomes accessible (see illustration).

7 Undo the four retaining nuts, and remove the circuit board from the rear of the tachometer (see illustration).

8 Slacken and remove the three screws from the front face of the tachometer, and remove the tachometer from the case.

9 Refitting is a reverse of the removal procedure. Do not overtighten the instrument panel fasteners, as the plastic is easily cracked.

Temperature gauge

10 Remove the front cover and the rear cover, as described in paragraphs 2 and 6.

11 Undo the three retaining nuts from the rear, and the single screw from the front, of the temperature gauge, and withdraw the gauge from the case (see illustration).

12 Refitting is a reverse of the removal procedure. Do not overtighten the instrument panel fasteners, as the plastic is easily cracked.

Fuel gauge

13 Remove the front cover as described in paragraph 2.

14 Slacken and remove the three nuts from the rear, and undo the single retaining screw from the front face of the gauge, and withdraw the gauge from the case.

15 Refitting is a reverse of the removal procedure. Do not overtighten the instrument panel fasteners, as the plastic is easily cracked.

Printed circuit

16 Remove all the panel instruments as described above.

17 Remove all the bulbholders from the rear of the case, by twisting them in an anti-clockwise direction. Slacken and remove all the circuit retaining screws, then release the printed circuit from its retaining pins, and remove it from the rear of the case.

18 Refitting is a reversal of the removal procedure, ensuring that the printed circuit is correctly located on all the necessary retaining pins.

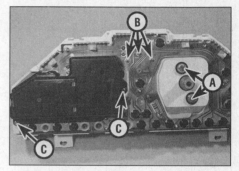

10.3b Instrument panel component rear fasteners

A Speedometer bolts
B Fuel gauge nuts
C Rear cover screws

11 Clock - removal and refitting

Removal

1 Disconnect the battery negative terminal.

2 Using a flat-bladed screwdriver, carefully prise the clock out of the facia panel, taking great care not mark the clock or facia (see illustration).

10.6 Instrument panel rear cover wiring connector

10.7 Tachometer rear retaining nuts and printed circuit board

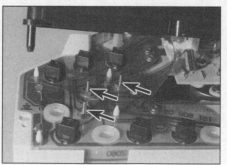

10.11 Temperature gauge retaining nuts (arrowed)

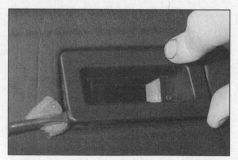

11.2 Carefully prise the clock out of the facia (note the use of padding under the screwdriver, to avoid damage) . . .

11.3 . . . and disconnect its wiring connector

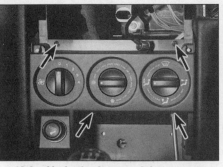

13.3a Undo the four retaining screws (arrowed) . . .

13.3b . . . then withdraw the centre vent panel, disconnecting the wiring connectors from the cigarette lighter

3 Disconnect the wiring connector, and remove the clock **(see illustration)**.

Refitting

4 Reconnect the wiring connector, then clip the clock into the position in the facia.
5 Reconnect the battery negative terminal, then reset the clock.

12 Door-open warning display - general information

Some models covered in this manual are equipped with a door-open warning display in the instrument panel. If a door is not correctly shut, the relevant door on the warning panel will be illuminated.

The system consists of switches which are built into the door lock assemblies and the panel in the instrument cluster. The panel bulbs are the same as the other instrument panel bulbs, and can be renewed as described in Section 6. The switches are an integral part of each door lock assembly.

13 Cigarette lighter - removal and refitting

Removal

1 Remove the centre console as described in Chapter 11.
2 Where a radio/cassette player is fitted, remove it as described in Section 21, then undo the two retaining screws and remove the mounting bracket from the radio aperture. Where no radio/cassette player is fitted, carefully prise out the storage box from the centre of the facia panel.
3 Undo the four centre vent panel retaining screws (two located above the heater controls, and two directly below), then unclip the panel and withdraw it from the facia. Disconnect the wiring connectors from the cigarette lighter and ashtray illumination bulb, and remove the centre vent panel assembly from the vehicle **(see illustrations)**.
4 Remove the lighter element, release the retaining tangs and push out the metal insert,

13.4a Release the retaining tangs, then withdraw the metal insert . . .

then remove the plastic outer section of the lighter **(see illustrations)**.

Refitting

5 Refitting is a reversal of the removal procedure.

14 "Lights-on" warning system - general information

1 Most vehicles covered in this manual are equipped with a "lights-on" warning system. The purpose of the system is to inform the driver that the lights have been left on once the ignition switch has been turned off; the buzzer will sound when a door is opened. The system consists of a buzzer unit which is linked to the door courtesy light switches.

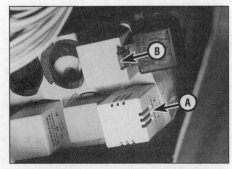

14.2 "Lights-on" warning buzzer (A) is situated behind the main fusebox

B Flasher relay

13.4b . . . followed by the plastic outer section of the cigarette lighter

2 To gain access to the buzzer unit, release the three fasteners by rotating them through 90°, then remove the driver's side lower facia panel. The buzzer unit is situated in the relay panel located directly behind the fusebox. The buzzer unit is a push-fit in the panel, and can easily be identified by the slots in its cover **(see illustration)**.
3 Refer to Section 4 for information on courtesy light switch removal.

15 Horn - removal and refitting

Removal

1 Jack up the front of the vehicle, and support it on axle stands.

Electric horn

2 Undo the nut securing the horn to its mounting bracket, then lower the horn out of position, and disconnect it from its wiring connector.

Air horn

3 Slacken and remove the nut and bolt securing the horn mounting bracket to the vehicle body, then remove the horn, disconnecting it from its air supply pipe **(see illustrations)**.
4 Disconnect the wiring connector from the air compressor, then undo the retaining nut and withdraw the compressor from underneath the vehicle **(see illustrations)**.

Recover the spacer from the compressor mounting bolt.

Refitting

5 Refitting is a reverse of the removal procedure.

16 Speedometer drive cable - removal and refitting

General

1 The drive cable is in two parts; the lower cable runs from the transmission to a point just in front of the left-hand end of the bulkhead, while the upper cable runs from that point to the rear of the instrument panel. Each section can be removed individually, as follows.

Upper cable

Removal

2 On left-hand-drive models, remove the instrument panel as described in Section 9.
3 On right-hand-drive models, remove the complete facia assembly (see Chapter 11).
4 Working in the engine compartment, slacken the knurled retaining ring, and separate the upper and lower cable sections **(see illustration)**. Tie a length of string to the end of the upper section of the cable.
5 From inside the vehicle, withdraw the cable from the bulkhead. Once the cable is free, untie the string and leave it in position in the vehicle; the string can then be used to draw the new cable back into position.

Refitting

6 Tie the inner end of the string to the end of the cable, then use the string to draw the speedometer cable through into the engine compartment. Once the cable is through, untie the string.
7 On left-hand-drive models, position the cable so that approximately 145 mm of the cable protrudes into the engine compartment, then connect the end of the cable to the lower cable section, and securely tighten the retaining ring. Refit the instrument panel as described in Section 9.
8 On right-hand-drive models, position the cable so that approximately 100 mm of the cable protrudes into the engine compartment, then connect the end of the cable to the lower cable section, and securely tighten the retaining ring. Refit the facia assembly as described in Chapter 11.

Lower cable

Removal

9 Apply the handbrake, then jack up the front of the vehicle and support it on axle stands.
10 Working from underneath the vehicle, withdraw the rubber retaining pin, and detach the cable from the speedometer drive on the transmission.

15.3a Slacken and remove the retaining nut and bolt (arrowed) . . .

15.4a Disconnect the wiring connector . . .

11 Working in the engine compartment, slacken the knurled retaining ring, then detach the lower cable section from the upper section, and remove it from the vehicle.

Refitting

12 Examine the O-rings fitted to the cable lower-end fitting for signs of damage or deterioration, and renew if necessary. Apply a smear of clean engine oil to the O-rings, to aid installation.
13 Attach the lower cable to the upper cable, and securely tighten the retaining ring.
14 Ensuring that the cable is correctly routed, slide the lower end of the cable into position in the speedometer drive, and secure it in position with the rubber retaining pin. Lower the vehicle to the ground.

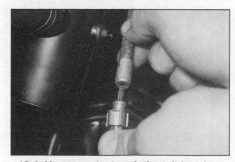

16.4 Unscrew the knurled retaining ring, and separate the upper and lower speedometer cable sections

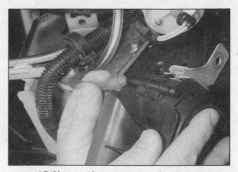

15.3b . . . then remove the horn, disconnecting it from its supply pipe

15.4b . . . then undo the retaining nut and remove the air compressor

17 Wiper arm - removal and refitting

Removal

1 Operate the wiper motor, then switch it off so that the wiper arm returns to the at-rest position.

> **HAYNES HINT** *Stick a piece of masking tape on the glass along the edge of the wiper blade to use as an alignment aid on refitting.*

2 Lift up the wiper arm spindle nut cover, then slacken and remove the spindle nut. Lift the blade off the glass, and pull the wiper arm off its spindle **(see illustrations)**. If necessary,

17.2a Raise the spindle cover, then undo the retaining nut . . .

17.2b ... and remove the wiper arm from the spindle

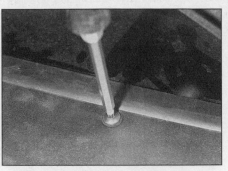

18.3a Undo the six retaining screws ...

18.3b ... then carefully ease the wiper motor/vent panel cover out from behind the windscreen sealing strip

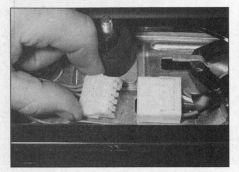

18.4 Disconnect the wiper motor wiring connector ...

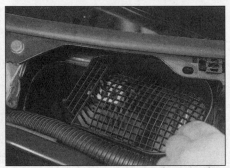

18.5 ... and remove the plastic cover from the blower motor intake duct

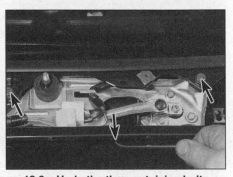

18.6a Undo the three retaining bolts (arrowed) ...

the arm can be levered off the spindle using a suitable flat-bladed screwdriver.

Refitting

3 Ensure that the wiper arm and spindle splines are clean and dry, then refit the arm to the spindle, aligning the wiper blade with the tape fitted on removal. Refit the spindle nut, tightening it securely, and clip the nut cover back in position.

18 Windscreen wiper motor and linkage - removal and refitting

Removal

1 Disconnect the battery negative terminal.
2 Remove the wiper arm as described in the previous Section.

3 Open the bonnet, and slacken and remove the six wiper motor cover/vent panel retaining screws. Carefully ease the cover out from behind the windscreen sealing strip, then disengage its front locating pegs, and manoeuvre the panel away from the vehicle **(see illustrations)**.
4 Disconnect the wiring connector from the front of the wiper motor **(see illustration)**.
5 Remove the plastic cover from the heater blower motor intake passage **(see illustration)**.
6 Undo the three wiper motor retaining bolts, then manoeuvre the wiper motor out of position, and remove it from the vehicle **(see illustrations)**.
7 If necessary, using a suitable flat-bladed screwdriver, carefully lever the wiper linkage off the motor spindle balljoint. Slacken and

remove the three motor retaining bolts, and separate the motor and linkage **(see illustration)**.

Refitting

8 Where necessary, assemble the motor and linkage, and securely tighten the motor retaining bolts. Clip the linkage onto the spindle balljoint, and check that it is securely retained.
9 Manoeuvre the motor assembly back into position, and refit the three retaining bolts, tightening them securely.
10 Reconnect the wiring connector to the motor, and refit the cover to the blower motor intake passage.
11 Manoeuvre the wiper motor/vent cover back into position, and engage its front locating pegs with their mounting rubbers **(see illustration)**. Starting at the centre and working outwards, carefully ease the top edge

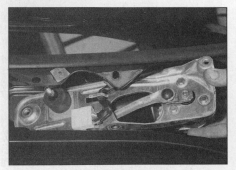

18.6b ... then remove the wiper motor from the vehicle

18.7 Windscreen wiper motor retaining bolts (arrowed)

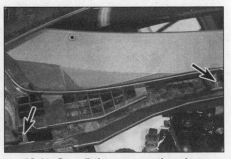

18.11 On refitting, ensure the wiper motor/vent cover locating pegs (arrowed) are correctly located

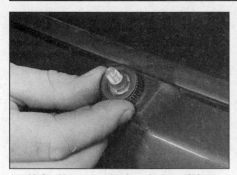

19.2a Unscrew the knurled retaining ring . . .

19.2b .... and remove the trim cover from the tailgate wiper motor spindle

19.3 Removing the wiper motor cover from the rear of the tailgate

of the cover behind the windscreen sealing strip. Once the cover is correctly seated behind the strip, secure it in position with its six retaining screws.

12 Refit the wiper arm as described in Section 17, and reconnect the battery negative terminal.

19 Tailgate wiper motor - removal and refitting

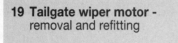

Removal

1 Remove the wiper arm as described in Section 17.

2 Unscrew the knurled retaining ring from the wiper spindle, and lift off the trim cover **(see illustrations)**.

3 Open up the tailgate. On Hatchback models, release the fasteners by rotating them through a quarter of a turn and remove the wiper motor cover from the centre of the tailgate **(see illustration)**. On Estate models, remove the tailgate inner trim panel complete.

4 Undo the three wiper motor retaining bolts, then withdraw the motor from the tailgate, disconnecting its wiring connectors as they become accessible **(see illustrations)**.

Refitting

5 Refitting is a reverse of the removal procedure. Ensure that the tailgate central locking servo motor (where fitted) is correctly engaged with the lock pin, prior to refitting the wiper motor retaining bolts.

19.4a Slacken and remove the three retaining bolts (arrowed) . . .

20 Windscreen/tailgate washer system components - removal and refitting

Washer system reservoir

Note: *To minimise fluid spillage, it is recommended that the washer reservoir is at least half-empty prior to removal.*

1 Jack up the front of the vehicle, and support it on axle stands. Remove the right-hand front roadwheel.

2 Open the bonnet, and disconnect the windscreen washer supply pipe from its non-return valve, situated on the right-hand side of the bonnet **(see illustration)**.

3 Undo the retaining screw from the front edge of the wheel arch liner, then work around the liner carefully, prising out all its retaining

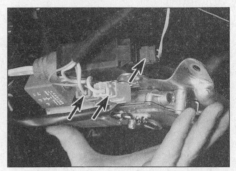

19.4b . . . then withdraw the motor, disconnecting the wiring connectors (arrowed) as they become accessible

clips, and remove the right-hand wheel arch liner and access cover from the vehicle **(see illustration)**.

4 Push the front direction indicator repeater light unit towards the rear of the vehicle, to free its retaining clips, then withdraw it from the wing.

5 Reach up behind the wing, and disconnect the wiring connector(s) from the washer pump(s).

6 Slacken and remove the two reservoir retaining bolts, then pull the top of the reservoir outwards, to release it from the reservoir filler neck **(see illustrations)**. Lower the reservoir out from underneath the wing, disconnecting the supply pipe(s) from the washer pump(s) as they become accessible.

7 Refitting is the reverse of removal, ensuring that the reservoir is correctly engaged with its filler neck.

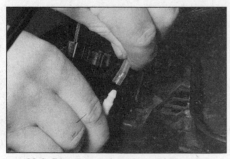

20.2 Disconnecting the windscreen washer supply pipe from its non-return valve

20.3 Removing the right-hand wheel arch liner

20.6a Undo the two retaining bolts (arrowed) . . .

20.6b . . . and lower the washer reservoir out from behind the wing

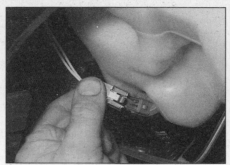

20.10a Disconnect the wiring connector . . .

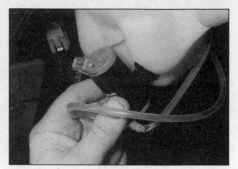

20.10b . . . then ease the washer pump out from the reservoir

Washer pump(s)

Note: *Prior to removing the pump(s), empty the contents of the reservoir, or be prepared for fluid spillage.*

8 Jack up the front of the vehicle, and support it on axle stands. Remove the right-hand front roadwheel.

9 Remove the wheel arch liner as described in paragraph 3.

10 Disconnect the wiring connector from the relevant pump, then carefully ease the pump out of its sealing grommet, and manoeuvre it out from behind the wing **(see illustrations)**. If necessary, to improve access to the pump, undo the mounting bolts, and lower the reservoir slightly. Note that, on models with a dual pump arrangement, the upper pump is tailgate washer pump, and the lower one is the windscreen washer pump.

11 Refitting is a reversal of the removal procedure.

Windscreen washer jet

12 Open the bonnet, then unclip the washer jet from the underside of the bonnet, and disconnect it from its supply pipe.

13 On refitting, ensure that the jet is clipped securely in position. If necessary, the jet nozzles can be adjusted using a pin; aim the spray to a point slightly above the centre of the wiper swept area.

Tailgate washer jet

14 Carefully prise the washer jet out of the top of the tailgate, and disconnect it from its supply pipe. Whilst the jet is removed, tape

the supply pipe in position, to ensure that it does not fall back into the tailgate.

15 On refitting, ensure that the jet is clipped securely in position. If necessary, the jet nozzle can be adjusted using a pin; aim the spray to the centre of the wiper swept area.

Non-return valves

16 If trouble is experienced at any time with the flow to the tailgate or windscreen washer jets, check that the relevant non-return valve is not blocked. The windscreen washer valve is situated in the supply pipe, next to the right-hand bonnet hinge; the tailgate washer valve is situated at the rear of the vehicle, tucked away underneath the top of the tailgate sealing strip.

17 To remove a non-return valve, simply disconnect the hoses from either end of it.

18 On refitting, ensure that the valve is installed the correct way around, so that it allows fluid to flow only in the direction of the washer jet(s).

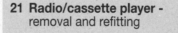

21 Radio/cassette player - removal and refitting

Note: *The following removal and refitting procedure is for the range of radio/cassette units which Citroën fit as standard equipment. Removal and refitting procedures for non-standard units may differ slightly.*

Removal

1 Disconnect the battery negative terminal.

2 Remove the two rubber plugs from the front

of the unit, to gain access to the radio/cassette unit retaining screws **(see illustration)**.

3 Undo the retaining screws, then withdraw the unit from the facia, and disconnect the wiring connectors and aerial from the rear of the unit **(see illustrations)**.

Refitting

4 Refitting is the reverse of the removal procedure. On completion, reconnect the battery, and enter the radio security code using the information given in *"Radio/cassette unit anti-theft system"* at the start of this manual.

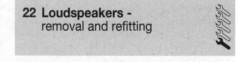

22 Loudspeakers - removal and refitting

Removal

1 The front speakers are located in the front door trim panels, in front of the door pull handles. On five-door models, the rear speakers are located at the bottom of the rear door trim panel; the rear speakers on three-door models are located in the rear seat side trim panels.

2 Carefully prise the speaker grille out from the trim panel **(see illustration)**.

3 Slacken and remove the speaker retaining screws and, on the front speaker, remove the retaining clip from the mounting peg. Withdraw the speaker from the panel, disconnecting its wiring connector as it becomes accessible **(see illustrations)**.

21.2 Remove the rubber plugs . . .

21.3a . . . and undo the two radio/cassette unit retaining screws

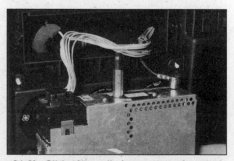

21.3b Slide the radio/cassette unit out of position, and disconnect the aerial connection and wiring connectors

22.2 Remove the grille to gain access to the relevant speaker

Refitting

4 Refitting is a reverse of the removal procedure.

---

23 Radio aerial -
removal and refitting

Removal

Aerial

1 Carefully prise the courtesy light out from the overhead console, and disconnect it from its wiring connector. Remove the two console retaining screws, then lower the console out of position, and disconnect it from its wiring connectors **(see illustrations)**.

2 Slacken and remove the nut from the base of the aerial, and disengage the aerial lead collar from its stud. The aerial can then be lifted away from the outside of the vehicle, noting the rubber seal which is fitted to its base **(see illustrations)**.

Aerial lead upper section

3 Remove the aerial as described above.

4 Unclip the trim panel from the right-hand windscreen pillar, to gain access to the aerial connection **(see illustration)**. Where necessary, release the alarm sensors from the clip on the top of the panel, and remove the panel. If the aerial connection is not situated behind the right-hand trim panel, remove the left-hand panel.

5 Disconnect the upper section of the lead, and tie a piece of string to it. Withdraw the aerial

22.3a Front speakers are retained by three screws and a retaining clip (arrowed)

lead through the overhead console aperture, and untie the string from its end. Leave the string in position - it can then be used to draw the lead back into position on refitting.

Aerial lead lower section

6 To remove the lower section of the aerial lead, linking the upper section to the rear of the radio/cassette unit, it is first necessary to remove the facia panel as described in Chapter 11. The lead can then be freed from all its relevant retaining clips, and removed from the vehicle.

Refitting

Aerial

7 Ensure that the rubber seal is in good condition, then refit it to the aerial base. Refit the aerial to the roof, ensuring that its locating pin is correctly located in its hole.

8 From inside the vehicle, locate the aerial

23.1a Undo the two retaining screws (arrowed) . . .

22.3b Rear speakers are retained by four retaining screws

22.3c Remove the speaker from the panel, and disconnect it from its wiring connector

lead collar on the aerial stud, and refit the retaining nut, tightening it securely.

9 Reconnect the wiring connectors to the overhead console, and locate the console in position in the headlining. Refit the two

23.1b . . . then lower out the overhead console, and disconnect it from its wiring connectors

23.2a Undo the aerial lead retaining nut from inside the vehicle . . .

23.2b . . . then remove the aerial from the roof of the vehicle

23.4 Aerial lead upper-to-lower section connection is located behind the windscreen pillar trim panel

console retaining screws, and tighten them securely. Reconnect the courtesy light to its wiring connector, and clip the light back into position in the console.

Aerial lead upper section

10 Tie the string to the end of the aerial lead, and use the string to draw the lead back into position. Untie the string, and reconnect the lead to the lower aerial section.

11 Where necessary, ensure that the alarm sensor wire is correctly routed, and refit the sensor to its retaining clip. Clip the panel back into position, ensuring that the pegs on the base of the panel are correctly located in the facia panel.

12 Refit the aerial as described above.

Aerial lead lower section

13 Refitting is a reversal of the removal procedure.

24 Anti-theft alarm system - general information

Note: *This information is applicable only to the anti-theft alarm system fitted by Citroën as standard equipment.*

Some models in the range are fitted with an anti-theft alarm system as standard equipment. The alarm is automatically armed and disarmed when the door locks are operated using the remote central locking transmitter.

Note that if the doors are operated using the key, the alarm will not be armed or disarmed (as applicable). If for some reason the remote central locking transmitter fails whilst the alarm is armed, the alarm can be disarmed using the key. To do this, open the door with the key, then enter the vehicle, noting that the alarm will sound as the door is opened, and switch on the ignition switch whilst depressing the small button on the alarm switch mounted in the facia. Note that the ignition switch must be turned on and the button depressed within 10 seconds of opening the door.

The alarm system has switches on the bonnet, tailgate and each of the doors. It also has ultrasonic sensing, which detects movement inside the vehicle, via the sensors mounted on the top of each windscreen pillar trim panel. If required, the ultrasonic sensing facility of the system can be switched off, whilst retaining the switched side of the system. To switch off the ultrasonic sensing, with the ignition switch off, depress the alarm switch on the facia for approximately 1 second, until the switch LED is continuously lit. Now, when the doors are locked using the remote central locking transmitter, and the alarm is armed, only the switched side of the alarm system is operational. This facility is useful, as it allows you to leave the windows/sunroof open, and still arm the alarm. If the windows/sunroof are left open with the ultrasonic sensing not switched off, the alarm may be falsely triggered by a gust of wind.

Should the alarm system become faulty, the vehicle should be taken to a Citroën dealer for examination.

25 "Dim-dip" lighting system (UK models only) - general information

1 To comply with UK regulations, a "dim-dip" lighting system is fitted to all UK models. The system is operates through a dim-dip relay, and a resistor unit situated at the front left-hand corner of the vehicle, above the horn assembly.

2 The dim-dip relay is supplied with current from the sidelight circuit, and energised by a feed from the ignition switch. When energised, the unit allows battery voltage to pass through the resistor unit to the headlight dipped-beam circuits; this lights the headlights with approximately one-sixth of their normal power, so that the car cannot be driven using sidelights alone.

26 Air bag system - general information, precautions and system de-activation

General information

Where fitted, the driver's side air bag is located in the steering wheel centre pad.

The air bag system is armed only when the ignition is switched on. However, a reserve power source maintains a power supply to the system in the event of a break in the main electrical supply. The system is activated by a 'g' sensor (deceleration sensor) and is controlled by an electronic control unit which is integral with the steering wheel.

The air bag is inflated by a gas generator, which forces the bag out from its location in the steering wheel.

Precautions

 Warning: The following precautions must be observed when working on vehicles equipped with an air bag system, to prevent the possibility of personal injury.

General

The following precautions **must** be observed when carrying out work on a vehicle equipped with an air bag:

(a) *Do not disconnect the battery with the engine running.*

(b) *Before carrying out any work in the vicinity of the air bag, removal of any of the air bag components, or any welding work on the vehicle, de-activate the system as described in the following sub-Section.*

(c) *Do not attempt to test any of the air bag system circuits using test meters or any other test equipment.*

(d) *If the air bag warning light comes on, or any fault in the system is suspected, consult a Citroën dealer without delay.* **Do**

not attempt to carry out fault diagnosis, or any dismantling of the components.

Handling the air bag unit

(a) *Transport the unit by itself, bag upward.*

(b) *Do not put your arms around the unit.*

(c) *Carry the unit close to the body, bag outward.*

(d) *Do not drop the unit or expose it to impacts.*

(e) *Do not attempt to dismantle the unit.*

(f) *Do not connect any form of electrical equipment to any part of the air bag circuit.*

Storing the air bag unit

(a) *Store the unit in a cupboard with the air bag upward.*

(b) *Do not expose the unit to temperatures above 80°C.*

(c) *Do not expose the unit to naked flames.*

(d) *Do not attempt to dispose of the unit - consult a Citroën dealer.*

(e) *Never refit a unit which is known to be faulty or damaged.*

De-activation of air bag system

The system must be de-activated before carrying out any work on the air bag components or surrounding area:

(a) *Switch off the ignition.*

(b) *Remove the ignition key.*

(c) *Switch off all electrical equipment.*

(d) *Disconnect the battery negative lead.*

(e) *Insulate the battery negative terminal and the end of the battery negative lead to prevent any possibility of contact.*

(f) *Wait for at least ten minutes before carrying out any further work.*

Activation of air bag system

To activate the system on completion of any work, proceed as follows:

(a) *Ensure that the vehicle is unoccupied and that there are no loose objects around the vicinity of the steering wheel. Close the vehicle doors and windows.*

(b) *Ensure that the ignition is switched off, then reconnect the battery negative lead.*

(c) *Open the driver's door and switch on the ignition without reaching in front of the steering wheel. Check that the air bag warning light in the steering wheel illuminates for approximately 3 seconds and then extinguishes.*

(d) *Switch off the ignition.*

(e) *If the air bag warning light does not operate as described in paragraph (c), consult a Citroën dealer before driving the vehicle.*

27 Air bag system components - removal and refitting

 Warning: Refer to the precautions given in Section 26 before attempting to carry out work on any of the air bag components.

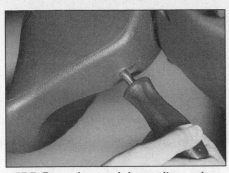

27.7 Removing an air bag unit securing screw

27.9 The air bag unit wiring connector (arrowed)

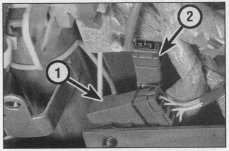

27.14 Disconnect the radio/cassette player remote control (1) and air bag unit (2) wiring connectors

General

1 The air bag system comprises the following.
 (a) Air bag unit
 (b) Warning light
 (c) Firing unit
 (d) Rotary switch
 (e) Vehicle wiring and sensor
2 Any suspected faults with the system components should be referred to a Citroën dealer. Under no circumstances attempt to carry out any work other than removal and refitting of the air bag unit and/or the rotary switch, as described in the following paragraphs.

Firing unit

3 The air bag firing unit is integral with the steering wheel and cannot be removed independently. Refer to Chapter 10 for details of steering wheel removal.

Air bag unit

Removal

4 The air bag unit is an integral part of the steering wheel centre boss.
5 De-activate the air bag system as described in Section 26.
6 Move the steering wheel as necessary for access to the two air bag unit securing screws. The screws are located at the rear of the steering wheel boss.
7 Remove the two air bag unit securing screws **(see illustration)**.
8 Unclip one edge of the air bag unit from the centre of the steering wheel and pivot away from the wheel, but do not pull it completely clear.
9 Carefully disconnect the wiring connector from the rear of the unit, then withdraw the unit from the steering wheel **(see illustration)**.
10 If the air bag unit is to be stored for any length of time, refer to the storage precautions given in Section 26.

Refitting

11 Refitting is a reversal of removal, bearing in mind the following points:
 (a) Do not strike the air bag unit, or expose it to impacts during refitting.
 (b) On completion of refitting, activate the air bag system as described in Section 26.

Rotary switch

Removal

12 Remove the air bag unit as described previously in this Section.
13 Remove the steering wheel and steering column shrouds.
14 Locate the two rotary switch wiring connectors beneath the steering column, and separate the two halves of each connector **(see illustration)**.
15 Remove the switch securing clip by using a screwdriver. Alternatively, remove the two switch securing screws. Pull the unit from the steering column **(see illustrations)**.
16 Feed the wiring harnesses up through the housing (if necessary remove the right-hand stalk switch to allow the wiring to pass through the housing).

Refitting

17 Refitting is a reversal of removal. Refit the steering wheel with reference to Chapter 10 and refit the air bag unit as described previously in this Section.

28 Wiring diagrams - explanatory notes

The wiring diagrams in this manual represent typical examples of those available. To assist you in using the diagrams, here is an explanation of the various letters and their use, in conjunction with the wiring diagram keys **(see illustration)**.
(a) **Large numbers** - identify the various components.
(b) **Capital letters printed in the middle of a wire** - indicate which harness the wire is located in.
(c) **Small letters located at the connection points** - indicates the colour of either of the wire itself, or of the marking on the wire. If the letter has a line drawn above it, then this shows it indicates the colour of the wire itself; if there is no line above the letter, it indicates the colour of the marking on the wire.
(d) **Connecting blocks** - the first number and letter(s) inside the box indicates the size and colour of the connecting block. The second letter (where applicable) and last number gives the exact location of the relevant wire in that connecting block; the letter indicates which row the wire is situated in, and the number denotes its location in that row. For example:
3 Bl 2 - shows that the wiring connector is blue in colour, and contains three wiring channels, the wire shown in the diagram being located in the second channel of the connector.
15 V A 2 - shows that the wiring connector is green in colour, and contains fifteen channels. The A shows that the wire shown in the diagram is in the upper row of the connector, and the 2 shows it to be in the second channel of that row.

27.15a Remove the rotary switch securing clip . . .

27.15b . . . and pull the switch from the steering column

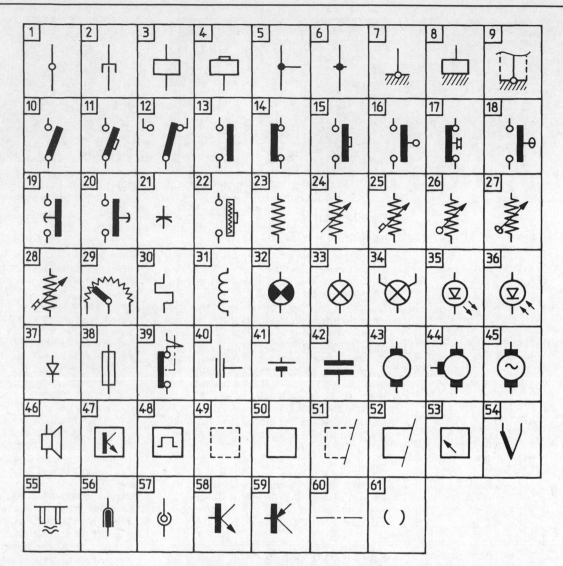

Symbols used in wiring diagrams - typical

No.	Description
1	Socket connection
2	Pin connection
3	Connector connection
4	Connector connection with index (for differentiation)
5	Junction not to be dismantled (splice)
6	Junction not to be dismantled (with other connection possibilities)
7	Socket earthing
8	Connector earthing
9	Part body earth connection
10	Switch (non-automatic return)
11	Manual switch
12	Selector switch
13	Switch on at-rest (automatic return)
14	Swithc off at-rest (automatic return)
15	Manual contact switch
16	Mechanical contact switch
17	Pressure contact switch
18	Thermal switch
19	Contact delayed on opening
20	Contact delayed on closing

No.	Description
21	Friction contact switch
22	Manual contact switch (cigar lighter) with resistance
23	Resistance
24	Rheostat
25	Manual rheostat
26	Mechanical rheostat
27	Temperature rheostat (thermistor)
28	Pressure rheostat
29	Rheostat
30	Shunt
31	Coil (relay-solenoid)
32	Warning light
33	Light bulb
34	Double-filament light bulb
35	Light-emitting diode (LED)
36	Photo-diode
37	Diode
38	Fuse
39	Thermal circuit breaker
40	Screening
41	Battery cell

No.	Description
42	Suppressor
43	Motor
44	Two-speed motor
45	Alternative power generator
46	Sound equipment (horn, loudspeaker)
47	Electronic control unit
48	Delay unit
49	Part framing (with its circuit diagram)
50	Part framing (without its circuit diagram)
51	Part extract
52	Part extract
53	Indicator
54	Thermocouple
55	Electrodes
56	Oxygen sensor
57	Supply socket
58	NPN transistor
59	PNP transistor
60	Connection indicating line
61	No extremity

Key to wiring diagrams
Not all items fitted to all models

No.	Description	No.	Description	No.	Description
5	Front cigar lighter	429	Fuel cut-off solenoid (stop solenoid)	715	LH headlight adjustment device motor
10	Ignition distributor	430	Canister discharge solenoid	716	RH headlight adjustment device motor
15	Alternator	431	Fast idling solenoid	720	Engine cooling fan (single, or LH of two)
20	LH horn	432	Idling actuator		
21	RH horn	434	Canister solenoid	721	RH engine cooling fan
35	Battery	437	Exhaust gas recirculation solenoid	742	Central interior light
40	Instrument cluster	441	Vacuum advance solenoid	743	Rear interior light
45	Ignition coil	443	Injection timing correction solenoid	750	LH front brake pads sensor
50	Supply connector box	480	LH rear light	751	RH front brake pads sensor
52	Junction box	481	RH rear light	755	Fuel pump
53	Water temperature control unit	482	LH front foglight	757	Windscreen washer pump
55	Central door locking control unit	483	RH front foglight	758	Rear screen washer pump
58	Remote control door locking receiver (PLIP)	484	LH rear foglight	765	Radio set
		485	RH rear foglight	770	Throttle spindle potentiometer
59	Pre-heater (glow plugs) control unit	486	LH dipped beams	772	Mixture adjustment potentiometer
62	Earth connection box	487	RH dipped beams	775	Pressure switch
100	Spark plugs	488	LH front direction indicator	779	TDC sensor plug (petrol) or Water temp. sensor (Diesel)
101	Glow plugs	489	RH front direction indicator		
130	Lights-on warning buzzer	490	LH rear direction indicator	781	ABS diagnostic socket
140	Anti-lock braking ECU	491	RH rear direction indicator	783	Injection diagnostic socket
141	Air conditioning ECU	492	LH sidelight	786	Headlight: LH main and dipped beams
142	Fuel injection ECU	493	RH sidelight	787	Headlight: RH main and dipped beams
144	Exhaust gas recirculation ECU	496	LH tail light	790	Air blower motor
152	Engine speed sensor	497	RH tail light	798	Injection timing cut-off relay
155	LH front wheel sensor (ABS)	498	LH reversing light	804	Air conditioning relay
156	RH front wheel sensor (ABS)	499	RH reversing light	805	Compressor cut-off relay (temperature)
157	LH rear wheel sensor (ABS)	500	LH direction indicator repeater	806	Front foglight relays
158	RH rear wheel sensor (ABS)	501	RH direction indicator repeater	807	Injection double relay
160	TDC sensor	502	LH headlight	809	Front window relay
170	Flasher unit	503	RH headlight	813	Engine cooling fan relay (fast speed)
180	Additional air control	504	LH stop-light	814	Engine cooling fan relay (slow speed)
183	Air blower control	505	RH stop-light	815	Engine cooling fan speed switchover relay
211	LH column switch (lights, indicators, horn)	550	LH front speaker		
		551	RH front speaker	819	Rear foglight relays
212	RH column switch (front and rear wipers)	554	LH rear speaker	820	Heated rear window relay
		555	RH rear speaker	822	Compressor cut-off relay (injection)
215	Exterior mirror switch	570	Injector	827	Dim-dip relay (UK only)
254	Air horn compressor	582	Refrigerated air switch	841	Window re-energising relay
255	Air con. compressor driving clutch	587	Front foglight switch	843	Air horn compressor relay
270	HT coil suppressor	588	Rear foglight switch	844	ABS main relay
300	Ignition switch	589	Hazard warning light switch	845	Hydraulic fluid motor relay
302	Boot light switch	590	Driver's window switch	849	Post-heating cut-off relay
305	Driver's door locking switch	591	Passenger's window switch (on driver's door)	857	Carburettor base heating resistance
306	Passenger's door locking switch			858	Dipped beams resistance (dim-dip)
307	LH rear door closing switch	592	Passenger's window switch (on passenger's door)	859	Air blower speed resistor
308	RH rear door closing switch			860	Coding resistance
310	LH front door pillar switch	597	Heated rear window switch	862	Injector additional resistance
311	RH front door pillar switch	608	Headlight adjustment device switch	876	RH rear view mirror
312	LH rear door pillar switch	650	Fuel gauge	880	Instrument lighting rheostat
313	RH rear door pillar switch	660	Map reading light	900	Oxygen sensor
314	Reversing light switch	671	Engine oil pressure switch	902	Engine oil level sensor
315	Handbrake switch	680	Ignition module	903	Injection air pressure sensor
317	Hydraulic fluid level switch	681	Air blower control module	904	Engine oil pressure sensor
318	Throttle butterfly switch	685	Digital clock	907	Injection air temperature sensor
319	Stop-light switch	694	Windscreen wiper motor	909	Injection water temperature sensor
322	Atmospheric pressure switch	695	Tailgate wiper motor	910	Water temp. sensor (control unit)
326	Starter motor switch	696	LH front window motor	912	Evaporator temperature sensor
330	Post-heater switch	697	RH front window motor	915	Water temperature switch sensor
340	Airflow meter	703	Driver's door locking motor	918	Engine oil temperature sensor
350	Starter motor	704	Passenger's door locking motor	962	Windscreen intermittent wipe timer
385	Front ashtray illumination	705	LH rear door locking motor	963	Tailgate intermittent wipe timer
389	Boot light	706	RH rear door locking motor	970	Coolant temp. warning thermal switch
391	Number plate LH light	708	Tailgate locking motor	971	Cooling fan thermal switch (radiator)
392	Number plate RH light	712	Idling control stepper motor	974	Water temperature switch
394	Air con. control illumination	714	ABS hydraulic pump motor	990	Heated rear window

Harness code

AB	ABS	PG	LH rear door
AV	Front	PJ	Headlight adjustment device
CL	Air conditioning	PL	Interior light
CN	Negative cable	PP	Passenger's door
CP	Positive cable	RD	RH rear
EF	Boot lighting	RG	LH rear
FR	Rear lights	RL	Direction indicator side repeater
HB	Interior	TJ	Headlight adjustment device switch
MT	Engine (and injection)	UD	RH brake pad wear
MV	Electric cooling fan	UG	LH brake pad wear
PB	Dashboard	VD	RH side tailgate
PC	Driver's door	VG	LH side tailgate
PD	RH rear door		

Colour code

B	White
Bl	Blue
G	Grey
Ic	Clear/transparent
J	Yellow
M	Brown
Mv	Purple
N	Black
Or	Orange
R	Red
Ro	Pink
V	Green
Vi	Lilac

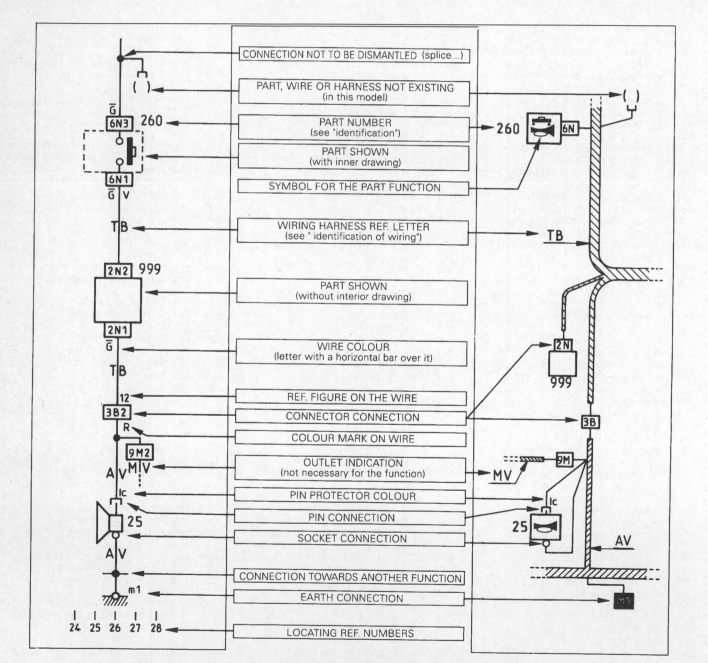

How to use the wiring diagrams

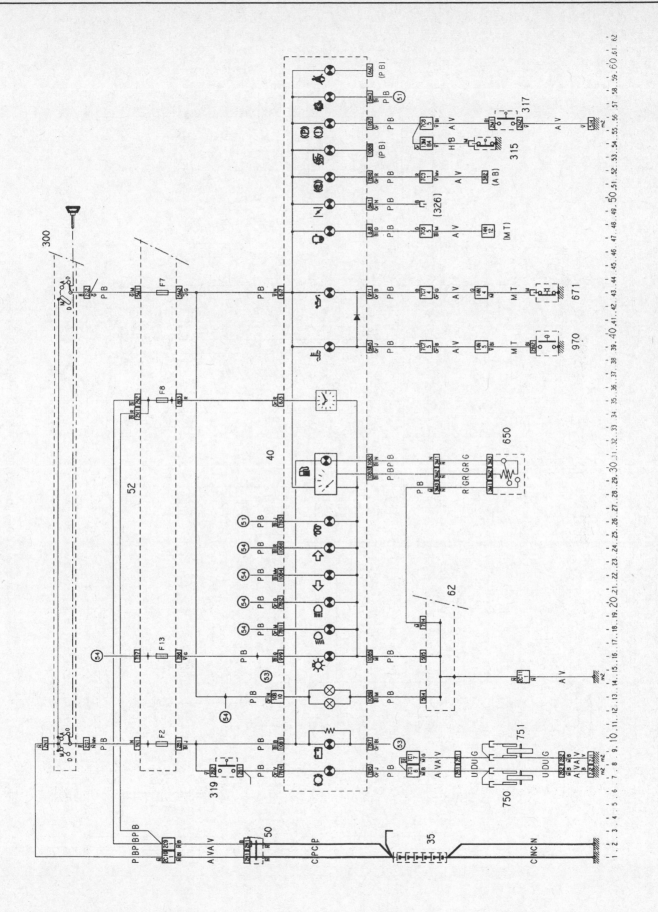

Instrument panel (low-specification models) - typical

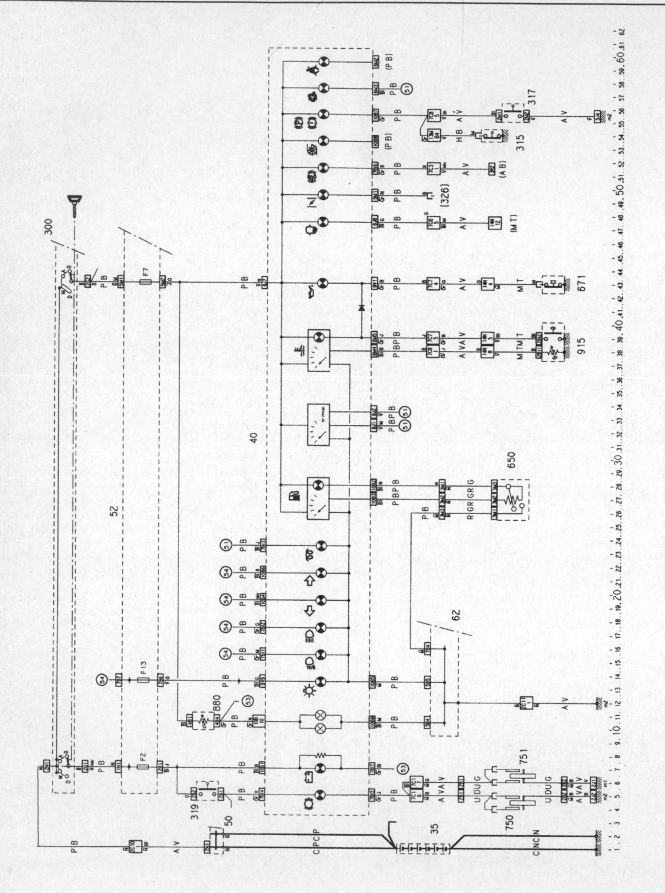

Instrument panel (low- to mid-specification models) - typical

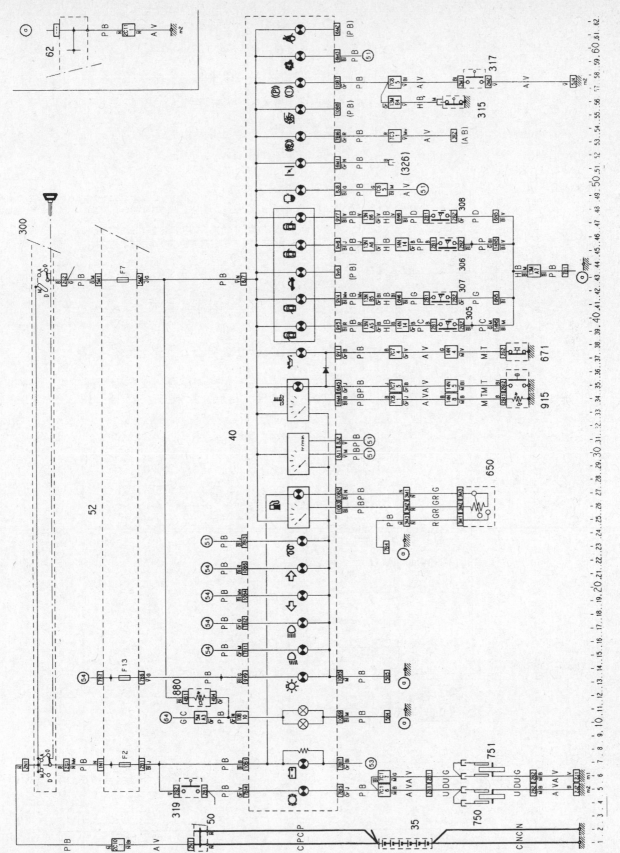

Instrument panel (mid- to high-specification models) - typical

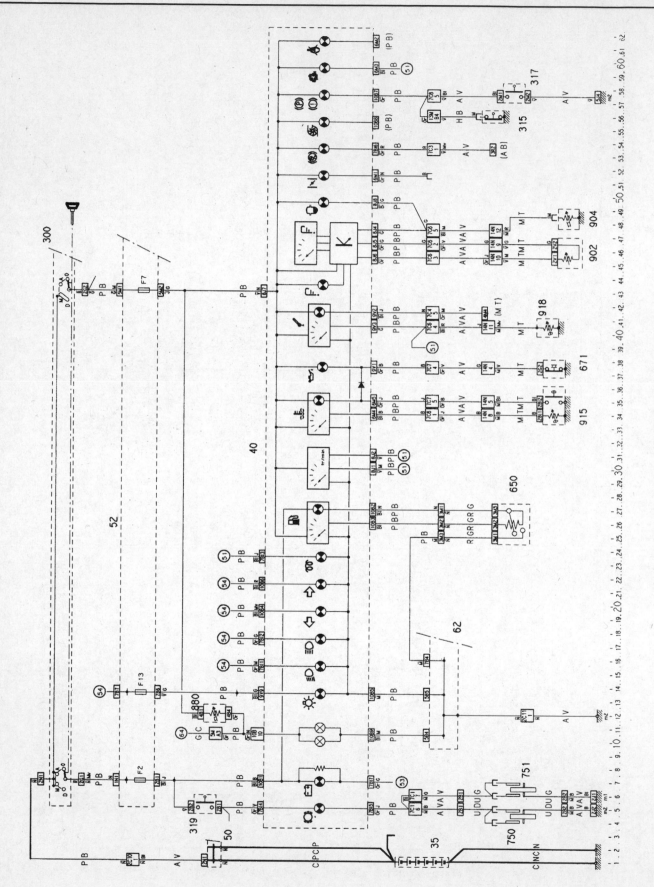

Instrument panel (high-specification models) - typical

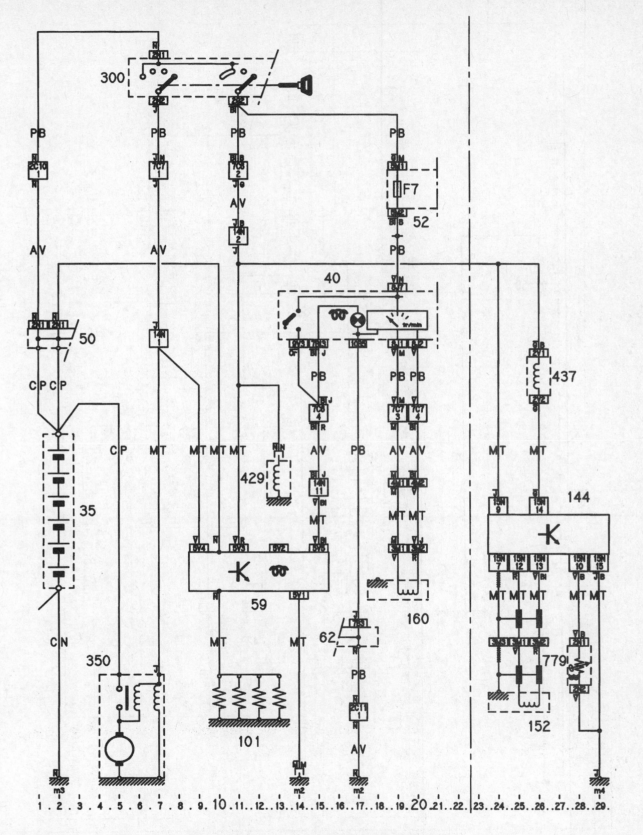

Engine electrical systems (non-Turbo models) - typical

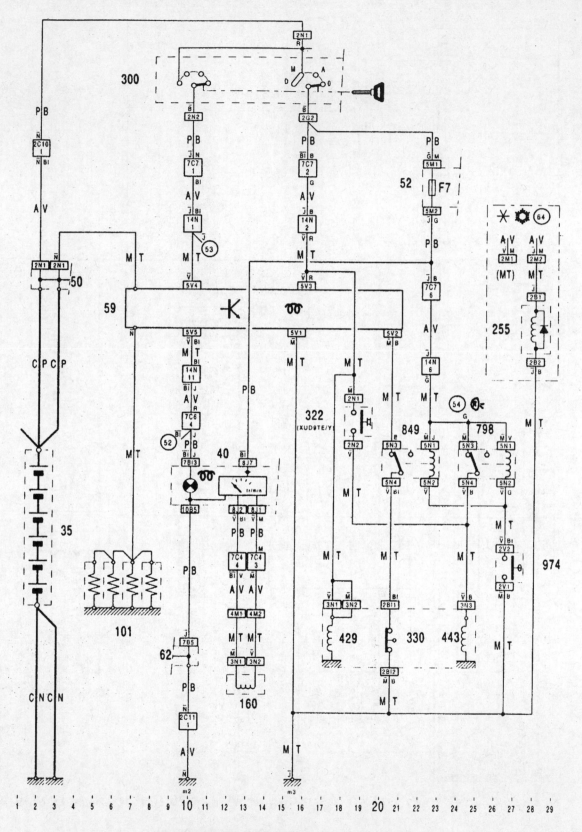

Engine electrical systems (Turbo models) - typical

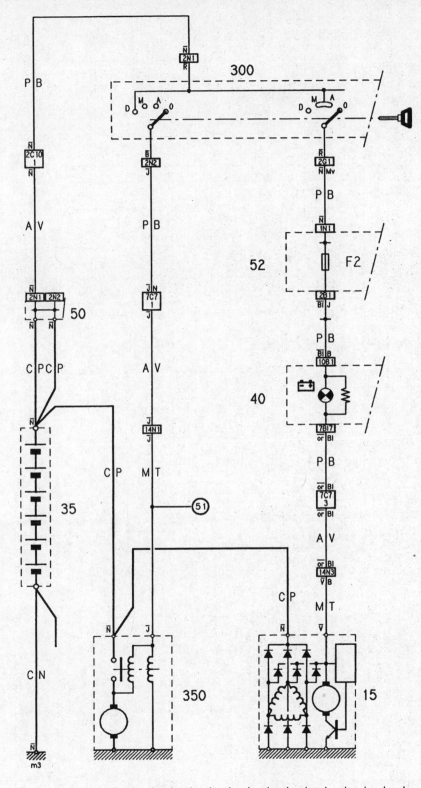

Starting and charging systems - typical

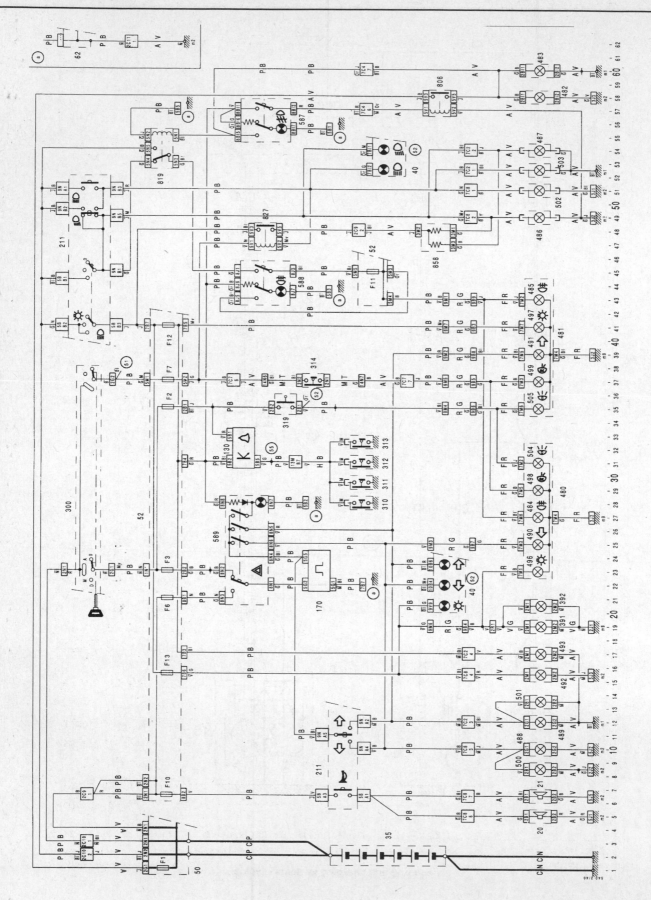

Exterior lighting, including "dim-dip" (UK models) - typical

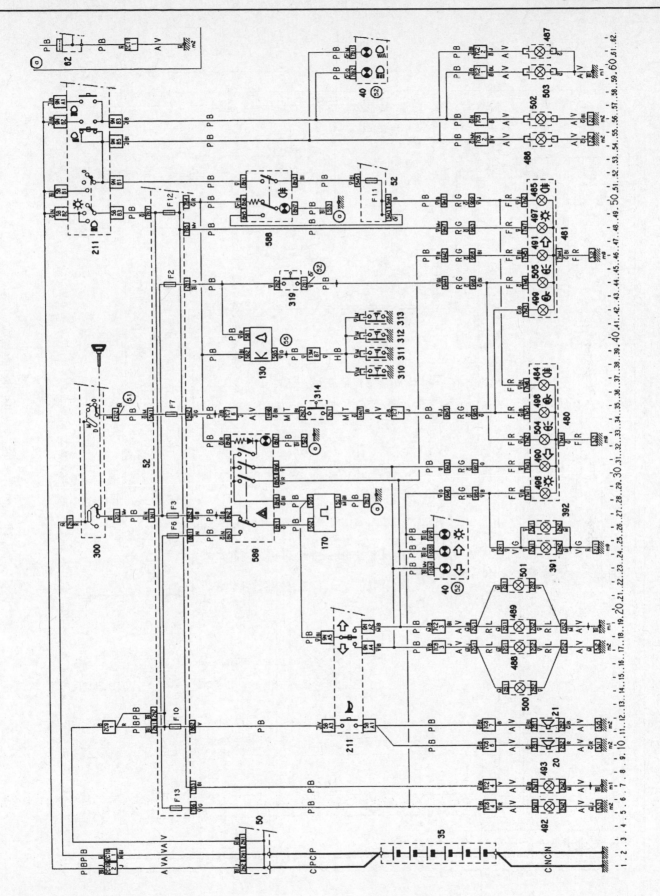

Exterior lighting (left-hand-drive low-specification models) - typical

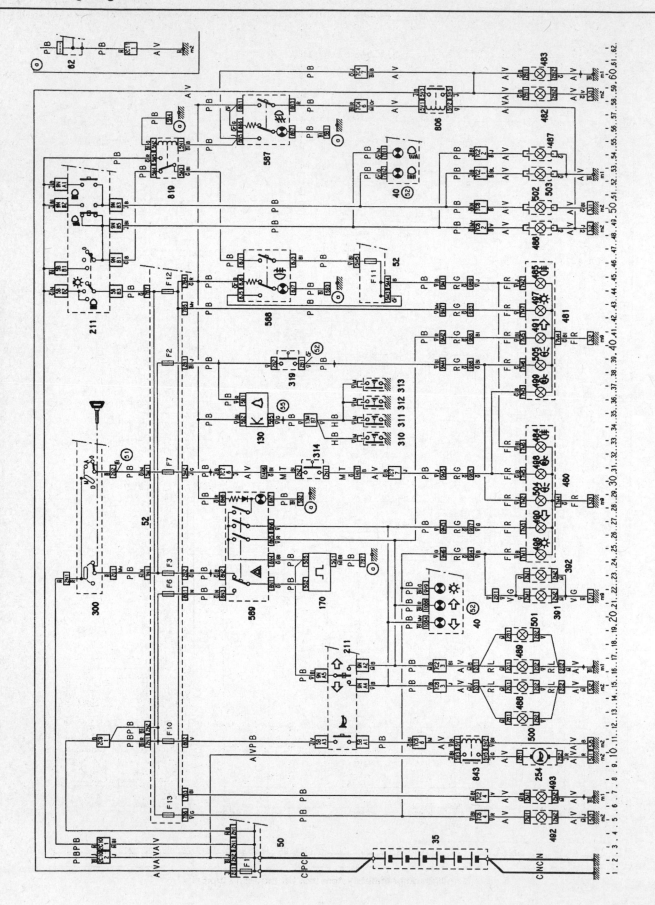

Exterior lighting (left-hand-drive high-specification models) - typical

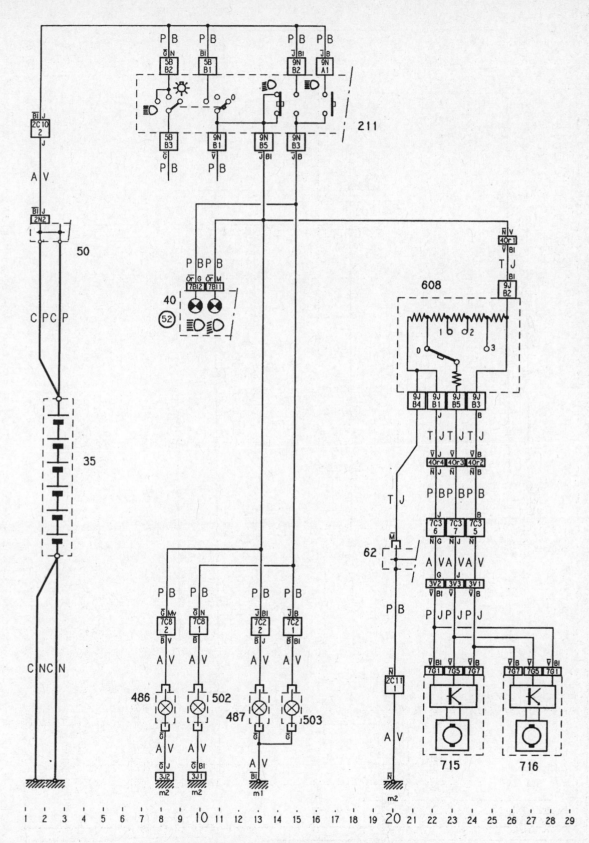

Headlight adjustment system (not UK models) - typical

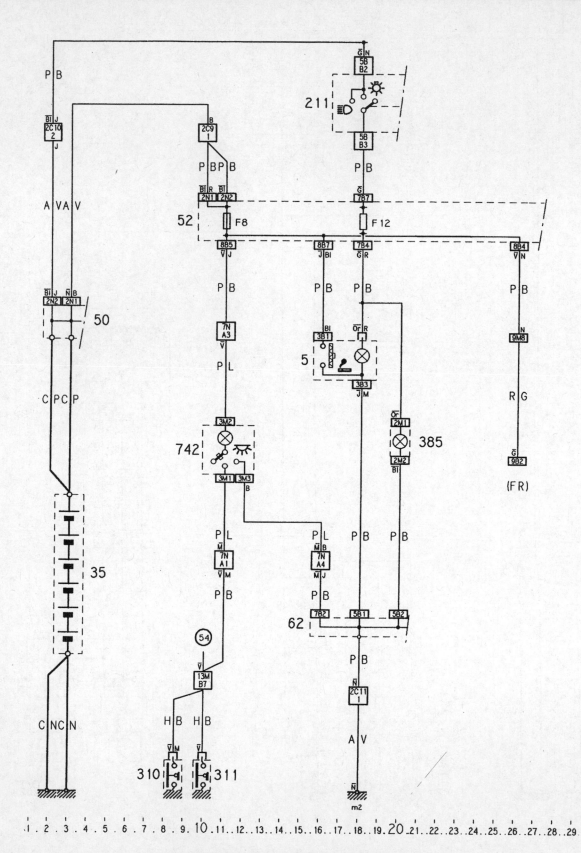

Interior lighting (low-specification models) - typical

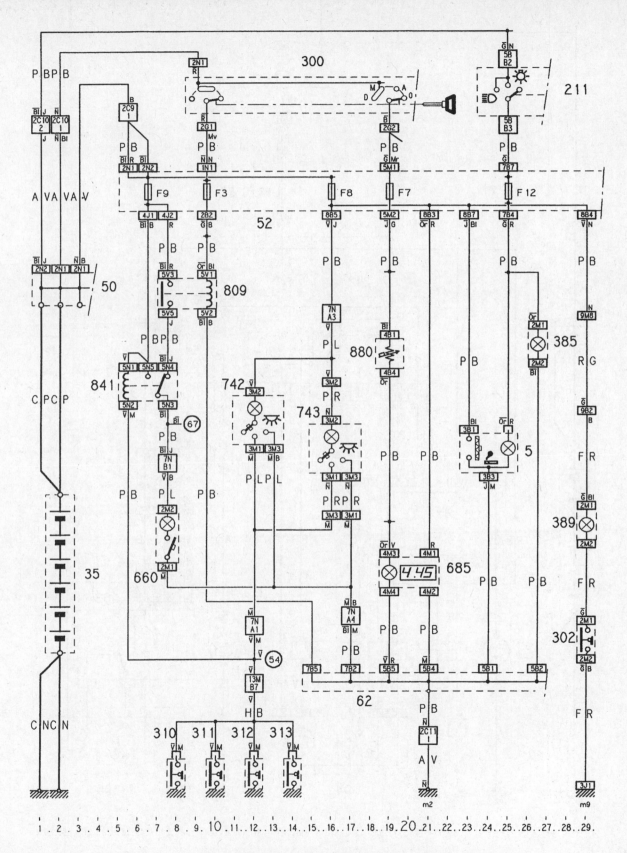

Interior lighting (high-specification models) - typical

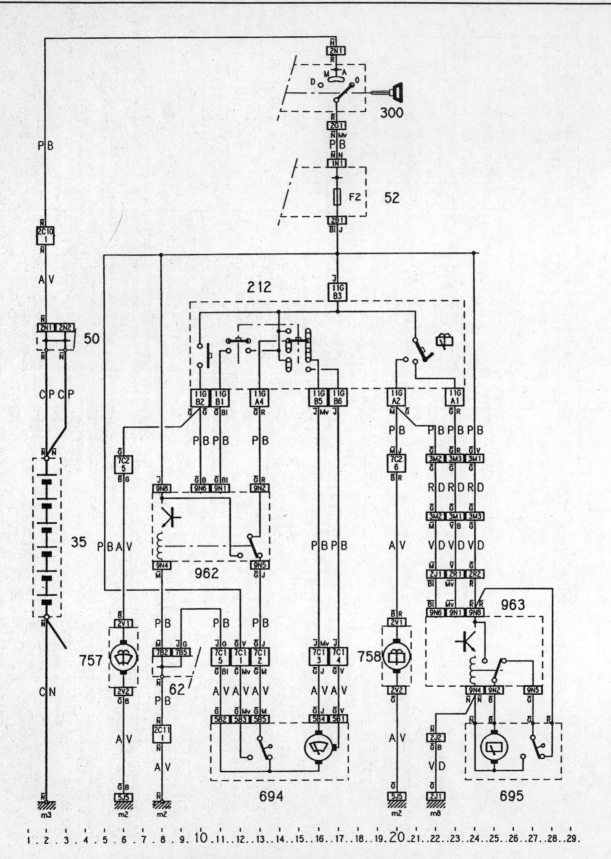

Wash/wipe systems (left-hand-drive models) - typical

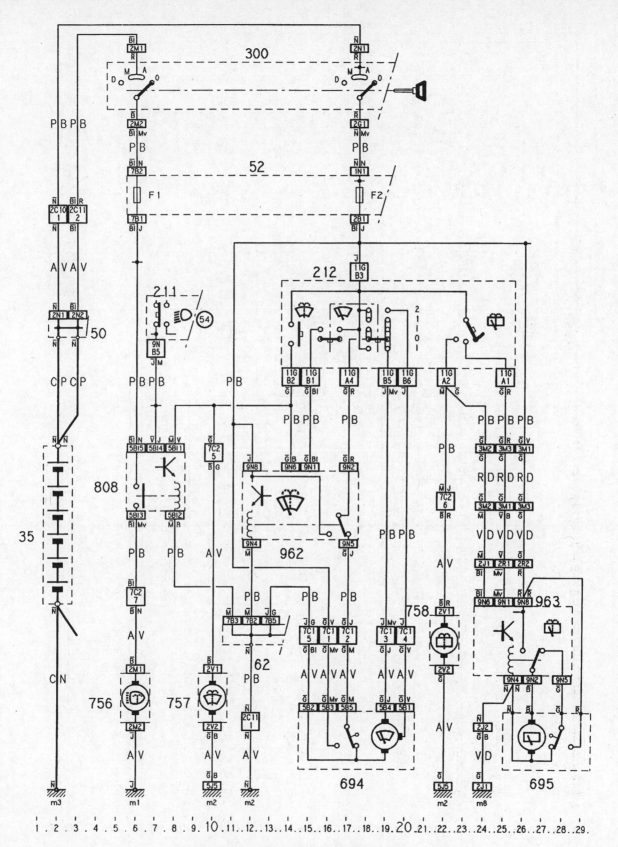

Wash/wipe systems (right-hand-drive models) - typical

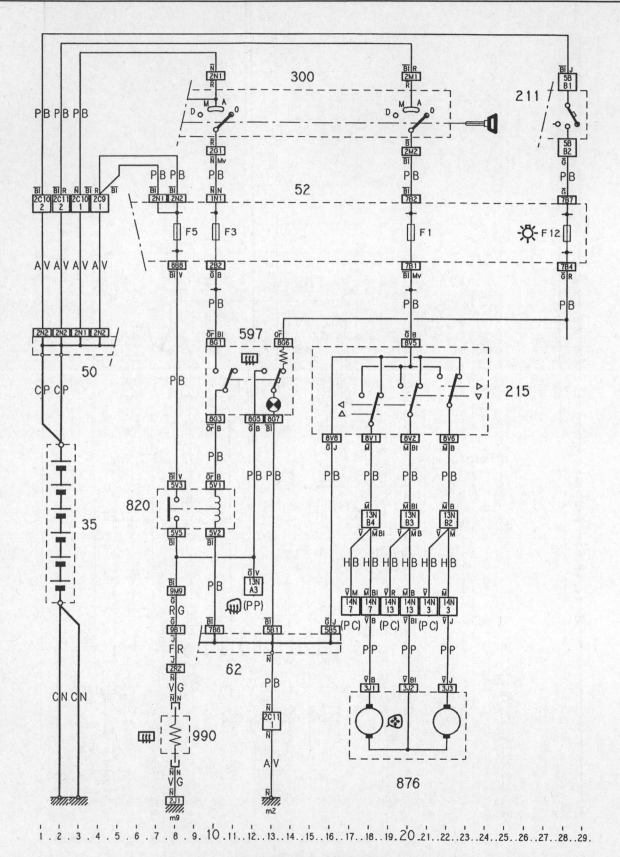

Heated rear window, electric mirror - typical

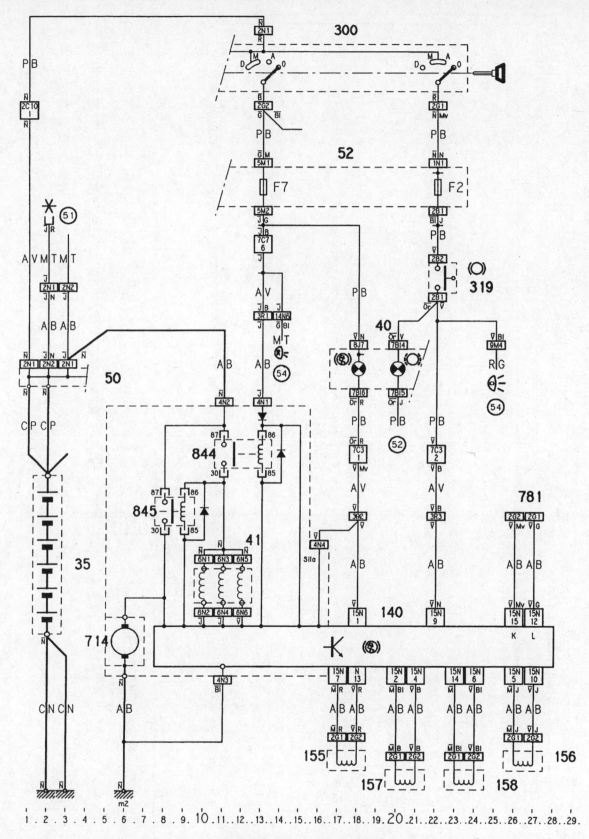

Anti-lock braking system - typical

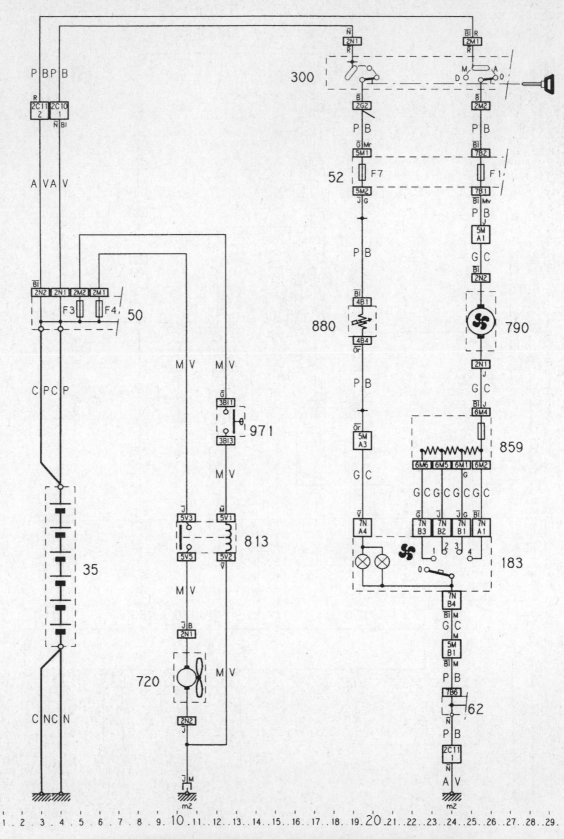

Engine cooling fan and heater blower (low-specification models) - typical

1 . 2 . 3 . 4 . 5 . 6 . 7 . 8 . 9 . 10 . 11 . 12 . 13 . 14 . 15 . 16 . 17 . 18 . 19 . 20 . 21 . 22 . 23 . 24 . 25 . 26 . 27 . 28 . 29 .

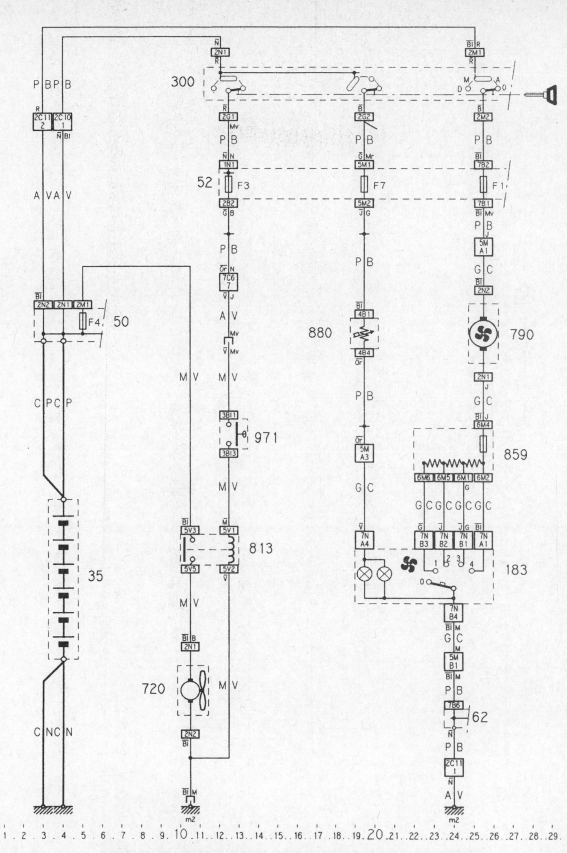

Engine cooling fan and heater blower (high-specification models) - typical

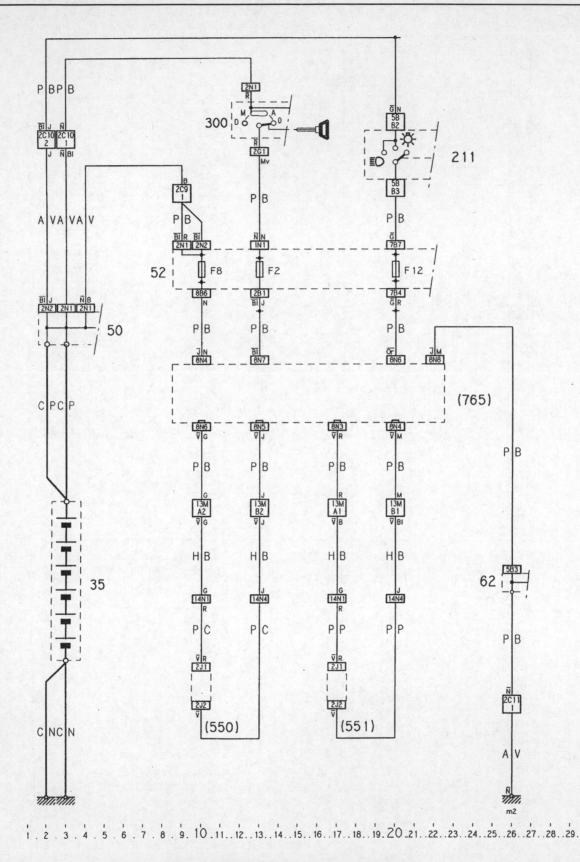

Radio/cassette unit (two-speaker type) - typical

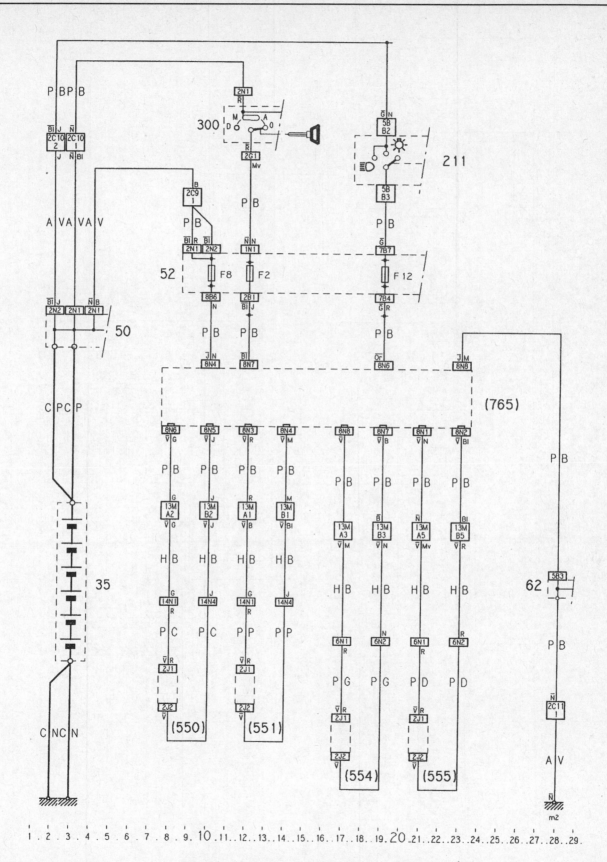

Radio/cassette unit (four-speaker type) - typical

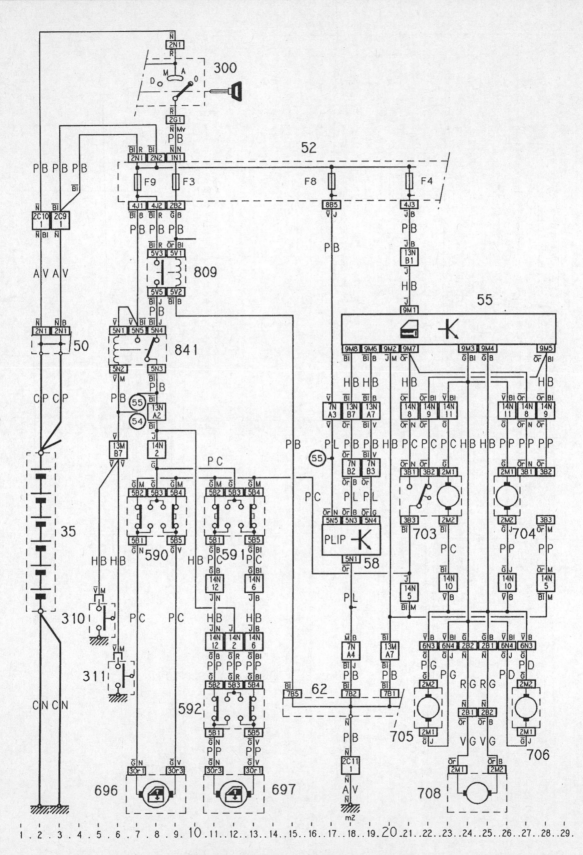

Electric windows and central locking - typical

Dimensions and weights . . . . **REF•1**
Conversion factors . . . . **REF•2**
Buying spare parts . . . . **REF•3**
Vehicle identification . . . . **REF•3**
General repair procedures . . . . **REF•4**
Jacking and vehicle support . . . . **REF•5**

Radio/cassette unit anti-theft system -
  precaution . . . . **REF•5**
Tools and working facilities . . . . **REF•6**
MOT test checks . . . . **REF•8**
Fault finding . . . . **REF•12**
Glossary of technical terms . . . . **REF•19**
Index . . . . **REF•23**

Dimensions and weights

Note: *All figures are approximate, and may vary according to model. Refer to manufacturer's data for exact figures.*

Dimensions

Overall length
Hatchback:
  All models except Volcane . . . . .4070 mm
  Volcane models . . . . .4090 mm
Estate . . . . .4260 mm

Overall width (excluding mirrors)
Hatchback:
  All models except Volcane . . . . .1700 mm
  Volcane models . . . . .1710 mm
Estate . . . . .1705 mm

Overall height
Hatchback:
  All models except Volcane . . . . .1400 mm
  Volcane models . . . . .1390 mm
Estate . . . . .1475 mm

Wheelbase
All models . . . . .2540 mm

Front and rear track
All models except Aura and Volcane Hatchback . . . . .1410 mm
Aura and Volcane Hatchback models . . . . .1420 mm

Turning circle
All models except Aura and Volcane Hatchback . . . . .10.5 m
Aura and Volcane Hatchback models . . . . .10.7 m

Weights

Maximum gross vehicle weight
Hatchback:
  Non-turbo models . . . . .1560 kg
  Turbo models:
    3-door . . . . .1580 kg
    5-door . . . . .1590 kg
Estate:
  Non-turbo models . . . . .1650 kg
  Turbo models . . . . .1665 kg

Weights (continued)

Kerb weight
Hatchback 3-door:
  Non-turbo models . . . . .1024 kg
  Turbo models . . . . .1087 kg
Hatchback 5-door:
  Non-turbo models:
    Manual transmission . . . . .1035 kg
    Automatic transmission . . . . .1068 kg
  Turbo models . . . . .1102 kg
Estate:
  Non-turbo models . . . . .1090 kg
  Turbo models . . . . .1150 kg

Maximum roof rack load
Hatchback . . . . .75 kg
Estate . . . . .100 kg

Maximum towing nose weight
All models . . . . .70 kg

Maximum towing weight
Braked trailer:
  Hatchback and Estate:
    Non-turbo models . . . . .1000 kg
    Turbo models . . . . .1100 kg
Unbraked trailer:
  Hatchback:
    Non-turbo models:
      3-door . . . . .510 kg
      5-door . . . . .515 kg
    Turbo models:
      3-door . . . . .540 kg
      5-door . . . . .550 kg
  Estate:
    Non-turbo models . . . . .545 kg
    Turbo models . . . . .575 kg

Conversion factors

Length (distance)

Inches (in)	x 25.4	= Millimetres (mm)	x 0.0394	= Inches (in)	
Feet (ft)	x 0.305	= Metres (m)	x 3.281	= Feet (ft)	
Miles	x 1.609	= Kilometres (km)	x 0.621	= Miles	

Volume (capacity)

Cubic inches (cu in; in^3)	x 16.387	= Cubic centimetres (cc; cm^3)	x 0.061	= Cubic inches (cu in; in^3)	
Imperial pints (Imp pt)	x 0.568	= Litres (l)	x 1.76	= Imperial pints (Imp pt)	
Imperial quarts (Imp qt)	x 1.137	= Litres (l)	x 0.88	= Imperial quarts (Imp qt)	
Imperial quarts (Imp qt)	x 1.201	= US quarts (US qt)	x 0.833	= Imperial quarts (Imp qt)	
US quarts (US qt)	x 0.946	= Litres (l)	x 1.057	= US quarts (US qt)	
Imperial gallons (Imp gal)	x 4.546	= Litres (l)	x 0.22	= Imperial gallons (Imp gal)	
Imperial gallons (Imp gal)	x 1.201	= US gallons (US gal)	x 0.833	= Imperial gallons (Imp gal)	
US gallons (US gal)	x 3.785	= Litres (l)	x 0.264	= US gallons (US gal)	

Mass (weight)

Ounces (oz)	x 28.35	= Grams (g)	x 0.035	= Ounces (oz)	
Pounds (lb)	x 0.454	= Kilograms (kg)	x 2.205	= Pounds (lb)	

Force

Ounces-force (ozf; oz)	x 0.278	= Newtons (N)	x 3.6	= Ounces-force (ozf; oz)	
Pounds-force (lbf; lb)	x 4.448	= Newtons (N)	x 0.225	= Pounds-force (lbf; lb)	
Newtons (N)	x 0.1	= Kilograms-force (kgf; kg)	x 9.81	= Newtons (N)	

Pressure

Pounds-force per square inch (psi; lbf/in^2; lb/in^2)	x 0.070	= Kilograms-force per square centimetre (kgf/cm^2; kg/cm^2)	x 14.223	= Pounds-force per square inch (psi; lbf/in^2; lb/in^2)	
Pounds-force per square inch (psi; lbf/in^2; lb/in^2)	x 0.068	= Atmospheres (atm)	x 14.696	= Pounds-force per square inch (psi; lbf/in^2; lb/in^2)	
Pounds-force per square inch (psi; lbf/in^2; lb/in^2)	x 0.069	= Bars	x 14.5	= Pounds-force per square inch (psi; lbf/in^2; lb/in^2)	
Pounds-force per square inch (psi; lbf/in^2; lb/in^2)	x 6.895	= Kilopascals (kPa)	x 0.145	= Pounds-force per square inch (psi; lbf/in^2; lb/in^2)	
Kilopascals (kPa)	x 0.01	= Kilograms-force per square centimetre (kgf/cm^2; kg/cm^2)	x 98.1	= Kilopascals (kPa)	
Millibar (mbar)	x 100	= Pascals (Pa)	x 0.01	= Millibar (mbar)	
Millibar (mbar)	x 0.0145	= Pounds-force per square inch (psi; lbf/in^2; lb/in^2)	x 68.947	= Millibar (mbar)	
Millibar (mbar)	x 0.75	= Millimetres of mercury (mmHg)	x 1.333	= Millibar (mbar)	
Millibar (mbar)	x 0.401	= Inches of water (inH$_2$O)	x 2.491	= Millibar (mbar)	
Millimetres of mercury (mmHg)	x 0.535	= Inches of water (inH$_2$O)	x 1.868	= Millimetres of mercury (mmHg)	
Inches of water (inH$_2$O)	x 0.036	= Pounds-force per square inch (psi; lbf/in^2; lb/in^2)	x 27.68	= Inches of water (inH$_2$O)	

Torque (moment of force)

Pounds-force inches (lbf in; lb in)	x 1.152	= Kilograms-force centimetre (kgf cm; kg cm)	x 0.868	= Pounds-force inches (lbf in; lb in)	
Pounds-force inches (lbf in; lb in)	x 0.113	= Newton metres (Nm)	x 8.85	= Pounds-force inches (lbf in; lb in)	
Pounds-force inches (lbf in; lb in)	x 0.083	= Pounds-force feet (lbf ft; lb ft)	x 12	= Pounds-force inches (lbf in; lb in)	
Pounds-force feet (lbf ft; lb ft)	x 0.138	= Kilograms-force metres (kgf m; kg m)	x 7.233	= Pounds-force feet (lbf ft; lb ft)	
Pounds-force feet (lbf ft; lb ft)	x 1.356	= Newton metres (Nm)	x 0.738	= Pounds-force feet (lbf ft; lb ft)	
Newton metres (Nm)	x 0.102	= Kilograms-force metres (kgf m; kg m)	x 9.804	= Newton metres (Nm)	

Power

Horsepower (hp)	x 745.7	= Watts (W)	x 0.0013	= Horsepower (hp)	

Velocity (speed)

Miles per hour (miles/hr; mph)	x 1.609	= Kilometres per hour (km/hr; kph)	x 0.621	= Miles per hour (miles/hr; mph)	

Fuel consumption*

Miles per gallon, Imperial (mpg)	x 0.354	= Kilometres per litre (km/l)	x 2.825	= Miles per gallon, Imperial (mpg)	
Miles per gallon, US (mpg)	x 0.425	= Kilometres per litre (km/l)	x 2.352	= Miles per gallon, US (mpg)	

Temperature

Degrees Fahrenheit = (°C x 1.8) + 32

Degrees Celsius (Degrees Centigrade; °C) = (°F - 32) x 0.56

It is common practice to convert from miles per gallon (mpg) to litres/100 kilometres (l/100km), where mpg x l/100 km = 282

Spare parts are available from many sources, including maker's appointed garages, accessory shops, and motor factors. To be sure of obtaining the correct parts, it may sometimes be necessary to quote the vehicle identification number. If possible, it can also be useful to take the old parts along for positive identification. Items such as starter motors and alternators may be available under a service exchange scheme - any parts returned should always be clean.

Our advice regarding spare part sources is as follows:

Officially-appointed garages

This is the best source of parts which are peculiar to your car, and are not otherwise generally available (eg badges, interior trim, certain body panels, etc). It is also the only place at which you should buy parts if the vehicle is still under warranty.

Accessory shops

These are very good places to buy materials and components needed for the maintenance of your car (oil, air and fuel filters, spark plugs, light bulbs, drivebelts, oils and greases, brake pads, touch-up paint, etc). Parts like this sold by a reputable shop are of the same standard as those used by the car manufacturer.

Motor factors

Good factors will stock all the more important components which wear out comparatively quickly and can sometimes supply individual components needed for the overhaul of a larger assembly. They may also handle work such as cylinder block reboring, crankshaft regrinding and balancing, etc.

Tyre and exhaust specialists

These outlets may be independent or members of a local or national chain. They frequently offer competitive prices when

compared with a main dealer or local garage, but it will pay to obtain several quotes before making a decision. Also ask what 'extras' may be added to the quote - for instance, fitting a new valve and balancing the wheel are both often charged on top of the price of a new tyre.

Other sources

Beware of parts of materials obtained from market stalls, car boot sales or similar outlets. Such items are not invariably sub-standard, but there is little chance of compensation if they do prove unsatisfactory. In the case of safety-critical components such as brake pads there is the risk not only of financial loss but also of an accident causing injury or death.

Second-hand components or assemblies obtained from a car breaker can be a good buy in some circumstances, but this sort of purchase is best made by the experienced DIY mechanic.

Vehicle identification

Modifications are a continuing and unpublicised process in vehicle manufacture, quite apart from major model changes. Spare parts manuals and lists are compiled upon a numerical basis, the individual vehicle identification numbers being essential to correct identification of the component concerned.

When ordering spare parts, always give as much information as possible. Quote the car model, year of manufacture, body and engine numbers as appropriate.

The *vehicle identification number* is stamped on a plate located under the bonnet on the right-hand wheel arch **(see illustration)**.

The *chassis number* is stamped on the body panel under the bonnet on the

right-hand side of the bulkhead on models produced up to 1993, or on the right-hand wheel arch on models produced from 1993.

The *paint code number* is located on the body panel under the bonnet on the left-hand upper wheel arch.

The *engine number* is stamped on the front of the cylinder block **(see illustration)**.

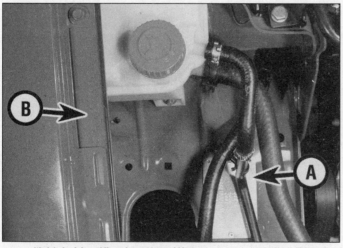

Vehicle identification plate (A) and chassis number (B)

Engine number on front of cylinder block

Whenever servicing, repair or overhaul work is carried out on the car or its components, observe the following procedures and instructions. This will assist in carrying out the operation efficiently and to a professional standard of workmanship.

Joint mating faces and gaskets

When separating components at their mating faces, never insert screwdrivers or similar implements into the joint between the faces in order to prise them apart. This can cause severe damage which results in oil leaks, coolant leaks, etc upon reassembly. Separation is usually achieved by tapping along the joint with a soft-faced hammer in order to break the seal. However, note that this method may not be suitable where dowels are used for component location.

Where a gasket is used between the mating faces of two components, a new one must be fitted on reassembly; fit it dry unless otherwise stated in the repair procedure. Make sure that the mating faces are clean and dry, with all traces of old gasket removed. When cleaning a joint face, use a tool which is unlikely to score or damage the face, and remove any burrs or nicks with an oilstone or fine file.

Make sure that tapped holes are cleaned with a pipe cleaner, and keep them free of jointing compound, if this is being used, unless specifically instructed otherwise.

Ensure that all orifices, channels or pipes are clear, and blow through them, preferably using compressed air.

Oil seals

Oil seals can be removed by levering them out with a wide flat-bladed screwdriver or similar implement. Alternatively, a number of self-tapping screws may be screwed into the seal, and these used as a purchase for pliers or some similar device in order to pull the seal free.

Whenever an oil seal is removed from its working location, either individually or as part of an assembly, it should be renewed.

The very fine sealing lip of the seal is easily damaged, and will not seal if the surface it contacts is not completely clean and free from scratches, nicks or grooves. If the original sealing surface of the component cannot be restored, and the manufacturer has not made provision for slight relocation of the seal relative to the sealing surface, the component should be renewed.

Protect the lips of the seal from any surface which may damage them in the course of fitting. Use tape or a conical sleeve where possible. Lubricate the seal lips with oil before fitting and, on dual-lipped seals, fill the space between the lips with grease.

Unless otherwise stated, oil seals must be fitted with their sealing lips toward the lubricant to be sealed.

Use a tubular drift or block of wood of the appropriate size to install the seal and, if the seal housing is shouldered, drive the seal down to the shoulder. If the seal housing is unshouldered, the seal should be fitted with its face flush with the housing top face (unless otherwise instructed).

Screw threads and fastenings

Seized nuts, bolts and screws are quite a common occurrence where corrosion has set in, and the use of penetrating oil or releasing fluid will often overcome this problem if the offending item is soaked for a while before attempting to release it. The use of an impact driver may also provide a means of releasing such stubborn fastening devices, when used in conjunction with the appropriate screwdriver bit or socket. If none of these methods works, it may be necessary to resort to the careful application of heat, or the use of a hacksaw or nut splitter device.

Studs are usually removed by locking two nuts together on the threaded part, and then using a spanner on the lower nut to unscrew the stud. Studs or bolts which have broken off below the surface of the component in which they are mounted can sometimes be removed using a stud extractor. Always ensure that a blind tapped hole is completely free from oil, grease, water or other fluid before installing the bolt or stud. Failure to do this could cause the housing to crack due to the hydraulic action of the bolt or stud as it is screwed in.

When tightening a castellated nut to accept a split pin, tighten the nut to the specified torque, where applicable, and then tighten further to the next split pin hole. Never slacken the nut to align the split pin hole, unless stated in the repair procedure.

When checking or retightening a nut or bolt to a specified torque setting, slacken the nut or bolt by a quarter of a turn, and then retighten to the specified setting. However, this should not be attempted where angular tightening has been used.

For some screw fastenings, notably cylinder head bolts or nuts, torque wrench settings are no longer specified for the latter stages of tightening, "angle-tightening" being called up instead. Typically, a fairly low torque wrench setting will be applied to the bolts/nuts in the correct sequence, followed by one or more stages of tightening through specified angles.

Locknuts, locktabs and washers

Any fastening which will rotate against a component or housing during tightening should always have a washer between it and the relevant component or housing.

Spring or split washers should always be renewed when they are used to lock a critical component such as a big-end bearing retaining bolt or nut. Locktabs which are folded over to retain a nut or bolt should always be renewed.

Self-locking nuts can be re-used in non-critical areas, providing resistance can be felt when the locking portion passes over the bolt or stud thread. However, it should be noted that self-locking stiffnuts tend to lose their effectiveness after long periods of use, and should then be renewed as a matter of course.

Split pins must always be replaced with new ones of the correct size for the hole.

When thread-locking compound is found on the threads of a fastener which is to be re-used, it should be cleaned off with a wire brush and solvent, and fresh compound applied on reassembly.

Special tools

Some repair procedures in this manual entail the use of special tools such as a press, two or three-legged pullers, spring compressors, etc. Wherever possible, suitable readily-available alternatives to the manufacturer's special tools are described, and are shown in use. In some instances, where no alternative is possible, it has been necessary to resort to the use of a manufacturer's tool, and this has been done for reasons of safety as well as the efficient completion of the repair operation. Unless you are highly-skilled and have a thorough understanding of the procedures described, never attempt to bypass the use of any special tool when the procedure described specifies its use. Not only is there a very great risk of personal injury, but expensive damage could be caused to the components involved.

Environmental considerations

When disposing of used engine oil, brake fluid, antifreeze, etc, give due consideration to any detrimental environmental effects. Do not, for instance, pour any of the above liquids down drains into the general sewage system, or onto the ground to soak away. Many local council refuse tips provide a facility for waste oil disposal, as do some garages. If none of these facilities are available, consult your local Environmental Health Department, or the National Rivers Authority, for further advice.

With the universal tightening-up of legislation regarding the emission of environmentally-harmful substances from motor vehicles, most vehicles have tamperproof devices fitted to the main adjustment points of the fuel system. These devices are primarily designed to prevent unqualified persons from adjusting the fuel/air mixture, with the chance of a consequent increase in toxic emissions. If such devices are found during servicing or overhaul, they should, wherever possible, be renewed or refitted in accordance with the manufacturer's requirements or current legislation.

OIL CARE
FOLLOW THE CODE
OIL BANK LINE
0800 66 33 66
www.oilbankline.org.uk

Note: It is antisocial and illegal to dump oil down the drain. To find the location of your local oil recycling bank, call this number free.

The jack supplied with the vehicle tool kit should only be used for changing the roadwheels - see *Wheel changing* at the front of this manual. When using the jack, position it on firm ground and locate its head in the relevant vehicle jacking point **(see illustrations)**.

When carrying out any other kind of work, raise the vehicle using a hydraulic jack and always supplement the jack with axle stands positioned under the vehicle jacking points.

When using a hydraulic jack or axle stands, always position the jack head or axle stand head under one of the relevant jacking points. Note that the jacking points for use with a hydraulic jack and axle stands are different to those for use with the vehicle jack **(see**

illustration). Do not jack the vehicle under the sump or any of the steering or suspension components.

Note the following when using a hydraulic jack:

a) *When raising the side of the vehicle, ensure that the load is taken by the raised jacking plates on the sill panels. Do not jack under the body panel behind the sill panels.*

b) *When raising the front of the vehicle, use a suitable metal or strong wooden bar and wooden spacer blocks under the front suspension subframe*

c) *When raising the rear of the vehicle, position the jack or axle stands under the rear suspension tubular crossmember.*

⚠️ **Warning: Never work under, around, or near a raised vehicle, unless it is adequately supported in at least two places.**

Locating jack head into vehicle jacking point

Raising vehicle with scissor jack

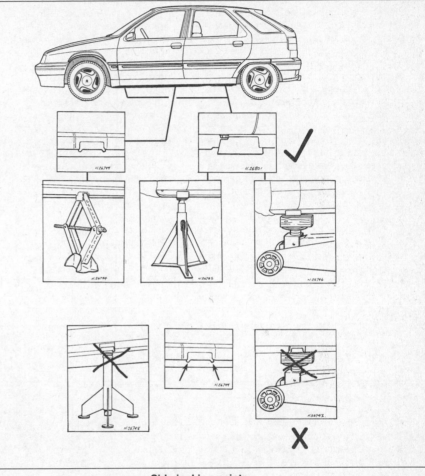

Side jacking points

Radio/cassette unit anti-theft system - precaution

The radio/cassette unit fitted as standard equipment by Citroën is equipped with a built-in security code to deter thieves. If the power source to the unit is cut, the anti-theft system will activate. Even if the power source is immediately reconnected, the radio/cassette unit will not function until the correct security code has been entered. Therefore, if you do not know the correct security code for the radio/cassette unit, do not disconnect either of the battery terminals or remove the radio/cassette unit from the vehicle.

To enter the security code, first switch the unit on - the display will show 'Cod'. The security

code can then be entered using buttons 1 to 4 on the unit. Each button alters the corresponding digit of the code. Note that there is no facility on the radio display to show the number 0 for the first digit of the security code. For the first digit, 0 is indicated by a blank. Once the correct code is displayed, press the 'up' section of the four-way tuning button to enter the code.

If an incorrect code is entered, the display will show three dashes, after which the radio will be locked for 10 seconds. On the first two attempts, after 10 seconds the radio display will show the 'Cod' prompt again and allow you to enter the security code again.

However, if the correct security code is not entered on the third attempt, the unit will be locked for 1 hour. To make any further attempts, the unit must be switched on and left untouched for approximately 1 hour before the display shows the 'Cod' prompt again and allows you to re-enter the security code. Note that after twenty attempts, the unit will become permanently locked.

If this happens, or if the security code is lost or forgotten, seek the advice of your Citroën dealer. On presentation of proof of ownership, a Citroën dealer will be able to unlock the unit and provide you with a new security code.

Introduction

A selection of good tools is a fundamental requirement for anyone contemplating the maintenance and repair of a motor vehicle. For the owner who does not possess any, their purchase will prove a considerable expense, offsetting some of the savings made by doing-it-yourself. However, provided that the tools purchased meet the relevant national safety standards and are of good quality, they will last for many years and prove an extremely worthwhile investment.

To help the average owner to decide which tools are needed to carry out the various tasks detailed in this manual, we have compiled three lists of tools under the following headings: *Maintenance and minor repair*, *Repair and overhaul*, and *Special*. Newcomers to practical mechanics should start off with the *Maintenance and minor repair* tool kit, and confine themselves to the simpler jobs around the vehicle. Then, as confidence and experience grow, more difficult tasks can be undertaken, with extra tools being purchased as, and when, they are needed. In this way, a *Maintenance and minor repair* tool kit can be built up into a *Repair and overhaul* tool kit over a considerable period of time, without any major cash outlays. The experienced do-it-yourselfer will have a tool kit good enough for most repair and overhaul procedures, and will add tools from the *Special* category when it is felt that the expense is justified by the amount of use to which these tools will be put.

Maintenance and minor repair tool kit

The tools given in this list should be considered as a minimum requirement if routine maintenance, servicing and minor repair operations are to be undertaken. We recommend the purchase of combination spanners (ring one end, open-ended the other); although more expensive than open-ended ones, they do give the advantages of both types of spanner.

☐ *Combination spanners:*
  Metric - 8 to 19 mm inclusive
☐ *Adjustable spanner - 35 mm jaw (approx.)*
☐ *Spark plug spanner (with rubber insert) - petrol models*
☐ *Spark plug gap adjustment tool - petrol models*
☐ *Set of feeler gauges*
☐ *Brake bleed nipple spanner*
☐ *Screwdrivers:*
  Flat blade - 100 mm long x 6 mm dia
  Cross blade - 100 mm long x 6 mm dia
  Torx - various sizes (not all vehicles)
☐ *Combination pliers*
☐ *Hacksaw (junior)*
☐ *Tyre pump*
☐ *Tyre pressure gauge*
☐ *Oil can*
☐ *Oil filter removal tool*
☐ *Fine emery cloth*
☐ *Wire brush (small)*
☐ *Funnel (medium size)*
☐ *Sump drain plug key (not all vehicles)*

Repair and overhaul tool kit

These tools are virtually essential for anyone undertaking any major repairs to a motor vehicle, and are additional to those given in the *Maintenance and minor repair* list. Included in this list is a comprehensive set of sockets. Although these are expensive, they will be found invaluable as they are so versatile - particularly if various drives are included in the set. We recommend the half-inch square-drive type, as this can be used with most proprietary torque wrenches.

The tools in this list will sometimes need to be supplemented by tools from the *Special* list:

☐ *Sockets (or box spanners) to cover range in previous list (including Torx sockets)*
☐ *Reversible ratchet drive (for use with sockets)*
☐ *Extension piece, 250 mm (for use with sockets)*
☐ *Universal joint (for use with sockets)*
☐ *Flexible handle or sliding T "breaker bar" (for use with sockets)*
☐ *Torque wrench (for use with sockets)*
☐ *Self-locking grips*
☐ *Ball pein hammer*
☐ *Soft-faced mallet (plastic or rubber)*
☐ *Screwdrivers:*
  Flat blade - long & sturdy, short (chubby), and narrow (electrician's) types
  Cross blade - long & sturdy, and short (chubby) types
☐ *Pliers:*
  Long-nosed
  Side cutters (electrician's)
  Circlip (internal and external)
☐ *Cold chisel - 25 mm*
☐ *Scriber*
☐ *Scraper*
☐ *Centre-punch*
☐ *Pin punch*
☐ *Hacksaw*
☐ *Brake hose clamp*
☐ *Brake/clutch bleeding kit*
☐ *Selection of twist drills*
☐ *Steel rule/straight-edge*
☐ *Allen keys (inc. splined/Torx type)*
☐ *Selection of files*
☐ *Wire brush*
☐ *Axle stands*
☐ *Jack (strong trolley or hydraulic type)*
☐ *Light with extension lead*
☐ *Universal electrical multi-meter*

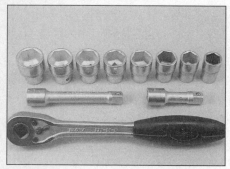

Sockets and reversible ratchet drive

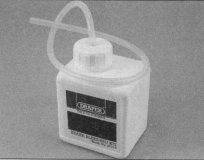

Brake bleeding kit

Torx key, socket and bit

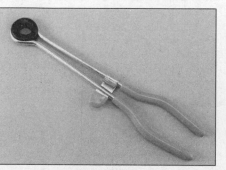

Hose clamp

Angular-tightening gauge

Special tools

The tools in this list are those which are not used regularly, are expensive to buy, or which need to be used in accordance with their manufacturers' instructions. Unless relatively difficult mechanical jobs are undertaken frequently, it will not be economic to buy many of these tools. Where this is the case, you could consider clubbing together with friends (or joining a motorists' club) to make a joint purchase, or borrowing the tools against a deposit from a local garage or tool hire specialist. It is worth noting that many of the larger DIY superstores now carry a large range of special tools for hire at modest rates.

The following list contains only those tools and instruments freely available to the public, and not those special tools produced by the vehicle manufacturer specifically for its dealer network. You will find occasional references to these manufacturers' special tools in the text of this manual. Generally, an alternative method of doing the job without the vehicle manufacturers' special tool is given. However, sometimes there is no alternative to using them. Where this is the case and the relevant tool cannot be bought or borrowed, you will have to entrust the work to a dealer.

☐ Angular-tightening gauge
☐ Valve spring compressor
☐ Valve grinding tool
☐ Piston ring compressor
☐ Piston ring removal/installation tool
☐ Cylinder bore hone
☐ Balljoint separator
☐ Coil spring compressors (where applicable)
☐ Two/three-legged hub and bearing puller
☐ Impact screwdriver
☐ Micrometer and/or vernier calipers
☐ Dial gauge
☐ Stroboscopic timing light
☐ Dwell angle meter/tachometer
☐ Fault code reader
☐ Cylinder compression gauge
☐ Hand-operated vacuum pump and gauge
☐ Clutch plate alignment set
☐ Brake shoe steady spring cup removal tool
☐ Bush and bearing removal/installation set
☐ Stud extractors
☐ Tap and die set
☐ Lifting tackle
☐ Trolley jack

Buying tools

Reputable motor accessory shops and superstores often offer excellent quality tools at discount prices, so it pays to shop around.

Remember, you don't have to buy the most expensive items on the shelf, but it is always advisable to steer clear of the very cheap tools. Beware of 'bargains' offered on market stalls or at car boot sales. There are plenty of good tools around at reasonable prices, but always aim to purchase items which meet the relevant national safety standards. If in doubt, ask the proprietor or manager of the shop for advice before making a purchase.

Care and maintenance of tools

Having purchased a reasonable tool kit, it is necessary to keep the tools in a clean and serviceable condition. After use, always wipe off any dirt, grease and metal particles using a clean, dry cloth, before putting the tools away. Never leave them lying around after they have been used. A simple tool rack on the garage or workshop wall for items such as screwdrivers and pliers is a good idea. Store all normal spanners and sockets in a metal box. Any measuring instruments, gauges, meters, etc, must be carefully stored where they cannot be damaged or become rusty.

Take a little care when tools are used. Hammer heads inevitably become marked, and screwdrivers lose the keen edge on their blades from time to time. A little timely attention with emery cloth or a file will soon restore items like this to a good finish.

Working facilities

Not to be forgotten when discussing tools is the workshop itself. If anything more than routine maintenance is to be carried out, a suitable working area becomes essential.

It is appreciated that many an owner-mechanic is forced by circumstances to remove an engine or similar item without the benefit of a garage or workshop. Having done this, any repairs should always be done under the cover of a roof.

Wherever possible, any dismantling should be done on a clean, flat workbench or table at a suitable working height.

Any workbench needs a vice; one with a jaw opening of 100 mm is suitable for most jobs. As mentioned previously, some clean dry storage space is also required for tools, as well as for any lubricants, cleaning fluids, touch-up paints etc, which become necessary.

Another item which may be required, and which has a much more general usage, is an electric drill with a chuck capacity of at least 8 mm. This, together with a good range of twist drills, is virtually essential for fitting accessories.

Last, but not least, always keep a supply of old newspapers and clean, lint-free rags available, and try to keep any working area as clean as possible.

Micrometers

Dial test indicator ("dial gauge")

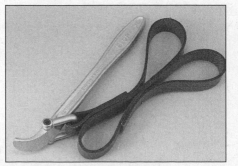

Strap wrench

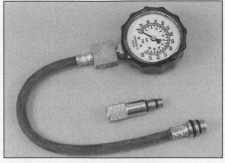

Compression tester

Fault code reader

This is a guide to getting your vehicle through the MOT test. Obviously it will not be possible to examine the vehicle to the same standard as the professional MOT tester. However, working through the following checks will enable you to identify any problem areas before submitting the vehicle for the test.

Where a testable component is in borderline condition, the tester has discretion in deciding whether to pass or fail it. The basis of such discretion is whether the tester would be happy for a close relative or friend to use the vehicle with the component in that condition. If the vehicle presented is clean and evidently well cared for, the tester may be more inclined to pass a borderline component than if the vehicle is scruffy and apparently neglected.

It has only been possible to summarise the test requirements here, based on the regulations in force at the time of printing. Test standards are becoming increasingly stringent, although there are some exemptions for older vehicles.

An assistant will be needed to help carry out some of these checks.

The checks have been sub-divided into four categories, as follows:

1 Checks carried out **FROM THE DRIVER'S SEAT**

2 Checks carried out **WITH THE VEHICLE ON THE GROUND**

3 Checks carried out **WITH THE VEHICLE RAISED AND THE WHEELS FREE TO TURN**

4 Checks carried out on **YOUR VEHICLE'S EXHAUST EMISSION SYSTEM**

---

1 Checks carried out **FROM THE DRIVER'S SEAT**

Handbrake

☐ Test the operation of the handbrake. Excessive travel (too many clicks) indicates incorrect brake or cable adjustment.

☐ Check that the handbrake cannot be released by tapping the lever sideways. Check the security of the lever mountings.

Footbrake

☐ Depress the brake pedal and check that it does not creep down to the floor, indicating a master cylinder fault. Release the pedal, wait a few seconds, then depress it again. If the pedal travels nearly to the floor before firm resistance is felt, brake adjustment or repair is necessary. If the pedal feels spongy, there is air in the hydraulic system which must be removed by bleeding.

☐ Check that the brake pedal is secure and in good condition. Check also for signs of fluid leaks on the pedal, floor or carpets, which would indicate failed seals in the brake master cylinder.

☐ Check the servo unit (when applicable) by operating the brake pedal several times, then keeping the pedal depressed and starting the engine. As the engine starts, the pedal will move down slightly. If not, the vacuum hose or the servo itself may be faulty.

Steering wheel and column

☐ Examine the steering wheel for fractures or looseness of the hub, spokes or rim.

☐ Move the steering wheel from side to side and then up and down. Check that the steering wheel is not loose on the column, indicating wear or a loose retaining nut. Continue moving the steering wheel as before, but also turn it slightly from left to right.

☐ Check that the steering wheel is not loose on the column, and that there is no abnormal

movement of the steering wheel, indicating wear in the column support bearings or couplings.

Windscreen, mirrors and sunvisor

☐ The windscreen must be free of cracks or other significant damage within the driver's field of view. (Small stone chips are acceptable.) Rear view mirrors must be secure, intact, and capable of being adjusted.

290mm

☐ The driver's sunvisor must be capable of being stored in the "up" position.

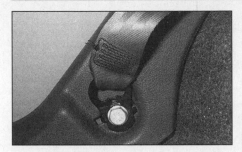

Seat belts and seats

Note: *The following checks are applicable to all seat belts, front and rear.*

☐ Examine the webbing of all the belts (including rear belts if fitted) for cuts, serious fraying or deterioration. Fasten and unfasten each belt to check the buckles. If applicable, check the retracting mechanism. Check the security of all seat belt mountings accessible from inside the vehicle.

☐ Seat belts with pre-tensioners, once activated, have a "flag" or similar showing on the seat belt stalk. This, in itself, is not a reason for test failure.

☐ The front seats themselves must be securely attached and the backrests must lock in the upright position.

Doors

☐ Both front doors must be able to be opened and closed from outside and inside, and must latch securely when closed.

2 Checks carried out WITH THE VEHICLE ON THE GROUND

Vehicle identification

☐ Number plates must be in good condition, secure and legible, with letters and numbers correctly spaced – spacing at (A) should be at least twice that at (B).

☐ The VIN plate and/or homologation plate must be legible.

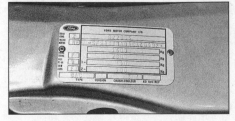

Electrical equipment

☐ Switch on the ignition and check the operation of the horn.

☐ Check the windscreen washers and wipers, examining the wiper blades; renew damaged or perished blades. Also check the operation of the stop-lights.

☐ Check the operation of the sidelights and number plate lights. The lenses and reflectors must be secure, clean and undamaged.

☐ Check the operation and alignment of the headlights. The headlight reflectors must not be tarnished and the lenses must be undamaged.

☐ Switch on the ignition and check the operation of the direction indicators (including the instrument panel tell-tale) and the hazard warning lights. Operation of the sidelights and stop-lights must not affect the indicators - if it does, the cause is usually a bad earth at the rear light cluster.

☐ Check the operation of the rear foglight(s), including the warning light on the instrument panel or in the switch.

☐ The ABS warning light must illuminate in accordance with the manufacturers' design. For most vehicles, the ABS warning light should illuminate when the ignition is switched on, and (if the system is operating properly) extinguish after a few seconds. Refer to the owner's handbook.

Footbrake

☐ Examine the master cylinder, brake pipes and servo unit for leaks, loose mountings, corrosion or other damage.

☐ The fluid reservoir must be secure and the fluid level must be between the upper (A) and lower (B) markings.

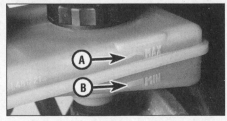

☐ Inspect both front brake flexible hoses for cracks or deterioration of the rubber. Turn the steering from lock to lock, and ensure that the hoses do not contact the wheel, tyre, or any part of the steering or suspension mechanism. With the brake pedal firmly depressed, check the hoses for bulges or leaks under pressure.

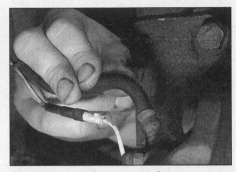

Steering and suspension

☐ Have your assistant turn the steering wheel from side to side slightly, up to the point where the steering gear just begins to transmit this movement to the roadwheels. Check for excessive free play between the steering wheel and the steering gear, indicating wear or insecurity of the steering column joints, the column-to-steering gear coupling, or the steering gear itself.

☐ Have your assistant turn the steering wheel more vigorously in each direction, so that the roadwheels just begin to turn. As this is done, examine all the steering joints, linkages, fittings and attachments. Renew any component that shows signs of wear or damage. On vehicles with power steering, check the security and condition of the steering pump, drivebelt and hoses.

☐ Check that the vehicle is standing level, and at approximately the correct ride height.

Shock absorbers

☐ Depress each corner of the vehicle in turn, then release it. The vehicle should rise and then settle in its normal position. If the vehicle continues to rise and fall, the shock absorber is defective. A shock absorber which has seized will also cause the vehicle to fail.

Exhaust system

☐ Start the engine. With your assistant holding a rag over the tailpipe, check the entire system for leaks. Repair or renew leaking sections.

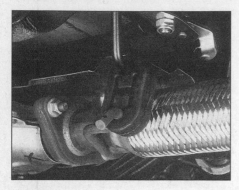

3 Checks carried out **WITH THE VEHICLE RAISED AND THE WHEELS FREE TO TURN**

Jack up the front and rear of the vehicle, and securely support it on axle stands. Position the stands clear of the suspension assemblies. Ensure that the wheels are clear of the ground and that the steering can be turned from lock to lock.

Steering mechanism

☐ Have your assistant turn the steering from lock to lock. Check that the steering turns smoothly, and that no part of the steering mechanism, including a wheel or tyre, fouls any brake hose or pipe or any part of the body structure.
☐ Examine the steering rack rubber gaiters for damage or insecurity of the retaining clips. If power steering is fitted, check for signs of damage or leakage of the fluid hoses, pipes or connections. Also check for excessive stiffness or binding of the steering, a missing split pin or locking device, or severe corrosion of the body structure within 30 cm of any steering component attachment point.

Front and rear suspension and wheel bearings

☐ Starting at the front right-hand side, grasp the roadwheel at the 3 o'clock and 9 o'clock positions and rock gently but firmly. Check for free play or insecurity at the wheel bearings, suspension balljoints, or suspension mountings, pivots and attachments.
☐ Now grasp the wheel at the 12 o'clock and 6 o'clock positions and repeat the previous inspection. Spin the wheel, and check for roughness or tightness of the front wheel bearing.

☐ If excess free play is suspected at a component pivot point, this can be confirmed by using a large screwdriver or similar tool and levering between the mounting and the component attachment. This will confirm whether the wear is in the pivot bush, its retaining bolt, or in the mounting itself (the bolt holes can often become elongated).

☐ Carry out all the above checks at the other front wheel, and then at both rear wheels.

Springs and shock absorbers

☐ Examine the suspension struts (when applicable) for serious fluid leakage, corrosion, or damage to the casing. Also check the security of the mounting points.
☐ If coil springs are fitted, check that the spring ends locate in their seats, and that the spring is not corroded, cracked or broken.
☐ If leaf springs are fitted, check that all leaves are intact, that the axle is securely attached to each spring, and that there is no deterioration of the spring eye mountings, bushes, and shackles.

☐ The same general checks apply to vehicles fitted with other suspension types, such as torsion bars, hydraulic displacer units, etc. Ensure that all mountings and attachments are secure, that there are no signs of excessive wear, corrosion or damage, and (on hydraulic types) that there are no fluid leaks or damaged pipes.
☐ Inspect the shock absorbers for signs of serious fluid leakage. Check for wear of the mounting bushes or attachments, or damage to the body of the unit.

Driveshafts (fwd vehicles only)

☐ Rotate each front wheel in turn and inspect the constant velocity joint gaiters for splits or damage. Also check that each driveshaft is straight and undamaged.

Braking system

☐ If possible without dismantling, check brake pad wear and disc condition. Ensure that the friction lining material has not worn excessively, (A) and that the discs are not fractured, pitted, scored or badly worn (B).

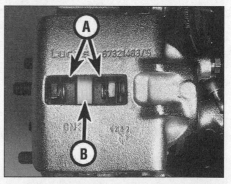

☐ Examine all the rigid brake pipes underneath the vehicle, and the flexible hose(s) at the rear. Look for corrosion, chafing or insecurity of the pipes, and for signs of bulging under pressure, chafing, splits or deterioration of the flexible hoses.
☐ Look for signs of fluid leaks at the brake calipers or on the brake backplates. Repair or renew leaking components.
☐ Slowly spin each wheel, while your assistant depresses and releases the footbrake. Ensure that each brake is operating and does not bind when the pedal is released.

□ Examine the handbrake mechanism, checking for frayed or broken cables, excessive corrosion, or wear or insecurity of the linkage. Check that the mechanism works on each relevant wheel, and releases fully, without binding.

□ It is not possible to test brake efficiency without special equipment, but a road test can be carried out later to check that the vehicle pulls up in a straight line.

Fuel and exhaust systems

□ Inspect the fuel tank (including the filler cap), fuel pipes, hoses and unions. All components must be secure and free from leaks.

□ Examine the exhaust system over its entire length, checking for any damaged, broken or missing mountings, security of the retaining clamps and rust or corrosion.

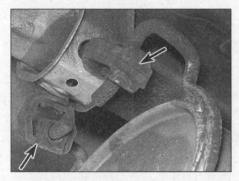

Wheels and tyres

□ Examine the sidewalls and tread area of each tyre in turn. Check for cuts, tears, lumps, bulges, separation of the tread, and exposure of the ply or cord due to wear or damage. Check that the tyre bead is correctly seated on the wheel rim, that the valve is sound and properly seated, and that the wheel is not distorted or damaged.

□ Check that the tyres are of the correct size for the vehicle, that they are of the same size and type on each axle, and that the pressures are correct.

□ Check the tyre tread depth. The legal minimum at the time of writing is 1.6 mm over at least three-quarters of the tread width. Abnormal tread wear may indicate incorrect front wheel alignment.

Body corrosion

□ Check the condition of the entire vehicle structure for signs of corrosion in load-bearing areas. (These include chassis box sections, side sills, cross-members, pillars, and all suspension, steering, braking system and seat belt mountings and anchorages.) Any corrosion which has seriously reduced the thickness of a load-bearing area is likely to cause the vehicle to fail. In this case professional repairs are likely to be needed.

□ Damage or corrosion which causes sharp or otherwise dangerous edges to be exposed will also cause the vehicle to fail.

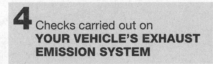

4 Checks carried out on **YOUR VEHICLE'S EXHAUST EMISSION SYSTEM**

Petrol models

□ Have the engine at normal operating temperature, and make sure that it is in good tune (ignition system in good order, air filter element clean, etc).

□ Before any measurements are carried out, raise the engine speed to around 2500 rpm, and hold it at this speed for 20 seconds. Allow the engine speed to return to idle, and watch for smoke emissions from the exhaust tailpipe. If the idle speed is obviously much too high, or if dense blue or clearly-visible black smoke comes from the tailpipe for more than 5 seconds, the vehicle will fail. As a rule of thumb, blue smoke signifies oil being burnt (engine wear) while black smoke signifies unburnt fuel (dirty air cleaner element, or other carburettor or fuel system fault).

□ An exhaust gas analyser capable of measuring carbon monoxide (CO) and hydrocarbons (HC) is now needed. If such an instrument cannot be hired or borrowed, a local garage may agree to perform the check for a small fee.

CO emissions (mixture)

□ At the time of writing, for vehicles first used between 1st August 1975 and 31st July 1986 (P to C registration), the CO level must not exceed 4.5% by volume. For vehicles first used between 1st August 1986 and 31st July 1992 (D to J registration), the CO level must not exceed 3.5% by volume. Vehicles first

used after 1st August 1992 (K registration) must conform to the manufacturer's specification. The MOT tester has access to a DOT database or emissions handbook, which lists the CO and HC limits for each make and model of vehicle. The CO level is measured with the engine at idle speed, and at "fast idle". The following limits are given as a general guide:

At idle speed -
CO level no more than 0.5%
At "fast idle" (2500 to 3000 rpm) -
CO level no more than 0.3%
(Minimum oil temperature 60°C)

□ If the CO level cannot be reduced far enough to pass the test (and the fuel and ignition systems are otherwise in good condition) then the carburettor is badly worn, or there is some problem in the fuel injection system or catalytic converter (as applicable).

HC emissions

□ With the CO within limits, HC emissions for vehicles first used between 1st August 1975 and 31st July 1992 (P to J registration) must not exceed 1200 ppm. Vehicles first used after 1st August 1992 (K registration) must conform to the manufacturer's specification. The MOT tester has access to a DOT database or emissions handbook, which lists the CO and HC limits for each make and model of vehicle. The HC level is measured with the engine at "fast idle". The following is given as a general guide:

At "fast idle" (2500 to 3000 rpm) -
HC level no more than 200 ppm
(Minimum oil temperature 60°C)

□ Excessive HC emissions are caused by incomplete combustion, the causes of which can include oil being burnt, mechanical wear and ignition/fuel system malfunction.

Diesel models

□ The only emission test applicable to Diesel engines is the measuring of exhaust smoke density. The test involves accelerating the engine several times to its maximum unloaded speed.

Note: *It is of the utmost importance that the engine timing belt is in good condition before the test is carried out.*

□ The limits for Diesel engine exhaust smoke, introduced in September 1995 are:
Vehicles first used before 1st August 1979: Exempt from metered smoke testing, but must not emit "dense blue or clearly visible black smoke for a period of more than 5 seconds at idle" or "dense blue or clearly visible black smoke during acceleration which would obscure the view of other road users".
Non-turbocharged vehicles first used after 1st August 1979: 2.5m⁻¹
Turbocharged vehicles first used after 1st August 1979: 3.0m⁻¹

□ Excessive smoke can be caused by a dirty air cleaner element. Otherwise, professional advice may be needed to find the cause.

Engine

- ☐ Engine fails to rotate when attempting to start
- ☐ Starter motor turns engine slowly
- ☐ Starter motor spins without turning engine
- ☐ Starter motor noisy or excessively-rough in engagement
- ☐ Engine rotates but will not start
- ☐ Engine fires but will not run
- ☐ Engine difficult to start when cold
- ☐ Engine difficult to start when hot
- ☐ Engine idles erratically
- ☐ Engine misfires at idle speed
- ☐ Engine misfires throughout the driving speed range
- ☐ Engine stalls
- ☐ Engine lacks power
- ☐ Oil pressure warning light illuminated with engine running
- ☐ Engine runs-on after switching off
- ☐ Engine noises

Cooling system

- ☐ Overheating
- ☐ Overcooling
- ☐ External coolant leakage
- ☐ Internal coolant leakage
- ☐ Corrosion

Fuel and exhaust systems

- ☐ Excessive fuel consumption
- ☐ Fuel leakage and/or fuel odour
- ☐ Excessive noise or fumes from exhaust system

Clutch

- ☐ Pedal travels to floor - no pressure or very little resistance
- ☐ Clutch fails to disengage (unable to select gears)
- ☐ Clutch slips (engine speed increases with no increase in vehicle speed)
- ☐ Judder as clutch is engaged
- ☐ Noise when depressing or releasing clutch pedal

Manual transmission

- ☐ Noisy in neutral with engine running
- ☐ Noisy in one particular gear
- ☐ Difficulty engaging gears
- ☐ Jumps out of gear
- ☐ Vibration
- ☐ Lubricant leaks

Automatic transmission

- ☐ General gear selection problems
- ☐ Fluid leakage
- ☐ Transmission fluid brown, or has burned smell
- ☐ Transmission will not downshift (kickdown) with accelerator fully depressed
- ☐ Engine will not start in any gear, or starts in gears other than Park or Neutral
- ☐ Transmission slips, shifts roughly, is noisy, or has no drive in forward or reverse gears

Driveshafts

- ☐ Clicking or knocking noise on turns (at slow speed on full-lock)
- ☐ Vibration when accelerating or decelerating

Braking system

- ☐ Vehicle pulls to one side under braking
- ☐ Noise (grinding or high-pitched squeal) when brakes applied
- ☐ Excessive brake pedal travel
- ☐ Judder felt through brake pedal or steering wheel when braking
- ☐ Brake pedal feels spongy when depressed
- ☐ Excessive brake pedal effort required to stop vehicle
- ☐ Brakes binding
- ☐ Rear wheels locking under normal braking

Suspension and steering systems

- ☐ Vehicle pulls to one side
- ☐ Wheel wobble and vibration
- ☐ Excessive pitching and/or rolling around corners or during braking
- ☐ Excessive play in steering
- ☐ Lack of power assistance
- ☐ Wandering or general instability
- ☐ Excessively-stiff steering
- ☐ Tyre wear excessive

Electrical system

- ☐ Battery will not hold a charge for more than a few days
- ☐ Alternator (no-charge) warning light remains illuminated with engine running
- ☐ Alternator (no-charge) warning light fails to come on
- ☐ Lights inoperative
- ☐ Instrument readings inaccurate or erratic
- ☐ Horn inoperative, or unsatisfactory in operation
- ☐ Windscreen/tailgate wipers inoperative, or unsatisfactory in operation
- ☐ Windscreen/tailgate washers inoperative, or unsatisfactory in operation
- ☐ Electric windows inoperative, or unsatisfactory in operation
- ☐ Central locking system inoperative, or unsatisfactory in operation

Introduction

The vehicle owner who does his or her own maintenance according to the recommended service schedules should not have to use this section of the manual very often. Modern component reliability is such that, provided those items subject to wear or deterioration are inspected or renewed at the specified intervals, sudden failure is comparatively rare. Faults do not usually just happen as a result of sudden failure, but develop over a period of time. Major mechanical failures in particular are usually preceded by characteristic symptoms over hundreds or even thousands of miles. Those components which do occasionally fail without warning are often small and easily carried in the vehicle (eg bulbs).

With any fault finding, the first step is to decide where to begin investigations. Sometimes this is obvious, but on other occasions a little detective work will be necessary. The owner who makes half a dozen haphazard adjustments or replacements may be successful in curing a fault (or its symptoms), but will be none the wiser if the fault recurs, and ultimately may have spent more time and money than was necessary. A calm and logical approach will be found to be more satisfactory in the long run. Always take into account any warning signs or abnormalities that may have been noticed in the period preceding the fault - power loss, high or low gauge readings, unusual smells, etc - and remember that failure of certain components such as fuses may only be pointers to some underlying fault.

The pages which follow provide an easy reference guide to the more common problems which may occur during the operation of the vehicle. These problems and their possible causes are grouped under headings denoting various components or systems, such as Engine, Cooling system, etc. The Chapter and/or Section which deals with the problem is also shown in brackets. Whatever the fault, certain basic principles apply. These are as follows:

Verify the fault. This is simply a matter of being sure that you know what the symptoms are before starting work. This is particularly important if you are investigating a fault for someone else, who may not have described it very accurately.

Don't overlook the obvious. For example, if the vehicle won't start, is there fuel in the tank? (Don't take anyone else's word on this particular point, and don't trust the fuel gauge either!) If an electrical fault is indicated, look for loose or broken wires before digging out the test gear.

Cure the disease, not the symptom. Substituting a flat battery with a fully-charged one will get you off the hard shoulder, but if the underlying cause is not attended to, the new battery will go the same way.

Don't take anything for granted. Particularly, don't forget that a 'new' component may itself be defective (especially if it's been rattling around in the boot for months), and don't leave components out of a fault diagnosis sequence just because they are new or recently fitted. When you do finally diagnose a difficult fault, you'll probably realise that all the evidence was there from the start.

Engine

Engine fails to rotate when attempting to start

☐ Battery terminal connections loose or corroded (*Weekly checks*).
☐ Battery discharged or faulty (Chapter 5).
☐ Broken, loose or disconnected wiring in the starting circuit (Chapter 5).
☐ Defective starter solenoid or switch (Chapter 5).
☐ Defective starter motor (Chapter 5).
☐ Starter pinion or flywheel ring gear teeth loose or broken (Chapter 5 or Chapter 2, Part A).
☐ Engine earth strap broken or disconnected (Chapter 5).
☐ Automatic transmission not in Park/Neutral position or starter inhibitor switch faulty (Chapter 7, Part B).

Starter motor turns engine slowly

☐ Partially-discharged battery (recharge, use jump leads, or push start) (Chapter 5).
☐ Battery terminals loose or corroded (*Weekly checks*).
☐ Battery earth to body defective (Chapter 5).
☐ Engine earth strap loose (Chapter 5).
☐ Starter motor (or solenoid) wiring loose (Chapter 5).
☐ Starter motor internal fault (Chapter 5).

Starter motor spins without turning engine

☐ Starter motor reduction gears stripped (Chapter 5).
☐ Starter motor mounting bolts loose (Chapter 5).

Starter motor noisy or excessively-rough in engagement

☐ Starter pinion or flywheel ring gear teeth loose or broken (Chapter 5 or Chapter 2, Part A).
☐ Starter motor mounting bolts loose or missing (Chapter 5).
☐ Starter motor internal components worn or damaged (Chapter 5).

Engine rotates but will not start

☐ Fuel tank empty.
☐ Battery discharged (engine rotates slowly) (Chapter 5).
☐ Battery terminal connections loose or corroded (*Weekly checks*).
☐ Air in fuel (Chapter 4).
☐ Wax formed in fuel (in very cold weather).
☐ Faulty stop solenoid (Chapter 4).
☐ Low cylinder compressions (Chapter 2, Part A).
☐ Fuel system or preheating system fault (Chapters 4 and 5).
☐ Major mechanical failure (eg camshaft drive) (Chapter 2, Part A).

Engine fires but will not run

☐ Preheating system fault (Chapter 5).
☐ Air in fuel (Chapter 4).
☐ Wax formed in fuel (in very cold weather).
☐ Other fuel system fault (Chapter 4).

Engine difficult to start when cold

☐ Battery discharged (Chapter 5).
☐ Battery terminal connections loose or corroded (*Weekly checks*).
☐ Air in fuel (Chapter 4).
☐ Air filter element dirty or clogged (Chapter 1).
☐ Wax formed in fuel (in very cold weather).
☐ Preheating system fault (Chapter 5).
☐ Other fuel system fault (Chapter 4).
☐ Low cylinder compressions (Chapter 2, Part A).

Engine difficult to start when hot

☐ Battery discharged (Chapter 5).
☐ Battery terminal connections loose or corroded (*Weekly checks*).
☐ Air filter element dirty or clogged (Chapter 1).
☐ Air in fuel (Chapter 4).
☐ Low cylinder compressions (Chapter 2, Part A).

Engine idles erratically

☐ Incorrectly-adjusted idle speed (Chapter 1).
☐ Air filter element clogged (Chapter 1).
☐ Incorrectly-adjusted valve clearances (Chapter 2, Part A).
☐ Uneven or low cylinder compressions (Chapter 2, Part A).
☐ Camshaft lobes worn (Chapter 2, Part A).
☐ Timing belt incorrectly tensioned (Chapter 2, Part A).
☐ Incorrect fuel injection pump timing (Chapter 4).

Engine misfires at idle speed

☐ Air in fuel (Chapter 4).
☐ Wax formed in fuel (in very cold weather).
☐ Other fuel system fault (Chapter 4).
☐ Incorrectly-adjusted valve clearances (Chapter 2, Part A).
☐ Uneven or low cylinder compressions (Chapter 2, Part A).
☐ Disconnected, leaking or perished crankcase ventilation hoses (Chapters 1 and 4).
☐ Incorrect fuel injection pump timing (Chapter 4).

Engine misfires throughout the driving speed range

☐ Fuel filter choked (Chapter 1).
☐ Fuel tank vent blocked or fuel pipes restricted (Chapter 4).
☐ Uneven or low cylinder compressions (Chapter 2, Part A).
☐ Incorrect fuel injection pump timing (Chapter 4).

Engine stalls

☐ Incorrectly-adjusted idle speed (Chapter 1).
☐ Fuel filter choked (Chapter 1).
☐ Fuel tank vent blocked or fuel pipes restricted (Chapter 4).

Engine (continued)

Engine lacks power

- [ ] Air in fuel (Chapter 4).
- [ ] Incorrect fuel injection pump timing (Chapter 4).
- [ ] Timing belt incorrectly fitted or tensioned (Chapter 2, Part A).
- [ ] Fuel filter choked (Chapter 1).
- [ ] Uneven or low cylinder compressions (Chapter 2, Part A).
- [ ] Brakes binding (Chapters 1 and 9).
- [ ] Clutch slipping (Chapter 6).
- [ ] Automatic transmission fluid level incorrect (Chapter 1).

Oil pressure warning light illuminated with engine running

- [ ] Low oil level or incorrect oil grade (*Weekly checks*).
- [ ] Faulty oil pressure switch (Chapter 5).
- [ ] Worn engine bearings and/or oil pump (Chapter 2, Part B).
- [ ] High engine operating temperature (Chapter 3).
- [ ] Oil pressure relief valve defective (Chapter 2, Part B).
- [ ] Oil pick-up strainer clogged (Chapter 2, Part B).

Note: *Low oil pressure in a high-mileage engine at tickover is not necessarily a cause for concern. Sudden pressure loss at speed is far more significant. In any event, check the warning light sender before condemning the engine.*

Engine runs-on after switching off

- [ ] Faulty stop solenoid (Chapter 4).

Engine noises

Note: *To inexperienced ears, the diesel engine can sound alarming even when there is nothing wrong with it, so it may be prudent to have an unusual noise expertly diagnosed before making renewals or repairs.*

Whistling or wheezing noises

- [ ] Leaking manifold gasket (Chapter 4).
- [ ] Leaking vacuum hose (Chapters 1 and 4).
- [ ] Blowing cylinder head gasket (Chapter 2, Part A).

Tapping or rattling noises

- [ ] Incorrect valve clearances (Chapter 2, Part A).
- [ ] Worn valve gear or camshaft (Chapter 2, Part A).
- [ ] Worn oil pump chain (Chapter 2, Part A).
- [ ] Broken piston ring (ticking noise) (Chapter 2, Part B).
- [ ] Ancillary component fault (water pump, alternator etc) (Chapters 3 and 5).

Knocking or thumping noises

- [ ] Air in fuel (Chapter 4).
- [ ] Worn drivebelt (Chapter 1 and Chapter 2, Part A).
- [ ] Fuel injector(s) leaking or sticking (Chapter 4).
- [ ] Worn big-end bearings (regular heavy knocking, perhaps less under load) (Chapter 2, Part B).
- [ ] Worn main bearings (rumbling and knocking, perhaps worsening under load) (Chapter 2, Part B).
- [ ] Piston slap (most noticeable when cold) (Chapter 2, Part B).
- [ ] Ancillary component fault (alternator, water pump etc) (Chapters 3 and 5).

Cooling system

Overheating

- [ ] Insufficient coolant in system (*Weekly checks*).
- [ ] Thermostat faulty (Chapter 3).
- [ ] Radiator core blocked, or grille restricted (Chapter 3).
- [ ] Electric cooling fan or thermo-switch faulty (Chapter 3).
- [ ] Pressure cap faulty (Chapter 3).
- [ ] Timing belt worn, or incorrectly adjusted (Chapter 2, Part A).
- [ ] Inaccurate temperature gauge sender unit (Chapter 3).
- [ ] Air lock in cooling system (Chapter 1).

Overcooling

- [ ] Thermostat faulty (Chapter 3).
- [ ] Inaccurate temperature gauge sender unit (Chapter 3).

External coolant leakage

- [ ] Deteriorated or damaged hoses or hose clips (Chapter 1).
- [ ] Radiator core or heater matrix leaking (Chapter 3).
- [ ] Pressure cap faulty (Chapter 3).
- [ ] Water pump seal leaking (Chapter 3).
- [ ] Boiling due to overheating (Chapter 3).
- [ ] Core plug leaking (Chapter 2, Part B).

Internal coolant leakage

- [ ] Leaking cylinder head gasket (Chapter 2, Part A).
- [ ] Cracked cylinder head or cylinder bore (Chapter 2, Parts A and B).

Corrosion

- [ ] Infrequent draining and flushing (Chapter 1).
- [ ] Incorrect antifreeze mixture or inappropriate antifreeze type (Chapter 1).

Fuel and exhaust systems

Excessive fuel consumption

- [ ] Air filter element dirty or clogged (Chapter 1).
- [ ] Preheating system fault (Chapter 5).
- [ ] Incorrect idle speed (Chapter 1).
- [ ] Incorrect fuel injection pump timing (Chapter 4).
- [ ] Brakes binding (Chapter 9).
- [ ] Tyres under-inflated (*Weekly checks*).

Fuel leakage and/or fuel odour

- [ ] Damaged or corroded fuel tank, pipes or connections (Chapters 1 and 4).

Excessive noise or fumes from exhaust system

- [ ] Leaking exhaust system or manifold joints (Chapter 4).
- [ ] Leaking, corroded or damaged silencers or pipe (Chapter 4).
- [ ] Broken mountings causing body or suspension contact (Chapter 4).

Clutch

Clutch fails to disengage (unable to select gears)

☐ Incorrect clutch adjustment (Chapter 6).
☐ Friction plate sticking on transmission input shaft splines (Chapter 6).
☐ Friction plate sticking to flywheel or pressure plate (Chapter 6).
☐ Faulty pressure plate assembly (Chapter 6).
☐ Transmission input shaft seized in crankshaft spigot bearing - where applicable (Chapter 2, Part A).
☐ Clutch release mechanism worn or incorrectly assembled (Chapter 6).

Judder as clutch is engaged

☐ Friction plate linings contaminated with oil or grease (Chapter 6).
☐ Friction plate linings excessively worn (Chapter 6).
☐ Clutch cable sticking or frayed (Chapter 6).
☐ Faulty or distorted pressure plate or diaphragm spring (Chapter 6).
☐ Worn or loose engine or transmission mountings (Chapter 2, Part A).
☐ Friction plate hub or transmission input shaft splines worn (Chapter 6).

Pedal travels to floor - no pressure or very little resistance

☐ Broken clutch cable (Chapter 6).
☐ Incorrect clutch adjustment (Chapter 6).
☐ Broken clutch release bearing or fork (Chapter 6).
☐ Broken diaphragm spring in clutch pressure plate (Chapter 6).

Clutch slips (engine speed increases with no increase in vehicle speed)

☐ Incorrect clutch adjustment (Chapter 6).
☐ Friction plate linings excessively worn (Chapter 6).
☐ Friction plate linings contaminated with oil or grease (Chapter 6).
☐ Faulty pressure plate or weak diaphragm spring (Chapter 6).

Noise when depressing or releasing clutch pedal

☐ Worn clutch release bearing (Chapter 6).
☐ Worn or dry clutch pedal bushes (Chapter 6).
☐ Faulty pressure plate assembly (Chapter 6).
☐ Pressure plate diaphragm spring broken (Chapter 6).
☐ Broken friction plate cushioning springs (Chapter 6).

Manual transmission

Noisy in neutral with engine running

☐ Input shaft bearings worn (noise apparent with clutch pedal released but not when depressed) (Chapter 7, Part A).*
☐ Clutch release bearing worn (noise apparent with clutch pedal depressed, possibly less when released) (Chapter 6).

Noisy in one particular gear

☐ Worn, damaged or chipped gear teeth (Chapter 7, Part A).*

Difficulty engaging gears

☐ Clutch fault (Chapter 6).
☐ Worn or damaged gear linkage (Chapter 7, Part A).
☐ Incorrectly-adjusted gear linkage (Chapter 7, Part A).
☐ Worn synchroniser units (Chapter 7, Part A).*

Jumps out of gear

☐ Worn or damaged gear linkage (Chapter 7, Part A).
☐ Incorrectly-adjusted gear linkage (Chapter 7, Part A).
☐ Worn synchroniser units (Chapter 7, Part A).*
☐ Worn selector forks (Chapter 7, Part A).*

Vibration

☐ Lack of oil (Chapter 1).
☐ Worn bearings (Chapter 7, Part A).*

Lubricant leaks

☐ Leaking oil seal (Chapter 7, Part A).
☐ Leaking housing joint (Chapter 7, Part A).*

*Although the corrective action necessary to remedy the symptoms described is beyond the scope of the home mechanic, the above information should be helpful in isolating the cause of the condition, so that the owner can communicate clearly with a professional mechanic.

Automatic transmission

Note: *Due to the complexity of the automatic transmission, it is difficult for the home mechanic to properly diagnose and service this unit. For problems other than the following, the vehicle should be taken to a dealer service department or automatic transmission specialist. Do not be too hasty in removing the transmission if a fault is suspected, as most of the testing is carried out with the unit still fitted.*

General gear selection problems

☐ Chapter 7, Part B deals with checking and adjusting the selector cable on automatic transmissions. The following are common problems which may be caused by a poorly-adjusted cable:
a) *Engine starting in gears other than Park or Neutral.*
b) *Indicator panel indicating a gear other than the one actually being used.*
c) *Vehicle moves when in Park or Neutral.*
d) *Poor gear shift quality or erratic gear changes.*
☐ Refer to Chapter 7, Part B for the selector cable adjustment procedure.

Fluid leakage

☐ Automatic transmission fluid is usually dark in colour. Fluid leaks should not be confused with engine oil, which can easily be blown onto the transmission by airflow.
☐ To determine the source of a leak, first remove all built-up dirt and grime from the transmission housing and surrounding areas using a degreasing agent, or by steam-cleaning. Drive the vehicle at low speed, so airflow will not blow the leak far from its source. Raise and support the vehicle, and determine where the leak is coming from. The following are common areas of leakage:
a) *Oil pan (Chapter 1 and Chapter 7, Part B).*
b) *Dipstick tube (Chapter 1 and Chapter 7, Part B).*
c) *Transmission-to-fluid cooler pipes/unions (Chapter 7, Part B).*

Transmission fluid brown, or has burned smell

☐ Transmission fluid level low, or fluid in need of renewal (Chapter 1).

Automatic transmission (continued)

Transmission will not downshift (kickdown) with accelerator pedal fully depressed

☐ Low transmission fluid level (Chapter 1).
☐ Incorrect selector cable adjustment (Chapter 7, Part B).

Engine will not start in any gear, or starts in gears other than Park or Neutral

☐ Incorrect starter/inhibitor switch adjustment (Chapter 7, Part B).
☐ Incorrect selector cable adjustment (Chapter 7, Part B).

Transmission slips, shifts roughly, is noisy, or has no drive in forward or reverse gears

☐ There are many probable causes for the above problems, but the home mechanic should be concerned with only one possibility - fluid level. Before taking the vehicle to a dealer or transmission specialist, check the fluid level and condition of the fluid as described in Chapter 1. Correct the fluid level as necessary, or change the fluid and filter if needed. If the problem persists, professional help will be necessary.

Driveshafts

Clicking or knocking noise on turns (at slow speed on full-lock)

☐ Lack of constant velocity joint lubricant - possibly due to split rubber gaiter (Chapter 8).
☐ Worn outer constant velocity joint (Chapter 8).

Vibration when accelerating or decelerating

☐ Worn inner constant velocity joint (Chapter 8).
☐ Bent or distorted driveshaft (Chapter 8).

Braking system

Note: *Before assuming that a brake problem exists, make sure that the tyres are in good condition and correctly inflated, the front wheel alignment is correct, and the vehicle is not loaded with weight in an unequal manner. Apart from checking the condition of all pipe and hose connections, any faults occurring on the anti-lock braking system should be referred to a Citroën dealer for diagnosis.*

Vehicle pulls to one side under braking

☐ Worn, defective, damaged or contaminated front or rear brake pads/shoes on one side (Chapter 9).
☐ Seized or partially-seized front or rear brake caliper/wheel cylinder piston (Chapter 9).
☐ A mixture of brake pad/shoe lining materials fitted between sides (Chapter 9).
☐ Brake caliper mounting bolts loose (Chapter 9).
☐ Rear brake backplate mounting bolts loose (Chapter 9).
☐ Worn or damaged steering or suspension components (Chapter 10).

Noise (grinding or high-pitched squeal) when brakes applied

☐ Brake pad or shoe friction lining material worn down to metal backing (Chapter 9).
☐ Excessive corrosion of brake disc or drum. (May be apparent after the vehicle has been standing for some time (Chapter 9).

Judder felt through brake pedal or steering wheel when braking

☐ Excessive run-out or distortion of front discs or rear drums (Chapter 9).
☐ Brake pad or brake shoe linings worn (Chapter 9).
☐ Brake caliper or rear brake backplate mounting bolts loose (Chapter 9).
☐ Wear in suspension or steering components or mountings (Chapter 10).

Excessive brake pedal travel

☐ Inoperative rear brake self-adjust mechanism (Chapter 9).
☐ Faulty master cylinder (Chapter 9).
☐ Air in hydraulic system (Chapter 9).
☐ Faulty vacuum servo unit (Chapter 9).
☐ Faulty brake vacuum pump (Chapter 9).

Brake pedal feels spongy when depressed

☐ Air in hydraulic system (Chapter 9).
☐ Deteriorated flexible rubber brake hoses (Chapter 9).
☐ Master cylinder mounting nuts loose (Chapter 9).
☐ Faulty master cylinder (Chapter 9).

Excessive brake pedal effort required to stop vehicle

☐ Faulty vacuum servo unit (Chapter 9).
☐ Disconnected, damaged or insecure brake servo vacuum hose (Chapters 1 and 9).
☐ Faulty brake vacuum pump (Chapter 9).
☐ Primary or secondary hydraulic circuit failure (Chapter 9).
☐ Seized brake caliper or wheel cylinder piston(s) (Chapter 9).
☐ Brake pads or brake shoes incorrectly fitted (Chapter 9).
☐ Incorrect grade of brake pads or brake shoes fitted (Chapter 9).
☐ Brake pads or brake shoe linings contaminated (Chapter 9).

Brakes binding

☐ Seized brake caliper or wheel cylinder piston(s) (Chapter 9).
☐ Incorrectly-adjusted handbrake mechanism or linkage (Chapter 9).
☐ Faulty master cylinder (Chapter 9).

Rear wheels locking under normal braking

☐ Rear brake shoe linings contaminated (Chapter 9).
☐ Faulty brake pressure regulator (Chapter 9).

Suspension and steering

Note: *Before diagnosing suspension or steering faults, be sure that the trouble is not due to incorrect tyre pressures, mixtures of tyre types or binding brakes.*

Vehicle pulls to one side

- ☐ Defective tyre (*Weekly checks*).
- ☐ Excessive wear in suspension or steering components (Chapter 10).
- ☐ Incorrect front wheel alignment (Chapter 10).
- ☐ Accident damage to steering or suspension components (Chapter 10).

Wheel wobble and vibration

- ☐ Front roadwheels out-of-balance (vibration felt mainly through the steering wheel) (*Weekly checks*).
- ☐ Rear roadwheels out-of-balance (vibration felt throughout the vehicle) (*Weekly checks*).
- ☐ Roadwheels damaged or distorted (*Weekly checks*).
- ☐ Faulty or damaged tyre (*Weekly checks*).
- ☐ Worn steering or suspension joints, bushes or components (Chapter 10).
- ☐ Wheel bolts loose (Chapter 10).

Excessive pitching and/or rolling around corners or during braking

- ☐ Defective shock absorbers (Chapter 10).
- ☐ Broken or weak coil spring and/or suspension component (Chapter 10).
- ☐ Worn or damaged anti-roll bar or mountings (Chapter 10).

Excessive play in steering

- ☐ Worn steering column universal joint(s) or intermediate coupling (Chapter 10).
- ☐ Worn steering track-rod end balljoints (Chapter 10).
- ☐ Worn rack-and-pinion steering gear (Chapter 10).
- ☐ Worn steering or suspension joints, bushes or components (Chapter 10).

Lack of power assistance

- ☐ Broken or incorrectly-adjusted auxiliary drivebelt (Chapter 1).
- ☐ Incorrect power steering fluid level (*Weekly checks*).
- ☐ Restriction in power steering fluid hoses (Chapter 1).
- ☐ Faulty power steering pump (Chapter 10).
- ☐ Faulty rack-and-pinion steering gear (Chapter 10).

Wandering or general instability

- ☐ Incorrect front wheel alignment (Chapter 10).
- ☐ Worn steering or suspension joints, bushes or components (Chapter 10).
- ☐ Roadwheels out-of-balance (*Weekly checks*).
- ☐ Faulty or damaged tyre (*Weekly checks*).
- ☐ Wheel bolts loose (Chapter 10).
- ☐ Defective shock absorbers (Chapter 10).

Excessively-stiff steering

- ☐ Lack of steering gear lubricant - possibly due to split rubber gaiter (Chapter 10).
- ☐ Seized track-rod end balljoint or suspension balljoint (Chapter 10).
- ☐ Broken or incorrectly-adjusted auxiliary drivebelt (Chapter 1).
- ☐ Incorrect front wheel alignment (Chapter 10).
- ☐ Steering rack or column bent or damaged (Chapter 10).

Tyre wear excessive

Tyres worn on inside or outside edges

- ☐ Tyres under-inflated (wear on both edges) (*Weekly checks*).
- ☐ Incorrect camber or castor angles (wear on one edge only) (Chapter 10).
- ☐ Worn steering or suspension joints, bushes or components (Chapter 10).
- ☐ Excessively-hard cornering.
- ☐ Accident damage.

Tyre treads exhibit feathered edges

- ☐ Incorrect toe setting (Chapter 10).

Tyres worn in centre of tread

- ☐ Tyres over-inflated (*Weekly checks*).

Tyres worn on inside and outside edges

- ☐ Tyres under-inflated (*Weekly checks*).

Tyres worn unevenly

- ☐ Tyres out-of-balance (*Weekly checks*).
- ☐ Excessive wheel or tyre run-out (*Weekly checks*).
- ☐ Worn shock absorbers (Chapter 10).
- ☐ Faulty tyre (*Weekly checks*).

Electrical system

Note: *For problems associated with the starting system, refer to the faults listed under 'Engine' earlier in this Section.*

Battery will not hold a charge for more than a few days

- ☐ Battery defective internally (Chapter 5).
- ☐ Battery electrolyte level low - where applicable (*Weekly checks*).
- ☐ Battery terminal connections loose or corroded (*Weekly checks*).
- ☐ Auxiliary drivebelt worn or incorrectly adjusted (Chapter 1).
- ☐ Alternator not charging at correct output (Chapter 5).
- ☐ Alternator or voltage regulator faulty (Chapter 5).
- ☐ Short-circuit causing continual battery drain (Chapter 5).

Alternator (no-charge) warning light remains illuminated with engine running

- ☐ Auxiliary drivebelt broken, worn, or incorrectly adjusted (Chapter 1).
- ☐ Alternator brushes worn, sticking, or dirty (Chapter 5).
- ☐ Alternator brush springs weak or broken (Chapter 5).
- ☐ Internal fault in alternator or voltage regulator (Chapter 5).
- ☐ Broken, disconnected, or loose wiring in charging circuit (Chapter 5).

Electrical system (continued)

Alternator (no-charge) warning light fails to come on

☐ Warning light bulb blown (Chapter 12).
☐ Broken, disconnected, or loose wiring in warning light circuit (Chapter 12).
☐ Alternator faulty (Chapter 5).

Lights inoperative

☐ Bulb blown (Chapter 12).
☐ Corrosion of bulb or bulbholder contacts (Chapter 12).
☐ Blown fuse (Chapter 12).
☐ Faulty relay (Chapter 12).
☐ Broken, loose, or disconnected wiring (Chapter 12).
☐ Faulty switch (Chapter 12).

Instrument readings inaccurate or erratic

Instrument readings increase with engine speed

☐ Faulty voltage regulator (Chapter 12).

Fuel or temperature gauges give no reading

☐ Faulty gauge sender unit (Chapters 3 or 4).
☐ Wiring open-circuit (Chapter 5).
☐ Faulty gauge (Chapter 12).

Fuel or temperature gauges give continuous maximum reading

☐ Faulty gauge sender unit (Chapters 3 or 4).
☐ Wiring short-circuit (Chapter 5).
☐ Faulty gauge (Chapter 12).

Horn inoperative, or unsatisfactory in operation

Horn operates all the time

☐ Horn push either earthed or stuck down (Chapter 12).
☐ Horn cable-to-horn push earthed (Chapter 12).

Horn fails to operate

☐ Blown fuse (Chapter 12).
☐ Cable or cable connections loose, broken or disconnected (Chapter 12).
☐ Faulty horn (Chapter 12).

Horn emits intermittent or unsatisfactory sound

☐ Cable connections loose (Chapter 12).
☐ Horn mountings loose (Chapter 12).
☐ Faulty horn (Chapter 12).

Windscreen/tailgate wipers inoperative, or unsatisfactory in operation

Wipers fail to operate, or operate very slowly

☐ Wiper blades stuck to screen, or linkage seized or binding (Chapter 1 or Chapter 12).
☐ Blown fuse (Chapter 12).
☐ Cable or cable connections loose, broken or disconnected (Chapter 12).
☐ Faulty relay (Chapter 12).
☐ Faulty wiper motor (Chapter 12).

Wiper blades sweep over too large or too small an area of the glass

☐ Wiper arms incorrectly positioned on spindles (Chapter 12).
☐ Excessive wear of wiper linkage (Chapter 12).
☐ Wiper motor or linkage mountings loose or insecure (Chapter 12).

Wiper blades fail to clean the glass effectively

☐ Wiper blade rubbers worn or perished (Weekly checks).
☐ Wiper arm tension springs broken or arm pivots seized (Chapter 12).
☐ Insufficient windscreen washer additive to adequately remove road film (Weekly checks).

Windscreen/tailgate washers inoperative, or unsatisfactory in operation

One or more washer jets inoperative

☐ Blocked washer jet (Chapter 12).
☐ Disconnected, kinked or restricted fluid hose (Chapter 12).
☐ Insufficient fluid in washer reservoir (Weekly checks).

Washer pump fails to operate

☐ Broken or disconnected wiring or connections (Chapter 12).
☐ Blown fuse (Chapter 12).
☐ Faulty washer switch (Chapter 12).
☐ Faulty washer pump (Chapter 12).

Washer pump runs for some time before fluid is emitted from jets

☐ Faulty one-way valve in fluid supply hose (Chapter 12).

Electric windows inoperative, or unsatisfactory in operation

Window glass will only move in one direction

☐ Faulty switch (Chapter 11).

Window glass slow to move

☐ Regulator seized or damaged, or in need of lubrication (Chapter 11).
☐ Door internal components or trim fouling regulator (Chapter 11).
☐ Faulty motor (Chapter 11).

Window glass fails to move

☐ Blown fuse (Chapter 12).
☐ Faulty relay (Chapter 12).
☐ Broken or disconnected wiring or connections (Chapter 12).
☐ Faulty motor (Chapter 11).

Central locking system inoperative, or unsatisfactory in operation

Complete system failure

☐ Blown fuse (Chapter 12).
☐ Faulty relay (Chapter 12).
☐ Broken or disconnected wiring or connections (Chapter 12).

Latch locks but will not unlock, or unlocks but will not lock

☐ Faulty master switch (Chapter 11).
☐ Broken or disconnected latch operating rods or levers (Chapter 11).
☐ Faulty relay (Chapter 12).

One solenoid/motor fails to operate

☐ Broken or disconnected wiring or connections (Chapter 12).
☐ Faulty solenoid/motor (Chapter 11).
☐ Broken, binding or disconnected latch operating rods or levers (Chapter 11).
☐ Fault in door latch (Chapter 11).

A

ABS (Anti-lock brake system) A system, usually electronically controlled, that senses incipient wheel lockup during braking and relieves hydraulic pressure at wheels that are about to skid.

Air bag An inflatable bag hidden in the steering wheel (driver's side) or the dash or glovebox (passenger side). In a head-on collision, the bags inflate, preventing the driver and front passenger from being thrown forward into the steering wheel or windscreen.

Air cleaner A metal or plastic housing, containing a filter element, which removes dust and dirt from the air being drawn into the engine.

Air filter element The actual filter in an air cleaner system, usually manufactured from pleated paper and requiring renewal at regular intervals.

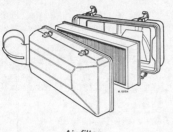

Air filter

Allen key A hexagonal wrench which fits into a recessed hexagonal hole.

Alligator clip A long-nosed spring-loaded metal clip with meshing teeth. Used to make temporary electrical connections.

Alternator A component in the electrical system which converts mechanical energy from a drivebelt into electrical energy to charge the battery and to operate the starting system, ignition system and electrical accessories.

Ampere (amp) A unit of measurement for the flow of electric current. One amp is the amount of current produced by one volt acting through a resistance of one ohm.

Anaerobic sealer A substance used to prevent bolts and screws from loosening. Anaerobic means that it does not require oxygen for activation. The Loctite brand is widely used.

Antifreeze A substance (usually ethylene glycol) mixed with water, and added to a vehicle's cooling system, to prevent freezing of the coolant in winter. Antifreeze also contains chemicals to inhibit corrosion and the formation of rust and other deposits that would tend to clog the radiator and coolant passages and reduce cooling efficiency.

Anti-seize compound A coating that reduces the risk of seizing on fasteners that are subjected to high temperatures, such as exhaust manifold bolts and nuts.

Asbestos A natural fibrous mineral with great heat resistance, commonly used in the composition of brake friction materials.

Asbestos is a health hazard and the dust created by brake systems should never be inhaled or ingested.

Axle A shaft on which a wheel revolves, or which revolves with a wheel. Also, a solid beam that connects the two wheels at one end of the vehicle. An axle which also transmits power to the wheels is known as a live axle.

Axleshaft A single rotating shaft, on either side of the differential, which delivers power from the final drive assembly to the drive wheels. Also called a driveshaft or a halfshaft.

B

Ball bearing An anti-friction bearing consisting of a hardened inner and outer race with hardened steel balls between two races.

Bearing The curved surface on a shaft or in a bore, or the part assembled into either, that permits relative motion between them with minimum wear and friction.

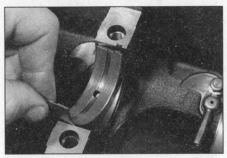

Bearing

Big-end bearing The bearing in the end of the connecting rod that's attached to the crankshaft.

Bleed nipple A valve on a brake wheel cylinder, caliper or other hydraulic component that is opened to purge the hydraulic system of air. Also called a bleed screw.

Brake bleeding Procedure for removing air from lines of a hydraulic brake system.

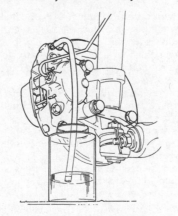

Brake bleeding

Brake disc The component of a disc brake that rotates with the wheels.

Brake drum The component of a drum brake that rotates with the wheels.

Brake linings The friction material which contacts the brake disc or drum to retard the vehicle's speed. The linings are bonded or riveted to the brake pads or shoes.

Brake pads The replaceable friction pads that pinch the brake disc when the brakes are applied. Brake pads consist of a friction material bonded or riveted to a rigid backing plate.

Brake shoe The crescent-shaped carrier to which the brake linings are mounted and which forces the lining against the rotating drum during braking.

Braking systems For more information on braking systems, consult the *Haynes Automotive Brake Manual*.

Breaker bar A long socket wrench handle providing greater leverage.

Bulkhead The insulated partition between the engine and the passenger compartment.

C

Caliper The non-rotating part of a disc-brake assembly that straddles the disc and carries the brake pads. The caliper also contains the hydraulic components that cause the pads to pinch the disc when the brakes are applied. A caliper is also a measuring tool that can be set to measure inside or outside dimensions of an object.

Camshaft A rotating shaft on which a series of cam lobes operate the valve mechanisms. The camshaft may be driven by gears, by sprockets and chain or by sprockets and a belt.

Canister A container in an evaporative emission control system; contains activated charcoal granules to trap vapours from the fuel system.

Canister

Carburettor A device which mixes fuel with air in the proper proportions to provide a desired power output from a spark ignition internal combustion engine.

Castellated Resembling the parapets along the top of a castle wall. For example, a castellated balljoint stud nut.

Castor In wheel alignment, the backward or forward tilt of the steering axis. Castor is positive when the steering axis is inclined rearward at the top.

Catalytic converter A silencer-like device in the exhaust system which converts certain pollutants in the exhaust gases into less harmful substances.

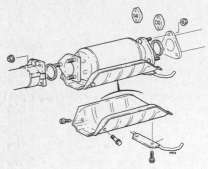

Catalytic converter

Circlip A ring-shaped clip used to prevent endwise movement of cylindrical parts and shafts. An internal circlip is installed in a groove in a housing; an external circlip fits into a groove on the outside of a cylindrical piece such as a shaft.

Clearance The amount of space between two parts. For example, between a piston and a cylinder, between a bearing and a journal, etc.

Coil spring A spiral of elastic steel found in various sizes throughout a vehicle, for example as a springing medium in the suspension and in the valve train.

Compression Reduction in volume, and increase in pressure and temperature, of a gas, caused by squeezing it into a smaller space.

Compression ratio The relationship between cylinder volume when the piston is at top dead centre and cylinder volume when the piston is at bottom dead centre.

Constant velocity (CV) joint A type of universal joint that cancels out vibrations caused by driving power being transmitted through an angle.

Core plug A disc or cup-shaped metal device inserted in a hole in a casting through which core was removed when the casting was formed. Also known as a freeze plug or expansion plug.

Crankcase The lower part of the engine block in which the crankshaft rotates.

Crankshaft The main rotating member, or shaft, running the length of the crankcase, with offset "throws" to which the connecting rods are attached.

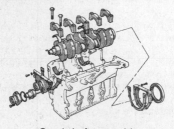

Crankshaft assembly

Crocodile clip See Alligator clip

D

Diagnostic code Code numbers obtained by accessing the diagnostic mode of an engine management computer. This code can be used to determine the area in the system where a malfunction may be located.

Disc brake A brake design incorporating a rotating disc onto which brake pads are squeezed. The resulting friction converts the energy of a moving vehicle into heat.

Double-overhead cam (DOHC) An engine that uses two overhead camshafts, usually one for the intake valves and one for the exhaust valves.

Drivebelt(s) The belt(s) used to drive accessories such as the alternator, water pump, power steering pump, air conditioning compressor, etc. off the crankshaft pulley.

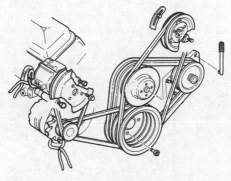

Accessory drivebelts

Driveshaft Any shaft used to transmit motion. Commonly used when referring to the axleshafts on a front wheel drive vehicle.

Drum brake A type of brake using a drum-shaped metal cylinder attached to the inner surface of the wheel. When the brake pedal is pressed, curved brake shoes with friction linings press against the inside of the drum to slow or stop the vehicle.

E

EGR valve A valve used to introduce exhaust gases into the intake air stream.

Electronic control unit (ECU) A computer which controls (for instance) ignition and fuel injection systems, or an anti-lock braking system. For more information refer to the *Haynes Automotive Electrical and Electronic Systems Manual*.

Electronic Fuel Injection (EFI) A computer controlled fuel system that distributes fuel through an injector located in each intake port of the engine.

Emergency brake A braking system, independent of the main hydraulic system, that can be used to slow or stop the vehicle if the primary brakes fail, or to hold the vehicle stationary even though the brake pedal isn't depressed. It usually consists of a hand lever that actuates either front or rear brakes mechanically through a series of cables and linkages. Also known as a handbrake or parking brake.

Endfloat The amount of lengthwise movement between two parts. As applied to a crankshaft, the distance that the crankshaft can move forward and back in the cylinder block.

Engine management system (EMS) A computer controlled system which manages the fuel injection and the ignition systems in an integrated fashion.

Exhaust manifold A part with several passages through which exhaust gases leave the engine combustion chambers and enter the exhaust pipe.

F

Fan clutch A viscous (fluid) drive coupling device which permits variable engine fan speeds in relation to engine speeds.

Feeler blade A thin strip or blade of hardened steel, ground to an exact thickness, used to check or measure clearances between parts.

Feeler blade

Firing order The order in which the engine cylinders fire, or deliver their power strokes, beginning with the number one cylinder.

Flywheel A heavy spinning wheel in which energy is absorbed and stored by means of momentum. On cars, the flywheel is attached to the crankshaft to smooth out firing impulses.

Free play The amount of travel before any action takes place. The "looseness" in a linkage, or an assembly of parts, between the initial application of force and actual movement. For example, the distance the brake pedal moves before the pistons in the master cylinder are actuated.

Fuse An electrical device which protects a circuit against accidental overload. The typical fuse contains a soft piece of metal which is calibrated to melt at a predetermined current flow (expressed as amps) and break the circuit.

Fusible link A circuit protection device consisting of a conductor surrounded by heat-resistant insulation. The conductor is smaller than the wire it protects, so it acts as the weakest link in the circuit. Unlike a blown fuse, a failed fusible link must frequently be cut from the wire for replacement.

G

Gap The distance the spark must travel in jumping from the centre electrode to the side electrode in a spark plug. Also refers to the spacing between the points in a contact breaker assembly in a conventional points-type ignition, or to the distance between the reluctor or rotor and the pickup coil in an electronic ignition.

Adjusting spark plug gap

Gasket Any thin, soft material - usually cork, cardboard, asbestos or soft metal - installed between two metal surfaces to ensure a good seal. For instance, the cylinder head gasket seals the joint between the block and the cylinder head.

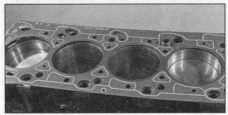

Gasket

Gauge An instrument panel display used to monitor engine conditions. A gauge with a movable pointer on a dial or a fixed scale is an analogue gauge. A gauge with a numerical readout is called a digital gauge.

H

Halfshaft A rotating shaft that transmits power from the final drive unit to a drive wheel, usually when referring to a live rear axle.

Harmonic balancer A device designed to reduce torsion or twisting vibration in the crankshaft. May be incorporated in the crankshaft pulley. Also known as a vibration damper.

Hone An abrasive tool for correcting small irregularities or differences in diameter in an engine cylinder, brake cylinder, etc.

Hydraulic tappet A tappet that utilises hydraulic pressure from the engine's lubrication system to maintain zero clearance (constant contact with both camshaft and valve stem). Automatically adjusts to variation in valve stem length. Hydraulic tappets also reduce valve noise.

I

Ignition timing The moment at which the spark plug fires, usually expressed in the number of crankshaft degrees before the piston reaches the top of its stroke.

Inlet manifold A tube or housing with passages through which flows the air-fuel mixture (carburettor vehicles and vehicles with throttle body injection) or air only (port fuel-injected vehicles) to the port openings in the cylinder head.

J

Jump start Starting the engine of a vehicle with a discharged or weak battery by attaching jump leads from the weak battery to a charged or helper battery.

L

Load Sensing Proportioning Valve (LSPV) A brake hydraulic system control valve that works like a proportioning valve, but also takes into consideration the amount of weight carried by the rear axle.

Locknut A nut used to lock an adjustment nut, or other threaded component, in place. For example, a locknut is employed to keep the adjusting nut on the rocker arm in position.

Lockwasher A form of washer designed to prevent an attaching nut from working loose.

M

MacPherson strut A type of front suspension system devised by Earle MacPherson at Ford of England. In its original form, a simple lateral link with the anti-roll bar creates the lower control arm. A long strut - an integral coil spring and shock absorber - is mounted between the body and the steering knuckle. Many modern so-called MacPherson strut systems use a conventional lower A-arm and don't rely on the anti-roll bar for location.

Multimeter An electrical test instrument with the capability to measure voltage, current and resistance.

N

NOx Oxides of Nitrogen. A common toxic pollutant emitted by petrol and diesel engines at higher temperatures.

O

Ohm The unit of electrical resistance. One volt applied to a resistance of one ohm will produce a current of one amp.

Ohmmeter An instrument for measuring electrical resistance.

O-ring A type of sealing ring made of a special rubber-like material; in use, the O-ring is compressed into a groove to provide the sealing action.

Overhead cam (ohc) engine An engine with the camshaft(s) located on top of the cylinder head(s).

Overhead valve (ohv) engine An engine with the valves located in the cylinder head, but with the camshaft located in the engine block.

Oxygen sensor A device installed in the engine exhaust manifold, which senses the oxygen content in the exhaust and converts this information into an electric current. Also called a Lambda sensor.

P

Phillips screw A type of screw head having a cross instead of a slot for a corresponding type of screwdriver.

Plastigage A thin strip of plastic thread, available in different sizes, used for measuring clearances. For example, a strip of Plastigage is laid across a bearing journal. The parts are assembled and dismantled; the width of the crushed strip indicates the clearance between journal and bearing.

Plastigage

Propeller shaft The long hollow tube with universal joints at both ends that carries power from the transmission to the differential on front-engined rear wheel drive vehicles.

Proportioning valve A hydraulic control valve which limits the amount of pressure to the rear brakes during panic stops to prevent wheel lock-up.

R

Rack-and-pinion steering A steering system with a pinion gear on the end of the steering shaft that mates with a rack (think of a geared wheel opened up and laid flat). When the steering wheel is turned, the pinion turns, moving the rack to the left or right. This movement is transmitted through the track rods to the steering arms at the wheels.

Radiator A liquid-to-air heat transfer device designed to reduce the temperature of the coolant in an internal combustion engine cooling system.

Refrigerant Any substance used as a heat transfer agent in an air-conditioning system. R-12 has been the principle refrigerant for many years; recently, however, manufacturers have begun using R-134a, a non-CFC substance that is considered less harmful to the ozone in the upper atmosphere.

Rocker arm A lever arm that rocks on a shaft or pivots on a stud. In an overhead valve engine, the rocker arm converts the upward movement of the pushrod into a downward movement to open a valve.

Rotor In a distributor, the rotating device inside the cap that connects the centre electrode and the outer terminals as it turns, distributing the high voltage from the coil secondary winding to the proper spark plug. Also, that part of an alternator which rotates inside the stator. Also, the rotating assembly of a turbocharger, including the compressor wheel, shaft and turbine wheel.

Runout The amount of wobble (in-and-out movement) of a gear or wheel as it's rotated. The amount a shaft rotates "out-of-true." The out-of-round condition of a rotating part.

S

Sealant A liquid or paste used to prevent leakage at a joint. Sometimes used in conjunction with a gasket.

Sealed beam lamp An older headlight design which integrates the reflector, lens and filaments into a hermetically-sealed one-piece unit. When a filament burns out or the lens cracks, the entire unit is simply replaced.

Serpentine drivebelt A single, long, wide accessory drivebelt that's used on some newer vehicles to drive all the accessories, instead of a series of smaller, shorter belts. Serpentine drivebelts are usually tensioned by an automatic tensioner.

Serpentine drivebelt

Shim Thin spacer, commonly used to adjust the clearance or relative positions between two parts. For example, shims inserted into or under bucket tappets control valve clearances. Clearance is adjusted by changing the thickness of the shim.

Slide hammer A special puller that screws into or hooks onto a component such as a shaft or bearing; a heavy sliding handle on the shaft bottoms against the end of the shaft to knock the component free.

Sprocket A tooth or projection on the periphery of a wheel, shaped to engage with a chain or drivebelt. Commonly used to refer to the sprocket wheel itself.

Starter inhibitor switch On vehicles with an automatic transmission, a switch that prevents starting if the vehicle is not in Neutral or Park.

Strut See MacPherson strut.

T

Tappet A cylindrical component which transmits motion from the cam to the valve stem, either directly or via a pushrod and rocker arm. Also called a cam follower.

Thermostat A heat-controlled valve that regulates the flow of coolant between the cylinder block and the radiator, so maintaining optimum engine operating temperature. A thermostat is also used in some air cleaners in which the temperature is regulated.

Thrust bearing The bearing in the clutch assembly that is moved in to the release levers by clutch pedal action to disengage the clutch. Also referred to as a release bearing.

Timing belt A toothed belt which drives the camshaft. Serious engine damage may result if it breaks in service.

Timing chain A chain which drives the camshaft.

Toe-in The amount the front wheels are closer together at the front than at the rear. On rear wheel drive vehicles, a slight amount of toe-in is usually specified to keep the front wheels running parallel on the road by offsetting other forces that tend to spread the wheels apart.

Toe-out The amount the front wheels are closer together at the rear than at the front. On front wheel drive vehicles, a slight amount of toe-out is usually specified.

Tools For full information on choosing and using tools, refer to the *Haynes Automotive Tools Manual*.

Tracer A stripe of a second colour applied to a wire insulator to distinguish that wire from another one with the same colour insulator.

Tune-up A process of accurate and careful adjustments and parts replacement to obtain the best possible engine performance.

Turbocharger A centrifugal device, driven by exhaust gases, that pressurises the intake air. Normally used to increase the power output from a given engine displacement, but can also be used primarily to reduce exhaust emissions (as on VW's "Umwelt" Diesel engine).

U

Universal joint or U-joint A double-pivoted connection for transmitting power from a driving to a driven shaft through an angle. A U-joint consists of two Y-shaped yokes and a cross-shaped member called the spider.

V

Valve A device through which the flow of liquid, gas, vacuum, or loose material in bulk may be started, stopped, or regulated by a movable part that opens, shuts, or partially obstructs one or more ports or passageways. A valve is also the movable part of such a device.

Valve clearance The clearance between the valve tip (the end of the valve stem) and the rocker arm or tappet. The valve clearance is measured when the valve is closed.

Vernier caliper A precision measuring instrument that measures inside and outside dimensions. Not quite as accurate as a micrometer, but more convenient.

Viscosity The thickness of a liquid or its resistance to flow.

Volt A unit for expressing electrical "pressure" in a circuit. One volt that will produce a current of one ampere through a resistance of one ohm.

W

Welding Various processes used to join metal items by heating the areas to be joined to a molten state and fusing them together. For more information refer to the *Haynes Automotive Welding Manual*.

Wiring diagram A drawing portraying the components and wires in a vehicle's electrical system, using standardised symbols. For more information refer to the *Haynes Automotive Electrical and Electronic Systems Manual*.

A

ABS computer - 9•21
Accelerator cable - 4•11
Accelerator pedal - 4•12
Accessory shops - REF•3
Acknowledgements - 0•4
Aerial - 12•19
Air bags - 0•5, 12•20
Air conditioning - 1•6, 1•10, 3•11, 3•12, 12•5
Air distribution housing - 4•18
Air filter - 1•15
Air horn - 12•14
Air temperature sensor - 3•7
Alarm - 12•5, 12•20
Alternator - 5•3, 5•4
Antifreeze - 0•13, 0•16, 1•1, 1•19
Anti-lock braking system (ABS) - 9•19, 9•20
Anti-roll bar - 10•9, 10•15
Anti-stall speed - 1•11
Anti-theft alarm system - 12•20
Asbestos - 0•5
Ashtray - 12•9
ATF - 0•16, 1•1, 1•8, 1•17
Atmospheric pressure correction system - 4•20
Automatic transmission - 2A•18, 2B•6, 7B•0 *et seq*
   fault finding - REF•15
Automatic transmission fluid - 0•16, 1•1, 1•8, 1•17
Axle assembly - 10•17

B

Badges - 11•14
Battery - 0•5, 0•15, 1•6, 5•2, 5•3
Big-end bearings - 2B•15, 2B•19
Bleeding
   brakes - 9•2
   fuel system - 4•20
   power steering - 10•22
Body electrical systems - 12•1 *et seq*
Bodywork and fittings - 11•1 *et seq*
Bonnet - 1•4, 11•5
Brake fluid - 0•12, 0•16, 1•17

Brake pressure compensator - 9•19
Brake pressure regulating valves - 9•18
Braking
   system - 1•6, 1•15, 9•1 *et seq,* REF•10
   fault finding - REF•16
Bulbs - 12•6, 12•8
Bumpers - 11•3, 11•4
Burning - 0•5
Buying spare parts - REF•3

C

Cables - 3•9, 4•11, 6•2, 7B•1, 7B•2, 7B•3, 9•18, 11•5, 12•15
Calipers - 9•11, 9•12
Camshaft - 2A•10
   cover - 2A•5
   oil seals - 2A•17
   sprocket - 2A•7
Carpets - 11•2, 11•18
Catalytic converter - 4•3
Central locking - 11•11
Centre console - 11•18
Charging system - 5•3
Cigarette lighter - 12•9, 12•14
Clock - 12•9, 12•13
Clutch - 1•14, 6•1 *et seq*
   fault finding - REF•15
Compression test - 2A•4
Connecting rods - 2B•11, 2B•14, 2B•19
Contents - 0•2
Conversion factors - REF•2
Coolant - 0•13, 0•16, 1•1, 1•18
Coolant pump - 2A•9, 3•7
Cooling, heating and ventilation systems - 3•1 *et seq*
   fault finding - REF•14
Corrosion - REF•11
Courtesy lights - 12•5, 12•8
Crankcase - 2B•12
Crankcase emission control system - 4•19
Crankshaft - 2B•11, 2B•15, 2B•17
   oil seals - 2A•16, 2A•17
   pulley - 2A•5
   sprocket - 2A•8
Crushing - 0•5
Cylinder block - 2B•12

Cylinder
   head - 2A•13, 2A•14, 2B•8, 2B•9, 2B•10

D

Dents in bodywork - 11•2
Diesel injection equipment - 0•5
Dim-dip lighting system - 12•20
Dimensions - REF•1
Direction indicators - 1•6, 12•7, 12•11
Discs - 9•9, 9•10
Door-open warning display - 12•14
Doors - 11•5, 11•6, 11•7, 11•8, REF•9
Drivebelts - 1•12, 1•14, 5•3
Driveplate - 2A•18
Driveshafts - 8•1 *et seq,* REF•10
   fault finding - REF•16
   gaiter - 1•9
   oil seals - 7A•3, 7B•3
Drivetrain - 1•14
Drums - 9•10

E

Earth fault - 12•4
EGR system coolant temperature sensor - 3•7
Electric cooling fan - 3•6
Electric shock - 0•5
Electric windows - 11•12, 12•6
Electrical equipment - 1•14, REF•9
Electrical systems - 0•15
   fault finding - REF•17
Electrolyte - 1•6
Emission control system - 1•12, 4•19, 4•20, REF•11
Engine electrical systems - 5•1 *et seq*
Engine fault finding - REF•13
Engine oil - 0•11, 0•16, 1•1, 1•7
Engine removal and general engine overhaul procedures - 2B•1 *et seq*
Exhaust emission control system - 4•19, 4•20
Exhaust gas recirculation system - 4•19, 4•20
Exhaust manifold - 4•15
Exhaust specialists - REF•3
Exhaust system - 4•18, REF•10, REF•11

F

Facia panel - 11•19
Facia vents - 3•11
Fan - 3•6
Fast idle thermostatic sensor - 4•4
Fault finding - REF•12 *et seq*
  automatic transmission - REF•15
  braking system - REF•16
  clutch - REF•15
  cooling system - REF•14
  driveshafts - REF•16
  electrical system - 5•2, 12•3, REF•17
  engine - REF•13
  fuel and exhaust systems - REF•14
  manual transmission - REF•15
  suspension and steering systems - REF•17
Filling - 11•2
Filters
  air - 1•15
  fuel - 1•7, 1•16, 3•8
  oil - 1•7
Fire - 0•5
Fluid cooler - 7B•4
Fluids - 0•16
Flywheel - 2A•18
Foglight - 12•7, 12•8, 12•11
Footbrake - REF•8, REF•9
Fuel filter - 1•7, 1•16, 3•8
Fuel gauge - 12•13
Fuel injection pump - 4•6
  sprocket - 2A•8
Fuel injectors - 4•10
Fuel level sender - 4•12
Fuel pick-up unit - 4•13
Fuel system - REF•11
Fuel tank - 1•1, 4•13
Fuel, exhaust and emission control systems - 4•1 *et seq*
  fault finding - REF•14
Fume or gas intoxication - 0•5
Fuses - 12•4

G

Gaiters - 1•9, 8•3, 10•22
Gashes in bodywork - 11•2
Gearchange linkage - 7A•2, 7A•3
General repair procedures - REF•4
Glossary of technical terms - REF•19 *et seq*
Glovebox - 11•18
Glow plugs - 5•7

H

Handbrake - 9•17, 9•18, REF•8
  warning light switch - 12•6
Handles - 11•7
Headlight - 12•6, 12•10
  beam alignment - 12•11
  washer fluid - 0•13
Headlining - 11•18
Heater - 3•4, 3•8, 3•9, 3•10, 3•11
  control panel illumination bulb - 12•10
Hinges - 1•6, 1•16

Horn - 1•6, 12•14
Hose and fluid leak check - 1•8
Hubs - 10•4, 10•5, 10•10, 10•11
Hydraulic pipes and hoses - 9•3
Hydrofluoric acid - 0•5

I

Idle speed - 1•10
Ignition switch - 5•6, 10•21, 12•4
In-car engine repair procedures - 2A•1 *et seq*
Indicators - 1•6, 12•7, 12•11
Injection timing - 4•8, 4•9
Inlet manifold - 4•14
Input shaft oil seal - 7A•4
Instrument panel - 12•11, 12•12
  dimmer switch - 12•5
  lights - 12•9
Instrument shroud switches - 12•5
Instruments - 1•14
Intercooler - 4•17
Introduction to the Citroën ZX Diesel - 0•4

J

Jacking and vehicle support - REF•5
Jump starting - 0•7

K

Kickdown cable - 7B•3

L

Latches - 1•6
Leakdown test - 2A•4
Leaks - 0•9, 1•8
Lights - 1•6, 12•10
Lights-on warning system - 12•14
Locks - 1•6, 1•16, 10•21, 11•5, 11•7, 11•11, 12•4
Loudspeakers - 12•18
Lower arms - 10•8
Lubricants and fluids - 0•16
Luggage compartment light - 12•5, 12•9

M

Main bearings - 2B•15, 2B•17
Maintenance schedule - 1•3
Manifolds - 4•14
Manual transmission - 2A•18, 2B•3, 7A•1 *et seq*
  fault finding - REF•15
  oil - 0•16, 1•1, 1•16, 1•19
Map reading light - 12•9
Master cylinder - 9•14
Maximum speed - 4•3
Mirrors - 11•12, 12•5, REF•8
MOT test checks - REF•8 *et seq*
Motor factors - REF•3
Mountings - 2A•9, 2A•18

N

Number plate light - 12•8, 12•11

O

Oil cooler - 2A•19
Oil
  engine - 0•11, 0•16, 1•1, 1•7
  manual transmission - 0•16, 1•1, 1•16, 1•19
Oil filter - 1•7
Oil level sensor - 2A•18, 5•7
Oil pressure warning light switch - 5•6
Oil pump - 2A•15, 2A•16
Oil seals - 2A•16, 2A•17, 7A•3, 7B•3
Open-circuit - 12•3

P

Pads - 1•9, 1•14, 9•4, 9•6
Pedals - 4•12, 6•2, 9•15
Pistons - 2B•11, 2B•14, 2B•19
  rings - 2B•16
Plastic components - 11•3
Poisonous or irritant substances - 0•5
Power steering - 10•22
  fluid - 0•11, 0•16, 1•1
  pump - 10•23
Pre-heating system - 5•7, 5•8
  coolant temperature sensor - 3•7
Pressure compensator - 9•19
Pressure regulating valves - 9•18
Pressure sensor - 2A•18
Priming fuel system - 4•20
Printed circuit - 12•13
Puncture - 0•8

Q

Quarter window - 11•13

R

Radiator - 3•3, 3•4, 3•5
Radio/cassette player - 12•18
  anti-theft system - precaution - REF•5
Rear light cluster - 12•8, 12•11
Relays - 9•22, 12•4
Reluctor rings - 9•22
Repair procedures - REF•4
Respraying - 11•2
Reversing light switch - 7A•5, 7B•4
Ride height - 10•17
Road test - 1•14
Roadside repairs - 0•6 *et seq*
Routine maintenance and servicing - 1•1 *et seq*
  bodywork and underframe - 11•1
  upholstery and carpets - 11•2
Rubber gaiters - 8•3, 10•22
Rust holes in bodywork - 11•2

S

Safety first! - 0•5, 0•11, 0•12
Scalding - 0•5
Scratches in bodywork - 11•2
Seat belts - 1•6, 11•15

Seats - 11•14
Selector (automatic transmission) - 7B•1, 7B•2, 7B•5
  display bulbs - 12•9
Selector shaft oil seal - 7A•4, 7B•3
Servo unit - 9•16, 9•17
  vacuum pump - 1•14
Shock absorbers - 1•9, 10•12, REF•9, REF•10
Shoes - 1•14, 9•7
Short-circuit - 12•3
Sidelight - 12•7
Spare parts - REF•3
Speedometer - 7A•5, 7B•3, 12•11, 12•14
Springs - REF•10
Starter inhibitor switch - 7B•4
Starter motor - 5•5
Starting system - 5•4
Steering - 1•8, 1•14, REF•9, REF•10
  angles - 10•24
  column - 10•19, 12•4, REF•8
    combination switches - 12•4
    lock - 10•21
  gear - 10•21
  wheel - 10•18, REF•8
Stop solenoid - 4•5
Stop-light switch - 9•19
Strut/shock absorbers - 1•9
Struts - 10•6, 11•10
Subframe - 10•10
Sump - 2A•15
Sunroof - 11•13, 12•5
Suspension - 1•8, 1•14, REF•9, REF•10
Suspension and steering - 10•1 et seq
  fault finding - REF•17
Switches - 3•6, 5•6, 7A•5, 7B•5, 9•19, 10•21, 12•4, 12•5, 12•10
Swivel hub - 10•4

T

Tachometer - 12•13
Tailgate - 11•10, 11•11, 11•13
  wiper motor - 12•17
Tamperproof screws - 4•3
Tappets - 2B•10
Temperature gauge - 3•6, 12•13
Temperature sensor - 2A•18
Thermostat - 3•5
  housing - 3•8
Timing belt - 1•19, 2A•6, 2A•7
  covers - 2A•6
  idler roller - 2A•10
  tensioner - 2A•9
Toe setting - 10•25
Tools and working facilities - REF•6 et seq
Top dead centre (TDC) for No 1 piston - 2A•4
Torsion bar - 10•12
Towing - 0•9
Track rod - 10•23, 10•24
Trailing arm - 10•14
Transmission - See Manual and Automatic transmission
Trim panels/strips - 11•6, 11•14, 11•16
Turbocharger - 4•3, 4•15, 4•16, 4•17
Tyres - REF•11
  condition - 0•14
  pressure - 0•14, 0•16
  specialists - REF•3

U

Underbonnet check points - 0•10
Underframe - 11•1
Under-panels - 11•14
Upholstery - 11•2

V

Vacuum pump - 1•14, 9•22, 9•23
Vacuum servo unit - 9•16, 9•17
Valves - 2B•9, 2B•10
  clearances - 2A•12
Vehicle identification - REF•3, REF•9
Vehicle support - REF•5
Ventilation - 3•8, 3•11

W

Warning light sender - 3•6
Washer system - 12•17
  fluid - 0•13
Water pump - 3•7
  sprocket - 2A•9
Weekly checks - 0•10 et seq
Weights - REF•1
Wheel alignment - 10•24
Wheel arch liners - 11•14
Wheel bearings - REF•10
Wheel changing - 0•8
Wheel cylinder - 9•14
Wheel sensor - 9•21
Wheels - REF•11
Window glass - 11•8
Window regulator - 11•8
Windows - 11•12
Windscreen - 11•13, 12•16, 12•17, REF•8
Wiper arm - 12•15
Wiper blades - 0•12
Wiper motor and linkage - 12•16, 12•17
Wiring diagrams - 12•21 et seq
Working facilities - REF•6 et seq

Haynes Manuals – The Complete UK Car List

Title	Book No.
ALFA ROMEO Alfasud/Sprint (74 - 88) up to F *	0292
Alfa Romeo Alfetta (73 - 87) up to E *	0531
AUDI 80, 90 & Coupe Petrol (79 - Nov 88) up to F	0605
Audi 80, 90 & Coupe Petrol (Oct 86 - 90) D to H	1491
Audi 100 & 200 Petrol (Oct 82 - 90) up to H	0907
Audi 100 & A6 Petrol & Diesel (May 91 - May 97) H to P	3504
Audi A3 Petrol & Diesel (96 - May 03) P to 03	4253
Audi A4 Petrol & Diesel (95 - 00) M to X	3575
Audi A4 Petrol & Diesel (01 - 04) X to 54	4609
AUSTIN A35 & A40 (56 - 67) up to F *	0118
Austin/MG/Rover Maestro 1.3 & 1.6 Petrol (83 - 95) up to M	0922
Austin/MG Metro (80 - May 90) up to G	0718
Austin/Rover Montego 1.3 & 1.6 Petrol (84 - 94) A to L	1066
Austin/MG/Rover Montego 2.0 Petrol (84 - 95) A to M	1067
Mini (59 - 69) up to H *	0527
Mini (69 - 01) up to X	0646
Austin/Rover 2.0 litre Diesel Engine (86 - 93) C to L	1857
Austin Healey 100/6 & 3000 (56 - 68) up to G *	0049
BEDFORD CF Petrol (69 - 87) up to E	0163
Bedford/Vauxhall Rascal & Suzuki Supercarry (86 - Oct 94) C to M	3015
BMW 316, 320 & 320i (4-cyl) (75 - Feb 83) up to Y *	0276
BMW 320, 320i, 323i & 325i (6-cyl) (Oct 77 - Sept 87) up to E	0815
BMW 3- & 5-Series Petrol (81 - 91) up to J	1948
BMW 3-Series Petrol (Apr 91 - 99) H to V	3210
BMW 3-Series Petrol (Sept 98 - 03) S to 53	4067
BMW 520i & 525e (Oct 81 - June 88) up to E	1560
BMW 525, 528 & 528i (73 - Sept 81) up to X *	0632
BMW 5-Series 6-cyl Petrol (April 96 - Aug 03) N to 03	4151
BMW 1500, 1502, 1600, 1602, 2000 & 2002 (59 - 77) up to S *	0240
CHRYSLER PT Cruiser Petrol (00 - 03) W to 53	4058
CITROËN 2CV, Ami & Dyane (67 - 90) up to H	0196
Citroën AX Petrol & Diesel (87 - 97) D to P	3014
Citroën Berlingo & Peugeot Partner Petrol & Diesel (96 - 05) P to 55	4281
Citroën BX Petrol (83 - 94) A to L	0908
Citroën C15 Van Petrol & Diesel (89 - Oct 98) F to S	3509
Citroën C3 Petrol & Diesel (02 - 05) 51 to 05	4197
Citroën CX Petrol (75 - 88) up to F	0528
Citroën Saxo Petrol & Diesel (96 - 04) N to 54	3506
Citroën Visa Petrol (79 - 88) up to F	0620
Citroën Xantia Petrol & Diesel (93 - 01) K to Y	3082
Citroën XM Petrol & Diesel (89 - 00) G to X	3451
Citroën Xsara Petrol & Diesel (97 - Sept 00) R to W	3751
Citroën Xsara Picasso Petrol & Diesel (00 - 02) W to 52	3944
Citroën ZX Diesel (91 - 98) J to S	1922
Citroën ZX Petrol (91 - 98) H to S	1881
Citroën 1.7 & 1.9 litre Diesel Engine (84 - 96) A to N	1379
FIAT 126 (73 - 87) up to E *	0305
Fiat 500 (57 - 73) up to M *	0090
Fiat Bravo & Brava Petrol (95 - 00) N to W	3572
Fiat Cinquecento (93 - 98) K to R	3501
Fiat Panda (81 - 95) up to M	0793
Fiat Punto Petrol & Diesel (94 - Oct 99) L to V	3251
Fiat Punto Petrol (Oct 99 - July 03) V to 03	4066
Fiat Regata Petrol (84 - 88) A to F	1167
Fiat Tipo Petrol (88 - 91) E to J	1625
Fiat Uno Petrol (83 - 95) up to M	0923
Fiat X1/9 (74 - 89) up to G *	0273
FORD Anglia (59 - 68) up to G *	0001
Ford Capri II (& III) 1.6 & 2.0 (74 - 87) up to E *	0283
Ford Capri II (& III) 2.8 & 3.0 V6 (74 - 87) up to E	1309

Title	Book No.
Ford Cortina Mk I & Corsair 1500 ('62 - '66) up to D*	0214
Ford Cortina Mk III 1300 & 1600 (70 - 76) up to P *	0070
Ford Escort Mk I 1100 & 1300 (68 - 74) up to N *	0171
Ford Escort Mk I Mexico, RS 1600 & RS 2000 (70 - 74) up to N *	0139
Ford Escort Mk II Mexico, RS 1800 & RS 2000 (75 - 80) up to W *	0735
Ford Escort (75 - Aug 80) up to V *	0280
Ford Escort Petrol (Sept 80 - Sept 90) up to H	0686
Ford Escort & Orion Petrol (Sept 90 - 00) H to X	1737
Ford Escort & Orion Diesel (Sept 90 - 00) H to X	4081
Ford Fiesta (76 - Aug 83) up to Y	0334
Ford Fiesta Petrol (Aug 83 - Feb 89) A to F	1030
Ford Fiesta Petrol (Feb 89 - Oct 95) F to N	1595
Ford Fiesta Petrol & Diesel (Oct 95 - Mar 02) N to 02	3397
Ford Fiesta Petrol & Diesel (Apr 02 - 05) 02 to 54	4170
Ford Focus Petrol & Diesel (98 - 01) S to Y	3759
Ford Focus Petrol & Diesel (Oct 01 - 05) 51 to 05	4167
Ford Galaxy Petrol & Diesel (95 - Aug 00) M to W	3984
Ford Granada Petrol (Sept 77 - Feb 85) up to B *	0481
Ford Granada & Scorpio Petrol (Mar 85 - 94) B to M	1245
Ford Ka (96 - 02) P to 52	3570
Ford Mondeo Petrol (93 - Sept 00) K to X	1923
Ford Mondeo Petrol & Diesel (Oct 00 - Jul 03) X to 03	3990
Ford Mondeo Petrol & Diesel (July 03 - 07) 03 to 56	4619
Ford Mondeo Diesel (93 - 96) L to N	3465
Ford Orion Petrol (83 - Sept 90) up to H	1009
Ford Sierra 4-cyl Petrol (82 - 93) up to K	0903
Ford Sierra V6 Petrol (82 - 91) up to J	0904
Ford Transit Petrol (Mk 2) (78 - Jan 86) up to C	0719
Ford Transit Petrol (Mk 3) (Feb 86 - 89) C to G	1468
Ford Transit Diesel (Feb 86 - 99) C to T	3019
Ford 1.6 & 1.8 litre Diesel Engine (84 - 96) A to N	1172
Ford 2.1, 2.3 & 2.5 litre Diesel Engine (77 - 90) up to H	1606
FREIGHT ROVER Sherpa Petrol (74 - 87) up to E	0463
HILLMAN Avenger (70 - 82) up to Y	0037
Hillman Imp (63 - 76) up to R *	0022
HONDA Civic (Feb 84 - Oct 87) A to E	1226
Honda Civic (Nov 91 - 96) J to N	3199
Honda Civic Petrol (Mar 95 - 00) M to X	4050
Honda Civic Petrol & Diesel (01 - 05) X to 55	4611
Honda Jazz (01 - Feb 08) 51 - 57	4735
HYUNDAI Pony (85 - 94) C to M	3398
JAGUAR E Type (61 - 72) up to L *	0140
Jaguar MkI & II, 240 & 340 (55 - 69) up to H *	0098
Jaguar XJ6, XJ & Sovereign; Daimler Sovereign (68 - Oct 86) up to D	0242
Jaguar XJ6 & Sovereign (Oct 86 - Sept 94) D to M	3261
Jaguar XJ12, XJS & Sovereign; Daimler Double Six (72 - 88) up to F	0478
JEEP Cherokee Petrol (93 - 96) K to N	1943
LADA 1200, 1300, 1500 & 1600 (74 - 91) up to J	0413
Lada Samara (87 - 91) D to J	1610
LAND ROVER 90, 110 & Defender Diesel (83 - 07) up to 56	3017
Land Rover Discovery Petrol & Diesel (89 - 98) G to S	3016
Land Rover Discovery Diesel (Nov 98 - Jul 04) S to 04	4606
Land Rover Freelander Petrol & Diesel (97 - Sept 03) R to 53	3929
Land Rover Freelander Petrol & Diesel (Oct 03 - Oct 06) 53 to 56	4623
Land Rover Series IIA & III Diesel (58 - 85) up to C	0529
Land Rover Series II, IIA & III 4-cyl Petrol (58 - 85) up to C	0314

Title	Book No.
MAZDA 323 (Mar 81 - Oct 89) up to G	1608
Mazda 323 (Oct 89 - 98) G to R	3455
Mazda 626 (May 83 - Sept 87) up to E	0929
Mazda B1600, B1800 & B2000 Pick-up Petrol (72 - 88) up to F	0267
Mazda RX-7 (79 - 85) up to C *	0460
MERCEDES-BENZ 190, 190E & 190D Petrol & Diesel (83 - 93) A to L	3450
Mercedes-Benz 200D, 240D, 240TD, 300D & 300TD 123 Series Diesel (Oct 76 - 85)	1114
Mercedes-Benz 250 & 280 (68 - 72) up to L *	0346
Mercedes-Benz 250 & 280 123 Series Petrol (Oct 76 - 84) up to B *	0677
Mercedes-Benz 124 Series Petrol & Diesel (85 - Aug 93) C to K	3253
Mercedes-Benz C-Class Petrol & Diesel (93 - Aug 00) L to W	3511
MGA (55 - 62) *	0475
MGB (62 - 80) up to W	0111
MG Midget & Austin-Healey Sprite (58 - 80) up to W *	0265
MINI Petrol (July 01 - 05) Y to 05	4273
MITSUBISHI Shogun & L200 Pick-Ups Petrol (83 - 94) up to M	1944
MORRIS Ital 1.3 (80 - 84) up to B	0705
Morris Minor 1000 (56 - 71) up to K	0024
NISSAN Almera Petrol (95 - Feb 00) N to V	4053
Nissan Almera & Tino Petrol (Feb 00 - 07) V to 56	4612
Nissan Bluebird (May 84 - Mar 86) A to C	1223
Nissan Bluebird Petrol (Mar 86 - 90) C to H	1473
Nissan Cherry (Sept 82 - 86) up to D	1031
Nissan Micra (83 - Jan 93) up to K	0931
Nissan Micra (93 - 02) K to 52	3254
Nissan Primera Petrol (90 - Aug 99) H to T	1851
Nissan Stanza (82 - 86) up to D	0824
Nissan Sunny Petrol (May 82 - Oct 86) up to D	0895
Nissan Sunny Petrol (Oct 86 - Mar 91) D to H	1378
Nissan Sunny Petrol (Apr 91 - 95) H to N	3219
OPEL Ascona & Manta (B Series) (Sept 75 - 88) up to F *	0316
Opel Ascona Petrol (81 - 88)	3215
Opel Astra Petrol (Oct 91 - Feb 98)	3156
Opel Corsa Petrol (83 - Mar 93)	3160
Opel Corsa Petrol (Mar 93 - 97)	3159
Opel Kadett Petrol (Nov 79 - Oct 84) up to B	0634
Opel Kadett Petrol (Oct 84 - Oct 91)	3196
Opel Omega & Senator Petrol (Nov 86 - 94)	3157
Opel Rekord Petrol (Feb 78 - Oct 86) up to D	0543
Opel Vectra Petrol (Oct 88 - Oct 95)	3158
PEUGEOT 106 Petrol & Diesel (91 - 04) J to 53	1882
Peugeot 205 Petrol (83 - 97) A to P	0932
Peugeot 206 Petrol & Diesel (98 - 01) S to X	3757
Peugeot 206 Petrol & Diesel (02 - 06) 51 to 06	4613
Peugeot 306 Petrol & Diesel (93 - 02) K to 02	3073
Peugeot 307 Petrol & Diesel (01 - 04) Y to 54	4147
Peugeot 309 Petrol (86 - 93) C to K	1266
Peugeot 405 Petrol (88 - 97) E to P	1559
Peugeot 405 Diesel (88 - 97) E to P	3198
Peugeot 406 Petrol & Diesel (96 - Mar 99) N to T	3394
Peugeot 406 Petrol & Diesel (Mar 99 - 02) T to 52	3982
Peugeot 505 Petrol (79 - 89) up to G	0762
Peugeot 1.7/1.8 & 1.9 litre Diesel Engine (82 - 96) up to N	0950
Peugeot 2.0, 2.1, 2.3 & 2.5 litre Diesel Engines (74 - 90) up to H	1607
PORSCHE 911 (65 - 85) up to C	0264

* Classic reprint

Title	Book No.
Porsche 924 & 924 Turbo (76 - 85) up to C	0397
PROTON (89 - 97) F to P	3255
RANGE ROVER V8 Petrol (70 - Oct 92) up to K	0606
RELIANT Robin & Kitten (73 - 83) up to A *	0436
RENAULT 4 (61 - 86) up to D *	0072
Renault 5 Petrol (Feb 85 - 96) B to N	1219
Renault 9 & 11 Petrol (82 - 89) up to F	0822
Renault 18 Petrol (79 - 86) up to D	0598
Renault 19 Petrol (89 - 96) F to N	1646
Renault 19 Diesel (89 - 96) F to N	1946
Renault 21 Petrol (86 - 94) C to M	1397
Renault 25 Petrol & Diesel (84 - 92) B to K	1228
Renault Clio Petrol (91 - May 98) H to R	1853
Renault Clio Diesel (91 - June 96) H to N	3031
Renault Clio Petrol & Diesel (May 98 - May 01) R to Y	3906
Renault Clio Petrol & Diesel (June '01 - '05) Y to 55	4168
Renault Espace Petrol & Diesel (85 - 96) C to N	3197
Renault Laguna Petrol & Diesel (94 - 00) L to W	3252
Renault Laguna Petrol & Diesel (Feb 01 - Feb 05) X to 54	4283
Renault Mégane & Scénic Petrol & Diesel (96 - 99) N to T	3395
Renault Mégane & Scénic Petrol & Diesel (Apr 99 - 02) T to 52	3916
Renault Megane Petrol & Diesel (Oct 02 - 05) 52 to 55	4284
Renault Scenic Petrol & Diesel (Sept 03 - 06) 53 to 06	4297
ROVER 213 & 216 (84 - 89) A to G	1116
Rover 214 & 414 Petrol (89 - 96) G to N	1689
Rover 216 & 416 Petrol (89 - 96) G to N	1830
Rover 211, 214, 216, 218 & 220 Petrol & Diesel (Dec 95 - 99) N to V	3399
Rover 25 & MG ZR Petrol & Diesel (Oct 99 - 04) V to 54	4145
Rover 414, 416 & 420 Petrol & Diesel (May 95 - 98) M to R	3453
Rover 45 / MG ZS Petrol & Diesel (99 - 05) V to 55	4384
Rover 618, 620 & 623 Petrol (93 - 97) K to P	3257
Rover 75 / MG ZT Petrol & Diesel (99 - 06) S to 06	4292
Rover 820, 825 & 827 Petrol (86 - 95) D to N	1380
Rover 3500 (76 - 87) up to E *	0365
Rover Metro, 111 & 114 Petrol (May 90 - 98) G to S	1711
SAAB 95 & 96 (66 - 76) up to R *	0198
Saab 90, 99 & 900 (79 - Oct 93) up to L	0765
Saab 900 (Oct 93 - 98) L to R	3512
Saab 9000 (4-cyl) (85 - 98) C to S	1686
Saab 9-3 Petrol & Diesel (98 - Aug 02) R to 02	4614
Saab 9-5 4-cyl Petrol (97 - 04) R to 54	4156
SEAT Ibiza & Cordoba Petrol & Diesel (Oct 93 - Oct 99) L to V	3571
Seat Ibiza & Malaga Petrol (85 - 92) B to K	1609
SKODA Estelle (77 - 89) up to G	0604
Skoda Fabia Petrol & Diesel (00 - 06) W to 06	4376
Skoda Favorit (89 - 96) F to N	1801
Skoda Felicia Petrol & Diesel (95 - 01) M to X	3505
Skoda Octavia Petrol & Diesel (98 - Apr 04) R to 04	4285
SUBARU 1600 & 1800 (Nov 79 - 90) up to H *	0995
SUNBEAM Alpine, Rapier & H120 (67 - 74) up to N *	0051
SUZUKI SJ Series, Samurai & Vitara (4-cyl) Petrol (82 - 97) up to P	1942
Suzuki Supercarry & Bedford/Vauxhall Rascal (86 - Oct 94) C to M	3015
TALBOT Alpine, Solara, Minx & Rapier (75 - 86) up to D	0337

Title	Book No.
Talbot Horizon Petrol (78 - 86) up to D	0473
Talbot Samba (82 - 86) up to D	0823
TOYOTA Avensis Petrol (98 - Jan 03) R to 52	4264
Toyota Carina E Petrol (May 92 - 97) J to P	3256
Toyota Corolla (80 - 85) up to C	0683
Toyota Corolla (Sept 83 - Sept 87) A to E	1024
Toyota Corolla (Sept 87 - Aug 92) E to K	1683
Toyota Corolla Petrol (Aug 92 - 97) K to P	3259
Toyota Corolla Petrol (July 97 - Feb 02) P to 51	4286
Toyota Hi-Ace & Hi-Lux Petrol (69 - Oct 83) up to A	0304
Toyota Yaris Petrol (99 - 05) T to 05	4265
TRIUMPH GT6 & Vitesse (62 - 74) up to N *	0112
Triumph Herald (59 - 71) up to K *	0010
Triumph Spitfire (62 - 81) up to X	0113
Triumph Stag (70 - 78) up to T *	0441
Triumph TR2, TR3, TR3A, TR4 & TR4A (52 - 67) up to F *	0028
Triumph TR5 & 6 (67 - 75) up to P *	0031
Triumph TR7 (75 - 82) up to Y *	0322
VAUXHALL Astra Petrol (80 - Oct 84) up to B	0635
Vauxhall Astra & Belmont Petrol (Oct 84 - Oct 91) B to J	1136
Vauxhall Astra Petrol (Oct 91 - Feb 98) J to R	1832
Vauxhall/Opel Astra & Zafira Petrol (Feb 98 - Apr 04) R to 04	3758
Vauxhall/Opel Astra & Zafira Diesel (Feb 98 - Apr 04) R to 04	3797
Vauxhall/Opel Astra Petrol (04 - 07) 04 - 07	4732
Vauxhall/Opel Astra Diesel (04 - 07) 04 - 07	4733
Vauxhall/Opel Calibra (90 - 98) G to S	3502
Vauxhall Carlton Petrol (Oct 78 - Oct 86) up to D	0480
Vauxhall Carlton & Senator Petrol (Nov 86 - 94) D to L	1469
Vauxhall Cavalier Petrol (81 - Oct 88) up to F	0812
Vauxhall Cavalier Petrol (Oct 88 - 95) F to N	1570
Vauxhall Chevette (75 - 84) up to B	0285
Vauxhall/Opel Corsa Diesel (Mar 93 - Oct 00) K to X	4087
Vauxhall Corsa Petrol (Mar 93 - 97) K to R	1985
Vauxhall/Opel Corsa Petrol (Apr 97 - Oct 00) P to X	3921
Vauxhall/Opel Corsa Petrol & Diesel (Oct 00 - Sept 03) X to 53	4079
Vauxhall/Opel Corsa Petrol & Diesel (Oct 03 - Aug 06) 53 to 06	4617
Vauxhall/Opel Frontera Petrol & Diesel (91 - Sept 98) J to S	3454
Vauxhall Nova Petrol (83 - 93) up to K	0909
Vauxhall/Opel Omega Petrol (94 - 99) L to T	3510
Vauxhall/Opel Vectra Petrol & Diesel (95 - Feb 99) N to S	3396
Vauxhall/Opel Vectra Petrol & Diesel (Mar 99 - May 02) T to 02	3930
Vauxhall/Opel Vectra Petrol & Diesel (June 02 - Sept 05) 02 to 55	4618
Vauxhall/Opel 1.5, 1.6 & 1.7 litre Diesel Engine (82 - 96) up to N	1222
VW 411 & 412 (68 - 75) up to P *	0091
VW Beetle 1200 (54 - 77) up to S	0036
VW Beetle 1300 & 1500 (65 - 75) up to P	0039
VW 1302 & 1302S (70 - 72) up to L *	0110
VW Beetle 1303, 1303S & GT (72 - 75) up to P	0159
VW Beetle Petrol & Diesel (Apr 99 - 01) T to 51	3798
VW Golf & Jetta Mk 1 Petrol 1.1 & 1.3 (74 - 84) up to A	0716
VW Golf, Jetta & Scirocco Mk 1 Petrol 1.5, 1.6 & 1.8 (74 - 84) up to A	0726

Title	Book No.
VW Golf & Jetta Mk 1 Diesel (78 - 84) up to A	0451
VW Golf & Jetta Mk 2 Petrol (Mar 84 - Feb 92) A to J	1081
VW Golf & Vento Petrol & Diesel (Feb 92 - Mar 98) J to R	3097
VW Golf & Bora Petrol & Diesel (April 98 - 00) R to X	3727
VW Golf & Bora 4-cyl Petrol & Diesel (01 - 03) X to 53	4169
VW Golf & Jetta Petrol & Diesel (04 - 07) 53 to 07	4610
VW LT Petrol Vans & Light Trucks (76 - 87) up to E	0637
VW Passat & Santana Petrol (Sept 81 - May 88) up to E	0814
VW Passat 4-cyl Petrol & Diesel (May 88 - 96) E to P	3498
VW Passat 4-cyl Petrol & Diesel (Dec 96 - Nov 00) P to X	3917
VW Passat Petrol & Diesel (Dec 00 - May 05) X to 05	4279
VW Polo & Derby (76 - Jan 82) up to X	0335
VW Polo (82 - Oct 90) up to H	0813
VW Polo Petrol (Nov 90 - Aug 94) H to L	3245
VW Polo Hatchback Petrol & Diesel (94 - 99) M to S	3500
VW Polo Hatchback Petrol (00 - Jan 02) V to 51	4150
VW Polo Petrol & Diesel (02 - May 05) 51 to 05	4608
VW Scirocco (82 - 90) up to H *	1224
VW Transporter 1600 (68 - 79) up to V	0082
VW Transporter 1700, 1800 & 2000 (72 - 79) up to V *	0226
VW Transporter (air-cooled) Petrol (79 - 82) up to Y *	0638
VW Transporter (water-cooled) Petrol (82 - 90) up to H	3452
VW Type 3 (63 - 73) up to M *	0084
VOLVO 120 & 130 Series (& P1800) (61 - 73) up to M *	0203
Volvo 142, 144 & 145 (66 - 74) up to N *	0129
Volvo 240 Series Petrol (74 - 93) up to K	0270
Volvo 262, 264 & 260/265 (75 - 85) up to C *	0400
Volvo 340, 343, 345 & 360 (76 - 91) up to J	0715
Volvo 440, 460 & 480 Petrol (87 - 97) D to P	1691
Volvo 740 & 760 Petrol (82 - 91) up to J	1258
Volvo 850 Petrol (92 - 96) J to P	3260
Volvo 940 petrol (90 - 98) H to R	3249
Volvo S40 & V40 Petrol (96 - Mar 04) N to 04	3569
Volvo S40 & V50 Petrol & Diesel (Mar 04 - Jun 07) 04 to 07	4731
Volvo S70, V70 & C70 Petrol (96 - 99) P to V	3573
Volvo V70 / S80 Petrol & Diesel (98 - 05) S to 55	4263

AUTOMOTIVE TECHBOOKS

Automotive Electrical and Electronic Systems Manual	3049
Automotive Gearbox Overhaul Manual	3473
Automotive Service Summaries Manual	3475
Automotive Timing Belts Manual – Austin/Rover	3549
Automotive Timing Belts Manual – Ford	3474
Automotive Timing Belts Manual – Peugeot/Citroën	3568
Automotive Timing Belts Manual – Vauxhall/Opel	3577

DIY MANUAL SERIES

The Haynes Air Conditioning Manual	4192
The Haynes Car Electrical Systems Manual	4251
The Haynes Manual on Bodywork	4198
The Haynes Manual on Brakes	4178
The Haynes Manual on Carburettors	4177
The Haynes Manual on Diesel Engines	4174
The Haynes Manual on Engine Management	4199
The Haynes Manual on Fault Codes	4175
The Haynes Manual on Practical Electrical Systems	4267
The Haynes Manual on Small Engines	4250
The Haynes Manual on Welding	4176

* Classic reprint

Preserving Our Motoring Heritage

< The Model J Duesenberg Derham Tourster. Only eight of these magnificent cars were ever built – this is the only example to be found outside the United States of America

Almost every car you've ever loved, loathed or desired is gathered under one roof at the Haynes Motor Museum. Over 300 immaculately presented cars and motorbikes represent every aspect of our motoring heritage, from elegant reminders of bygone days, such as the superb Model J Duesenberg to curiosities like the bug-eyed BMW Isetta. There are also many old friends and flames. Perhaps you remember the 1959 Ford Popular that you did your courting in? The magnificent 'Red Collection' is a spectacle of classic sports cars including AC, Alfa Romeo, Austin Healey, Ferrari, Lamborghini, Maserati, MG, Riley, Porsche and Triumph.

A Perfect Day Out

Each and every vehicle at the Haynes Motor Museum has played its part in the history and culture of Motoring. Today, they make a wonderful spectacle and a great day out for all the family. Bring the kids, bring Mum and Dad, but above all bring your camera to capture those golden memories for ever. You will also find an impressive array of motoring memorabilia, a comfortable 70 seat video cinema and one of the most extensive transport book shops in Britain. The Pit Stop Cafe serves everything from a cup of tea to wholesome, home-made meals or, if you prefer, you can enjoy the large picnic area nestled in the beautiful rural surroundings of Somerset.

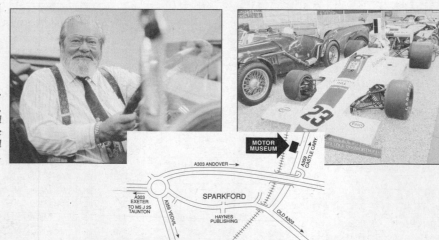

> John Haynes O.B.E., Founder and Chairman of the museum at the wheel of a Haynes Light 12.

< Graham Hill's Lola Cosworth Formula 1 car next to a 1934 Riley Sports.

The Museum is situated on the A359 Yeovil to Frome road at Sparkford, just off the A303 in Somerset. It is about 40 miles south of Bristol, and 25 minutes drive from the M5 intersection at Taunton.
Open 9.30am - 5.30pm (10.00am - 4.00pm Winter) 7 days a week, *except Christmas Day, Boxing Day and New Years Day*
Special rates available for schools, coach parties and outings Charitable Trust No. 292048